Access Controlled

WITHDRAWN

I.C.C. LIBRARY

DEMCO

Information Revolution and Global Politics
William J. Drake and Ernest J. Wilson III, editors

Access Controlled

The Shaping of Power, Rights, and Rule in Cyberspace

Ronald Deibert, John Palfrey, Rafal Rohozinski, and Jonathan Zittrain, editors

I.C.C. LIBRARY

The MIT Press
Cambridge, Massachusetts
London, England

Hm
851
.A254
2010

© 2010 Massachusetts Institute of Technology

All rights reserved. No part of this book may be reproduced in any form by any electronic or mechanical means (including photocopying, recording, or information storage and retrieval) without permission in writing from the publisher.

For information about special quantity discounts, please email special_sales@mitpress.mit.edu

This book was set in Stone Serif and Stone Sans on 3B2 by Asco Typesetters, Hong Kong.

Printed and bound in the United States of America.

Library of Congress Cataloging-in-Publication Data

Access controlled : the shaping of power, rights, and rule in cyberspace / edited by Ronald Deibert ... [et al.] ; foreword by Miklos Haraszti.
    p.   cm. — (Information revolution and global politics)
Report from the OpenNet Initiative.
Includes bibliographical references and index.
ISBN 978-0-262-01434-2 (hardcover : alk. paper) — ISBN 978-0-262-51435-4 (pbk. : alk. paper)
1. Cyberspace—Government policy. 2. Internet—Government policy. 3. Computers—Access control. 4. Internet—Censorship. I. Deibert, Ronald. II. OpenNet Initiative.
HM851.A254   2010
005.8—dc22   2009049632

10 9 8 7 6 5 4 3 2 1

The views expressed by the authors in this publication are their own and do not necessarily reflect the views of the OSCE.

Contents

8/11 Amazon 21.00

Preface

Access Controlled: The Shaping of Power, Rights, and Rule in Cyberspace is the latest report from the OpenNet Initiative (ONI), which is a collaboration of the Citizen Lab at the Munk Centre for International Studies, University of Toronto; the Berkman Center for Internet and Society at Harvard University; and the SecDev Group (Canada). The country profiles and regional overviews provided in this volume have been substantially updated and revised to reflect recent events since our last publication, *Access Denied*. In addition, *Access Controlled* includes six newly authored thematic chapters that analyze the themes of our investigations and grapple with the theoretical and public policy implications.

With *Access Controlled*, we take on new themes emerging from our research and concentrate on the countries that make up the Organization for Security and Cooperation in Europe (OSCE), as it is there, primarily, where some of the most important techniques of next-generation Internet controls are emerging and a normative terrain is being set. While the *Access Controlled* volume focuses on the OSCE region as an important locus of norms and emerging techniques, the ONI conducted tests in more than 65 countries over the last year and a half. We have included a selection of these regional overviews and country profiles in this volume on the basis of two criteria: first, we included countries that either border on or have strategic significance to the OSCE region; second, we included countries that are significant stories in and of themselves and on which we wanted to report. China and Iran are included in both categories, for example, but we also included Egypt, Tunisia, and South Korea (which are OSCE "partner in cooperation" states), as well as Australia and New Zealand, and all our regional overviews. As with *Access Denied*, all our country profiles and regional overviews are accessible in full on our Web site: http://opennet.net/, as well as the thematic chapters of this book.

Ronald Deibert and Rafal Rohozinski

Acknowledgments

The OpenNet Initiative would not exist without the vital contributions of dozens of very talented and often courageous researchers from around the world. The ONI's regional deputies primarily wrote the country profiles and regional overviews: Vesselina Haralampieva (CIS/Europe), Helmi Noman (Middle East and North Africa), and Stephanie Wang (Asia). Masashi Crete-Nishihata (Citizen Lab), provided invaluable written and editorial inputs to the entire book. Jillian York, Rebekah Heacock, and Robert Faris (Berkman) provided editorial input and writing assistance for the country profiles and regional overviews. Other written contributions were made by Fabian Pregel (Germany), Andrea Glorioso (Italy), Sangamitra Ramachander (Europe Overview), Brendan Ballou (Europe Overview), Amina Waheed (Europe Overview, Middle East and North Africa), Natalie Senst (Australia and New Zealand), Dan Larsen (Nordic Overview), Jessica Walch (France).

Robert Faris and Jillian York help to manage the ONI research enterprise on an ongoing basis. Their professional stewardship keeps the ONI on track. Primary research in the CIS was conducted in partnership with the Eurasia i-Policy network and coordinated by Tattugul Mambetalieva. Technical support for testing in the region was provided by Aleksei Bebinov (Civil Initiative for Internet policy, Kyrgyzstan). Jonathan Doda (Citizen Lab) acted as the lead technical engineer and analyst for the ONI in 2008 and 2009; Shishir Nagaraja (Cambridge) did the same in 2007. Jane Gowan (Citizen Lab) designed the cover art for *Access Controlled*, and provided additional design input to the ONI project.

The ONI would like to acknowledge the contributions of the ONI Asia group, and in particular the regional coordinators, Francois Fortier and Al Alegre, the project manager Deirdre Collings, and research assistants Arnav Marchanda and Antoine Nouvet. The ONI is grateful to the University of Amsterdam Digital Methods Team, especially Professor Richard Rogers, Erik Borra, Esther Weltevrede, and Anat Ben-David for participating in the ONI's April 2009 analysis workshop at the Citizen Lab.

The ONI is grateful to MIT Press: William Drake, Ernest Wilson III, Marguerite Avery, and Ellen Sklar.

The Citizen Lab would like to thank Laird Brown, Francois Cadieux, Sarah Boland, Jessica Daggers, Jakub Dalek, Sahar Golshan, Robert Guerra, Gus Hosein, Michael Hull, Dylan Jones, Andrej Karpathy, Elana Koren, Lucinda Li, Daniel Lister, Jamie Liu, Rebecca Mackinnon, Margaret McKone, Kay Nguyen, David Naylor, Palantir Technologies, Psiphon, Inc., Wilhelmina Peter, Janice Stein, James Tay, Jeremy Vernon, Nart Villeneuve, and Greg Walton.

The Berkman Center would like to thank Nagib AlHadi, Renata Avila, Catherine Bracy, Andrea Calderaro, Rafik Dammak, J. C. DeMartin, Zsuzsa Detrekői, Alexey Dolinskiy, Eric Fish, Charles Frentz, Effi Fuks, Urs Gasser, Joshua Goldstein, Cicek Gurkan, Sanjana Hattotuwa, Eric Johnson, Ismael Kahtan, Mohamed Keita, Colin Maclay, Ladan Mahabadi, Persephone Miel, Katitza Rodriguez Pereda, Elfine Peterson, Daniel Rosenberg, Anas Qtiesh, Amin Sabeti, Zinta Saulkalns, Gbenga Sesan, Chris Soghoian, Firuzeh Shookoh Valle, Kanupriya Tehawari, Shiham Thabreez, Kate von Achen, Sally Walkerman, Seth Young, Ethan Zuckerman, Yushu Zhou.

The SecDev Group would like to thank the Eurasia i-Policy Network who carried out the primary field research and technical testing in the CIS, and who prepared country situation reports upon which the country profiles in this volume are based: Emin Akhundov (Azerbaijan), Asmudin Atoev (Tajikstan), Galiya Baltina (Kazakhstan), Aleksandra Belyaeva (Citizen's Initiative for Internet Policy – Russia), Vadim Dryganov (Belarus), Movses Hakobyan (Internews Centre for Law and Policy – Armenia), Parvina Ibodova (Tajikistan), Igor Kozachkov (technical contributor – Ukraine), Nino Kuntseva-Gabashvili (Business Intelligence and Valuation Group (BVG), Ltd – Georgia), Aleksei Marchuk (Informational Policy Institute – Russia), Andrei Marusov (Ukraine), Pervin Pavel, ("Microtest", technical contributor – Russia), Andrei Pazuk (Ukraine), and Zviad Sulaberidze (Georgia).

The ONI is very grateful for financial support from the following institutions: The John D. and Catherine T. MacArthur Foundation, The International Development Research Centre (Canada), and the Donner Canada Foundation.

Production of this volume was made possible through the generous support of the Office of the Representative on Freedom of the Media Organization for Security and Cooperation in Europe.

The ONI would like to especially acknowledge numerous researchers and contributors to our research and other activities who have chosen to remain anonymous. We dedicate this volume to their courage.

Author Biographies

Ronald Deibert is an associate professor of political science and director of the Citizen Lab at the Munk Centre for International Studies, University of Toronto. He is a cofounder and principal investigator of the OpenNet Initiative and the Information Warfare Monitor.

Colin Maclay is the Managing Director of the Berkman Center for Internet and Society at Harvard University. He works on new media, institutions, and international development, and helped start the Global Network Initiative.

John Palfrey is a professor of law at Harvard Law School and a faculty codirector of the Berkman Center for Internet and Society at Harvard University. He is a co principal investigator of the OpenNet Initiative.

Hal Roberts is a fellow at the Berkman Center for Internet and Society. He studies a range of issues related to the control and flow of information online, including surveillance, filtering circumvention, and digital media.

Rafal Rohozinski is a principal with the SecDev Group and CEO of Psiphon, Inc. He is a co–principal investigator of the OpenNet Initiative and the Information Warfare Monitor.

Nart Villeneuve is the CTO of Psiphon, Inc., and the Psiphon Research Fellow at the Citizen Lab at the Munk Centre for International Studies, University of Toronto.

Ethan Zuckerman is a senior researcher at the Berkman Center for Internet and Society, where he focuses on digital media in the developing world. He is the cofounder of the international citizen media community Global Voices.

Foreword

Imagine if an unknown person entered your home on a regular basis and removed books from your bookshelves. You would never be told which books were being taken away, and you would never be given a reason except that someone, somewhere, somehow, deemed them "extremist," "indecent," or simply "insulting," or felt that they might "incite" some form of hatred. Imagine if the books removed included historical research on disputed facts, secular depictions of religious images, and irreverent accounts of the conduct or policies of political leaders.

Couldn't happen in a democracy? Guess again.

Under the guise of protecting citizens from "smut" and "offensiveness," Internet filtering programs routinely block access to thousands of World Wide Web search results, home pages, chat rooms, newsgroups, and other Internet options—in democratic countries as well as in authoritarian states. In most cases the criteria are based on an arbitrary and politicized understanding of what is "smut" or "offensive."

Online surveillance and censorship are growing in scale, scope, and sophistication around the world. This growth is not surprising given the importance of the medium. But there is increasing cause for concern about the implications of these trends for media freedom, for unhampered discussion of matters of public interest, and even for political activism.

In charting these developments, surveys carried out by the OpenNet Initiative (ONI) are indispensable tools in my own daily job of reminding governments of the Organization for Security and Cooperation in Europe (OSCE) of their commitments concerning the free flow of information.

Published in 2007, ONI's first global survey of Internet filtering, *Access Denied: The Practice and Policy of Global Internet Filtering*, revealed that "state-mandated net filtering" was carried out in a only "a couple" of countries in 2002—but by 2007, it was under way in 25 out of the 41 countries scrutinized.

In its new publication, *Access Controlled: The Shaping of Power, Rights, and Rule in Cyberspace*, ONI goes further.

It shines a spotlight on filtering to help make the practice more transparent, or at least to divulge it as an acknowledged fact. And it also predicts a rise in more "subtle" forms of Internet censorship, such as blocking certain political Web sites during election periods or waging cyberwarfare campaigns such as those recently witnessed in the Russian-Georgian conflict.

One of the most regrettable aspects of net filtering is the fact that it is often invisible— and almost always happens out of public control. As a citizen, there is no place you can turn to get answers from your state authorities about how and why they are filtering, and about what is being blocked.

In the early days of the Web, a decade or so ago, it was taken for granted that freedom of expression online would inexorably evolve and progress. It was assumed that governments that did not uphold the fundamental human right to speak and write freely would be powerless against the spread of those values over the Internet.

By now, though, those early dreams have been dashed. The reality today is that Internet censorship is a growing practice both east and west of Vienna, with the filtering of Internet content carried out by both established Western democracies and transitional ones. Indeed, the countries where Internet matters the most as the sole carrier of real news media are the same countries whose governments, posing as "defenders" of the public, filter and block the most online content.

No one can rely on the Internet anymore as a self-healing mechanism that can defeat censorship or blocking on its own. It is for that reason that the Freedom of the Media office will continue to actively promote guarantees for freedom of the media on the Internet.

Let us be clear. The benefits of the Internet far outweigh the dangers of misuse. In some countries, the Internet is the only source of pluralistic and independent information, even if Internet penetration may still be low. Let us make sure that this unique source of unguided information does not dry out.

In light of these issues, I dedicate this foreword to Magomed Yevloyev, the publisher of the independent news Web site Ingushetiya.ru, who was shot dead on August 31, 2008, while in police custody. The Ingushetiya.ru Web site has been a torchbearer of what a free Internet stands for: access to a plurality of information and opinion.

I am grateful for the partnership with the ONI, as well as for the timely publication of this book, which would not have been possible without the generous contribution of the government of Ireland, for which I also express my gratitude.

Miklos Haraszti
OSCE Representative on Freedom of the Media

Part I Access Controlled: Theory and Analysis

1 Beyond Denial

Introducing Next-Generation Information Access Controls

Ronald Deibert and Rafal Rohozinski

Introduction

It is hard to imagine the world before the Internet. A generation of digital natives has grown up with ubiquitous connectivity, where neither borders nor language seems a barrier to communication.[1] And yet, less than 20 years ago the global information environment was a much more controlled and regulated space, organized around sovereign states. Throughout much of modern history, governments have wrestled with the tensions of the relentless drive to build new technologies and the unpredictable and often counterproductive consequences that flow from them for their power and authority.[2] No less of a historical figure than Stalin captured this tension between the quest for modernity and the compulsion to control. When presented with a proposal to build a modern telephone system for the new Soviet state, he reportedly replied, "I can imagine no greater instrument of counterrevolution in our time."

The rise of the Internet coincided with a major set of political upheavals that culminated with the collapse of the Soviet Union and communist bloc. In the euphoria that ensued, the idea of technological redemption, inevitable democratization, and for some, the end of history, coalesced into a popular ideology that equated technology with empowerment. This idea was far from new. Indeed, the telegraph, electrical lighting, and telephony all emerged at similarly transformational historical junctures, leading to a long pedigree of speculation regarding the democratizing role of technology in social and political change.[3]

There is no doubt that the Internet has unleashed a wide-ranging and globally significant shift in communications—a shift that has led to the empowerment of individuals and nonstate actors on an unprecedented scale. At times, the Internet seems uncontrollable, a constantly evolving and dynamic virtual realm, reshaped continuously by a growing number of users at edge points of the network. But Newtonian physics is as relevant in politics and cyberspace as it is in the physical realm. Just as with previous technological developments, as the Internet has grown in political significance, an architecture of control—through technology, regulation, norms, and political calculus —has emerged to shape a new geopolitical information landscape.

In 2008, the OpenNet Initiative (ONI) published its first global study—*Access Denied: The Practice and Policy of Global Internet Filtering*[4]—which documented how states are seeking to establish borders in cyberspace. Our snapshot of 41 countries discovered that states were busy constructing defensive perimeters to deny access to unwanted content. For the most part, these methods consisted of building firewalls at key Internet choke points. The People's Republic of China was among the first to adopt national filtering systems at the backbone of the country's Internet—popularly known as the "Great Firewall of China"—and it has become a paradigm of Internet censorship ever since. "Chinese-style" filtering—as we call it here—represents the *first generation* of Internet control techniques.

In Chinese-style filtering, lists of Internet protocol (IP) addresses, keywords, and/or domains are programmed into routers or software packages that are situated at key Internet choke points, typically at international gateways or among major Internet service providers (ISPs).[5] Requests that are made for any information contained in the block lists are denied for citizens living within those jurisdictions. The latter can happen in a variety of ways, with greater and lesser degrees of transparency, but it is almost always static, fixed in time, and relatively easy to discern using the methods developed over time by the OpenNet Initiative's researchers (see box on ONI's methodology). Moreover, determined Internet users can circumvent them with relative ease.

Not all countries have been as forthright with their rationale for filtering Internet content as China. Our research for *Access Denied* also found coyness on the part of many states to admit seeking to control Internet content. In many cases, denial of access occurred extralegally, or under the guise of opaque national security laws. Often, ISPs were simply asked or told to block access to specific content without any reference to existing law. Other times, blockages were difficult to distinguish from network errors or other technical problems, like denial of service attacks, but seemed suspiciously connected to political events. Many of the countries listed in our first report denied that they were in fact blocking access to Internet content or had any connection to attacks on services. We saw these events as anomalies insofar as they did not fit the paradigm of Chinese style filtering and largely eluded the methodologies that we had developed to test for Internet censorship.[6]

We have subsequently come to learn that these anomalies were, in fact, emerging norms. Since our research for *Access Denied* was conducted, a sea change has occurred in the policies and practices of Internet controls. States no longer fear pariah status by openly declaring their intent to regulate and control cyberspace. The convenient rubric of terrorism, child pornography, and cyber security has contributed to a growing expectation that states should enforce order in cyberspace, including policing unwanted content. Paradoxically, advanced democratic states within the Organization for Secu-

Box 1.1

The ONI employs a unique "fusion" methodology that combines field investigations, technical reconnaissance, and data mining, fusion, analysis, and visualization. Our aim is to uncover evidence of Internet content filtering in countries under investigation. The ONI's tests consist of running special software programs within countries under investigation that connect back to databases that contain lists of thousands of URLs, IPs, and keywords. The lists are broken down into two categories: global lists include URLs, IPs, and keywords that are tested in every country, and which help us make general comparisons of accessibility across countries. Global lists also provide a "snapshot" of accessibility to content typically blocked by filtering software programs, and can help us understand whether particular software programs are being used in a specific context. Local lists are unique for each country and are usually made up of content in local languages. These are high-impact URLs, IPs, and keywords, meaning they are content that is likely to, or has been reported to have been, targeted for filtering. Our aim is to run tests on each of the main ISPs in a country over an extended period of time—typically at least two weeks on at least two occasions. Our accessibility depends very much on our in-country testers, and for security and other reasons we are not always able to perform comprehensive tests, meaning in some cases we have only partial results on which to make inferences. Our specially designed software checks access both within the country and from one or more control locations simultaneously. Anomalies are analyzed and determinations are made as to whether a site is accessible or not, and if the latter, how the inaccessibility occurs. In some instances, block-pages— Web sites that explicitly confirm blocking—are yielded for requests for banned content. In other instances, connections are simply broken. In some cases, special filtering software is employed, while in others routers are manually configured to block.

rity and Cooperation in Europe (OSCE)—including members of the European Union (EU)—are (perhaps unintentionally) leading the way toward the establishment of a global norm around filtering of political content with the introduction of proposals to censor hate speech and militant Islamic content on the Internet. This follows already existing measures in the UK, Canada, and elsewhere aimed at eliminating access to child pornography. Recently and amid great controversy, Australia announced plans to create a nationwide filtering system for Internet connectivity in that country. Although the proposal has ultimately languished, it shows the extent of this growing norm. No longer is consideration of state-sanctioned Internet censorship confined to authoritarian regimes or hidden from public view. Internet censorship is becoming a global norm.

At the same time, states have also become more cognizant of the strategic importance of cyberspace (of which the Internet is an important constituent component). Cyberspace has become militarized. A clever use of the Internet by insurgents and militants in Iraq and other parts of the Middle East, the significance of the Internet in conflicts such as the 2008 Russia-Georgia war, and revelations concerning large-scale cyber-espionage networks,[7] has emphasized the impact of cyberspace on the *sweat and muscle* aspects of war fighting, and geopolitical competition among states and nonstate actors. Reflecting on these recent incidents, many states' armed forces and policymakers have engaged in a fundamental rethinking of assumptions about the importance of the informational domain to conflict and competition. As a consequence, states are now openly pursuing a cyber arms race with leading powers such as the United States, Russia, and China unashamedly making their intentions clear in doctrines for military engagement in cyberspace. The quest for information control is now *beyond denial*.

The present volume aims to document, analyze, and explore these emerging next-generation techniques, what they mean for relationships between citizens and states, and how they will shape cyberspace as a domain for civic interaction into the future. The title of our volume—*Access Controlled: The Shaping of Power, Rights, and Rule in Cyberspace*—suggests how the *center of gravity* of practices aimed at managing cyberspace has shifted subtly from policies and practices aimed at denying access to content to methods that seek to *normalize* control and the exercise of power in cyberspace through a variety of means.

This volume differs from its predecessors in two ways. First, our focus is primarily on the 56 countries that make up the OSCE. This is a deliberate choice, as many of the legal mechanisms that legitimate control over cyberspace, and its militarization, are led by the advanced democratic countries of Europe and North America. Likewise, many of the more innovative means by which laws and techniques used to silence voices in cyberspace are emerging from the postcommunist countries of the Commonwealth of Independent States (CIS). In this respect, the industrialized North is establishing norms that are only too readily propagated and adopted by repressive and authoritarian regimes elsewhere.

Second, *Access Controlled* focuses on the new generations of Internet controls that go beyond mere denial of information. Whereas Chinese-style national filtering schemes represent the first generation of Internet filtering, second- and third-generation techniques are more subtle, flexible, and even offensive in character. These next-generation techniques employ the use of legal regulations to supplement or legitimize technical filtering measures, extralegal or covert practices, including offensive methods, and the outsourcing or privatizing of controls to "third parties," to restrict what type of information can be posted, hosted, accessed, or communicated online. Examples of next-generation techniques include the infiltration and exploitation of computer systems by targeted viruses and the employment of distributed denial-of-service (DDoS) attacks, surveillance at key choke points of the Internet's infrastructure, legal takedown notices, stifling terms-of-usage policies, and national information-shaping strategies, all of which are highlighted in one way or another in the chapters that follow. Although these measures may have the same aim as Chinese-style filtering, they reflect a maturation of methods resulting from a growing colonization of cyberspace by states and other actors. They emerge from a desire to *shape* and *influence* as much as tightly *control* national and global populations that are increasingly reliant on cyberspace as their main source of information. These next-generation controls raise important and sometimes troubling public policy issues—particularly for the relationship between citizens and states.

Chapter Overview

Second- and third-generation controls are carefully defined in our subsequent chapter in this volume, *Control and Subversion in Russian Cyberspace*. Second-generation controls create a legal and normative environment and technical capabilities that enable actors to deny access to information resources as and when needed, while reducing the possibility of blowback or discovery. These controls have an overt and covert track. The overt track aims to legalize content controls by specifying the conditions under which they can be denied. Instruments here include the doctrine of information security as well as the application of existent laws, such as slander and defamation, to the online environment. The covert track establishes procedures and technical capabilities that allow content controls to be applied "just in time," when the information being targeted has the highest value (e.g., during elections or public demonstrations), and to be applied in ways that assure plausible deniability.

Third-generation controls take a highly sophisticated, multidimensional approach to enhancing state control over national cyberspace and building capabilities for competing in informational space with potential adversaries and competitors. The key characteristic of third-generation controls is that the focus is less on denying access than successfully competing with potential threats through effective counterinformation campaigns that overwhelm, discredit, or demoralize opponents. Third-generation controls also focus on the active use of surveillance and data mining as means to confuse and entrap opponents.

We argue that while the countries of the CIS are often seen as lagging behind Europe, North America, and the technological tigers of Asia, they may be leaders in the development of next-generation controls. Some of the first, and most elaborate, forms of just-in-time blocking, terms-of-usage policies, surveillance, and legal takedown notices occurred among the countries of the CIS over the last several years. Examining that region in detail may give us insight into the future of information controls elsewhere.

Computer network attacks and exploitation—what we called "just-in-time" blocking in *Access Denied*—are perhaps the starkest of examples of next-generation techniques. Computer network attacks describe the range of controls that target and "take down" strategically important sources of information or services at key moments in time through computer-based information attacks. Although there are several tactics that can be employed within this rubric—deliberate tampering with domain name servers, virus and Trojan horse insertion, and even brute physical attacks—the most common is the use of DDoS attacks. These attacks flood a server with illegitimate requests for information from multiple sources—usually from so-called "zombie" computers that are infected and employed as part of a "botnet." The ONI has monitored an increasing number of just-in-time blocking incidences using DDoS attacks, going back to our first acquaintance during the Kyrgyzstan parliamentary elections of 2005. In that episode, the Web sites of opposition newspapers came under a debilitating attack that left them unable to communicate during the critical period leading up to and during the Kyrgyz election.[8] Since the Kyrgyz case, DDoS attacks have featured prominently in the dispute between Russia and Estonia in May 2007, during the Russia-Georgia conflict of 2008, and in numerous cases involving the Web sites of human rights and political opposition groups.

These tactics are particularly difficult to monitor using traditional ONI methods because of their temporary and fleeting duration, and because their perpetrators can disguise their involvement through distribution and anonymity. Today, organized criminal networks operate commercial botnets with significant powers of disruption. Perpetrators can simply contract out a DDoS attack and benefit by the convenience of an electronic assault that from the outside may look as though it is a random attack or a series of unfortunate network errors. Attributing such attacks to their source is difficult because the vectors are distributed and the transactions are done through criminal activity and illicit shadow markets. Although much of what the ONI has observed in terms of computer network attacks and just-in-time blocking has occurred in the developing world, it is noteworthy the military use of botnets is being debated in NATO countries and elsewhere.[9] The prospect of an arms race in cyberspace looms large.

Among many countries in the industrialized world, a major impetus to filter is the desire to control access to information relating to the sexual exploitation of children, otherwise known as child pornography. In almost all countries, possession and distribution of child pornography is illegal. In some countries, laws have been enacted to restrict distribution of child pornography online. In some countries, private ISPs have entered into voluntary arrangements to filter access to lists of child pornographic material, while in others entire nationwide filtering schemes have been proposed. In all cases, the proposals have been the subject of considerable public debate and controversy. Although only a few very extreme minority groups, such as libertarians, question the right to access child pornography, many have raised questions about the transparency of the processes being followed or the mechanisms put in place for oversight and review. For the ONI, for example, the mere test for access to this material is prohibited because a simple connection to such a site would constitute a crime in most jurisdictions. This situation leaves many researchers in a quandary as to how to verify that lists are accurate and do not contain collateral filtering problems or categorization mistakes common to filtering software. Nart Villeneuve's chapter provides a historical overview of online child pornography controls and examines the range of policy responses that have been employed. As Villeneuve explains, many governments have adopted national filtering policies rather than developing international information-sharing arrangements that would involve police cooperation and the removal of information at its source.

Another example of next-generation information controls prominent among the countries of the OSCE is the extensive use and application of surveillance. As Hal Roberts and John Palfrey outline in their chapter, surveillance can happen at numerous points throughout the infrastructure of cyberspace and can be collected by a variety of public and private actors who have access to those choke points. States' intelligence and law enforcement agencies are increasingly extracting precious information flows through the installation of permanent eavesdropping equipment at key Internet choke points, such as Internet exchanges, ISPs, or major international peering facilities, and combining such information with new tools of reconnaissance drawn from data sources such as CCTVs, satellite imagery, and powerful systems of geo-locational mapping. To be sure, electronic surveillance is nothing new, having a long history shrouded with secrecy. Throughout the cold war, both superpowers assembled globe-spanning electronic surveillance systems that operated in the most highly classified realms. However, today's surveillance systems are much more extensive and penetrating, and are legitimized by permissive antiterror legislation that removes many previous operational constraints. They are also increasingly operated and controlled not by the state but by private actors. As with just-in-time blocking, surveillance eludes the ONI's methods and is generally quite difficult to monitor using technical means. It is, however, a very powerful force of information control and can create a stifling climate of self-censorship.

Another control beyond denial that is profiled in *Access Controlled* relates to the growing and widespread prevalence of cyberspace as a communications environment, and the ways in which third-party intermediaries, including private companies and public institutions, host, service, and ultimately control that environment. At one point in time, it might have been fair to characterize cyberspace as largely a separate and distinct realm—something people "enter into" when they turn on their computers or play video games. Today, however, with always-on portable devices that are fully connected to the Internet, and much of society's transactions mediated through information and communication technologies—including business, work, government, and play—cyberspace is not so much a distinct realm as it is the very environment we inhabit. Our lives have been digitally disassembled, disaggregated, and dispersed into multiple digital domains. Our "private" information now traverses through cables and spectrum owned and operated by numerous private and public institutions located in numerous legal jurisdictions. The same is true of government and business information. It is hosted on servers each of which may have unique terms-of-service, data-retention, and use policies. Depending on the territorial jurisdiction in which they are located, they may be subject to the pressures of law enforcement and intelligence to turn over that information, either overtly or covertly. And they are subject to a bewildering variety of local, national, and international laws, some of which may conflict.

Issues of censorship that involve terms-of-use policies, takedown notices, and other commercial compliance and service issues are taken up in both the Ethan Zuckerman and Colin Maclay chapters. Zuckerman outlines some of the ways in which competitive market forces can create unintended consequences leading to censorship by ISPs and online service providers (OSPs). Unwilling or afraid to bear the burden of legal and other costs of hosting controversial information, ISPs and OSPs may simply err on the side of caution, leading to a situation where the spaces for hosting content deemed objectionable anywhere are progressively winnowed. As much of what happens online today, from e-mail to documentation to chats, flows through or otherwise depends on these large "cloud" services managed by private companies, such a chilling effect could have profound consequences on freedom of speech and access to information.

Maclay's chapter focuses on issues of accountability and transparency around OSPs and ISPs that operate or provide services in jurisdictions where Internet censorship takes place. In many countries, Internet companies are either pressured or legally compelled to censor their services or turn over user data, with search engines being among the most common of them. In China, for example, major search engine companies all filter their search results, and at least one has turned over personal data to Chinese authorities, resulting in arrests. These practices have garnered significant controversy, particularly in the United States where the largest of them—Microsoft, Yahoo!, Google—are based. In an effort to forestall legislation that would restrict their investment practices abroad, these companies have entered into a self-regulation pact, called the Global Network Initiative, which Maclay analyzes and discusses. Given that much of cyberspace is operated by the private sector, such self-regulation pacts may become a more common feature of cyberspace governance, as will undoubtedly the policing of Internet content controls.

Conclusion

The trends and findings analyzed in *Access Controlled* reveal a rapidly emerging normative terrain that should be of concern to policymakers, advocacy and rights networks, and academics. Given the strategic importance of the OSCE, in terms of relative military capabilities, wealth, and diplomatic influence, the norms emerging from this region are bound to have unintended consequences all over the world. Understanding those impacts will be of paramount importance for Internet governance at all levels in years to come.

Probably the most important norm is the "security first" orientation toward Internet governance, driven in part by the fear of terrorism and in part by concerns of protecting vulnerable populations (particularly children) from exploitation. Across the OSCE, communities of practice in law enforcement, intelligence, and the private sector are working, often in uncoordinated, discrete, but like-minded ways, leading to a normalization of Internet surveillance and censorship across all sectors of cyberspace. It is perhaps ironic that these norms so antithetical to basic rights and freedoms are being propagated from many countries that just over a decade ago were responsible for the expansion of liberal democratic principles and market capitalism across the globe. And yet upon closer consideration such trends conform to what have been called "governmentality practices" in general that characterize these societies, as techniques of control become progressively more refined, technologically rigorous, and bureaucratically complex. Although not "socially sinister," as David Lyons puts it, what he calls "everyday surveillance" has routinized itself into ordinary life in so many myriad ways that it has become the taken-for-granted context within which modern industrialized society operates.[10] The security-first norm around Internet governance can be seen, therefore, as but another manifestation of these wider developments. Internet censorship and surveillance—once largely confined to authoritarian regimes—is now fast becoming the global norm.

But there is a second characteristic of this newly emerging normative terrain that is unique to cyberspace and the speed with which such changes are being wrought, in particular to the long-standing pillars of modern citizen-state relations. The "social contract" that has set the basic framework for citizen-state relations in the modern industrialized period has been shaped by decades of technological and social change and institutional innovations. One must be careful, therefore, to ascribe to contemporary events unique and epochal challenges. However, the way in which citizen-state relations are being upset in a very compressed time frame is worth noting, and may be comparable only to that which happened at the height of the industrial revolution itself. In such a context of rapid technological and social change, the margin for error and unintended consequence around laws and regulations is enormous as path dependencies open up around fast-moving developments that only in hindsight can be identified as such.

The salience of such impacts can be seen in the practices surrounding the distributed ownership infrastructure of cyberspace. Today, peoples' everyday lives are mediated not only through the state per se, but dispersed through clouds of digital-electronic telecommunications owned and operated by private entities. Each of these clouds—often spanning multiple national jurisdictions—represents potential, and often actual, loci of private authority. As shown throughout each of the chapters in this volume, the decisions they make on when to retain, filter, monitor, and share the information they control (and with whom) are increasingly having important political ramifications for citizens the world over. The normative terrain outlined in *Access Controlled* thus offers a compelling example of the privatization of authority.

Perhaps the most important unintended consequences may come from new conflicts and offensive operations documented in this volume. The growing acceptance of the militarization of cyberspace, by states and by third-party actors, risks significant blowbacks as these techniques—once hidden from view or confined to marginalized contexts—become an entrenched characteristic of global relations. Societies around the world—none more so than those of the OSCE—are heavily dependent on globally networked technologies. They have been locked in and interpenetrated by a digital web of their own spinning.[11] And so from a rational perspective, an arms race in cyberspace is to no one's advantage; a collapse of one information infrastructure would undoubtedly affect others—perhaps even the perpetrator. But as so often is the case in the competitive dynamics of world politics, the logic of security dilemmas can easily overwhelm and entrap rational decision-making processes. Today, governments are responding to the threats of cyberwar not by pursuing norms of mutual restraint but by endorsing new techniques of offensive operations, including outsourcing to third-party actors and criminal organizations.

Last, this newly emerging normative terrain of next-generation Internet controls presents major challenges to monitoring organizations, including the ONI itself. The technical investigations that informed our country studies and that are reported on here represent a methodology borne out of the need to monitor first-generation technical filtering techniques. If the trends identified in *Access Controlled* are accurate, then these first-generation filtering techniques may be gradually superseded by a variety of next-generation controls that are more subtle and fluid and deeply integrated into social relations rather than fixed at specific choke points. This possibility suggests that the ONI itself must now respond with a new suite of methodologies if it hopes to remain relevant to the challenges of cyberspace governance that lay ahead.

Notes

1. John Palfrey and Urs Gasser, *Born Digital: Understanding the First Generation of Digital Natives* (New York: Basic Books, 2008).

2. Unpredictable consequences of technological change is a theme explored in Ronald J. Deibert, *Parchment, Printing and Hypermedia: Modes of Communication in World Order Transformation* (New York: Columbia University Press, 1997).

3. Tom Standage, *The Victorian Internet: The Remarkable Story of the Telegraph and the Nineteenth Century's On-line Producers* (New York: Berkeley Books, 1998).

4. Ronald J. Deibert, John Palfrey, Rafal Rohozinski, and Jonathan Zittrain, eds., *Access Denied: The Practice and Policy of Global Internet Filtering* (Cambridge, MA: MIT Press, 2008).

5. Steven J. Murdoch and Ross Anderson, "Tools and Technology of Internet Filtering," in *Access Denied: The Practice and Policy of Global Internet Filtering*, ed. Ronald J. Deibert, John Palfrey, Rafal Rohozinski, and Jonathan Zittrain (Cambridge, MA: MIT Press, 2008), 57–72.

6. Ronald J. Deibert and Rafal Rohozinski, "Good for Liberty, Bad for Security? Global Civil Society and the Securitizaton of the Internet," in *Access Denied: The Practice and Policy of Global Internet Filtering*, ed. Ronald J. Deibert, John Palfrey, Rafal Rohozinski, and Jonathan Zittrain (Cambridge, MA: MIT Press, 2008), 123–149.

7. Information Warfare Monitor, "Tracking GhostNet: Investigating a Cyber Espionage Network," Citizen Lab/the SecDev Group, March 29, 2009, http://www.tracking-ghost.net.

8. OpenNet Initiative, "Special Report: Kyrgyzstan, Election Monitoring in Kyrgyzstan," April 15, 2005, http://www.opennetinitiative.net/special/kg/.

9. For example, see Col. Charles W. Williamson III, "Carpet Bombing in Cyberspace: Why America Needs a Military Botnet," *Armed Forces Journal* (May 2008), http://www.armedforcesjournal.com/2008/05/3375884.

10. David Lyons, *Surveillance Society: Monitoring Everyday Life* (Buckingham, UK: Open University Press, 2001).

11. Ronald J. Deibert, "Network Power," in *The Political Economy of a Changing Global Order*, 2nd ed., ed. Richard Stubbs and Geoffrey Underhill (New York: Oxford University Press, 1999).

2 Control and Subversion in Russian Cyberspace

Ronald Deibert and Rafal Rohozinski

Introduction

It has become a truism to link censorship in cyberspace to the practices of authoritarian regimes. Around the world, the most repressive governments—China, Burma, North Korea, Cuba, Saudi Arabia—are the ones that erect digital firewalls that restrict citizens' access to information, filter political content, and stymie freedom of speech online. When we turn to the countries of the former Soviet Union—Russia and the Commonwealth of Independent States (CIS)—we should expect no different. The Economist *index of democracy* paints a bleak picture of political freedoms in the CIS (see Table 2.1; numbers represent the country's rank in the world).[1] Only two countries, Ukraine and Moldova, rank as *flawed democracies*, with the remaining 10 countries of the region described as either *hybrid regimes* or *authoritarian*.

Throughout the CIS, this creeping authoritarianism is evident in just about every facet of social and political life. Independent media are stifled, journalists intimidated, and opposition parties and civil society groups harassed and subject to a variety of suffocating regulations. And yet, in spite of this increasingly constrained environment, the Internet remains accessible and relatively free from filtering. The ONI has tested extensively through the CIS region, far deeper and more regularly in fact than in any other region in the world. To date we have documented traditional "Chinese-style" Internet filtering—the deliberate and static blocking of Internet content and services by state sanction—only in Uzbekistan and Turkmenistan. For the rest of the region, while connectivity may be poor and unreliable, and suffer from the usual rent-seeking distortions found in other developing country environments, the same basic content is available there as in the most open country contexts.

In our chapter, we explore this seeming disjuncture between authoritarianism in the CIS and the relative freedom enjoyed in Russian cyberspace, commonly known as RUNET. We argue that attempts to regulate and impose controls over cyberspace in the CIS are not necessarily absent (as ONI testing results may suggest) but are *different* than in other regions of the world. We hypothesize that CIS control strategies have

Table 2.1

INDEX OF DEMOCRACY		
Less Authoritarian	World Ranking	
Ukraine	53	Flawed democracy
Moldova	62	
Georgia	104	Hybrid regime
Russia	107	
Armenia	113	
Kyrgyzstan	114	
Kazakhstan	127	Authoritarian
Belarus	132	
Azerbaijan	135	
Tajikistan	150	
Uzbekistan	164	
Turkmenistan	165	
More Authoritarian		

Source: The Economist Intelligence Unit, "The Economist Intelligence Unit's Index of Democracy 2008," 2008, http://graphics.eiu.com/PDF/Democracy%20Index%202008.pdf.

evolved several generations ahead of those used in other regions of the world (including China and the Middle East). In RUNET, control strategies tend to be more subtle and sophisticated and designed to *shape and affect* when and how information is received by users, rather than denying access outright.

One reason for this difference may be the prior experiences of governments and opposition groups in the region. State authorities are aware of the Internet's potential for mobilizing opposition and protest that goes far beyond the nature of content that can be downloaded from Web sites, chat rooms, and blogs. These technologies have the potential to enable *regime change*, as demonstrated by the eponymous color revolutions in Ukraine, Georgia, and Kyrgyzstan. By the same token, state actors have also come to recognize that these technologies make opposition movements vulnerable, and that disruption, intimidation, and disinformation can also cause these movements to fragment and fail. The failure of opposition movements in Belarus and Azerbaijan to ignite a wider social mobilization, along with the role that targeted information controls played in fragmenting and limiting the effectiveness of these movements, also points to the possible trajectory in which controls aimed at Russian cyberspace may be moving.

Our chapter unfolds in several steps. We begin by describing some of the unique characteristics of the "hidden" information revolution that has taken place in Russian cyberspace since the end of the cold war. Contrary to widespread perceptions outside of the region, Russian cyberspace is a thriving and dynamic space, vital to economics, society, and politics. Second, we outline *three generations* of cyberspace controls that emerge from the research conducted by the ONI in this region. *First-generation controls*—so-called Chinese-style filtering—are unpopular and infrequently applied. While instances of filtering have been identified in just about all CIS countries, wide-scale national filtering is only pursued as a matter of state policy in two of the CIS states. Rather, information control seems to be exercised by way of more subtle, hidden, and temporally specific forms of denial. These controls can involve legal and normative pressures and regulations designed to inculcate an environment of self-censorship. Others, like denial-of-service attacks, result in Web sites and services becoming unavailable, often during times of heightened political activity. Still others, like mass blogging by political activists on opposition Web sites, cannot be characterized as an attack per se, although the outcome of silencing these Web sites is as effective as traditional filtering (if not more so).

These *second-* and *third-generation* controls are increasingly widespread, and they are elusive to traditional ONI testing methods. They are difficult to measure and often require in-depth fieldwork to verify. Consequently, many of the examples in this chapter are based on field investigations carried out by our ONI regional partners where technical testing was used to establish the characteristics of controls, rather than measure the extent of them. We hypothesize that, although these next-generation controls emerged in the CIS, they may in fact be increasingly practiced elsewhere. In the next section of the chapter we turn our lens beyond the CIS to find examples of second- and third-generation controls.

We conclude by arguing that, contrary to initial expectations, first-generation filtering techniques may become increasingly rare outside of a few select content categories, raising serious public policy issues around accountability and transparency of information controls in cyberspace. The future of cyberspace controls, we argue, can be found in RUNET.

RUNET

On July 6, 2006, Russian President Vladimir Putin fielded questions from the Internet at an event organized by the leading Russian Web portal Yandex.[2] It was the first time a Russian leader directly engaged and interacted with an Internet audience. The event itself made few headlines in the international media, but in Russia it marked an important milestone. The Internet had graduated to the mainstream of Russian politics and was being treated by the highest levels of state authority as equal in importance to television, radio, and newspapers. The question put to President Putin by the Internet audience also revealed a sense of the informal, irreverent culture of Russian cyberspace. Over 5,640 *netizens* wrote in to ask when the President first had sex. More surprising, perhaps, was that Putin replied.[3]

The rise of the Internet to the center of Russian culture and politics remains poorly understood and insufficiently studied. With the end of the cold war and the demise of the USSR, Russia and the CIS entered into a long period of decline. Economies stagnated, political systems languished, and the pillars of superpower status—military capacities and advanced scientific and technological potential—rapidly ebbed away. Overnight, the CIS become less relevant and dynamic. The precipitously declining population rates in the Slavic heartland, a wholesale free-for-all of *mafiya*-led privatization, growing impoverishment, and failing public infrastructure, all made the distant promise of a knowledge revolution led by information technologies seem highly improbable.

Moreover, the prospects for Russia and the CIS keeping up with the Internet and telecom boom of the late 1990s and early 2000s seemed, for many, a distant reality. By the time the USSR finally collapsed in 1991, it had the lowest teledensity of any industrialized country. Its capacity for scientific development, particularly in the field of PCs (which the USSR had failed to develop) and computer networking (which was based on reverse-engineered systems pirated from European countries) was weak to nonexistent. Moreover, Russian seemed to be a declining culture and language as newly independent CIS countries adopted national languages and scripts, and preferred to send their youth to study at Western institutions. In almost every major indicator of economic progress, political reform, scientific research, and telecommunications capacity, the countries of the CIS seemed headed for the dustheap of history. Not surprisingly, scholarly and policy interest in the effects and impact of the information revolution in the CIS waned, as attention focused on the rising behemoths in Asia (particularly China and India), and the need and potential of bridging the *digital divide* in Africa and the Middle East. And yet, during the last decade the CIS has undergone a largely unnoticed information revolution. Between 2000 and 2008 the Russian portion of cyberspace, or RUNET, which encompasses the countries of the CIS, grew at an average rate of 7,208 percent, or over five times the rate of the next faster region (Middle East) and 15 times faster than Asia (see Table 2.2).

More than 55 million people are online in the CIS, and Russia is now the ninth-largest Internet country in terms of its percentage of world users, just ahead of South Korea.[4] By latest official estimates, 38 million Russians, or a third of the population of the Russian Federation, are connected, with over 60 percent of those surfing the Internet from home on broadband connections. And these figures may be low. Russian cyberspace also embraces the global Russian diaspora that, through successive waves of emigration, is estimated at above 27 million worldwide. Many Russian émigrés reside in developed countries, but tend to live *online* in the RUNET. Statistics to back this claim are methodologically problematic, but anecdotal evidence suggests that this is the case. The popular free mail service mail.ru, for example, boasts over 50 million user accounts, suggesting that the number of inhabitants in Russia cyberspace may be significantly above the 57 million users resident in the CIS. And these figures are

Table 2.2

	Population	Number of	Internet	Internet Growth
PROFILE OF INTERNET USE, PENETRATION, AND GROWTH IN THE CIS				
Country	(2008)	Internet Users	Penetration (2008)	(2000–2008)
Armenia	2,968,586	172,800	5.8%	476%
Azerbaijan	8,177,717	1,500,000	18.3%	12,400%
Belarus	9,685,768	2,809,800	29%	1,461%
Georgia	4,630,841	360,000	7.8%	1,700%
Kazakhstan	15,340,533	1,900,600	12.4%	2,615.1%
Kyrgyzstan	5,356,869	750,000	14%	1,353.5%
Moldova	4,324,450	700,000	16.2%	2,700%
Tajikistan	7,211,884	484,200	6.7%	24,110%
Turkmenistan	4,829,332	70,000	1.4%	3,400%
Russia	140,702,094	38,000,000	27%	1,125.8%
Ukraine	45,994,287	6,700,000	14.6%	3,250%
Uzbekistan	27,345,026	2,400,000	8.8%	31,900%
Totals	267,567,387	55,847,400	20% (average 13.5%)	7,208%

Source: Miniwatts Marketing Group, "Internet World Statistics, 2009," http://www.internetworldstats.com.

set to rise—dramatically. By official predictions, Russia's Internet population is set to double to over 80 million users by 2012.[5]

Paradoxically, the very *Russianness* of the RUNET may have contributed to hiding this "cyber revolution." Unlike much of the Internet, which remains dominated by English and dependent on popular applications and services that are provided by U.S.-based companies (such as Google, Yahoo, and Hotmail), RUNET is a self-contained linguistic and cultural environment with well developed and highly popular search engines, Web portals, social network sites, and free e-mail services. These sites and services are modeled on services available in the United States and the English-speaking world but are completely separate, independent, and only available in Russian.[6] In a recent ranking of Internet search engines, the Russian Web portal Yandex was one of only three non-English portals to make the top ten, and was only beaten out by a Baidu (China) and NHK (Korea), both of which have much larger absolute user base.[7] Within RUNET, Russian search engines dominate with Yandex (often called the Google of Russia), beating out Google with 70 percent of the market (Google has between 18 and 20 percent).[8]

The RUNET is also increasingly central to politics. Elections across the CIS are now fought online, as the Internet has eclipsed all the mass media in terms of its reach, readership, and especially in the degree of free speech and opportunity to mobilize that it provides. By 2008, Yandex could claim a readership larger than that of the popular mainstream newspapers *Izvestia, Komsomolskaya Pravda*, and *Moskovsky Komso-molets* combined.[9] The Russian-language *blogosphere*—which currently makes up 3 percent of the world's 3.1 million blogs—grows by more than 7,000 new blogs per day.[10] There are currently more Russian-language blogs than there are French, German, or Portuguese, and only marginally fewer than Spanish,[11] which is spoken by a larger percentage of the world population.[12]

This shift has been fueled as much by the growing state control over the traditional mass media as it has been by the draw of what the new online environment has to offer. Well-known journalists, commentators, and political figures have all turned to the RUNET as the off-line environment suffers through more severe restrictions and sanctions. Across the CIS, especially in the increasingly authoritarian countries of Uzbekistan, Belarus, and Kazakhstan, the RUNET has become the last and only refuge of public debate. Given its rapid ascent to the popular mainstream, it is paradoxical— and certainly a puzzle—that RUNET has elided filtering controls of the kind imposed by China on its Internet in all but a few countries. In the next section, we explore why that is the case.

Next-Generation Information Controls in the CIS

Although RUNET is a wild hive of buzzing online activity, it is not completely unregulated. Since its emergence in the early 1990s, RUNET has been subject to a variety of controls. Some controls have been commercial in motivation and represent crude attempts to use formal authority to create what amounts to a monopoly over secure communications and as means to seek rents.[13] This form of control has not been unique to RUNET and has extended to every other facet of post-Soviet life, from car registration through to the supply of gasoline, as an aspect of the great scramble to *prihvatizatsia* public assets that occurred during the early to mid 1990s.[14] Other controls have emerged from a legal system inherited from the Soviet era, which criminalized activities without necessarily seeking prosecution, except selectively. These forms of control effectively form the rules of the game for all informal networks. Their emergence in the virtual online world of the RUNET is transparent and natural.

But during the late 1990s, and especially following the color revolutions that swept through the CIS region, states began to think seriously about the security implications of RUNET, and in particular its potential to enable mobilization of mass social unrest. The first attempts at formally controlling cyberspace were legal, beginning with legislation enabling surveillance (SORM-II),[15] and later in 2001 with the publication of Russia's *Doctrine of Information Security*. While the doctrine addressed mass media and did not focus on RUNET specifically, it declared the information sphere to be a vital national asset that required state protection and policing. The doctrine used strong language to describe the state's right to guide the development of this space, as well as its responsibility to ensure that information space respects "the stability of the constitutional order, sovereignty, and the territorial integrity of Russian political, economic and social stability, the unconditional ensuring of legality, law and order, and the development of equal and mutually beneficial international cooperation."[16]

The intent of the doctrine was as much international as it was domestic, establishing demarcated borders in cyberspace, at least in principle. The international intent of the doctrine appears to have been driven by a growing concern that Russia was falling behind its major adversaries in developing a military capability in cyberspace; efforts by countries such as the United States, China, India, and others to develop covert computer network attack capabilities risked creating a strategic imbalance.[17] Domestically, the doctrine was aimed at the use of the Internet by militant groups to conduct information operations, specifically the Chechen insurgency. Within a few years, most other CIS countries had followed suit, adopting variations of the Russian doctrine.

ONI Tests for Internet Controls in RUNET

The controls outlined previously are qualitatively different from the usual types of controls for which the ONI tests. Establishing empirical evidence of the effects of policies like SORM and the Doctrine of Information Security is challenging, since their application is largely contextual, their impact at times almost metaphysical. Such controls do not yield a technological "fingerprint" in the way that a filtering system blocking access to Internet content does. However, they may be just as effective, if not more so, in achieving the same outcomes. In its 2007 study of the policy and practice of Internet filtering, the ONI found that substantial and pervasive attempts to technically filter content on RUNET did not begin until 2004, and even then were isolated to Turkmenistan and Uzbekistan, with lesser attempts at filtering found in most other CIS countries (see Table 2.3)[18]

These reports have remained consistent in more recent rounds of ONI tests. And yet persistent *anecdotal* reports, as well as special monitoring efforts mounted by the ONI, reveal in the majority of CIS countries that *information denial* and *access shaping* is occurring, and on a significant scale, especially around critical events such as elections. The ONI carried out a number of special investigations, including mounting monitoring efforts during the 2005 parliamentary elections in Kyrgyzstan[19] and the March 2006 Belarus presidential elections.[20] These efforts yielded the first technically verified results that the RUNET was being deliberately tampered with to achieve a political effect.

The results obtained by ONI in the CIS are unique, and they differ significantly from the results obtained in ONI's global survey. They demonstrate that information controls in the CIS have developed in different ways and using different techniques than those found in other areas of the world. They suggest a much more sophisticated approach to managing networks through denial that is highly selective and event based, and that *shapes* access to the sources of information and means of

Table 2.3

SUMMARY RESULTS FOR ONI TESTING FOR INTERNET FILTERING, 2007–2008				
	No Evidence	Suspected	Selective	Substantial	Pervasive
Armenia			•		
Azerbaijan			•		
Belarus			•		
Georgia			•		
Kazakhstan			•		
Kyrgyzstan			•		
Moldova	•				
Tajikistan			•		
Turkmenistan					•
Russia			•		
Ukraine	•				
Uzbekistan			•	•	

communication in a manner that could plausibly be explained by errant technical failures or other random network effects. In the following sections, we define the three different generations of cyberspace controls and provide examples for each from our research in the CIS region. The three generations of controls are also summarized in Table 2.4.

First-Generation Controls

First-generation controls focus on denying access to specific Internet resources by directly blocking access to servers, domains, keywords, and IP addresses. This type of filtering is typically achieved by the use of specialized software or by implementing instructions manually into routers at key Internet choke points. First-generation filtering is found throughout the world, in particular among authoritarian countries, and is the phenomenon targeted for monitoring by the ONI's methodology. In some countries, compliance with first-generation filtering is checked manually by security forces, who physically police cybercafés and ISPs.

In the CIS, first-generation controls are practiced on a wide scale only in Uzbekistan and Turkmenistan. In Uzbekistan, a special department of the SNB (KGB) monitors the Internet and develops block lists that are then conveyed to individual ISPs who in turn implement blocking against the specific resources or domain names. The filtering is universal across all ISPs, and the SNB spot-checks ISPs for compliance. In Turkmenistan, filtering is centralized on the country's sole ISP (operated by Turkmentelekom), and access is heavily filtered. Up until late 2007, Internet access in Turkmenistan was severely restricted and expensive, limiting its access and impact.

Table 2.4

SPECTRUM OF CYBERSPACE CONTENT CONTROLS IN THE CIS

	First Generation			Second Generation				Third Generation		
	Internet Filtering	Policing Cybercafés	Legal Environment for Information Control[1]	Informal Removal Requests	Technical Shutdowns	Computer Network Attack	Warrantless Surveillance	National Cyberzones	State-Sponsored Information Campaigns	Direct Action
Armenia			●	●	●	●[2]				
Azerbaijan			●	●		●[2]				●
Belarus	●		●	●	●	●	●	●	●	●
Georgia			●							
Kazakhstan	●		●	●				●	●	●
Kyrgyzstan			●	●		●[3]				
Moldova			●				●	●		
Tajikistan			●	●				●		
Turkmenistan	●	●	●					●		
Russia	●		●	●		●	●			●
Ukraine			●							●
Uzbekistan	●	●					●			

1. Legal and Normative Environment for Information Control includes the following:

a. Compelling Internet sites to register with authorities and using noncompliance as grounds for filtering "illegal" content.

b. Strict criteria pertaining to what is "acceptable" within the national media space, leading to the de-registration of sites that do not comply.

c. Expanded use of defamation, slander, and "veracity" laws to deter bloggers and independent media from posting material critical of the government or specific government officials.

d. Evoking national security concerns, especially at times of civic unrest, as the justification for blocking specific Internet content and services.

e. Legal regime for Internet surveillance.

2. CNA has been used by both Azeri and Armenian hackers in an ongoing series of attacks. It is unclear whether these are the actions of individual hackers, or whether these groups receive tacit or direct support from the state. Attacks are directed against the Web sites of the opposing country, so are not a content control mechanism.

3. The DDoS attacks were outsourced to commercial "black hat" hackers in Ukraine. The party ordering attacks is unknown, but suspicion falls on rogue elements inside the security services.

A second practice associated with first-generation blocking is policing and surveillance of Internet cafés. In Uzbekistan, SNB officers monitor Internet cafés, often enlisting café owners to notify them of individual users who try to access "banned" sites. Many Uzbek Internet cafés now openly post notices that viewing illegal sites is subject to fine and arrest. On several occasions, ONI researchers have manually verified the surveillance.

Second-Generation Controls

Second-generation controls aim to create a legal and normative environment and technical capabilities that enable state actors to deny access to information resources as and when needed, while reducing the possibility of blowback or discovery. Second-generation controls have an overt and a covert track. The overt track aims to legalize content controls by specifying the conditions under which access can be denied. Instruments here include the doctrine of information security as well as the application of existent laws, such as slander and defamation, to the online environment. The covert track establishes procedures and technical capabilities that allow content controls to be applied "just in time," when the information being targeted has the highest value (e.g., during elections or public demonstrations), and to be applied in ways that assure plausible deniability.

The legal mechanisms used by the overt track vary from country to country, but most share the characteristic of establishing double jeopardy for RUNET users, making requirements such that compliance sets the grounds for prosecution, and noncompliance establishes a legal basis for sanction.

The following are among the more common legal mechanisms being applied:

Compelling Internet sites to register with authorities and to use noncompliance as grounds for taking down or filtering "illegal" content, and possibly revoking service providers' licenses. This tack is effectively used in Kazakhstan and Belarus, and it is currently being considered in Russia. The mechanism is particularly effective because it creates multiple disincentives for potential Web site owners who must go through the hassle of registering with authorities, which leaves them open to legal sanction should their site be deemed to be carrying illegal content. It also creates double jeopardy for international content providers (such as the BBC, CNN, and others) and opens the question whether they should register their services locally. In practice, the registration requirement applies to them so long as their audience is local, and a failure to comply leaves open the option to filter their content for "noncompliance" with local registration requirements. On the other hand, registering would make the content they carry subject to local laws, which may deem their content "unacceptable" or "slanderous" and could lead to legally sanctioned filtering.

Strict criteria pertaining to what is "acceptable" within the national media space, leading to the de-registration of sites that do not comply. In Kazakhstan, opposition Web sites or Web sites carrying material critical of the government are regularly de-registered from the national domain. This includes a large number of opposition sites and, notably, the *Borat* Web site, ostensibly because the owners of the site were not resident in Kazakhstan as required by the Kazakh domain authority. In Belarus, the popular portal tut.by refused to put up banners advertising opposition Web sites, possibly for fear of reprisals (although those fears were not made explicit).[21]

Expanded use of defamation, slander, and "veracity" laws, to deter bloggers and independent media from posting material critical of the government or specific government officials, however benignly (including humor). In Belarus, slander laws were used to prosecute an owner of a Web site posting cartoons of the president. In both Belarus and Uzbekistan, the law on mass media requires that reporting passes the "objectivity test." Journalists and editors are held responsible for the "veracity" of publications and postings, leading to a high degree of self-censorship. In Kazakhstan, there are several cases of oppositional and independent media Web sites being suspended for providing links to publications about corruption among senior state offices and the president.

Evoking national security concerns, especially at times of civic unrest, as the justification for blocking specific Internet content and services. Most recently, this justification was evoked in Armenia when the opposition demonstrations that followed the February 2008 presidential elections turned to violence leading to the death and injury of several dozen protesters. A 20-day state of emergency was declared by President Kocharian, which also led to the de registration of popular Armenian political and news sites, including a site carrying the Armenian-language BBC service and the filtering of YouTube (ostensibly because of allegations that footage of the rioting had been posted to the popular video sharing site).[22] Similar filtering occurred during the Russian-Georgian crisis of 2008 when Georgia ordered ISPs to block access to Russian media. The blocks had the unintended consequence of creating panic in Tbilisi, as some Georgians perceived the blocks as a signal of impending Russian invasion of the capital.

The technical capabilities typical of second-generation controls are calibrated to effect "just-in-time" or event-based denial of selected content or services.[23] These techniques can be difficult to verify, as they can be made to look like technical errors. One of the more common techniques involves formal and informal requests to ISPs. Providers in the CIS are under constant pressure to comply with government requests or face any number of possible sanctions if they do not, from visits from the taxation police to revocations of their licenses. Such pressures make them vulnerable to requests from authorities, especially those that are conveyed informally. In Russia, top-level ISPs are in the hands of large telecommunication companies, such as Trans-TeleKom and Rostelecom, with strong ties to the government. These providers appear responsive to informal requests to make certain content inaccessible, particularly when information could prove embarrassing to the government or its officials. In one such case, the popular Russian site—Kompromat.ru—known for publishing documents and photographs of corrupt or illegal practices (roughly analogous to the Web site wikileaks.com) was de-registered or filtered by several top-level ISPs (including TransTeleKom and Rostelekom). Service was later restored, and the blocking of the site was deemed "accidental." Nonetheless, the Web site was inaccessible throughout the February 2008 Russian presidential poll.[24] Similar incidents have been documented in Azerbaijan, where Web sites critical of President Ilham Aliyev were filtered by ISPs, apparently at the request of the security department of the office of the president. [25] A similar dynamic is found in Kazakhstan, where a number of Web sites are inaccessible on a regular basis, with no official reason ever being given.[26]

Other, less subtle but nonetheless effective technical means include shutting down Internet access, as well as selected telecommunications services such as cell phone services and especially short message services (SMS). Temporary outages of the Internet and SMS services were employed by Belarus authorities during the February 2006 presidential elections as a means to limit the ability of the opposition to launch street demonstrations of the type that precipitated the color revolutions in Ukraine, Georgia, and Kyrgyzstan. At first, authorities denied that any interruptions had taken place, and later they attributed the failures to technical reasons.[27] Similar instances were reported (although not verified) to have occurred during the 2007 elections in Azerbaijan.

Second-generation techniques also make extensive use of computer network attacks, especially the use of distributed denial of service (DDoS) attacks, which can overwhelm ISPs and selected sites, and which make tracking down perpetrators difficult, since the attacks themselves are sold and engineered by "black hat hackers" and can be ordered by anyone. Such attacks were used extensively during the 2005 Kyrgyz presidential elections that precipitated the Tulip revolution.[28] They were also used during the 2006 Belarus elections against opposition political and news sites. In 2008, presidential and parliamentary elections in many parts of the region saw the significant use of DDoS attacks against the Web sites of major opposition leaders as well as prominent human rights groups. Recently, computer network attacks have been conducted by state-sanctioned "patriotic hackers" who act as vigilantes in cyberspace. A Russian hacker who admitted that officers from the FSB encouraged him brought down the pro-Chechen Web site "Kavkaz center" repeatedly.[29] There is strong suspicion that the May 2007 DDoS attacks that brought down most of Estonia's networks were the work of state-sanctioned "patriotic hackers" responding to unofficial calls from the FSB to "punish" Estonia over the removal of a monument to Soviet soldiers in Tallinn. Such attacks were also a prominent feature of the Russian-Georgian crisis of 2008. Several prominent investigations have been undertaken to determine attribution in this case—including an ongoing one by the ONI's sister project, the *Information Warfare Monitor*—and to date no definitive evidence has been found linking the attacks to the Russian security forces.

Third-Generation Controls

Unlike the first two generations of content controls, third-generation controls take a highly sophisticated, multidimensional approach to enhancing state control over national cyberspace and building capabilities *for competing in informational space* with potential adversaries and competitors. The key characteristic of third-generation controls is that the focus is less on *denying* access than successfully *competing* with potential threats through effective counterinformation campaigns that overwhelm, discredit, or demoralize opponents. Third-generation controls also focus on the active use of surveillance and data mining as means to confuse and entrap opponents.

Third-generation controls include enhancing jurisdiction over national cyberspace and expanding the powers of state surveillance. These include warrantless monitoring of Internet users and usage. In 2008, Russia expanded the powers previously established by SORM-II, which obliged ISPs to purchase and install equipment that would also permit local FSB offices to monitor the Internet activity of specific users. The new legislation makes it possible to monitor all Internet traffic and personal usage without specific warrants. The legislation effectively brings into the open covert powers that were previously assigned to FAPSI, with the twist of transferring to the ISPs the entire costs associated with installing the necessary equipment. The SORM-II law was widely used as a model for similar legislation in other CIS counties, and it is expected that the new law will likewise become a standard in the CIS. Although it is difficult to verify the use of surveillance in specific incidences, inferences can be drawn from specific examples. In July 2008, a Moldovan court ordered the seizure of the personal computers of 12 individuals for allegedly posting critical comments against the governing party. The people were accused of illegally inciting people "to overthrow the constitutional order" and "threaten the stability and territorial integrity of the Republic of Moldova." It is unknown how the authorities obtained the names of the people, but some suggest that an ISP provided them with the IP addresses of the users.[30]

Several CIS countries are also pursuing the creation of national cyberzones. Countries such as Kazakhstan, Tajikistan, and Russia are investing heavily into expanding Internet access to schools. These institutions are being tied to special Internet connections, which limit access only to resources found in the national Internet domain. These "national zones" are popular among some Tajik and Kazakh ISPs because they allow the ISPs to provide low-cost connectivity, as traffic is essentially limited to the national segment. In 2007, Russian authorities floated the idea of creating a separate Cyrillic cyberzone, with its own domain space and addressing scheme. National cyberzones are appealing because they strengthen the degree of national control over Internet content. They also appeal to consumers, since access to them is less costly and the resources that can be found there are almost exclusively in the local language.

Other aspects of third-generation controls, such as state-sponsored information campaigns in cyberspace, are difficult to document, as they use surveillance, interaction, and direct physical action to achieve a disruption of target groups or networks. The intent of these campaigns is to effect cognitive change rather than to deny access to online information or services. The ultimate source of these campaigns is also difficult to attribute and can only be established through careful research or insider knowledge, since they are designed to render opaque the role of state actors. These techniques include employing "Internet Brigades" to engage, confuse, or discredit individuals or sources. Such action can include the posting of prepackaged propaganda, *kompromat*, and disinformation through mass blogging and participation in Internet polls, or harassment of individual users, including the posting of personal information.[31] This technique, along with the use of surveillance of Internet traffic to affect direct action, saw a marked increase in the run-up to parliamentary and presidential polls in Russia. Numerous accounts allege that progovernment forces monitored opposition Web sites and disrupted planned rallies and marches. In some cases, members of the opposition were warned by cell phone not to participate in rallies or risk being beaten. In other cases, false information was disseminated by progovernment forces, leading to confusion among opposition supporters and, in one documented case, leading them into an ambush by progovernment supporters where several were severely beaten.

Assessing the Evolution of Next-Generation Controls in the CIS

The three generations of controls are not mutually exclusive, and several can exist concurrently. Taken together, they form a pattern of control that is both unique to each country and generalizable to the region as a whole. However, the degree to which a country is more or less authoritarian does seem to influence the choice of "generational mix" applied. Countries with stronger authoritarian tendencies tend to apply more comprehensive information controls in cyberspace, often using all three generations of controls. Conversely, countries that are "more democratic" tend to favor second- and third-generation strategies. None of the six countries scoring as "hybrid regimes" or "flawed democracies" applied first-generation controls (see Figure 2.1).

Several factors can explain this pattern. The most obvious explanation of the general tendency is that authoritarian states will seek to dominate the public sphere. These states tend to be the most vulnerable to mass unrest, prompting additional efforts by security forces to ensure that all channels of potential mobilization are controlled. A second factor worth noting is that these six counties are also experiencing the fastest rates of Internet growth and, with the exception of Belarus, have among the lowest

Less Authoritarian			First Generation	Second Generation	Third Generation
Ukraine	53	Flawed Democracy			
Moldova	62				
Georgia	104	Hybrid Regime			
Russia	107				
Armenia	113				
Kyrgyzstan	114				
Kazakhstan	127	Authoritarian			
Belarus	132				
Azerbaijan	135				
Tajikistan	150				
Uzbekistan	164				
Turkmenistan	165				

More Authoritarian

Figure 2.1

Spectrum of cyberspace content controls in the CIS (clustered by generation and EIU Index of Democracy)

Source: The Economist Intelligence Unit, "The Economist Intelligence Unit's Index of Democracy 2008," 2008, http://graphics.eiu.com/PDF/Democracy%20Index%202008.pdf.

levels of Internet penetration in the region. This latter explanation, which suggests that the RUNET in these counties has not become the locus for informal networks that it has in some of the less authoritarian countries, may make it more vulnerable and a target for filtering controls than what would be the case elsewhere in the CIS where the RUNET is more central to the political mainstream. In this respect, the maturity of the network itself seems to influence the degree to which filtering controls will be applied. This observation begs the obvious question—will the RUNET remain open even as countries in the CIS slide toward a new authoritarianism?

While the possibility of greater direct content controls being applied in the RUNET certainly exists, there is a far greater potential that information controls will continue to evolve along the evolutionary trajectory, toward strategies that seek to compete, engage, and dominate opponents in the informational battle space through persistent messaging, disinformation, intimidation, and other tactics designed to divide, confuse, and disable. In this respect, the patterns of information control in the CIS may in fact represent a model that will evolve elsewhere as governments are faced with the choice of imposing harsh controls and being labeled pariahs or doing nothing and risking that the technologies could become enablers of hyperdemocracy and undesired regime change.

Conclusion: Next-Generation Controls Beyond the CIS?

There are several obvious and not so obvious reasons to believe that second- and third-generation controls will become more common outside of the CIS and in fact may presage the future of cyberspace controls as a whole. First, the experience from other regions suggests that first-generation filtering is easy to circumvent. The "Great Firewall of China" is easily breached, as evidenced by the growing number of circumvention technology solutions, from Tor to Psiphon and others. As such techniques become more common, enabled and supported by large-scale and distributed efforts in the United States and Europe, the incentives to rely on less technologically static and temporally fixed methods characteristic of next-generation controls will likely grow.

It is also questionable whether first-generation controls in countries like Burma, North Korea, and China are really sustainable in the long run. In China's case, the floodgates may open sooner rather than later as the Chinese Internet itself becomes much more central to popular culture. First-generation filtering practices can produce economic and other social costs through collateral filtering and disincentives for foreign direct investment and tourism. As countries become more dependent on cyberspace for research, business, and other international communications, the friction introduced by filtering becomes increasingly unpopular, costly, and impractical.

More important than these factors, however, is the growing legitimization and frequent practice of policing the Internet through indirect and distributed means, and in particular through third parties, including the entities that actually support the cyberspace infrastructure, from connectivity to hosting to social networking platforms. Since much of cyberspace is operated by the private sector, there are practical and legal limits to the direct reach of government controls. Controls have thus evolved downward and in a distributed fashion, in a significant privatization of authority, in conformity with second- and third-generation controls outlined previously. Naturally, the scope for second- and third-generation controls differs among authoritarian and democratic countries, but examples of each can be found in both contexts.

In China, for example, while much of the attention focuses on the technologies of the Great Firewall of China filtering access to the Internet, at least as much, if not more, of the information controls exercised in that country happen in a more distributed fashion and by private actors. Web hosting and social networking services are now routinely obliged to sign self-discipline pacts and follow rigid hosting protocols that limit what can be communicated online; search engines—including those owned by American companies like Google, Microsoft, and Yahoo!—routinely filter their search results, often more aggressively than the government does itself; and in the most extreme example, volunteer citizen groups—sometimes known in China as *50 cent brigades* for the amount they are purportedly paid for each post—swarm the Internet's chat rooms, blogs, and other public forums making statements favorable to the government.[32] The latter was dramatically demonstrated, in a clear example of third-generation controls, during the time of the Olympics, when thousands of Chinese bloggers posted aggressively to counter what they perceived as anti-Chinese propaganda.[33] Whether the volunteer posts were managed or encouraged by the state, or simply benefited the state coincidentally, or some combination, is a vexing question nearly impossible to untangle. Such attribution problems are, in fact, one of the key characteristics of second- and third-generation controls and one of their greatest challenges for research projects like the ONI.

Outside of authoritarian contexts and among democratic countries, it is now common to hear of legal and market pressures being invoked to remove content from Web hosting and social networking platforms, and there is also a very noticeable trend to offload policing activities to ISPs, particularly in the areas of content controls around pornography, hate speech, and copyright violations. In fact, most industrialized democratic countries have passed far-reaching surveillance measures that enable widespread eavesdropping on e-mail, cellular phone, and other communications activities by requiring ISPs to retain and, when required, turn over such information to legal authorities.

Perhaps the strongest impetus toward second- and third-generation controls has emerged from a growing emphasis on cyber security and the recognition of cyberspace as a domain of military action. Military actors have come to understand cyberspace as a domain equal in importance to land, air, sea, and space, requiring a full spectrum of capabilities. This has meant developing weapons and tactics designed to disrupt, destroy, and confuse potential adversaries. For the most part, these capabilities have been kept quiet and under classification, but they are similar in intent and execution to the network attacks characteristic of second-generation information controls. Russia, China, and the United States have all developed doctrines and capabilities for operations in cyberspace that include computer network attacks, as well as psychological operations designed to shape the domain through selective filtering, denial of access to information, and information engagement. The intent and effect of these emerging doctrines is the same as those we have documented in second- and third-generation controls in the CIS—to silence information that is strategically threatening and sow confusion and doubt among opponents dependent on cyberspace for information and organization.

Overall, the lexicon of cyber security is shifting norms around acceptable behavior for intervention into cyberspace and generating new incentives for technological development. Pervasive surveillance, including deep packet inspection, is now an acceptable part of compliance with good security practices, despite the impacts on privacy protections. Similarly, the political rush to secure cyberspace is generating economic opportunities not seen since the Internet boom of the 1990s. However, unlike the 1990s when the rush was led by companies seeking to open up cyberspace, the current momentum is in the other direction. The fact that defense contractors are now lining up to compete in this domain only raises the troubling concerns that some of the valuable freedoms gained over the last 15 years in cyberspace will be sacrificed at the altar of security.

These are troubling tendencies, and ones with implications far outside of the democratic countries of the OSCE. The confluence of second- and third-generation controls, the militarization of cyberspace, and the legitimization of surveillance are contributing to a dangerous brew. The cyberspace enjoyed by the next generation of users may be a very different, more regulated, and less empowering domain than that which was taken for granted in the past.

Notes

1. The Economist Intelligence Unit, *The Economist Intelligence Unit's Index of Democracy 2008* (The Economist, 2008), http://graphics.eiu.com/PDF/Democracy%20Index%202008.pdf.

2. Radio Free Europe, "Putin Quizzed by Internet Users," July 6, 2006, http://www.rferl.org/featuresarticle/2006/07/40C4C298-C619-4FCC-9D9D-D24787E10EAB.html.

3. "When did you start to have sex?" asked Kommersant reporter Andrei Kolesnikov on behalf of 5,640 Internet users. "I don't remember when I started. But I can remember the last time," Putin replied. *St Petersburg Times*, "Putin Weighs In on Robots, Sex Following Internet Conference," July 11, 2006, http://www.sptimes.ru/index.php?action_id=2&story_id=18178.

4. As of March 31, 2009, the top five countries with the highest number of Internet users, in order are China, United States, Japan, India, and Brazil. See Miniwatts Marketing Group, "Top 20 Countries with the Highest Number of Internet Users," March 31, 2009, http://www.internetworldstats.com/top20.htm.

5. Between 2005 and 2007 Internet use in the Russian Federation jumped from 15% to over 28% of the population.

6. Popular sites include rutube, a Russian version of the popular U.S. site YouTube, as well as the social network sites odnoklassniki.ru and vkontakte.ru, which are modeled after Classmates.com and Facebook.com.

7. China has an estimated 298 million Internet users, while Korea possesses over 48 million users and a 76.1 percent Internet penetration. Miniwatts Marketing Group, "Top 20 Countries with Highest Number of Internet Users," March 31, 2009, http://www.internetworldstats.com/top20.htm.

8. More significant yet than its impressive growth has been the emergence of RUNET at the center of Russian popular culture. Internet memes and jokes once marginalized to the community of computer specialists and aficionados are now in the mainstream of popular culture. For example, *Preved Medved*, an allusion to primitive cartoon of a bear surprising a couple having sex in a field and shouting *preved* (a deliberate misspelling of *privet*—a greeting, and *medved*—bear) has become a cultural icon, showing up on the cover of mainstream journals, in advertisements, and even, as a joke, in a question put to President Putin. Similarly, the *Olbanian* language, once an obscure Internet in-joke is now mainstream enough to have warranted a joke by President-elect Medvedev, who, when asked whether it should become a school subject, replied, "One cannot ignore the

necessity of learning the Olbanian language." The slang it inspired has also led to political neo-logisms, such as *Putings*, which refers to political meetings in support of former President Putin, and whose usage on-air (as opposed to online) landed a Russian TV journalist a stiff fine.

9. LiveInternet, "Report: From Search Engines, 2009," http://www.liveinternet.ru/stat/ru/searches.html?slice-ru.

10. Nick Wilsdon, "Yandex Releases Autumn Report on Russian Blogosphere," Multilingual Search, November 12, 2007, http://www.multilingual-search.com/yandex-releases-autumn-report-on-russian-blogosphere/12/11/2007.

11. Yandex, "*Sostoyaniye Blogosfery Rossiykogo Interneta*," [The State of the Russian Blogosphere], 2007, http://download.yandex.ru/company/yandex_on_blogosphere_autumn_2007.pdf.

12. Raymond Gordon, Jr., ed., *Ethnologue: Languages of the World*, 15th ed. (Dallas: SIL International, 2005).

13. For example, in mid-1995 the Federal Agency for Communication and Information (FAPSI) announced a joint venture with Relcom to create a secure business network. But FAPSI's interests in Relcom had less to do with security than with its growing business interests. FAPSI recognized that the Internet was becoming an important channel for business transactions. It wanted part of this market. Its intervention was part of a broader effort aimed at using its special position with respect to responsibility for state communications and security as means to seek rents from Russian and foreign businesses. By the time the Relcom deal had been announced, FAPSI had already secured legislation that required all use of cryptography in Russia to be licensed by FAPSI. Similarity, it had won the exclusive right to produce smart cards for the Russian market. Both moves had essentially given it a monopoly over the critical technologies required by the banking sector in Russia, as well as a future stake in all e-commerce. FAPSI was also present in the telecommunications market more broadly. The legislation creating Sviazinvest, the state-dominated holding company that owned shares in Russian telecommunications companies, required that senior officers from the service were present on the board of every major telecommunications player. Before long, the boards of most telecommunications companies were filling up with retired ex-FAPSI generals. In 1997 the FAPSI–Relcom deal collapsed, as the agency itself was disbanded over allegations of corruption by its leadership. Its assets, which included most of Russia's signal intelligence capacity, were reabsorbed into the FSB. But by that time, Relcom's dominance of the Internet market in Russia and the CIS was on the wane. The Internet was becoming a profitable business, and telecom operators where quickly entering the Internet market and putting former Relcom nodes out of business.

14. The term "prihvatizatsia" is slang, and a neologism of the Russian word for "theft" and the English term "privatize."

15. See the Russia country profile in this volume.

16. Security Council of the Russian Federation, *Information Security Doctrine of the Russian Federation*, 2000, http://www.scrf.gov.ru/documents/5.html.

17. Two years prior to the publication of this doctrine, Russia began actively working through the UN to establish an arms control regime in cyberspace. A. A. Streltsov, "International Information Security: Description and Legal Aspects," *Disarmament Forum* 3 (2007), 5–13.

18. Ronald J. Deibert, John Palfrey, Rafal Rohozinski, and Jonathan Zittrain, eds., *Access Denied: The Practice and Policy of Global Internet Filtering* (Cambridge, MA: MIT Press, 2008).

19. OpenNet Initiative, "Special Report: Kyrgyzstan," April 15, 2005, http://opennet.net/special/kg/.

20. OpenNet Initiative, "The Internet and Elections: The 2006 Presidential Election in Belarus (and Its Implications)," April 2006, http://opennet.net/sites/opennet.net/files/ONI_Belarus_Country_Study.pdf.

21. Mikhail Doroshevich, "Major Belarusian Internet Portal TUT.BY Introduces Restrictions for Internet Forums," E-Belarus.Org, June 28, 2005, http://www.e-belarus.org/news/200506281.html.

22. OpenNet Initiative Blog, "Armenia Imposes Internet Censorship as Unrest Breaks Out Following Disputed Presidential Elections," March 11, 2008, http://opennet.net/blog/2008/03/armenia-imposes-internet-censorship-unrest-breaks-out-following-disputed-presidential-e.

23. Ronald J. Deibert and Rafal Rohozinski, "Good for Liberty, Bad for Security? Global Civil Society and the Securitization of the Internet," in *Access Denied: The Practice and Policy of Global Internet Filtering*, ed. Ronald J. Deibert, John Palfrey, Rafal Rohozinski, and Jonathan Zittrain (Cambridge, MA: MIT Press, 2008), 123–149.

24. As reported by ONI field researchers.

25. See the Azerbaijan country profile in this volume.

26. Reuters, "Kazakh Bloggers Say Can't Access Popular Website," October 10, 2008, http://ca.reuters.com/article/technologyNews/idCATRE4995D020081010.

27. OpenNet Initiative, "The Internet and Elections: The 2006 Presidential Election in Belarus (and Its Implications)," April 2006, http://opennet.net/sites/opennet.net/files/ONI_Belarus_Country_Study.pdf.

28. OpenNet Initiative, "Special Report: Kyrgyzstan," April 15, 2005, http://opennet.net/special/kg/.

29. John Varoli, "In Bleak Russia, a Young Man's Thoughts Turn to Hacking," New York Times, June 29, 2000, http://www.nytimes.com/2000/06/29/technology/in-bleak-russia-a-young-man-s-thoughts-turn-to-hacking.html."

30. Sami Ben Gharbia, "Moldavia: Sequestration of Personal Computers of 12 Young People for Posting Critical Comments Online," Global Voices Advocacy, June 13, 2008, http://advocacy.globalvoicesonline.org/2008/06/13/moldavia-destruction-of-personal-computers/.

31. Anna Polyanskaya, Andrei Krivov, and Ivan Lomko, "Commissars of the Internet: The FSB at the Computer," Vestnik Online, April 30, 2003, http://www.vestnik.com/issues/2003/0430/win/polyanskaya_krivov_lomko.htm.

32. David Bandurski, "China's Guerrilla War for the Web," *Far Eastern Economic Review*, July 2008, http://www.feer.com/essays/2008/august/chinas-guerrilla-war-for-the-web.

33. See the China country profile in this volume.

3   The EU Data Retention Directive in an Era of Internet Surveillance

Hal Roberts and John Palfrey

Introduction

The European Union (EU) enacted a directive on data retention in 2007 that requires all member countries to mandate the retention by telecom companies of the sender, recipient, and time of every Internet or other telecom communication. The directive requires the collection of the Internet Protocol (IP) address, user ID, phone number, name, and address of every sender and recipient, but explicitly excludes (but does not forbid) the monitoring of content itself. All the monitored data must be retained for a period ranging between six months and two years, contingent upon the local law of each member state. Telecom companies must promptly give these data to law enforcement authorities upon request to assist with serious crimes, overseen by a national public authority monitoring the data retention practices.[1] As of its effective date of April 2009, all Internet service providers (ISPs) in EU countries must comply with the relevant national implementations of the directive.

The monitoring required by the EU data retention directive amounts to a form of surveillance. The directive does not take the form of surveillance that most quickly leaps to mind: the two men in a van with headphones listening to phone conversations of an unwitting crook in a seedy apartment. But it has functional similarities. The directive requires that the participating states collect personal data about their citizens without the citizens' consent. It enables states to use these data to control some of the subjects of monitoring (including by arresting them). What matters most about the directive and its relationship to surveillance is its impact on citizen activity and its place in the growing constellation of surveillance activities online.

The Internet is a "surveillance-ready" technology. There is a wide range of choices for any state that wishes to know more about its citizens. This digital information comes in the form of bits of data that flow through rivers and into oceans of data. These rivers are full of information that passes by a given point, or series of points, in a network and can be intercepted; these oceans are stocked with information that can be searched after the fact; and the rivers arise from springs that can be watched at the source. The data involved are held in private hands as well as public.

This chapter paints a simplified picture of the technical landscape of Internet surveillance, as well as the place of the EU data retention directive within that landscape, by taking up a series of short cases about surveillance. We examine how these cases inform (and are informed by) the technical questions of what *data* are being *actually* and *potentially* monitored on the Internet and whom we are *trusting* to access that data.

We break Internet surveillance into three broad categories: network, server, and client. The Internet is composed of clients and servers, in essence a series of devices that talk to one another through the network. Every bit of data on the Internet is traveling or residing at one or more of these locations at any given time. As such, any given Internet activity must happen at one (or more) of these locations. We treat any surveillance happening on the end user device as client-side surveillance, including both software tools like workplace keylogging systems and hardware tools like keyboard tapping devices. We treat any surveillance happening on a machine that predominantly accepts requests, processes them, and returns responses as server-side surveillance. And for simplicity, we treat everything between the client and the server as the network, including the wires over which the data travel and the routers that direct the traffic.

We argue in this chapter that the EU data retention directive introduces new risks related to the networks of trust created by each category of surveillance. In the section on network surveillance we argue that trust can only be rerouted around the network, rather than removed from it, and that the EU data retention directive may cause users to reroute trust in the network in ways that both reduce the amount of useful data available to law enforcement and encourage users to expose more of their network data to non-EU states. In the section on server surveillance we argue that users struggle to evaluate how the data they submit to servers are used and combined and that the EU data retention directive is likely to increase this problem by requiring ISPs to store more server data (which will be used and combined in ways opaque to most users). In the section on client surveillance we argue that the client has become an intensely complicated battleground of trust played out by sophisticated actors with their own agendas, resulting in widespread leaks of data from the client. This section argues that the EU data retention directive will place a large new set of private data onto this battleground—to the detriment of people from around the world.

Network Surveillance

The most obvious kind of Internet surveillance takes place on the network between the clients and servers. Government agencies collect data from within network ISPs, including not only wiretap-like data about specific subjects with warrants but also entire streams of data for mining without judicial oversight. But the network is a diverse place. There are a wide variety of different actors with different access to data. As a result, there are a wide variety of other cases of network surveillance: about users who try to get around surveillance but end up exposing themselves to different sorts of surveillance in unexpected ways, about the collection of extensive user data without meaningful consent for targeted advertising, and about how criminal organizations exploit the trust model of the network to facilitate illegal surveillance.

The U.S. Communications Assistance for Law Enforcement Act (CALEA) requires that telecommunications companies have the ability to respond quickly and fully to wiretap requests even when using the newly digital telephone switches. The current interpretation of this law includes not only traditional telephone service but also Internet telephone services like Skype and, pending a ruling by the Federal Communications Commission, maybe even sender and recipient data for all Internet traffic. Such a ruling would render CALEA in a sense analogous to the EU data retention directive. The FCC has ruled that ISPs can forward their entire data stream to independent "trusted third parties" to handle the wiretapping implementation, exposing data streams of entire ISPs to these third parties.[2]

More intrusively, the National Security Agency (NSA) is apparently mining the full stream of data passing through major ISP backbones in the United States.[3] There are limits to our understanding, as laypersons, of this process, for obvious national security reasons. We know that the equipment used for this surveillance is capable of executing highly sophisticated queries on the data passing through the backbone. We know that the NSA is engaged in some level of warrantless surveillance of the international communications of U.S. citizens, but we do not know precisely what is being done with the data.[4] We are left with indeterminate, circumstantial evidence about the existence and function of the surveillance that leaves unanswerable questions about what data the NSA is making available to whom.

Relakks is one of many proxy tools available on the Internet that encrypts and reroutes traffic to avoid monitoring or filtering by anyone, such as the NSA, monitoring the user's local ISP. When someone in China uses Relakks to request a page from the BBC, the connection goes from the user's ISP in China to Relakks in Sweden (where Relakks is hosted) and then from Relakks in Sweden to the BBC in Britain (and back along the same route). The Chinese ISP can only see a connection to Relakks in Sweden, hiding the ultimate destination of the request (and bypassing any filtering as well). But in 2008, Swedish lawmakers authorized the the Försvarets Radioanstalt (FRA), or National Defense Radio Establishment, a government agency responsible for signals intelligence, to monitor the content of all international Internet and phone traffic (including that of Relakks) without a warrant, requiring all Swedish ISPs to install FRA monitoring equipment.[5] Now, Relakks users (at least, those who do not follow Swedish politics) are unwittingly handing their complete Internet data streams over to the Swedish government as they seek to avoid monitoring on their own local networks.

Users have reason to be concerned about forms of surveillance on their local networks beyond government monitoring. In June and July of 2007, several British Telecom (BT) Internet customers noticed strange problems with their Internet connections that they tracked down to a spyware company, 121media.[6] BT insisted that it had nothing to do with the suspicious behavior, and 121media refused to comment on the grounds of customer (BT's) privacy.[7] But in 2008, 121media, renamed Phorm, publicly announced a deal with BT to target advertising at the ISP's customers.[8] Phorm soon afterward admitted, in response to media reports of the 2007 activity related to 121media and BT, that it had already tried its targeted advertising on tens of thousands of users on the BT network with BT's help but without the knowledge of the users.[9] Phorm claims that it does not store any personally identifying information or browsing histories in the process of targeting ads; Phorm says it only stores information about the kinds of sites each user visits (expensive cars, rugby sites, and so on) connected to the user only by a randomly generated unique ID.[10] Privacy advocates have reacted strongly against Phorm's announcement and justifications, but BT continues to push for a full rollout of the system.[11]

As with the Relakks case, user efforts to circumvent network monitoring can have unpredictable results on the network of trusted relationships that tie together Internet activity. In February 2008, a Pakistani ISP responded to a government request to ban a video on YouTube.com by (probably accidentally) blocking a majority of the entire Internet from accessing the whole site for a few hours.[12] During the few days Pakistan was blocking YouTube.com locally, many Pakistanis bypassed the block using a tool called Hotspot Shield.[13] AnchorFree describes Hotspot Shield as a privacy tool: "You remain anonymous and protect your privacy."[14] But AnchorFree makes money by injecting ads into Web pages, and users of the tool give AnchorFree complete access to all data exchanged while Web browsing with the tool. AnchorFree implies (but never explicitly says) that it does not monitor its users' traffic, but it nonetheless has both the ability to snoop on the data at any time and a business model based on processing user data for advertisers. Thus, Pakistan is monitoring its citizens' Internet traffic to block content it does not like, and citizens are accessing the blocked content by using a tool that circumvents Pakistan's filters. But the circumvention tool is at least potentially just a monitoring tool for the different purpose of advertising.

To make sense of these cases, we need to understand what data are available on the network and to whom they are accessible. Three sorts of data are vulnerable to surveillance on the network: routing information, the actual content of the data stream, and contextual signatures. All Internet data packets must include the IP address of the ultimate recipient, and most data packets (including all Web and e-mail traffic) also include the IP address of the sender. Users can hide routing information on the network by using proxies, like Relakks or HotSpot Shield, which forward communication between a client and a server. In addition to the routing data, the packets contain both protocol-specific data (data about the URL requested, the referring URL, the user agent, and so on for Web requests; data about the originating e-mail server, the "from:" e-mail address, the date, and so on for e-mails) and the content proper of the communication. This content includes, but is not limited to, any data submitted to Web sites, any Web pages retrieved, and any e-mails sent or received.

Users can encrypt the content of their network communications to hide their activities from network monitoring. Encryption is most effective when it is applied end-to-end, as by using Hypertext Transfer Protocol Secure (HTTPS). In this case, the entire stream of data from the client to the server is encrypted, allowing no one on the network between the sender and the receiver to read the content. But end-to-end encryption has to be supported by both the client and the server, and many servers do not support encrypted communication at all or for all pages. In these cases, a user can connect through a proxy like Relakks or HotSpot Shield to encrypt the data from the client to the proxy. But such encrypting proxies still use unencrypted channels to talk to servers that do not support encryption. As a result, the proxied content remains readable to any intervening routers on the network. For instance, even though content between Relakks and the user is encrypted, the requests and responses between Relakks and Google.com are not encrypted.

These apparently secure connections between Internet users leak other, contextual forms of information as well. The information about those requests and responses—think of it as "metadata" to the "data" of the communication itself—can be observed by anyone on the network in between. Communications that are both encrypted and proxied can hide both the routing information for, and the content of, a communication from the network between the client and the proxy. But even proxied and encrypted data leaks some of its metadata: information about the timing, number, and size of the packets as well as the fact that the communication is proxied and encrypted, may be observed. Different sorts of traffic generate different signatures of packet size and timing that can allow easy identification of the nature of the communication. These signature-based monitoring methods have reportedly been used, for example, to block proxied file-sharing traffic.

The Internet consists of billions of links between clients, servers, and routers, making comprehensive surveillance of the entire network very difficult. But in practice, all Internet traffic flows through a much smaller number of links between routers, and those routers are controlled by a much smaller yet number of autonomous systems (ASs). These ASs are the independent entities (mostly ISPs) that have the ability to route traffic on the Internet. There are fewer than 100,000 of these ASs in the world. In practice, the vast majority of Internet traffic flows through an even much smaller number of those ASs. For instance, virtually all 300 million Internet users in China connect to the Internet through only five big ISP ASs.[15] For a combination of technical, business, and policy reasons, a disproportionate amount of global Internet traffic flows through a few very large ASs in the United States, including most traffic between Europe and Asia.[16] Traffic between ASs within a given country (or sometimes even a given city) often flows through an Internet exchange point (IXP), a physical network node that connects geographically close ASs. There are fewer than 200 major IXPs in the world, which together carry much of the Internet's local traffic.[17] IXPs keep local traffic local, so unlike the ASs responsible for routing intracountry and intracontinental traffic, most IXPs are located in (and therefore potentially under the jurisdictional control of) the country whose traffic they carry.

This topology of the Internet has several implications for the actors trusted with access to Internet data. The first is that a large majority of users need to access the Internet through an AS (usually an ISP). The situation should be familiar by now: data from these users is therefore vulnerable to surveillance by someone controlling that AS. The second is that there are a relatively small number of these ASs within any given country and an even smaller number of IXPs, so monitoring all the network traffic in a given country is a manageable task of making the small number of ASs and IXPs monitor their networks (though some of these ASs can be big complex organizations in themselves). This rule applies doubly for international Internet traffic, which is controlled by an even smaller number of ASs disproportionately located in the United States.[18] And the United States is capable of monitoring a large portion of international Internet traffic through a few ASs based in the United States, including even traffic flowing between non-U.S. countries.

A user can move her trust around from provider to provider. In the end, though, she must ultimately trust someone on the network (barring the unlikely event of widespread adoption of end-to-end encryption of networked digital communications). In practice, almost every user of digital networked technologies ends up trusting more actors over time. A user who tries to get around surveillance of her local ISP connection, for instance by Phorm, has only a few choices of ISPs in the United Kingdom, most of whom have been reported to be considering adding Phorm monitoring to their networks. A user may choose to stay on the possibly monitored local network but use a service like Relakks to proxy and encrypt her data as it travels through the local, Phorm monitoring, ISP. The user will avoid Phorm monitoring in the process, but at the cost of trusting not only Relakks but also the Swedish ISP through which Relakks talks to the Internet *and* the Swedish government that monitors the data flowing through all Swedish ISPs. And her local ISP will still be able to tell that she is proxying and encrypting all her data through a third party, which fact itself might prove suspicious to a law enforcement agency. Finally, the user's data are vulnerable to network monitoring at any point along which they travel, from her local ISP to the server's ISP to any ISPs between. A portion of her data is likely to travel outside of Europe through one of a few ISPs in the United States that process a disproportionate share of international Internet traffic.

Against the backdrop of these forms of network surveillance, we can see that the EU data retention directive has the potential to distort the network of trust through which Internet data flows. The precise effects of these distortions are difficult to predict. Some number of EU users may react to the increased monitoring by using encrypted proxies in non-EU countries to avoid local ISP surveillance, maybe to hide illegal activity but maybe to hide legal but sensitive personal activity. The directive may encourage these proxy users to route their connections through non-EU countries to avoid the data retention mandate altogether.

The net effect of this process may very well be that law enforcement has less access to useful data. Likewise, smart users may proxy their data through autocratic countries like China that are least likely to share data with EU countries to avoid monitoring by another EU country compliant with the data retention directive. If enough users resist monitoring through the use of proxies, ISPs will be pressured to try to block such proxied traffic. If ISPs were to take this step, they would likely start an arms race between proxy tools and proxy blocking tools analogous to the current arms race between malware and antivirus software (as has happened in China with its attempts to block filtering circumvention tools). This arms race could further strain the network through the same sort of knock-on effects of the malware arms race: users wanting to avoid monitoring would become increasingly dependent on increasingly sophisticated anonymizing tools and therefore become increasingly vulnerable to the developers of such tools (some with good, some with bad intentions as with the current developers of antivirus tools). We have already seen this process with music downloading tools, which have become a vector for malware infections as the music industry has driven them underground.[19]

The popularity of tools that circumvent various sorts of filtering of music downloading tools points to the possibility that large numbers of users will attempt to route around the monitoring, particularly if authorities brand illegal music downloading a "serious crime." But users also have a tendency to accept gradual erosions of privacy without resorting to resistance.[20] Even relatively small-scale usage of proxy tools could have the strong effect of making those few users very susceptible to false suspicion by law enforcement authorities. Given the widespread availability of proxying tools and widespread publication of the EU data retention directive, it seems safe to assume that many of the most serious criminals will use such tools, reducing the effectiveness of the monitoring of such users. Internet service providers can use contextual information about connections to detect the use of proxies and will be tempted to track which users are resisting monitoring. This possibility raises the risk that merely resisting monitoring will label a user as suspicious.

Server Surveillance

As with the network, the collection of data on Internet servers is highly concentrated among a few big actors. Even though there are hundreds of millions of servers on the Internet, a few large entities like Google, Yahoo, Facebook, and Wikipedia capture a large proportion of Internet traffic. Virtually all these big sites collect data about their users. For example, Google and Yahoo collect search queries (among many other sorts of data), Facebook collects the social maps of its users, Wikipedia collects the editing histories of its users, and so forth. The collection of these sorts of data does not look like the typical Internet surveillance performed by the NSA and other government actors, but it represents a second type of surveillance on the network, equivalent in scope to the collection of data flowing across the network.

Google in particular (but not alone) has collected a tremendously large and intrusive amount of personal data about its users through the operation of its various services. Google argues that users should not be overly concerned about Google's data collection: "we remember some basic information about searches. Without this information, our search engine wouldn't work as well as it does or be as secure. [What this information] doesn't tell Google is personal stuff about you like where you live and what your phone number is.... Logs don't contain any truly personal information about you."[21]

User search data surely help in the way Google says they do ("improve our search results," "maintain security," and "prevent fraud"). And their explanations of the privacy implications of the data usage of Google's engineers are accurate in a narrowly technical sense. But the importance of data is determined by the larger world in which it exists—by the other data that it connects to. Google's statement that a cookie does not tell them "personal stuff about you like where you live" is only true in the narrow sense that your driver's license number does not tell the police where you live. Even though the cookie itself is just a random string of gibberish letters, it can indeed be used to look up personal information "like where you live." For example, the cookie connects to all searches performed by a single person. Many people search for their own names at some point and for their own addresses at some point (if for no other reason than to see their houses in Google Maps). The cookie connects those two searches to the same (otherwise anonymous) person, thus potentially identifying the name and address of the person behind the random gibberish of a particular cookie. Researchers have consistently shown the ability to crack the identity of individual users in these kinds of data collections with anonymous but individually unique identifiers.[22]

It is likely that Google's collection of search terms, IP addresses, and cookies represents one of the largest and most intrusive single collections of personal data online or off-line. Google may or may not choose to do the relatively easy work necessary to translate its collection of search data into a database of personally identifiable data, but it does have the data and the ability to query personal data out of the collection at will. Even assuming perfect security to prevent data leaks, Google is still subject to many sorts of government requests for its data. Witness, for instance, the success of Viacom in subpoenaing the complete log of every video ever viewed on YouTube.com (which is owned by Google) in the context of copyright litigation.[23]

In addition to its search engine, Google's AdWords displays ads on about 35 percent of all advertising Web pages.[24] Google logs instances of consumers clicking on ads through its AdWords system and watches the advertisers through AdWords auctions that determine the value of advertising topics. Content providers track the value of those advertising topics to determine which sorts of content to publish. The advertisers use the AdWords system as a stateless form of market research to target consumers without knowing anything about them. Content providers watch consumers to determine which sorts of content generate the most interest. All this monitoring happens in real time. Google adjusts the placement of ads in real time according to the current results of an ad auction; content providers watch the profitability of their content in real time and make adjustments to attract more ad-clicking customers; advertisers adjust their bids and update their ads in real time to attract more users. The effect of the system is continuous but stateless market research that is constantly adjusting to the current interests of users rather than the historical interests over time tracked by user profiling organizations like comScore, Phorm, and NebuAd.

Google and other service providers only have access to data that is sent directly to them over the network: the client address, the request itself, and any content explicitly submitted by the user. All these server-collected data, other than the client address, may be encrypted while traveling over the network, giving the end server access to some data that are not available on the network. For Web servers, the protocol data may include cookies, which are often used to assign a pseudonymous identity that persists between separate requests. Users voluntarily (and knowingly, at least in theory) submit vast amounts of such data to Internet servers. Users are aware that they are submitting names, addresses, and credit card numbers to Amazon when buying merchandise, personal e-mail to Microsoft through Hotmail, and movie preferences to Netflix when renting videos.

What determines the risk of privacy intrusions—and what ties this case to the narrative of online surveillance—is not just the collection of data but rather what the actors controlling the servers do with the data, with whom they share the data, and how the data are combined with other data. The act of collecting a credit card number to execute a purchase for a user is presumably acceptable and necessary in the modern global economy. But using the credit card number to request data about a user's purchase history from the credit card company in order to target advertising at him may not be so acceptable. Likewise, it is fine for Microsoft to collect personal e-mails through Hotmail, but it would become a concern if Microsoft were to sell its users' e-mail content to a consumer research company. And Netflix seems innocuous when using video preference information for its own recommendation engine, but many users would be uncomfortable if they found out Netflix was combining its users' video rental history with (even public) information from users' social networking pages to make video recommendations.

The issue of combining data is particularly relevant (but not unique) to server-based surveillance because, in comparison to network and client surveillance, the domain of the data collected is generally much more limited. However, these domains of data can almost always be combined either with themselves or with other domains to create a much more personal, intrusive set of combined data—for instance, by combining the Google search data with the Google search cookies to identify users by cookie, or by combining the Google search IP addresses with ISP logs (as required by the EU data retention directive) to identify users by IP address.

All these different possible uses and combinations of data represent networks of trust. A rational user ought to evaluate these decisions about trust carefully, though in practice few have the time to do so with any level of sophistication. The example of Google demonstrates the complexity of these issues of trust—about how data are collected, who has access to it, and what is done with it. Google is collecting vast amounts of information from users in ways that are not clear to most users, yet most users eagerly accept the arrangement that Google offers them. Most users presumably understand that they are giving Google access to their search terms, but some may not understand that Google is storing these data. Yet other users are likely not to understand that Google generates its revenue through its advertising brokerage business. It is not at all clear that clicking on any Google AdWords ad takes you to a Google server first and only then redirects you to the clicked ad. Nor is it clear that by clicking on a Google AdWords ad, you are sharing with the advertiser the fact that you searched for or browsed content about a given subject. The potential of Google's vast store of user data creates a serious risk of disclosure throughout this network of trust regardless of whether Google's intentions are in fact good for its customers.

The exchange of data between user and server establishes a relationship of trust. A survey by the Internet security company WebSense found that 60 of the 100 most popular sites on the Internet had hosted malicious code at some point in the past year.[25] The examples that WebSense cites are attacks on the Web pages displayed to users rather than the back-end servers, so they do not give direct access to user data stored on the servers. But they do hijack the identity of the server on behalf of the attacker, allowing the attacker to present a portion of the Web page as if it is coming from the trusted server. The result is a variety of attacks that collect data on behalf of an attacker posing as the trusted server. These widely prevalent Web site attacks allow attackers to insert themselves into users' networks of trusted actors by way of the infected sites.

Google tried to use the EU data retention directive as part of the rationale behind its eighteen-month data retention period for certain user data, though some observers contend that the directive does not apply to Google as a "content provider," as opposed to a "communication service."[26] EU commissioners beat back that particular argument and have aggressively lobbied for Google to reduce the amount of data it keeps and how long it keeps the data under its privacy directive.[27] This exchange demonstrates precisely the problem at the intersection of the EU data retention directive and the way that surveillance works in the networked public sphere today. The same EU authority that is responsible for guarding against the retention of personal data by service providers like Google is at the same time requiring ISPs to increase the amount of data they are storing and the length of time over which they are storing it. ISPs are companies just like Google, and requiring that they store the data required by the data retention directive imposes the same sorts of risks of unwarranted surveillance.

Client Surveillance

In addition to surveillance on the network and on servers, there is a range of different actors directly watching users' machines in various ways. The number of different actors trying to control access to the client has turned the end user's computers into a constant battleground of surveillance. Malware creators try to infect machines to steal valuable personal information. Anti-virus developers watch computers to find these malware and other sorts of snooping software, including sophisticated family and workplace surveillance systems. Even personal computing equipment—say, a laptop— can itself be turned into a surveillance system, through the use of keyboard logging devices that are installed inside the box of the computer, making them virtually impossible for the casual user to detect.

SpectorSoft was selected as *PC Magazine*'s editor's choice for "monitoring" software and is the largest provider of such software for home, small business, and corporate use. It captures virtually every kind of activity on the client computer and can send all of the monitored data to a remote computer for viewing.[28] Since becoming the market leader in 2004, SpectorSoft has stopped advertising to spouses, citing legal ambiguity and spousal abuse, but it continues to market itself for use monitoring minors and employees, neither of whom are legally protected from such monitoring in the U.S.[29] SpectorSoft reported in 2007 that its software was installed on over 400,000 desktops, 60 percent of which were home users.[30] All major anti-virus products classify SpectorSoft as spyware and attempt to remove it, but SpectorSoft actively avoids detection by either the monitored subject or anti-virus or other anti-spyware software.[31]

In addition to these monitoring products like SpectorSoft, which take the form of software, a variety of companies make hardware keyboard logging devices. These devices are generally small plugs that sit between the USB plug of the logged keyboard and the USB plug of the logged computer but can also be cards that sit inside the computer case. The devices record every key pressed on the keyboard and can be used to capture passwords, emails, typed documents, and any such information entered on the keyboard. Relative to software keyloggers, these devices are much easier to install given physical access and are impossible to detect via anti-virus software. The only way to detect some of these devices is physically to open the computer case.[32]

The most intrusive and prevalent example of client-side surveillance software is the collection of various bots, viruses, worms, trojans, and other malware that infect a significant chunk all Internet connected computers. As a whole, the set of malware-infected computers have the ability to collect all of the client data of hundreds of millions of computers, though in practice data collected is usually limited to obviously profitable data like credit card numbers.[33] Most of these infected computers are organized into large botnets—networks of infected computers remotely controlled by a single entity. The Conficker botnet, one of the biggest currently, now controls several million infected computers.[34] Botnets like Conficker perform a variety of illicit activities including sending spam, committing click fraud, subjecting servers to denial of service attacks, and stealing financial information. One recent study of spam distribution determined that the Storm botnet was responsible for twenty percent of all spam sent in the first quarter of 2008, and Storm was just the biggest of many botnets at the time.[35]

The direct impact of most of these activities on any given infected user is usually relatively small: outgoing spam only costs the user bandwidth, credit card theft is generally insured by the credit card company, and click fraud costs a user nothing directly. But the potential for greater abuse of personal data, both individually and collectively, is difficult to overstate given the vast number of malware-infected computers, the complete access of the malware to the infected computers' data, and the increasing sophistication of the criminal organizations that run them.[36] A recent report by two of this volume's co-editors, Ron Deibert and Rafal Rohozinski, and their respective teams, on the use of a small botnet to surveil a wide variety of embassies and other highly sensitive sites in southeast Asia, demonstrates the potential for harm represented by the botnet surveillance. The Information Warfare Monitor found clear evidence that the botnet, which they call GhostNet, had wide ranging abilities on the client: from copying locally stored files to watching the physical spaces through the webcams.[37] The study presented only circumstantial evidence pointing to Chinese involvement—the servers commanding the botnet were mostly located in China, and the infected sites were all of high, regional value to China. But the documentation of this particular botnet demonstrates that it would be straightforward for China or another state (or private) actor to perform wide-scale client-side surveillance through a botnet.

To protect oneself from viruses, bots, worms, and other such malware, most experts recommend installing anti-virus systems on all client computers. But this anti-virus software is itself highly intrusive, operating at the most fundamental levels of the operating system, incurring significant performance penalties, and attempting to avoid the notice of malware (which is itself trying to detect the anti-virus systems to disable them). Anti-virus tools have the capability to do the same sorts of harm that a piece of malware can do, including both stealing data from and disabling the host computer. Trust in Symantec and the other anti-virus vendors not to snoop or harm the computer is mostly well founded, but fake anti-virus systems have now become one of the most common types of malware precisely because of the need to trust anti-virus systems and the difficulty of determining which anti-virus systems to trust.

Various other sorts of actors surveil users through their clients as well. ComScore is one of the biggest of several companies that collect data about Internet users for market research. It collects the entire Web browsing stream, including encrypted requests, from the 2 million members of its worldwide "consumer panel." ComScore connects its online data with a variety of sources of off-line data, including supermarket purchases and automobile registrations. ComScore has admitted to using its collected data to log in to its members' online banking accounts to verify reported incomes.[38] ComScore recruits these panel members from a wide variety of countries, including many from Europe and Asia, through a combination of sweepstakes, network performance improvement tools, claims of antimalware protection, and (according to ComScore) a sincere desire by panel members to improve the efficiency of the Internet. ComScore discloses to the panel members that the software is monitoring their Web browsing activities, but it also keeps a strong separation between the company itself and the operations that collect the data—currently OpinionSquare and PermissionResearch—by not directly naming the tools or the organizations that operate them anywhere on ComScore.com or even in its SEC annual report filing. And it has had to recreate those operations at least once to evade detection by antispyware tools.[39] ComScore sells access to these data, estimated by ComScore at 28 terabytes collected per month in 2007, as market research to many of the largest companies in the world. The U.S. Privacy Act of 1974 prohibits the U.S. federal law enforcement and other government agencies from importing data from ComScore (or LexisNexis or other private database) en masse, but the law does allow the agencies to perform queries through ComScore or other private data sources about specific people.[40]

Governments have various levels of access to data collected through anti-virus software market research, and malware. Some governments allegedly also use their own client software to collect data directly. Direct evidence of government client surveillance is rare, but examples occasionally pop up. For instance, the U.S. Drug Enforcement Agency (DEA) has been documented as installing a keylogger on a suspect's machine to capture the encryption keys necessary to read the suspect's PGP-encrypted email.[41] And we know major anti-virus companies have complied with court orders to ignore such U.S. government spyware.[42] There is strong evidence that the German police are aggressively pursuing the use of client-side software to tap calls on Skype.[43] In Denmark, parliament approved a law that explicitly gives law enforcement agencies the authority to install keylogging software on a suspect's computer.[44] And, thanks to researchers at the Citizen Lab, the world knows that a Chinese version of Skype was logging sensitive messages to servers as mandated by the Chinese government.[45] The software used by government agencies for surveillance in all these examples is functionally indistinguishable from client malware—the whole point of the software is to collect data from the subject without knowledge or consent.

Client-side surveillance provides the most complete access to user data in comparison to network or server surveillance. Every bit of data sent, received, viewed, played, or typed on a computer is vulnerable to client-side surveillance, though most client surveillance tools collect all possible data. Malware mostly targets various sorts of directly profitable data, including e-mail addresses and bank account information. The most sophisticated anti-virus tools monitor all data stored on and transmitted to the computer, checking the data for malware signatures, but not keyboard or screen activity. Market research tools like ComScore typically monitor all network traffic, whether encrypted or not, but not stored data or keyboard or screen activity. Workplace and family monitoring tools usually monitor keystrokes and periodic screenshots of the activity on the computer screen but not stored or network data. The GhostNet report demonstrated that active malware is even capable of activating and recording the webcams and microphones of infected computers.

Indeed, the biggest problem for client surveillance tools is often dealing with the sheer amount of data. For example, even one screenshot a minute on a single computer can generate a daunting amount of data. This problem is magnified when applied over a large set of monitored clients. Botnets (networks of malware-infected computers controlled from a single point) only search for a limited set of data, like credit card numbers, which they can easily sell, presumably because of the difficulty (and therefore unprofitability) of sifting through the vast trove of other sorts of data on infected computers. Likewise, a primary challenge of corporate anti-virus systems that must manage entire networks of clients is to manage the resulting flood of data about infections and vulnerabilities in a network of clients.

Nonetheless, any client-side program has at least the *potential* to access every sort of data that resides on or passes through the computer. So, a keylogger may only monitor keystrokes, but that restriction is mostly the choice of the tool (and its developers) once it has been installed. Even non-surveillance-oriented programs (screen savers, games, chat programs, and so on) potentially have complete access to data once they have been installed. Most computers try to make it difficult for an arbitrary program to take over a computer, but a constant stream of vulnerabilities gives client programs access to the entire computer. And this same level of access applies to most hardware devices installed on the computer as well. Even devices that do not directly have the ability to access a shared bus or run a driver may have the ability to infect clients with malware, as shown by cases like virus-carrying digital photo frames.[46]

Unlike server and network surveillance, client surveillance is always theoretically detectable. Any change in the client behavior (whether processing data, storing it, or sending it over a network) requires some detectable change to the client. In practice, there is a long history of surveillance tools using increasingly sophisticated methods to hide themselves, including through rootkits that embed themselves into the deepest layers of the client operating system. But even with these sophisticated methods, there are always small changes in behavior that at least theoretically make the tools detectable. But detecting these small changes in the large number of malware, spyware, and other surveillance tools is beyond the capabilities of even the most sophisticated user.

Detection of the most advanced client surveillance tools requires the use of some other monitoring tool, such as an anti-virus system, designed specifically for this purpose. The latest versions of malware and other surveillance tools change themselves constantly to avoid detection even by sophisticated anti-virus systems. This cycle of increasingly sophisticated detection and evasion requires constant monitoring of every networked client, by anti-virus tools, by mal- or spyware, or often by both.

In a strict sense, the EU data retention directive applies directly only to network and server monitoring. But the routers that will be used in the implementation of the directive to collect network data are client devices themselves. As such, they are vulnerable to a stack of hardware, operating system, and applications just like any other client. Any actor within that network may potentially have access to the data, so adding the monitoring box to the ISP network potentially adds all those actors to the network trusted with the client data. Most of those actors (including hardware manufacturers, operating system developers, application developers) have access to all the data potentially collected through network surveillance and not just the legally monitored data, so we have to consider the flow of both the actual and potential data mandated by the directive through this network of trust around the monitoring tools. The sophistication of client surveillance tools at both collecting data and hiding themselves from detection demonstrates the possibility of an attacker installing such code undetected on a data retention tool. The number of well-publicized, active exploits against a range of routers (not to mention counterfeit routers) means that the risk of this occurring is high.

Conclusion

This chapter provides a typology of the different sorts of Internet surveillance through cases about Internet surveillance tools. For each set of cases, it is important to focus on the *actual* and *potential data* monitored and *networks of trust* through which the data necessarily flow. This typology is intended to serve as a starting point for analysis of the steady stream of cases about Internet surveillance; for the analysis of those cases not only from a technical frame but also from social, political, legal, and other frames; and for the application of the resulting road map to specific questions about surveillance that arise over time. As new stories about surveillance emerge, this road map can provide a context for determining whether and in what ways those stories tell us anything new about Internet surveillance. For example, one might ask whether recently reported iPhone viruses represent a new sort of surveillance or how the monitoring required for Comcast's BitTorrent throttling (described in the U.S.-Canada Overview presented later in this book) compares to existing examples of surveillance.

This typology also provides a frame for considering the impact of the EU data retention directive, which is likely to have important effects beyond its explicit scope. These effects apply both to the data potentially accessible to monitoring and to the way users will relate to the networks of trusted actors who have access to these data. As the cases about client tools show, surveillance is both widespread and very difficult to detect on a range of client devices, including the routers and other computers necessary to implement the EU directive. As a result, an unintended outcome of the directive will be that both the mandated data (senders, recipients, and time stamps) and the potentially collected data (the content of the whole data stream) will be exposed to potential access by a whole network of new actors. The cases about server tools and surveillance show that the directive's requirements, when applied to server-side companies like Google, will have the effect of increasing the data stored by those companies and thereby further pushing the already strained trust relationship between users and servers. Similar mandates related to data retention should be viewed in a similar context of growing Internet surveillance practices in the OSCE member states and elsewhere around the world.

Finally, the cases about network surveillance show that many users, including many of the serious criminals that the directive is meant to track, have an incentive to choose to use available rerouting methods to avoid monitoring. The increased use of rerouting proxies will both pose a privacy risk to those users and potentially route a significant portion of EU Internet traffic through countries unfriendly (at least in terms of data sharing) to the EU. As a result, the intended purpose of the EU data retention directive may be thwarted in dangerous ways. The unintended consequences of the EU data retention directive are likely to prove costly.

Notes

1. European Union, *Directive 2006/24/EC of the European Parliament and of the Council of 15 March 2006 on the retention of data generated or processed in connection with the provision of publicly available electronic communications services or of public communications networks and amending Directive 2002/58/EC*, 2006.

2. Federal Communications Commission, *Order FCC 06–56* (Federal Communications Commission, May 12, 2006).

3. John Markoff and Scott Shane, "Documents Show Link between AT&T and Agency in Eavesdropping Case," *New York Times*, April 13, 2006, http://www.nytimes.com/2006/04/13/us/nationalspecial3/13nsa.html.

4. Ibid.

5. Sara Sundelius, "Sweden Adopts Controversial Law to Allow Secret Tapping of E-mails, Phone Calls," *International Herald Tribune*, June 18, 2008; DW-World Staff, "Swedish Government Clears Hurdles to Pass Surveillance Bill," *DW-World.de*, June 19, 2008, http://www.dw-world.de/dw/article/0,2144,3421627,00.html.

6. Frank Rizzo, "thinkbroadband: sysip.net (BT and 121Media)," discussion forum, thinkbroadband.com, July 2, 2007, http://forums.thinkbroadband.com/bt/3047764-sysipnet-bt-and-121media.html; Filippo Spike Morelli, "To Own, To Be Owned, or What Else? BT and Its Proxies," *SpikeLab.org*, July 9, 2007, http://www.spikelab.org/blog/btProxyHorror.html; Ryan Naraine, "Spyware, Rootkit Maker Stops Distribution," *eWeek.com*, May 10, 2006, http://www.eweek.com/c/a/Security/Spyware-Rootkit-Maker-Stops-Distribution/.

7. Chris Williams, "ISP Data Deal with Former 'Spyware' Boss Triggers Privacy Fears," *The Register*, February 25, 2008, http://www.theregister.co.uk/2008/02/25/phorm_isp_advertising/.

8. Phorm, Inc., "BT PLC, TalkTalk and Virgin Media Inc Confirm Exclusive Agreements with Phorm," phorm.com, February 14, 2008, http://cyber.law.harvard.edu/pubrelease/accesscontrolled/phorm-launch-agrement.html.

9. Chris Williams, "ISP Data Deal with Former 'Spyware' Boss Triggers Privacy Fears," *The Register*, February 25, 2008, http://www.theregister.co.uk/2008/02/25/phorm_isp_advertising/; Chris Williams, "BT Admits Misleading Customers over Phorm Experiments," *The Register*, March 17, 2008, http://www.theregister.co.uk/2008/03/17/bt_phorm_lies/print.html.

10. Phorm, Inc., "Phorm: No Personal Information," phorm.com, http://privacy.phorm.com/no_personal_info.php.

11. Philip Stafford, "BT to Begin Further Trials of Ad Technology," *FT.com*, July 17, 2008, http://www.ft.com/cms/s/0/34c59420-5356-11dd-8dd2-000077b07658.html.

12. Ethan Zuckerman, "How a Pakistani ISP Briefly Shut Down YouTube," My Heart's in Accra, February 25, 2008, http://www.ethanzuckerman.com/blog/2008/02/25/how-a-pakistani-isp-briefly-shut-down-youtube/.

13. Sylvie Barak, "Pakistan Becomes VPN Routing Hot-spot," *The Inquirer*, February 26, 2008, http://www.theinquirer.net/gb/inquirer/news/2008/02/26/pakistan-becomes-vpn-routing.

14. AnchorFree, Inc., "AnchorFree History," anchorfree.com, 2008, http://anchorfree.com/about/history/.

15. Berkman Center for Internet and Society, "Mapping Local Internet Control," http://cyber.law.harvard.edu/netmaps.

16. Cooperative Association for Internet Data Analysis, *IPv4 Internet Topology Report as Internet Graph* (Cooperative Association for Internet Data Analysis, August 1, 2007), http://www.caida.org/research/topology/as_core_network/.

17. Jacco Tunnissen, "Global Internet Exchange Points / BGP Peering Points / IXP," Bgp4.as, 2008, http://www.bgp4.as/internet-exchanges.

18. Josh Karlin, Stephanie Forrest, and Jennifer Rexford, "Nation-State Routing: Censorship, Wiretapping, and BGP," arXiv.org (March 18, 2009), http://arxiv.org/abs/0903.3218.

19. Ryan Naraine, "Spyware Floods in through BitTorrent," *eWeek.com*, June 15, 205, http://www.eweek.com/index2.php?option=content&task=view&id=9664; Dan Ilett, "CA Slaps Spyware

Label on Kazaa," *CNET News.com*, http://news.cnet.com/CA-slaps-spyware-label-on-Kazaa/2100 -1025_3-5467539.html.

20. Gary T. Marx, "Soft Surveillance: The Growth of Mandatory Volunteerism in Collecting Personal Information—'Hey Buddy Can You Spare a DNA?,'" in *Surveillance and Security: Technological Power and Politics in Everyday Life*, ed. Torin Monahan (New York: Routledge, 2006), 37–56; Daniel J. Solove, *The Digital Person* (New York: New York University Press, 2004).

21. Google Inc., "Google Search Privacy: Plain and Simple," August 8, 2007, http://www .youtube.com/watch?v=kLgJYBRzUXY.

22. Michael Barbaro and Tom Zeller, Jr., "A Face Is Exposed for AOL Searcher No. 4417749," *New York Times*, August 9, 2006, http://www.nytimes.com/2006/08/09/technology/09aol.html; Arvind Narayanan and Vitaly Shmatikov, "How to Break Anonymity of the Netflix Prize Dataset," arXiv.org, October 18, 2006, http://arxiv.org/abs/cs/0610105.

23. Miguel Helft, "Google Told to Turn Over User Data of YouTube," *The New York Times*, July 4, 2008, http://www.nytimes.com/2008/07/04/technology/04youtube.html.

24. Attributor Corporation, "Get Your Fair Share of the Ad Network Pie," March 30, 2008, http:// www.attributor.com/blog/get-your-fair-share-of-the-ad-network-pie/.

25. Websense Security Labs, *Websense Security Labs: State of Internet Security Q1–Q2, 2008* (Websense Security Labs, 2008), http://www.websense.com/securitylabs/docs/WSL_Report_1H08 _FINAL.pdf.

26. Google Inc., "Google Log Retention Policy FAQ," March 14, 2007, http://www.seroundtable .com/google_log_retention_policy_faq.pdf; Kevin J. O'Brien and Thomas Crampton, "E.U. Probes Google Over Data Retention Policy," *New York Times*, May 26, 2007, http://www.nytimes.com/ 2007/05/26/business/26google.html.

27. European Commission Article 29 Data Protection Working Party, "Opinion 1/2008 on Data Protection Issues Related to Search Engines," April 4, 2008, ec.europa.eu/justice_home/fsj/privacy/ docs/wpdocs/2008/wp148_en.pdf.

28. SpectorSoft, "Spector Pro 2008 for Windows," http://www.spectorsoft.com/products/ SpectorPro_Windows/.

29. Camille Calman, "Spy v. Spouse: Regulating Surveillance Software on Shared Marital Computers," *Columbia Law Review 105*, no. 2097 (2005), http://www.columbialawreview.org/pdf/ Calman-Web.pdf.

30. Ellen Messmer, "Spouse-vs.-Spouse Cyberspying Dangerous, Possibly Illegal," *Network World*, August 16, 2007, http://www.networkworld.com/news/2007/081607-spouse.html?page=2.

31. Computer Associates, "eTrust PestPatrol, EBlaster," August 16, 2004, http://www.ca.com/ securityadvisor/pest/pest.aspx?id=55479.

32. KeyCarbon, "Record Keystrokes on Laptop Keyboard with Tiny 50 × 60mm Device. Software Free—Plug Device into Base of Laptop, It Begins to Record Immediately," keycarbon.com, http:// www.keycarbon.com/products/keycarbon_laptop/overview/.

33. Tim Weber, "Criminals 'May Overwhelm the Web'," *BBC News*, January 25, 2007, http://news.bbc.co.uk/1/hi/business/6298641.stm; PandaLabs, *Quarterly Reports PandaLabs* (April—June 2008), (PandaLabs, July 1, 2008).

34. John Markoff, "Worm Infects Millions of Computers Worldwide," *New York Times*, January 23, 2009, http://www.nytimes.com/2009/01/23/technology/internet/23worm.html.

35. MessageLabs, *MessageLabs Intelligence: Q1/March 2008:* "One Fifth of All Spam Springs from Storm Botnet," (MessageLabs, April 1, 2008).

36. Nicholas Ianelli and Aaron Hackworth, *Botnets as a Vehicle for Online Crime*, (CERT Coordination Center, December 1, 2005), http://www.cert.org/archive/pdf/Botnets.pdf.

37. Information Warfare Monitor, "Tracking GhostNet: Investigating a Cyber Espionage Network" (Citizen Lab/the SecDev Group, March 29, 2009), http://www.tracking-ghost.net.

38. ComScore, Inc., "ComScore Methodology," ComScore.com, http://cyber.law.harvard.edu/pubrelease/accesscontrolled/comscore-tech.html; Evan Hansen, "Net Privacy and the Myth of Self-regulation," *CNET News.com*, October 16, 2001, http://www.news.com/Net-privacy-and-the-myth-of-self-regulation/2010-1071_3-281580.html.

39. ComScore, Inc., *SEC Filing, 10-K Annual Report*, 2008; Stefanie Olsen, "ComScore: Spyware or 'Researchware'?," *CNET News.com*, December 20, 2004, http://news.cnet.com/ComScore-Spyware-or-researchware/2100-1032_3-5494004.html.

40. Electronic Privacy Information Center, "EPIC Privacy Act of 1974 Page 5 U.S.C. § 552a," epic.org, August 26, 2003, http://epic.org/privacy/1974act/.

41. Declan McCullagh, "Feds Use Keylogger to Thwart PGP, Hushmail," *CNET News.com*, July 10, 2007, http://news.cnet.com/8301 10784_3 9741357-7.html

42. Declan McCullagh and Anne Broache, "Will Security Firms Detect Police Spyware?" *CNET News.com*, July 17, 2007, http://news.cnet.com/Will-security-firms-detect-police-spyware/2100-7348_3-6197020.html.

43. Louis Charboneau, "Skype Encryption Stumps German Police," *Global and Mail*, November 22, 2007; Kim Zetter, "Leaked Documents Show German Police Attempting to Hack Skype," *Wired.com*, January 29, 2008, http://blog.wired.com/27bstroke6/2008/01/leaked-document.html.

44. Privacy International, *PHR2006—Kingdom of Denmark* (Privacy International, December 18, 2007), http://www.privacyinternational.org/article.shtml?cmd%5B347%5D=x-347-559545.

45. Nart Villeneuve, "Breaching Trust: An Analysis of Surveillance and Security Practices on China's TOM-Skype Platform" (Information Warfare Monitor/ONI Asia, October 1, 2008), http://www.nartv.org/mirror/breachingtrust.pdf; Josh Silverman, "Answers to Some Commonly Asked Questions about the Chinese Privacy Breach," Skype Blogs, October 4, 2008, http://share.skype.com/sites/en/2008/10/answers_to_some_commonly_asked.html.

46. David Goldsmith, "Digital Hitchhikers," SANS Internet Storm Center, December 25, 2007, http://isc.sans.org/diary.html?storyid=3787.

4 Barriers to Cooperation

An Analysis of the Origins of International Efforts to Protect Children Online

Nart Villeneuve

Introduction

While providing an innovative platform for global communications and economic transactions, the Internet brings some of society's worst ailments, such as the proliferation of images of child abuse, into the public sphere. Every day, children are sexually abused, and graphic images of this exploitation are transferred over the Internet to a global audience.[1] Despite a near worldwide consensus on the illegality of the trafficking of images of child abuse (often referred to as child pornography) on the Internet, effective international cooperation on this issue remains elusive.[2] Instead, an increasing number of countries are simply hiding online child sexual abuse through the cosmetic practice of Internet filtering—the technical blocking of Internet content within a country's territorial boundaries—rather than cooperating internationally to remove such content at its (foreign) source and subsequently prosecuting those who produce and traffic in images of the sexual abuse of children.

However, there was an early recognition among diverse international actors that tackling the problems posed by new information communication technologies (ICT) would require potentially new forms of cooperation. These forms of cooperation emphasize sustained communication and interaction among a community of diverse actors spanning supranational institutions such as the European Union, national governments, law enforcement, private industry including Internet service providers (ISPs), and nongovernmental organizations. This concept of "dynamic cooperation" constitutes not just the outcome of an agreement reached through bargaining, but the ongoing practice of cooperation in which actors must rely on each others' capabilities for continual implementation in situations where compliance cannot be achieved solely through unilateral means.

While the prospect of dynamic cooperation was consistently raised in international deliberations concerning the challenges of combating child pornography and ICTs, it is not reflected in official outcomes such as declarations and conventions. Moreover, preliminary evidence indicates that the introduction of Internet filtering, to prevent *accidental* access to child pornography, correlates with decreasing efforts to have images of child abuse removed at the source. As a result, child pornography identified and filtered by one country remains available on the Internet and is accessible in other countries. This situation occurs among countries that participate in institutions designed to facilitate cooperation targeting the source of the child pornography. Thus, countries that participate in the institutions dedicated to removing child pornography—such as international law enforcement task forces, including the Virtual Global Task Force and the Innocent Images International Task Force, as well as the INHOPE association of "hot line" providers—filter Internet content located within each other's territorial boundaries.

This evidence suggests that traditional cooperative mechanisms may have unintended consequences that conflict with rather than complement dynamic cooperation. This potential conflict raises the concern that contemporary cooperative institutions do not have the capacity to meet the global challenges posed by the proliferation of ICTs. This chapter argues that the dominant conception of cooperation, the domestic implementation of the results of bargaining, obscures potentially new forms of dynamic cooperation at the international level. A conceptual shift in the understanding of what constitutes cooperation is required to capture this emergent practice.

In this chapter, I present an analysis of the widespread adoption of filtering as the primary solution to combating the proliferation of child pornography on the Internet. While international agreements concerning the protection of children played a role in spurring state action, the emphasis on domestic implementation over dynamic cooperation facilitated the preference for filtering as the solution to the problem of Internet child pornography. Internet filtering is a solution that states can implement domestically irrespective of international agreements, and it does not require sustained cooperation. The goal of filtering is to block domestic access to Internet content located in another country. Dynamic cooperation—in contrast to blocking domestic access to foreign-hosted child pornography—refers to the continual cooperation necessary to have foreign-hosted content removed at its source.

Within this context, I trace how filtering has been constituted as a solution to the problem of Internet child pornography and how its implementation was made possible by delinking the issue from three key factors: the interpretation of filtering mandated by the state as a form of censorship, the effect of filtering on freedom of expression as a result of technical deficiencies, and the overall effectiveness of filtering technology itself in combating Internet child pornography. I present a preliminary analysis of the ways in which the continued emphasis on domestic implementation may be affecting attempts to move toward dynamic cooperation on this issue. Finally, I suggest areas for further research that result from treating cooperation as a dynamic practice rather than an instance of bargaining and domestic implementation.

Following the methodology outlined by Richard Price, this chapter does not focus on causal explanations, but emphasizes historical contingencies that reflect ideational contests and defining moments in international agreements, conferences, and events concerned with the issue of child pornography.[3] The chapter will employ a genealogical method as a means of understanding how the conception of cooperation as domestic implementation emerged in the international arena concerning the issue area of the protection of children. It will trace how the discourse of domestic implementation overshadowed that of dynamic cooperation and thus enabled the practice of filtering. It examines the role of discourses and power in redefining filtering from an ineffective tool of state censorship to one of effective cooperation. The following is not a comprehensive history of international efforts to protect children or of Internet filtering but, following Price, an analysis of events that "provide discursive moments" and reflect "crucial dimensions."[4] Such an analysis detects the unsuccessful attempts to constitute cooperation as more than an outcome of bargaining but as a dynamic practice based on sustained communication and interaction.

Competing Perceptions of Cooperation

An analysis of the texts of key international agreements and conferences focused on the rights of children highlights a tension between perspectives that view cooperation as the implementation of domestic laws and procedures by states and those that see it as constituting the continual practice of interaction and information sharing between a diverse set of actors. This becomes particularly evident with the rise of new communications technologies and the complex set of problems, including the proliferation of child pornography, that result. It also reflects a dynamic between state and nonstate actors that emerged as a result of the prominent role that nongovernmental organizations (NGOs) played in international conferences and agreements concerning the rights of children.

While given an arguably low priority in international political affairs, children have constituted an important issue at the international level.[5] Primarily framed in terms of human rights, children have been singled out for protection in international agreements as far back as the Declaration of Geneva, which was adopted by the League of Nations in 1924.[6] A more specific emphasis on children followed with the United Nations' (UN) Declaration on the Rights of the Child adopted in 1959. This declaration put forward ten principles that emphasized diverse issues such as the child's right to nutrition, education, and nationality. The protection of children from forms of exploitation was also explicitly raised, as was a prohibition on any forms of trafficking in children.[7] Although these Declarations firmly entrenched the issue of children on the international agenda they were not legally binding on states and did not "lay down precise obligations for states."[8]

The UN Convention on the Rights of the Child (UNCRC) was adopted in 1989 after 11 years of negotiation among the UN and its related bodies such as UNICEF, as well as the International Committee for the Red Cross and many NGOs.[9] In fact, NGOs were instrumental in the development and adoption of both the 1924 and 1959 declarations as well as the 1989 convention. Nongovernmental organizations played a critical role in ensuring that a legally binding agreement was reached. Moreover, particular elements including "articles which give the child protection against sexual and other exploitation, traffic, torture, and armed conflicts" would have not been included were it not for the determined efforts of NGOs.[10] However, while the role of international cooperation was acknowledged, the convention relied heavily on domestic mechanisms and little on the "international machinery" required to enforce these rights.[11]

The United Nations created the Special Rapporteur on the sale of children, child prostitution, and child pornography in 1990, but its emphasis was also domestic implementation. However, by 1994 an increasing awareness emerged concerning the lack of international cooperation, including a UN General Assembly resolution calling for the "need to adopt efficient international measures" in addition to domestic solutions.[12] The Special Rapporteur began to highlight the international character of the problem of child sexual exploitation by framing the issue in terms of states that fall on the demand or supply side of the problem.[13] By 1995, the Special Rapporteur began to note the impact of new communications technology on legislation and jurisdiction, noting that "new technology gave birth to concepts and applications like cyberporn or audio-pornography, not envisaged by most legislation" and that when "materials cross national boundaries the determination of the forum having jurisdiction over the offence will also pose a problem."[14] The Special Rapporteur represented an early attempt to sustain cooperation after the UNCRC was adopted in 1989; however, it was confined to an advisory role. Although the ability to make recommendations helped in terms of agenda setting and raising the profile of the issue, it fell well short of facilitating sustained cooperation.

The 1996 World Congress against Commercial Sexual Exploitation of Children (CSEC) was the result of the considerable efforts of End Child Prostitution in Asian Tourism (ECPAT), a child advocacy NGO, and UNICEF. The congress centered on the UNCRC and culminated in the Stockholm Declaration and Agenda for Action. Despite the growing awareness of the challenges posed by the rapid expansion of Internet technology, the Stockholm Declaration and Agenda for Action contains no mention of the Internet. Instead, they focus on the promotion of national laws and policies that would allow states to meet their obligations under the UNCRC. The Stockholm Declaration encourages states to develop national plans of action to combat child exploitation. Despite some recommendations focused on increasing communication and cooperation among states, civil society, and international organizations, the primary emphasis of the document is on domestic state action. In fact the document explicitly states that the "primary task of combating the commercial sexual exploitation of children rests with the State and families."[15]

However, the extensive background paper on child pornography presented at the conference as well as the congress's child pornography panel all highlighted the role of new technologies, particularly the Internet, and the global character of the problem. It was argued that, whereas domestic legislation and increased enforcement led to a reduction in the production of child pornography in the 1980s, video and Internet technologies were dramatically changing the production and distribution of images of child sexual abuse. The background report concluded that domestic efforts, such as updating legislation to cover criminal activities made possible by new technologies, must be "supported by global cooperation of an enormous magnitude."[16] Although increased enforcement of domestic legislation led to a decrease in child pornography in the 1980s, such methods would not be sufficient to deal with the problems posed by new technologies:

Regulation of child pornography in the computer age presents special challenges that require considerable technical expertise.... The establishment of an international resource organisation which would employ a team of specialists in the areas of investigation, law enforcement, behavioural science, prosecution, law and computer technology could be an invaluable resource for the global community.[17]

Although it does not explicitly suggest reconceptualizing cooperation as a sustained practice, it does strongly indicate that the problems posed by new technologies require more than domestic implementation by states. It does clearly articulate that past practices, such as domestic legislation, would be insufficient. These debates are not reflected in the formal outcome of the congress.

The International Conference on Combating Child Pornography on the Internet in 1999 focused almost exclusively on child pornography and new communications technologies. This conference also marked the introduction of filtering as an option to deal with the problem. However, the discussion of filtering was limited to applications at the individual level in order to "empower Internet users." Efforts at the national and international level focused on increasing international cooperation, since Internet child pornography "does not know or respect borders."[18]

The fight against this abuse cannot be done alone but only through strong international cooperation, among governments, particularly law enforcement agencies, but equally important between States and the Internet industry, hotlines and non-governmental organizations.[19]

The result of the conference, the Vienna Commitment, called for "common measures to speed up and enable the transborder use of coercive powers such as transborder computer search and seizure" in conjunction with government, law enforcement, and the Internet industry.[20] It explored the relationship between law enforcement organizations, Internet service providers, and "hotlines" to which illegal content could be reported. These "hotlines" had recently formed an association known as INHOPE in order to increase sustained cooperation based on the development of "common good practices" to facilitate the "exchange of reports internationally."[21] The heavy focus on technology and the inclusion of diverse actors signaled the emergence of a conception of cooperation as a sustained practice.

While the Vienna Commitment was explicitly recognized by the UN's Optional Protocol to the Convention on the Rights of the Child on the sale of children, child prostitution, and child pornography, which was introduced in 2000, its emphasis on sustained cooperation as a response to the challenges of new technologies was not. While noting challenges posed by the Internet in the preamble, the actual text of the document does not explicitly mention new technologies, nor does it provide for mechanisms of sustained cooperation. Instead, the Optional Protocol focuses primarily on domestic implementation by highlighting issues of legislating criminal offenses into national law. The Optional Protocol, which has been the basis of action against child pornography since 2000, constitutes cooperation as a form of domestic implementation and does not reflect the diversity of discourse on the issue of child pornography.[22]

Recognizing the challenges posed by new communications technologies, nonstate actors devoted considerable efforts toward broadening the conception of cooperation to include practices that leveraged the continual and coordinated efforts of multiple actors. However, these efforts are not reflected in official declarations and conventions. The official discourse thus heavily favors solutions that can be domestically implemented.

The Emergence of Filtering

Filtering technology emerged in 1995, and by 1999 authoritarian states had already implemented such technology to block access to political content at the national level.[23] Inspired by these developments, studies concerning the role of the state in regulating access to Internet content at the national level through technical means began to emerge in democratic states. However, these studies concluded that filtering technologies deployed at the national level would be ineffective and would have the unintended consequence of harming freedom of expression online.[24]

At the international level, deliberation on the role that technology could play in combating Internet child pornography was also taking place. The Second World Congress against Commercial Sexual Exploitation of Children held in 2001 resulted in the Yokohama Global Commitment, which encouraged states to "take adequate measures to address negative aspects of new technologies, in particular child pornography on the Internet."[25] However, the specific measures to be taken are not specified. While articles emphasizing cooperation reflect the need to include diverse actors, their role is confined to one of supporting state actors in increasing the effectiveness of domestic measures taken to protect children. However, documents presented during the conference reflect a broader debate.

The Theme Paper on Child Pornography presented at the conference does focus on the challenges of sustained interaction. It highlights the successes and challenges of coordinated efforts of law enforcement agencies from multiple states to arrest and prosecute those involved with the production and exchange of child pornography. It noted that "closer working relationships" were required between law enforcement agencies worldwide to further "greater co-operation within the international law enforcement community."[26] In conjunction with the need to cooperate, the paper also makes clear that technology can play a role. The technological focus of the paper was devoted to technologies that can identify and remove, as opposed to filter, child pornography online.

Software developers have a particular responsibility to develop technologies which can locate child pornographic images on the Internet more swiftly, and allow for their rapid identification and removal.[27]

The report noted the increased use of filtering technology at the individual level but warned that "none of this software is perfect and it would be wrong if parents thought of it as being a substitute for sound advice and appropriate supervision."[28] Moreover, the report noted that increasing public demand to do something about the problem of child pornography online was leading to the preference of restrictive technologies, such as filtering at the national level, and warned of possible negative unintended consequences:

Unless the Internet industry, Governments and the civil society can find a convincing way of assuaging these strong concerns which are beginning to surface, public opinion will sooner or later force politicians to consider forms of intervention which could rob us of much that it is truly marvellous, dynamic and revolutionary about the Internet.[29]

With the exception of a growing number of authoritarian countries using filtering to impose political censorship, democratic states had not implemented filtering at the national level.[30] In 2004 the role of filtering technology was thrust into the international spotlight. In the United States, the Pennsylvania state legislature passed a law in 2002 that required ISPs to block access to Web sites suspected of hosting child pornography. When the Pennsylvania attorney general's office identified Web sites containing child pornography, they issued an informal notice to ISPs requiring that access to these Web sites be blocked. The ISPs subsequently blocked access to these Web sites. Because of the nature of ISP networks, these ISPs blocked access nationally, since they were technically unable to differentiate users located in Pennsylvania.[31]

However, civil liberties organizations challenged the law in court, arguing that these informal notices constituted "secret blocking orders" issued by the state and thus violated the First Amendment of the U.S. Constitution. Moreover, they argued that the technical filtering process implemented by ISPs resulted in large-scale overblocking that further violated free speech rights. Ultimately, the Federal District Court in Philadelphia ruled that the law violated the First Amendment. This ruling details the process, both legal and technical, that led to the blocking of 1.5 million legitimate Web sites while trying to block access to approximately 400 Web sites suspected of containing child abuse images. The decision by Judge Jan E. duBois stated:

There is little evidence that the Act has reduced the production of child pornography or the child sexual abuse associated with its creation. On the other hand, there is an abundance of evidence that implementation of the Act has resulted in massive suppression of speech protected by the First Amendment.[32]

The decision explicitly confirmed what had been implicitly noted by NGOs throughout their involvement in international agreements and conferences on child pornography: state-mandated national filtering was technically ineffective and posed a threat to the right of freedom of expression. While the case of the United States may be exceptional given the strong preference for the First Amendment guaranteeing the right to freedom of speech, the events in Pennsylvania did not go unnoticed. A report published in 2004 by UNESCO after the World Summit on the Information Society in 2003 noted that some countries were beginning to follow the legislative approach of the United States by introducing their own legislative efforts to "require the implementation of filtering at ISPs and gateways."[33] However, these attempts were plagued by the same issues faced in the United States, and widespread adoption did not occur until filtering was reconstituted as a legitimate practice.

The Legitimization of Filtering

The legitimization of filtering centers on three interlocking developments: a model of implementation in which the role of the state is reduced, the delinking of filtering and free speech concerns through technological developments, and a reframing of the effectiveness of filtering.

In 2004, British Telecom (BT), the largest ISP in the United Kingdom, and the Internet Watch Foundation (IWF), a "tip line" for reporting illegal online content, developed a partnership in consultation with the government.[34] British Telecom agreed to block access to a list of Web sites compiled by the IWF. This model of private partnership removes the need for government to implement legislation requiring ISPs to filter—it is a voluntary private initiative. This development changed the perception of filtering from one of state imposition to one of private initiative. While technically a private arrangement, the state's involvement in the process leading to the implementation of filtering allowed it to retain some influence.[35] British Telecom's filtering system, known as Cleanfeed, was designed to be extremely precise and cost effective.[36] Cleanfeed elegantly avoids the pitfall of overblocking, the key objection that was consistently raised with respect to filtering. This innovative system created a flood of interest from ISPs worldwide and received an endorsement from the leading child advocacy group ECPAT.[37]

The Cleanfeed filtering system was promoted as a method to block inadvertent access to child pornography. The reduction of the scope of the mandate to simply inadvertent access protected Cleanfeed from the charges of ineffectiveness that plagued earlier filtering technologies. While those determined to access such content could easily circumvent the filtering system, Cleanfeed is in fact effective at blocking inadvertent access.[38] The advocacy group ECPAT, whose background documents submitted to the World Congress against Commercial Sexual Exploitation of Children had been critical of filtering, now added filtering to its model National Action Plan. The National Action Plan, which has its roots in the first World Congress against Commercial Sexual Exploitation of Children held in 1996, now recommends "cooperation arrangements between ISPs and police in place to block illegal content."[39] Following the UK's lead, numerous countries began implementing national filtering systems, including Norway (September 2004), Germany[40] (February 2005), Sweden (May 2005), Denmark (October 2005), Canada (November 2006), Switzerland (January 2007), Italy[41] (January 2007), the Netherlands[42] (September 2007), and Finland (January 2008).[43]

The rapid spread of filtering across numerous democratic countries was enabled by conceptual and technological changes that legitimized filtering.[44] Countries that had previously shunned the practice now embraced it. From a traditional perspective the introduction of filtering technologies can be seen as the successful domestic implementation of agreements such as the UNCRC. However, such a "thin" conception of cooperation obscures the calls for sustained interaction that emerged within the competing discourses in and around international conferences and agreements. Dominant discourses and key events sidelined conceptions of dynamic cooperation that key non-state participants advocated as a response to the challenges posed by new ICTs.

Prospects for Dynamic Cooperation

International cooperation often produces unintended consequences. These "side effects" may be positive or negative.[45] Empirical evidence is beginning to emerge that suggests that domestic filtering efforts may be acting as a disincentive to cooperate. Consistent with a conception of cooperation as domestic implementation, filtering is perceived as cooperation, thus conceptually negating the need to engage in dynamic cooperation.

INHOPE is an international organization founded in 1999 comprising state-delegated NGOs that operate "hotlines" that deal with the issue of child exploitation. While distinct from the state, these organizations were empowered with authority and legitimacy by their strong connections to the state. These domestic organizations accept tips from the public and act to remove images of child abuse if located within their territorial jurisdiction. They may also act within the INHOPE organization to have the content removed at the source by their international counterpart within INHOPE. One of INHOPE's major objectives is "to ensure rapid and effective response to illegal content reports around the world by developing consistent, effective and secure mechanisms for exchanging reports between hotlines internationally and ensuring a coordinated approach is taken."[46] It has been argued that "cooperation between members of INHOPE has facilitated the removal of illegal content from the Internet and avoided the 'difficulties in the complex diplomatic procedures necessary for cross border cooperation of law enforcement authorities.'"[47]

Save the Children is an NGO and a key member of INHOPE. In a 2003 position paper, Save the Children outlined a vision of dynamic cooperation that centered on INHOPE. INHOPE is the nexus that links intergovernmental organizations, such as the European Union, primarily through national law enforcement organizations, the Internet industry, and child advocacy NGOs. The report provides examples of interaction across these actors but particularly emphasizes the relationship between INHOPE and law enforcement leading to "high profile police-operations [that] have led to the infiltration [of] and legal action against international child pornography/abuse networks."[48] The vision of INHOPE before the proliferation of filtering technologies in 2004 was clearly on the dynamic cooperation necessary to remove Internet child pornography at its source and arrest and convict those found responsible for trafficking in such content.

Many countries with representation in INHOPE have subsequently implemented national filtering technology to block access to foreign-host Internet child pornography. Some, but not all, members of INHOPE are now filtering such content, including content hosted within the territorial boundaries of other INHOPE members.[49] INHOPE reports that between September 2004 and December 2006 reports sent through the network between "hotlines" has decreased by 11 percent per year.[50] This decrease correlates with the increase in the number of INHOPE countries that implemented filtering, although for a variety of reasons it does not indicate causation.[51] Further research is required to determine precisely why this decrease in cooperation is occurring within the organization.

However, even when there is cooperation to have content removed at its source (rather than filtered), there are still significant delays and limited effectiveness. In 2006, the IWF, an INHOPE member, conducted a six-week test in which they found that 20 percent of the sites in their database remained active after having been reported to the relevant authorities in other countries.[52] Moore and Clayton obtained 2,585 suspect domains from the IWF and noted that nearly all of them had been previously reported and had removed images of child sexual abuse. They found that "child sexual abuse image websites fare worse than other types of offending content," such as phishing and copyright violations, when it comes to removal, with most lasting 719 hours after being reported.[53] While the IWF has been successful within the United Kingdom, their own jurisdiction, they acknowledge that there are Web sites that have been reported to relevant national authorities outside the United Kingdom that continue to remain active.

One site, for example, has been reported to us 224 times since 2002; another has been reported to us 54 times since 2000 and in that time has been found on seven different servers in different countries; yet another has been reported by us to the relevant authorities 32 times since 2005.

Some of the most prolific of these commercial child abuse websites have remained "live" for long periods of time, despite our concerted efforts to the contrary. 94 of these websites reported by us to relevant authorities in 2006 are known to have been actively selling child abuse images in 2005. Indeed, 33 were "live" in 2004 and 32 were "live" prior to that.

We regularly pass details of the websites and other intelligence to Interpol via our own police agency links, to international hotlines and the apparent host countries' own police services to enable them to launch a united assault on the organised criminals selling images of child abuse. However, the ever-changing jurisdictions, the differing laws, priorities and police responses as well as the varying cooperation of internet service providers around the world, mean that some countries face challenges to remove content.[54]

The factors that the IWF highlights as barriers to removing images of child sexual exploitation online illustrate the conception of cooperation as domestic implementation. Once the report has been handed off to the relevant domestic authorities, no further action is taken. After analyzing takedown regimes in a variety of different circumstances, including defamation, copyright violation, phishing, and child pornography, Moore and Clayton argue that incentives rather than differences in law, penalties, and other factors influence the rate at which takedown successfully occurs. In cases of phishing, banks have a high level of incentive to have the offending content removed and work with a variety of actors to achieve the takedown of such sites almost always without the use of courts or official channels. In contrast, the responsibility for the removal of child abuse images is delegated to the relevant national authorities and is subject to delay and neglect despite strong legal regimes.[55] Moore and Clayton argue:

The Internet is multi-national. Almost everyone who wants content removed issues requests to ISPs or website owners throughout the world, believing—not always correctly—that the material must be just as illegal "there" as "here." Unexpectedly, in the one case where the material is undoubtedly illegal everywhere, the removal of child sexual abuse image websites is dealt with in a rather different manner. The responsibility for removing material has been divided up on a national basis, and this appears to lead directly to very long website lifetimes.[56]

Not only do the domestic organizations charged with compiling lists of offending child pornography Web sites lack the willingness (or ability) to reach out to relevant nonstate actors across national boundaries, but they also have a reduced incentive to do so because their own population is "protected" from the offending foreign content through the use of filtering.

Conclusion

This chapter presented competing conceptions of cooperation that emerged from a genealogical analysis of the developments that led to the implementation of filtering to combat the proliferation of child exploitation on the Internet. In contrast to dominant perspectives that view cooperation as the state's domestic implementation of international agreements, this chapter presented the concept of dynamic cooperation. Dynamic cooperation constitutes a sustained practice in which actors, both state and nonstate, must continually interact to achieve implementation. While not reflected in official declarations, the behind-the-scenes debates surrounding international efforts to protect children online reflected a concern that the problems posed by ICTs required potentially new forms of cooperation. These approaches emphasized continual interaction among a diverse set of participants in order to take down images of child abuse at their source. However, this conception of cooperation was unable to unseat the dominant discourse, and Internet filtering was ultimately legitimized and implemented.

The result is a situation in which domestic organizations that have been delegated authority to combat the proliferation of child abuse images online lack the willingness or institutional capacity for dynamic cooperation. The introduction of filtering technology reduces the incentive for organizations with an already narrow conception of cooperation to further engage with relevant counterparts across international boundaries. Those engaging in the proliferation of images of child abuse online remain largely unaffected by filtering technology, as well as takedown and removal efforts. They are able to exploit the lack of cooperation among international actors. Unlike the forms of cooperation emerging in other areas of content removal, such as those targeting phishing Web sites, efforts to combat child pornography are framed and narrowly understood as the domain of states. There remain considerable barriers to dynamic forms of cooperation as a result.

Problematizing cooperation contributes to a better understanding of the complex challenges facing the international community in the 21st century. It suggests that our existing institutions may be unable to cope with the demands of problems exacerbated by the proliferation of ICTs. It suggests that new norms and mechanisms designed to promote a deeper form of dynamic cooperation may be necessary.

Notes

1. R. Barri Flowers, "The Sex Trade Industry's Worldwide Exploitation of Children," *Annals of the American Academy of Political and Social Science* 575 (2001): 147–157.

2. Marie Eneman, "The New Face of Child Pornography," in *Human Rights in the Digital Age*, ed. M. Klang and A. Murray (London: Cavendish Publishing, 2005); Steven Hick and Edward Halpin,

"Children's Rights and the Internet," *Annals of the American Academy of Political and Social Science* 575 (2001): 56–70.

3. Richard M. Price, *The Chemical Weapons Taboo* (Ithaca, NY: Cornell University Books, 1997).

4. Ibid., 10.

5. Alison Watson, "Children and International Relations: A New Site of Knowledge?" *Review of International Studies* 32 (2006): 237–250.

6. The Declaration of Geneva articulated the principle of "children first" with regard to access to emergency relief and signaled the beginning of an international emphasis on children. See Thomas Hammarberg, "The UN Convention on the Rights of the Child—And How to Make It Work," *Human Rights Quarterly* 12, no. 1 (1990): 97–105.

7. United Nations, *Declaration of the Rights of the Child*, 1959, http://www.unhchr.ch/html/menu3/b/25.htm.

8. Thomas Hammarberg, "The UN Convention on the Rights of the Child—And How to Make It Work," *Human Rights Quarterly* 12, no. 1 (1990): 98.

9. David A. Balton, "The Convention on the Rights of the Child: Prospects for International Enforcement," *Human Rights Quarterly* 12, no. 1 (1990): 120–129.

10. Cynthia P. Cohen, "The Role of Nongovernmental Organizations in the Drafting of the Convention on the Rights of the Child," *Human Rights Quarterly* 12, no. 1 (1990): 137–147.

11. David A. Balton, "The Convention on the Rights of the Child: Prospects for International Enforcement," *Human Rights Quarterly* 12, no. 1 (1990): 129.

12. United Nations, *Need to Adopt Efficient International Measures for the Prevention and Eradication of the Sale of Children, Child Prostitution and Child Pornography*, 1994, http://www.un.org/documents/ga/res/49/a49r210.htm.

13. Ofelia Calcetas-Santos, "Promotion and Protection of the Rights of Children," 1995, http://daccess-ods.un.org/access.nsf/Get?OpenAgent&DS=A/50/456&Lang=E.

14. Ibid.

15. World Congress against Commercial Sexual Exploitation of Children, *Stockholm Declaration and Agenda for Action*, 1996, http://www.csecworldcongress.org/PDF/en/Stockholm/Outome_documents/Stockholm%20Declaration%201996_EN.pdf.

16. World Congress against Commercial Sexual Exploitation of Children, *Child Pornography: An International Perspective*, 1996, http://www.csecworldcongress.org/PDF/en/Stockholm/Background_reading/Theme_papers/Theme%20paper%20Pornography%201996_EN.pdf.

17. Ibid.

18. International Conference on Combating Child Pornography, *Vienna Commitment against Child Pornography on the Internet*, 1999.

19. Ibid.

20. Ibid.

21. Ibid.

22. United Nations, *Optional Protocol to the Convention on the Rights of the Child on the Sale of Children, Child Prostitution and Child Pornography*, 2000, http://www.un.org/documents/ga/res/49/a49r210.htm.

23. Ronald J. Deibert, "Black Code: Censorship, Surveillance, and the Militarisation of Cyberspace," *Millennium: Journal of International Studies* 32, no. 3 (2003): 501–530.

24. In 1999, Industry Canada commissioned a report to explore "from a technological perspective, issues arising from attempts to regulate content on the Internet and to control access by individuals to Internet sites and facilities." The report analyzed the efforts by Singapore and China to block access to Internet content for political reasons as part of a censorship strategy and explored the possibility of introducing such technologies to block Canadians' access to undesirable content such as child pornography. The report focused on evaluating the effectiveness of filtering and concluded that filtering technologies are subject to underblocking (the inability to block all or most of the content one intends to block), overblocking (the accidental blocking of content that was never intended to be blocked), and circumvention (the ability to easily bypass the restrictions). Concerning the implementation of filtering at the national level, the report concluded that filtering was unreliable and would have a "negative impact on Canada's place in the global Information Economy." Gerry Miller, Gerri Sinclair, David Sutherland, and Julie Zilber, "Regulation of the Internet: A Technological Perspective" (commissioned by Industry Canada from EXCITE, Simon Fraser University, 1999), http://www.ic.gc.ca/epic/site/smt-gst.nsf/vwapj/005082_e.pdf/$FILE/005082_e.pdf.

25. World Congress against Commercial Sexual Exploitation of Children, *The Yokohama Global Commitment*, 2001, http://www.csecworldcongress.org/PDF/en/Yokohama/Outcome_documents/YOKOHAMA%20GLOBAL%20COMMITMENT%202001_EN.pdf.

26. World Congress against Commercial Sexual Exploitation of Children, *Child Pornography*, 2001, http://www.csecworldcongress.org/PDF/en/Yokohama/Background_reading/Theme_papers/Theme%20paper%20Child%20Pornography.pdf.

27. Ibid.

28. Ibid.

29. Ibid.

30. However, legislation such as the Children's Internet Protection Act (CIPA), which was passed in 2000 in the United States, did require schools and libraries to implement filtering technology. See Lisa M. Bowman, "Supreme Court Backs Library Net Filter," *CNET News.com*, June 23, 2003, http://www.news.com/Supreme-Court-backs-library-Net-filters/2100-1028_3-1019952.html.

31. Gus Hosein, "Politics of the Information Society: The Bordering and Restraining of Global Data Flows," United Nations Educational, Scientific and Cultural Organization (2004): 29, http://unesdoc.unesco.org/images/0013/001375/137516e.pdf.

32. *Center for Democracy & Technology v. Pappert, G. J.*, 03-5051 U.S. District Court for the Eastern District of Pennsylvania, 2004, http://www.cdt.org/speech/pennwebblock/20040910memorandum.pdf.

33. Gus Hosein, "Politics of the Information Society: The Bordering and Restraining of Global Data Flows," United Nations Educational, Scientific and Cultural Organization (2004): 16.

34. Martin Bright, "BT Puts Block on Child Porn Sites," *The Observer*, June 6, 2004, http://www.guardian.co.uk/technology/2004/jun/06/childrensservices.childprotection.

35. Gus Hosein, "Politics of the Information Society: The Bordering and Restraining of Global Data Flows," United Nations Educational, Scientific and Cultural Organization (2004): 23.

36. Richard Clayton, "Failures in a Hybrid Content Blocking System" (paper presented at Workshop on Privacy Enhancing Technologies, Dubrovnik, Croatia, 2005), http://www.cl.cam.ac.uk/~rnc1/cleanfeed.pdf.

37. John Carr, "Internet Safety Must Be a Priority," *ECPAT Newsletter*, 3, (2004): 3–4, http://www.make-it-safe.net/eng/pdf/ECPAT_Newsletter48_Jul2004.pdf.

38. Clayton raises failures within the system including security vulnerabilities and identification of blocked content but none that impinge of freedom of expression. Clayton, "Failures in a Hybrid Content Blocking System" (paper presented at Workshop on Privacy Enhancing Technologies, Dubrovnik, Croatia, 2005), http://www.cl.cam.ac.uk/~rnc1/cleanfeed.pdf.

39. ECPAT, "Model of a National Plan," http://www.ecpat.net/EI/Global_npaModel.asp

40. The German system differs from most others because it focuses on having search engines block sites, rather than ISPs.

41. Although filtering has been announced, the status of the actual implementation is unclear.

42. Only one of several national ISPs participate in the filtering system.

43. Irene Graham, "ISP 'Voluntary'/Mandatory Filtering," libertus.net, February 20, 2008, http://libertus.net/censor/ispfiltering-gl.html.

44. Some of these countries do not implement a hybrid system such as the one in the United Kingdom and thus continue to overblock content.

45. Oran R. Young, *International Governance: Protecting the Environment in a Stateless Society* (Ithaca, NY: Cornell University Press, 1994), 151.

46. INHOPE, "Mission and Objectives of INHOPE," 2008, https://www.inhope.org/en/about/mission.html.

47. Australian Communications and Media Authority (ACMA), *Developments in Internet Filtering Technologies and Other Measures for Promoting Online Safety*, 2008, http://www.acma.gov.au/webwr/ _assets/main/lib310554/developments_in_internet_filters_1streport.pdf.

48. Save the Children, "Position Paper on Child Pornography and Internet-Related Sexual Exploitation of Children," 2003, https://www.inhope.org/system/files/stc-pp-cp.pdf.

49. Technical testing by the author as part of a research project on Internet filtering indicates that ISPs in Canada are blocking access to Web sites hosted in the United States. At this time definitive conclusions cannot be reached about why these sites are being filtered instead of being removed at the source. In another case a Dutch blogger found that the Dutch National Police were adding domestically hosted child pornography sites to their block list rather than taking legal action against the owners. See Karin Spaink, "Child Pornography: Fight It or Hide It?" February 19, 2008, Spaink.net, http://www.spaink.net/2008/02/19/child-pornography-fight-it-or-hide-it/.

50. INHOPE, "2007 Global Internet Trend Report: Trends Associated with Illegal Content on the Internet Based on the Experiences of the INHOPE International Network of Internet Hotlines," 2007, https://www.inhope.org/en/system/files/inhope_global_internet_trend_report_v1.0.pdf.

51. It is unclear what actions are taken within the countries found to be hosting such content. Are international sites forwarded to the relevant domestic hotlines through the INHOPE network? Are the INHOPE members receiving the content not taking action? In addition, it remains unclear how reports of action taken (or not taken) are passed back through INHOPE to the organization that initially reported the content.

52. Tyler Moore and Richard Clayton, "The Impact of Incentives on Notice and Take-down," Computer Laboratory, University of Cambridge, 2008, http://www.cl.cam.ac.uk/~rnc1/ takedown.pdf; Internet Watch Foundation, "Annual and Charity Report 2006," April 2007, http://www.iwf.org.uk/documents/20070412_iwf_annual_report_2006_(web).pdf.

53. Ibid.

54. Internet Watch Foundation, "Annual and Charity Report 2006," April 2007, http://www .iwf.org.uk/documents/20070412_iwf_annual_report_2006_(web).pdf.

55. Tyler Moore and Richard Clayton, "The Impact of Incentives on Notice and Take-down," Computer Laboratory, University of Cambridge, 2008, http://www.cl.cam.ac.uk/~rnc1/ takedown.pdf.

56. Ibid.

5 Intermediary Censorship

Ethan Zuckerman

Introduction

When academics, journalists, or Internet users discuss "Internet censorship," they are usually referring to the inability of users in a given country to access a specific piece of online content. For instance, when Internet policymakers from around the world came to Tunisia for the 2005 World Summit on the Information Society, they discovered that the Tunisian government was blocking access to several sites, including Yezzi.org, an online freedom of speech campaign.[1]

This model of Internet filtering, where Internet service providers (ISPs) implement directives issued by government authorities and block connections to selected Web addresses, has been extensively documented by the OpenNet Initiative using in-country testing. Identifying potential cases of filtering by ISPs is likely to be easier in the future with the advent of tools like Herdict (www.herdict.org), which invite end users to be involved with in-country testing on a continuing basis.

Given aggressive national filtering policies implemented in countries like Saudi Arabia, China, and Vietnam, state-sponsored ISP-level Web filtering has been an appropriate locus for academic study. However, ISPs are only one possible choke point in a global Internet. As the Internet increases in popularity around the world, we are beginning to see evidence of Internet filtering at other points in the network. Of particular interest are online service providers (OSPs) that host social networking services, blogs, and Web sites. Because so many Internet users are dependent on OSPs to publish content, censorship by these entities has the potential to be a powerful control on online speech.

In this chapter, I look at recent developments in intermediary censorship in China, where unclear government directives mandate censorship by blogging hosts, but provide little guidance for what content must be filtered. Confusion over U.S. trade restrictions is having a chilling effect on speech in the United States, where some OSPs are removing the accounts of users from sanctioned nations, including sensitive human rights Web sites. I examine the incentives and costs OSPs face surrounding removal of online content and argue that protection of online speech rights by these intermediaries will require an affirmation of their role as free speech providers and clarification of applicable laws and regulations.

Points of Control

While filtering by ISPs was well documented as early as 2002, and commercial tools to filter Internet access in schools, libraries, and businesses have been available since the late 1990s, filtering at other points in the network is a more recent phenomenon. Skype's Chinese-language client, built in cooperation with TOM Online, demonstrated that Internet filtering could be implemented at the client software level. In April 2006, Skype admitted that the co-branded Chinese version of the Skype text chat product filtered users' messages based on a list of banned keywords.[2] In 2008, Internet researcher Nart Villeneuve discovered that the TOM Skype software was not merely blocking keywords, but surveilling users, storing conversations where specific keywords had been mentioned.[3]

Examples like this indicate that scholars of Internet filtering and censorship need to develop methods to monitor and study filtering at other points in the network: an end user's operating system, application software and hardware; intermediate nodes in networks, beyond ISPs and boundary routers; Web hosting providers; and providers of social media services.

Companies that provide Web hosting services or social media platforms are becoming increasingly important as possible choke points as Web users publish content on Web servers they do not control. In the early days of the World Wide Web, most Web sites were managed by organizations that controlled the content posted on the sites, the server software that delivered Web pages, and the server hardware that ran the code. While some Web sites are still vertically integrated and managed, the vast majority of Web site developers rent server space from Web hosting companies or use free Web hosting services like Tripod.com or Wordpress.com.

These OSPs provide services to millions of users, most of whom would lack the means and technical skill to maintain their own Web servers. Sites that allow publishing in the context of more complex community interactions, like Facebook or LiveJournal, would be extremely difficult for even a sophisticated user to reproduce. The unique dynamics of those communities require thousands or millions of users to share a single platform managed by a community host. While the ease of use of these platforms has been a great boon for online free speech, it has put a great deal of power in the hands of companies that provide Web site or community hosting services.

Under pressure from local legal authorities, these companies can reveal sensitive information about users. Yahoo!'s Hong Kong office complied with Chinese government requests for the identity of a user who forwarded a memo documenting government pressure on Chinese journalists to an overseas Web site. Armed with information from Yahoo!, Chinese authorities arrested journalist Shi Tao and eventually sentenced him to ten years on charges of leaking state secrets.[4] These companies can also act as censors, removing material that governments deem unacceptable in local jurisdictions. More unsettlingly, they may also remove material based on misunderstandings of local laws or based on calculations of fiscal and legal risk.

Host-Based Censorship in China

Studies of ISP-based Internet filtering have characterized Chinese Internet filtering that was pervasive as early as 2002.[5] Bloggers and journalists refer to China's complex set of filtering practices as the Great Firewall. It should not be a surprise, then, that China has pioneered censorship at the Web and community hosting level, as well as filtering content by means of ISPs.

In March 2004, Chinese authorities closed down three blog hosts—blogcn.com, blogbus.com, and blogdriver.com—because of concerns that sensitive content was being published on these sites.[6] After these sites reopened, the OpenNet Initiative found evidence that Chinese-based blogging providers were using lists of sensitive keywords to prevent controversial content from being posted to their Web servers.[7] In June 2005, Rebecca MacKinnon demonstrated that Microsoft was using similar techniques to block content on their Chinese-language version of MSN Spaces—her attempts to start a blog titled "I love freedom of speech, human rights and democracy" (in Chinese) yielded an error message that she translates as "You must enter a title for your space. The title must not contain prohibited language, such as profanity. Please type a differ ent title."[8]

A report by Reporters Without Borders (RSF) and China Human Rights Defenders, released in October 2007, was compiled with the help of an anonymous technician (Mr. Tao) working for a Chinese Internet company, presumably a company involved with hosting user-generated content. The report, "A Journey to the Heart of Internet Censorship,"[9] details training efforts to ensure that employees of content hosting companies censor sensitive content, and describes a weekly meeting at the Internet Information Administrative Bureau of the employees of Beijing's 19 leading Web sites. The meetings outline sensitive topics likely to be discussed in the coming week and provide instructions on which topics are to be censored.

While RSF's report details efforts aimed at coordinating content censorship in China, subsequent research by MacKinnon reveals that such censorship is extremely unpredictable and subjective. In "China's Censorship 2.0: How Companies Censor Bloggers,"[10] MacKinnon and students tested censorship systems on 15 Chinese blogging providers, using a variety of potentially sensitive texts taken from Chinese-language blogs and news sites. Her team posted the text to author accounts on the 15 platforms, and checked to see whether (1) they were able to successfully post the material, (2) whether it remained posted 24–48 hours later, and (3) whether they could view the posted content from a Chinese ISP without using circumvention software.

Results varied widely. One of the blogging service providers tested blocked 60 of 108 tested texts. Another blocked only one. MacKinnon was unable to find a single text blocked by all blogging providers, though she concluded that current news topics, which she terms "sudden incidents" were far more likely to be blocked than other sensitive topics. She observes, "The wide variation in levels of censorship confirms that censorship of Chinese user-generated content is highly decentralized, and that implementation is left to the Web companies themselves."

While many countries block access to social media sites,[11] the vast majority of these blocked sites are managed and hosted in the United States. China's unusual approach of filtering access to sensitive sites and requiring social media providers to censor their users reflects the large number of social media companies based in China, catering to a huge domestic market. The history of filtering and censorship in China may have led to an especially effective model. Since many popular online publishing platforms are filtered by Chinese ISPs, Chinese netizens have gravitated to hosts located in China. Because these sites provide interfaces in Chinese, they are easier to use than U.S.-based sites. And while these sites engage in censorship to avoid government sanctions, most users will not notice the censorship until they try to post about sensitive topics.

It is somewhat surprising that we have not seen other countries that filter the Internet by means of ISPs implement China's model of platform-based censorship. However, Chinese companies have taken leadership in the social media world, while leading platforms for social media in many other countries that filter the Internet are located outside national control, generally within the United States.

OSP-Based Censorship in the United States

There is no evidence that the U.S. government is demanding censorship of OSPs in the same way that the Chinese government has attempted to control social media. However, unclear U.S. laws may have led to situations in which U.S.-based OSPs have removed user accounts, effectively silencing those users, based on legal misinterpretations.

Brenda Burrell is used to worrying about censorship. As one of the cofounders of Kubatana, a civil-society organization based in Harare, Zimbabwe, she works with human rights organizations whose members are routinely harassed and imprisoned for speaking in public or online. In a blog post, she notes that she is used to fielding questions about what might happen if the Mugabe regime shut down her Internet operations. But on February 6, 2009, she was surprised to hear from BlueHost, an American Web-hosting company, that Kubatana's Web site, along with the Web sites of Women of Zimbabwe Arise and Island Hospice and Bereavement Service, would be disabled so that BlueHost would remain in compliance with U.S. Treasury Department restrictions.[12]

BlueHost, which had hosted Kubatana's Web site, told Burrell that her site was in contravention of section 13 of their terms of service, which read in part:

Sanctioned Countries presently include, among others, Balkans, Belarus, Burma, Cote d'Ivoire (Ivory Coast), Cuba, Democratic Republic of the Congo, Iran, Iraq, former Liberian Regime of Charles Taylor, North Korea, Sudan, Syria, and Zimbabwe. 'Sanctioned Countries' shall be deemed automatically to be added to or otherwise modified from time to time consistent with the determination(s) of the government of the United States, and shall include all other countries with respect to which commercial activities are prohibited, embargoed, sanctioned, banned and/or otherwise excluded by determination(s) of the government of the United States from time to time.

1. Each Sanctioned Country, all governmental, commercial, or other entities located therein, and all individuals located in any Sanctioned Country are hereby prohibited from registering or signing up with, subscribing to, or using any service of BlueHost.Com.[13]

These are not the terms of service Burrell agreed to when opening an account with BlueHost. Archived copies of the BlueHost terms of service, retrieved via Archive.org, do not contain section 13—the section was evidently added sometime after February 8, 2008 (the last date BlueHost's terms of service is available via Archive.org).[14] Burrell was unaware of the change in terms of service until BlueHost alerted her that she would need to remove her Web site or face its removal.

Burrell challenged BlueHost's decision, not by arguing that she was in compliance with their terms of service—she clearly was not—but by arguing that these terms of service misrepresented the U.S. Treasury Department's sanctions. The sanctions Zimbabwe faces are targeted to the Mugabe regime, not toward all Zimbabweans. The U.S. Treasury Department's Office of Foreign Assets Control (OFAC) is quite specific about who the sanctions target:

Executive Order 13391 prohibits U.S. persons, wherever located, or anyone in the United States from engaging in any transactions with any person, entity or organization found to: 1.) be undermining democratic institutions and processes in Zimbabwe; 2.) have materially assisted, sponsored, or provided financial, material, or technological support to these entities; 3.) be or have been an immediate family member of a sanctions target; or 4.) be owned, controlled or acting on behalf of a sanctions target. Persons, entities and organizations referenced in Annex A of the Executive Order are all incorporated into OFAC's list of Specially Designated Nationals (SDNs).[15]

It would be difficult for a company like BlueHost to evaluate whether Burrell and Kubatana were engaged in undermining democratic institutions. Fortunately, OFAC maintains a list of Specially Designated Nationals that U.S. companies are banned from doing business with—checking against this list is significantly simpler.

Burrell forwarded the relevant OFAC sanctions documents to BlueHost's abuse department, sought assistance from the U.S. Embassy in Zimbabwe, and mounted an online campaign to pressure BlueHost to change its policies.[16] Neither the explanatory e-mails nor public campaign swayed BlueHost or their CEO Matt Heaton. Burrell reports that Heaton communicated with her directly on the matter of the campaign, telling her that her supporters were "spamming" him and that he was unwilling to help her resolve the situation given this external pressure.[17]

Pressure from the Treasury Department, however, was ultimately successful. Burrell received an e-mail from BlueHost on February 18 stating:

Per request from the Treasury Dept, we have reactivated your account with Bluehost. With the release from the Treasury Department received today from Rachel Nagle of the Treasury Department via telephone and email confirming on February, 18, 2009 that you do not appear on OFAC's list of Specially Designated Nationals and Blocked Persons we will continue hosting your website.

We apologize for any inconvenience this may have caused you.

Burrell and Kubatana decided that the "inconvenience" was significant enough that they moved their Web sites to a hosting company based in New Zealand and exempt from U.S. Treasury Department sanctions—the managing director of that company was alerted to Kubatana's status as a Zimbabwean nonprofit and affirmed his willingness to host their Web sites.

Zimbabwean human rights organizations were not the only ones affected by Blue-Host's interpretation of U.S. Treasury regulations. Yaraslau Kryvoi, a Belarusian activist based in Washington, DC, saw his blog, promoting the Belarusian American Association, taken down by BlueHost.[18] 1 Fathi, a prominent Persian blogger, reported that his blog, as well as several other Persian blogs, were being removed by BlueHost as they contravened Section 13 of the company's terms of service.[19]

Evgeny Morozov, reporting on the situation in *Newsweek*, suggests that BlueHost's decision was based on expediency: "Although BlueHost is one of the world's biggest hosting companies, it probably does not have the time or resources to match the OFAC list with its own customer ranks. Banning everyone from Belarus takes much less time and effort." He notes that BlueHost's terms of service are surprisingly sloppy—there's no nation called "the Balkans," and Morozov wonders whether Blue-Host plans on removing Romanian and Slovenian sites as well.[20] It is worth noting that, despite Burrell's successful protest and Morozov's article, BlueHost's terms of service still include a blanket block on usage from 11 nations, one region, and one long-deposed regime.

The removal of Iranian, Belarusian, and Zimbabwean content is deeply ironic, given that the sites that were removed were critical of the governments being sanctioned by the United States. The actions taken by BlueHost, either at the encouragement of the Treasury Department or because of their misinterpretation of Treasury regulations, had an effect opposite to what was intended by those sanctions—by silencing criticism, the removal of these sites benefits the sanctioned governments.

An Emerging Trend?

It is possible that BlueHost may be on the leading edge of a new trend. Social networking site LinkedIn.com began blocking Syrian users from connecting to their site in April 2009. Anas Marrawi reported that LinkedIn began blocking Syrian users based on their IP in late March, but that Syrian users continued to use the site through filtering-circumvention software. On April 19, Marrawi reported that the site delivered a message to any users who had listed their home country as Syria when they logged on: "Access to this account has been suspended. Please contact Customer Service to resolve this problem." He contacted customer service and was told that LinkedIn could no longer provide services to Syrian users.[21]

Like Kubatana targeting BlueHost, Syrian LinkedIn users and their supporters began an online campaign to convince LinkedIn to reevaluate their policies. Jillian York,[22] a U.S.-based blogger with strong ties to the Syrian online community, helped coordinate the effort, writing about the block on the Huffington Post[23] and promoting the cause on Twitter. Through Twitter, she got in touch with LinkedIn's senior director of corporate communications, who quickly issued a mea culpa and promised a swift reversal of the decision.[24] Shortly after, LinkedIn issued the following statement: "Some changes made to our site recently resulted in Syrian users being unable to access LinkedIn. In looking into this matter, it has come to our attention that human error led to over compliance with respect to export controls. This issue is being addressed tonight and service to our Syrian users should be restored shortly."[25]

It is unclear what has motivated U.S. Web hosting and social media companies to ensure they are in compliance with Treasury restrictions and export controls. Like Blue-Host, LinkedIn has recently changed their terms of service. The current terms of service references export controls in its opening section: "Your use of LinkedIn services, including its software, is subject to export and reexport control laws and regulations, including the the Export Administration Regulations ('EAR') maintained by the United States Department of Commerce and sanctions programs maintained by the Treasury Department's Office of Foreign Assets Control."[26] An archived version of their terms of service,[27] from January 3, 2008, makes no reference to export controls or sanctioned countries. Users of hosting and social media tools who live in nations subject to U.S. export controls or sanctions face an extremely confusing situation. LinkedIn, MySpace, and Blogger make reference to U.S. export laws, while YouTube, Facebook, Wikipedia, Rapidshare, and Wordpress do not.[28]

Web hosting companies are similarly divided—of the 22 top hosting sites, as tracked by Webhosting.info,[29] BlueHost, sister company Hostmonster, and hosting company One and One require users to certify that they are not from a list of specified countries. Network Solutions and BCentral offer a general caution that users must comply with U.S. export laws, and the other hosts do not mention export controls or sanctions in their terms of service. (Based on an examination of current terms of service of the 22 top sites as listed by Webhosting.info. One of the top sites does not offer a formal terms of service—it controls hundreds of thousands of domains itself, but has no customer relationships. Two sites serving China did not have terms of service available on their Web sites. Evaluation covers the remaining 19 sites.)

In contrast to BlueHost's decision to deny service to over 300 million potential customers, sanctioned or not, other companies are taking a de minimis approach to compliance with U.S. government restrictions. Andrew McLaughlin, senior policy counsel for Google, notes, "We do the minimum to comply with the export restrictions and sanctions regimes. Primarily, this means (1) we don't allow downloads of software (Google Earth, e.g.,) containing cryptography from IPs believed to be in restricted countries (Cuba, Iran, North Korea, Syria, Sudan)—this includes the Google download server and code.google.com; and (2) we don't engage in any sort of money transactions into or out of restricted countries. We do not, though, block access to publicly available sites where there are no downloads."[30] Perhaps in reaction to the criticism the company took for filtering search results in the Chinese market, Google has demonstrated a willingness to challenge government-mandated filtering measures. When South Korea passed a law requiring online postings to be accompanied by the author's real name and ID card number, Google's YouTube division disabled commenting and video uploads from South Korea, but allows Korean users to state that they are posting from another country and post anonymously.[31]

The Economics of Intermediary Censorship

Google may have decided to disable comments in South Korea to make a statement about how requiring identification systems limits online speech. Or they may have been making a smart business decision—it would have required a major engineering effort for Google to build an identity authentication system for YouTube in Korea. The decisions BlueHost, LinkedIn, and others have made make more sense in a context of business risk and reward, rather than in a free speech and human rights context.

BlueHost advertises entry-level Web hosting for an annual cost of USD 83.40. Web hosting is a highly competitive business, and profit margins tend to be quite tight. With professional legal counsel experienced in U.S. export and sanctions law charging hundreds of dollars an hour for advice, it is an easy decision for BlueHost to sacrifice a handful of customer relationships in exchange for avoiding legal review. It is possible that LinkedIn made a similar evaluation and reversed course when public pressure indicated that LinkedIn's cost in terms of public relations damage might be substantial for removing Syrian users.

Wendy Seltzer identifies the problem of "unbalanced incentives" as a major concern in the United States' administration of the Digital Millennium Copyright Act (DMCA).

Section 512(c) of the DMCA provides "safe harbor" from liability due to copyright infringement if online service providers follow a prescribed procedure to remove copyrighted content when alerted by the copyright's owner.[32] On receiving a properly completed notice, an OSP should promptly remove the content in question and alert the individual who posted it, giving her an opportunity to respond with a counternotice to the party claiming infringement—on receipt of this counternotice, the OSP should restore the material to the Internet within 14 business days.

Seltzer argues that OSPs have a great incentive to take down potentially infringing material (the threat of litigation from movie studios or record companies), but significantly less incentive to protect the First Amendment rights of users. Providers do not generally alert their users that they might have a fair use argument to defend their use of a piece of content or direct users to sites like Chilling Effects (www.chillingeffects .org), a clearinghouse of information on takedown notices developed by Seltzer and others. The incentives for removing content are large, and they are small—and perhaps negative—for OSPs to encourage their users to fight takedown notices. If an OSP develops a reputation for aggressively defending user rights, it is likely to attract more users who generate infringement claims. Each one of these claims requires time and legal resources from an OSP to respond to—as a result, OSPs have an incentive to rapidly remove potentially infringing users and, perhaps, to discourage them from returning.

Sjoera Nas and the Dutch nonprofit Bits of Freedom wondered whether Netherlands ISPs would defend user rights against complaints of copyright infringement, so they mounted an experiment. In 2004, they opened accounts with ten Dutch OSPs and posted the same public domain text written by Eduard Douwes Dekker, better known by the pen name Multatuli. Then, they sent complaints in the name of a fictitious Mr. Johan Droogleever, legal advisor to the E. D. Dekker Society, which claimed to hold copyright to the works and demanded their removal. Seven of ten OSPs complied swiftly, without challenging the claim or demanding further information, despite the fact that the e-mail came from a Hotmail address. However, ISPs generally alerted the fictitious customer to the takedown request. Nas concludes, "It only takes a Hotmail account to bring a website down, and freedom of speech stands no chance in front of the cowboy-style private ISP justice."[33]

Whether Seltzer or Nas is correct in being concerned that copyright infringement complaints favor IP owners rights over user rights, the mechanisms for removing content suggest key weaknesses that censors could exploit. During the 2008 presidential election, both the Obama and McCain camps found that campaign videos were frequently removed from YouTube. The videos in question generally featured small excerpts from broadcast television newscasts, and takedown notices were issued by those broadcasters. The campaigns challenged the takedowns, arguing that their use of excerpts represented fair use.[34] Given the rapid-fire nature of political campaigns, the 14 business days it can take to restore a video to YouTube may effectively constitute censorship. It seems likely that we will see political rivals attempt to disable each other's online speech using spurious copyright claims, even though these claims run the risk of exposing a complainant to penalties for acting in bad faith.

We are already beginning to see attacks on online speech that attempt to trigger an "immune system response" from hosting companies. Irrawaddy, a leading Web site for Burmese dissidents, suffered a series of distributed denial of service (DDoS) attacks in September 2008. Other pro-dissident sites, including the Oslo-based Democratic Voice of Burma and the New Era Journal, based in Bangkok, were rendered inaccessible by DDoS attacks, prompting speculation that the attacks were the work of hackers hired by the Burmese government.[35] As Irrawaddy struggled to fend off the DDoS attacks, its hosting provider became increasingly agitated, since the DDoS attack affected their other customers. For a period of time, the attack was so severe that Thailand's primary Internet connection was overloaded with DDoS traffic. The attack had the immediate effect of making the site unreachable, as well as the longer-term effect of forcing Irrawaddy to find a new ISP.[36]

As with copyright takedown notices, OSPs have a strong incentive to remove "troublesome" users—DDoS attacks can require hours of expensive system administration time to fend off. For hosting accounts that generate little revenue, the cost of fending off even a small DDoS is likely to exceed profit margins, and OSPs have an incentive to remove customers who have come under attack. Providers that develop a reputation for protecting their users from DDoS attacks are likely to attract customers who come under DDoS attacks, increasing their costs. As such, some OSPs are comfortable removing customers because they have come under attack. A libel lawsuit between Colocation America and Archie Garga-Richardson, whose Web site came under DDoS attack while hosted by Colocation America, makes it clear that OSPs are sometimes willing to remove customers generating thousands of dollars of revenue.[37]

Implications for Researchers

While the underlying threats to speech are deeply different between the case of Chinese blogging hosts studied by MacKinnon and U.S.-based OSPs outlined here, a common theme emerges: threats to online speech come not just from government action, but from the needs of OSPs to interpret and follow government regulations and to turn an operating profit. If this trend persists and grows, it has implications for scholars and activists focused on this issue.

Scholars need to develop tools and methods to study corporate filtering of Internet content. These methods might incorporate the techniques pioneered by MacKinnon in testing Chinese Web sites for automated censorship, perhaps with development of more robust tools to help automate testing. They could also include a site like Chilling Effects focused on collecting reports of corporate censorship of content, or an expansion of the work of the Citizen Media Law Project to thoroughly document filtering and censorship by online service providers beyond the United States. Global Voices Advocacy, which now maps the accessibility of social media Web sites in different countries, may need to start mapping Web sites that ban users from certain countries.

To the extent that confusion over U.S. Treasury and export restrictions is leading toward the removal of Web sites and the understandable uncertainty of users in sanctioned countries, it may be worth pursuing clarifications from the U.S. government. Clinical students at the Berkman Center at Harvard are pursuing a formal request to the U.S. Treasury's Office of Foreign Asset Control to clarify the restrictions that social media and Web hosting companies face in providing services to users in sanctioned countries. If the Berkman Center receives useful clarifications, it will need to develop a strategy to communicate these guidelines to the affected companies.

Intermediary censorship by U.S. companies appears to be experiencing a steep and sudden rise. In May 2009, Vineetha Menon reported that Microsoft had turned off its Windows Live Messenger service in Iran, Syria, Sudan, Cuba, and North Korea, citing OFAC sanctions.[38] It is likely that Microsoft, BlueHost, and LinkedIn are not acting entirely independently—they may all be coming under pressure from the U.S. Treasury Department or another government authority. It would be useful for journalists or researchers to determine whether there is an organized campaign to remove users from these five sanctioned countries from U.S.-based tools. Given the use of these tools by human rights activists and ordinary citizens, a policy of removing all users in sanctioned nations from these tools merits careful public debate. It is possible that the most interested opponent of U.S. Treasury policy might be the U.S. State Department, anxious to hear opposition voices in repressive nations.

Imbalanced Incentives and Free Speech

So long as it continues to be possible for for-profit OSPs to terminate difficult clients for arbitrary reasons, it is likely that we will see providers "optimizing" their client base, providing services to customers who do not attract DDoS attacks or copyright or trade complaints. In a recent *New York Times* article, Brad Stone and Miguel Helft introduce the troubling idea that social media sites may start restricting memberships for users in developing nations because they are finding it difficult to target ads to these users.[39]

If these trends increase, organizations dedicated to free and open speech, especially in developing nations, may find themselves needing to create OSPs specifically oriented toward the needs of users who are less fiscally appealing to social media and Web hosting companies. We can imagine supporters of human rights creating OSPs explicitly to provide services for human rights organizations.

This is probably a poor idea. The cost structures of these organizations will be significantly higher than for traditional hosting providers, as they are likely to attract users who come under attack by DDoS or who introduce complex legal questions. Furthermore, when human rights activists congregate on a small subset of servers, traditional ISP-level filtering becomes a more effective tool for censoring sensitive speech. If all sites critical of Burmese government policy are located on a single group of servers, that server is certain to be blocked at a national level, and is likely to come under sustained DDoS attack. By utilizing OSPs used by nonactivists, activists raise the social cost of traditional censorship—a country that chooses to block the Blogger.com domain to prevent access to a subset of blogs removes access from millions of uncontroversial Web sites, alienating citizens. Individuals who were not interested in the censored content become aware of the censorship when they can no longer access other Blogger.com sites.

Rather than creating a subset of Web sites that protect speech, it would be vastly better to see OSPs affirm their roles as providers of free speech tools to users throughout the world. As discussed earlier, this is a difficult decision for an organization, particularly a for-profit company, to make in isolation. At the moment, companies seem to be choosing a legally cautious path, disabling access for users in sanctioned countries before experiencing pressure from activists.

The experience of the successful protest against LinkedIn's block of Syrian users suggests that one powerful tool activists have is public protest. While companies may make a calculated financial decision to discontinue services to certain users, public pressure can add another factor into the equation—the potential lost business from bad publicity. While the LinkedIn protest shows the power of this strategy, BlueHost's decision not to reconsider their terms of service shows that the influence of public pressure may be limited.

Given the importance of OSPs as a space for open, public speech, it is necessary to consider their responsibilities as common carriers. For OSPs to limit their liabilities as common carriers, they should be required to provide services to anyone legally using these services, even if their usage is likely to attract DDoS attacks. To do otherwise is to allow attackers a "heckler's veto," an ability to silence speech by creating a damaging and expensive response to that speech. If OSPs are required to provide services to any law-abiding users, an appropriate response to this form of intermediary censorship is legal action to address discrimination, not public protest. An affirmation of OSPs' role as common carriers would not resolve the situation Iranian and Syrian users are facing, but it might invite legal action that would force clarification of U.S. Treasury sanctions.

Conclusion

In countries like China, where online speech is carefully monitored and controlled, we are likely to see intermediary censorship emerge as an increasingly important component of a censorship apparatus. Filtering at the OSP level blocks content from reaching both local and international audiences, allowing more thorough control of online content. The phenomenon is most developed in China, in part because existing Internet filtering strategies drive local users to publish on locally hosted sites, and in part because linguistic constraints drive Chinese-speaking users to a particular set of tools. If filtering and language constraints drive users in the Middle East toward locally hosted tools, we might expect to see similar systems of OSP-based filtering emerge.

As users around the world look to online services hosted in less controlled countries to find unfiltered venues to publish their content, other forms of content filtering are emerging. Online service providers have compelling financial incentives not to host content likely to provoke DDoS attacks or raise complex legal issues. While clarification of relevant regulations may help reduce uncertainty about what content can and cannot be hosted, there is a danger that OSPs will stop providing services to some users. This tendency needs to be counterbalanced by the sorts of public protest that called attention to BlueHost's and LinkedIn's actions, but user's rights will only be guaranteed by an affirmation of common carrier status that explicitly protects rights to publish on these platforms.

Notes

1. Rebecca MacKinnon, "Tunisian Online Protest Blocked," Global Voices, October 4, 2005, http://globalvoicesonline.org/2005/10/04/tunisian-online-protest-blocked/.

2. Ben Charny, "Chinese Partner Censors Skype Text Messages," PCmag.com, April 20, 2006, http://www.pcmag.com/article2/0,2817,1951637,00.asp.

3. Nart Villeneuve, "Breaching Trust: An Analysis of Surveillance and Security Practices on China's TOM-Skype Platform" (Information Warfare Monitor/ONI Asia, October 1, 2008), http://www.nartv.org/mirror/breachingtrust.pdf.

4. Reporters Without Borders, "Information Supplied by Yahoo! Helped Journalist Shi Tao Get 10 Years in Prison," September 6, 2005, http://www.rsf.org/article.php3?id_article=14884.

5. Jonathan Zittrain and Benjamin Edleman, "Empirical Analysis of Internet Filtering in China" (Berkman Center for Internet and Society, Harvard Law School, March 2003), http://cyber.law.harvard.edu/filtering/china/.

6. Mat Honan, "Little Red Blogs," Salon, June 4, 2004, http://dir.salon.com/story/tech/feature/2004/06/04/china_blogs/index.html.

7. OpenNet Initiative, "OpenNet Initiative: Bulletin 008, Filtering by Domestic Blog Providers in China," January 20, 2005, http://opennet.net/bulletins/008/.

8. Rebecca MacKinnon, "Screenshots of Censorship," RConversation Blog, June 17, 2005, http://rconversation.blogs.com/rconversation/2005/06/screenshots_of_.html.

9. Reporters Without Borders, "A 'Journey to the Heart of Internet censorship' on Eve of Party Congress," October 10, 2007, http://www.rsf.org/article.php3?id_article=23924.

10. Rebecca MacKinnon, "China's Censorship 2.0: How Companies Censor Blogs," *First Monday* 14, no. 2 (2009), http://firstmonday.org/htbin/cgiwrap/bin/ojs/index.php/fm/article/view/2378/2089.

11. See Global Voices Advocacy for a map of social media censorship. Global Voices Advocacy, "Access Denied Map," October 29, 2008, http://advocacy.globalvoicesonline.org/projects/maps/.

12. Bev Clark, "Curve Balls and Blue Beards," Kubanta.net, February 17, 2009, http://www.kubatanablogs.net/kubatana/?p=1261.

13. BlueHost, "Bluehost.com Terms of Service," 2009, http://www.bluehost.com/cgi/info/terms.html.

14. BlueHost, "Bluehost.com Terms of Service," archive.org, February 8, 2008, http://web.archive.org/web/20080201055355/www.bluehost.com/terms_of_service.html.

15. U.S. Department of the Treasury, Office of Foreign Assets Control, "Zimbabwe: What You Need to Know about U.S. Economic Sanctions—An Overview of O.F.A.C. Regulations Involving Sanctions against Zimbabwe," November 13, 2005, http://www.treas.gov/offices/enforcement/ofac/programs/ascii/zimb.txt.

16. The author was involved in this online campaign and advised Burrell on her dealings with BlueHost.

17. Bev Clark, "Curve Balls and Blue Beards," Kubanta.net, February 17, 2009, http://www.kubatanablogs.net/kubatana/?p=1261.

18. Evgeny Morozov, "Do-It-Yourself Censorship," *Newsweek*, March 7, 2009. http://www.newsweek.com/id/188184.

19. Kanmangir, "Persian Blogs on Bluehost Will Be Going Down," February 23, 2009, http://kamangir.net/2009/02/23/persion-blogs-on-bluehost-will-be-going-down/.

20. Evgeny Morozov, "Do-It-Yourself Censorship," *Newsweek*, March 7, 2009. http://www.newsweek.com/id/188184.

21. ArabCrunch, "LinkedIn Kicks Off Syrian Users!," April 17, 2009, http://arabcrunch.com/2009/04/breaking-linkedin-kicks-off-syrian-users.html; Morozov, "Do-It-Yourself Censorship."

22. York works for the Berkman Center for Internet and Society at Harvard University, focused on the OpenNet Initiative.

23. Jillian York, "LinkedIn Alienates Syrian Users: Why Now?" Huffington Post, April 20, 2009, http://www.huffingtonpost.com/jillian-york/linkedin-alienates-syrian_b_188629.html.

24. Mary Joyce, "Why LinkedOut Syrians Are LinkedIn Again," Digiactive, April 21, 2009, http://www.digiactive.org/2009/04/21/why-linkedout-syrians-are-linkedin-again/.

25. Jillian York, "LinkedIn Alienates Syrian Users: Why Now?" Huffington Post, April 20, 2009, http://www.huffingtonpost.com/jillian-york/linkedin-alienates-syrian_b_188629.html.

26. LinkedIn, "User Agreement," January 22, 2009, http://www.linkedin.com/static?key=user _agreement.

27. LinkedIn, "User Agreement," archive.org, January 3, 2008, http://web.archive.org/web/ 20080103101839/http://www.linkedin.com/static?key=user_agreement.

28. Current terms of service were examined for the top social media sites, as listed by Alexa.com.

29. Webhosting.info, "Top Web Hosts Worldwide," 2009, http://www.webhosting.info/ webhosts/tophosts/global/.

30. Andrew McLaughlin, personal communication, April 2008.

31. Martyn Williams, "Google Disables Uploads, Comments on YouTube Korea," PCWorld.com, April 13, 2009, http://www.pcworld.com/article/162989/google_disables_uploads_comments _on_youtube_korea.html.

32. Wendy Seltzer, ""Intermediaries, Incentive Misalignments, and the Shape of Online Speech?" (unpublished manuscript, Berkman Center for Internet and Society, Harvard Law School, 2009).

33. Sjorea Nas, "The Multatuli Project: ISP Notice and Takedown," October 1, 2004, http:// 74.125.45.132/search?q=cache:lKhZFWp5TkcJ:www.bof.nl/docs/researchpaperSANE.pdf.

34. Fred von Lohmann, "McCain Campaign Feels DMCA Sting," Electronic Frontier Foundation, October 14, 2008, http://www.eff.org/deeplinks/2008/10/mccain-campaign-feels-dmca-sting.

35. Lwin Aung Soe, "Request Mail from Irrawaddy Website Due to Cyber Attack; Hoping to Defeat Hackers Soon," Save Burma, September 19, 2008, http://antidictatorship.wordpress.com/2008/09/ 19/request-mail-from-irrawaddy-website-due-to-cyber-attack/.

36. Irrawaddy system administrators, e-mail message to author, May 2008.

37. Citizen Media Law Project, "Colocation America v. Garga-Richardson (Letter)," April 1, 2009, http://www.citmedialaw.org/threats/colocation-america-v-garga-richardson-letter.

38. Vineetha Menon, "US Sanctions Sees Live Messenger Blocked in Syria," itp.net, May 25, 2009, http://www.itp.net/news/556637-us-sanctions-sees-live-messenger-blocked-in-syria.

39. Brad Stone and Miguel Helft, "In Developing Countries, Web Grows without Profit," New York Times, April 26, 2009, http://www.nytimes.com/2009/04/27/technology/start-ups/27global.html.

6 Protecting Privacy and Expression Online

Can the Global Network Initiative Embrace the Character of the Net?

Colin M. Maclay

Introduction

When Yahoo! became interested in building upon the surprise success of its services in Vietnam, it was not simply a matter of finding an established partner or setting up local servers, but began with a human rights impact assessment. This process sought to anticipate the potential risks to freedom of expression and privacy in Vietnam that might result from expanded operations, and to develop strategies to mitigate them. What could happen if the Vietnamese authorities determined a blog post to be illegal and demanded its removal, also requesting the author's name? Ultimately, Yahoo! decided to make its data harder to reach by hosting servers offshore (in Singapore), to reduce vulnerability to external pressure by minimizing the number and responsibilities of staff (hiring only a local sales team, rather than people with operational control), and to implement a series of other policies intended to limit avenues used by government to abridge human rights.[1]

Although the decisions implied slower service and less robust operations, Yahoo! placed those costs in perspective of previous very difficult and public lessons, most notably, the ugly aftermath of having provided Chinese authorities with information used in the 2005 imprisonment of Chinese journalist Shi Tao.[2] This trade of near-term profits for principles (and hopefully, long-term gain) was informed—and required—by a nascent multistakeholder effort called the Global Network Initiative (GNI),[3] of which Yahoo! is a founding member. Participants evaluate human rights risks and seek opportunities to mitigate them when considering whether and how to enter a new market. Yahoo!'s motivations were likely diverse, but the actions were aligned with their mission, corporate health and profitability,[4] and the preferences of at least some shareholders.[5]

GNI's collaborative approach to compensating for the lack of effective legal and policy measures to protect and advance online privacy and expression extends far beyond these assessments, recognizing that genuine progress requires a context of conscious corporate commitment to meaningfully integrate the protection of freedom of expression and privacy into both business practice and corporate culture. For its part, in 2008, Yahoo! created the Business and Human Rights Program, supported by corporate leadership, guided by principles and internal process, staffed by cross-functional teams, tracking an inventory of rights issues, informed by stakeholder engagement, and subject to outside monitoring and accountability.[6] These internal developments are complemented, informed, and reinforced by Yahoo!'s participation in the GNI.

From recent postelection violence in Kenya and Moldova facilitated by mobile devices to vibrant online expression in Vietnam, ongoing battles over culturally sensitive (and legally prohibited) imagery online in Turkey and Thailand, and the record proportion of online journalists detained worldwide in 2008, digital tools are associated with voice and power, and governments realize it. Whether as part of the normal sociopolitical milieu or in a moment of crisis, they are increasingly aware not only of the power of new media, but also of the role of private companies in providing—and potentially limiting—that power.

Governments also seem to be more cognizant of the unique characteristics of the Net as compared to traditional media, not only in terms of how these traits might allow it to threaten the status quo, but also where associated weaknesses can lie. However mistakenly, many people have come to understand this vulnerability of information and communication technologies (ICT) companies to government interference as *the China Problem*, owing in large measure to publicized instances in which Microsoft, Yahoo!, and Google have failed to adequately protect their users' rights to freedom of expression and privacy. Unfortunately, similar challenges are emerging around the world, oftentimes at the hands of democratic governments, and not only in the Global South, but also in the West.[7]

In response to these tensions and understanding the complexity of resolving them, a group of companies, civil society organizations, investors, and academics spent over two years creating a collaborative approach to protect and advance freedom of expression and privacy in the ICT sector, and formed an initiative to take this work forward. Proposed by my colleagues John Palfrey and Jonathan Zittrain in the book *Access Denied* and elsewhere,[8] the GNI released foundational documents in October 2008 and publicly launched in December 2008 on the 60th anniversary of the Universal Declaration of Human Rights. The group includes Google, Microsoft, and Yahoo!, along with numerous noncompany participants, such as Human Rights Watch, Human Rights in China, Committee to Project Journalists, Human Rights First, Calvert Investments, Center for Democracy and Technology (CDT), and the Berkman Center for Internet and Society, where I work.

The process has been rewarding and challenging, seeking to move beyond mistrust, hostility, and competition, drawing upon human rights experiences in sectors as far afield as labor and security, and balancing the perspectives and needs of the diverse participants. It began as three separate processes, driven respectively by companies, scholars, and non-governmental organizations. In early 2006, a group of companies first met to draft an industry code of conduct under the joint facilitation of Business for Social Responsibility (BSR) and the Berkman Center. That spring, Orville Schell and Xiao Qiang of the University of California-Berkeley's Graduate School of Journalism initiated the creation of a code of conduct by academics, in collaboration with the Berkman Center. Meanwhile, CDT convened a third set of actors to deepen understanding, raise issue awareness, and seek solutions. Participants from the three processes met in Oxford in July 2006 and soon agreed to work together.

This chapter examines the context in which GNI has emerged, describes its structure and intentions, explores some concerns, and highlights some of the challenges GNI must address to fulfill its intended purpose. Issues that will impact success include the tensions among structure and flexibility, aspiration and practicality, and refining known approaches and creating new ones. While these considerations play into many elements of the initiative, they are particularly salient with respect to accountability and governance. I offer these thoughts as objectively as possible, recognizing my personal participation throughout the process, to support collective understanding of both this process and emerging institutional approaches to governance in the knowledge society.

Government and Business Collide: Expression and Privacy at Risk

All over the world, companies in the ICT sector face increasing government pressure to comply with domestic laws and practices in ways that conflict with both core elements of their business and their users' fundamental rights to privately impart and access information and communication. Whether law enforcement officials request a user's personal information for unknown reasons or a takedown of content that is acceptable in other jurisdictions, companies find themselves in an untenable position in which they must balance their obligation to respect local law with their responsibility to protect the rights of their users. Companies know that resisting a government is costly, perhaps placing their operating license and local employees at risk, but that acceding blindly can have terrible implications for them and their users, and that this tension is ever more part of their business. A (more) sustainable solution is essential.[9]

Described most comprehensively by Palfrey and Zittrain in *Access Denied* and informed by the OpenNet Initiative's research, the problem has been framed in many ways, whether as an ethical issue, a reckless drive for appealing markets, an international legal question, a matter of Internet governance, a trade barrier,[10] or an organizational deficit. It is clear that ICT companies (broadly interpreted) face very real challenges with respect to freedom of expression and privacy. Left unchecked, governments seem likely to chip away at these fundamental freedoms, potentially leading companies into a proverbial race to the bottom, with a possibly daunting impact upon these liberties and the other rights they help to protect. Responsible international companies might also choose to withdraw from such markets in order to protect themselves against complicity, thereby further limiting the options of local users and sacrificing the opportunity to engage troublesome governments constructively.

Under the guidance of the Special Representative of the Secretary-General of the United Nations on business and human rights, John Ruggie, the United Nations has developed the Protect, Respect, and Remedy Framework: "Each principle is an essential component of the framework: the state duty to protect because it lies at the very core of the international human rights regime; the corporate responsibility to respect because it is the basic expectation society has of business; and access to remedy, because even the most concerted efforts cannot prevent all abuse, while access to judicial redress is often problematic, and non-judicial means are limited in number, scope, and effectiveness. The three principles form a complementary whole in that each supports the others in achieving sustainable progress."[11]

Ruggie's work recognizes the tremendous power of business but points out that markets work best when they exist in the context of rules and institutions. While he identifies governance gaps created by globalization as a root cause of the often uneasy and sometimes negative relationship between business and human rights, he also notes that most businesses do not actually have systems to know when they are causing harm.

Government Steps In: Policy and Regulatory Responses

While business has focused its requests on the executive branch, requesting bilateral assistance in individual cases and on trade issues, civil society has been more likely to call for proscriptive legal solutions, spurring significant legislative interest.[12] Such approaches face many challenges, including law's tendency to trail technology because of its rapid pace of change, evolving business models, unanticipated user behavior, and unpredictable government action, to say nothing of the cultural differences and jurisdictional issues associated with globalization and the Internet. These factors, combined with the desire to support continued innovation and creativity in the ICT space, suggest that specific legal interventions or policy prescriptions may be premature, or may even risk taking a step backward.

A varied group of supporters within the U.S. Congress has harnessed members who are rights supporters and China-watchers, liberals and conservatives, to raise issue awareness. Holding frequent hearings and considering the Global Online Freedom Act (GOFA)[13] annually for the past three years, their actions may occur at the intersection of policy and politics, but they have created invaluable urgency for companies to take action. Amid many other legitimate concerns, CDT has criticized GOFA for creating an adversarial relationship with companies, rather than a collaborative one.[14] For its part, the U.S. Department of State created the Global Internet Freedom Task Force to track the issue and engage with foreign governments, but along with the Department of Justice, the State Department also expressed concern over GOFA.[15] The shortest version of our analysis at the Berkman Center is that GOFA is simply too blunt, impractical, and inflexible: although the GNI may provide the basis for law over time, we simply do not yet have a clear enough sense of the answers to mandate any particular approach, let alone the proposed one.[16]

European policymakers have likewise been active on issues related to online expression and privacy on both the substantive and the political fronts. The Council of Europe has offered actionable insights, including fostering understanding and developing useful guidance for the interactions between ICT service providers and law enforcement[17] and providing clear and detailed guidance on human rights issues for ICT providers.[18] The European Parliament weighed in on security and freedom online, calling for sustained engagement and expressing interest in developing a multistakeholder initiative.[19] It has also recommended the creation of a code of conduct for freedom of expression.[20] Parliamentarians from across Europe also introduced a version of GOFA,[21] leading Viviane Reding, European Commission Lead Member on the Information Society, to express concern over the "heavy" nature of the instruments (including the prospect of forcing companies to withdraw and leave markets to less scrupulous competitors) and to place promise in the GNI.[22]

Sadly, even as some governments seek to address this problem globally, numerous competing government efforts are under way that will abridge the human rights others are seeking to preserve.[23] While problems in developing and transitioning countries first caught the public eye, it is the disconcerting legislation among early Internet adopters that has received attention recently. From proposals for national filtering in Australia to the South Korean government's requirement for real name legislation, efforts to rein in perceived Internet dangers represent troubling examples for countries that are just beginning their policymaking efforts related to the Internet.

Stakeholders Unite: Global Network Initiative

Recognizing profound challenges associated with the broad spectrum of laws and practices related to freedom of expression and privacy in states around the world, as well as the laws and standards of home countries, employees, shareholders, and the international community, some ICT companies decided not to continue down this path in isolation. The initial framing was inspired substantially by the Sullivan Principles,[24] introduced in 1977 as a code of conduct for U.S. companies doing business in apartheid South Africa. An industry-code approach offered the potential to set a higher standard than if companies were left to fend for themselves, allowed them to benefit from the strength of their numbers, and it recognized the need for even dread competitors to unite around certain values—all while retaining control of the expectations.

But given the complexity of the current situation—that it is not simply about companies following the law (or divesting), but also about companies understanding when and how to challenge the law and avoiding conflicts and mitigating risk in the first place—increased expectations alone would have limited impact. Gaining a deeper and wider understanding of the pressures, developing supportive internal process and structure, advancing global transparency, and engaging other stakeholders were judged equally important—and best accomplished collectively. The perspective was not based simply on altruism, but established by recognizing the broader business case, including the fundamental social obligations of which companies have been clearly reminded by human rights organizations, academics, investors, shareholders, and U.S. and European policymakers through protest, legislation, shareholder resolutions, and public criticism. Ultimately, the companies recognized that they faced a serious business problem with profound implications for all human rights.

Conversations about developing a response began in early 2006, with a consensus emerging that underscored the importance of collaboration across sectors, each recognizing that it required the other for understanding, implementation, legitimacy, experience, access, and so on. There was consensus that law and regulation were not currently attending to the challenges that individual companies confronted in seeking to respond responsibly to government requests. An unlikely family was born, including former colleagues, current competitors, and long-time critics, and in which each group needed the other to accomplish its goals and across which there was (perhaps) surprising overlap. There was also a great diversity of views, in particular, on how best to achieve those goals, what to take as givens, and so on.

Beginnings
As the group moved from research and brainstorming to drafting, clear questions emerged. What was the proper balance between aspiration (as manifest in documents and language) and realistic, operational, and evaluable results? How high should the bar be set? How would the noncompany partners (and the world) know whether the company partners were implementing (and maintaining) their commitments? What was the scope of the effort, in terms of company types, technologies, and business models? Should focus go beyond freedom of expression and privacy, extending to other rights, or to rule of law? What were the primary activities in which the group could begin to see results in the near term and create value over time?

The group was able to exploit its institutional and individual differences, using them to flesh out alternatives and implications, and to identify the intersections of ambitious, realistic, meaningful, and sustainable solutions, based on interests and compromise, rather than positions and claiming. Many of these key tensions are discernible within the structure and letter of the GNI, some largely resolved, others to be informed by future learning—an expectation built into the GNI. While the participants brought a wealth of knowledge and experience to the process, our collectively limited understanding was also acknowledged and is reflected in GNI's adaptive stance.

Beyond identifying common cause, reaching rough consensus for an operating approach was essential for the development of supportive strategies and tactics. These positions are apparent in the documents, both by their presence and their absence. As with the rest of the group decisions, they do not necessarily represent agreement, except in the collaborative context of the GNI. The consensus included support for corporate engagement, the development of tools that accounted for the complexity of the situation, and the notion that we would actively develop understanding and responses over time.

The group, for instance, took the perspective that on balance it was better to have companies operating responsibly even in potentially repressive markets, both in terms of services rendered and the leverage of positive engagement (around transparency and rule of law, in particular). Platforms that many consider self-indulgent or worse, including Twitter (and its 140-character "what are you doing?"), Facebook, and YouTube, have proven to be powerful platforms for activists. (Indeed, in the lead-up to the 20th anniversary of the Tiananmen Square protests, these and others were blocked in China.[25]) The tools they provide to potentially advance social, economic, and political democracy are especially important in information- and communications-poor settings, as artfully argued by my colleague Ethan Zuckerman.[26]

Just as we note the power of new technologies to support human rights, it is equally essential to recognize the potential influence of company relationships and process on government behavior. After Microsoft removed Michael Anti's blog based on a less-than-formal request from Chinese law enforcement, for instance, the company implemented new policies with respect to content takedowns. In addition to limiting removal to the local jurisdiction, Microsoft began requiring "legally binding notice from the government indicating that the material violates local laws," as well as requiring assurance "that users know why that content was blocked, by notifying them that access has been limited due to a government restriction."[27] Google's launch of Google.cn, criticized by many for its willingness to censor results, also initiated the practice of appending a warning to filtered search results that notes the removal of certain results according to local law, subsequently instituted by Microsoft and Yahoo!, and later followed by Chinese services including market-leader Baidu.[28] Moving forward, strong corporate process may indeed be a great resource for supporting rule of law and fostering increased transparency on free expression and privacy.

Participants

Global Network Initiative participants include ICT companies, nongovernmental organizations, investors, and academics. The founding group of *companies* comprises Google, Microsoft, and Yahoo!. *Academic participants* in the GNI are Annenberg School for Communication (University of Southern California); Deirdre Mulligan, Berkeley School of Information (University of California); Berkman Center for Internet and Society (Harvard University); Rebecca MacKinnon, Journalism and Media Studies Centre (University of Hong Kong); and Research Center for Information Law (University of St. Gallen). *Investors* participating in the GNI are Boston Common Asset Management, Calvert Group, Domini Social Investments LLC, F&C Asset Management, KLD Research & Analytics, Inc., and Trillium Asset Management. *Nongovernmental organizations* participating in the GNI are Center for Democracy and Technology, Committee to Protect Journalists, Electronic Frontier Foundation, Human Rights First, Human Rights in China, Human Rights Watch, International Business Leaders Forum, Internews, and World Press Freedom Committee. The United Nations Special Representative to the Secretary General on business and human rights enjoys *observer* status. The *drafting* group also included Amnesty International, Reporters Without Borders, France Telecom, Teliasonera, and Vodafone, none of whom continued to participate in the GNI after launch.

Foundational Elements

The structure and overall approach that emerged from the multiyear process are largely defined by three documents: the Principles,[29] the Implementation Guidelines,[30] and the Governance, Accountability, and Learning Framework,[31] which were released in October 2008 and will be supplemented by the Governance Charter, slated for final approval in September 2009. At the most fundamental, aspirational, and stable level lie the Principles, which express overarching support for international standards centered on expression and privacy, and a commitment to act upon them. The associated Implementation Guidelines provide concrete guidance to companies regarding the realization of the Principles in practice and are intended to reflect developing institutional knowledge and respond to the challenges companies and users face. The Framework describes the initial expectations regarding a supporting organization and the general design of the accountability and learning regime, which both ensures that companies are complying with the Principles and fosters learning within and across GNI participants.

Principles

While implementation will surely prove to be the greatest challenge, the audacious first task of the 20-odd participating organizations—and the essential first step toward orienting the Initiative's values and goals—was to articulate a common understanding of global principles for freedom of expression and privacy online. In doing so, the GNI drew heavily upon the Universal Declaration of Human Rights (UDHR), the International Covenant on Civil and Political Rights (ICCPR), and the International Covenant on Economic, Social, and Cultural Rights (ICESCR), which together constitute the

International Bill of Human Rights.[32] Within this broad frame, the document high-lights the undergirding role of government in respecting, protecting, and promoting human rights, along with the complementary responsibility—and opportunity—of ICT companies to do likewise.

The Principles include a preamble and sections on freedom of expression; privacy; responsible company decision making; multistakeholder collaboration; and gover-nance, accountability, and transparency. The structure and tone balance lofty state-ments with more actionable commitments within each of these areas, acknowledging the elements of aspiration and implementation in the GNI.

While the GNI limits its explicit focus to online expression and privacy, the Princi-ples recognize the interdependence of all human rights. They call out the particularly important role of expression and privacy in realizing other rights and as guarantors of human dignity. On the more active side, GNI participants commit to protect expres-sion and privacy rights both generally and in the face of laws and government demands that seek to undermine them.

They also acknowledge "narrow" but potentially substantial exceptions to the rights outlined in the ICCPR, including "actions necessary to preserve national security and public order, protect public health or morals, or safeguard the rights or reputations of others,"[33] related interpretations issued by international human rights bodies, and the Johannesburg Principles on National Security, Freedom of Expression, and Access to Information.

The sections that describe the key elements of the GNI's approach—including re-sponsible company decision making; multistakeholder collaboration; and governance, accountability, and transparency—include reference to both higher-level vision and operational commitments. Companies agree to integrate the Principles within their mission, decisions, and culture, and to that end, commit to senior-level involvement, to anticipate risks and opportunities centered on expression and privacy, and to make best efforts to encourage partners and related businesses to also implement the Principles. In recognition of the novel challenges associated with ICT, the Princi-ples point to the value of collaborative strategies that reach across sectors, and agree to engage jointly to advance expression and privacy. The final, and perhaps most notable, element is the commitment to public transparency and accountability in im-plementation of the Principles—including independent assessment and evaluation of compliance.

Implementation Guidelines

While accounting for the limitations of the GNI's current incipient understanding of effective strategies and tactics, the Guidelines promise actionable steps for ICT compa-nies that constitute compliance with the Principles and provide an initial framework for collaboration among participants. Drawing upon collective experience to date, they are designed as a starting point, prepared to incorporate lessons as the GNI and its participants discern them.

The expectations cover roughly the same terrain as the Principles, but place "responsible company decision making" first, suggesting the overall frame within which the activities occur. Companies are expected to form internal cross-functional teams to lead implementation, to train employees (and the board) on approaches and procedures, to provide whistle-blowing mechanisms for employees, and to encourage business partners and others to adopt the Principles.

With a priority placed on preventing incidents, participants will undertake human rights impact assessments to identify circumstances when expression and privacy rights may be jeopardized or advanced (e.g., entering new markets; designing and introducing new technologies, products, or services; selecting partners; responding to policy change) and develop steps to mitigate risks and to leverage opportunities. Companies will elaborate procedures and policies that govern these occurrences and the possible issues that arise within them.

The Guidelines state that authorities seeking to limit expression or privacy will be expected to do so in writing along with the legal basis for the restriction and the name of the requesting official, and that when required by governments to limit access to information and ideas, companies will interpret laws and requests narrowly and communicate actions to users when legally permissible. When they are confronted with a practice that appears inconsistent with domestic law and procedures or international human rights laws and standards on expression or privacy, companies will challenge it. Companies will document these requests and demands to permit tracking and review.

Governance, Learning, and Accountability Framework

Much of the value of the collective is created by means of the activities described in the Framework, which include the GNI's organizational structure and responsibilities, along with those of the participating companies and the independent assessors. The Framework covers basic institution-building responsibilities including recruiting of new participants and outreach, fostering learning and collaboration on policy issues, offering a communications channel for external parties and users, publishing an annual report, and creating an accountability mechanism.

Independent monitoring, which begins with an orientation toward process and becomes increasingly comprehensive over the GNI's first five years (ultimately including incident review), supports corporate accountability, remediation where necessary, development of good practice among participants, and continued evolution and refinement of the GNI. The accountability process moves from capacity building (2009–2010), to independent process review (2011), and independent process and case review (2012 and beyond). The phasing process was designed to accommodate the lack of existing capacity to conduct monitoring and assessment in the ICT space, with the recognition that assessment would have to parallel a gradual learning process, evolving alongside the GNI and company implementation. During the *first phase*, the board develops independence and competence criteria for monitor selection as well as operational guidance for assessors, while the companies initiate implementation of the Principles, and the organization focuses on learning and outreach.

The *second phase* expects the companies to have fully implemented the Principles and provided a detailed report of its internal processes to the organization. Based on this report, an assessor (or team, more likely) who meets the GNI's criteria and is selected by a company will review that company's processes in operation. In preparing their report, assessors draw upon other relevant materials from the company, except in cases of reasonable legal limits to disclosure, preservation of attorney-client privilege, or protection of trade secrets.

In addition to facilitating the assessment process, the organization will review the accountability process with an eye to necessary improvements, while also informing the board of the results of individual assessments. In conjunction with GNI participants, the organization develops "clear, achievable guidelines" for compliance with the next phase of assessment based on experience to date.

In the *third phase*, the board accredits a pool of eligible assessors, identifying any concerns related to independence for particular companies, and companies draw from this pool, with the board resolving any resulting concerns. With GNI's guidance, the assessor goes beyond process, examining actual incidents and company responses to government requests, providing recommendations for improvement and a detailed report to the GNI on the company's implementation of the Principles. Based on this and accounting for any changes the company has made in response to the findings, the board will determine whether the company meets GNI expectations and share that finding publicly.

As in the previous phase, companies may choose to withhold certain information based on legal limitation (as in the case of a national security letter), for the preservation of attorney-client privilege, or to protect trade secrets, but will be expected to provide as much information as possible as to any specific limitations on their responses. Withholding and the reasoning behind it will be reported and factored into the findings and may render the assessor unable to certify compliance.

Criticisms and Challenges

Lackluster Participation

As varied as the group is in many respects, the Global Network Initiative clearly lacks culturally and geographically diverse participation, and is likewise limited in terms of the range of participating organizations within sectors, and companies in particular, which is surprising given the expectation of diverse corporate approaches to business and technology and the avoidance of techno-deterministic solutions. For instance, with the tremendous influence of telecommunications companies and recent issues to date (e.g., warrantless wiretaps or TOM-Skype surveillance),[34] their absence represents an important and missing piece of the puzzle. Their participation throughout the drafting process suggests that the model should be fairly well suited to their interests, and yet they chose not to continue. Likewise, given the potential for explosive growth and expansion within the ICT space, the lack of small companies is notable—and troubling. From a strategic perspective, their inclusion is important to ensure diversity of perspective and practicability of approach, to say nothing of orienting them to human rights issues at the stages when integration with corporate functioning may be easier.

These deficits do not necessarily reflect a lack of GNI commitment to identifying additional partners and are likely a result of some combination of its early stage of organizational development, a market reaction, and limited outreach capacity. In each case, however, GNI must ask what it needs to do to attract these groups, and also whether their absence has some larger significance. Legislators, shareholders, and other stakeholders should also consider whether they offer a sufficiently ample reward—and urgency—for companies to make the investments necessary to participate in GNI. Given that neither non-Western nor start-up companies took part in the drafting process (a path passively taken and reluctantly accepted by the group for expediency), it seems possible that some adaptation of the GNI may be necessary to facilitate their participation, especially those in markets less welcoming to the GNI.

Accommodations could conceivably take many forms, whether some manner of onboarding or associate membership for those unable to implement the principles immediately, or a private form of participation, either to avoid government scrutiny or to simply focus on collective activities rather than make a public statement. While these types of arrangements might extend participation, they might also diminish the GNI brand and its value to current participants, and will require careful consideration.

Accountability
While Internet companies are new to accountability (perhaps reflecting their libertarian outlook, propensity for confidentiality, and relative corporate immaturity), a reasonable, meaningful, and ambitious approach to accountability was widely viewed within GNI as essential to its success and was a necessity for retaining the diverse coalition that comprises the GNI. Participants were deeply aware of Ruggie's observation, "The Achilles heel of self-regulatory arrangements is to date their underdeveloped accountability mechanisms. Company initiatives increasingly include rudimentary forms of internal and external reporting.... But no universally—or even widely—accepted standards yet exist for these practices.... Beyond certain multi-stakeholder systems,

like the Fair Labor Association, or third-party verification processes, such as Social Accountability 8000, social audits currently enjoy only limited credibility among external stakeholders."[35] With the credibility of the GNI, and the importance of accountability for learning and behavior change, the GNI spent a great deal of energy examining diverse voluntary initiatives and industry practices, and developing its own regime.

Taking inspiration from researchers[36] and practitioners[37] who have identified the limits to accountability and proposed a more integrated model, the GNI has sought not to be an organization that is primarily based on accountability, but one that integrates a strong regime alongside and in conjunction with other activities. Only as reports and information are generated, however, will we learn what this means in practice.

Beyond the more common challenges of nonexistent metrics (although relevant ones are perhaps now on offer),[38] various needs for confidentiality, and resistant corporate culture, the process is made more complex by GNI's particular characteristics and the unique attributes of the risks it seeks to mitigate—these include the tension between evaluating aspiration and implementation, the scale and scope of the Internet, and the expectation that responsible companies will sometimes need to resist the law, rather than comply with it. (Companies will choose to comply on some occasions, based on the context, implications, and likelihood of success.) Moving forward, these issues will remain in discussion, because the solutions—whether best or only good practices—do not yet exist. Thus, the accountability process cannot only compare behavior with the model, but must go deeper to separate company implementation of the Principles from the outcome, because the former may have limited efficacy.

As the structure that undergirds the GNI by informing learning and earning public trust, the accountability regime has rightly received a good deal of attention. Indeed, it is complex and important enough that discussions are ongoing within the GNI and will likely be a significant internal focus for years to come. There are specific critiques: the Electronic Frontier Foundation (EFF), Amnesty International, and Reporters Without Borders have publicly questioned whether a company will have undue influence on its assessment teams and whether the companies will withhold potentially damaging information from assessors. The companies are uncomfortable, concerned with the prospect of allowing outsiders to access and share intimate secrets, and eager to find trustworthy and competent assessors. There is broad consensus that it will not be a "gotcha" process, wherein the assessors are trying to "catch" the company, but one in which they work together to identify and address issues over time to keep the company in compliance. The current approach seeks to achieve balance by having the board set independence criteria for the assessors and the GNI assist in resolving concerns, likely along with an elaborate contracting and compensation scheme, but only in implementation will fears be deemed justified or overblown. Indeed, at present, nobody has ever done such assessments, and it is not at all clear who might be both able and interested in doing them.

Ultimately, each of these concerns (and others like them) *must* be addressed by the accountability regime, as independent monitors report initially on company process and then on actual incidents, in evaluating a company's implementation of the Principles. This process will be complex, with the assessor needing to determine not only the more straightforward elements of compliance such as whether a training program is in place, but also the difference between lackluster recruitment efforts and GNI flaws. The matters only get weightier, in the case of bad outcomes, discerning between irresponsible company actions and good faith decisions, for instance, if the actions following a human rights impact assessment were sufficient or ill considered, in light of the impact.

The constraint on the accountability platform is that not only must it earn the public trust, but it must do so in a relatively lightweight, scalable, and affordable fashion that reinforces learning across the GNI. As participants, online activity, and government interventions all increase, the regime will need to evolve with the Internet. If it is unable or if it cannot be effective without being overly onerous, ICT companies will not embrace the GNI.

Public Communication and Remedy

As suggested by empirical experience and proposed in Ruggie's Protect, Respect, and Remedy Framework, offering transparent channels of communication and the potential for remedy is essential to addressing business and human rights concerns, and the GNI views them as essential for the purposes of information gathering and for its own credibility. A means for individual users and other parties to reliably access and communicate with the nascent GNI is still in the design phase and likely to be pilot tested in 2009–2010. While all GNI participants recognize the need for channels for communication, query, and complaint, the sheer number of Internet users is intimidating, and is orders of magnitude different from the equivalent community in the labor or extractive industries, for instance. The participatory expectations common to Internet culture further increase the likelihood of public interaction with the GNI (noting the grass-roots creation of a GNI Facebook group upon launch), suggesting the incorporation of a Web 2.0 approach that not only accepts complaints, but develops and shares information, perhaps even in real-time.

The GNI must be able to consider, review, utilize, or redirect large numbers of external submissions and do its best to keep contributors informed of the progress of their concerns. The GNI recognizes that it faces potential user submissions on any number of general topics, from critiques to requests for participation in GNI. Relevant distinctions must be made between those communications and submissions that concern noncompliance with the Principles. Problems may arise when, for example, poor service, terms-of-service violations (often interpreted as censorship), or the desire for an avenue of appeal is perceived as noncompliance.

According to the Governance Framework, the GNI complaints process should not be triggered until company channels are exhausted, and is for extraordinary circumstances. Complainants may also choose to seek redress through noncompany participants, which may or may not have systems in place to address such inquiries, potentially overloading them or yielding referrals to GNI without sufficient investigation. Given what are likely to be modest resources on the part of GNI, a robust system will be imperative to maintain public trust and access to the system. The pilot program will develop a mechanism that is credible, practical, and effective, while anticipating the challenges posed by the potential scale of complaints and the diversity of end users and issues.

Learning and Understanding

Limited knowledge of current practice among ICT companies and empirical understanding of the problems they face related to online free expression and privacy, in conjunction with the ceaseless changes in business, user behavior, and government responses, mean that learning is perhaps the greatest contribution that GNI can make for participants and other stakeholders. The GNI should leverage the tremendous collective resources and expertise of its participants, but will face the task of finding realistic ways to access and combine them—a task made difficult by legal concerns, secrecy, intellectual property, and other competing agendas. From the development of human rights impact assessments (a process long under way in the GNI) to the generation of useful data to identify emerging issues and trends, to the creation of relevant metrics to help track the state of expression and privacy online worldwide, the Initiative has the capacity to create novel outputs that can inform company and user behavior, as well as government intervention. While more attention has been paid to other areas of GNI, this zone holds the greatest potential to attract new participants and to change behavior in the long term.

Scope and Specificity

While the GNI has been cautiously welcomed, the participants in the process and others outside it have expressed a range of concerns. In many cases, it is simply too early to tell whether these apprehensions will be borne out by experience, but they serve as valuable markers for GNI guidance and evaluation. While all are of consequence, some relate to the core functioning of the initiative, while others relate to significant, but not necessarily essential, details. The EFF, for instance, has noted that the Principles lack a commitment by companies to develop technologies that support privacy and circumvent censorship, a practice that seems to be a reasonable extension of the GNI commitments.[39] A host of other such issues were left out for a variety of reasons, including data retention, user-notification on data storage locations and risks, statistics on government requests, and circumvention methods, which have technological, legal, practical, and business implications, and were deemed to be either outside GNI's scope or too involved to address within its initial phase.

As the GNI's capacity grows with the hiring of a dedicated staff, the inclusion of additional participants, and the development of robust systems, participants will need to revisit these ideas in greater depth. For those that remain outside its purview, the hope is that the GNI will be able to foster cross-fertilization among a variety of different forums, including governments, advocacy groups, and international organizations. Can EFF's ideas on technology tools, for instance, be taken up in a joint technology development group?

Of more cross-cutting concern, Amnesty International and Reporters Without Borders[40] point to language that they consider too open to interpretation, including companies' commitment to using "best efforts" to foster GNI adoption among joint ventures, subsidiaries, and the like, as well as the discretion afforded to companies to determine when and how to resist government requests. Responsible company behavior in each is of the utmost importance, and while the language was intended to be realistic and to provide companies with a degree of flexibility (e.g., not all suppliers are relevant, oral requests may be acceptable in cases of imminent harm, fighting every single government request is impractical), it most certainly also provides them with an escape clause, which underscores the role of the accountability process.

Criteria for Success

In order to accomplish the goals of the GNI, there are broad traits present in the design phase that should be retained over time. As the structure, process, and organization develop and respond to existing and emerging concerns, it will be essential to periodically revisit the values that inform the overall approach, especially with respect to its efficacy, adaptability, scalability, transparency, legitimacy, neutrality, and sustainability.

Efficacy Does the operationalization of the Principles recognize that expecting companies to resist government requires balance with respect for the legitimate aspects of government power over expression and privacy, including a spectrum of national standards? Will the accountability regime provide the correct incentives, encouraging company attention to specifics as well as larger and more aspirational activities?

Adaptability With the entire landscape shifting continually, presenting new challenges, opportunities, modes, and pressures, can the GNI create sufficient process to meet current needs while maintaining its flexibility to adapt and improve alongside, or ahead of, the path ahead? Will the organization be caught responding to the new terrain with the methods for traversing that of the past decade, whether in accountability, learning, or public remedy? Can the GNI adjust its vision and mode as the participants—and their needs and perspectives—change?

Scalability Does the approach scale alongside increasing users and uses of ICT, as well as the apparently concomitant increase in government affronts on expression and privacy? How will the GNI attract greater participation? How will the GNI's internal systems represent the interests of the current 1.6 billion Internet users[41] and 4 billion mobile subscribers,[42] and what will happen as those numbers grow?

Transparency With an accurate understanding of the issues essential for effective intervention on the part of the policymakers, advocacy organizations, business, and ultimately users (who decide what, if anything, they do online), will the GNI be capable of widely and faithfully conveying what is actually happening? Will statements be supported by data and directly informed by company experience, rather than by anecdote, to promote understanding of systemic issues and trends, contributing to a chain of accountability and building understanding of new/potential pressure points as they emerge over time?

Legitimacy Will the organization earn and keep the public's trust? Are the accountability processes perceived as both robust and reasonable, are there open channels for communications with the public, is the information shared with the public adequate? How does the GNI distinguish between the progress of the participants and its own advances? How will these developments be evaluated?

Neutrality Can the GNI become a truly global standard, and not be viewed as being unduly influenced or dominated by the interests of any nation, culture, or organization? Will its interventions or recommendations take into account cultural nuance and local knowledge while continuing to uphold high international standards for human rights?

Sustainability Will the GNI and its participants be able to generate the collective and internal resources necessary for implementation and ongoing effectiveness? Will the organization be able to sustain the level of activity to which it has committed, or come up with creative ways that involve others in this work?

Conclusion

The story has not yet ended for the GNI or for Yahoo!. In December 2008, the Vietnamese government passed a law limiting online political speech and requiring online service providers to report violators, publicly stating its expectations that Google and Yahoo! would contribute to a "healthy" Internet.[43] How the situation develops—

whether government rests on rhetoric or actually seeks to enforce the new law, and how Yahoo! (and Google and non-GNI companies) responds—will inform company and government strategy in Vietnam[44] and suggest the capacity of a self-governing initiative to require its participants to *not* comply with the law when it conflicts with international human rights standards.

As the GNI moves ahead, observers will rightly ask what to expect—how we will know we have begun to impact company behavior, government approaches, and user conduct online. Perhaps most importantly, they will ask what success will look like. These are hard questions. The GNI was designed by a relatively small group with limited resources, and the fact that it has come this far in a relatively short period of time is objectively impressive, but only when it is tested in the marketplace will the appropriateness of its design begin to become apparent. Initially, beyond reporting on basic commitment, output measures will help, such as growth in participants, creation of data and other learning resources, and policy engagement. Individual examples may also be helpful, for instance, if GNI helps a company address a tough decision or anticipate an emerging issue.

Over time, we must expect positive outcomes, but with so many factors affecting the protection and advancement of free expression and privacy—and the GNI—the causes of success and failure will not always be clear. Measuring impact is difficult in part because the GNI will be successful precisely when it avoids problems and goes unnoticed. Some useful proxies may be increased public awareness of the issues, enlightened government action, and ideally metrics for takedowns and information requests that suggest a combination of waning government abuse and avoidance of increased corporate restrictions.

We are caught between the proverbial rock and a hard place, particularly as society undergoes the complicated process of integrating, adapting, and shaping the role of new media. As it becomes integrated into our lives and livelihoods, the potential for both good and harm continues to grow, along with the responsibility of the businesses providing these services. Thus far, this adoption of the Internet and related technologies has brought not only new challenges, but new tools for addressing them. Rather than resisting change, we need to consider how to guide it using a combination of past experience and innovative approaches.

While there are other broad changes and trends with much deeper social, economic, and political importance, the combination of reach, speed, and accessibility of new media render it a poignant—and challenging—frontier for an increasingly globalized world. The particular contours may well be indicative of other pressing (or emerging) challenges, suggesting that our approach to addressing these challenges may also hold broader lessons for new kinds of institutions and new approaches to policymaking at the nexus of sectors and nations, economics and politics, culture and identity.

Notes

1. Michael Samway, "A Wired—and Safe—Vietnam," Yodel Anecdotal, March 12, 2009, http://ycorpblog.com/2009/03/12/a-wired-and-safe-vietnam/.

2. Rebecca MacKinnon, "Yahoo! Execs Called Moral 'Pygmies' in Congress," RConversation Blog, November 8, 2007, http://rconversation.blogs.com/rconversation/2007/11/yahoo-execs-cal.html.

3. Global Network Initiative, "Global Network Initiative," http://www.globalnetworkinitiative.org/.

4. Reo Research, *Managing Access Security and Privacy in the Global Digital Economy* (F&C Investments, January 2007), http://www.business-humanrights.org/Documents/FandC-study-tech-risks-Jan-2007.pdf.

5. Elinor Mills, "Pension Fund Nudges Google, Yahoo on Censorship," CNET News.com, December 14, 2006, http://news.cnet.com/8301-10784_3-6143860-7.html.

6. Michael Samway, "Business and Human Rights," Yodel Anecdotal, May 7, 2008, http://ycorpblog.com/2008/05/07/business-and-human-rights/.

7. Rebekah Heacock, "Australia's Conroy Named Internet Villain of the Year," OpenNet Initiative Blog, July 13, 2009, http://opennet.net/blog/2009/07/australias-conroy-named-internet-villain-year.

8. Jonathan Zittrain and John Palfrey, "Reluctant Gatekeepers: Corporate Ethics on a Filtered Internet," in *Access Denied: The Practice and Policy of Global Internet Filtering*, ed. Ronald J. Deibert, John Palfrey, Rafal Rohozinski, and Jonathan Zittrain (Cambridge, MA: MIT Press, 2008), 103–122.

9. Jeffrey Rosen, "Google's Gatekeepers," *New York Times Magazine*, November 28, 2008, http://www.nytimes.com/2008/11/30/magazine/30google-t.html?_r=1.

10. Tim Wu, "The World Trade Law of Internet Filtering" (working paper, Columbia University, Law School, May 3, 2006) http://ssrn.com/abstract=882459; Jack Goldsmith and Tim Wu, *Who Controls the Internet? Illusions of a Borderless World* (New York, NY: Oxford University Press, 2006).

11. United Nations Human Rights Council, *Promotion and Protection of All Human Rights, Civil, Political, Economic, Social and Cultural Rights, Including the Right to Development—Protect, Respect and Remedy: A Framework for Business and Human Rights*, April 7, 2008, http://www.reports-and-materials.org/Ruggie-report-7-Apr-2008.pdf.

12. Arvind Ganesan, "Viewpoint: Why Voluntary Initiatives Aren't Enough." *Leading Perspectives*, Spring 2009, http://www.bsr.org/reports/leading-perspectives/2009/LP_Spring_2009_Voluntary_Initiatives.pdf.

13. U.S. Congress, H.R. 275 [110th]: Global Online Freedom Act of 2007, 2d sess., Rep 110–481, February 22, 2008, http://www.govtrack.us/congress/bill.xpd?bill=h110-275.

14. Center for Democracy and Technology, "Analysis of the Global Online Freedom Act of 2008 [H.R. 275]: Legislative Strategies to Advance Internet Free Expression and Privacy Around the World," May 2, 2008, http://www.cdt.org/international/censorship/20080505gofa.pdf.

15. U.S. Department of State, "State Summary of Global Internet Freedom Task Force," December   20,   2006,   http://www.america.gov/st/freepress-english/2006/December/ 20061220173640xjsnommis0.7082331.html.

16. John Palfrey, "Testimony on Internet Filtering and Surveillance," John Palfrey Blog, May 20,   2008,   http://blogs.law.harvard.edu/palfrey/2008/05/20/testimony-on-internet-filtering-and -surveillance/.

17. Council of Europe, Directorate General of Human Rights and Legal Affairs, *Guidelines for the Cooperation between Law Enforcement and Internet Service Providers against Cybercrime*, April 2, 2008, http://www.coe.int/t/DGHL/cooperation/economiccrime/cybercrime/cy_activity_Interface2008/ 567_prov-d-guidelines_provisional2_3April2008_en.pdf.

18. Council of Europe, Directorate General of Human Rights and Legal Affairs, *Human Rights Guidelines for Internet Service Providers*, 2008, http://www.coe.int/t/dghl/standardsetting/media/ Doc/H-Inf(2008)009_en.pdf.

19. European Parliament Committee on Civil Liberties, Justice and Home Affairs, "Proposal for a European Parliament Recommendation to the Council on Strengthening Security and Fundamental Freedoms on the Internet," June 1, 2009, http://www.europarl.europa.eu/meetdocs/2004 _2009/documents/pr/755/755000/755000en.pdf.

20. European Parliament, "European Parliament Resolution on Freedom of Expression on the Internet," July 6, 2006, http://www.europarl.europa.eu/sides/getDoc.do?pubRef=-//EP//TEXT+TA +P6-TA-2006-0324+0+DOC+XML+V0//EN&language=EN.

21. Jules Maaten et al., "Proposal for a Directive of the European Parliament and of the Council Concerning the EU Global Online Freedom Act," 2008, http://www.julesmaaten.eu/_uploads/ EU%20GOFA.htm.

22. Viviane Reding, "Freedom of Speech: ICT Must Help, Not Hinder" (speech presented at the Event on the Idea of an EU "GOFA" EP Plenary Session, Strasbourg, February 3, 2009), http:// ec.europa.eu/commission_barroso/reding/docs/speeches/2009/strasbourg-20090203.pdf.

23. Art Brodsky, "Global Internet Freedom—What a Concept for America," TPMCafé, May 26, 2008, http://tpmcafe.talkingpointsmemo.com/2008/05/26/global_internet_freedom_what_a/.

24. John Palfrey and Jonathan Zittrain, "Perspective: Companies Need Guidance to Face Censors Abroad," CNET News.com, August 14, 2007, http://news.cnet.com/Catalysts-for-corporate -responsibility-in-cyberspace/2010-1028_3- 6202426.html.

25. Rebecca MacKinnon, "China Blocks Twitter, Flickr, Bing, Hotmail, Windows Live, etc. Ahead of Tiananmen 20th Anniversary," RConversation Blog, June 2, 2009, http://rconversation.blogs .com/rconversation/2009/06/china-blocks-twitter-flickr-bing-hotmail-windows-live-etc-ahead-of -tiananmen-20th-anniversary.html.

26. Ethan Zuckerman, "The Cute Cat Theory Talk at ETech," My Heart's in Accra, March 8, 2008, http://www.ethanzuckerman.com/blog/2008/03/08/the-cute-cat-theory-talk-at-etech/.

27. Jack Krumholtz, "Congressional Testimony: 'The Internet in China: A Tool for Freedom or Suppression'?" Committee on International Relations, Subcommittee on Africa, Global Human Rights and International Operations and the Subcommittee on Asia and the Pacific, February 16, 2006. http://www.microsoft.com/presspass/exec/krumholtz/02-15WrittenTestimony.mspx.

28. Nart Villeneuve, "Perspectives on Transparency," Nart Villeneuve: Internet Censorship Explorer, June 26, 2008, http://www.nartv.org/2008/06/26/perspectives-on-transparency/.

29. Global Network Initiative, "Principles," 2008, http://www.globalnetworkinitiative.org/principles/index.php.

30. Global Network Initiative, "Implementation Guidelines," 2008, http://www.globalnetworkinitiative.org/implementationguidelines/index.php.

31. Global Network Initiative, "Governance, Accountability and Learning Framework," 2008, http://www.globalnetworkinitiative.org/governanceframework/index.php.

32. United Nations General Assembly, *The International Bill of Human Rights*, 1948, http://www.unhchr.ch/html/menu6/2/fs2.htm.

33. Global Network Initiative, "Principles," 2008, http://www.globalnetworkinitiative.org/principles/index.php.

34. Nart Villeneuve, "Breaching Trust: An Analysis of Surveillance and Security Practices on China's TOM-Skype Platform" (Information Warfare Monitor/ONI Asia, October 1, 2008), http://www.nartv.org/mirror/breachingtrust.pdf.

35. John G. Ruggie, "Business and Human Rights: The Evolving International Agenda" (working paper, Corporate Social Responsibility Initiative, John F. Kennedy School of Government, Harvard University, 2007), http://www.hks.harvard.edu/m-rcbg/CSRI/publications/workingpaper_38_ruggie.pdf.

36. Richard Locke and Monica Romis, "Beyond Corporate Codes of Conduct: Work Organization and Labor Standards in Two Mexican Garment Factories" (working paper, MIT Sloan School of Management, 2006), http://mitsloan.mit.edu/newsroom/pdf/conduct.pdf.

37. Fair Labor Association, "2007 Annual Report," November 2007, http://www.fairlabor.org/images/WhatWeDo/2007_annualpublicreport.pdf.

38. Derek E. Bambauer, "Cybersieves," *Duke Law Journal*, 59 (2009), http://ssrn.com/abstract=1143582.

39. Danny O'Brien, "Sign on Letter," Electronic Frontier Foundation, http://www.eff.org/files/filenode/gni/signon_letter.txt.

40. Reporters Without Borders, "Why Reporters Without Borders Is Not Endorsing the Global Principles on Freedom of Expression and Privacy for ICT Companies Operating in Internet-Restricting Countries," October 28, 2008, http://www.rsf.org/article.php3?id_article=29117.

41. Miniwatts Marketing Group, "World Internet Usage Statistics News and World Population Stats," InternetWorldStats.com, March 31, 2009, http://www.internetworldstats.com/stats.htm.

42. International Telecommunications Union, "Press Release: Worldwide Mobile Cellular Subscribers to Reach 4 Billion Mark Late 2008," September 25, 2008, http://www.itu.int/newsroom/press_releases/2008/29.html.

43. Radio Free Asia, "Vietnam to Police Blogs," December 9, 2008, http://www.unhcr.org/refworld/docid/496234c3c.html.

44. Douglas MacMillan, "Yahoo's Delicate Dance in Vietnam," *BusinessWeek*, May 28, 2009, http://www.businessweek.com/technology/content/may2009/tc20090528_660986.htm.

Part II   Country Profiles and Regional Overviews

Introduction to the Country Profiles

The country profiles that follow offer a synopsis of the findings and conclusions of OpenNet Initiative (ONI) research into the factors influencing specific countries' decisions to filter or abstain from filtering the Internet, as well as the impact, relevance, and efficacy of technical filtering in a broader context of Internet censorship.

These profiles cover the countries where ONI conducted technical testing and analysis from 2007 to 2008. Countries selected for in-depth analysis are those in which it is believed that there is the most to learn about the extent and processes of Internet filtering.

Each country profile includes the summary results of the empirical testing for filtering. The technical filtering data alone, however, do not amount to a complete picture of Internet censorship and content regulation. A wide range of policies relating to media, speech, and expression also act to restrict expression on the Internet and online community formation. Legal and regulatory frameworks, including Internet law, the state of Internet access and infrastructure, the level of economic development, and the quality of governance institutions are central to determining which countries resort to filtering and how they choose to implement Internet content controls. A brief study of each of these factors is included in each of the country profiles. Together, these sections are intended to offer a concise, accurate, and unbiased view of Internet filtering and content regulation.

Each country is given a score on a five-point scale presented in the "Results at a Glance" table. The scores reflect the observed level of filtering in each of four themes:

1. *Political:* This category is focused primarily on Web sites that express views in opposition to those of the current government. Content more broadly related to human rights, freedom of expression, minority rights, and religious movements is also considered here.

2. *Social:* This group covers material related to sexuality, gambling, and illegal drugs and alcohol, as well as other topics that may be socially sensitive or perceived as offensive.

3. *Conflict and security:* Content related to armed conflicts, border disputes, separatist movements, and militant groups is included in this category.

4. *Internet tools:* Web sites that provide e-mail, Internet hosting, search, translation, Voice over Internet Protocol (VoIP) telephone service, and circumvention methods are grouped in this category.

The relative magnitude of filtering for each of the four themes is defined as follows:

1. *Pervasive filtering* is characterized by both its depth—a blocking regime that blocks a large portion of the targeted content in a given category—and its breadth—a blocking regime that includes filtering in several categories in a given theme.

2. *Substantial filtering* has either depth or breadth: either a number of categories are subject to a medium level of filtering, or a low level of filtering is carried out across many categories.

3. *Selective filtering* is narrowly targeted filtering that blocks a small number of specific sites across a few categories or filtering that targets a single category or issue.

4. *Suspected filtering* is indicated when connectivity abnormalities are present that suggest the presence of filtering, although diagnostic work was unable to confirm conclusively that inaccessible Web sites are the result of deliberate tampering.

5. *No evidence of filtering:* ONI testing did not uncover any evidence of Web sites being blocked.

The "Results at a Glance" table also includes a measure (low, medium, or high) of the observed transparency and consistency of blocking patterns. The transparency score given to each country is a qualitative measure based on the level at which the country openly engages in filtering. In cases where filtering takes place without open acknowledgment, or where the practice of filtering is actively disguised to appear as network errors, the transparency score is low. In assigning the transparency score, we have also considered the presence of provisions to appeal inappropriate blocking or report instances of it. Consistency measures the variation in filtering within a country across different ISPs—in some cases the availability of specific Web pages differs significantly depending on the ISP one uses to connect to the Internet.

An aggregate view of the level of development for each country is represented by the results of the first four indexes presented in the "Key Indicators" table: gross domestic product per capita, life expectancy, literacy rates, and the human development index.

The first three measures are drawn from the World Bank development indicators data set. The GDP measure, which captures the ability to purchase a standard basket of consumer goods, is expressed in constant 2005 international dollars. Life expectancy can be seen as a proxy for general health, and literacy an imperfect but reasonable indication of the quality of education. The human development index is constructed by the United Nations Development Program to reflect overall human well-being.

Governance is widely recognized to be a key determinant of economic success and human welfare. We therefore also include two measures of governance: rule of law and voice and accountability. These indexes are defined and compiled by researchers at the World Bank using an aggregation of the best available data. The authors of the indexes define them in the following way:

Rule of law includes several indicators that measure the extent to which agents have confidence in and abide by the rules of society. These include perceptions of the incidence of crime, the effectiveness and predictability of the judiciary, and the enforceability of contracts.

Voice and accountability includes a number of indicators measuring various aspects of the political process, civil liberties, and political and human rights, measuring the extent to which citizens of a country are able to participate in the selection of governments.

An aggregate view of the state of democracy is provided by the Economist Intelligence Unit's index of democracy. This index is based on five categories: electoral process and pluralism; civil liberties; the functioning of government; political participation; and political culture. The 165 states included in this index are placed within one of four regime type categories; full democracies, flawed democracies, hybrid regimes, and authoritarian regimes.

We also include two measures of Internet accessibility provided by the International Telecommunication Union: the digital opportunity index (DOI) and Internet users as a percentage of the population. The DOI is based on 11 core information and communication technology (ICT) indicators that are agreed upon by the International Telecommunication Union's Partnership on Measuring ICT for Development. These are grouped in three clusters by type: opportunity, infrastructure, and utilization. The DOI therefore captures the overall potential for and context of Internet availability rather than usage alone. The measure of Internet access, the Internet penetration rate, is simply the percentage of the population identified as active Internet users. Additional Internet penetration rate indicators are drawn from the Miniwatts Marketing Group, which compiles the latest Internet usage statistics from a range of reputable international and local sources including the ITU, Gfk Group, and Nielson Online.

Internet regulation and filtering practices are often dynamic processes, subject to frequent change, though we expect that the political climate and the aggregate view of the issues reflected in these profiles will change more slowly than the specific instances of filtering. As the context for content regulation and the practice of Internet filtering evolve, updates will be made to the country profiles, and new countries may be added. These updates will be available at http://www.opennet.net.

Sources for Key Indicators

GDP per capita, PPP (constant 2005 international dollars)

World Bank, "World Development Indicators Online," 2009, http://web.worldbank.org/WBSITE/EXTERNAL/DATASTATISTICS/0,,contentMDK:20398986~menuPK:64133163~pagePK:64133150~piPK:64133175~theSitePK:239419,00.html.

Life expectancy at birth (years)

World Bank, "Key Development Data and Statistics," 2009, http://www.worldbank.org/data/countrydata/countrydata.html.

Literacy rate

World Bank, "Key Development Data and Statistics," 2009, http://www.worldbank.org/data/countrydata/countrydata.html.

Human development index (value and ranking)

United Nations Development Program (UNDP). "2008 Statistical Update", 2008, http://hdr.undp.org/en/.

Rule of law

World Bank. "Worldwide Governance Indicators 1996–2008", 2009, http://info.worldbank.org/governance/wgi/index.asp.

Voice and accountability

World Bank. "Worldwide Governance Indicators 1996–2008", 2009, http://info.worldbank.org/governance/wgi/index.asp.

Democracy index

Economist Intelligence Unit. "Economist Intelligence Unit Democracy Index, 2008", 2008, http://www.eiu.com/site_info.asp?info_name=sovereign_ratings.

Digital opportunity index (value and ranking)

International Telecommunication Union (ITU), "World Information Society Report, 2007: Beyond WSIS", 2007, http://www.itu.int/osg/spu/publications/worldinformationsociety/2007/.

Internet penetration

International Telecommunication Union (ITU), "Internet Indicators: Subscribers, Users, and Broadband Subscribers," 2008, http://www.itu.int/ITU-D/icteye/Reporting/ShowReportFrame.aspx ?ReportName=/WTI/InformationTechnologyPublic&RP_intYear=2008&RP_intLanguageID=1.

Miniwatts Marketing Group, "Internet World Statistics," 2009, http://www.internetworldstats .com.

Commonwealth of Independent States

CIS Overview

Over the past four years the scale and reach of the Internet in the Commonwealth of Independent States (CIS) has continued to expand. As it has grown, a vibrant cyber culture has emerged, strengthened by a Soviet legacy, which has bequeathed the region with Russian as a lingua franca and common cultural and historical reference that continues to bridge the national boundaries between the former Soviet states.

Commensurate with its growth, the Internet domain in the CIS has emerged as a dynamic and complex environment in which states, cyber criminals, nongovernmental organizations, businesses, and individuals actively collude and compete. The region is currently driving the evolution of next-generation information controls encompassing legal regulation as well as innovative tactics such as the alleged use of third-party actors to generate crowd sourced denial of service attacks and other offensive means. These control tactics shape the information space through competition, rather than traditional filtering. There are also indications that these tactics and techniques are now being adopted in other regions.

Consequently, since the last OpenNet Initiative (ONI) volume, *Access Denied*, the CIS region has provided a number of new developments in information controls. The region witnessed two cyberwars. The first was a campaign by pro-Russian (and allegedly state-sponsored) hackers, which paralyzed the Estonian Internet in May 2007. The second was a similar campaign (also allegedly organized by nationalist pro-government Russian hackers) that occurred at the same time as major combat operations in Georgia (August 2008). The latter campaign targeting Georgian online media and government Web sites led Georgian authorities to filter access to Russian Internet sites (allegedly as a means of self-defense against Russian cyber propaganda) and resulted in an information vacuum in Tbilisi during the critical days where it was unclear whether Russian troops would stop their advance into Georgia.

Next-generation Internet controls have also been utilized during elections. For example, reports indicate that in Belarus, Kyrgyzstan and (allegedly) Russia[1] pro-government forces selectively used denial-of-service (DoS) attacks during elections in order to silence opposition and independent media. During periods of heightened political tensions, countries such as Armenia and Belarus have employed legal and technical means to seize control of domain space, or shut down access to the Internet.

In the last 20 years, rapid changes have been a constant phenomenon in the CIS, but Western-sponsored democratic reforms have only been partially successful. In recent years a new authoritarianism has emerged in the region, with many governments seeking to reassert control over the national information sphere.

At the same time, many countries of the CIS have adopted national development strategies that emphasize information technology (IT) as a means for economic growth, with some even declaring their intent to become regional "IT powerhouses." However, as a consequence of the color revolutions in the early to mid-2000s in Ukraine, Georgia, and Kyrgyzstan, many CIS states—particularly those with authoritarian tendencies—are aware of the consequences that this "technological empowerment" may prompt. Many in the region now see the Internet and other communications channels in national strategic terms, and these countries have increasingly turned to security-based arguments—such as the need to secure "national informational space"—to justify regulation of the sector. Consequently, the region is a leader in the development of next-generation information controls.

In 2007 and 2008, ONI tested for the presence of filtering in all CIS countries: Armenia, Azerbaijan, Belarus, Georgia, Kazakhstan, Kyrgyzstan, Moldova, Russia, Tajikistan, Turkmenistan, Ukraine, and Uzbekistan.

The results of ONI testing yield significant patterns of first-generation filtering in Uzbekistan and Turkmenistan. Uzbekistan pursued pervasive filtering of the kind found in China and Iran. Turkmenistan's Internet is even more tightly restricted, with access available only through a single government provider. In other countries, strong evidence of second- and third-generation controls is emerging, with filtering occurring at strategic junctures, as well as in indirect and less detectable ways often supported by restrictive legal regimes. In almost all countries, filtering also occurred on corporate networks (such as educational and research networks), where accepted usage policies (AUPs) dictated that inappropriate content was not permitted; or in "edge locations" such as Internet cafés, where the reasons for filtering were more benign (conserving bandwidth) or left to the discretion of the Internet café owners themselves.

The ONI methodology makes it difficult to detect second- or third-generation techniques, which often involve DoS attacks, or other means of eliminating or silencing Web sites that do not rely on filtering. In these cases, which include Kyrgyzstan, Armenia, Belarus, Estonia, and the Russian-Georgian war, the ONI relied on a network of researchers within these countries to run ad hoc and one-time tests, as well as to investigate specific instances where DoS attacks, or other forms of technical manipulation, were used to silence Web sites or other Internet-based communication tools.

The CIS Region: Ethnocultural Diversity and a Shared Historical Space

The CIS—a loose and largely ineffectual political organization—occupies most of the territory that once constituted the Union of Soviet Socialist Republics (USSR). Straddling a swath of Eurasia from the Pacific to the doorsteps of Europe, the Arctic Circle, and the deserts of Central Asia, this vast land mass encompasses 12 time zones, some 350 million people, and more than 100 distinct ethnic groups including all the world's major religions and at least three major linguistic communities (Slavic, Turkic, Farsi). The CIS remains dominated by the Russian Federation, which maintains its influence through economic, political, and defense ties, as well as popular culture that continues to predominate within the region. Russia is currently a major energy supplier to many CIS states, giving it considerable political muscle in the region.

The region's shared political heritage, together with the fact that many present-day leaders in the CIS governments and economies were also in positions of authority during the Soviet era, means that much formal and informal coordination continues to exist among and between member states, despite political differences that are at times difficult. On some occasions, this coordination has led to the adoption of similar approaches in legal and political development. Furthermore, the loose, informal coordination among officials is helped along by the fact that most countries share the same legal tradition, as well as similar organizational characteristics of the security forces and the distribution of powers among the judicial, executive, and legislative branches of government.

Notwithstanding their shared past, over the past few years CIS governments have not hesitated to challenge Russia's hegemony by seeking other political and military alliances with Western Europe and the United States. At an accelerating pace, governments are looking beyond their traditional partners to discover new international trade and economic routes. This approach even more distinctively defines the CIS as a quickly changing region: although CIS countries share a common cultural heritage, they are increasingly taking diverging paths in their political and economic development, mainly because of foreign influence and an emerging rivalry among them.

Access to the Internet in the CIS

Internet penetration rates in the CIS region have experienced significant growth over the last couple of years, though the figures are still low in comparison to Europe and other regions. Internet access is mainly clustered in urban areas and spread among youth. In contrast to gender penetration rates in most Asian and Middle East and North African (MENA) countries, the percentage of male and female users in the CIS is almost the same, perhaps reflecting the "equality" between sexes prevailing in the Soviet era.[2] Income levels in the CIS are generally low, while the costs of computers and connectivity are relatively high. Overall, Internet penetration in Russia lags behind that of other industrialized nations (27 percent as of 2008)[3] and is relatively high only in large cities (particularly Moscow and St. Petersburg). Among the CIS countries, Belarus has the highest Internet penetration rate, 29 percent for 2008. The popularity of the Internet in this country might be a response, at least in part, to the fact that Belarus is one of the countries with the toughest governmental control in the CIS. As a result, the Internet remains one of the few media where citizens can exchange viewpoints and obtain uncensored information from international sources.

Ukraine (with a 14.6 percent penetration rate) and Moldova (16.2 percent) have almost doubled their Internet access rates over the last couple of years. The states of Central Asia have also shown considerable growth in their Internet penetration rates: Kyrgyzstan (13.8 percent) has become a leader in this subgroup partly as a result of the state's policies aiming at further market liberalization. Kazakhstan (12.3 percent) follows closely. Uzbekistan and Tajikistan have measured a swift increase in the number of Internet users, with Uzbekistan at 8.8 percent and Tajikistan at 6.6 percent in 2008. Turkmenistan measures very low Internet penetration (1.4 percent), since until recently the Internet was a privilege only for elites. As of 2008 Azerbaijan had an Internet penetration rate of 18.3 percent, while Armenia and Georgia had penetration rates of 5.8 percent and 7.8 percent, respectively.[4]

Official figures, in most cases, are far from being accurate. Depending on the country, local sources show either higher Internet penetration rates or considerably lower (in Kyrgyzstan local sources show that only 7 percent of the population had access at the end of 2008).[5] Even among international organizations the estimates are strikingly different: the United Nations (UN) *e-Government Survey*[6] states that in Kyrgyzstan, Internet penetration was no more than 5.6 percent for 2008, while the International Telecommunications Union (ITU) provides figures almost three times higher for 2008. These discrepancies are partly due to difficulties in calculating the number of users in countries where most people share Internet access through their places of work or study (for example, workplaces account for over 51 percent of all users in Kyrgyzstan[7] and Belarus), as well as via Internet cafés, whose use is very high in some countries (around 30 percent for Uzbekistan). This shared use, and in some cases the creative use of networks such as Fidonet to route traffic to and from the Internet, may result in considerable underestimation of the actual number of users.[8] In addition, some Internet service providers (ISPs) do not reveal the real number of customers in order to conceal their proceeds.

The Role of New Technology in the CIS

The CIS region showcases examples of just how profoundly the Internet can affect social and political life. The importance of the Internet to political and social life is affected by the general openness of the media in the country. In Uzbekistan and Belarus, for example, where the government controls the media and stifles political opposition, the relevance of the Internet to political and social life is very high. In Tajikistan relevance remains low, while in Turkmenistan the Internet is still reined in by the government to such an extent that simple access remains a problem, leaving little room for the Internet to significantly influence political and social life.

The Internet constitutes an effective political tool in the hands of the people. During sensitive times, when governments attempt a tough crackdown on the media, the Internet remains the only available source of information, a fact that determines its high impact on shaping groups and affecting behavior. At times, when faced with a "state of emergency," governments attempt to shut down online news sources in order to limit the spread of oppositional materials. For example, in Armenia the president imposed severe restrictions on the media and the Internet after the presidential elections in February 2008. This situation by itself triggered waves of discontented reactions by bloggers and online media journalists, who were among the few who reported on these events outside the country. Their condemnation of the imposed restrictions was quickly taken on, spread on the Internet, and hence multiplied the effect of the government's critics both inside and outside the country.

The CIS demonstrates that information and communication technology (ICT) is not always deterred by low incomes, and its significance to political life grows quickly when people want to voice their opinion. Such examples were the Ukrainian Orange Revolution (November 2004),[9] the Rose Revolution in Georgia (2003), and recently the so-called Twitter Revolution in Moldova (April 2009). Even though Moldova is one of the poorest countries in Europe, Moldovans demonstrated that they are prepared to resort to the latest technologies when needed to unite and voice their discontent. Communicating by means of Twitter through the General Packet Radio Service (GPRS) on their mobile telephones, Moldovans revealed the growing role of social media in Eastern Europe as a political tool. Surprisingly, poor countries show a growing appetite for adopting new technology and catching up with the West. Turkmenistan is another example of how quickly technology can reach people when it is offered at competitive prices. For years operating only with one state ISP and limited access, the country has been showing the lowest Internet penetration rate in the region. When a license for a private operator was granted, MTS began offering new services (GPRS/EDGE for the country). More than 500,000 people joined for about half a year,[10] which is 9–10 percent of the population. Citizens in CIS countries have expressed a growing enthusiasm for the Internet and 3G mobile services and have manifested their "e-readiness" in politically sensitive times. This trend raises the concern that governments already accustomed to controlling media and communications may wish to develop means to close down free speech outlets any time they feel threatened.

Government officials recognize the power of the Internet to affect political and social life, and have actively moved to compete for influence in the space. In Moldova and Azerbaijan, for example, ministers and heads of agencies are now required to maintain Web sites and blogs, and regularly give interviews to student organizations, broadcasting them over YouTube or IPTV as an effective means to reach out to young people. This is a relatively new development that demonstrates an awareness among the political elites that the Internet is an important channel for exerting influence over domestic audiences.

Moreover, a key aspect of the Internet's political significance remains understudied: as a person-to-person back channel for communications and social networking essential to daily life in Russia, where personal contacts and an "informal economy of favors" remain keys to "getting ahead."[11] In this sense, it is interesting to note that in Uzbekistan information obtained from the Internet is accepted as being more accurate than that secured from other sources, reflecting the culture's strong social networking aspect.

Legal and Regulatory Mechanisms to Control the Internet in the CIS

In recent years, the trend in all CIS states has been toward greater regulation of the national information space, which includes the Internet. While the constitutions of (nearly) all countries enshrine the principles of freedom of information and freedom of expression, the authorities have taken various legal steps to regulate and shape participation in this space. Such measures are described in the following subsections.

Restrictions on Access to or Dissemination of Certain Types of Content

Restriction of Internet Content under State General Laws Freedom of expression is an important feature in almost all constitutions in the CIS. But increasingly, laws, decrees, and administrative orders are used to limit the extent of these freedoms, and in general the tendency is toward restrictions which contradict in spirit, if not in law, the rights enshrined in constitutional documents. For example, freedom of information can be restricted when necessary to protect moral values, public order, national security, state secrets, and other privileged data (Belarus, Russia, and Tajikistan). Uzbekistan goes even further to limit freedom of information to safeguard national, spiritual, cultural, and scientific potential. No specific laws explain satisfactorily the meaning behind such notions as "public order." By referring to broadly defined values, the text apparently leaves leeway for authorities to prosecute users for any type of content that it considers "illegal."

In some cases, government officials have demanded that the ISPs—formally or informally—temporarily suspend sites detrimental to "public order" (Tajikistan). Some of these sites remain suspended for an indefinite period of time (Kazakhstan).

Restrictions Envisioned in the Internet Service Agreements between the ISPs and their Customers Meant to be an open medium encouraging freedom of speech and expression, the Internet has increasingly become a target for strict regulation. Governments are frequently expanding the scope of content that is not to be allowed on the Internet. At times, ISPs are setting strict rules for the users, which, if not complied with, can lead to the termination of service agreements. Some providers set broad restrictive rules as preconditions in the contract with the user (e.g., TurkmenTelecom, Kazakhstan); others may decide to limit access if they subsequently decide that the accessed content is "inappropriate" (Uzbekistan). Such "inappropriate" content is not strictly defined and open to broad interpretations and arbitrary decisions by the ISPs, or state authorities.

In some cases, ISPs are part of the state administration and are directly instructed by the government to introduce such restrictive legal provisions in the customer agreement. One such example is TurkmenTelecom, which cautions its users that Internet is not a "place for unconsidered behavior" and provides an extensive list of types of content that users are forbidden to access or disseminate online, such as violent behavior, foul language, and defamatory remarks, among others.[12] On other occasions, ISPs have been directly instructed by the state to envision restrictions to accessing online content. In Kazakhstan, for example, ISPs prohibit their customers from disseminating pornographic, extremist, or terrorist materials or "any other information not in accordance with the country's laws" over the Internet.[13] Such vague categorization opens the door for authorities to prosecute online journalists and bloggers on a broad range of issues. Such uncertainty contributes to growing self-censorship.

In a third category of cases, ISPs may not have been instructed by authorities to apply measures against certain online behavior or types of content posted on the Internet, but based on the repressive climate encouraging self-censorship, these ISPs are attempting to anticipate what the authorities may find objectionable and act accordingly in order to avoid losing their license, as is the case in Russia.

Registration Requirements for Internet Web Sites
CIS states are increasingly requiring Web sites to register as mass media, making them subject to national legislation governing content, defamation, and copyright, criminal offense to the state and officials, and others. Officials increasingly speak in favor of

registering all information outlets, including the Internet, as a means to exert control over the quality and character of media content (e.g., Belarus, Russia, Kazakhstan). Requiring such registration for Web sites would have a chilling effect on anyone seeking to publish on the Internet. They would become vulnerable to criminal or civil liability and would be an easy target for government prosecution, especially as the laws describing "undesired content" weigh in favor of the state. Moreover, failure to register a Web site creates a valid legal pretext under which such content can be deemed "illegal" by state authorities, thus providing a legal case for filtering the content or suspending the licenses of the ISPs. Posting "illegal" content also carries the risk of prosecution for the site owner or the user who posted such material, contributing to a climate of self-censorship, and generally dissuading anyone from posting content on the Internet.

In Uzbekistan, the law on mass media that holds journalists and editors responsible for the "veracity" of published materials has already brought about self-censorship among journalists and bloggers. The "objectivity" test is applied also in Belarus, where independent journalists, editors, and opposition leaders are frequently subject to arbitrary prosecution and arrest. In Russia, online forums have been added to the definition of mass media, setting a precedent for prosecution of social networking sites.

Defamatory Provisions

Defamation laws have been used successfully to prosecute civil and criminal cases against Web site owners for allegedly hosting "defamatory" content. In Belarus, for example, the definition of defamation and slander laws has been expanded to selectively prosecute and deter bloggers, opposition leaders, and independent media from posting material critical of the government or specific government officials. On numerous occasions, Russian officials have spoken of the need to introduce specific legal measures that would allow them to prosecute online participants for defamation of members of the federal or regional state administration. In Russia, Uzbekistan, Kazakhstan, and Belarus, there are numerous cases of online journalists and bloggers being charged for defamation and subsequently jailed.

National Security Concerns

The need to develop ICT is a national priority in many CIS countries. Almost all CIS governments have adopted national ICT strategies that set ambitious targets for the development of the Internet in government, education, and industry. At the same time, most countries have also adopted national information security doctrines, which, on one hand, underline their understanding of the need to encourage development of the information sphere and, on the other, document their growing security concerns with regard to the Internet. Russia remains a significant influence in leading these tendencies within the region, and has been increasingly proactive in exporting its expertise to other CIS states. Since late 2000, Russia's "Doctrine of Information Security" has been adapted (in various forms and guises) as the basic precept defining the national strategic value of the Internet and the "national informational space" in most CIS countries.[14]

Governments see the Internet as a very direct and personal media that reaches into people's homes faster and deeper than traditional media. As it is subject to less regulation and less control than the traditional media, its potential impact on national security is seen as greater than that of mass media. Consequently, several governments have actively moved to restrict foreign influences ostensibly to safeguard the citizens from being exposed to any "damaging" and subversive content online. This is the case in Kazakhstan and Turkmenistan, and in 2009 the issue of designating the Internet as a national strategic sector of the economy was included in Russian legislation for a second time.[15] Such a designation would limit the percentage of foreign investment in Internet companies and would expose the sector to a number of usage restrictions.

Surveillance

Russia's legal approach to Internet surveillance for law enforcement (that is, the System for Operational-Investigative Activities or SORM-II, which allows security services unfettered physical access to ISP networks) has influenced the way in which other CIS countries have approached surveillance of the Internet.

At the regulatory and technical level, SORM-II, (which came into effect in Russia in 2000[16]) requires ISPs to provide the Federal Security Service (FSB) with statistics about all Internet traffic that goes through the ISP servers (including the time of an online session, the IP address of the user, and the data that were transmitted).[17] The ISPs themselves are responsible for the cost and maintenance of the hardware and connections. Providers' objections to SORM-II, which raised concerns about individual privacy, resulted in the ISPs being stripped of their licenses.[18]

In many respects, SORM-II is not unlike a combination of the United States' Communications Assistance to Law Enforcement Act (CALEA)[19] and the recent "warrantless" provisions for wiretapping, including the PATRIOT Act[20] passed after the attacks of 9/11. Russian legislation formally protects individual privacy, prohibiting wiretapping of any kind without a court order.[21] As a consequence, SORM-II requires government personnel to obtain a court order to intercept telephone conversations, electronic communications, or postal correspondence. In reality, however, the FSB does not bother to seek a warrant. Recently, a senior FSB official sought to apply similar registration requirements for all mobile phones with Internet capabilities. However, despite this formidable surveillance potential, there is doubt about the actual capacity of the FSB to analyze the data collected.[22]

Most CIS countries have followed Russia's lead in implementing Internet surveillance. These include the following:

• Kazakhstan followed the Russian example, requiring ISPs to install SORM-II in order to register and maintain electronic records of customers' Internet activities.
• Azerbaijan made an unsuccessful attempt to employ technologies similar to SORM-II. As of 2009, surveillance does occur, but mainly by way of visits to ISPs and Internet cafés by officials from the State Security Service.
• In Uzbekistan, the principal intelligence agency, the National Security Service (SNB), monitors the Uzbek segment of the Internet and works with the main regulatory body to impose censorship. As all ISPs must rent channels from the state monopoly provider, available evidence strongly suggests that Internet traffic is recorded and monitored by means of a centralized system. SNB officers frequently visit ISPs and Internet cafés to monitor compliance.
• In Ukraine, the security services have developed a capacity to monitor Internet traffic, and legislation has been proposed to limit access to "questionable" content for reasons of national security. The security services are also empowered to initiate criminal investigations and use wiretapping devices.
• In Belarus, special services conduct active and warrantless surveillance of Internet activities under the pretext of national security using a system similar to SORM-II.

Russia, Belarus, Moldova, and Ukraine have all established specialized units under the Ministry of Internal Affairs (Department "K") trained in combating cyber crime. Specialized technical units have also been established in other security services and ministries of defense in these countries.

Other Means to Control the Internet

The ONI has documented the use of a wide range of measures to control the Internet— legal, administrative, and technological, as well as psychological: threats and physical violence, which usually are designed to cultivate a culture of self-censorship among Internet users. In some cases these measures are used only at times of heightened political tensions and are limited in scope and duration, making them difficult to document and report.

The following subsections list some of the second- and third-generation techniques documented by the ONI during the last four years.

Event-Based Interventions   The CIS is the first region in which ONI research documented the presence of "event-based" filtering. This form of filtering differs in technical execution from more conventional filtering forms (such as those that rely on block lists) and is more difficult to track and definitively ascertain.

The Case of Kyrgyzstan (2005)   During Kyrgyzstan's 2005 parliamentary elections, two ISPs were disrupted by distributed denial of service (DDoS) attacks. Following the attacks, a "hacker for hire" posted threats to the affected ISPs' visitor logs, stating that unless these sites stayed off-line the attacks would continue.[23] The DDoS attacks effectively disrupted the ISPs' services because the hacker exploited the ISPs' narrow bandwidths and dependence on a single satellite-based connection. It remains unclear who hired the hackers responsible for the attack, although an investigation by ONI found that they were based in Ukraine (and were also responsible for an attack on a U.S. site using the same "bot" network). The opposition accused the government of ordering the attacks as a means of undermining them. The government responded by ordering the affected ISPs to keep their resources online, but it was impossible to do so because the DDoS attack had degraded their ability to provide any services. In the end, the attack was stopped as a result of U.S. legal action against the originating "botnet," which had also been attacking a U.S. site. When the "botnet" was taken down, the attacks against the Kyrgyz sites also stopped.

The Case of Belarus (2006)   During the March 2006 presidential elections in Belarus, several opposition Web sites became suddenly inaccessible, ostensibly because of innocuous network faults and domain name system (DNS) failures. Likewise, at the peak of protests against the election results, a major Minsk-based ISP ceased to provide dial-up services owing to "technical problems." These occurrences meant that important independent media and opposition political Web sites were not accessible at periods when the information they were conveying could have had political significance or acted as a catalyst for further political action. Although nothing transpired that could be identified as extralegal filtering, de facto access was not available when and where needed, with some evidence suggesting that tampering may have occured.[24]

This form of "event-based" information control, which temporally shapes Internet access, can be said to represent the emerging next-generation Internet controls. Not unlike the shorter supply-line chains that boosted manufacturing efficiencies under "just-in-time" production, event-based filtering can also be considered to be "just-in-time," as it offers greater efficiencies in denying access to information when and where it is needed. At the same time, the fact that this form of targeted and time-limited filtering is much harder to prove also removes the potential liabilities of being caught undertaking more deliberative filtering.

Crowd-Sourced Attacks: Pro-Government or Patriotic Hacktivists
During the August 2008 Russia-Georgia war over the breakaway territory of Ossetia, pro-government Russian hackers launched DDoS attacks against a wide range of Georgian ISPs and Web sites. As a consequence, the majority of Georgian government Web sites, as well as official media sites were inaccessible throughout the conflict. In response, Georgian ISPs filtered Russian Internet sites to prevent the dissemination of what they considered inaccurate and inflammatory reports by Russian media.[25] The effect of the Russian DDoS attacks and Georgian filtering was to create an information

vacuum in Georgia during crucial moments of the conflict, particularly as Russian troops crossed the Ossetian border and moved in the direction of the Georgian capital. While the Russian government denied responsibility for the cyber campaign, it did little to stop these activities, even though most of the attacks originated from crowd-sourcing on Russian Web sites and chat rooms.[26] In many respects, the cyber campaign against Georgia resembled a scaled-up version of techniques previously used against opposition Web sites and independent media during elections in the CIS, and the earlier cyber attack against Estonia.

The emergence of cross-border hacktivist activities, however, is not a new phenomenon within the CIS. Similar attacks—albeit on a much smaller scale—have taken place between Armenia and Azerbaijan for more than a decade, where the moribund conflict over the region of Nagorno Karabakh continues in cyberspace.

Administrative Mechanisms to Shut Down Access to the Internet

Legal Deregistration of Domain Names and Web Sites   Authorities often resort to various quasi-legal or "administrative" mechanisms to suppress "inappropriate" information or shut down oppositional domain names (e.g., Kazakhstan, Kyrgyzstan). In Armenia, the president created an unprecedented media and Internet blackout after announcing a state of emergency following public protests. Based on the president's instructions, the registrar of the top-level country domain suspended a number of independent media and opposition Web sites.

Pro-government and patriotic social activism has become a feature of politics in several CIS countries. In Russia, the pro-government *Nashi* youth movement ran an aggressive campaign in cyberspace in support of the government during the 2008 parliamentary and 2009 presidential elections.[27] The volume of blogs, online newspapers, and even posts to opposition and independent media sites overwhelmed and overmatched critical posts or articles, and has proven a more successful mechanism for silencing the opposition than resorting to Internet filtering or other more heavy handed repressive measures.

Self-Censorship   The constitutions of the CIS countries prohibit censorship. Nonetheless, the net effect of the various sanctions (legal, administrative, technological) is creating a general climate of self-censorship among ISPs in many CIS states, which are fearful of jeopardizing their licenses, and among individuals for whom prosecution or imprisonment is too high a price to pay for voicing criticism. Often, self-censorship is aided by opaque state practices. Many CIS countries deny that they filter the Internet or resort to extralegal methods. In Azerbaijan, for example, the author of Web sites critical of the government was detained on a number of occasions (on no legal grounds) without any follow-up or prosecution. In other cases, such as the pervasive filtering policies of Internet cafés throughout the region, the decision to limit content is formally controlled by the café owners, so it is difficult to argue whether their filtering results from a fear of sanction for allowing politically sensitive material to be accessed or from personal choice. Certainly, for most Internet café owners, the objective is to make a living, not to defy state policy. In Russia, self-censorship is sometimes perceived as a citizen's responsibility. In Tajikistan, however, research suggests that filtering is based on economic factors rather than fear of persecution from the security forces.

Emerging Second- and Third-Generation Controls in the CIS

Overt Internet filtering, such as that undertaken by China or Iran, is unlikely to occur in the CIS for several reasons. First, only in a very few cases (Uzbekistan, Turkmenistan) is the government disposed to effect an informational blockade of the country that could, in turn, jeopardize economic prospects and stifle the "scientific potential" of these technologies. Second, as noted earlier, governments generally have more subtle legal and quasi-legal methods for putting pressure on content and access providers to remove or otherwise eliminate "undesirable" content, so there is little need to resort to overt technical means such as filtering. Third, many CIS states are dependent on development aid and trade, and have oriented themselves toward integration with the global economy and are actively seeking to lower barriers on trade. Engaging in widespread filtering of the kind conducted by China or Iran would present the risk of being labeled as an "international human rights pariah," an eventuality that most CIS countries would rather avoid. Fourth, and perhaps most important, CIS states that are concerned about the Internet's empowering potential—that is, its potential to make possible further "color revolutions"—have found more subtle technical means for ensuring that these capacities are curtailed, if and when necessary.

Telecoms and ISP Market Players Until recently, almost all CIS governments preserved the monopoly right of the state telecommunication provider over international traffic. Under the pressure of international organizations (such as the European Bank for Reconstruction and Development, the World Bank, and the World Trade Organization), some CIS countries are abolishing the exclusivity provision over international traffic (Armenia). However, the need to demonopolize the service continues to be a significant problem in the rest (Kazakhstan, Turkmenistan, Uzbekistan). Since the traffic of all ISPs has to go through the state incumbent's channels, filtering can be achieved easily, without outside control, while using centralized resources. The ISPs may unknowingly receive filtered content because the main operator could install filters on any information that it deems inappropriate.

Russia, for example, does not require that the ISPs buy international traffic from a major state provider. Nonetheless, Russia has introduced other practices unprecedented for other industrialized countries. There are multiple players on the Internet market, but few of these are the major ISPs that provide international traffic to the groups of small regional providers. Interestingly, most of the big telecommunication operators (if not all) are owned or controlled by the large state company Svyazinvest. Control in Russia is not easily detectable but permeates the ownership and control structure of the operators. The Russian Internet (including operators and popular blog servers) remains a playground of interests for the state and pro-government oligarchs.

Upstream Filtering

For its size, the CIS region has a relatively underdeveloped telecommunications system, much of which remains centered on Russia. At the same time, the region itself is contiguous with (or borders) Europe, Asia, and—via the circumpolar route—North America. This centrality means that most countries in the region obtain connectivity from several different sources beyond Russia. This situation has created some interesting patterns in filtering behavior, such as similar content becoming inaccessible across several different countries, but with different filtering patterns among content providers within any single country.

Some of the CIS countries are buying connectivity from European and Asian operators. An interesting phenomenon that ONI confirmed is that private operators sometimes effectively influence online behavior of foreign operators. For example, in 2008, YouTube was not accessible in Georgia for a few days because the main ISP in the country was buying international traffic from TurkTelecom. The Turkish operator, however, often executes bans against the multimedia site in the implementation of the controversial Internet law.[28] Since the local ISP provides Internet service to more than 85 percent of the users, this block rendered YouTube inaccessible to the majority of Georgians.

Judging by common indicators appearing in almost all CIS countries, ONI research suggests that providers reselling connectivity to CIS countries may be providing prefiltered access, passing on filtered content either as part of their service offering or as a consequence of the policies they use to manage traffic on their own networks. This form of blocking, which we have dubbed "upstream" filtering (indicating that the filtering is happening in a jurisdiction other than that of the state in question), was first observed during ONI testing in Uzbekistan in 2004. At that time, the traffic of one Uzbek ISP was clearly filtered using a pattern similar to that employed by Chinese ISPs. Further investigation revealed that the Uzbek ISP was buying connectivity from China Telecom, which in this case may have sold access to its network as it would to a regular Chinese client. Testing conducted by the ONI in 2006, 2007, and 2008 reveals similar patterns of prepackaged filtering affecting Internet services within several other CIS states where ISPs had purchased their connectivity from a Russian provider.

Conclusion

The CIS region is experiencing a general trend toward greater regulation and control of the national information space, which includes the Internet. Although most CIS countries do not practice substantive or pervasive filtering—with the exception of Uzbekistan and Turkmenistan—Internet content control through regulation or intimidation is growing throughout the region. Countries deny allegations that filtering based on "official" requests is taking place. Governments are becoming more creative in designing new ways to influence the content posted online and to shape the information environment. At times, filtering is justified by national interests or by other broad notions like "public morals" that answer the needs of the ruling elite and submit the rest to self-censorship.

Moreover, the laws are often unevenly applied, with "flexible" implementation often paired with other more subtle (but effective) measures designed to promote self-restraint (or self-censorship) of both ISPs and content producers. Information control —in particular the protection of national informational space—is clearly an issue of concern throughout the CIS, and it has encouraged more stringent attention to telecommunications surveillance. In addition, measures to deny access to Internet content at sensitive times, flagged as "event-based filtering," to limit access to content geographically through "upstream filtering," or to influence accessed information in a neighboring country because of international control of the Internet traffic routes are indicative of a new seriousness with which strategies for information control are being developed. The CIS region is leading the world in the evolution of second- and third-generation information controls. The trend toward new authoritarianism, combined with shifts in regional power relations that include a relative decline in U.S. influence and Chinese ascendancy, suggests a tendency toward greater control. These are unlikely to manifest themselves in Internet filtering as overt censorship, but rather will take the form of attempts to shape the information space creating a growing climate of self-censorship. The success (or lack thereof) of this approach is likely to shape policy choices well beyond the CIS region.

Notes

1. The OpenNet Initiative did not conduct formal testing or monitoring during the 2008 Russian parliamentary elections or the 2009 presidential elections. However, persistent allegations of denial of service attacks being used against opposition Web sites, and the mobilization of pro-government hacktivism by pro-government groups such as *Nashi*, were widely reported in the press. These tactics are consistent with those observed and documented by the ONI in Kyrgyzstan and Belarus.

2. Internet users in the CIS are predominantly young, aged between 15 and 25. Around 55 percent of all users in Azerbaijan belong to this age group, compared with 60 percent in Kyrgyzstan

and similar percentages in Uzbekistan. The number of women using the Internet in Uzbekistan and Kazakhstan is equal to or larger than the number of their male counterparts. The proportion is slightly in favor of men in Ukraine, while in Tajikistan only 22.5 percent of the Internet users are women.

3. Miniwatts Marketing Group, "Internet World Statistics," 2009, http://www.internetworldstats .com.

4. Ibid.

5. Bishkek, "Isledovanie auditorii Internet v Kyrgyzstane" [Survey on the Internet Auditorium in Kyrgyzstan], 2009.

6. United Nations, *United Nations e-Government Survey 2008: From e-Government to Connected Governance*, http://unpan1.un.org/intradoc/groups/public/documents/UN/UNPAN028607.pdf.

7. "Obshtestvenyi Fond 'Grajdanskaya initsiativa internet politiki'" [Social Fund 'Civil Initiative for Internet Policy'].

8. Rafal Rohozinski, "Mapping Russian Cyberspace: Perspectives on Democracy and the Net," United Nations Research Institute for Social Development (UNRISD) Discussion Paper 115, October 1999, http://unpan1.un.org/intradoc/groups/public/documents/UNTC/UNPAN015092.pdf.

9. Joshua Goldstein, "The Role of Digital Networked Technologies in the Ukrainian Orange Revolution," Berkman Center Research Publication No. 2007-14, December 2007, http://cyber.law .harvard.edu/sites/cyber.law.harvard.edu/files/Goldstein_Ukraine_2007.pdf.

10. *Turkmenistan.ru*, "MTS Podlklychila Turkmenov k Internetu" [MTS Connected Turkmens to the Internet], April 18, 2008, http://www.turkmenistan.ru/?page_id=3&lang_id=ru&elem_id=12590 &type=event&sort=date_desc.

11. Alena Ledeneva, *How Russia Really Works: The Informal Practices That Shaped Post-Soviet Politics and Business* (Ithaca, NY: Cornell University Press, 2006).

12. TurkmenTelecom, http://www.online.tm.

13. See the general user agreement between Nursat, a major ISP, and its customers at "Public Contract," http://www.nursat.kz/?72.

14. Doctrine of the Information Security of the Russian Federation, September 9, 2000, No. Pr-1895, http://www.medialaw.ru/e_pages/laws/project/d2-4.htm.

15. An earlier attempt in 2008 to include the Internet in state legislation defining strategic sectors was removed upon second reading in the parliament.

16. Prikaz Minsviazi RF, Order of Ministry of Communications of the Russian Federation, 25 July 2000, http://www.libertarium.ru/libertarium/37988.

17. Freedom House, "Russia" in *Freedom on the Internet: A Global Assessment of Internet and Digital Media*, http://www.freedomhouse.org/printer_friendly.cfm?page=384&key=202&parent=19&report =79, (last accessed October 26, 2009).

18. Jeanette Borzo, "Russian ISP Finds Court Victory Sometimes Is No Victory at All," *Wall Street Journal Interactive Edition*, October 5, 1999, http://www.libertarium.ru/libertarium/14424/def _article_t?PRINT_VIEW=YES.

19. The Communications Assistance for Law Enforcement Act (CALEA), passed in 1994 (P.L. 103–414, 108 Stat. 4279).

20. Uniting and Strengthening America by Providing Appropriate Tools Required to Intercept and Obstruct Terrorism (USA PATRIOT) Act of 2001 (H.R. 3162), http://thomas.loc.gov/cgi-bin/query/ z?c107:H.R.3162.ENR:.

21. Article 23 of the Constitution of the Russian Federation, http://www.constitution.ru/en/ 10003000-01.htm.

22. Interview with Andrei Richter, Director, Media Law and Policy Institute, Moscow State University, in Moscow, Russia, March 28, 2006; Interview with Alexey Simonov, President, Glasnost Defense Foundation, in Moscow, Russia, March 27, 2006.

23. OpenNet Initiative, "Election Monitoring in Kyrgyzstan," February 15, 2005, http://opennet .net/special/kg/.

24. OpenNet Initiative, "The Internet and Elections: The 2006 Presidential Election in Belarus," April 2006, http://opennet.net/sites/opennet.net/files/ONI_Belarus_Country_Study.pdf.

25. For more information on the Russia-Georgia cyberwar, refer to the Information Warfare Monitor (http://www.infowar-monitor.net), which followed and analyzed developments.

26. Ibid.

27. For more information on this new phenomenon, please refer to the Russia country profile in this volume.

28. For more information, refer to the Turkey country profile in this volume.

Armenia

Access to the Internet in Armenia is largely unfettered, although evidence of second- and third-generation filtering is mounting. Armenia's political climate is volatile and largely unpredictable. In times of political unrest, the government has not hesitated to put in place restrictions on the Internet as a means to curtail public protest and discontent.

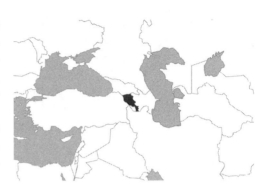

Background

Located in the heart of the Caucasus region, and situated between Turkey, Georgia, Azerbaijan, and Iran, Armenia relies on diplomacy in order to overcome political and economic isolation. Because of its unique geographical situation—and unlike most former Soviet countries—Armenia has traditionally been ethnically and religiously homogeneous. Armenia is a semipresidential republic where the president (currently, Serzh Sargsyan) holds a substantial amount of power, particularly in the areas of defense and national security. Like the other CIS republics, Armenia has experienced the hardships of switching from a centrally planned system to a market economy. The land locked status of this country coupled with poor transportation infrastructure has not

RESULTS AT A GLANCE					
Filtering	No Evidence of Filtering	Suspected Filtering	Selective Filtering	Substantial Filtering	Pervasive Filtering
Political				•	
Social			•		
Conflict and security			•		
Internet tools			•		

Other Factors	Low	Medium	High	Not Applicable
Transparency	•			
Consistency		•		

KEY INDICATORS	
GDP per capita, PPP (constant 2005 international dollars)	5,377
Life expectancy at birth (years)	72
Literacy rate (percent of people age 15+)	99
Human development index (out of 179)	83
Rule of law (out of 211)	125
Voice and accountability (out of 209)	145
Democracy index (out of 167)	113 (Hybrid regime)
Digital opportunity index (out of 181)	117
Internet users (percent of population)	5.8

Source by indicator: World Bank 2009a, World Bank 2009a, World Bank 2009a, UNDP 2008, World Bank 2009b, World Bank 2009b, Economist Intelligence Unit 2008, ITU 2007, Miniwatts Marketing Group 2009.

eased Armenia's economic transition. The Nagorno-Karabakh war with neighboring Azerbaijan and uneasy political relations with Turkey have further complicated this process. Russia remains Armenia's main strategic partner in the region, and the two countries are parties to a bilateral military agreement. Armenia is also seeking close political, economic, and strategic ties with the United States and NATO. Although the government has implemented far-reaching economic measures, including joining the World Trade Organization in 2002, poverty in Armenia remains widespread, and its economy is critically dependent on foreign support.

Internet in Armenia

The number of Internet users in Armenia increased from 161,000 in 2006 to 172,800 in 2008—the latter figure represents 5.8 percent of the population.[1] Armenia has 90,000 Internet subscribers, representing 2.97 percent of Armenia's population. Low-speed dialup access still dominates among private users (about 80–85 percent) and most companies use DSL and Wi-Fi broadband access. In addition, official sources suggest that Internet penetration is less than 4 percent.[2] In June 2007, the incumbent operator of the telephone network (Armentel) introduced DSL services—they represent approximately 76 percent of the capital city of Yerevan's population and 15 percent of the population of rural areas.[3] Local statistics show that fixed-line penetration amounted to around 18 percent,[4] while international sources point to 19.7 percent.[5]

Owing to the high level of urbanization in the country, the percentage of access to basic telephony appears high. While it has been officially estimated that 95 percent of households in the capital and 75 percent of households in other major cities have access to public telephone networks,[6] in reality only 40 percent of households have individual telephone connections, and the quality of service is extremely poor.

Most users access the Internet from home and work. Internet cafés, which grew rapidly in the 2000–2005 period, currently attract fewer users. During the last two years, the number of Wi-Fi hot spots has significantly increased, covering Yerevan's center and some residential areas. There is little Internet penetration outside Yerevan, mainly because of poor infrastructure, low income, and low levels of computer literacy. The most popular languages among Internet users are Russian, English, and Armenian. In 2005, 40 percent of Web sites visited from within Armenia were located in Russia, 30 percent were in Europe and the United States, 25 percent were local resources, and 5 percent were hosted in other countries.[7]

The high cost of Internet access for some years slowed down the entry of foreign providers into the market.[8] Over the last couple of years, the number of ISPs providing Wi-Fi and broadband connections has been increasing, resulting in price cuts. Despite the increased affordability, Internet access is still expensive in comparison to most European countries. Monthly unlimited dial-up access service costs AMD 7,500 (USD 24.50)[9] in Yerevan and about USD 30 in rural areas. The cost of dial-up of Beeline, however, is the same for rural and urban areas. If the user prefers megabyte services, connection speeds are not dedicated and can vary from 64 Kbps to 1 Mbps, depending on the area and time of day.[10]

Regulatory enforcement against dominant market players has been problematic. However, in July 2008, Armenia's antitrust regulator imposed a fine on Beeline for anticompetitive behavior.[11] In the wake of the regulator's decision, the market has enjoyed greater competitiveness, and Internet services have expanded.

Armenia was one of the first of the former Soviet countries to privatize its telecommunications industry.[12] In August 2007, the Russian VimpelCom[13] acquired a majority shareholding in ArmenTel, the incumbent telecommunications operator, and subsequently bought out the rest. In February 2008, VimpelCom registered the operator's license, allowing ArmenTel to use the Beeline brand on the territory of Armenia.[14] Until 2007 the incumbent operator enjoyed a monopoly over international connections and other services. Consequently, the liberalization of international Internet access introduced only in 2007 radically altered the Internet access market. The cost of international connections significantly decreased, but it is still higher than in European and some CIS markets.[15] The incumbent operator owns the main telecommunications infrastructure including the Trans-Armenian Optical System (the national fiber-optic backbone), satellite antennas, the entire fixed telephone infrastructure (PSTN), and most of the country's cellular infrastructure, which covers about 85 percent of Armenia.

The telecommunications regulation authority renewed ArmenTel's license, stripping it of its monopoly in some telecommunications services. However, ArmenTel has maintained its de facto monopoly of the fixed-line market. This situation may change, as two ISPs (Arminco and Cornet) announced they would start offering fixed-line communication services by the end of June 2009.[16] Nonetheless, as the networks of all operators are connected to ArmenTel's infrastructure, the incumbent will continue to dominate and benefit from interconnection fees.

Although ISPs are increasingly building their own fiber-optic networks, cable infrastructure is still underdeveloped in Armenia. Over the last three years, more than three ISPs have extended their network to cover the capital, while networks in rural areas have been developing at a much slower rate.

Satellite services are relatively well developed in Armenia; however, the demand for them is not significant because of their higher cost. Home users utilize satellite services almost exclusively for television. Downlink satellite services are widely used by ISPs in the capital city and rural areas because they provide the only means of supplying Internet services without requiring physical networks. Nonetheless, the development of two-way satellite services in Armenia has been affected not only by their high cost but also by administrative barriers to importing and using radio equipment.

The majority of the main ISPs are owned by Armenian entities. The main ISPs in the country are ArmenTel (operates under the Beeline brand),[17] Arminco LLC,[18] WEB LLC,[19] Xalt LLC,[20] Netsys LLC,[21] ADC CJSC,[22] Cornet-AM CJSC,[23] Fibernet Communication LLC,[24] and Freenet Armenia.[25] There are numerous small ISPs supplying Internet services to large companies or to certain geographic areas. However, their number is decreasing as a result of strong competition, and they recently introduced high license fees and state duties (regulated by the Law on State Duties), which have led to increasing consolidation in the market. At least two foreign ISPs are expected to enter the market in 2009.

Most ISPs gain access to the international backbone by way of ArmenTel's fiber-optic cable (Trans Armenia Optical System)[26] with 155 Mbps capacity, which connects to the Georgian Optical Highway and then to Russian and European channels. The second national backbone, routing through Iranian territory, commenced operations in September 2008. ArmenTel bought this cable, which connects to Sovintel (VimpelCom's subsidiary).[27] The third international route over the TRASEKA fiber-optic cable is owned by the state and is operated by Fibernet LLC on the basis of a 25-year concession agreement.

As an alternative route, ArmenTel utilizes the Teleglobe satellite connection, limited to 2 Mbps. Major ISPs such as Arminco and WEB LLC have built their own infrastructure, mainly fiber-optic networks and wireless networks, and also use satellite connections (usually via PlanetSkye and SatGate).

There are three nonprofit fiber-optic networks constructed with the assistance of foreign and international organizations that supply Internet services to scientific and educational institutions: ARENA Foundation, National Foundation for Science and Advanced Technologies, and Academic Scientific Research Computer Network of Armenia (ASNET-AM).

There is no Internet exchange point used by all Armenian ISPs. However, most ISPs are interconnected, and local traffic is not charged yet. The Armenian top-level domain ".am" is administrated by the Armenian Internet Society.[28]

The provision of VoIP services has raised a number of conflicts between the incumbent operator, new market players, and regulatory authorities. At present, ISPs and other private service providers are allowed to freely use the incumbent's fixed network for the provision of VoIP services. According to data provided by the Public Services Regulatory Commission, from May 2007 to May 2008, 108 companies were granted authorization to provide VoIP services.[29]

There are two mobile telephony operators in Armenia: Beeline and Vivacell-MTS, both controlled by Russian companies. Vivacell-MTS entered the market in 2005 under the name K-Telecom.[30] Each mobile operator in Armenia serves approximately 1 million users.[31] The cost of mobile communication services varies from USD 0.10 to 0.16 per minute. A third mobile operator (Orange France Telecom) recently obtained a license to operate in the country and is expected to enter the market by the end of 2009. Its entry might reduce mobile communication costs.

Legal and Regulatory Framework

In June 2001, the government issued a Concept Paper announcing that ICT is a priority for the country's economic development. Pursuant to a presidential decree, the government created the ICT Development Supporting Council (ITDSC), an advisory body chaired by the prime minister. The ITDSC was established as a communication platform for stakeholders to propose and discuss issues in the area of telecommunications policy and regulation. In 2003, the government launched the "E-Armenia" initiative. However, progress toward implementing the proposal and the Concept Paper was interrupted by the parliamentary election in 2003 and presidential election in 2004, and little progress has been made on relaunching either initiative since.[32]

Finally, in July 2008 the government approved the Concept Paper on Development of the ICT sector in Armenia. In contrast to the Concept Paper of 2001, the former lays out short- and long-term action plans with fixed timetables for fostering an information society and ensuring sector competitiveness.

The Law on Electronic Communications adopted in July 2005 regulates electronic communications in Armenia. The Ministry of Transport and Communications is responsible for formulating sector policy and setting universal service objectives.

In 2006, the Public Services Regulation Commission (PSRC) took on the role of the regulatory authority for telecommunications in line with the Law on Electronic Communications.[33] The Telecommunications Department of the PSRC develops and enforces a package of important regulations, including criteria for license holders and their reporting standards, standards for cost accounting and archiving, quality of service, and cost calculation standards for the incumbent operators and service providers. Even though the government does not have direct political influence on the decisions of the regulator, the PSRC is not entirely independent, as it is financed by the state and its members are appointed by the president upon nomination of the prime minister. The regulator frequently does not consult with operators on all important questions that affect them.

In the context of other CIS countries, Internet legislation in Armenia has demonstrated liberal trends. For example, Armenia was one of the first countries that opened the 2.4-GHz frequency band for free use by ISPs and end users. Data services have been fully liberalized since December 2006 and voice services since October 2007. There are four types of licenses for providing communication services: (1) a generic "network" license; (2) a license for the provision of electronic communications services (data transmission and Internet access); (3) a license for providing VoIP services; and (4) a license for utilization of radio frequencies.

Generally, the fees for obtaining a license are low. Electronic communications and VoIP licenses are obtained after a relatively simple procedure. By contrast, network licenses are granted through a rather complicated process.

The supply of leased-line services has always been an obligation of the incumbent operator in Armenia. Although the license requires the incumbent to provide leased-line services on a transparent and nondiscriminatory basis, communications providers have complained of the selective provision of leased-line services and alleged frequent refusals by the incumbent. The tariffs for leased-line services are subject to approval by the national regulator. The legal regime for local loops unbundling and access to the network still does not meet international standards, a fact which negatively affects market competition.

With regard to media rights, the Armenian constitution guarantees freedom of expression, media, and other means of mass information (Article 27) and freedom of entrepreneurship and ownership.[34] Armenian media have become increasingly restricted since 2003. Most newspapers act as a mouthpiece for official political agendas, and television stations are predominantly progovernment.[35] In practice, censorship is widespread among journalists.

In 2005, Armenia signed and ratified the Optional Protocol of the Convention on the Rights of the Child on the Sale of Children, Child Prostitution, and Child Pornography. Armenia's Criminal Code implemented these conventions, criminalizing, inter alia, the possession and distribution of child pornography on computer networks. Moreover, according to the Law on Mass Media (2003), the publication of any kind of pornographic material in mass media (including the Internet) is prohibited. Indeed, there have been at least two criminal convictions over the last three years related to the dissemination of pornographic materials on the Internet.

Surveillance

In Armenia, there are no express provisions to conduct monitoring of online content. Furthermore, ISPs and companies providing Web hosting services are not obliged to monitor the content of transmitted and stored content. In addition, under Armenian law it is necessary to prove gross negligence or actual knowledge in order to impose liability upon an Internet hosting company or ISP for hosting illegal content. However, ISPs must block access to particular content on request from law enforcement agencies for the purposes of crime prevention.

Following the February 2008 elections, widespread protests led the outgoing president, Robert Kocharyan, to sign a state-of-emergency decree imposing severe restrictions upon mass media and Internet publications for a 20-day period.[36] Consequently, Armenia faced both media censorship and Internet blocking for the first time since its independence. This blockage targeted Armenia-based sites, as well as YouTube after a video showing clashes between protesters and police was uploaded. The blocked Web sites included news portals, opposition Web sites, foreign media, and blogging services. The blocking was not extended beyond the original 20-day term because of international pressure. The media and Internet blackout created an unprecedented opportunity for bloggers to provide alternative viewpoints on the situation in Armenia, as during this period they were one of the few information outlets available.

Internet censorship has been implemented in two ways. First, the Armenian Internet Community simply froze several subdomains in the ".am" domain (such as aravot.am, hzh.am, echannel.am, azatutyun.am, and others). Thus, the Web sites were accessible only through their IP addresses. Only one week later, the Armenian Internet Community announced that this measure was to be enforced by the National Security Service (NSS). After the order from the NSS, some ISPs blocked access to a number of Web sites on a preselected blacklist.

Second, surveillance is regulated through the Code of Criminal Procedure of Armenia. The code provides that surveillance should be carried out only pursuant to a court warrant when applied to restrict legally guaranteed rights and freedoms (Article 284). The warrant must indicate grounds for the measures, the data that are being obtained, and the venue and duration of the surveillance and accompanying data substantiating the necessity for the warrant.

There are some exceptions to the need for a warrant—for instance, when a delay in the implementation of the search could lead to a terrorist attack or threats to national security, military, or environmental interests. The court has to be notified within 48 hours of the measures being taken. If the court finds that the grounds for the implementation of the search are insufficient, surveillance shall be immediately stopped, and the materials and data obtained deemed inadmissible as evidence.

Finally, Article 50 (3) of the Law on Electronic Communications sets forth an obligation on operators and ISPs to assist law enforcement investigators in conducting surveillance measures.

ONI Testing Results

In 2007 and 2008, the ONI ran tests on the first-tier ISPs in the country: Arminco, WEB, and Netsys. During Armenia's state-of-emergency, ONI monitored the media and Internet blackout in the country and concluded that pervasive filtering was occurring. The ONI detected a large number of blocked Web sites, including regional sites providing information on ethnic and religious freedom groups, Armenian opposition sites, Russian opposition sites and youth movements, personal blogs, an Armenian Internet portal, and a political and cultural site about Nagorno-Karabakh. A number of international and regional (mainly Russian) media sites, e-mail services, and search engines were also filtered. In addition, leading Armenian online media were intentionally blocked. Few pornographic, LGBTQ, and drug-related sites were blocked.

Conclusion

Armenia has struggled through political instability, regional conflict, and widespread poverty and unemployment. The new president has pledged to carry out reforms that would decrease corruption, improve living standards, and enhance foreign confidence in the economic development of the country. The crackdown on the media and the Internet in sensitive times, however, reveals that the government is likely to resort to such measures in order to stifle public criticism.

Notes

1. Miniwatts Marketing Group, "Internet World Statistics: Armenia," 2009, http://www .internetworldstats.com/asia/am.htm.

2. Ministry of Transport and Communications, http://www.mtc.am.

3. David Sandukhchyan, "Armenia," *Political Intelligence Internews, December, 2006*, http://ec .europa.eu/information_society/activities/internationalrel/docs/pi_study_rus_ukr_arm_azerb_bel _geor_kaz_mold/4_armenia.pdf.

4. Deliverable Report No.1: Inception Report (Tasks 1 through 4), "Design of Universal Services Fund for the Telecommunication Sector in Armenia," Prepared for World Bank Project WB 230–695/07.

5. International Telecommunication Union (ITU), "Internet Indicators: Subscribers, Users, and Broadband Subscribers," 2008, http://www.itu.int/ITU-D/icteye/Reporting/ShowReportFrame.aspx ?ReportName=/WTI/InformationTechnologyPublic&RP_intYear=2008&RP_intLanguageID=1.

6. David Sandukhchyan, "Armenia."

7. The Center for Information Law and Policy, http://www.gipi.am.

8. "High Prices for Internet in Armenia Scare Investors Away," PanARMENIAN.Net, July 2005, http://www.panarmenian.net/news/eng/?nid=14278.

9. Arminco ISP: http://www.arminco.com/en/dialup/.

10. Because of the requirement to provide basic coverage to a large number of rural villages envisaged by license conditions, Beeline has deployed CDMA450 infrastructure, and today it provides CDMA Internet services predominantly for rural inhabitants.

11. The State Commission for the Protection of Economic Competition fined Beeline USD 1 million for refusing to allow smaller ISPs to use its facilities to provide competitive service.

12. In 1994, 49 percent of ownership in the state telecommunications operator, Armenia Telecommunications Company (ArmenTel), was privatized and acquired by Trans World Telecom (TWT), allegedly an American-owned corporation. Very little is publicly known about the first phase of ArmenTel's privatization. In 1997, 90 percent of ArmenTel's shares, including TWT's and most of those owned by the Armenian government, were sold to OTE, a Greek company. In June 2006, OTE decided to sell most of its shares in ArmenTel and announced an open tender for the purchase of 90 percent of them. After a six-month evaluation of the commercial offers submitted by two Russian companies and a United Arab Emirates company, the Russian company VimpelCom was announced as the winning bidder. ArmenTel and VimpelCom announced and later signed a share sale-purchase agreement. The Armenian government announced that it would sell its shares in ArmenTel should the operator agree to abolish the monopoly on main telecommunication services.

13. VimpelCom is a leading mobile phone operator in the territory of Russia and the CIS, http://www.vimpelcom.com.

14. *ArmeniaNow.com*, "New Buzz in Mobile Service: ArmenTel becomes Beeline," April 11, 2008, http://www.armenianow.com/?action=viewArticle&IID=1182&CID=2894&AID=2965&lng=eng.

15. At present, 1 Mbps international connectivity costs for ISP are from EUR 1,500 to EUR 3,000 (depending on the type of connection, e.g., fiber-optic, satellite) against EUR 12,000 in 2006 and EUR 16,000 in 2005.

16. IHS Global Insight, "Armenia: Further Positive News in Armenian Fixed-Line Sector as Arminco Prepares to Launch Services," May 10, 2009.

17. The incumbent operator provides 90 percent of International uplink connections and provides dial-up and DSL services over PSTN, CDMA, and ISDN networks owned by the company all over the country. It provides dedicated copper lines (leased local loops) and ISDN lines to ISPs and private network owners. In May 2008, Beeline installed a 3G network in Yerevan. See Armentel, http://www.armentel.am; Beeline, http://www.beeline.am.

18. The operator is co-owned by a joint Russian-Armenian company and was founded in 1992. Arminco LLC owns about 45 percent of the Internet access market. It provides dial-up, xDSL,

dedicated broadband lines, ENUM registration, VoIP, IPTV (beta test phase), wireless access in 11 cities, Wi-Fi access, and fiber-optic connection as well as international Internet roaming. Arminco introduced prepaid Wi-Fi and dial-up Internet access cards, which do not require a contract. Services are available in the capital, major towns, and rural areas, as well as in Nagorno-Karabakh. The Arminco network is peered with the Netsys, Cornet, WEB, and Xalt ISP networks, as well as with the Armenian Freenet. The current bandwidth assigned is 10 Mbps per peer. Arminco is one of the seven official registrars of the ".am" domain. In 2003, Arminco attained the status of a Microsoft and VUE testing center. Arminco LLC, http://www.arminco.com/.

19. WEB LLC is controlled by an Armenian entity and owns approximately 12.2 percent of the Internet access market. It provides dial-up, dedicated broadband lines, DSL, Wi-Fi access, and fiber-optic connection in the capital city and rural areas, as well as in Nagorno-Karabakh. It is one of the official registrars of the ".am" domain. See WEB LLC, http://www.web.am/.

20. The operator is owned by a joint Armenian-Swiss company. Xalt LLC owns approximately 15 percent of the Internet access market. It provides dial-up, dedicated broadband lines, wireless and satellite Internet access, and Wi-Fi access services in Yerevan and rural areas. It is one of the official registrars of the ".am" domain. See Xalt LLC, http://www.xalt.am/, Xter.net, http://www.xternet .am/eng/.

21. The operator is owned by a joint Armenian-U.S. company and has approximately 12 percent of the Internet access market. It provides dial-up, dedicated-lines broadband access, Committed Information Rate Internet Connection (CIR), VoIP, and WiMAX access services mainly in Yerevan, but also in some rural cities. It is one of the official registrars of the ".am" domain. See NetSys LLC, http://www.netsys.am/.

22. The operator is owned by the Armenian-Norwegian Armenian Datacom Company (ADC) and provides cable broadband Internet services across the entire area of Yerevan city and suburbs. See Armenian Datacom Company, http://www.adc.am/.

23. Recently sold to a Russian investor, a subsidiary company of COMSTAR-Obyedinenniye Tele-Systems—Comstar United Telesystems—was established in the Armenian telecommunication market in 2000. It owns approximately 10 percent of the Internet access market. It provides dial-up, one-way (downstream) Internet access through satellite digital channels, roaming, dedicated-line broadband DSL and Wi-Fi, and WiMax access services mainly in Yerevan, as well as in some rural cities. It is one of the official registrars of the ".am" domain. See Coronet-AM CJSC, http://www.cornet.am/.

24. Provides broadband access to Internet through its own fiber-optic network, mainly to ISPs. See Fibernet Communications, http://www.fibernet.am/.

25. The Armenian Freenet (ArmFN) was created in the framework of the UNDP Armenia Internet Project in 1997. The project aims to support the development of Internet and information technologies in Armenia and provides free Internet services to individuals, as well as nonprofit, educational, and research organizations and government and other institutions. For local users the project provides free access to their servers through dial-up lines, as well as full access to national WWW resources, and to the computers in their two Public Access Sites. The ArmFN provides con-

nection to the server that activates the user's account using POP3, telnet, and FTP Internet protocols. See Armenian Freenet, http://www.freenet.am.

26. TAOS consists of a northern "ring" (Yerevan–Armavir–Gyumri–Vanadzor–Sevan–Yerevan) and a southern "tail" running from Yerevan to Meghri on the border with Iran. From Vanadzor the backbone has a northward extension to Georgia, and thence to Russia and the Black Sea submarine cable system. TAOS is the principal infrastructure providing national and international connectivity. TAOS passes through some 30 major cities in Armenia, serving approximately 60 percent of the population of Armenia. An additional component of TAOS is Beeline's metropolitan-area fiber-optic backbone network in Yerevan, comprising a logical ring and extensions that link the major telephone exchanges.

27. As to unofficial sources, Beeline is conducting negotiations with its Turkish counterparts in relation to the construction of its third alternative fiber-optic network (4 STU), which is expected to be put into operation during 2009.

28. There are seven country code domain names registrars in Armenia that are also major ISPs: Arminco LLC, http://www.arminco.com; ABCDomain LLC (formerly ARMINCO, Ltd.), http://www.abcdomain.am; WEB LLC, http://www.web.am; Xalt LLC (Xternet), http://www.xter.net; NetSys LLC, http://www.netsys.am; Dolphin LLC, http://www.dolphin.am; and Cornet-AM CJSC, http://www.cornet.am.

29. Public Services Regulatory Commission, Authorizations for Provision of Voice Services, http://www.psrc.am/en/?nid=198.

30. In 2007, a major Russian corporation, MTS, purchased 80 percent of shares in Vivacell, previously owned by K Tel A Lebanese company called Fatoush Group owns the remaining 20 percent of Vivacell shares

31. These figures are not accurate because they reflect dual subscriptions (some users use services of both operators) and a significant number of inactive users. Consequently, it is considered that the actual level of penetration of mobile telephony is less than 60 percent. The cost of mobile communication services varies from USD 0.10 to 0.16 per minute for both prepaid and contract services. Both operators are owned by Russian companies.

32. David Sandukhchyan, "Armenia."

33. The PSRC is also responsible for the regulation of electricity and water supply services and the supply of energy, fuel, and other vital goods.

34. Constitution of the Republic of Armenia, July 5, 1995, amended in November 2005.

35. Economist Intelligence Unit, "Armenia Country Profile," 2008, http://stone.eiu.com/product/50000205AM.html.

36. OpenNet Initiative Blog, "Armenia Imposes Internet Censorship as Unrest Breaks Out Following Disputed Presidential Elections," March 11, 2008, http://opennet.net/blog/2008/03/armenia-imposes-internet-censorship-unrest-breaks-out-following-disputed-presidential-e.

Azerbaijan

The Internet in Azerbaijan remains largely free from direct censorship despite the government's heavy-handed approach to political opposition and evidence of second- and third-generation controls. Azerbaijan has a growing Internet population, supported by a national strategy to develop the country into an information and communication technology 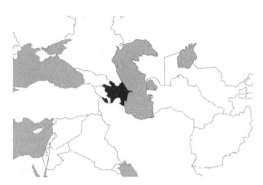 (ICT) hub for the Caucasus region. The Azerbaijani government actively seeks to attract foreign aid to help boost the telecommunications and ICT sectors.[1] Investment in the ICT sector has been prioritized, with ICT seen as an essential pillar for diversifying the country's oil-dependent economy—an important policy given that Azerbaijan's rich oil and gas reserves are expected to run out in the next 20 to 40 years. Azerbaijan's transition from war and instability in the 1990s under the charismatic former president, Heidar Aliev, has left the political opposition weak and fragmented and has led to certain authoritarian tendencies in the government. The Internet is also beginning to surface as an important medium and space for political communication, and there are some indications that restrictions on content may emerge in the future.

Background

After a decade of civil unrest and a disastrous war over the territory of Nagorno-Karabakh, Azerbaijan recovered and stabilized under the strong hand of former President Heidar Aliev (elected in 1993). Since then, the country's political life has remained dominated by the presidential apparatus. In 2003, Heidar Aliev was succeeded by his son Ilham Aliev in an election whose fairness is questioned by international observers.[2] In October 2008, President Ilham Aliev was re-elected. Transparency International has ranked Azerbaijan as one of the most corrupt countries in the world.[3]

The high economic growth in the country over the last several years is largely due to revenues coming in from oil and gas sales. Seeking to advance other sectors, the first President Aliev strongly promoted ICT as a pillar for national development, enacting a national ICT strategy in 2003 that set ambitious targets for the development of Internet in government, education, and the industrial sector.[4] However, the poor

RESULTS AT A GLANCE

Filtering	No Evidence of Filtering	Suspected Filtering	Selective Filtering	Substantial Filtering	Pervasive Filtering
Political			•		
Social			•		
Conflict and security	•				
Internet tools	•				

Other Factors	Low	Medium	High	Not Applicable
Transparency	•			
Consistency	•			

infrastructure and slow regulatory reforms in the country proved to be a challenge in developing medium-level local business and attracting foreign investors.

The Internet plays an increasingly important role in daily life, including politics. Opposition groups as well as individuals use the Internet as a communications platform, prompting sporadic crackdowns by authorities. The opposition in Azerbaijan is weak, and its leaders are often targets of government repression. A number of cases have been reported where journalists have been arrested for criticizing the government policies.[5]

Opposition groups in Azerbaijan are "seasonal" and not well coordinated. Most of the opposition and political media Web sites are created during elections and are not periodically updated. After the elections, domain names used in the campaigns are usually left to expire. Hardly any political media or opposition groups' Web sites have

KEY INDICATORS

GDP per capita, PPP (constant 2005 international dollars)	7,414
Life expectancy at birth (years)	67
Literacy rate (percent of people age 15+)	100
Human development index (out of 179)	97
Rule of law (out of 211)	161
Voice and accountability (out of 209)	177
Democracy index (out of 167)	135 (Authoritarian regime)
Digital opportunity index (out of 181)	101
Internet users (percent of population)	18.2

Source by indicator: World Bank 2009a, World Bank 2009a, World Bank 2009a, UNDP 2008, World Bank 2009b, World Bank 2009b, Economist Intelligence Unit 2008, ITU 2007, Miniwatts Marketing Group 2009.

been created since 2007 when elections were last held.[6] Even though there were expectations of increased political activity online from the opposition before the October 2008 presidential election, no notable political discussion was documented. By contrast, the president and the government update their Web sites periodically.[7]

Online groups are popular with young Internet users. Most of these groups focus on issues of practical interest—that is, free mailing lists, file-hosting services, forums, dating, blogs, and WAP services. A few opposition youth groups have focused on organizing public actions against corruption and freedom of speech (e.g., Dalga, OI). One example of such youth activist groups is the ANTV—the first organized and moderated Azerbaijani video channel on YouTube, which aims to reveal unpopular decisions taken by officials.[8] Based on the reaction of state officials to events highlighted by ANTV, it is likely that officials are tracking it regularly.

The Internet has also become a source of information for government bodies and the police. For example, at the beginning of 2008, the police tracked down online information from a car drivers' community Web site in relation to a forthcoming street race. As a result, the police arrested 17 young drivers for speeding.

The longstanding "cyberwar" over the unresolved Nagorno-Karabakh conflict between Azerbaijani and Armenian hackers continues to take place, although rather infrequently. No official sanctions have been imposed upon Azerbaijani hackers. The attacks do not appear to be part of a government-organized campaign, but rather the work of individuals acting on their own. Web site defacements and DoS attacks have also led to disruptions in the Azerbaijani Internet.

Internet in Azerbaijan

During the Soviet era, Azerbaijan was a major center for IT development, particularly in the area of process control systems. This legacy left the country with a reasonably large and well-developed technical infrastructure, including several research institutes and a political leadership savvy about the importance of the ICT sector. Internet development is following the pattern typical of many developing countries, with access centered on major cities, particularly the capital city Baku. Overall Internet penetration is rising as a result of the support of the government's ICT strategy as well as the large Azerbaijani diaspora, for whom the Internet is increasingly an important channel for maintaining contact with their homeland. The number of Internet users has grown over the last several years to 1.5 million users, or 18.2 percent of the population, as of March 2009, estimated by the Ministry of Communications[9] (or close to 17 percent for 2008 according to the latest estimates of ITU[10]).

Many Azerbaijanis access the Internet from shared connections, such as their place of work or study, or from Internet cafés (with the latter providing access for 19 percent of users in 2007). The rate of ownership of computers is low (2.4 units per

100 inhabitants), and Internet usage in homes is moderate—it accounts for 41.6 percent of the total usage for 2007, up from 36.4 percent for 2006. For connectivity, some individual subscribers rely on mobile telephony, though access remains expensive, with most using dial-up services as their primary means. Official survey results for 2007 indicate that economic and educational barriers are the main contributing factors for these low figures, with 31.4 percent blaming the high cost of computer equipment and 21.8 percent indicating a lack of necessary skills.[11]

The Ministry of Communications and Information Technologies (MCIT), together with the Ministry of Education, Microsoft, and Hewlett Packard, has started the pilot stage of the National PC Initiative aiming to provide conditions for a rapid increase of the PC penetration rate (up to 15 percent) and e-society development.[12] The state-backed Program on Information of the Education System (2008–2012) plans to provide Internet connectivity to all the schools of Azerbaijan. Currently, more than 200 secondary schools have been connected to the Internet (ADSL).

The cost of Internet service remains high for the average citizen: a DSL connection of 64 Kbps costs around USD 40–50 per month, and unlimited monthly access costs around USD 35. For comparison, the average salary in the country is slightly over USD 300 per month. While the cost of international traffic has gone down over the last several years, the cost for usage of the local infrastructure remains unchanged. Approximately 50 percent of the expenses of small ISPs are local connection costs paid to the state-owned company controlling the market. Because these expenses are the same for all providers, they have agreed among themselves to charge end users the same price for unlimited monthly dial-up service. Larger providers temporarily blocked the ISPs that tried to contravene the concerted practice. In December 2007, for example, two small providers—SuperOnline and AvirTel—were blocked by local ISPs (Adanet and IntraNS) while trying to provide service at a lower price for the customers. Shortly after the providers agreed to bring the price of their services into line, the block was lifted. For similar reasons, the larger ISPs blocked another smaller local ISP—Azeronline.

In Azerbaijan, fixed-line telephony is largely centralized in the hands of the state-owned telecom provider AzTelecom, which also acts as a commercial ISP. Delta Telecom (previously operating as AzerSat) is the main ISP in the country, supplying international connectivity to at least 90–95 percent of all users. Delta Telecom also owns the Internet international gateway and sells international traffic to almost all ISPs.

The nonprofit AZNET/AZRENA project provides connectivity to the educational and research community and benefits from a satellite channel built under NATO's "Silk Road" project. AzEuroTel started commercial activity as a telecommunications company and thus managed to establish a relatively wide network infrastructure. AzEuroTel and Adanet also have satellite channels to Russia. AzerOnline, which is funded predominantly by the largest mobile operator, AzerCell, has an additional satellite connection to Turkey. The cost of satellite connection is very high because of the monopoly regime set by the MCIT.

Since the second half of 2007, Azerbaijan does not have a free Internet Exchange Point (IXP). Delta Telecom controls the only IXP and charges the same amount for local and international traffic. Providers have not been able to agree on setting up another IXP. The external traffic of Azerbaijan is now 6 Gbps, which is a notable increase from the 155 Mbps capacity of 2006. Delta Telecom has external fiber-optic connections with Russia via TransTelecom and with Turkey via RosTelecom.[13] (Indirectly, Delta Telecom serves Georgian users because a local ISP, TransEuroCom, buys international traffic from Delta and carries it by fiber to Georgia. Through the TRACECA Fiber Optic Cable line, TransEuroCom is connected also to the TurkTelecom in Turkey.)

State control over domain name registration is limited. The assignment of the country code domain name ".az" is controlled by AzNic, Ltd., a joint venture between three Azerbaijani firms. The cost for a one-year registration is USD 34. Network Technologies (a subsidiary of IntraNS) is the company that carries out the registration and administration of the top-level domain level (TLD) in the country. Domain name registrations cannot be done online. Instead, a client is required in most cases to go in person to the offices of the domain name holder. Since 2002, the number of registered domain names has rapidly increased, with approximately 3,000 first-level and more than 6,000 second-level domains registered under the ".az" domain.

The Azerbaijani Internet population is young, mostly male, and largely concentrated in urban areas: more than 55 percent of the users are people in the age range of 16 to 24, and approximately 70 percent of the users are male. During the 1990s, the official language of Azerbaijan switched from Russian to Azerbaijani, and the script from Cyrillic to Latin. As a result, the number of Web sites using Azerbaijani language increased. Due to the increased use of blogs by young people, several local blog servers were created in the Azerbaijani language. However, most of the bloggers still post on Russian blog servers, and others on Western European and Turkish sites. The Azerbaijani language is currently used on all official government Web sites, as well as within mainstream media and the general Internet population.

Mobile telephony is increasingly popular among the younger population. This is especially the case in rural areas where the fixed-line infrastructure is poor and people are increasingly subscribing to mobile services. The major mobile operator in the country is Azercell with more than 35 percent MCIT participation. Bakcell, the second operator, is relatively small. Azercell recently started offering mobile e-mail services. Both operators provide coverage of the whole Azerbaijani territory (except the territory of Nagorno-Karabakh). In March 2006, the MCIT agreed to grant a license to a third GSM operator, Azerphone.[14] Catel[15] started operation earlier. The state telecom,

AzTelecom, has participation in the two new mobile operators. Azercell, Bakcell, and Azerphone provide WAP and GRPS services. Mobile providers also use Delta Telecom's external channel for Internet.[16]

Legal and Regulatory Frameworks

Even though Azerbaijan made telecommunications and Internet national development priorities, the telecom regulatory framework remains insufficiently developed. The MCIT acts as both regulator and operator. In 2008, the MCIT moved to separate the two functions but has not yet completed this process. Some telecommunications services must be licensed,[17] including VoIP.[18]

The major public telecom operators are the government-owned AzTelecom, Azeronline, IntraNS, Adanet, and AzEuroTel (50 percent owned by the MCIT and 50 percent by a British company). Around half of the telephone lines in Azerbaijan are analog, and more than 85 percent of the main lines are in urban areas. The MCIT has adopted a program for development of telecommunications aimed at modernizing the telecommunications infrastructure.

Under foreign pressure, the government has taken steps to liberalize the ISP market. Compulsory state licensing for ISPs was eliminated in 2002,[19] although the MCIT has continued to ignore this provision on isolated occasions. The MCIT continues to hold about a 50 percent share in a few of the leading ISPs in Azerbaijan. Azerbaijan applied for World Trade Organization (WTO) membership in 1997, and even though some progress in liberalization of services was made, the country still remains on the accession agenda. It has been suggested that there is not enough political will to join the WTO, mainly because local businesses fear the loss of their advantageous position in the internal market.

From a regulatory perspective, the Internet is treated as mass media[20] and included on the list of telecommunications services regulated by the 2005 Law on Telecommunications. Azerbaijani law does not provide for mandatory filtering or monitoring of Internet content. However, as Web sites that criticize governmental policies have emerged, the government has considered introducing a law that will impose restrictions on Web sites with obscene or antinational content, thereby strengthening already existing defamation laws. Content filtering is practiced by AZNET, the education and research ISP, but is regulated by an accepted usage policy and is restricted to filtering out pornographic content. Anecdotal accounts claim that filtering of specific Web sites occurs, which is seemingly the result of informal requests to ISP managers by state officials from the Ministry of National Security, MCIT, or the presidency. These instances have been infrequent, and the resulting public outcry has led to the swift unblocking of affected sites.

YouTube is also becoming increasingly popular among Azerbaijani Internet users. Several youth groups are posting videos online and are using YouTube as a platform to communicate with other YouTube members or members of the public at large. The popularity of the multimedia site prompted the head of the National Council on TV and Radio Broadcasting of Azerbaijan, Nushirevan Magerramli, to announce the government's intention to regulate Internet TV and Internet Radio.[21]

The Telecommunications Act is expected to prohibit the same legal entity from concentrating more than three publications under one TV and radio company. In 2007, the government announced that in some regions of the country, TV signals from neighboring Armenia and Iran are stronger than the national TV broadcast.[22] As a result, the National Television and Radio Council ordered a discontinuation of the broadcast of Russian and Turkish TV stations on Azerbaijani territory. In October 2008, the council announced its decision to suspend the licenses of some international radio channels, such as the BBC, Radio Liberty, and others.

The Azerbaijani defamation legislation has been a frequent subject of criticism by the international human rights community. The government has been under pressure to decriminalize libel, especially after prosecution against journalists and bloggers has intensified. For example, Eynulla Fatullayev, the editor of Azerbaijan's largest independent newspaper and an outspoken critic of the government, was sentenced to eight years and six months in prison on charges of terrorism and inciting ethnic hatred.[23] Fatullayev was sentenced earlier during the same year under the criminal libel provision to 30 months in prison for a posting attributed to him. The posting blamed the Azerbaijani government for one of the massacres in the Nagorno-Karabakh war in 1992.[24] Fatullayev denied writing the posting and argued that the charges were politically motivated. This case stirred massive protests in the country against the editor's conviction. The authorities shut down the publications in which Fatullayev participated. The hard disk drives of the computers of these publications were also seized.[25]

Another recent case shows that the government has exercised pressure on ISPs to take down specific Internet content. Sensitive videos considered offensive to Azerbaijani national feelings were uploaded online to cause a massive uproar in the society. In response, the Ministry of Foreign Affairs sent an official letter to the ISP to express its disapproval and have the videos removed.

Surveillance

Azerbaijani law does not include a formal legal foundation requiring Internet surveillance. Nevertheless, surveillance does occur, mainly by means of sporadic visits of the State Security Services to ISPs. In 2000–2001, there was an unsuccessful attempt to adopt the Russian SORM-II model for Internet surveillance, but the project was interrupted because of financial difficulties and opposition from ISPs and the Internet community.

In order to deal with cyber attacks, the MCIT is planning to establish a council dealing with Internet-related problems.[26] The Azerbaijani Internet community is hoping that the proposed council will be able to decrease cyber security risks without undermining the privacy of users. Another recent MCIT initiative is the launch of an Internet antihackers agency.

There are several reported cases of people arrested because of content posted online. The author of the Web site http://www.pur.gen.az, infamous for its biting humorous content, posted a caricature of the president of Azerbaijan in 2006. In 2007, the Ministry of National Security searched one of the Internet cafés in Baku and discovered this caricature on the cache page. The author and the webmaster of the site, as well as several café guests, were arrested and indicted for organized criminal activities. The individuals were released several days later, but the Web site was shut down by its owners in order to avoid further prosecution.

Another case followed the rapid increase of the price of petrol, gas, and electricity in the country in January 2007. The author of http://www.susmayaq.biz[27] published a protest letter to the president online. As a result, the author was arrested, and the Web site was temporarily inaccessible on ten Azerbaijani ISPs from January to March 2007.[28] After a protest by youth organizations, the author was released without charges.

ONI Testing Results

In 2007 and 2008, the OpenNet Initiative tested for content filtering on four ISPs—AzNet, DeltaTelecom, AzerOnline, and AzEuroTel, as well as several end user locations (such as Internet cafés). Most of the ISPs in the country purchase international traffic from Delta Telecom and utilize the infrastructure of AzTelecom for local traffic. It appears that most of the filtering occurs on Delta Telecom lines. The ONI found reverse filtering on a number of U.S. military sites.

Evidence of second-generation controls was also evident in the run-up to the 2008 parliamentary elections. The political section of the most popular online forum (http://www.day.az/forum) in Azerbaijan was removed around 20 days before the elections and was still inactive in May 2009.

The popular opposition Web blog Tinsohbeti.com was blocked in March 2008 after it published an article detailing the political and economic problems in Azerbaijan. Earlier, in 2006, the same Web site was blocked because it posted satirical cartoons of the president.[29] Before the presidential elections in October 2008, the Web site was unblocked, but by then the original domain registration had expired and no longer hosted the opposition Web blog.

The autonomous republic of Nakhchivan, an exclave of Azerbaijan, closed down Internet cafés for several days in March 2008, according to the Azerbaijani press.[30] The reasons behind the ban remain unclear, but restrictive policies on seeking and distributing information in the republic are not isolated cases. At the end of 2008, a number of Web sites were locally blocked in Nakhchivan.[31]

At the Internet café level, many owners impose restrictions that prevent users from downloading large attachments and visiting certain pornographic sites. But these policies are not universal, and they are implemented at the discretion of Internet café owners.

At the business level, most employers limit access to the Internet through the use of intelligent firewalls that restrict the downloading of files with certain extensions (.mp3, .avi, .mpg, .mov, etc.), as well as access to storage file servers and to the servers of instant messaging clients such as ICQ, MSN, Skype, and others.

The ongoing cyberwar between Azerbaijani and Armenian hackers has also caused disruptions to some Web sites and ISPs. In early 2007, five Armenian Web sites were inaccessible, and users were displayed a block page commenting on the political affiliation of the Nagorno-Karabakh region.[32] At the same time, the Web site of the Azerbaijani Public Television ITV was taken down.[33] Since most of the allegedly inaccessible sites contained oppositional political content, there are allegations that the Azerbaijani government was involved in the attacks. However, ONI testing could not confirm these suspicions. The ONI did not test for political issues related to the proclaimed independence of the Nagorno-Karabakh region.[34]

Conclusion

The Internet in Azerbaijan remains for the most part "free and open" as a result of the government's strong interest in converting the country into an "ICT hub" for the region. However, evidence of second- and third-generation controls is mounting. As the IT market is not yet fully liberalized, the commercial ISPs operate under economically inconvenient conditions set by the state monopolist, which stifle smaller competitors. Government pressure on content providers is not isolated and takes different manifestations ranging from surveillance to the shutting down of commercial activities. Instances of "just-in-time" filtering appeared to result from "informal" requests by state officials to ISP operators and were limited in duration and scope. Moreover, public pressure led to a swift reversal of the policies. That said, the filtering requests appear to be directed through informal channels. Given the prospect of increased use of the Internet by Azerbaijani opposition groups and the government's sensitivity to opposition, we may expect to see some attempts to regulate Internet content and further instances of "just-in-time" filtering affecting opposition Web sites.

Notes

1. Azerbaijan has signed grant agreements with the UNDP (National Information Communication Technologies Strategy for 2003–2012), the World Bank (for expanding telecommunications in the rural areas of the Southern Caucasian countries), and other international organizations.

2. Human Rights Watch, "Azerbaijan: Presidential Elections 2003," http://www.hrw.org/backgrounder/eca/azerbaijan/index.htm.

3. Transparency International, "Corruption Perceptions Index 2008," http://www.transparency.org/policy_research/surveys_indices/cpi/2008.

4. Decree 1146 on the Establishment of National Strategy on Information and Communication Technologies Aimed at the Development of the Republic Azerbaijan (2003–2012), signed by the President of the Republic of Azerbaijan on February 17, 2003.

5. Radio Free Europe/Radio Liberty, "Azerbaijan: RFE/RL Journalist Freed but Faces New Charges," December 10, 2007, http://www.rferl.org/featuresarticle/2007/12/0d8a4642-2e50-4135-a8c2-21bfbe12eefa.html; Radio Free Europe/Radio Liberty, "Azerbaijan: Activist Becomes First Female Political Prisoner to Die in Detention," November 29, 2007, http://www.rferl.org/featuresarticle/2007/11/6bd1a0ac-31ce-4874-bf46-f6d4525ce5ca.html.

6. Two previously active opposition news Web sites, http://www.times.az and http://www.kiv.az, were bought out by a U.K. media corporation and are no longer supported.

7. A local nonprofit multimedia center conducts regular monitoring of state Web sites and provides information about e-governance services, frequency of information updates, and accessibility (http://www.informasiya.org/).

8. ANTV is a product of an initiative of the Forum of Azerbaijani Students in Europe. ANTV encourages free speech, video sharing, and discussions using the YouTube platform. See http://www.youtube.com/user/vhsoy.

9. *BBC News*, "Country Profile: Azerbaijan," April 15, 2009, http://news.bbc.co.uk/2/hi/europe/country_profiles/1235976.stm.

10. International Telecommunication Union (ITU), "Internet Indicators: Subscribers, Users, and Broadband Subscribers," 2008, http://www.itu.int/ITU-D/icteye/Reporting/ShowReportFrame.aspx?ReportName=/WTI/InformationTechnologyPublic&RP_intYear=2008&RP_intLanguageID=1.

11. Transport, Communication, Information, and Communication Technologies, State Statistical Committee of the Republic of Azerbaijan. The latest published data are for 2006; The State Statistical Committee of the Republic of Azerbaijan, http://www.azstat.org/statinfo/communication/en/042_1.shtml.

12. The project targets selling more than 100,000 PCs in the country by 2010 and providing each Internet user with free Internet hours. *Trend*, "National PC Project Open for Cooperation: Azerbaijani IT Ministry," April 13, 2009, http://en.trend.az/capital/it/1455207.html.

13. Delta Telecom inherited the infrastructure of AzerSat with connections to TeliaSonera (Sweden) and preserves partnership with Eutelsat, Belgacom, SatGate, XANTİC, Hughes Network Systems, Pandatel, Siemens, and Motorola.

14. Azerphone is expected to cover 85 percent of the territory of the country by 2008, offering lower prices than the two preexisting operators and 3G technology. *Today.Az*, "Azerphone Company to Cover 85% Territory of Country in Following 2 Years," January 17, 2006, http://www.today.az/news/business/22128.html.

15. Catel is an entirely CDMA based mobile operator and also provides Internet services.

16. For operators, it is easier to obtain a license for CDMA services using transportable phone, rather than for a mobile operator. All CDMA operators provide Internet services, and their coverage is mainly in big cities. GPRS services in the country are expensive (in the range of 15 MB for USD 5).

17. As provided in Presidential Decree No. 861, March 19, 2003.

18. *Day.az*, "Azerbaidjanskie Internet—Provaideri Mogut Okazyvat' Uslugu IP-telefonii" [Azerbaijani Internet—ISPs Can Provide VoIP Services], February 5, 2007, http://www.day.az/news/hitech/69561.html.

19. "Pravilami Pol'zovaniya Uslugami Internet Svyazi" [Internet Service Use Rules], www.mincom.gov.az.

20. Under the provisions of the Law on Mass Media adopted on December 7, 1999.

21. *Day.az*, Nushirevan Maharramli, "Internet-radio i Internet-TV Doljny Regulirovatsya Zakonom" [Internet Radio and Internet TV Should Be Regulated by Law], July 27, 2007, http://www.day.az/news/hitech/87198 html.

22. *Regeneum.ru*, "V Azerbaijane ne Mogut Aaglushit' Armyanskie i Iranskie Telekanaly" [In Azerbaijan, Armenian and Iranian TV Cannot Be Drowned], January 17, 2008, http://www.regnum.ru/news/944030.html.

23. Human Rights Watch, "Azerbaijan: Outspoken Editor Sentenced to Eight Years and Six Months," October 29, 2007, http://hrw.org/english/docs/2007/10/30/azerba17204.htm.

24. Human Rights Watch, "Azerbaijan: Opposition Editor Sentenced to Prison," April 25, 2007, http://hrw.org/english/docs/2007/04/26/azerba15790.htm.

25. Several journalists were arrested during the last two years on different accusations. Six of them were released, and three remain in jail. The last police attack on journalists occurred on June 23, 2008, when the leader of the Institute of Freedom and Security of Journalists, Emin Huseynov, was arrested while filming a meeting dedicated to Che Guevara's birthday.

26. *Day.az*, "V Azerbaijane Sozdaetsya Sovet po Resheniyu Problem, Svyazannyh s Internetom" [In Azerbaijan, a Council to Address the Problems Associated with the Internet], December 24, 2007, http://www.day.az/news/hitech/102319.html.

27. The Web site, in translation from Azerbaijani, bears as its title the provocative slogan "Let's not be silent."

28. *Day.az*, "V Azerbaijane Arestovan Avtor Sajta, Vyrajavshego Protest Protiv Podnyatiya Tzen" [In Azerbaijan—the Author of a Web site Protesting Price Increases is Arrested], January 15, 2007, http://www.day.az/news/politics/68040.html.

29. The site was still blocked in July 2008. Reporters Without Borders report on a previous block. See Reporters Without Borders, "Blog that Satirizes President Aliev made Inaccessible," July 28, 2006, http://www.rsf.org/Blog-that-satirizes-President.html.

30. *Day.az*, "V Nahchyvane Vnov' Zarabotali Internet-kluby" [Internet-clubs are in Operation Again in Vahchivan], March 7, 2008, http://www.day.az/news/hitech/110584.html.

31. See http://nakhInternet.az, http://www.nakhchivan.org.az, http://www.turan.az, http://www
.azadliqradiosu.az, http://www.azadliq.org, http://www.irfs.az.

32. *Day.az*, "Azerbaijanskii Haker Vzlomal Pyat' Armyanskih Sajtov" [Azerbaijan Hacker Breaks Five Armenian Web sites], January 29, 2007, http://www.day.az/news/hitech/68996.html.

33. *Day.az*, "Spetzslujby Armenii Vzlomali Sajt Obshestvennogo Televiden'ya Azerbaijana" [Azerbaijani Public Television Web site Defaced by Armenian Secret Service], January 22, 2007, http://www.day.az/news/hitech/68493.html.

34. In an attempt to improve the hostile relations between Armenia and Azerbaijan, the first site in Armenian was launched last year in Azerbaijan. The purpose of this site is to inform Armenians about the real situation in Azerbaijan and the conflict from an Azeri viewpoint.

Belarus

The Belarus government has moved to second- and third-generation controls to manage its national information space. Control over the Internet is centralized with the government-owned Beltelecom managing the country's Internet gateway. Regulation is heavy with strong state involvement in the telecommunications and media market. Most users  who post online media practice a degree of self-censorship prompted by fears of regulatory prosecution. The political climate is repressive and opposition leaders and independent journalists are frequently detained and prosecuted.

Background

Under President Alexander Lukashenka, the Belarusian regime has been criticized for its repressive and increasingly authoritarian tendencies. In 2008, it was announced that Lukashenka would most likely run for a fourth term in 2011.[1] During his rule a number of independent and opposition leaders have been detained, opposition parties banned, and public demonstrations suppressed. The economic and political system remains highly centralized, with executive authority vested exclusively in the office of

RESULTS AT A GLANCE					
Filtering	No Evidence of Filtering	Suspected Filtering	Selective Filtering	Substantial Filtering	Pervasive Filtering
Political			•		
Social			•		
Conflict and security			•		
Internet tools			•		

Other Factors	Low	Medium	High	Not Applicable
Transparency	•			
Consistency	•			

KEY INDICATORS	
GDP per capita, PPP (constant 2005 international dollars)	10,238
Life expectancy at birth (years)	70
Literacy rate (percent of people age 15+)	100
Human development index (out of 179)	67
Rule of law (out of 211)	184
Voice and accountability (out of 209)	182
Democracy index (out of 167)	132 (Authoritarian regime)
Digital opportunity index (out of 181)	78
Internet users (percent of population)	29

Source by indicator: World Bank 2009a, World Bank 2009a, World Bank 2009a, UNDP 2008, World Bank 2009b, World Bank 2009b, Economist Intelligence Unit 2008, ITU 2007, Miniwatts Marketing Group 2009.

the president. Charges of election fraud have also been widespread. Human rights organizations have been extremely critical of the current regime, including its steadily increasing control over information during the last several years. Nevertheless, Lukashenka remains genuinely popular with many, particularly the middle-aged and rural populations who have benefited most from his protectionist economic policies and the overall stability that Belarus has enjoyed[2] (which contrasts with political instability in Ukraine, Georgia, and other CIS countries). Market analysts predict that economic hardship will force the privatization of state assets, but such a move would most likely benefit top Belarusian officials.[3]

Internet in Belarus

Steady economic growth in Belarus has stimulated the development of telecommunications in recent years. However, because of excessive regulation and state control of major participants in the telecommunications industry, the development of telecommunications remains low compared to the rest of the region. The state retains a dominant position over the telecommunications sector, with all external fixed-line connections passing through the state-owned operator Beltelecom. Taking into account both the increase in Internet users and the potential of the Internet to spread political ideas, the government is adopting restrictive policies, monitoring content, and placing temporary limitations on access to politically sensitive Web sites, particularly during times of public protest.

The cost of Internet access in Belarus has decreased in recent years prompting a notable rise in Internet usage and a growing ISP market. As of 2008, Belarus had an Internet penetration rate of approximately 29 percent.[4] Prices for Internet access remain higher than those of neighboring countries. In 2008, the cost of dial-up Internet access through Beltelecom was around USD 0.68 per hour, while an ADSL connection (512 Kbps) cost around USD 122 per month,[5] placing the latter beyond the reach of most citizens, given that the average salary was around USD 436 per month as of July 2008. Private operators are attempting to break into the market by offering lower prices.

Because Beltelecom controls the market, tariffs for residential local calls are below cost. The government is preserving this policy in order to ensure that fixed voice services are affordable for all.[6] At the same time, Beltelecom is keeping prices high for international calls and Internet access service, a policy that allows the operator to subsidize local call services and remain a revenue-generating enterprise. This policy, however, hinders the establishment of a competitive market.

In recent years, broadband Internet services have developed rapidly. Beltelecom has announced plans to provide broadband Internet service to a large number of its subscribers and to launch Wi-Fi service. In April 2008, the Ministry of Communications estimated that 170,000 Internet users were using broadband services and forecast that by 2010 this number would reach 500,000 users.[7]

The most active Internet users in Belarus belong to the 17–22 age group (38 percent), followed by users in the 23–29 age group.[8] Internet access in Belarus is predominantly urban, with 60 percent of users living in the capital Minsk. The profile of the average Internet user is male, university educated, living in the capital, and working in a state enterprise. The Ministry for Statistics and Analysis estimates that one in four families in Belarus owns a computer at home.[9] In 2005, 58 percent of schools in Belarus had computers, and 25 percent of the schools had Internet access. The popularity of Internet cafés has fallen in recent years, as most users prefer to access the Internet from home or work. Russian is the most widely used language by Belarusians on the Internet, followed by Belarusian, English, and Polish.

As Internet usage has risen, related services have developed into fast-growing and profitable businesses in Belarus. According to ministry data, 150 ISPs had licenses to operate in the country, while only 41 were active at the beginning of 2008.[10] Conditional on obtaining a license, ISPs and mobile operators can apparently enter the market without facing any serious barriers. Fixed-line operators, however, are awaiting further liberalization of the market. There are four mobile operators, and the government owns stakes in all of them. The country's first deputy IT and communications minister, Ivan Rak, has announced that the tender for 3G licenses in Belarus would be held by September 1, 2009.[11] The state-controlled operator Beltelecom holds the biggest market share, with 187 public Internet access points in the country. Beltelecom's subsidiary Belpak is the main ISP in the country. Beltelecom holds exclusive rights over the external channels of communications,[12] and all ISPs are required to run their traffic through its infrastructure, often at high prices.

Only the network of the National Academy of Sciences of Belarus (BasNet) has its own independent satellite connection,[13] but it provides Internet access exclusively to academic institutions. In 2008, the speed of Beltelecom's internal Internet channel was significantly increased to 5.2 Gbps, with prospects to increase to 8 Gbps in 2010 (from a mere 1.5 Gbps in 2006). In comparison, BasNet's speed is 12 Mbps. Beltelecom routes its traffic predominantly through Russian operators (70 percent) to connect to the Internet.[14]

Second-tier ISPs have the right to build their own infrastructure, except for the construction of external liaison channels. Providers are also required to use Beltelecom channels to connect users (so-called last mile).

Despite the state-proclaimed "liberalization" of the Belarusian mobile market, the government continues to own a significant stake in four operators.[15] The main ISPs in the country apart from the state operator are Aichyna, Belinfonet, BN, and Solo. Because VoIP services are considered international services over which Beltelecom has exclusive rights, the state operator is the only operator licensed to provide commercial VoIP services in Belarus. The high prices maintained by the monopoly encourage the emergence of illegal VoIP providers, which are criminally prosecuted. Under decree of the Ministry of Communications and Informatization, IP telephony is permitted only for noncommercial purposes.[16] Regulation of P2P connections is currently not a priority for the government.

Beltelecom controls the main IXP and charges other ISPs for using it.[17] Nonetheless, a large number of second-tier ISPs are using the IXP because it significantly cuts down traffic costs. Interconnection tariffs between telecommunications operators are still not regulated.

There are more than 22,300 Belarusian Web sites, of which around 13,500 domain names were registered with the country-code top-level domain name ".by" by mid-2008.

Legal and Regulatory Frameworks

Extensive governmental regulation, a strict licensing regime, and Beltelecom's monopoly are major impediments to the development of competitive Internet services in Belarus. Beltelecom is under the direct supervision of the Ministry of Communications and Informatization. This arrangement could change as a result of the WTO's accession requirements, which demand that Beltelecom be privatized and end its monopoly on external communication channels. The ministry declared that Beltelecom's control over external communication channels would remain after privatization, with licenses given only to those operators that have built their own external communication infrastructure. Belarusian legislation has established a license-based regime for the following types of telecommunications activities: fixed local/national telephony, mobile telephony, radio trunk transmission, and data transmission.[18]

The Ministry of Communications and Informatization is the main regulatory authority of the telecommunications sector and is divided into six main departments: statistics, telecommunications, postal communications, television and broadcasting, certification, and technical regulation and standardization. The ministry is frequently accused of placing unjustified limitations on commercial operators to reinforce Beltelecom's monopoly. The ministry is a founder of Beltelecom and regulates the activities of the operator. This setup undermines regulatory independence, a principle essential for the efficient functioning of the communications sector. Policy relating to ICT appears to be created mostly on an ad hoc basis by President Lukashenka and his administration. The president frequently holds special meetings to issue directives regarding ICT regulation and the implementation of particular policies. The Security Council, chaired by the president, decides on a wide range of questions related to the security of the regime, including information security. Additionally, a number of state entities have significant power to influence and control the Internet. The Operational Analytics Center (formerly the State Center for Information Security), under the supervision of the president and initially a subdivision of the special security services (KGB), is a specialized body responsible for protecting state secrets. The center has preserved its close collaboration with the KGB. The center also manages the administration of the country's top-level domain (".by"). The State Inspection on Electronic Communications is a subunit of the Ministry of Communications and Informatization and exercises wide authority with regard to the Internet. The Inspection supervises the electronic communications sector, and in the event of a violation of the rules, it can impose sanctions on operators or propose the revocation of a wrongdoer's license.

Department "K"—a division of the Ministry of Internal Affairs—is responsible for investigating cyber crime (arts. 212, 349–355 of the Penal Code). The department coordinates its work with the police and other authorities. Department "K" keeps 1,500 Belarusian hackers on its records. Records show that 4,642 criminal cases related to usage of computer technologies commenced in the period of 1998 to 2006, of which 2,826 were registered in 2005. Belarus has witnessed a rapid growth of cyber crimes, and authorities have estimated a 30 percent increase for the first half of 2007 in comparison to the whole of the previous year.[19] The most common cyber crimes in the country are unauthorized appropriation of information through usage of computer technology (72 percent) and modification of computer information (13 percent).[20]

Although Belarus lacks a well-developed Internet regulatory framework, the authorities appear anxious to achieve control over the Internet. Conscious of the popularity of the Internet among opposition groups and private media, authorities compel self-censorship through frequent threats and prosecutions. In addition, in order to avoid public debate of pending legal measures, authorities often delay publishing laws before their final promulgation.

A number of laws refer to the Internet, such as the Law on Informatization of 1995,[21] the Law on SORM of 1999,[22] and the Law on Electronic Communications of 2005.[23] The Internet is within the ambit of regulation of the Law on Informatization, which subjects Internet activities to a number of media restrictions. The Law on the Media of June 2008 provides a similar regime for Web sites and media. The legal framework allows for the application of restrictive measures on Web sites, such as blocking of content or the cessation of operation. This is a result of increasing intent on the part of a number of state officials to control the Internet.

In 2006, the government approved the Program on Protection of Information. The main objective of this program is to prevent illegal access to information by the special services, to protect information systems, and to counteract excessive investigative measures. A new center was created in support of this program, but many activists have questioned its independence and effectiveness.[24]

E-commerce is also regulated by the state. All Internet retailers are legally obligated to register domain names with the State Center of Information Security, as well as to obtain a license for retail trade by e-commerce activities. International electronic payment systems are seriously limited in Belarus. All international monetary transfers must occur through banks that notify the tax authorities of all fund transfers from abroad.

Surveillance

Officially, Internet filtering and monitoring of telecommunications networks are illegal in Belarus. However, authorities conduct surveillance of Internet activities under the pretext of protecting national security. In 2001, the president extended the concept of "national security" to include the Internet as a potential threat to the information security of the country.[25]

Under the Law on Operational and Investigative Activities (SORM) and the Law on Authorities of National Security in the Republic of Belarus, the Ministry of Internal Affairs and the KGB have the right to monitor information carried through any communication channel in order to "fight criminal activity" and "guarantee national security."[26] Such activity may be carried out only as provided for in the law; however, the law gives the KGB the right to obtain any data from state entities and from private or public organizations considered to be "necessary" for accomplishing the KGB's objectives, and gives it unlimited access to the information systems and databases (including log files and so on) of communication providers. Article 17 of SORM establishes that all persons who are providing any type of electronic communications services should integrate additional certified equipment and program mechanisms into their systems, as specified by the KGB.

Belarus does not have systems monitoring Internet traffic analogous to the Russian SORM-II. However, it is likely that the Belarusian and Russian special services cooperate in this sphere. More than 70 percent of Belarusian Internet traffic goes through Russia, and part of it is processed through the Russian system SORM-2. Nonetheless, some providers confirm that the authorities have unofficially requested that all user IDs be kept for a few months and be turned over to the security services on demand.

On November 21, 2005, the leader of one of the opposition parties (Anatoliy Lebedko) was called to the prosecutor's office in relation to material published on his party's Web site (ucpb.org).[27] Lebedko was subsequently interrogated about the source of the information posted online and the person responsible for the article's content. Such examples of surveillance over Internet activities are not isolated.

ONI Testing Results

In 2007 and 2008, the ONI tested seven main ISPs: Atlant, Aichyna, BASNET, Belinfonet, Belpak (Beltelecom), BN, and Solo. The testing confirmed blocking by almost all ISPs. Many Web sites tested on the academic network BASNET were inaccessible in Belarus, among which were opposition Web sites and local and global freedom-of-expression Web sites, including a number of Web sites of international organizations, some dedicated to Belarus. International social networking, hosting, e-mail, P2P, and translation and multimedia Web sites were also filtered on BASNET, in addition to Web sites containing information on drug and alcohol consumption, as well as terrorist activities. Anonymizer Web sites were blocked on commercial ISPs and on the academic network. Several LGBTQ Web sites have been filtered openly since the beginning of 2005, on the basis that they contain pornographic material.[28] Interestingly, these Web sites were inaccessible on some ISPs but accessible on the state-owned Beltelecom. Some erotic Web sites were blocked as well. Access to U.S. military Web sites appears to be restricted through reverse filtering.[29]

Since April 2008, an association focused on promoting freedom of expression among ISPs has started gaining popularity in Belarus.[30] Nonetheless, most of the large operators are limiting access to the Internet when necessary to serve specific objectives. A study carried out in the spring of 2008 compiled a list of Web sites that are currently blocked by Belarusian companies. The results of this local survey are presented in the following table.[31]

Internet access is forbidden in military and national security agencies, as well as in the banking sector. Beltelecom's monopoly control over international connections provides the state with an effective and enforceable system for regulating and restricting Internet traffic. During presidential elections, access to opposition and independent media Web sites was temporarily blocked. During the February 2006 presidential

Position	Restriction of Access to Certain Internet Content	Percentage
1	Multimedia and P2P sites	28
2	No restrictions of Internet access	22
3	Access allowed only to a limited number of Web sites	20
4	Systems allowing for an instant exchange of messages	16
5	Erotic and porn sites	12
6	Limited traffic	10
7–8	Limitations on upload of large files	8
7–8	Social networks, Internet journals	8
9	Speed of download of information affected	6
10	Complete restriction of Internet access	4

elections, ONI documented second-generation techniques, including "just-in-time" filtering of opposition Web sites, which included DNS tampering, network disconnection, and allegations of DoS attacks.[32] Some specialists have suggested that, during presidential elections, Beltelecom established so-called traffic-shaping practices—that is, deliberately slowing down access to specific IP addresses. Beltelecom allegedly received special requests from authorities to block certain Web sites for a limited period of time.

Self-censorship by Internet users has become a pervasive phenomenon. In 2005, the popular Belarusian portal tut.by refused to put up banners advertising opposition Web sites. It is unknown whether this activity was a result of pressure by the authorities or merely an attempt to protect its own business.[33]

Researchers at ONI confirmed that most Internet cafés restrict access to Web sites containing pornographic, terrorist, and proxy-related material. Internet cafés install software that either blocks URLs in the list of forbidden Web sites or alerts the administrator if such a URL is visited. The restricted URL list includes Web sites forbidden for distribution by the Republic Committee on Prevention of Pornography, Violence, and Cruelty Propaganda. Administrators often require passport identification of customers. Some Internet cafés also limit the volume of Internet traffic and decrease download speeds when exceeded. On the request of state security services, administrators keep logs of users' network activity.

Conclusion

As Internet use in Belarus has risen significantly in recent years, the government is intent on extending its firm control over the national information space. The level of online piracy in the country is very high, but the government does not adequately confront such activity. Instead, it heavily regulates market participants and is taking a sluggish approach to technological innovation. All ISPs in Belarus must connect to the Internet through channels of the state-owned ISP Beltelecom, thus facilitating the government's control over all Internet traffic. The president has established a strong and elaborate information security policy and has declared his intention to exercise strict control over the Internet under the pretext of national security. Based on periodic testing, ONI has detected sporadic but sophisticated blocking of Internet content, prompted by political events in the country, suggesting that the regime is inclined toward using second- and third-generation techniques.

Notes

1. In the earlier redaction of the Belarus constitution, it was provided that the president cannot remain the head of state for more than two terms. A referendum in 2004, however, abolished that restriction, opening the doors for the current president to stay in power for an unlimited time.

2. The World Bank has acknowledged the high levels of growth of the Belarusian economy in recent years. Nonetheless, the bank has emphasized that the economy is highly dependent on the price of Russian gas and the industries are subject to strict state regulations.

3. IHS Global Insight, "Belarus," May 2009, http://www.globalinsight.com/.

4. Miniwatts Marketing Group, "Internet World Statistics: Belarus," 2009, http://www.internetworldstats.com/europa2.htm#by. Note that the Ministry of Communication and Informatization estimates that the Internet users are only around 3.3 million; Interfax News Agency "Minsvyazi Prognoziruet 500 Tysyach Polzovateley Shirokopolsnogo Interneta v Belorussii v 2010 Godu" [Communication Ministry Forecasts 500 Thousand in Belarus by 2010], http://it.tut.by/news/96876.html.

5. *ByFly*, "2 Khoroshie Novosti Dlya Nashikh Abonentov" [Two Pieces of Good News for Our Subscribers], December 15, 2008, http://www.byfly.by/bnews/26518/.

6. European Bank for Reconstruction and Development, *Communications Sector Assessment 2008*, http://www.ebrd.com/country/sector/law/telecoms/assess/belarus.pdf.

7. *It.Tut.by*, "Ministr Svyazi: v Belorussii 170 Tysyach Polzovateley Shirokopolosnogo Interneta" [Minister of Communications: There are 170 Thousand Broadband Subscribers in Belarus], April 21, 2008, http://it.tut.by/news/96647.html.

8. *Tut.by*, "Issle dovanie auditorii interneta v Belarusi, 2009," [Investigation of the Internet Audience in Belarus, 2009], April 2009, http://tutby.com/service/advert/statistics/.

9. *It.Tut.by*, "Minstat: v 2007 Godu Kompiuter Byl v Kazhdoy Chetvertoy Belorusskoy Semye" [Ministry of Statistics: in 2007 Every Fourth Belarusian Family had a Computer], March 12, 2008, http://it.tut.by/news/96941.html.

10. *It.Tut.by*, "Ministr Svyazi: v Belorussii 170 Tysyach Polzovateley Shirokopolosnogo Interneta" [Communications Minister: There are 170 Thousand Broadband Subscribers in Belarus], http://it.tut.by/news/96647.html.

11. IHS Global Insight, "Belarus," May 2009, http://www.globalinsight.com/.

12. Beltelecom's legal monopoly is established in article 44 of the Law on Telecommunications of July 19, 2005.

13. The BASNET satellite connection is provided by the Norwegian company Taide. ISP BASNET also has a 34 Mbps connection to the European network. It does not have its own land connection to GEANT and connects through the Polish scientific network PIONIER.

14. Beltelecom connects through four foreign operators: RosTelecom (Russia) with 2 Gbps, Peter-Star (Russia) with 1.2 Gbps, Teleglobe (Canada) with 0.6 Gbps, and Sprint (USA) with 0.6 Gbps.

15. European Bank for Reconstruction and Development, *Communications Sector Assessment 2008*, http://www.ebrd.com/country/sector/law/telecoms/assess/belarus.pdf.

16. *ByBanner.com*, "Ministerstvo Svyazi i Informatizatsii Razreshaet Skype" [The Ministry of Communications and Informatization Allows Skype], March 3, 2006, http://www.bybanner.com/article/1747.html.

17. Beltelecom National ISP, "Dostup k Natsionalnoy Tochke Obmena Traficom" [National IXP Access], http://www.beltelecom.by/services/internet/.

18. Licensing terms and conditions, depending on the communications services provided by the licensee, are defined in the regulation on licensing of activities in communications adopted by the Resolution of the Council of Ministers of Belarus dated October 20, 2003, No. 1387 (revised resolution of the Council of Ministers of Belarus dated December 29, 2007, No. 1903).

19. *It.Tut.by*, "Za Polgoda Prestupleniy v Sfere Informatsionnoy Bezopasnosti Bolshe, Chem za ves Proshly God" [In the First Half Year 30% More Crimes in the Field of Information Security than in the Last Year], October 5, 2007, http://it.tut.by/news/97906.html.

20. Based on the materials of the Ministry of Internal Affairs, available at http://mvd.gov.by/modules.php?name=Content&pa=showpage&pid=259, (Accessed May 19, 2009).

21. "Zakon Respubliki Belarus ob Informatizatsii" [Belarus Law on Informatization], http://pravo.by/webnpa/text.asp?start=1&RN=V19503850 (accessed May 19, 2009).

22. "Zakon Respubliki Belarus ob Operativno-rozysknoy Deyatelnosti" [Belarus Law on Investigative Activities], http://pravo.by/webnpa/text_txt.asp?RN=H19900289 (accessed May 19, 2009).

23. "Zakon Respubliki Belarus ob Electrosvyazi" [Belarus Law on Telecommunications], http://pravo.by/webnpa/text.asp?start=1&RN=H10500045 (accessed May 19, 2009).

24. *Delovaya Gazeta*, "Chto Skryvayut Spetssluzhby?" [What Do Special Services Conceal?], January 31, 2006, http://www.bdg.by/news/news.htm?81714,1.

25. "Zakon Respubliki Belarus ob Utverzhdenii Kontseptsii Natsionalnoy Bezopasnosti" [Law of the Republic of Belarus on Implementing the Concept of National Security], http://pravo.by/webnpa/text_txt.asp?RN=P30100390 (accessed May 19, 2009).

26. The Law on Operational and Investigative Activities (09.07.1999) and the Law on the Authorities of State Security of the Republic of Belarus (03.12.1997).

27. *ByBanner.com*, "Belorusskaya Prokuratura Zainteresovalac Saytom OGP" [The Belarussian Prosecutor's Office Showed an Interest in the OGP's Web site], November 12, 2005, http://www.bybanner.com/article/1301.html.

28. Filtering has been acknowledged by Beltelecom's current representative Andrey Saborov. See *Bybanner.com* "Beltelecom Potverdil Nalichie Blokirovki Dlia 'Golubyih' Saytov" [Beltelecom Confirmed the Blocking of Gay Sites], http://www.bybanner.com/article/647.html.

29. Reverse filtering occurs on the Web server hosting the content, as opposed to at a point along the way of the traffic flow, and is based on restricting requests based on geographical location of the originating Internet Protocol address. Copyright holders who want to restrict access to their content in certain markets often use reverse filtering. Examples include hulu.com, BBC.com, and other sites that syndicate commercial video and audio content that is subject to licensing. The ONI has detected that many U.S. military sites are inaccessible outside the United States. We strongly suspect that this may be as a result of reverse filtering.

30. *Tut.It.by*, "V Belarusi Poyvitsya Assotsiatsiya Otvetstvennykh Internet-izdatele" [An Association of Responsible Internet Publishers will be Created in Belarus], April 30, 2008, http://it.tut.by/news/96572.html.

31. *Tut.It.by*, "Top 10 Korporativnykh Setevikh Zapretov v Belarusi" [Top 10 Corporate Net Bans in Belarus], March 6, 2008, http://it.tut.by/news/96984.html.

32. OpenNet Initiative, "The Internet and Elections: The 2006 Presidential Elections in Belarus (and Its Implications)," April 2006, http://opennet.net/sites/opennet.net/files/ONI_Belarus_Country_Study.pdf.

33. *Obedinennaya Grazhdanskaya PartiyaSvaboda, Sobstvenocst Zakonnost*, "Na Belorusskikh Forumakh Vvodyat Tsensuru" [Censorship on Belarus Forums], April 20, 2005, http://www.ucpb.org/index.php?lang=rus&open=2799.

Georgia

Access to Internet content in Georgia is largely unrestricted as the legal constitutional framework, developed after the 2003 Rose Revolution, established a series of provisions that should, in theory, curtail any attempts by the state to censor the Internet. At the same time, these legal instruments have not been sufficient to prevent limited filtering. The ONI detected filtering on corporate and educational networks. Evidence also shows that Internet cafés limit access to some download sites (reportedly to conserve bandwidth and cut down on costs). During the Russia-Georgia war of August 2008, Georgian ISPs systematically filtered Russian Internet content. Georgian end users were also affected by the March 2008 blocking of YouTube by Turkish Telecom. Internet penetration remains low despite a liberal telecom market and comparatively moderate service prices, and it is influenced by an unstable political climate that has discouraged investment.

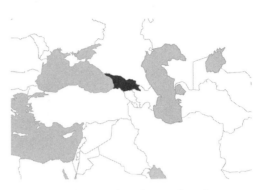

Background

Since 2003, Georgia has been governed by the reformist administration of President Mikheil Saakashvili, who came to power in the wake of the Rose Revolution. During

RESULTS AT A GLANCE					
Filtering	No Evidence of Filtering	Suspected Filtering	Selective Filtering	Substantial Filtering	Pervasive Filtering
Political			•		
Social	•				
Conflict and security			•		
Internet tools	•				

Other Factors	Low	Medium	High	Not Applicable
Transparency	•			
Consistency	•			

KEY INDICATORS	
GDP per capita, PPP (constant 2005 international dollars)	4,403
Life expectancy at birth (years)	71
Literacy rate (percent of people age 15+)	100
Human development index (out of 179)	93
Rule of law (out of 211)	120
Voice and accountability (out of 209)	120
Democracy index (out of 167)	104 (Hybrid Regime)
Digital opportunity index (out of 181)	88
Internet users (percent of population)	7.8

Source by indicator: World Bank 2009a, World Bank 2009a, World Bank 2009a, UNDP 2008, World Bank 2009b, World Bank 2009b, Economist Intelligence Unit 2008, ITU 2007, Miniwatts Marketing Group 2009.

this time, the government implemented tax reforms and liberalized the economy. These measures resulted in significant foreign investment, including investments from neighboring Russia and Kazakhstan. Georgia's strategic position makes the country an important route for the oil and gas pipelines connecting the Caspian Sea with the West—one of which is the strategic Baku-Tbilisi-Ceyhan (BTC) pipeline.[1] The country's unemployment rate is high (12.6 percent), with more than a million Georgians living outside the country.

Georgia has demonstrated a clear commitment to reform its economic and regulatory environment by enhancing transparency and efficiency as a means to improve the business climate. These reforms have positioned the country among the world leaders in the "ease of doing business" index prepared by the World Bank.[2] Georgia has also surpassed other CIS countries by obtaining the highest level of compliance with international standards with regard to its telecommunications sector.[3]

In August 2008, Georgia and Russia were embroiled in an armed conflict in South Ossetia (a semi-autonomous breakaway region bordering Russia). Georgia's strained relations with Russia have important economic and political consequences for the country's future.

Internet Infrastructure

In 2007, the government initiated a liberalization of the radio and television industry. This effort resulted in an increase in the number of independent newspapers and cable TV channels, several dozen of which now operate in the country. The state retains controlling interest in a number of key television stations, which has led to some criticism from international observers. Such criticism was especially apparent following the government's decision to revoke the license of Imedi—a major private TV channel which was strongly aligned with opposition parties.[4] This and other unilateral acts by the government have led to accusations that the administration is attempting to exert influence over the independent media.[5]

The fixed-line telecommunications network in Georgia remains outdated and is in need of significant investment. The network has very limited coverage outside Tbilisi—Georgia's capital—but even inside the capital the quality of telecommunications varies greatly. In urban areas, there are around 20 lines per 100 inhabitants, but in rural areas there are only around four lines per 1,000 inhabitants. At the same time, the number of fixed-line customers dropped in 2006 to 553,000, compared to their level in 2004 (596,000).[6] In 2005, the main telecommunications operator, Georgian Telecom, was privatized. There are currently three mobile phone operators in the country: Geocell (TeliaSonera), MagtiCom, and Beeline (VimpelCom).

The Internet emerged in Georgia in 1994 as an off-line e-mail service. By 1996, Sanet Networks (one of the early Georgian ISPs) attracted U.S. financial support and was the first entity in Georgia to provide full Internet services. In 1997, four more companies started to provide Internet services using dial-up technology. In 2002, ADSL services were introduced into the market.

During the 2000–2007 period, revenues earned by Internet operators increased from 3.7 million Georgian lari (GEL) to 42.5 million.[7] In 2006, their combined annual profits increased by 32 percent. Within the telecommunications market, the Internet is the second fastest growing segment after mobile services. Georgian sources estimate that by the end of 2007 the total number of Internet users of ADSL technologies went beyond 41,000.[8]

In 2006, a Kazakh investor acquired the state-owned telecom operator and established United Georgian Telecom (UGT). This operator is the owner of the cable infrastructure in the country, which it leases to other ISPs. Using its monopoly position, UGT charges higher rents on access to its network. Moreover, UGT frequently rejects requests by some ISPs to install or terminate their fiber-optic lines at UGT operated facilities and charges a fee for each DSL user.

In 2006, three of the largest ISPs on the market—Georgia Online, Sanet, and Caucasus Networks—merged to form Georgia's largest ISP, Caucasus Online. The company is the Internet market monopolist providing service to more than 80 percent of the population. Caucasus Online has begun laying down its own fiber-optic metropolitan network in Tbilisi. This development should lessen the dependence on the main fixed-line operator, UGT, which leases the underground right-of-ways that carry cable to Caucasus Online for USD 110 per kilometer.

A major countrywide survey on Internet use has not been carried out in Georgia. Consequently, reliable statistics on average Internet use are unavailable. However, isolated evidence can be gathered through small-scale surveys. Based on these sources, it is estimated that in 2008 there were approximately 360,000 Internet users in Georgia, which represents 7.8 percent of the population.⁹ The majority of Georgian Internet users are under 30 years of age.

The languages most commonly used among Georgian Internet users are English (90 percent), Russian (8 percent), and Georgian (2 percent). It is estimated that 50 percent of users access the Internet from their workplace, 40 percent from their homes, and 10 percent from other places (such as schools, universities, Internet cafés, and mobile networks). The monthly price of ADSL varies from USD 20 to USD 200 depending largely on bandwidth. The local backbone connection varies from 3 to 20 Mbps. Internet service is usually available in urban areas, with around 80 percent of the services provided in Tbilisi.

The Georgian market for Internet services consists of the following companies: Caucasus Online (covering 80 percent of the market), UGT (10–15 percent), and others that make up a combined 5 percent share of the market (Geonet, Service Net, Egrisi, Maximali [WiMAX provider], Magti, Geocell, and Beeline). Magti signed a contract with the Ministry of Education and Science of Georgia to connect 2,000 public schools (including schools in rural and high-mountain areas) to the Internet by the end of 2011. This will contribute to the growth of country's Internet audience, with approximately 700,000 new users. Georgian Research and Educational Networks Association (GRENA) is a noncommercial ISP that provides Internet access to academic and educational institutions. The market is open for foreign ISPs. At the end of 2008, Caucasus Online established a new fiber-optic channel, which goes from Tbilisi to Poti and through the Black Sea to Bulgaria and Romania, and connects to Cogent. The new channel gave Caucasus Online the ability to offer speeds up to 20 Mbps. Other ISPs route their commercial traffic through Turkey via Turk Telecom, Sweden via Baku, and Rostelecom via Novorosiisk.

All ministries and almost all government agencies have Web sites. The number of blogs is rapidly rising in the country, mainly among young people. No blogs are supported by opposition parties.

Legal and Regulatory Framework

The Constitution of August 24, 1995,¹⁰ enshrines freedom of expression and freedom of information. The primary legislation that regulates the electronic communications sector is the Law on Electronic Communications No. 1514 of June 6, 2005.¹¹

The law establishes the principles for development of a competitive environment in the communications sector; specifies the rights and obligations of persons owning, using, or providing services by means of electronic communications networks and facilities; and defines the scope of competence of the national regulatory authority in the sector—the Georgian National Communications Commission (herein referred to as the Commission). The provisions of the law step up the process of liberalization of the electronic communications market by (a) introducing a simple system of general authorization instead of an individual licensing regime; (b) identifying operators having significant market power in order to prevent the abuse of power and determining the usage of methodological approaches when carrying out competition analysis on the market segments; (c) recognizing principles of convergence and technological neutrality; and (d) setting out a sanctions regime in the event of violations of the legislation or the Commission's decisions. Articles 41 and 42 of the law establish the procedures for dealing with interconnection disputes.

The government has also implemented a strategic program for ensuring the decentralization of power in the regions, furthering transparency of governance, and promoting ICT for maintaining sustainable democracy in the country. The ICT development framework program has been elaborated under the initiative of the government and the Commission with the support of the UNDP and the World Bank. With its program for 2004–2009, the government has recognized that the development of the telecommunications sector and of the information society constitutes a main priority for the country's strategic economic development. One of the main objectives of the program is to overcome the uneven urban/rural coverage as communication system operators and service providers focus mainly on the big cities and settlements with little interest in developing networks for rural areas. As part of the National Strategy for ICT Development, among others, the government plans on creating a single information and communication network with integrated services, expanding the telephone network and transfer to digital systems, converting to digital TV-radio broadcasting, and increasing Internet usage among the population.

The Ministry of Economic Development, in particular its Telecommunications and Information Technology Department, sets out the government policy in the electronic communications sector and is responsible for monitoring communications and ICT policy implementation. The sector regulator, the Commission, was established on July 1, 2000. The Commission members are appointed for a period of six years by the president, a fact which may affect their political independence. Otherwise, the Commission is not financed by the state budget, and its source of revenue consists of the license and regulation fees it collects from licensees. The Commission regulates legal, technical, and economic issues on interconnection among telecommunications network operators. Other statutes providing for the Commission's regulatory authority are the Georgian Law on Broadcasting[12] and the Law on Independent Regulating Authorities.[13]

The regulations of the Commission promote innovation in the communications service sector, for example, by easing the procedures when consumers bring disputes against operators and forbidding suspensions of service in the event of a dispute.[14] Other decisions[15] revise the legal regime to guarantee a consumer's rights with regard to the protection of personal information, higher accountability and responsibilities of

---

the operators, effective complaint procedures, and better service. The Commission plans to expand the market of broadband communications service to ensure competition in local access networks, in order to decrease bandwidth rates and to promote VoIP technologies.

Any activity in the telecommunication sector in Georgia requires proper authorization.[16] In order to obtain an authorization,[17] the operator must register with the Commission and provide the required company information and type of services it intends to offer. Receiving authorization is not a burdensome process, with 25 ISPs receiving authorization to operate in 2007 alone.[18] To ensure compliance with active legislation, the Commission exerts direct control over the activities of operators in the electronic communications sector.[19]

According to Article 24 of Georgia's Constitution, any person has the right to receive and disseminate information in writing or any other form. Media restrictions and censorship are prohibited. The rights provided for in Article 24 may be restricted by law only to the extent needed to ensure the state's security and territorial integrity, prevent crimes, protect the rights and dignity of individuals, prevent the dissemination of information that has been considered confidential, or ensure the independence and impartiality of justice. Furthermore, the principle of freedom to disseminate information is also enshrined in Article 13 of the Criminal Code of Georgia.

The Law on Freedom of Speech and Expression of 2004[20] elaborates on the content of freedom of expression originally enshrined in the Constitution. This law also details the narrow circumstances under which freedom of speech and expression may be restricted.

Internet Filtering during the 2008 Russia-Georgia War

Despite the existence of legal safeguards that prohibit Internet censorship, the August 2008 conflict between Russia and Georgia witnessed unprecedented censorship of Russian Web sites by Georgian ISPs. According to Georgian sources interviewed by the ONI, Georgian ISPs filtered access to Russian media Web sites in the ".ru" domain to prevent the dissemination of what was described as "inaccurate and inflammatory reports by the Russian media."[21] Whether these actions were legal under Georgia law has not been adequately determined. From a factual perspective, President Saakashvili declared a state-of-emergency based on Article 46 of the Constitution during the onset of the conflict. As required by Georgian law, his decision was approved by Parliament within 48 hours. Consequently, media rights and freedom of expression were temporarily restricted in line with Article 46(2) of the Georgian Constitution. The law does not explicitly cover the Internet, however, at least two Georgian ISPs implemented limited filtering aimed at "protecting the population" during the state-of-emergency. ONI testing confirmed this filtering had occurred. One of the two ISPs, the GRENA, connects many of the country's schools. Its director claimed that the decision to filter content on the GRENA was taken by its leadership, and not a result of any government orders or pressure. Filtering was also detected on Caucasus Online, the largest ISP in the country.

During the conflict, Georgian authorities alleged that the Russian government supported DoS attacks by Russian hackers and cyber criminals against Georgian ISPs and Web sites. An investigation carried out by the Information Warfare Monitor, a sister project of the ONI, detected attacks against a variety of Georgian Internet resources, including Web sites belonging to the government, media, blogs, and Internet forums. This cyberwar received significant attention in the Western media, which implied Russian government involvement, noting that the cyber attacks occurred at the same time as Russian troops crossed the border and deployed in South Ossetia. In the aftermath of the conflict, independent experts did not find conclusive evidence that the Russian government was directly involved in planning or carrying out cyber attacks on Georgia. At the same time, it is clear that the Russian government did little to curtail the activity of pro-government hackers and activists who used Russian online forums and Web sites to coordinate denial-of-service attacks against Georgian Web sites and Internet infrastructure.[22]

Surveillance

Article 20 of the Constitution of Georgia provides for the inviolability of private records, correspondence, and telephone and other kinds of communications conducted through technical means. These rights can be restricted only with an appropriate court warrant, except for urgent cases as provided in certain statutes. Government authorities have been reported to engage in the conduct of targeted and selective surveillance. Allegations in the press point to illegal surveillance that is said to include interception of mobile phones, landline phones, and e-mails.

ONI Testing Results

Despite existing legal restrictions, filtering and monitoring of the Internet has been documented at Georgian ISPs. Evidence of filtering has also been documented on academic networks. In addition to the blocking of Web sites during the conflict with Russia in August 2008, the media reported that some Russian sites hosted on ".ru" were blocked again after the state-of-emergency was lifted.[23]

Limited cases of filtering in Georgia were detected by ONI. Over the course of several months during 2007 and 2008, ONI tested the main ISPs: Caucasus Online, GRENA, and Iberiapac. Several international gambling sites are filtered by most Georgian ISPs. In addition, a global blogging site has been blocked. Sporadic filtering has also been observed on GRENA, where Web sites carrying pornography and drug, violence, and hate speech are actively blocked.[24]

Commercial entities and public organizations filter some content mainly as a way of reducing Internet traffic. Often, online gaming services and instant messaging services are also affected. Researchers for ONI have observed that, in some Internet cafés, limited access to bandwidth is the result of intensive downloading.

Georgia is also subject to upstream filtering. The main Georgian ISP buys its international connectivity from Turk Telecom. Consequently, the access ban imposed by Turk Telecom to YouTube in March 2008 caused a temporary blocking of the popular video-sharing site in Georgia.

Conclusion

At present, Internet filtering in Georgia appears to be limited to corporate and educational networks. With the exception of the Russia-Georgia war, which witnessed limited state-sanctioned filtering of Russian Internet resources, access to Internet content remains largely unfettered. Georgia's dependence on international connectivity makes it vulnerable to upstream filtering, evident in the March 2008 blocking of YouTube by Turk Telecom. It is unlikely that the government would look to impose further controls over Internet content (or force ISPs to do so) given its strong public desire to forge stronger links with NATO, the European Union, and the United States.

Notes

1. Georgia, a Soviet republic until 1991, is strategically situated at the crossroads between Europe and Asia. Spreading over parts of the Caucasus Mountains with an outlet on the Black Sea, the country has historically been the object of a struggle for influence among Russia, Turkey, and, more recently, the United States.

2. World Bank, "Doing Business," http://www.doingbusiness.org/EconomyRankings.

3. European Bank for Reconstruction and Development, *Telecommunications Assessment, 2008*, http://www.ebrd.com/country/sector/law/telecoms/assess/index.htm.

4. *BBC News*, "Georgia Country Profile," August 10, 2009, http://news.bbc.co.uk/1/hi/world/europe/country_profiles/1102477.stm.

5. Economist Intelligence Unit, "Georgia Country Profile," 2009, http://store.eiu.com/country/GE.html?ref=lef_nav.

6. Ibid.

7. Annual Reports of the Georgian National Communications Commission, http://www.gncc.ge/.

8. Ibid.

9. Miniwatts Marketing Group, "Internet World Statistics: Georgia," 2009, http://internetworldstats.com/asia.htm#ge.

10. Constitution of Georgia, August 24, 1995, http://www.parliament.ge/files/68_1944_951190_CONSTIT_27_12.06.pdf.

11. The Law of Georgia on Electronic Communications, June 6, 2005, No. 1514, http://www.gncc.ge/files/7050_3555_376651_eleqtr.eng.pdf.

12. Law of Georgia on Broadcasting, December 23, 2004, No. 780-RS, http://www.parliament.ge/index.php?lang_id=ENG&sec_id=69&info_id=16087.

13. Law of Georgia on Independent Regulating Authorities, September 13, 2002, No. 1666—IS.

14. GNCC Resolution No. 3 of 2006: On Approval of Regulations on Service Providing and Protection of Consumers' Rights in the Sphere of Electronic Communications.

15. GNCC Resolution No. 8 of 2006: On Amendments to the Regulations for Service Providing and Consumers Rights Protection in the Sphere of Electronic Communications; GNCC Resolution No. 7 and No. 9 of 2007: On Introducing Changes and Amendments to the Resolution No. 3 of March 17, 2006, On Approval of the Rules and Regulations (Regulation) for Providing Services and Protecting Customer Rights in the Sphere of Electronic Communications.

16. The Law of Georgia on Electronic Communications, Chapter III, "Authorization of Undertakings in the Electronic Communications Sector: General Rights and Obligations of Authorized Undertakings."

17. The Law of Georgia on Electronic Communications, Article 2(i).

18. The ISPs need to provide the necessary information to the Commission related to their activities, according to the Law of Georgia on Electronic Communications, Article 19(2).

19. The Law of Georgia on the Control of Entrepreneurial Activity, Art. 3.1.

20. The Law on Freedom of Speech and Expression, June 24, 2004, No. 220-RS, http://www.parliament.ge/index.php?lang_id=GEO&sec_id=69&kan_det=det&kan_id=72.

21. For more information on the cyberwar conflict, refer to Information Warfare Monitor (http://www.infowar-monitor.net), which followed and analyzed the development of events.

22. Ibid.

23. *Lenta.ru*, "V Gruzii vnov Zablokirovan Dostup k Rynety" [In Georgia Access to the RuNet has been Blocked Again], September 10, 2008, http://lenta.ru/news/2008/09/10/notopen/.

24. Blacklists are mainly maintained using SquidGuard lists.

Kazakhstan

The Kazakh government has extended its control over the Internet, even as it seeks to liberalize the telecommunications market and position itself as a major IT power in the region. The state uses its significant regulatory authority to ensure that all Internet traffic passes through infrastructure controlled by the dominant telecommunications provider KazakhTelecom. 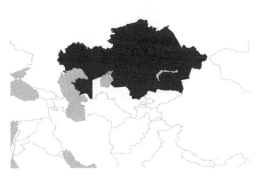 Selective content filtering is widely used, and second- and third-generation control strategies are evident. Independent media and bloggers reportedly practice self-censorship for fear of government reprisal.

Background

Kazakhstan has taken an authoritarian turn under the rule of President Nazarbayev, who has served as head of state since national independence in 1991. Nazarbayev is widely alleged to have manipulated results of elections and suppressed opposition to remain in power.[1] Although press freedom is enshrined in the Constitution, the government controls mass media outlets and exerts influence over most printing and distribution establishments.[2] Anecdotal evidence points to online media and bloggers

RESULTS AT A GLANCE					
Filtering	No Evidence of Filtering	Suspected Filtering	Selective Filtering	Substantial Filtering	Pervasive Filtering
Political			•		
Social			•		
Conflict and security	•				
Internet tools	•				

Other Factors	Low	Medium	High	Not Applicable
Transparency	•			
Consistency	•			

KEY INDICATORS	
GDP per capita, PPP (constant 2005 international dollars)	10,259
Life expectancy at birth (years)	66
Literacy rate (percent of people age 15+)	100
Human development index (out of 179)	71
Rule of law (out of 211)	160
Voice and accountability (out of 209)	171
Democracy index (out of 167)	127 (Authoritarian regime)
Digital opportunity index (out of 181)	94
Internet users (percent of population)	12.4

Source by indicator: World Bank 2009a, World Bank 2009a, World Bank 2009a, UNDP 2008, World Bank 2009b, World Bank 2009b, Economist Intelligence Unit 2008, ITU 2007, Miniwatts Marketing Group 2009.

practicing self-censorship for fear of prosecution by the state under highly restrictive defamation laws.

Pressed by growing domestic discontent and international criticism, President Nazarbayev agreed to a constitutional reform. In May 2007, the Parliament adopted amendments to the Constitution, including cutting the presidential mandate from seven to five years and increasing the role of Parliament. These changes are not expected to enter into force until the next presidential elections in 2012. The proposed reforms remove restrictions on how many terms a head of state may serve. Consequently, President Nazarbayev can stay in power indefinitely.

Internet in Kazakhstan

The Kazakh Internet community is growing rapidly. Between 2001 and 2005, the number of Internet users increased from 200,000 to 1 million. By 2007, Kazakhstan reported Internet penetration levels of 8.5 percent, rising to 12.4 percent in 2008.[3] The National Statistical Agency reports that 73 percent of users access the Internet by dial-up, 15 percent by means of ADSL, and 6 percent using satellite access. Over 50 percent of users accessed the Internet from home in 2008.[4] Forty-two percent of families living in towns with populations of at least 70,000 people have a personal computer. KazakhTelekom (KT) reported an increase in its broadband subscriber base from 270,000 to 456,000 in 2008.[5] Despite these increases, Internet usage is concentrated in urban centers, while outside those centers access remains beyond the reach of most Kazakhs.[6]

The official language in the country is Kazakh, spoken by 64 percent of the population. Russian, spoken by 95 percent, is recognized as the official language of international communication. Russian is the most popular language used on the Internet

(94.1 percent), followed by Kazakh (4.5 percent), and English (1.4 percent), a figure which may account for the high percentage of Kazakh Web sites hosted in Russia (including those on the country-code domain name ".kz"). Six percent of ".kz" domain Web sites are hosted in Kazakhstan, with the remainder hosted in Russia and elsewhere.

The cost of Internet access remains high relative to the average salary (54,500 tenge in 2008, or USD 363).[7] KazakhTelecom's tariffs for unlimited ADSL access with capacity of 128 Kbps were USD 30. However, as a result of the ongoing liberalization in the telecommunications sector in 2007, the operators' tariffs fell considerably. Since 2007, schools in Kazakhstan are provided with free dial-up access, which is being expanded to include broadband connections (although access is restricted to Web sites and other Internet resources within the ".kz" domain).[8]

Liberalization of the telecommunications market in 2004 increased competition among the five licensed operators: KazakhTelecom (the former state monopoly, now with 51 percent state participation), Transtelecom, Kaztranscom, Arna (DUCAT), and Astel. The first-tier ISPs with international Internet connections and their own infrastructure are KazakhTelecom, Nursat, Transtelecom, Kaztranscom, Arna, Astel, and TNS Plus. There are approximately 100 second-tier ISPs that are purchasing Internet traffic from the first-tier ISPs. Market liberalization has not been completely carried out, as there are restrictions on foreign ownership for fixed-line operators providing long-distance and international services. In addition, KazakhTelecom retains dominance over the telecommunications market, making it difficult for other operators to compete.[9]

One of the largest ISPs, Arna (DUCAT), accused KazakhTelecom of breaching the Law for Promoting Competition and Limiting Monopolist Activities. Arna claimed that KazakhTelecom used uncertified systems that monitor and interfere with the telecommunications of customers who are using services offered by competing companies. An investigation of the Kazakh government revealed that such systems indeed existed and were used by KazakhTelecom, but no evidence was found to prove KazakhTelecom was intentionally interfering with competitor activities.

KazakhTelecom is the operator of the national data transfer network, which connects the major cities of Kazakhstan with a total bandwidth of 957 Mbps[10] and carrying capacity in separate local segments of up to 10 Gbps.[11] KazakhTelecom had about 2.5 million fixed-line subscribers in 2005 and accounted for approximately 90 percent of the country's fixed-line market. It also controls 49 percent of the country's leading mobile operator, GSM Kazakhstan, and 50 percent of another cellular operator, Altel.[12] KazakhTelecom is also launching an interactive IP TV service, as it attempts to maintain its dominance in the fixed-line market.[13] Other leading first-tier ISPs, Nursat and Astel, operate terrestrial and satellite-based infrastructure. There are five mobile operators in the country. Three operators are offering GSM services and two CDMA. The government estimates that 60 percent of the population uses mobile services.

Legal and Regulatory Frameworks

The Kazakh government exhibits an ambiguous and at times contradictory approach to the Internet. The long-term development strategy of Kazakhstan for 2030[14] demonstrates the government's strong commitment to create a modern national information infrastructure. The government has announced plans to develop e-government as a part of a 2005–2007 program.[15] Since 2008, government officials have been encouraged to create their own personal blogs.[16] At the same time, the government follows a multilevel information security policy, which maintains surveillance of telecommunications and Internet traffic in the country.

The Ministry of Transport and Communications (MTC) is the main policymaker and regulator in the telecommunications market. The Agency for Informatization and Communication (AIC), a central executive body in the IT field, is authorized to implement state policy in telecommunications and information technology development industries, exercise control in these sectors, and issue licenses to every type of telecommunications service.[17] The Security Council (SC), a body chaired by the president, is responsible for drafting decisions and providing assistance to the head of state on issues of defense and national security.[18] The SC also prepares a list of Web sites every six months that should be blocked or forbidden from distribution. A 2005 SC decision made it illegal for key national security bodies to connect to the Internet (namely, the Ministries of Emergency Situations, Internal Affairs, and Defense, and the National Security Committee). However, despite this prohibition, ONI field researchers found evidence that state officials access forbidden Web sites using dial-up accounts and anonymizer applications.

The security system in Kazakhstan is complex and multilayered. The Inter-Departmental Commission is charged with coordinating and developing the national information infrastructure. The National Security Committee (NSC) monitors presidential, government, and military communications. The Office of the Prime Minister is an authorized state body responsible for the protection of state secrets and maintenance of information security. Broadly defined, a "state secret" encompasses various government policies as well as information about the president's private life, health, and financial affairs. The NSC has issued a general license to the private Agency on Information Security to establish and organize facilities for cryptographic protection of information, as well as to formulate proposals on information security to state organizations, corporate clients, banks, and other large commercial companies.

The Kazakh Ministry of Internal Affairs operates Department "K", which bears the functions of its counterpart in the Russian Federation. This department is tasked with investigating and prosecuting cyber crime and cyber attacks. At present, ISPs are required to prohibit their customers from disseminating pornographic, extremist, or terrorist materials or any other information that is not in accordance with the country's laws.[19] Kazakh officials are also considering additional laws to further regulate the Kazakh Internet.[20] One draft law presently under consideration envisions liability for owners of Web sites hosting weblogs and forums, as well as users of chat rooms. The draft law equates Internet sites to media outlets and applies similar regulations with respect to content. The authors of the law justified tighter oversight by the need to fight cyber crime and provide greater accountability for Internet users.

The Kazakhstan Association of IT Companies is the officially recognized administrator of the ".kz" domain. It is registered as a NGO, but it has 80 percent government ownership. The rules of registration and management of the ".kz" domain were issued by the State Agency on Informatization and Communication of the Republic of Kazakhstan in 2005. In recent years, the cost for registering and maintaining a domain name have significantly decreased, thereby boosting the development of the Kazakh portion of the Internet. Registrations are subject to strict regulation. Applications may be denied if the server on which they are located resides outside Kazakhstan. Even though the primary legislation guarantees freedom of speech and prohibits censorship, the government often resorts to various legal mechanisms to suppress "inappropriate" information or to ensure that domain names used by opposition groups are frozen, or withdrawn. As a result, very few political parties in Kazakhstan use the Internet, and few opposition or illegal parties have an online presence (at least within the ".kz" domain).

The ICT sector in Kazakhstan is overregulated, as evidenced by some 300 legislative acts that expressly or implicitly control the ICT environment. All telecommunications operators are legally obliged, as part of the licensing requirement, to connect their channels to a public network controlled by KazakhTelecom. The so-called Billing Center of Telecommunication Traffic, established by the government in 1999, helps monitor the activity of private companies and strengthen the monopolist position of KazakhTelecom in the IT sphere. In the past, some telecommunications operators circumvented such regulations by using VoIP for their interregional and international traffic, but the imposition of VoIP telephony tariffs eliminated this option.

Surveillance

The government has established systems to monitor and filter Internet traffic. Since the traffic of all first-tier ISPs goes through KazakhTelecom's channels, surveillance and filtering is centralized. The ONI suspects that state officials informally ask Kazakh-Telecom to filter certain content. KazakhTelecom, along with some Russian companies, has openly signed an agreement to provide filtering, censorship, and surveillance on the basis of Security Council resolutions. There are several recorded cases of journalists and Web site owners that have been prosecuted under broad media and criminal provisions.[21] Oppositional and independent media sites have been permanently suspended, allegedly for providing links to publications concerning corruption among senior state officers and the president.[22]

In 2004, the chairs of the National Security Committee and the Agency for Informatization and Communications approved Rules Providing for Mechanisms for Monitoring the Telecommunications Operators and Networks. These rules prescribe full collaboration and information sharing between the government agencies. This system is similar to that of the Russian SORM, introduced to monitor activities of users and any related information. The rules oblige ISPs to register and maintain electronic records of customer Internet activity. Providers are required to install special software and hardware equipment in order to create and store records for a specified amount of time, including log-in times, connection types, transmitted and received traffic between parties of the connection, identification number of the session, duration of time spent online, IP address of the user, and speed of data receipt and transmission.

ONI Testing Results

The OpenNet Initiative conducted testing on two main ISPs: KazakhTelecom and Nursat. KazakhTelecom blocks opposition groups' Web sites, regional media sites that carry political content, and selected social networking sites. A number of proxy sites providing anonymous access to the Internet have also been blocked. The ONI suspects that filtering practices in Kazakhstan are evolving and are performed at the network backbone by KazakhTelecom, which filters traffic it provides to downstream operators. Consequently, Kazakh ISPs may unknowingly receive pre-filtered content. At the same time, not all incoming and outgoing traffic passes through KazakhTelecom's centralized network, resulting in inconsistent patterns of blocking.

The majority of Internet users are on "edge" networks, such as Internet cafés and corporate networks. Kazakhstan companies apply filtering mechanisms at the user level to prevent employees from accessing pornography, music, film, and dating Web sites. However, ONI testing found that Kazakhstan does not block any pornographic content or sites related to drug and alcohol use.

Conclusion

The Kazakh government has harnessed efforts to modernize the IT sector, promote ICTs, and encourage e-government in order to spur social development. Nevertheless, the lack of a competitive fixed-line market and the partial market liberalization leaves the growing demand unsatisfied and slows down development of the IT sector in the country. The government has put in place a complex security system that is capable of state surveillance of Internet traffic and suppression of undesirable Internet content. Given government pressure on opposition media, self-censorship may also be an issue among online media publishers and bloggers. The technical sophistication of the Kazakhstan Internet environment is evolving and the government's tendency toward stricter online controls warrant closer examination and monitoring.

Notes

1. Commission on Security and Cooperation in Europe, "Missed Opportunity in Kazakhstan: Fraud and Intimidation Spoil Election Promised to Be 'Free and Fair,'" December 15, 2005, http://www.csce.gov/index.cfm?Fuseaction=ContentRecords.ViewDetail&ContentRecord_id=107& ContentType=G.

2. Article 20, paragraphs 1 and 2 of the Constitution of the Kazakhstan Republic and the Law on Media and Telecommunications (with last amendments of January 2006), Article 2, paragraph 1.

3. Miniwatts Marketing Group, "Internet World Statistics: Kazakhstan," 2009, http://www .internetworldstats.com/asia/kz.htm.

4. Statistics Agency of Kazakhstan, "Ispolzovaniye Tekhniki Svyazi dlya Dostupa v Internet," [Using Communication Technologies to Access the Internet], http://www.stat.kz/.

5. Ibid.

6. "Sovmestnyi Proekt Isledovatelskoy Kompanii 'Komkon-2 Evraziya' i Informacionnogo Portala 'Centr Tyazhesti'" [Joint Project of the Research Companies "Komkon-2 Eurasia" and the Information Portal "Center Tyajesti"], 2008.

7. *National News Agency KazInform*, "Srednyaya Zarplata v Kazakhstane" [Average Salary in Kazakhstan], April 15, 2008, http://www.zakon.kz/our/news/news.asp?id=301/3385.

8. Economist Intelligence Unit, "Kazakhstan Telecoms and Technology Report: Internet," October 15, 2008, http://store.eiu.com/product/1597096959KZ.html.

9. European Bank for Reconstruction and Development, *Assessment Report Kazakhstan*, 2008, http://www.ebrd.com/country/sector/law/telecoms/assess/kazak.pdf.

10. For comparison, by the end of 2002 the total Internet bandwidth capacity for Kazakhstan was 46 Mbps; by the end of 2003 it was 189 Mbps, and in June 2006 it was 665 Mbps. Paul Budde Communications, Pty., Ltd.,"Kazakhstan—Telecoms Market Overview, Statistics and Forecasts," November 17, 2008.

11. This investment is part of the USD 110 million loan from the European Bank for Reconstruction and Development. Lucent Worldwide Services and Winncom Technologies are providing support for the project. In 2006, KazakhTelecom began construction of a next-generation network (NGN) and plans to deploy fixed wireless access (FWA) platforms such as Wi-Fi and WiMAX.

12. Paul Budde Communications Pty., Ltd., "Kazakhstan—Telecoms Market Overview, Statistics and Forecasts."

13. The basic package on offer comprises 55 channels and will be available to broadband subscribers.

14. Republic of Kazakhstan (RK) Agency for Informatization and Communication, "Strategy: Kazakhstan–2030," http://www.aic.gov.kz/?mod=static&lng=rus&id=2.

15. RK Agency for Informatization and Communication, "The Program for Establishing Electronic Governance," http://www.aic.gov.kz/?mod=static&lng=rus&id=4.

16. *Interfax*, "Premier Kazahstana Poruchil Ministram Vesti Blogi" [The Kazakh Prime Minister Has Instructed the Ministers to Maintain Blogs], January 12, 2009, http://interfax.ru/news.asp?id=56332.

17. Resolution No. 724 of the Kazakh government, dated July 22, 2003.

18. The SC was founded by the president of Kazakhstan, according to the provisions of the Constitution (item 20 of Article 44).

19. See the general user agreement between Nursat, a major ISP, and its customers at "Public Contract" (in Russian) at http://www.nursat.kz/?72.

20. *Zakon.kz*, "Dosye na Proekt Zakona Respubliki Kazakhstan, 'O Regulirovanii Kazakhstanskogo Segmenta seti Internet'" [Dossier on the Draft Law of the Republic of Kazakhstan, 'On Regulation of the Kazakhstan Segment of the Internet'], August 21, 2008, http://www.zakon.kz/our/news/news.asp?id=30199882&NP=2#m1.

21. Reporters Without Borders, "Kazakhstan—Annual Report 2008," http://www.rsf.org/article.php3?id_article=25492; *Ferghana.ru*, "Kazahstan: Predstavitel OBSE Prizval Osvobodit Glavnogo Redaktora 'Alma-Ata Info'" [Kazakhstan: The Representative of OSCE Called for the Liberation of the Editor in Chief of 'Alma-Ata Info'], January 15, 2009, http://www.ferghana.ru/news.php?id=11062.

22. OpenNet Initiative blog, "Opposition Web Sites Shut Down in Kazakhstan,", October 28, 2007, http://opennet.net/blog/2007/10/opposition-web-sites-shut-down-kazakhstan; OpenNet Initiative blog, "Central Asian Governments Continue to Clamp Down on the Internet—II," February 4, 2008, http://opennet.net/blog/2008/02/central-asian-governments-continue-clamp-down-internet-%E2%80%93-ii.

Kyrgyzstan

Access to the Internet in Kyrgyzstan has deteriorated as heightened political tensions have led to more frequent instances of second- and third-generation controls. The government has become more sensitive to the Internet's influence on domestic politics and enacted laws that increase its authority to regulate the sector. Recent liberalization of the telecommu-

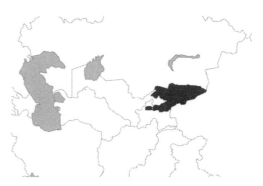

nications market in Kyrgyzstan has made the Internet affordable for the majority of the population. However, Kyrgyzstan is an effectively cyberlocked country dependent on purchasing bandwidth from Kazakhstan and Russia. The increasingly authoritarian regime in Kazakhstan is shifting toward more restrictive Internet controls, which is leading to instances of "upstream filtering" affecting ISPs in Kyrgyzstan.

Background

In 2005, Kurmanbek Bakiev won the presidential elections after the violent downfall of the 14-year authoritarian regime of the former president, Askar Akayev. The new head of state vowed to distribute more powers to the parliament, encourage free speech,

RESULTS AT A GLANCE					
Filtering	No Evidence of Filtering	Suspected Filtering	Selective Filtering	Substantial Filtering	Pervasive Filtering
Political			•		
Social			•		
Conflict and security	•				
Internet tools	•				

Other Factors	Low	Medium	High	Not Applicable
Transparency	•			
Consistency	•			

KEY INDICATORS	
GDP per capita, PPP (constant 2005 international dollars)	1,894
Life expectancy at birth (years)	68
Literacy rate (percent of people age 15+)	99
Human development index (out of 179)	122
Rule of law (out of 211)	191
Voice and accountability (out of 209)	149
Democracy index (out of 167)	114 (Hybrid regime)
Digital opportunity index (out of 181)	135
Internet users (percent of population)	13.8

Source by indicator: World Bank 2009a, World Bank 2009a, World Bank 2009a, UNDP 2008, World Bank 2009b, World Bank 2009b, Economist Intelligence Unit 2008, ITU 2007, Miniwatts Marketing Group 2009.

fight corruption, and tackle poverty. However, Bakiev's enthusiasm to introduce democratic constitutional amendments seemed to have died away soon after his inauguration. The political shift in power did not result in significant economic improvements in Kyrgyzstan, as the country entered economic stagnation and two-thirds of the population remained below the poverty line. International observers predict that new civil conflicts may erupt if the country does not adopt urgent economic measures.[1]

The Internet is one of the few free outlets for expressing public criticism in Kyrgyzstan, and it has been used as an instrument to mobilize protest and opposition against the government. Kyrgyzstan's UN global ranking for e-government for 2008 (0.4195) has deteriorated; however, compared to its Central Asian neighbors, the country remains in second place after Kazakhstan.[2]

Internet Infrastructure

Kyrgyzstan has one of the highest Internet penetration rates in Central Asia, although the figures gathered from different sources vary widely. According to local sources, around 7 percent of the population had access at the end of 2008 (760,664 people).[3] The ITU reports a high figure for Internet penetration for 2008 (13.8). The government estimated that Internet penetration would reach 10 percent by 2008,[4] while the United Nations *e-Government Survey* states that Internet penetration was no more than 5.6 percent for 2008.[5] Broadband users in Kyrgyzstan are estimated to be only 0.05 percent for 2008.[6] Personal computers (PCs) remain unaffordable for the vast majority: only 1.9 percent of the population own a PC.[7] There are more than 150 public Internet access centers in the country, including commercial Internet cafés and free-access centers sponsored by NGOs. The majority (51 percent) of users access the Internet from their workplace, 21 percent through their mobile telephone, 20 percent from Internet cafés, and only 8 percent from home.[8] Development of the Internet infrastructure still targets only the urban markets, in particular the two largest cities—Bishkek (in which 77 percent of the Internet users are concentrated) and Osh.

There are slightly more female than male users. Forty percent of all users are aged between 10 and 20, 35 percent are aged 20 to 30, and 16 percent are between 30 and 40. Most of the users are students (50 percent), and they prevail over the users who work (34 percent of users are employees in private companies, and 9 percent are employees in the state administration). Interestingly, the 25 percent of users who have defined themselves as unemployed make up the third largest group of Internet users. Russian sites remain the most visited among Kyrgyz Internet users (90 percent), compared with only 8 percent Kyrgyz and 2 percent English-language sites.[9] In spite of the popularity of the Russian language in everyday life, the Kyrgyz language portion of the Internet is expanding.

Kyrgyzstan has made relatively early progress in the liberalization of its economy compared to other CIS countries. The republic joined the WTO in the second half of 1998. In order to comply with the requirements for liberalization of the telecom sector in 2006, the government agreed to put more than 77 percent of the incumbent KyrgyzTelecom up for sale. Nonetheless, only 10 percent of the shares were transferred to private hands by 2007, and 77.84 percent of the incumbent is still owned by the state. In 2008, around 61 percent of all users connected to the Internet through KyrgyzTelecom.[10]

Notwithstanding the pending privatization of the main incumbent, the liberalization of telecommunications services, driven by foreign investment and financial assistance, has resulted in an increasingly competitive, profitable, and growing Internet sector in the last few years. The Law on Electronic and Postal Communications, drafted on the basis of sector best practices, has opened the market for competition. The communications regulator has developed and implemented new access, interconnection, and tariff regulations after extensive consultations with stakeholders.[11] The competitive market has provided a wide choice of telephone connection service, Internet access, mobile connection, and television and radio channels to the population. This has led to increased competition among the operators, and in particular Internet service providers. In 1996, there were only two operators—AsiaInfo and Elcat—that charged USD 2.50 per hour for Internet use. By 2000, there already were 16 companies providing Internet access for USD 0.90 an hour, and finally in 2005 there were 38 companies on the market, which dropped the cost for Internet access to USD 0.30 an hour. To win competitive advantage on the market, ISPs have introduced Internet cards, and these have become very popular.

Out of the 38 active ISPs, only three have independent external connections to the international Internet (KyrgyzTelecom, Saima Telecom, and Elcat). Also, only three providers own the infrastructure they use (KyrgyzTelecom, Saima Telecom, and Elcat).

The others lease lines and cables from the state-controlled top-tier ISP KyrgyzTelecom. The government has a major stake (50 percent) in Elcat, another top-tier ISP. All other ISPs are private except for the research and educational networks. All ISPs are based in the capital and very few of them operate in other regions. The majority of ISPs connect to the Russian portion of the Internet by fiber-optic cable. In addition to its major Russian connection, KyrgyzTelecom has built external connection ports to China and Kazakhstan. On a number of occasions, KyrgyzTelecom has been affected by KazakhTelecom's filtering practices, since it is buying international traffic from the foreign provider. For Internet data transfer, two of the largest ISPs—AsiaInfo and Totel— use fiber-optic lines financed by the Soros Foundation and extend parts of the infrastructure themselves where necessary. There are a number of Internet cafés in the capital, and although Internet cafés can be found in the regions, the connection is often unreliable.

The Soros Foundation also financed the national Internet Traffic Exchange Point (IXP). This IXP is governed by the Association of Telecommunications Operators and distributes local traffic among the local ISPs. The international Internet bandwidth in the country is 300 Mbps, and the most popular means for Internet access is through dial-up connection. Leased lines with transfer speeds of up to 64 Kbps are widely available for businesses, while higher-speed broadband access lines are very limited.[12] A private company, AsiaInfo, administers the country's top-level domain zone ".kg."[13] There are around 1,500 top-level domain names registered in the Kyrgyz Internet zone. The two most-visited Web sites are local media sites, while most information sought online is education related.

In recent years, the mobile sector in Kyrgyzstan has grown significantly. As a result, the government has expressed its intention to exert control over the mobile services. The number of mobile users in 2006 topped 1,000,000 (or 20 percent of the population), which is an increase of almost 50 percent compared to the previous year. As of September 2007, there were five mobile operators in the country. The dominant operator is Bitel GSM, which owns 78 percent of the market. The other operators, MegaCom, FONEX, and Katel, have a limited presence with 10 percent, 8 percent, and 4 percent, respectively.[14] A new operator, NEXI (offering CDMA service), became active in 2007.

Overall, state regulation in the communications sector created favorable conditions for establishing a competitive communications market. By 2008, the government issued 429 licenses to over 280 telecommunication companies.

VoIP licenses are readily available. To obtain a license, companies are required to contribute 20 million som (approximately USD 517,000) to a national IT development fund. Once an applicant obtains the license, they are licensed as an operator, or can resell their services to other companies. There are no restrictions on the provision of P2P services in the country.

Legal and Regulatory Frameworks

Compared with its neighbor Kazakhstan, Kyrgyzstan does not compel local ISPs to work with the state-owned provider and respects the rules of competition in the market. Previously, in order to ensure that a USD 500 million loan from the World Bank to build Kyrgyzstan's telecom infrastructure was repaid, a state decree granted KyrgyzTelecom the exclusive rights to international long-distance services until 2003.[15] This decree has since been overruled, and ISPs now have independent channels for international connections. Operators have built their own data transmission networks within the capital, Bishkek, providing an alternative to the incumbent KyrgyzTelecom's infrastructure. Outside of Bishkek, however, IT development is hindered by poor infrastructure, and only the incumbent KyrgyzTelecom provides Internet access. Internet companies are not investing in building their own networks, leading to very low Internet availability outside the capital. A retail-tariff-rebalancing plan was proposed in 2008, which is expected to begin improving investment in local infrastructure.

In 2002, the state declared ICT development a priority by way of the National Strategy on Information and Communication Technologies for Development of the Kyrgyz Republic. The national ICT plan was reviewed by the ICT Council and approved by the president in 2003. Eager to harness Internet capabilities in order to stimulate economic growth, the government is implementing action plans and ICT strategies to encourage development of e-government, e-education, and the e-economy. Moreover, under a joint program between the government and international organizations, 95 percent of central government bodies, as well as 50 percent of local ones, were connected to the Internet and now provide online information about their services.[16] However, the cyber presence of political opposition is limited. Only three Kyrgyz Web sites belonging to political parties were detected by ONI.[17]

The communications regulator in the country is the National Communications Agency (NCA) whose chairman is appointed by the president of Kyrgyzstan. The NCA is financed by fixed-percentage contributions from operators, and therefore it is not dependent on the state budget. The NCA regulates and supervises postal and electronic communication companies, issues licenses, monitors the Internet, and settles disputes among operators. The Ministry for Transport and Communications is the policy-making body in the communications sector, responsible for formulating the sector development policy, including designing privatization programs, enhancing competition, and exercising monitoring functions. Although the functions of NCA and the ministry are legislatively separate, the two entities often enter into disputes with regard to their authority to regulate some activities, in particular licensing, radio frequencies, telephone number capacity, and tariffs. The process is quite political and there are frequent disagreements concerning the development of communications regulatory programs and regulations. Since 2008, the legal framework has been under revision as a working group is debating new amendments to the 1998 Law on Electronic and Postal Communications. At the same time, the government has introduced new restrictions on the media. The recently introduced amendments to the Media Law have attracted criticism from local journalists.[18]

The presidential administration has made efforts to introduce restrictive measures to control Internet content. In the spring of 2005, members of the government proposed amendments to the Law on Mass Media that would have led to blocking all ".ru" domain sites containing content "offensive" to Kyrgyzstan. In turn, these amendments would have limited Kyrgyz access to sources solely on the ".kg" domain, which is regulated by local authorities, effectively creating a national "intranet." Although this proposal was rejected, it revealed a shift in official attitudes toward reigning in Internet development in the country.[19]

Kyrgyz national security laws do not directly apply to Internet activities. Nevertheless, in 2003 the National Security Council proposed the creation of specialized communication and information security within the Security Council. The Security Council would be, inter alia, responsible for examining internal and external policy questions in the field of information security. In 2005, a government resolution on the Program for Information Security was adopted. The program's main objective is to create protection for the individual, the society, and the state in the information space, but even after its amendments of 2005 it continues to lack precise definitions for what constitutes commercial secrets, state secrets, and private information. This absence of clear terminology may lead to variable interpretations, which could create space for potential abuse. Furthermore, the program does not explicitly define what information can be restricted, which broadens the scope for potential abuse, including the possibility that these provisions will be used as a justification for filtering Internet content.

Surveillance

There is no legislation in Kyrgyzstan that allows national security bodies to organize surveillance over the Internet. KyrgyzTelecom itself launched a technical investigation to prevent "gray traffic" generated by other ISPs, meaning spam or other illegitimate requests for information.

Proposals have been made for conducting state-led surveillance activities at the ISP level. In July 2006, the State Agency for Intellectual Property proposed the creation of an "Inter-Departmental Commission on State Regulation of the Kyrgyz Segment of the Internet." This institution, based on an existing Russian model, would have coordinated the activity of the executive power bodies and organizations participating in the Kyrgyz segment of the Internet. The proposal was rejected.

On a few isolated occasions, the government has attempted to track down the IP addresses of users accessing forums or chats.

ONI Testing Results

In 2007 and 2008, the OpenNet Initiative conducted testing from various access points on four main first-tier ISPs: AsiaInfo, Elcat, KyrgyzTelecom, and Saima Telecom. The ONI could not officially detect filtering by the providers at the time testing was carried out.

In 2008 and 2009, ONI observed a number of Web sites periodically unavailable on KyrgyzTelecom and Saima Telecom, such as http://www.kyrgyzpress.com, http://www.prezident.kg (a site containing materials derisive to Kyrgyz state officials), and http://www.24.kg (a media site). The reasons why these sites were targeted have not been clarified, although these observations are consistent with second-generation controls. In 2005, during the parliamentary elections, ONI documented the extensive use of DDoS attacks against opposition and media Web sites and Kyrgyz ISPs.[20]

Filtering by upstream providers (upstream filtering) was also detected in early 2009, with a number of Web sites blocked by the Kazakh state Internet provider, which included http://www.livejournal.com (a popular blogging site), http://www.internews.fr, http://www.posit.ru, and others. Access to these sites was inaccessible for the majority of users in Kyrgyzstan because of filters implemented by the main Kazakh telecommunication operator, which sells its services to KyrgyzTelecom. Filtering also exists at the enterprise level (i.e., NGOs, corporate clients) in order to block access to content deemed irrelevant and to economize on Internet traffic.

Conclusion

The Kyrgyz government has implemented policies aimed at fostering the development of the communications sector, which is seen as an instrument for attracting foreign investment. Potential limits in Internet freedom are posed by generally poor access and "upstream filtering" resulting from dependence on Kazakh and Chinese connections. There is also evidence of emerging second-generation methods, which are employed during periods of heightened political tension in the country. While the Kyrgyz government has shown determination in opening up the market to competition and abolishing measures leading to state-controlled access, much remains to be done in order to establish stable mechanisms guaranteeing media freedom and freedom of information. Kyrgyzstan is unlikely to follow the example of its neighbors that have introduced first-generation controls on Internet access, but second- and third-generation controls are likely to continue to evolve as the government grapples with the increasing significance of the Internet in domestic politics.

Notes

1. Kunduz Jenkis, "The Kyrgyz Revolution: One Step Ahead or Two Steps Back?" International Eurasian Institute for Economic and Political Research, September 21, 2005, http://www.iicas.org/libr_en/kg/libr_06_10_05kg.htm.

2. Compared to Kyrgyzstan's e-government readiness ranking in 2005 (0.4417). See United Nations, *United Nations e-Government Survey 2008: From e-Government to Connected Governance*, http://unpan1.un.org/intradoc/groups/public/documents/UN/UNPAN028607.pdf.

3. Bishkek, "Issledovanie Auditorii Internet v Kyrgyzstane" [Survey on the Internet Auditorium in Kyrgyzstan], 2009.

4. Paul Budde Communication Pty., Ltd., "Asian—Internet Market, 2008."

5. United Nations, *United Nations e-Government Survey 2008: From e-Government to Connected Governance*, http://unpan1.un.org/intradoc/groups/public/documents/UN/UNPAN028607.pdf.

6. International Telecommunication Union (ITU), "Internet Indicators: Subscribers, Users, and Broadband Subscribers," 2008, http://www.itu.int/ITU-D/icteye/Reporting/ShowReportFrame.aspx?ReportName=/WTI/InformationTechnologyPublic&RP_intYear=2008&RP_intLanguageID=1.

7. United Nations, *United Nations e-Government Survey 2008: From e-Government to Connected Governance*, http://unpan1.un.org/intradoc/groups/public/documents/UN/UNPAN028607.pdf.

8. Bishkek, "Obshestvenyi Fond 'Grajdanskaya Initsiativa Internet Politiki'" [Social Fund 'Civil Initiative for Internet Policy'], 2009.

9. Ibid.

10. Ibid.

11. European Bank for Reconstruction and Development, *Comparative Assessment of the Telecommunications Sector in the Transition Countries. Assessment Report: Kyrgyz Republic*, 2008, http://www.ebrd.com/country/sector/law/telecoms/assess/kyrgyz.pdf.

12. Paul Budde Communication Pty., Ltd., "Asian—Internet Market, 2008."

13. Kyrgyzstan Domain Registration Service, http://www.domain.kg/.

14. Sotovik Research Agency, August 2007, http://www.sotovik.ru.

15. Paul Budde Communication Pty., Ltd., "Kyrgyzstan—Telecoms Market Overview and Statistics," September 2008.

16. Kyrgzstan Government Gate Portal, http://www.govservices.kg.

17. These parties are the Moia Strana Party, the Democratic Party Turan, and the Ar-Namys Party, whose previous leader is the current prime minister, F. Koulov.

18. Bruce Pannier, "Kyrgyzstan: Rights Groups Assail Restrictive New Media Law," Radio Free Europe/Radio Liberty, June 17, 2008, http://www.rferl.org/content/article/1144636.html.

19. Before liberalization, KyrgyzTelecom carried out filtering of voice traffic in order to limit access to non-Kyrgyz providers offering IP-telephony service, to thereby compel the use of local providers. Voice traffic was filtered in all the standard ports on all popular non-Kyrgyz providers of IP telephony. Allegedly, Cisco (Pix) and Huawei (EuDemon) products were used for filtering voice content.

20. OpenNet Initiative, "Special Report: Kyrgyzstan: Election Monitoring in Kyrgyzstan," February 2005, http://www.opennetinitiative.net/special/kg/.

Moldova

Internet users in Moldova enjoy largely unfettered access despite the government's restrictive and increasingly authoritarian tendencies. Evidence of second- and third-generation controls is mounting. Although filtering does not occur at the backbone level, the majority of filtering and surveillance takes place at the sites where most Moldovans access the Internet:  Internet cafés and workplaces. Moldovan security forces have developed the capacity to monitor the Internet, and national legislation concerning "illegal activities" is strict.

Background

Moldova is a parliamentary republic with a president at the head of the state. A newly sovereign state as of the early 1990s, Moldova experienced both political and economic turmoil. Separatist movements erupted in the Transnistria region, which operates as an independent (albeit unrecognized) state with separate telecommunications and broadcasting networks.

RESULTS AT A GLANCE					
Filtering	No Evidence of Filtering	Suspected Filtering	Selective Filtering	Substantial Filtering	Pervasive Filtering
Political			•		
Social	•				
Conflict and security	•				
Internet tools	•				

Other Factors	Low	Medium	High	Not Applicable
Transparency	•			
Consistency	•			

KEY INDICATORS	
GDP per capita, PPP (constant 2005 international dollars)	2,409
Life expectancy at birth (years)	69
Literacy rate (percent of people age 15+)	99
Human development index (out of 179)	113
Rule of law (out of 211)	148
Voice and accountability (out of 209)	132
Democracy index (out of 167)	62 (Flawed democracy)
Digital opportunity index (out of 181)	111
Internet users (percent of population)	16.2

Source by indicator: World Bank 2009a, World Bank 2009a, World Bank 2009a, UNDP 2008, World Bank 2009b, World Bank 2009b, Economist Intelligence Unit 2008, ITU 2007, Miniwatts Marketing Group 2009.

Moldova has one of the lowest Internet development levels in Eastern Europe and ranks 93rd worldwide on the United Nations e-Readiness Survey of 2008.[1] The government has prioritized information and communication technology (ICT) as a means for national development and adopted a national ICT strategy designed to harmonize the sector with European standards by means of the European Union–sponsored Electronic South Eastern Europe initiative (eSEE). The telecommunications sector in Moldova is formally liberalized, but the government has faced problems privatizing the main operator. Privatization of the national operator is still under discussion.

Internet in Moldova

Internet penetration in Moldova has increased significantly in the past few years. According to the ITU, at the end of 2006 approximately 10.6 percent of the country's population had Internet access. By 2008, penetration rates had risen to 16.2 percent.[2] Despite this high rate of growth, development of the Internet has been constrained by a lack of quality infrastructure, low affordability, and the slow development of the fixed-line sector. In 2007, the number of subscribers to Internet access services at fixed locations increased by 33.2 percent, amounting to 110,200.[3]

More than 93 percent of ADSL access is provided by a single ISP, Moldtelecom.[4] Broadband usage is increasing, driven by rising demand and falling prices.[5] The cost for unlimited Internet ADSL access is approximately USD 11 a month (February 2009)[6] compared to EUR 25 a month a couple of years earlier. Broadband subscriber penetration reached 3.23 percent, up 1.86 percent, with two-thirds of the subscriptions concentrated in the capital, Chisinau, where household penetration was 30.8 percent.

Ownership of personal computers is also increasing, with 15.3 percent penetration as of 2006.[7] Most users are under 35 years.[8] Nearly half access the Internet from their place of work, 33.6 percent use Internet at home, and 8.1 percent use public access

points. The Internet subscriber statistics follow news that the growth of fixed-line telephony penetration in the country dropped to 3 percent in 2008 while mobile penetration rose by 28.7 percent over the same period. [9] Nearly 85 percent of Internet access
connections are mobile phone connections. In 2008, the Moldovan regulator reported
that the number of mobile Internet connections rose by 115.4 percent to 1,437,000.[10]

Moldova has five tier-one providers: Moldtelecom, Telemedia Group,[11] Dynamic
Network Technologies (DNT), Relsoft, and Riscom. A further 11 ISPs provide access
to all regions of the country. The telecommunications market is dominated by Moldtelecom, which retains its near monopoly position in the market (98 percent). Market
liberalization in Moldova started before 2004, partly as a result of pressure to join the
WTO and harmonize its standards with the EU telecommunications legal framework.
Most of the ISPs rent infrastructure from Moldtelecom. Almost all ISPs exchange traffic
through an IXP controlled by Moldtelecom. Interdnestrcom is the only ISP offering
services on a wide scale throughout the breakaway region, Transnistria.

Fixed-line remains underdeveloped compared to other European nations, much like
Internet and broadband penetration. However, communications have recorded solid
growth, reaching more than 10 percent of the country's GDP in 2007 (9.11 percent in
2008).[12] International Internet bandwidth in the country is currently 4,500 Mbps.[13]
Between 2004 and 2007, mobile phone ownership increased from to 790,000 (23.2
percent) to 1,880,000 (55 percent).[14] There are more than 14 operators providing
VoIP services on the international voice market, although Moldtelecom has retained
the largest share.[15] The taxes on VoIP operators were reduced several times in recent
years. Operators need to obtain a license in order to offer IP services.

Approximately 5,000 domain names are registered in the ".md" domain, some of
which are foreign Web sites.[16] The most popular languages accessed by Internet users
are Romanian, Russian, and English. The most-visited local Web sites are local media
sites, forums, and advertising sites. The most-used local search engines are google.md,
ournet.md, super.md, and mail.ru. The main purposes for accessing the Internet,
according to respondents to a local survey, are sending and receiving e-mails, reading
political news, and looking up educational information.[17]

Opposition groups have recognized the importance of the Internet. Most Moldovan
political parties have a solid online presence and frequently update their Web sites.[18]
The government has invested in the Internet and actively supports an effort to ensure
that ministries and other public bodies maintain Web sites in order to bring more
transparency to their operation. More than 40.6 percent of Internet users report that
they frequently access government Web sites.[19]

Legal and Regulatory Frameworks

In order to meet requirements for WTO and the EU accession, the telecommunications
market has been liberalized and no exclusive rights remain.[20] Moldtelecom—the

incumbent telecom operator—decreased its tariffs, allowing other providers into the market. However, low computer penetration rates and inconsistent government policy remain major impediments to Internet growth.

The state has officially committed to developing Moldova as an information society, although many of its policies undermine this objective. Moldtelecom, which is also the major national ISP, remains under state control despite large-scale criticism and four failed privatization attempts. Moldtelecom also controls Unite, one of the four mobile operators created in 2007. At present, ISPs are forced to rent access from Moldtelecom's well-developed infrastructure, a necessity which increases their costs and diminishes their competitiveness. Moldtelecom provides the nondiscriminatory Reference Interconnection Offer, the last version having been approved by the regulator after much delay in December 2007. Even though some interconnection agreements are now agreed between the incumbent and IP and data transmission operators, some new entrants have complained about insufficient access to Moldtelecom's network leading to inefficient usage of infrastructure.[21] In April 2009, the Moldovan regulator introduced new guidelines on interconnection tariffs. The regulation addresses the issues of obligations imposed on operators, with emphasis on transparency and non-discriminatory stances toward competitors.[22] It remains to be seen in practice how the new guideline will be applied by Moldtelecom.

The Ministry of Information Development is the main policymaker in the field of information and communications and was drafting new Policy Strategy 2009–2011. The ministry's objective is to implement the National Strategy and Program on establishing "e- Moldova."

The main law regulating the Internet is the 2007 Law on Electronic Communication. The law established the National Agency for Telecommunications and Information Regulation (NATIR) as the telecommunications regulator in Moldova. This law mandates the government to harmonize national legislation with European standards. The law is intended to give NATIR full autonomy over the sector and replaces the licensing regime. Internet service providers can now start operating immediately after notifying NATIR.[23]

This agency is responsible for monitoring ISPs' compliance with the law and keeping the Public Register of Electronic Communications Network and Service Providers. The law specifically provides for the possibility of introducing anticompetitive restrictions on service providers. The agency can demand that ISPs provide additional accounting information, can make them change to cost-oriented tariffs, and can introduce other measures in order to stimulate efficient market competition; and NATIR also regulates the management of the country's highest-level Internet domain (".md"). The National Security Doctrine of Moldova as of 1995 did not include the Internet. The Supreme Security Council (SSC), which oversees implementation of the president's decrees related to national security, monitors ministries' and state agencies' various activities to ensure national security. The Ministry of Information Development carries out government policies related to information and communications and encourages collaboration between state and private organizations. The Moldovan legislation does not provide for comprehensive regulation of information security. Rather, the National Security and Information Service is endowed with broad authority to monitor and gather information on Internet usage and data transmission related to national security issues.

In July 2008, a Moldovan court ordered the seizure of the PCs of 12 young Internet users for posting critical comments online against the governing party. The suspects were accused of illegally inciting people "to overthrow the constitutional order" and "threaten the stability and territorial integrity of the Republic of Moldova." It is unknown how the authorities obtained the names of the people, but some suggest that an ISP provided them with the IP addresses of the users.[24]

Even though Moldova is one of the poorest countries in Europe, Internet and cell phones are used extensively by opposition and civil society groups to organize protests and voice their opinion. After the parliamentary elections on April 5, 2009, thousands of Moldovans attempted to gather in Chisinau's main square to protest the results. The protesters set the Parliament and president's offices on fire, images of which were broadcast around the world. As the guarantees for press freedom are still weak, Moldovan state television continued to show regular TV programming rather than broadcasting events occurring in the capital.[25] The authorities disconnected cell phone coverage in the main square. More than 10,000 Moldovans joined in on Twitter (some with GPRS technology on their mobiles) to share their opinions and spread the news of Chisinau's political protests. The authorities attempted to shut down a number of Web sites for a few days, demonstrating a resolute hand in dealing with protesters. This incident, like others that have transpired in the region (e.g., the Ukrainian Orange Revolution), reveals the growing role of the social media in Eastern Europe as a tool for organizing protests and diffusing them online.[26] At the same time, it creates the concern that governments in the region, aware of the increasing importance of social media, might attempt to close down free speech outlets anytime they feel threatened.

Surveillance

The National Security and Information Service is authorized to monitor the Internet and collect any information necessary to prevent infringements of the laws. Surveillance in Moldova is permitted only after obtaining a court order. There is no special legal act providing for Internet surveillance per se. Nevertheless, surveillance may effectively be carried out on the provider level or at companies. The Parliament is deliberating on legislative proposals, including changes to the Law on Operative-Investigative Activities and the Law on Telecommunications that would allow government agencies to carry out surveillance on telephone and electronic communications. The law is still under consideration, but if it is approved, it is expected that it might follow the Russian Law on Surveillance (SORM).

Moldova has established two departments responsible for overseeing the activities of participants in the ICT sector. The first structure, within the Ministry of Internal Affairs, is charged with prevention of interregional and informational infringements. The other body, within the Center on Prevention of Economic Crimes and Corruption, has special powers to prevent infringements in the IT and other fields.

Moldova also possesses a comprehensive centralized database of information on all its citizens. This system, called *registru* (registry), has been heavily criticized by human rights groups for being too comprehensive and lacking oversight. Privacy rights are poorly developed in Moldova, and not yet defined in law. The information held by registru is extremely comprehensive and brings together data collected by all state agencies. Consequently, human rights groups fear that it represents unwarranted and unprecedented surveillance. The system has proven highly successful, and it is a model for governments in the CIS. It has been exported to several other countries in the region. The current Moldovan president, a former internal ministry general, supports registru—in part because it was originally developed within the Ministry of Internal Affairs.

ONI Testing Results

In 2007 and 2008, the OpenNet Initiative carried out testing on three first-tier ISPs in Moldova: Moldtelecom, Telemedia, and DNT SunCommunications. Results did not reveal any filtering carried out on the Internet backbone.

In Internet cafés, access is limited more by surveillance than by direct filtering. Specific content is prohibited, and, if it is accessed, the user is fined. Approximately 56 percent of Internet cafés' administrators surveyed by ONI admitted to filtering and surveillance activities in 2006. Other administrators stated that they noted that some Web sites were inaccessible, but would not confirm that they used any specific filtering system in the Internet cafés.

Conclusion

Moldovan authorities have recognized the political and social importance of the Internet. State authorities have interfered with mobile and Internet connections in an attempt to silence protestors and influence the results of elections. Generally, the Internet remains largely unfettered. Previous research by ONI revealed that at "edge" locations, such as Internet cafés and some enterprises, monitoring or filtering of certain content and services occasionally occurs. Research also suggests that Moldovan security forces have developed mechanisms to monitor Internet content. Given the low implementation of the laws protecting citizen's rights and privacy, as well as the insufficient independence of the regulator and the courts with regard to the state-owned Moldtelecom, there are few checks and balances in place to prevent authorities from taking a more aggressive stance on policing Internet content or from hindering new entrants on the market.

Notes

1. United Nations, *United Nations e-Government Survey 2008*, http://unpan1.un.org/intradoc/groups/public/documents/un/unpan028607.pdf.

2. Miniwatts Marketing Group, "Internet World Statistics: Moldova," 2009, http://www.internetworldstats.com/europa2.htm#md.

3. Of those, about 63,000 were dial-up subscribers and 47,200 were broadband Internet users. The number of dial-up users increased by only 3.4 percent in 2007, with a 23 percent rise outside the capital and a 9 percent decrease in Chisinau resulting from competition from broadband service providers. At the same time, broadband access grew from 36,000 to about 47,200 (80 percent, ADSL access; 15.9 percent, FTTH/LAN; and 6 percent, cable TV Internet).

4. National Regulatory Agency for Electronic Communications and Information Technology, *Report on Activity and Developments of the Electronic Communications Market in 2007*, 2008, http://www.anrti.md/en/Rapoarte/2007%20RAPORT%20ANUAL.pdf.

5. Moldtelecom has cut cross-subsidies on its services in an effort to rebalance its tariffs.

6. Moldtelecom National Operator, "MaxDSL," http://www.moldtelecom.md/ru/persons/internet/maxdsl/.

7. Ministry of Information Development, "Computer Utilization," 2007, http://www.mdi.gov.md/stat10_en/stat10_3_en/.

8. Center of Sociological, Politological and Psychological Analysis and Investigations (CIVIS), *Role of the Internet in Internet Users' Lives*, 2005, http://www.mdi.gov.md/img/pdf/3_ICT_en.pdf.

9. IHS Global Insight, "Annual Fixed-Line Growth in Moldova Drops to 3 Percent on Continued Mobile Growth," March 12, 2009, http://www.globalinsight.com/.

10. Ibid.

11. At the end of 2008, the French GSM company acquired the Moldovan mobile and Internet service provider Telemedia. Telemedia Group has its own fiber-optic network, developed radio network, main radio-relay TV channel, and information center for network control and monitoring.

12. National Regulatory Agency for Electronic Communications and Information Technology, *Report on Activity and Developments of the Electronic Communications Market in 2007*; Ancerti, *Report on Activity and Developments of the Electronic Communications Market in 2008*, 2008, http://en.anrceti.md/files/filefield/RAPORT_anual_2008_engl_fin_publ.pdf.

13. National Operator Moldtelecom, "Uslugi Dostupa v Internet ot Moldtelecom" [Internet Service by Moldtelecom], http://www.moldtelecom.md/ru/persons/internet.

14. National Regulatory Agency for Electronic Communications and Information Technology, *Report on Activity and Developments of Electronic Communications Market in 2007.*

15. Ibid.

16. Ournet, "Moldova Internet Resources," http://www.ournet.md/en.html.

17. Ministry of Information Development, "Computer Utilization," 2007, http://www.mdi.gov.md/stat10_en/stat10_3_en/.

18. "Partide Politice şi Alte Organizacii Social-politice din Republica Moldova" [Political Parties and Other Political Organizations of Moldova], http://www.parties.e-democracy.md/.

19. Center of Sociological, Politological and Psychological Analysis and Investigations (CIVIS), *Role of the Internet in Internet Users' Lives,* 2005, http://www.mdi.gov.md/img/pdf/3_ICT_en.pdf.

20. National data have been liberalized since 1993, international data since 1998, local fixed voice since 2001, domestic and long-distance fixed voice since 2004.

21. European Bank for Reconstruction and Development, *Comparative Assessment of the Telecommunications Sector in the Transition Countries,* http://www.ebrd.com/country/sector/law/telecoms/assess/moldova.pdf.

22. IHS Global Insight, "New Interconnection Regulation Instituted in Moldova," 2009, http://www.globalinsight.com/.

23. "The notification shall contain a minimum of information necessary for the Agency to keep the Public Register of electronic communications network and service providers and shall have attached a card containing an abstract description of the network and/or service, which shall be an integral part of the notification." See. Article 23 (3) of the Electronic Communications Act of November 15, 2007 at http://www.anrti.md.

24. *Curaj.net,* "Young People from Republic of Moldova Are Accused by Prosecutors of Expressing 'Dangerose' Opinions on the Web," June 11, 2008, http://www.curaj.net/?p=3945; Sami Ben Gharbia, "Moldavia: Sequestration of Personal Computers of 12 Young People for Posting Critical Comments Online," *Global Voices Advocacy,* June 13, 2008, http://advocacy.globalvoicesonline.org/2008/06/13/moldavia-destruction-of-personal-computers/.

25. Corneliu Rusnac, "Moldovans Outwit Communists with Twitter," Associated Press, April 8, 2009, http://www.itworld.com/node/66095.

26. Evgeny Morozov, "Moldova's Twitter Revolution in NOT a Myth," *Foreign Policy: Net Effect,* April 10, 2009, http://neteffect.foreignpolicy.com/posts/2009/04/10/moldovas_twitter_revolution_is_not_a_myth.

Russia

The absence of overt state-mandated Internet filtering in Russia has led some observers to conclude that the Russian Internet represents an open and uncontested space. In fact, the opposite is true. The Russian government actively competes in Russian cyberspace employing second- and third-generation strategies as a means to shape the national information  space and promote pro-government political messages and strategies. This approach is consistent with the government's strategic view of cyberspace that is articulated in strategies such as the doctrine of information security. The DoS attacks against Estonia (May 2007) and Georgia (August 2008) may be an indication of the government's active interest in mobilizing and shaping activities in Russian cyberspace.

Background

Under Vladimir Putin, the federal government of the Russian Federation (RF) has consolidated its power, stripping regional government representatives of some of their

RESULTS AT A GLANCE					
Filtering	No Evidence of Filtering	Suspected Filtering	Selective Filtering	Substantial Filtering	Pervasive Filtering
Political			•		
Social			•		
Conflict and security	•				
Internet tools	•				

Other Factors	Low	Medium	High	Not Applicable
Transparency	•			
Consistency	•			

KEY INDICATORS	
GDP per capita, PPP (constant 2005 international dollars)	13,873
Life expectancy at birth (years)	68
Literacy rate (percent of people age 15+)	100
Human development index (out of 179)	73
Rule of law (out of 211)	175
Voice and accountability (out of 209)	166
Democracy index (out of 167)	107 (Hybrid regime)
Digital opportunity index (out of 181)	51
Internet users (percent of population)	27

Source by indicator: World Bank 2009a, World Bank 2009a, World Bank 2009a, UNDP 2008, World Bank 2009b, World Bank 2009b, Economist Intelligence Unit 2008, ITU 2007, Miniwatts Marketing Group 2009.

authority.[1] Putin abolished the principle of electing regional heads by regional parliaments and channeled a number of legal and institutional reforms that demonstrate a gradual tendency to reintroduce a more centralized form of governance over its subjects. These shifts have been felt in all sectors of public life.

Putin's administration after eight years in power brought Russia back to the international scene as a strong global player, and this success has inspired a wave of nationalism fueled by government policies. Putin enjoyed high approval ratings in Russia up to 87 percent (July 2006)[2] largely because of the improved economic indicators of the country. The economy has performed well under his watch, especially in comparison to the period between 1991 and 1999. It has been growing steadily, bolstered by high global energy prices. The growing popularity for Putin, however, was coupled with a significant drop in political rights and civil liberties.[3] Putin's administration effectively silenced the opposition, cracked down on antigovernment protests, reimposed control over the media, and concentrated power in the presidency. The policy line introduced by Putin remains largely unchallenged during the first year of Dmitri Medvedev's presidency. Putin and his supporters refer to the current system of governance in Russia as "sovereign democracy." International observers disagree, describing the established system of government as an increasingly authoritarian state, albeit one that is supported "with the consent of the governed."[4]

As President, Putin strengthened state control over major outlets, focusing especially on media owned at the time by Russian oligarchs. As a sanction for unpaid debts, Putin took away owners' shares in television channels and placed the media under state control. This action sharply influenced the flow of information and the management of the outlets. Major federal television channels are either directly or indirectly controlled by the government, with the sole exception of RenTV, which openly criticizes the government but, ironically, is owned by a Kremlin supporter, Vladimir Potanin.[5] Print media are the least controlled part of the Russian media, but their influence may not be as strong as that of other media. The control on the media tightened particularly during and after the 2004 "Beslan Crisis," in which 1,100 students were taken hostage in Beslan in the North Caucasus by terrorists demanding an end to the second Chechen war.[6]

The Russian government has deliberately created mechanisms to centralize power in the Kremlin and influence major information outlets. This policy has been expanded to reach the Internet through a range of approaches from censorship to propaganda, resulting in self-censorship.

Although Putin admittedly has never sent an e-mail in his life,[7] his administration has been increasingly interested in regulating the Internet. Under Medvedev's presidency (since May 2008), Putin, now as the prime minister, continues to have significant influence over the internal and foreign politics of the state.

Dmitri Medvedev has demonstrated familiarity with Internet communications. During the election campaign, he addressed questions about the Russian blogosphere, promising clement conditions for its development. In October 2008, Medvedev launched his own video blog.[8] However, no significant changes have been introduced to promote media freedom and freedom of expression in Russia. Nonetheless, Russian media have surmised that Medvedev's involvement has led to the removal of the restrictions on foreign participation in ISPs, which were envisioned in the Draft Bill for Amendments to the Law "On the Order of Foreign Investment in Companies and Organizations Having Strategic Importance for National Security."

Internet Infrastructure

Internet use grew in Russia in the 1990s with a regime unprepared to deal with new information and communication technology (ICT) challenges. The post-Soviet government seemed to prefer to have strong control over the Internet, similar to the way it already controlled traditional media, but left it alone for lack of viable approaches. Internet penetration in Russia was low during this period, and access was difficult, factors that may explain why the Internet was not a major government concern.[9]

With the election of President Putin came a new focus on regulating the Internet. He issued the Information Security Doctrine in 2000, which outlined Russia's desire to encourage development of the information space amid growing security concerns. This document regulates traditional media but also indirectly positions the Internet at the core of national security policies.[10] Within a few years, the majority of other CIS countries adopted laws similar to Russia's Information Doctrine.

As of December 2008, the number of Internet users in Russia had reached 38 million.[11] Internet penetration is growing notably, though it remains predominantly two-tiered, with much higher Internet and PC penetration rates in Moscow and

St. Petersburg than in the rest of the country. The "e-readiness" standing of Russia as measured by the Economist Intelligence Unit[12] is 59th out of 70 countries surveyed in 2008.[13] The Ministry of Education and Science has initiated national programs for providing Internet access to all general educational institutions in the country.[14] Fifty thousand schools were connected to the Internet by the end of 2007.[15] Moreover, the government has announced its plans to install open-source software on every school computer by 2009.

The majority of Russian Internet users are connected by broadband (40 percent), followed by dial-up (27 percent), and ADSL (23 percent). Seven million PCs were sold in Russia in 2006, of which 1.9 million were laptops, representing a 62 percent annual increase from the year before.[16]

A significant portion of the telecom market has remained under state control. Telecommunication Investment Joint Stock Company SvyazInvest is one of the largest telecommunications holding companies in the world. It was created during the market transition by a regulation providing for the merger of a majority of the regional state telecommunications enterprises.[17] About 89 percent of the Russian telecommunications infrastructure now belongs to SvyazInvest,[18] with the remaining 11 percent divided among several other operators.[19] The main shareholder of SvyazInvest is the Russian government through the Federal Property Agency (75 percent minus 1 share), and Comstar-UTS owns 17.31 percent plus 1 share. Some of the main regional ISPs are SvyazInvest's subsidiaries: Central Telecommunication Company, North-West Telecom, VolgaTelecom, Southern Telecom, Uralsvyazinform, Sibirtelecom, Dalsvyaz, and Central Telegraph.[20]

Rostelecom is another large telecommunications operator and ISP. Despite strong international pressure for privatization, SvyazInvest continues to hold 51 percent of Rostelecom shares. Historically, Rostelecom has been the primary long-distance and international telephone operator, collecting mandatory intermediary fees from other providers. Before the adoption of the new regulatory framework on communications, Rostelecom had a monopoly over the provision of international long-distance services. Under the new regime, providers of long-distance services may offer their services directly to users without paying intermediary charges, provided certain prerequisites apply. These include that the providers "are in technical conformity with the local and long-distance network operators, with a point of presence in every Russian administrative region, and are operationally ready to provide long-distance services to any local network subscriber."

Russia has more than a dozen main first-tier ISPs, which have independent connections to foreign networks, and several other influential ISPs. First-tier ISPs in the Russian Federation are Rostelecom,[21] GoldenTelecom,[22] TransTeleCom,[23] Makomnet,[24] TeliaSonera,[25] Comstar-Direct (previously MTU-Intel),[26] Metrocom,[27] Corbina,[28] ER-Telecom, CentrTelecom,[29] RTComm,[30] RETN.net,[31] and RiNet.[32] The major ISPs in

Russia either are state owned or include significant state participation. State participation is either direct or through a state-controlled entity.

There are hundreds of ISPs throughout the country functioning on a divided market of well-connected big cities and underdeveloped infrastructure in towns and villages. The established fixed-line providers have been traditionally the largest ISPs, though many small ISPs have started to emerge. Under a regulation that entered into force at the beginning of 2006, all companies that control more than 25 percent of the capacity of communication traffic need to publish a list of prices for interconnection and data transmission within 20 days for the inspection and approval of the regulatory agency.[33]

There are several Internet exchange points (IXP) in Russia. The main ones are Moscow IX,[34] independent, comprising various locations in Moscow;[35] SPB-IX in St. Petersburg, jointly with the MSK-IX; SAMARA-IX in Samara; NSK-IX in Novosibirsk; and KRS-IX in Krasnoyarsk. Other IXPs are the North-West Internet Exchange based in St. Petersburg and Ural-IX in Ekaterinburg and Perm.

The cable television market and broadband Internet access market significantly increased penetration to around 40 percent in 2007.[36] Broadband connections are growing as operators invest in modernized networks. However, broadband is emerging mainly in large urban areas (ADSL, cable, and FttH/FttB-based services). A large portion of residential areas use Ethernet local area networks (LANs), followed by dial-up (27 percent), and ADSL (23 percent). Wireless broadband networks have become popular mainly in large tourist cities, especially St. Petersburg and Moscow, and some operators have announced plans to launch Wi-Fi coverage on a large scale. Also, IPTV services have been launched.[37]

In remote regions, satellite connection is very attractive to the Russian population, in comparison to fixed-line charges. Two main educational networks in Russia (Radio-MSU and the university network RUNET) are supported by satellite.

There are about 250 mobile operators on the Russian market. The mobile market represents about 40 percent of telecom revenue. As of September 2006, the market was divided as follows: MTS, 34 percent; Vimpelcom, 32 percent; Megafon, 19 percent; and others, 15 percent. According to studies, some 40 percent of the population does not have a mobile phone. Russia's three biggest operators were issued 3G licenses in 2007.

The importance of the blogosphere to Russians is increasing rapidly. The Russian-language part of the Internet, or the RUNET, is an active and vibrant environment. As a Russian-language platform, the RUNET has grown as the center of modern culture connecting Internet users from Russia and the rest of the CIS region, and ethnic Russians in Germany, Israel, and the United States. It brings together people sharing the same language and similar history and culture, and is a self-sufficient online environment with its own search engines, Web portals, free e-mail services, and social network

Web sites (most of them modeled after U.S. services). The most popular blog servers are LiveJournal.com and LiveInternet.ru. The Russian site of LiveJournal has more than 2 million[38] registered users, while the site's readership amounts to nearly 10 million people, according to Anton Nossik, one of the RUNET pioneers.[39]

The Russian blogosphere operates within an environment where the state directly competes with other actors for influence. During election times, the Kremlin maintains a network of supportive bloggers and online media experts, similar to China's so-called *fifty cent party*. This squadron of Kremlin bloggers has engaged in public discussions, trying to keep the level of political criticism low, to nurture nationalism, and to flood the Russian blogosphere with blogs that favor the regime during times of oppositional protests.[40] Instead of giving publicity to its efforts to control the Internet through direct censorship, the government has turned to these soft approaches to combat undesired content.

Recently, the Russian government has implemented an unprecedented, and so far surprisingly effective, initiative to engage with political dissent in order to weaken it. A number of pro-Kremlin blogs have been created; in number, they overshadow blogs not favoring the regime, and they were especially prevalent toward the end of 2007, when national political campaigns were under way for parliamentary and presidential elections. This strategy could also be intended to drown out the voices of opposition blogs.

Effective strategic blogging has been seen to have an impact. In April 2007, for example, an opposition movement held a march in Moscow. To interfere with the information about the march, blogger Pavel Danilin, a Putin supporter, together with his team, started blogging about a smaller pro-Kremlin march being held the same day. European Digital Rights noted, "they blogged so much and linked to each other so effectively, that they crowded out all the items about the opposition march from the very influential top-five blog post listing on the Yandex Web portal."[41] A consistent and motivated group of supporters is likely to channel the Kremlin's message to large online communities. According to Masha Lipman, a political expert at the Moscow Carnegie Center, "The Kremlin has lots of sites under its control, financed by businesses associated with the Kremlin or otherwise, which create an environment in which those more independent ones are easily dissolved. This [dissolution of independent sites] . . . is one thing that the Kremlin is using to counter or neutralize the potentially stirring effect."[42] The blogs are not based on simple propaganda, and some of the bloggers are not even necessarily loyal; "they may be critical themselves, but this will be criticism that the Kremlin itself sort of oversees."[43]

Legal and Regulatory Frameworks

The Constitution of the Russian Federation guarantees free speech and prohibits any restraint on the freedom of expression (Article 29). The constitution recognizes the rights to privacy and data protection, the right to information, and secrecy of communications (Articles 23, 24, and 25).

The Law on Communications of 2003[44] further protects the secrecy of communications and guarantees that restrictions on individual privacy are allowed only after a court order, unless otherwise envisioned by federal law.[45] To meet its obligations as a member of the Council of Europe, Russia adopted the Law on Personal Data in 2006.[46] Although the law guarantees the privacy of the individual, it provides for broad exemptions to the government in processing personal data. Also in 2006, Russia modified its information law, adopting the new Law on Information, Information Technologies, and Protection of Information.[47] The new laws, together with the Labor Law, establish a legal framework for handling personal data, including employee data. Russian experts claim that even though the new law on information guarantees citizens' access to public information held by federal or regional authorities, not more than 23.6 percent of the relevant information is publicly available.[48]

A presidential decree titled "Measures Providing Information Security to the Russian Federation in the Information Exchange Area," signed in May 2004, restricts the access of officials' computers to the Internet.[49] The decree prevents computers and communication networks from connecting to the Internet if they hold (have on their servers) state and official secrets, as well as other classified information.

The Internet in Russia is largely seen as an extension of media space. The mass media regime carries certain responsibilities, such as registration, necessary attestation, and others. The Internet escaped regulation in the Law on Mass Media, No.2124-1,[50] as the Law entered into force in 1991. However, it is held that the Internet should be regulated under this law anyway. Article 2 of the law states that it shall cover "other forms of periodic distribution of mass information" as purported by officials.[51] This interpretation has given grounds for detaining and prosecuting Web site owners and bloggers by authorities on the grounds of violation of media laws. Officials view Internet proliferation as increasing the government's responsibility for regulating the Internet space and ensuring that users act in accordance with legal and ethical norms of society. In at least one instance, the court included an online forum in the definition of mass media, setting a precedent for prosecution under mass media provisions.

On several occasions, the authorities have expressed interest in subjecting content on the Internet, specifically online media, to media law. Federation Council member Vladimir Slutsker initiated amendments to the Law on Mass Media: one of the amendments provides that Web sites visited more than 1,000 times a day should be subjected to registration as mass media outlets.[52] However, it was deemed impossible to find all applicable sites and force Web site owners to register. For this reason, unofficially, it was agreed that the Web sites would register only voluntarily as mass media.[53]

According to its supporters, the envisioned proposal would give official recognition to the registered Web sites and would be important for controlling child pornography and defamatory materials, and even for providing information about terrorist and extremist organizations. There are incentives for Web sites to register as mass media outlets, including an official stamp of legitimacy and permission to attend press conferences, request information from authorities, and be present at sites of emergencies or mass protests. Another push for registration came in 2004 when the head of the Federal Agency for Print and Mass Communications, Michail Seslavinski, called for "important" Web sites to register as mass media.[54] In 2004, there were 1,296 registered Web sites, a figure which had increased to nearly 20,000 registered Web sites by 2009.[55]

There have been several proposals to introduce ISP liability for content found on their servers.[56] In March 2008, a new initiative was suggested by the Russian prosecutor general's office to hold ISPs jointly liable with extremists for extremist content posted online.[57] However, currently no draft law is known to have been proposed.

The ICT sector does not have an independent regulatory authority. Until 2007, the regulation of the sector was managed by the Ministry of Communications and Informatization through RosSvyazNadzor (the Federal Service on the Supervision of Communications), which reported directly to it. After the Russian Television and Radio Broadcasting Network (RTDN) lodged complaints in court against RosSvyazNadzor that the control it was exercising exceeded the limits provided by law, the agencies were reorganized. RosSvyazNadzor merged with another regulatory agency, the Federal Service on the Supervision of the Mass Media and the Protection of Cultural Inheritance. In addition to current responsibilities, the newly formed agency will also be responsible for protecting personal data and monitoring the processing of such data.

The Federal Law on Communications of 2003 provides a simplified licensing regime for ISPs. In order to conduct business in Russia, operators need to obtain two licenses: one for data transfer and another for "telematic" (data transmission and storage) services. In 2005, the Ministry of Communications introduced a licensing regime for VoIP services. Any VoIP service must be processed through a licensed long-distance telephone operator.

Libel incurred through the media is a crime regulated by the Criminal Code. It is also addressed in the Law on Mass Media. Articles 43 through 45 of the law describe the circumstances for publishing a refutation in libel suits when the information spread through the mass medium does not correspond to reality and denigrates honor and dignity.[58] Registered Web sites and producers of online content can be liable for defamation for published information under the Criminal Code and in the Law on Mass Media. In at least one instance, the court included an online forum in the definition of mass media, setting a precedent for prosecution under mass media provisions.[59]

In December 2007, the Russian Supreme (Arbitrazh) Court upheld the seizure of media archives. According to the Internet outlet Regnum.ru, the court did not apply Article 57, which provides a media libel exception for published information.[60] This precedent establishes that Internet outlets do not receive the protection of the law, since they are not treated as mass media outlets, thus leaving the door open to any potential defamatory claims.

At present, the Criminal Code includes numerous provisions that may be grounds for criminal charges in connection with Internet activities. Article 278, for example, criminalizes "forced assumption of and retention of authority." The Criminal Code provides for government officials to prosecute individuals for posting objectionable content online. The text against terrorist activities in Article 282, in the section "Crimes against the Government," can be applied to online activities. The text states, "incitement of national, racial, or religious enmity, abasement of human dignity, and also propaganda of the exceptionality, superiority, or inferiority of individuals by reason of their attitude to religion, national, or racial affiliation, if these acts have been committed in public or with the use of mass media" are punishable by fines equaling up to two years of salary and up to two years imprisonment. This broad language leaves space for open interpretation of the statute, as it can apply to anything ranging from commentary on the infamous Danish cartoons,[61] to racial slurs and hate speech. Insulting a government official is an aggravated crime covered in Article 319, which may bring a fine of up to one month of salary or corrective labor of up to one year.[62]

The government and private individuals can and do attempt to find broad interpretations of the laws in order to silence independent Web sites. For example, the content provider Bankfax was charged under Article 282 with insulting a group of people by referring to them as "oligarchs."

The government has adopted the Law against Extremist Activities.[63] Under this law, effectively any Web site hosting a forum section is vulnerable. An individual needs only to post hate or extremist (or other objectionable) speech in a forum and report it to the authorities before a moderator notices it to kick off legal prosecution. Violations are not uniformly prosecuted—most reported content does not lead to penalties, making the Internet a source of information that is not found in print media. If such speech is detected, however, owners risk closure of their Web sites or fines.[64]

Censorship has not been legally introduced in the country, though informally it has been applied as a tool for use during a national crisis. Internet censorship has occurred or been discussed in several other ways—for example, interference with the work of oppositional and independent Web sites and restrictions imposed by a court.

Russia's government officials are sensitive to offensive speech posted online. The Criminal Code and the Law against Extremist Activities establish individual liability for a broad range of "illegal" content. A special enforcement agency, Department "K," was established within the Ministry of Internal Affairs to monitor for compliance with the regulations in cyberspace. Department "K" has branches in various regions and is mandated to investigate crimes in the sphere of information technologies, including online hate speech and defamation. Aside from monitoring for possible defamation of officials online, the "cyber police" deal with unauthorized access to computer systems and networks, and the distribution of pirated software.

An example of the activities of this cyber police department was the September 2007 case involving the sports site hc-rodina.ru.[65] The ISP of the sports Web site stopped maintaining service following an order from Department "K." The reasons for this censorship were "inaccurate" comments about representatives of the government posted on the Web site's forum section. In another example, a blogger was sentenced to a year in jail for posting a caricature of Putin depicted as a skinhead.[66]

On several occasions, Russian politicians have proposed establishing a legal framework that would directly control the Internet. At the end of January 2007, the Federation Council Commission on Information Policy discussed the possibility of introducing a law regulating the Internet in order to establish a "safe" online environment to protect people against the growing cases of illegal activities.[67]

In July 2007, Putin spoke of making Russia "a global information technology powerhouse." Following his statement, the Kremlin announced plans to create a Cyrillic Web for Russia and the rest of the CIS and Bulgaria. The Russian Federation is the only country other than China that has decisively announced plans to launch a self-contained and independent language Web parallel to the World Wide Web. At the end of June 2008, ICANN spoke in favor of proposals to establish Cyrillic and Chinese language-based domains. Although this idea moves toward further development of the Internet, there are shared fears that this step might also lead to the division of the Internet and facilitate state censorship through the registration and management process. If the administration of Russian Web sites is concentrated in the hands of a government agency, it could have chilling effects on independent-minded online media and bloggers.

In the past few years, Russia's government has recognized the need to develop a favorable environment for information technology by providing legal and tax incentives for companies in this market. The development of the ICT sector has risen to become a national policy priority. Yet, while the government is hoping to attract foreign investment, it is not ready to abandon centralized decision making and end its monitoring of ISPs.

Surveillance

The Russian government has been advancing justifications for surveillance, ostensibly to aid in the investigation of crimes and the prevention of terrorism. The Law on Systems for Operational Investigation Activity (SORM)[68] of 1995 authorized the FSB monitoring of telecommunication transmission. In 1999, formulated as an amendment to SORM, SORM-II was enacted to allow for the monitoring of Internet traffic. SORM-II is still effective and "reinforced," and in April 2008, Leonid Reiman, the Minister of Communications, signed an order that essentially restated the obligations of ISPs under SORM-II to allow monitoring of users' Internet activities.

Under SORM-II, ISPs are required to provide the FSB with statistics on all Internet traffic that passes through their servers. In addition, ISPs are required to install monitoring devices on their servers and route all transmissions in real time through the FSB's local offices, which would allow the FSB to track all users' transactions, e-mail communications, and online browsing. Even though the FSB still needs to obtain a warrant to read the contents, many doubt that they would obtain the warrant beforehand consistently, since there is no mechanism to prevent the FSB from having unauthorized access. Providers must also provide the FSB with information on users' names, telephone numbers, e-mail addresses, one or more IP addresses, key words, user identification numbers, and users' ICQ number (instant messaging client), among others.

Under Putin, Minister of Communications Reiman entered an order stating that the FSB officials shall not provide information to the ISPs either on users who are being investigated or regarding the decision on the grounds of which such investigations are made.[69] Consequently, this Order offered a "carte blanche" to the Special Services to police the activities of Internet users without supplying any further information to the provider or any other interested party.

Only a few days after assuming office, President Putin expanded the list of state agencies that can monitor communications under SORM to include the tax police, Ministry of Internal Affairs, Border Guards, Kremlin Security Service, Presidential Security Service, parliamentary security services, and Foreign Intelligence Service.

SORM places the substantial financial burden of installing routers on the FSB servers on the balance sheets of ISPs, with minimal benefit to them for the technology. The cost of equipment at the time the regulation was adopted was close to USD 25,000.[70] This expense has caused many small and independent ISPs to shut down. In one recorded case a small regional ISP in Volgograd, Bayard-Slaviya Communications, resisted the new law and refused to install the required equipment. As a result, the Ministry of Communications suspended the provider's license. However, when the ISP brought the question to court, the ministry renewed its license.

SORM-II drastically expanded the ability of the FSB to carry out surveillance of operators and individuals. Some reports reveal that ISP owners prefer to negotiate their own confidential agreements with the FSB office rather than take on the cost of complying with SORM-II or risk losing their licenses.[71]

In reality, however, many doubt that the FSB possesses the capability of monitoring all Internet traffic.[72] Increased Internet traffic renders ubiquitous surveillance practically impossible. Unless the authorities know ahead of time what they are searching for, random surveillance is unlikely to produce any meaningful results.[73] Nevertheless, as there is no independent authority that controls or supervises the FSB, their activities are not publicly known.

ONI Testing Results

The OpenNet Initiative tested from different locations and several access points on a number of main ISPs in the major cities and regions. The ONI tested on the following ISPs: AltaiTelecom, ASN-Yartelecom, Comstar, Corvette, Metrocom, North-West Telecom (ASN SPBNIT), Rosnet, RiNet, St. Petersburg State University (ASN-SPBGU), and Wiland. The ONI found first-generation filtering that targeted erotic and pornographic content. Second-generation filtering methods were largely undetected by the ONI, as they occur only during significant political events. The ONI did not monitor the 2007 parliamentary or 2008 presidential elections, during which numerous instances of second-generation and third-generation controls were reported in the Russian and foreign press.

Conclusion

Control of media has a long-established history in Russia. As the Internet has proliferated, the government has moved to design suitable control mechanisms. Compared to other countries, the Russian approach represents a notably different method of controlling Internet activity. Instead of utilizing Chinese-style filtering to control Internet access, the Russian government prefers to employ second- and third-generation techniques such as legal and technical instruments and national information campaigns to shape the information environment and stifle dissent and opposition.

As many countries around the world struggle with Internet regulation, it is likely that this Russian model will be emulated by other governments, in the CIS and beyond.

Notes

1. Helen Womack, "Russia's Governors Reluctantly Accept Putin Curbs on Power," *The Independent*, July 27, 2000, http://www.independent.co.uk/news/world/europe/russias-governors-reluctantly-accept-putin-curbs-on-power-707944.html; Nikolay Petrov and Michael A. McFaul, "How Much Has Federal Power Increased Under Putin?" Carnegie Endowment for International Peace, September 8, 2004, http://www.carnegieendowment.org/events/index.cfm?fa=eventDetail &id=747.

2. Centre for the Study of Public Policy (University of Aberdeen) and Levada Center (Moscow), "Russia Votes," January 22, 2009, http://www.russiavotes.org/president/presidency_performance _trends.php#190.

3. Freedom House sets Russia's country status as "nonfree" for 2006 and 2007.

4. Clifford J. Levy, "Is Russia's Economy a Threat to Putin's Power?" *The Seattle Times*, February 1, 2009, http://seattletimes.nwsource.com/html/nationworld/2008694591_worldweek01.html ?syndication=rss.

5. Only one radio station, Echo Mosckvy, is considered independent, but it actually belongs to the state-owned company Gazprom, which itself implies that any criticism of the government broadcast over its networks is "pre-approved." In a recent interview, the editor in chief Alexei Venediktov admitted that "The Kremlin is our real stockholder." See Alexi Venediktov: "'The Kremlin is our real stockholder.'" *Novaya Gazeta*, April 17, 2008, http://en.novayagazeta.ru/data/2008/25/08.html.

6. The federal TV channels did not report the tragedy, and it was only through print media and the Internet that the Russian population obtained information. See Organization for Security and Cooperation in Europe, *Report on Russian Media Coverage of the Beslan Tragedy: Access to Information and Journalists' Working Conditions*, September 16, 2004, http://www.osce.org/documents/rfm/2004/09/3586_en.pdf; Stephen Dalziel, "Russia 'Impeded Media' in Beslan," *BBC News*, September 16, 2004, http://news.bbc.co.uk/1/hi/world/europe/3662124.stm.

7. Adi Ignatius, "A Tsar is Born," *Time*, http://www.time.com/time/specials/2007/personoftheyear/article/0,28804,1690753_1690757_1690766-1,00.html.

8. Weblog of Dmitri Medvedev, President of the Russian Federation, http://blog.kremlin.ru/.

9. For an analysis of the development of the Internet in the Russian Federation in the early and mid-1990s and services provided by the main e-mail provider, please consult Chapter 2 in this volume.

10. Security Council of the Russian Federation, *Information Security Doctrine of the Russian Federation*, 2000, http://www.scrf.gov.ru/documents/5.html.

11. Miniwatts Marketing Group "Internet World Stats: Russia," 2009, http://www.internetworldstats.com/europa2.htm#ru.

12. Economist Intelligence Unit, "e-Readiness Rankings 2008: Maintaining Momentum," http://a330.g.akamai.net/7/330/25828/20080331202303/graphics.eiu.com/upload/ibm_ereadiness_2008.pdf.

13. Political Intelligence and Internews, *Russia*, 2006, http://ec.europa.eu/information_society/activities/internationalrel/docs/pi_study_rus_ukr_arm_azerb_bel_geor_kaz_mold/2_russia.pdf.

14. Russian Ministry of Education, "Ensure All Russia's Schools Access to the Internet," http://mon.gov.ru/pro/pnpo/int/.

15. *C News*, "Bum: Glava "Moego Banka" Stroit WiMax-set" [BUM: The Head of 'My Bank' Is Building a WiMAX Connection], May 2006, http://www.cnews.ru/news/top/index.shtml?2009/06/05/349841.

16. Paul Budde Communication Pty., Ltd., "Russia—Internet, Broadband and Convergence Overview and Statistics," November 8, 2007.

17. SyvazInvest, "Investor Relations," http://eng.svyazinvest.ru/investor-relations/fdir/.

18. By the end of 2003, the five largest ISPs (54 percent) have been the SvyazInvest interregional companies. RTComm.ru, a branch of Rostelecom and SvyazInvest that took over Rostelecom's wholesale ISP business, has become an undisputed leader with 28 percent market share.

Transtelecom came second with 18 percent, and interregional companies had 17 percent. Golden Telecom and MTU-Intel had 11 and 9 percent, respectively.

19. There are several groups besides SvyazInvest that own large shares of the telecommunications business and to a large extent influence the development of Russia's telecom industry: AFK Systema, Alfa Group/Altima, and Telecominvest.

20. SyvazInvest, "Investor Relations," http://eng.svyazinvest.ru/investor-relations/fdir/.

21. It is one of the leading operators. The company "owns and operates a 150,000 km nationwide fiber optic backbone network" as well as satellite connection. Rostelecom provides services in many regions of Russia but is focused on major cities. It owns a 31.59 percent significant share of RTComm and provides service for second-tier operators. See Rostelecom, "General Information," http://www.rt.ru/en/about/info/ and Rostelecom, "Rostelecom at a Glance," http://www .rostelecom.ru/en/serv-operators/info/.

22. It is the largest of the alternative fixed-line operators and one of the largest ISPs in Russia, offering access in over 60 locations, including Moscow, St. Petersburg, and the CIS region (Kiev, Tashkent, Almaty, etc.). GoldenTelecom is connected to all the mobile and fixed telephony service providers in the Russian Federation. It has many international points of presence including London, Stockholm, New York, Frankfurt, and Hong Kong. In March 2008, VimpelCom (under the trade name Beeline) acquired GoldenTelecom (http://msk.b2b.beeline.ru). The ISP announced further plans to invest USD 1.5 billion in Russia aiming to build a new broadband Internet network serving 65 Russian cities by 2010.

23. TransTeleCom is a backbone telecommunications provider with a 50,000 km network of communication lines stretching through all 11 zones of the country. It connects to the Euro-Asian telecommunication route, going through Western Europe and Asia. The network is based on the communication lines of the Russian railroad systems. TransTeleCom mostly provides service for second-tier ISPs. The operator is owned by the state-run JSC Russian Railways.

24. Makomnet possesses an internationally linked fiber-optic network. In November 2006, it put into operation its fourth international 100 Mbps Moscow-Stockholm cable. The operator provides more than 1 Gbps capacity to Frankfurt (MCI/UUNet), New York (MCI/UUNet), Helsinki, and Stockholm (TeliaSonera). It maintains a total capacity of more than 4 Gbps with leading Russian ISPs via MSK-IX and direct connections. Shareholders include state-owned Moscow Metro and Moseleset. See Macomnet, "Internet Access," http://www.macomnet.com/services/internet and Macomnet, "4th International Main 100 Mbps Moscow-Stockholm Was Put into Operation," November 1, 2006, http://www.macomnet.com/press/news/text?newsid=47.

25. TeliaSonera is an international ISP operating in Russia and connected to the Russian Internet Exchange MSK-IX. It has the largest communication network in Europe and connects Russian networks with European and American operators. See ISP Review, "TyeliaSonyera Intyernyeshinal Kerriyer Rasha" [TeliaSonera Russian International Carrier], http://www.ispreview.ru/company1109.html.

26. MTU-Intel was renamed Comstar-Direct in December 2006 after it grew to become one of the largest ISPs in Moscow and the largest broadband ISP in Moscow. It provides a 30 Gbps channel

Moscow-Europe and is connected to more than 200 Western ISPs at a couple of European Internet exchanges. Comstar-Direct is a subsidiary of Comstar, one of the largest telecoms in Russia. For international Internet connection, see http://www.comstar-uts.com/ru/services/internet/. Also see http://www.comstar-direct.ru.

27. Metrocom operates predominantly in the northwest of Russia. It is owned in majority by the city of St. Petersburg and closed joint stock company MST.

28. Corbina is one of the largest Russian ISPs. It has coverage in more than 20 regions, but it operates mostly in the Moscow region. Corbina does not have its own independent network and is connected to foreign networks through TeliaSonera's and GoldenTelecom's lines. The controlling shareholder is GoldenTelecom. See Corbina ISP, http://home.corbina.ru/news/2007/05/29/1653 .html.

29. CentrTelecom is one of the largest ISPs operating in the central part of Russia. It currently provides broadband connection, including xDSL, to more than 120,000 users. CentrTelecom is state run, and the majority shareholder is SvyazInvest. European Communications, "Russian Operator Center Telecom Selects Italtel for Implementation of Broadband and VoIP," July 3, 2007, See http://www.eurocomms.com/online_press/111822/Russian_operator_Center_Telecom_selects_Italtel _for_implementation_of_broadband_and_VoIP_.html.

30. RTComm was founded by SvyazInvest and Rostelecom; now it is now part of the Sinterra group, which is part of PromSvyazCapital, a private investment and media holding company. See RTComm, http://www.rtcomm.ru/geo/net/.

31. RETN.net operates a network joining Russian and Western ISPs. It serves over 140 national and foreign companies having some 500 direct connections between the Russian and international ISPs. It has points of presence in New York, London, Amsterdam, Stockholm, Helsinki, and Frankfurt, as well as in Moscow, St. Petersburg, and other Russian cities. RETN.net is connected to Internet exchanges in New York, London, Washington, D.C., Amsterdam, and Moscow. See RETN.net, "About Company," http://www.retn.net/about.

32. RiNet is owned by Sibirtelecom, http://www2.sibirtelecom.ru.

33. Order No. 127 on the Organization of Activities Concerned with the Consideration of Telecommunications Carriers' Requests Concerning the Issues of Telecommunication Networks Interconnection and Interaction issued by the Minister of Information Technologies and Communications on November 10, 2005.

34. Moscow Internet Exchange, http://www.msk-ix.ru/; Russia IP Traffic Exchange, http://www .ripn.net:8080/ix/.

35. Moscow Internet Exchange, http://www.msk-ix.ru/; graphs of traffic at http://www.msk-ix.ru/ network/traffic.html.

36. PMR IT & Telecoms in Russia, http://www.ictrussia.com.

37. J'son and Partners, "Forecast about IPTV Development in Russia (2007–2010)," *Rumetrika*, June, 16, 2007, http://rumetrika.rambler.ru/publ/article_show.html?article=3221.

38. See http://ru-news.livejournal.com/.

39. Galina Stolyarova, "Working the Net," *Transitions Online*, June 14, 2007, http://www.tol.cz/look/TOL/article.tpl?IdLanguage=1&IdPublication=4&NrIssue=222&NrSection=3&NrArticle=18778.

40. Anna Polyanskaya, Andrei Krivov, and Ivan Lomko, "Commissars of the Internet: The FSB at the Computer," *Vestnik Online*, April 30, 2003, http://www.vestnik.com/issues/2003/0430/win/polyanskaya_krivov_lomko.htm.

41. European Digital Rights, "Putin wants Control of Russian Internet," November 7, 2007, http://www.edri.org/edrigram/number5.21/putin-russia-internet.

42. Global Integrity, "Russia: Integrity Indicators Scorecard," 2007, http://report.globalintegrity.org/Russia/2007/scorecard/7.

43. Ibid.

44. Russia Federal Law on Communication, N 126-FZ, July 7, 2003, http://minkomsvjaz.ru/5878/7687.shtml.

45. The text of the law is at http://www.rg.ru/oficial/doc/federal_zak/126-03.shtm (in Russian). A few amendments were introduced in 2006: http://www.rg.ru/2006/07/27/svyaz.html.

46. Federal Law No. 152-FZ of July 27, 2006. See the text of the law at http://www.rg.ru/printable/2006/07/29/personaljnye-dannye-dok.html (in Russian). The law follows the Council of Europe Convention for the Protection of Individuals with Regard to Automatic Processing of Personal Data and incorporates it into national law. The Russian law provides for the establishment of a data protection authority, which, instead of being independent, is envisioned as an agency within the Ministry of Communications.

47. Federal Law No. 149-FZ of July 27, 2006. See the text of the law at http://www.rg.ru/2006/07/29/informacia-dok.html.

48. Ivan Pavlov, "Access to Information is Obstructed in Russia," Robert Amsterdam Blog, March 29, 2007, http://www.robertamsterdam.com/2007/03/ivan_pavlov_access_to_informat.htm.

49. No. 611 of May 12, 2004.

50. Federal Law on Mass Media No. 2124–1of 1991 with amendments of 1995, 2000, 2001, 2002, 2003, 2004, 2006, 2007. See http://www.rg.ru/1991/12/27/smi-zakon.html (in Russian).

51. Elena Kupriyanova, "Saity, kak Sredstva Massovoi Informatsii" [Sites as Means for Mass Information], *smi.ru*, February 12, 2008, http://www.smi.ru/08/02/12/908335250.html.

52. This number was determined based on the legal provision requiring registration for print media with a distribution of 1,000 or more copies per day.

53. *GZT.ru*, "Klevetnikam Rossii" [Slanderers of Russia], February 11, 2008, http://gzt.ru/society/2008/02/11/220201.html.

54. GIPP, "M. Seslavinskyi: 'Serieznyie Rossiiskie Internet Saityi Doljnyi Registrirovat Sebya kak Sredstva Massovoy Informacii'," ["M. Seslavinskyi: 'The Serious Russian Internet Sites Must Regis-

ter Themselves as Mass Media Outlets'"], September 28, 2004, http://www.gipp.ru/opennews.php ?id=3686.

55. As estimated by Rosokhrankultury. See Rosokhrankultury, "Intyernyet: Svobodniy i byez Rye-gistratsii" [Internet: Free and Without Registration], March 3, 2008, http://www.finmarket.ru/z/ nws/hotnews.asp?id=794793. Quoting the increased rate of voluntary registration, Rosokhrankul-tury (the regulatory federal agency) reasons against the proposed bill because it is not prepared to meet a large number of registrations. Rosokhrankultury, "Rossvyaz' Ohrankool' toori protiv Ofitsial'noy Ryegistratsii Saytov kak SMI" [Rosokhrankultury Against the Official Registration Sites as Media], March 12, 2008, http://www.rian.ru/society/20080312/101150561.html.

56. One such proposal was defeated in 2002, but the idea has resurfaced in a set of proposals known as Kroshennikov's amendments to existing laws.

57. *Lenta.ru*, "Genprokuratura Predlozhila Provaideram Razdelit' Vinu s Ekstremistami" [Prosecu-tor's Office Requested Providers to Share the Blame with Extremists], March 17, 2008, http://lenta .ru/news/2008/03/17/provider1/.

58. Law on Mass Media, translation (without amendments) at http://www.medialaw.ru/e_pages/ laws/russian/massmedia_eng/massmedia_eng.html.

59. A moderator of Fontanka.ru took down comments threatening migrants in Russia, saved them, and passed them on to authorities. Records traced the posts to an Internet café, where sur-veillance tapes made it possible to identify the poster. The poster was subsequently charged with threatening murder or infliction of grave injury under Article 119 of the criminal code. The court ruled that forum activity online is part of media activities and sentenced the poster to 18 months in prison.

60. Regnum, sued by a large dairy producer for defamation, claims that the information they used against the claimant was obtained from a regional authority for consumer protection, and thus protection under the Mass Media Law should be applied. The exception under Article 57 states that a mass media outlet should be absolved from liability when disseminating information that "does not conform to the reality and denigrates the honor and dignity of private citizens and organizations," in cases where inter alia the information was received from a public authority. As the court rejected the defense statement, it upheld censorship over the Internet in practice, according to the information outlet. Regnum, "Nasilstvennyi Zahvat Vlasti ili Nasilstvennoe Uder-janie Vlasti" [The Supreme Arbitration Court of Russia Instituted Review Proceedings on the Com-plaint Regnum], http://www.regnum.ru/news/933514.html.

61. A series of cartoons portraying the Prophet Mohammed were published in a Danish news-paper in late 2005. The cartoons were reprinted in several papers in early 2006, sparking riots throughout the Muslim world protesting the visual representation of Mohammed.

62. Article 319, Russian Federation Criminal Code with latest amendments as of 2007, http:// www.rg.ru/2007/11/12/ukrf-dok.html (in Russian). English translation without amendments is available at http://www.russian-criminal-code.com.

63. See the text of the law "O Protivodeystvii Eksstremistskoy Deyatelnosti" [Law against Extrem-ist Activities], http://www.rg.ru/oficial/doc/federal_zak/114-fz.shtm.

64. Interview with Sergey Smirnov, director, Human Rights Online, in Moscow, Russia (March 29, 2006); interview with Alexey Simonov, president, Glasnost Defense Foundation, in Moscow, Russia (March 27, 2006).

65. *Pingvinov.net*, " Bespredel v Runete. Kiberpolitseiskie Zakryvaiut Sportivnye Saity" [Lawlessness in Ru.net, Kiberpolitseyskie Closes Sports Web Sites], http://pingvinov.net/2007/09/25/Bespredel-v-Runete-Kiberpoliceiskie-zakryvajut-sportivnye-saity.html.

66. *CNews*, "Za Virtualnoe Oskorblenie Putina Dali Realnyi Srok" [For a Virtual Offence of Putin Was Given a Prison Sentence], November 1, 2008, http://internet.cnews.ru/news/top/index.shtml?2008/11/01/325760.

67. The text of the bill is published on the oppositional site Forum.msk.ru. See http://forum.msk.ru/material/lenty/433019.html.

68. Federal Law No. 144-FZ of August 12, 1995; amended in 1997, 1998, 1999, 2001, 2003, 2004, 2005, 2007.

69. Order No. 130 in July 2000 of the Ministry of Communications; see http://www.lenta.ru/internet/2000/08/21/sorm.

70. Jeanette Borzo, "Russian ISP Finds Court Victory Sometimes Is No Victory at All," *Wall Street Journal Interactive Edition*, http://www.libertarium.ru/libertarium/14424/def_article_t?PRINT_VIEW=YES.

71. Jeanette Borzo, "Russian ISP Finds Court Victory Sometimes Is No Victory at All," *Wall Street Journal Interactive Edition*, http://www.libertarium.ru/libertarium/14424/def_article_t?PRINT_VIEW=YES; Sharon LaFraniere, "Russian Spies, They've Got Mail," *Washington Post*, March 7, 2002, http://www.washingtonpost.com/wp-dyn/articles/A51550-2002Mar6.html.

72. Interview with Andrei Richter, Director, Media Law and Policy Institute, Moscow State University, in Moscow, Russia (March 28, 2006); interview with Alexey Simonov, President, Glasnost Defense Foundation, in Moscow, Russia (March 27, 2006).

73. Rafal Rohozinski, "How the Internet Did Not Transform Russia," *Current History* (2000) 58, 1: 334–338.

Tajikistan

Internet access in Tajikistan remains largely unrestricted, but emerging second-generation controls have threatened to erode these freedoms just as Internet penetration is starting to have an impact on political life in the country. In the run-up to the 2006 presidential elections, ISPs were asked to voluntarily censor access to an opposition Web site, and recently other second-generation controls have begun to emerge. Internet penetration remains low because of widespread poverty and the relatively high cost of Internet access.

Background

Tajikistan constitutional law gives the president unprecedented authority over the media. The incumbent president, Emomali Rahmon, who is presently in his third seven-year mandate,[1] suppresses opposition through prosecutions based on broad and inconsistent interpretations of Tajik laws.[2] Three of Tajikistan's eight political parties are represented in parliament, but few are politically active because of the increasingly authoritarian practices of the regime.[3]

RESULTS AT A GLANCE					
Filtering	No Evidence of Filtering	Suspected Filtering	Selective Filtering	Substantial Filtering	Pervasive Filtering
Political			•		
Social	•				
Conflict and security	•				
Internet tools	•				

Other Factors	Low	Medium	High	Not Applicable
Transparency	•			
Consistency	•			

KEY INDICATORS	
GDP per capita, PPP (constant 2005 international dollars)	1,657
Life expectancy at birth (years)	67
Literacy rate (percent of people age 15+)	100
Human development index (out of 179)	124
Rule of law (out of 211)	188
Voice and accountability (out of 209)	186
Democracy index (out of 167)	150 (Authoritarian regime)
Digital opportunity index (out of 181)	143
Internet users (percent of population)	6.6

Source by indicator: World Bank 2009a, World Bank 2009a, World Bank 2009a, UNDP 2008, World Bank 2009b, World Bank 2009b, Economist Intelligence Unit 2008, ITU 2007, Miniwatts Marketing Group 2009.

Government claims of an improving economic and political situation and investor confidence in the telecommunications and Internet market[4] are difficult to substantiate given that the majority of the population live below the poverty line.[5] The unemployment rate is high, and remittances from economic migrants form the backbone of the economy. According to World Bank statistics, in 2008 Tajikistan received USD 1.25 billion in remittances from workers abroad, while unofficial sources claim that this figure amounts to 60 percent of the country's GDP.[6]

Opposition parties are only beginning to explore the Internet's potential, in part owing to the low levels of Internet penetration throughout the country. None of the registered opposition parties have domain names registered in the ".tj" Internet zone, and only one party has its Web site available in Tajik.[7]

Internet in Tajikistan

The Internet in Tajikistan emerged as the country was ending a bloody civil war that followed the demise of Soviet rule in the early 1990s. The resulting fragmentation of power also meant that Internet services developed largely without state interference and the Ministry of Transport and Communications played a weak role in the development of the sector as a whole. Telecommunications remained fragmented up until the end of the 1990s, with several companies failing to interconnect because of fierce (and at times violent and armed) competition. During this period of instability, ISPs were aligned with feuding political and criminal interests that spilled over to the competition among the ISPs themselves.

Since the end of the civil war, the government has taken steps to attract investors and liberalize the sector prompted by expectations of accession to the WTO. However, important steps are still pending, such as the privatization of Tajiktelecom (the national operator) and the establishment of an independent regulatory authority.[8] In recent years, the telecommunications sector has boosted Tajikistan's GDP, and the number of licensed Internet and mobile operators has been increasing. In 2008, more than 180 companies were licensed in the ICT market.[9]

Internet penetration in Tajikistan is estimated at 6.6 percent (2008).[10] In 2009, the cost of accessing the Internet increased, further restricting development of the sector. Access costs of USD 73 per hour at Internet cafés and up to USD 300 for unlimited Wi-Fi traffic compare poorly with average wages of USD 35 per month and a minimum salary of USD 7 per month. The price for one hour of Internet access in Internet cafés is USD 0.73; unlimited monthly traffic by dial-up access costs USD 26.41; xDSL with capacity of 128/64 Kbps amounts to USD 200; and Wi-Fi unlimited traffic per month with the same capacity is USD 300.[11]

One respected Tajik NGO estimates that 1 percent of households own personal computers and that most people access the Internet from home by way of dial-up connections.[12] Access with DSL and wireless (Wi-Fi and WiMAX) technologies is limited by relatively high costs, and therefore restricted to a small number of commercial companies.

In 2009, there are ten main ISPs in Tajikistan actively providing Internet services to all major cities in the country.[13] The state-owned telecommunications company Tajiktelecom, which provides local, long-distance, and international telephone, mobile telephony, and Internet services, lost its unrivaled dominance of the telecoms market in 2007, when Babilon Mobile seized more than 30 percent of the market.

Tajikistan remains dependent on satellite-based connections, as the cost of fiber remains high—approximately 30 percent higher than using the same-capacity channel over VSAT. The country is connected to the Trans-Asia-Europe (TAE)[14] fiber optic high way passing through Uzbekistan, and a second connection is under construction to Kyrgyzstan. In part to overcome this bottleneck, both Tajiktelecom and Babilon-T have an ambitious plan to expand their fiber-optic infrastructure across the country and establish connections with China.[15]

The ISPs are reluctant to share information about their bandwidth because of the concern that the data would be used by their competitors to undermine their market position. They are also reluctant to discuss their international points of connection from which they buy bandwidth. The ONI data reveal that with the exception of TARENA (an educational network), all Tajik ISPs maintained two international points of access, one located in Russia and the other in Western Europe. Tajik providers are aggressive in adopting new technologies. Three of the operators, Babilon-T, Telecom Technology, and Eastera, provide a commercial Next Generation Network (NGN) service.[16]

In 2005, the Association of Tajik ISPs established a national Internet exchange point (IXP) that connected only four of the ten commercial ISPs (Babilon-T, Compuworld,

Eastera, and MKF Networks), as well as TARENA.[17] At the time of writing, the IXP is not operational as ISPs prefer to maintain bilateral peering connections between them.

Most Internet users are young and access the Internet through Internet cafés close to schools and universities. In January 2006, the Ministry of Transport and Communications estimated that some 400 Internet cafés, mostly concentrated in large cities, operated in the country. Many Internet cafés act as second-tier ISPs and buy their bandwidth from the first-level ISPs (i.e., main ISPs in the country with independent international connection). Recent changes in licensing regulations require Internet cafés operating as ISPs to obtain a license from the Ministry, a requirement which has brought about a decrease of the overall number of Internet cafés.[18]

Although more than 70 percent of the population resides in rural areas, Internet access is mainly restricted to urban areas because of poor infrastructure and low affordability. A 2005 study by the local Civil Initiative on Internet Policy (CIPI) shows a great disparity between the percentage of men accessing Internet (77.5) and that of women (22.5).[19] About 12 percent of users are secondary school students, with around 100 schools across the country connected to the Internet. The most active users are university students, employees of international organizations, commercial companies, and public sector institutions.

Tajik is the official national language. Nevertheless, Russian remains the most popular language for Internet use. According to data obtained from the national information portal (TopTJ.com), the top-ten most-visited Web sites in October 2007 were informational and analytical portals (AsiaPlus, Varorud, Watanweb, Ariana), a commercial bank, and entertainment sites. Other popular Web sites include mail.ru; popular research engines are rambler.ru, google.com, yahoo.com, and yandex.ru. Among Tajik youth, the most popular applications include instant messenger, followed by social networking sites (odnokassniki.ru, my.mail.ru), and online educational resources.

Local Tajik content on the Internet is poorly developed. Most Internet content is available in Russian, but the knowledge of Russian among the younger generation is gradually decreasing. A survey conducted among 342 students and professors from nine universities showed 60 percent of respondents saw the Internet as an informational and educational resource, but not as a means to create local information resources.[20]

The Tajik top-level domain name was registered with the Internet Assigned Numbers Authority (IANA) in 1997, but the domain name was later suspended because it was used mainly for registering pornography sites. In 2003, the domain name registration was delegated to the Information and Technical Center of the President of Tajikistan Administration, a state entity that now supervises registrations within the ".tj" domain.[21] Any operator that has a license for providing telecommunication services (including Internet) is eligible to act as a domain registrar. By January 19, 2008, 4,894 second-level domain names were registered within the ".tj" domain.[22]

Legal and Regulatory Frameworks

All Tajik ISPs operate under a license from the Tajik Ministry of Transport and Communication. Internet service providers are permitted to operate VoIP services under an IP-telephony license, although the ministry has introduced amendments that require VoIP providers to obtain a special license, presumably as a means to further regulate the sector.[23] In Tajikistan, P2P services are not popular, and the government has not shown ambitions to regulate them at this time.

The main state entities regulating the Internet in Tajikistan are the Security Council (SC), the ICT Council, and the MTC (an entity established in February 2007, replacing the former Ministry of Communications). The Communications and Informatization Department of the MTC is the main regulator in the telecommunications industry and is empowered to issue licenses for any related activities.[24] In 2003, the government adopted the Conception on Information Security,[25] which serves as a platform for proclaiming official views and policy directions to preserve state information security.

The president remains the key authority that ratifies the main legal documents in the IT sector and directs ICT policy in the country. The SC controls the implementation of the State Strategy on Information and Communication Technologies for Development of the Republic of Tajikistan (e-Strategy),[26] aimed at developing the information society and exploiting the country's ICT potential. The SC monitors telecommunications, including the Internet, for national security reasons. The ICT Council,[27] where the president sits as chairman alongside members of the government, is responsible for implementing and coordinating work under the e-Strategy and advising the president. However, although the council was established in February 2006, it has yet to be convened.

The government restricts the distribution of state secrets and other privileged data intending to "discredit the dignity and honor of the state and the President," or that which contains "violence and cruelty, racial, national and religious hostility ... pornography ... and any other information prohibited by law."[28] The provisions of this regulation are broad and allow state bodies wide discretion in their application. The control over information security is assigned to the Main Department of State Secrets and the Ministry of Security.

The lower chamber (Majlisi Namoyandagon) and the president ratified the Law on Changes and Amendments to the Criminal Code in June and July 2007, respectively. The changes introduced, inter alia, provisions on defamation (Article 135, part 2, Slander) and provisions on illegal collection and distribution of private data (Article 144, part 1). Defamation incurred over "mass media or Internet" is prosecuted according to local laws when it contains "intentional distribution via the Internet of knowingly false, libelous and insulting information, as well as expletive words and phrases which denigrate the dignity of human personality."

Tajikistan does not have an official policy on Internet filtering. However, state authorities have been known to restrict access to some Web sites at politically sensitive times by communicating their "recommendations" to all top-level ISPs—an example of second-generation controls. Prior to the 2006 presidential election, the government-controlled Communications Regulation Agency issued a "Recommendation on Filtering" that advised ISPs that, "for the purpose of information security," they should "engage in filtering and block access to Web sites that aim to undermine the state policy in the sphere of information."[29] As a result, several oppositional news Web sites hosted in Russia or Tajikistan were inaccessible to Tajik users for several days.[30] Although officials offered unclear reasons for shutting down the Web sites, independent media sources believe that the block list will grow in the future.[31]

Surveillance

Several government agencies possess the right to inspect ISPs' activities and premises, and require information on their users. The rights and obligations of ISPs in this regard are envisioned in the Annex to the "Internet Services Provision Rules within the Republic of Tajikistan" (herein referred to as the Rules). According to Section 4, paragraph 15, of the Rules, the provider is obliged to "render its activity in accordance with the current Rules" and "provide an easy access to its facilities for employees of the State Communications Inspectorate of the Ministry of Transport and Communications, Ministry of Security and other state agencies granted under the corresponding rules, provide on their demand information, for which they are authorized to ask and fulfill their instructions on time."

In 2006, the government signaled its intention to create an agency under the auspices of the Ministry of Transport and Communications that would control the ISP sector. All telecoms and ISPs were required to provide direct access to the state inspectorate in a manner similar to Russian surveillance legislation (SORM). In 2009, the high cost of the project as well as lobbying from telecom operators halted its realization.[32]

ONI Testing Results

In 2007 and 2008, the OpenNet Initiative tested in Tajikistan on four key ISPs: Babilon-T, Eastera, Tajiktelecom, and TARENA. Testing in Tajikistan yielded no evidence of Internet filtering. This extends to pornographic content, and with the exception of TARENA (which services schools and universities), the major ISPs do not filter such content on the backbone level. However, accessing pornographic content at Internet cafés is illegal. Any persons caught accessing such content is subject to a fine ranging from USD 15 to USD 100, and violators may be criminally prosecuted. The ONI's investigation concluded that currently most Internet cafés do not filter access to pornographic content. However, they do employ monitoring software that notifies them when a client is attempting to retrieve such content.

Conclusion

The Tajik government has adopted an e-strategy aimed at developing an information society and employing ICT potential for spurring economic growth. At the same time it does not seek to encourage independent online publishers, journalists, and bloggers. Media freedom is widely challenged and subject to de facto censorship, although the constitution provides that "state censorship and prosecution for criticism are forbidden."[33] State filtering is unlikely to be officially supported as ISPs remain independent, often linked to political or criminal interests with influence within state bodies. Tajikistan is also dependent on international aid, which has some influence over the direction of state policy in this sector, although this may change as Tajikistan moves closer to the Shanghai Cooperation Organization (discussed further below). The Tajik government, however, has in place policies and instruments to maintain firm control over the distribution of information, particularly before elections. The government is engaged in developing programs aimed at restricting citizens' Internet access, following on from President Rahmon's message that "Western values aren't always applicable" to Eastern countries.[34]

Future tendencies on the political agenda include the increasing role of regional organizations such as the Shanghai Cooperation Organization and the Eurasian Economic Union, which may lead to a harmonization of more repressive laws. This possibility combined with the regime's authoritarian tendencies may lead to the emergence of further second-generation controls (especially event-driven filtering and legal restrictions on categories of content).

Notes

1. Joanna Lillis, "Tajikistan: No Surprises in Presidential Elections," *Eurasia Insight*, November 6, 2006, http://www.eurasianet.org/departments/insight/articles/eav110606a.shtml; *Deutsche Welle*, "Nigora Buhari-zade, "Oppositsionery v Tajikistane Protestuyut" [The Opposition Raises Protests], August 29, 2006, http://www.dw-world.de/dw/article/0,2144,2150509,00.html.

2. In 2005, the State Licensing Commission formally denied BBC a license, basing its argumentations on a complex interpretation of the Law on Licensing Certain Types of Activities. In addition, in 2005 the leader of the main opposition party, Iskandarov, was convicted on terrorism and corruption charges and sentenced to a 23-year prison term. See *Eurasia Insight*, "Tajik Government 'Tightening the Screws' on Independent Media," August 25, 2006, http://www.eurasianet.org/departments/insight/articles/eav082506a.shtml.

3. Massoumeh Torfeh,"Tajikistan: Opposition Disorganized as Presidential Election Nears," *Radio Free Europe/Radio Liberty*, August 24, 2006, http://www.rferl.org/featuresarticle/2006/08/ce926b40-a58f-4215-8171-025bd977ebce.html.

4. Tajikistan State Statistics Committee, "Makroekomicheskie Pokasately 2004–2005" [Macroeconomic Indicators 2004–2005], http://www.stat.tj/russian/macroeconomic_indicators1.htm.

5. *NBCentralAsia*, "Migrant Workers Rescue Families from Poverty," September 14, 2007, http://www.iwpr.net/?p=btj&s=b&o=338726&apc_state=henb; European Bank for Reconstruction and Development, *Investments 1991–2007 Tajikistan*, http://www.ebrd.com/country/country/taji/sign.pdf.

6. Konstantin Parshin, "Tajikistan: World Bank Cautions Dushanbe against Tough Economic Times Ahead," *EurasiaNet*, November 13, 2008, http://www.eurasianet.org/departments/insightb/articles/eav111308a.shtml.

7. "Narodno-Demokraticheskaya Partiya Tajikistana Popolnila Svoy Web Resours" [People's Democratic Party of Tajikistan has Boosted Its Online Capacity], *SNGnews*, http://sngnews.ru/frame_article/5/67577.html (accessed May 21, 2009).

8. Privatization of Tajiktelecom has been planned for several years. The last target was the end of 2007, but the government did not meet it.

9. Data from the Main Department on Communications and Informatization of the Ministry of Transport and Communication, April 2008.

10. Miniwatts Marketing Group, "Internet World Statistics: Tajikistan," 2009, http://internetworldstats.com/asia.htm#tj.

11. State Statistics Committee, http://www.stat.tj; Internet access tariffs of ISP Intercom, http://www.intercom.tj; ISP Babilon-T, http://www.tojikiston.com.

12. Internews Network, http://www.khoma.tj.

13. A joint Tajik-American company, TACOM, stopped providing Internet service in the summer of 2006 but it is still a licensee.

14. TAE: Trans-Asia-Europe Fiber Optic Communications Line project envisions the laying of a 27,000-kilometer global telecommunications cable through 20 countries from Frankfurt to Shanghai.

15. A potential investor in this endeavor is the Chinese Development Bank.

16. In 2005, Tajiktelecom became the first when it contracted ZTE Corporation to install Central Asia's first commercial NGN.

17. Public Fund Civil Initiative on Internet Policy (CIPI), http://www.cipi.tj/.

18. Data from the Main Department on Communications and Informatization of the Ministry of Transport and Communication, April 2008.

19. CIPI, http://www.cipi.tj/.

20. Survey conducted in 2008 by Public Fund Centre of ICT (http://www.centreict.tj/) in partnership with CIPI.

21. See the Tajikistani TLD hosting organization, Information and Technical Centre of the President of Tajikistan Administration, http://www.nic.tj.

22. Ibid.

23. See the Ministry of Communications, http://www.mincom.tj, and the Law on Electronic Telecommunications adopted on May 3, 2002.

24. The government had earlier plans to create an independent regulatory authority. This goal was not accomplished, and instead the Communications Regulatory Agency, which remained under government control during the years of its operation, was set up in 2005.

25. The "Conception" was ratified by Presidential Decree No. 1175 of November 2003.

26. The "e-Strategy" was ratified by Presidential Decree No. 1174 of November 2003.

27. The ICT Council was established by Presidential Decree No. 1707 of February 27, 2006.

28. Points 2 and 3 of Regulation No. 389 of the government from August 8, 2001, On Creating a Republican Network of Data Transfer and Measures to Order Access to Global Information Networks (unofficial translation from Russian).

29. Recommendation on Filtering sent to ISPs by the Communications Regulatory Agency (unofficial translation), obtained by ONI researchers. December 2006.

30. *Deutsche Welle*, "V Tajikistane Zajroyut Dustup k Oppositsionnim Jurnalistskim Sitam" [Access to Opposition Media Web Sites is Blocked in Tajikistan], October 8, 2006, http://www.dw -world.de/dw/article/0,2144,2198763,00.html; *Fergana News*, "Ozvucheny Adresa Websitov Ofitsialno Zablokirovannykh v Tajikistane—Ferghana.ru Sredi Nikh" [The Web Sites Officially Blocked in Tajikistan were Announced: Among Them—Ferghana.ru], October 9, 2006, http://www .ferghana.ru/news.php?id=3633&mode=snews.

31. *SNGnews*, "Internet Service Providers in Tajikistan are Prepared for Filtering of 'Unsafe' Web Sites," http://sngnews.ru/articles/5/68051.html (accessed May 3, 2007).

32. Paul Budde Communication Pty., Ltd., "Tajikistan—Telecoms Market Overview and Statistics," July 2007.

33. Article 30 of the Constitution of the Republic of Tajikistan, 1994.

34. Joanna Lillis, "Tajikistan: No Surprises in Presidential Elections," *Eurasia Insight*, November 6, 2006, http://www.eurasianet.org/departments/insight/articles/eav110606a.shtml.

Turkmenistan

Turkmenistan ranks among the most repressive and closed societies in the world. The Internet is heavily regulated and available only to a small fraction of the population. Among the countries of the CIS, it has the lowest penetration rate of Internet access and the highest degree of first-generation controls. Censorship is ubiquitous and extensive. Surveillance is significant, and the few citizens who benefit from access to the Internet are closely monitored by state agencies.

Background

A Central Asian republic with a population of around 5 million and land area of 488,100 square kilometers,[1] Turkmenistan is a country rich in natural gas and oil resources.[2] The government has undertaken efforts to develop the gas and cotton industry but has failed to encourage development in other economic sectors.

Turkmenistan was a closed society under the proclaimed "President for Life," Saparmurat Niyazov.[3] To nourish his personality cult, Niyazov—in power for 15 years—frequently rotated, dismissed, or brought charges against government officials and

RESULTS AT A GLANCE					
Filtering	No Evidence of Filtering	Suspected Filtering	Selective Filtering	Substantial Filtering	Pervasive Filtering
Political					•
Social			•		
Conflict and security			•		
Internet tools			•		

Other Factors	Low	Medium	High	Not Applicable
Transparency	•			
Consistency			•	

KEY INDICATORS	
GDP per capita, PPP (constant 2005 international dollars)	4,677
Life expectancy at birth (years)	63
Literacy rate (percent of people age 15+)	100
Human development index (out of 179)	108
Rule of law (out of 211)	195
Voice and accountability (out of 209)	205
Democracy index (out of 167)	165 (Authoritarian regime)
Digital opportunity index (out of 181)	139
Internet users (percent of population)	1.4

Source by indicator: World Bank 2009a, World Bank 2009a, World Bank 2009a, UNDP 2008, World Bank 2009b, World Bank 2009b, Economist Intelligence Unit 2008, ITU 2007, Miniwatts Marketing Group 2009.

judicial representatives to create a situation of permanent instability in the society.[4] The death of Niyazov in December 2006 brought about a glimmer of hope for those pining for reform.[5] In February 2007, Gurbanguly Berdymukhamedov won the country's largely symbolic presidential elections. The post-Niyazov transition was surprisingly smooth, with Berdymukhamedov promptly securing support from the most important behind-the-scenes players, whom he then removed once becoming president. During the time of Niyazov, the president headed both the legislative and judicial branches of the state. Berdymukhamedov pledged to introduce democratic reforms and separation of powers. In September 2008, a new constitution entered into force that dissolved the People's Council (the highest representative body, which included parliament and cabinet members) and divided its powers between the president and the new 125-member parliament.

During Niyazov's rule, all opposition parties were banned. Dissenters were harassed or exiled, and a small and weakened opposition existed either underground or abroad.[6] By contrast, the new constitution promotes multiparty politics, thus formally legalizing opposition. However, in the 2008 parliamentary elections, the Democratic Party—the current ruling party—was the only one registered to participate. The leaders of the main political opposition parties—the Social and Political Movement of Watan and the Turkmenistan Republican Party—continue to reside abroad to avoid potential repression.

The people of Turkmenistan were positive about some of the reforms promised by Berdymukhamedov, including reinstating the recently abolished ten-year mandatory period of education, reversing measures aimed at denying pensions for the elderly, and guaranteeing Internet access to all.[7]

The ethnic composition of the population is Turkmen (85 percent), Russian (7 percent), Uzbek (5 percent), and other minorities (3 percent).[8] The largest percentage of the population shares orthodox Turkmen and Islamic values (89 percent), although Muslim traditions have been, to some extent, modulated by local customs and the country's Soviet past. Important factors in determining one's position in the Turkmen society remain kinship, regional links, and tribal affiliation. The state traditionally marginalizes ethnic and religious groups. Except for officially recognized Sunni Muslim and Russian Orthodox denominations, religious activities are severely limited. Religious congregations are required to register with the government to gain legal status.[9]

Internet Infrastructure

The telecommunications sector in Turkmenistan is developing slowly, encumbered by heavy government subsidies of basic services, contradictory procedures for obtaining licenses, and low levels of foreign investment.[10] In the late 1990s, two German companies, Siemens and Alcatel, were approved by the government to develop the telecommunications system. In addition, the TurkmenTelecom Company and the U.S.-based Verizon have agreed to provide Turkmenistan with direct access to the Internet.[11] Chinese telecommunication companies, financially supported by the Chinese government, have also entered the market. According to the U.S. Embassy in Turkmenistan, prior to 2004 there were no broadband fixed wireless service providers in the country, and the difficulties involved in obtaining operating licenses from the Ministry of Communications made the involvement of foreign companies impossible.[12]

Since the emergence of the Internet, the government has sought to establish complete control of the Internet to avoid any potential threat that unmonitored access may pose to the regime. In 2001, the largest ISP, Arlana, struggled to survive for months while appealing the revocation of its license. It continued to provide free Internet access to NGOs until the government finally closed it down. Thereafter, only the state-run provider, TurkmenTelecom, continued operations. Under the former administration, there was very little public Internet access. It was available only to those who could afford to pay USD 8 per hour at the few hotels catering to foreigners and less than ten public access points in the country, all sponsored by foreign aid programs. Private use was restricted to a few foreign-owned businesses that could acquire two-way satellites or the few USD 1,000 a month DSL lines, a few dozen universities and institutions connected through the NATO-established Virtual Silk Highway project, and a small number of local individuals and businesses that managed to acquire dial-up access accounts.[13]

There is only one legal provider of Internet in Turkmenistan, the official government body, TurkmenTelecom. All channels pass through TurkmenTelecom's central hub, and all are thoroughly monitored by the security services. TurkmenTelecom offers a small range of service connections for individuals and organizations, all of which are officially limited to the holder of the account. It remains illegal for a private organization, for-profit or otherwise, to open an Internet café. Should an organization manage to acquire a dial-up account, it would be presented with a contract obligating it to use the account solely for private personal use and not to share it with anyone. Those in breach of the rules are sanctioned.

In order to receive Internet access, users must register with TurkmenTelecom by submitting a declaration and their passport. In addition, TurkmenTelecom warns users on its Web site that the Internet is not a "place for unconsidered behavior." Accordingly, users have to refrain from undertaking a wide array of broadly defined activities when they are online—for example, posting materials containing foul language, showing "inappropriate behavior" online, posting information that conflicts with the standard norms of behavior and legislation, and uploading pornographic materials.[14] The contract signed by the operator and user contains even more restrictions, such as a ban on accessing Web sites that contain violent content and Web sites that disseminate "untruthful and defamatory information" (a definition that includes opposition Web sites). If, after a warning, a user insists on accessing forbidden Web sites, the operator shuts down his or her Internet service. Users are liable for any actions that might cause damage to the government or "anyone else."

Foreign aid organizations and expensive hotels continue to provide Internet access, though there is consensus among users that the speed of connections provided by TurkmenTelecom has declined over the last two years. These organizations and hotels, as a self-imposed measure, filter some opposition and freedom-of-expression Web sites. They defend such policies as necessary in order for them to continue providing Internet services. Their activities, as well as those of their patrons, continue to be monitored by the authorities.

Similar self-censorship behavior has been observed in schools. After Niyazov's death, the new president promised to install Internet access in every school and demanded that no new school or kindergarten be opened without Internet access.[15] This massive state computerization program led to the purchase of thousands of computers for the country's schools. However, lack of training in ICT among teachers and remaining fears among administrators that access to the Internet may lead to repression have left many of the computer rooms locked.

The results of the computerization program have been far more modest than the rhetoric behind it, and the country has largely failed to implement policies guaranteeing free and accessible Internet. The president legalized Internet cafés in 2007, but they continue to number only a few, are not advanced technologically, and are closely monitored by the state security service.[16] Since February 2007, 15 TurkmenTelecom-operated Internet cafés have been opened in the country's six largest cities.[17] Their hours of operation were limited to normal government business hours, and the price in 2007 was set at about USD 4 per hour (at this time the average salary in Turkmenistan was less than USD 100 a month).[18] All Internet café users are required to present a passport, and their activities are recorded and logs are sent to a government server.

Nearly two years after the transition several of the 15 official access points were closed, and all have suffered repeated service outages and closures. In 2007, President Berdymukhamedov reprimanded the minister of communications for the high prices at Internet cafés.[19] As a consequence, access prices dropped by more than 60 percent, and Internet access at Internet cafés now costs around USD 2. Aside from the obvious submission to monitoring inherent in presenting one's passport, Internet cafés are staffed mostly by youth; furthermore, anyone who uses an Internet café is mindful of what he or she accesses. Nevertheless, administrators report that most Internet cafés receive only up to ten visitors a day.

Contact with the outside world is still difficult in Turkmenistan. Prices for home access to the Internet are steep, creating an additional economic barrier to widespread Internet use. Thus, the Internet largely remains a privilege to those working for foreign companies, the government, and, in a small number of cases, those studying or working at universities. International organizations are trying to improve the local climate by providing regional centers and administrations with modern computer equipment and Internet access, as well as establishing satellite connections of Turkmen science centers to the worldwide network.[20]

In March 2008, the official government Web site Turkmenistan.ru announced that TurkmenTelecom was finally offering dial-up home Internet connection to the public. The rates were set at USD 42 to open an account, a flat USD 5 per month fee, and USD 4 per hour for browsing, with speeds of 45 Kbps.[21] These rates are unaffordable for the vast majority of the population and more than six times higher than in neighboring Uzbekistan. New leased lines were also to be connected starting immediately, at high monthly rates of USD 1,000–USD 2,000.

Internet use in the CIS region has increased significantly in the last several years in all countries except for Turkmenistan. Various attempts at measuring Internet penetration have posited that between 0.17 and 4 percent of the population use the Internet, with ITU estimates being 1.4 percent.[22] Notwithstanding the low level of penetration, the number of users has increased significantly since the offer of home Internet access. Fixed-line penetration is less than 10 percent, with negligible broadband. Permission has now been given for broadband national WiMAX frequencies. There are fewer than 500 Web sites hosted in the country under the top-level domain ".tm," more than half by a foreign-funded development project. The rest consist almost entirely of official Web sites of government entities. Nearly 95 percent of regular Internet users are in the capital, Ashgabat.

There are two mobile operators in the country. Atlyn Asyr is wholly controlled by the state, with roughly 160,000 subscribers. In November 2007, MTS, a Russian mobile service provider (100 percent privately owned), began offering GPRS/EDGE service to its corporate clients in Turkmenistan. In May 2008, the same service was offered to individual users for USD 50/Mbit plus a one-time fee of USD 5. As of 2008, MTS had around 500,000 users in Turkmenistan.[23] The service provided by MTS is considerably cheaper than TurkmenTelecom's: it costs USD 5 to connect (one-time fee); 1 MB is 58 cents (day) and 29 cents (night). For users who live in rural areas where fixed lines are not modernized, MTS remains the only option to connect to the Internet. Interestingly, MTS's introduction of GPRS Internet seems not to have been supported by the government, and the service was never announced in official media. The price is still quite high for most users, the service slow and unreliable, and Internet traffic still monitored and filtered through TurkmenTelecom. Focusing on GPRS, however, would herald a leap forward in public access to the Internet, bypassing the high-cost infrastructure of land and telephone lines. If the state does not encourage the establishment of independent networks, however, the service could remain slow, expensive, and unreliable, and will most likely remain filtered.[24]

Turkmenistan recently sold the rights of administration of top-level ".tm" domains to a U.S.-based contractor. Foreign companies are willing to pay high prices for ".tm" domain names because the abbreviation evokes the term "trademark." The vast majority of Turkmenistan-based Web sites are within second-level domains of international or official government bureaus, such as ".gov.tm" or ".edu.tm."

Legal and Regulatory Frameworks

The president and the Cabinet of Ministers are the policymakers in the communications sector. The Ministry of Communications implements policy; it is the sector's regulator, issuing licenses to operators, approving tariffs, and carrying out investigations to ensure that operators conform to all laws and regulations. The ministry supervises eight bodies in the post and telecommunications sectors: TurkmenTelecom (fixed operator), Ashgabat City Network, Altyn Asyr (GSM), TV Radio/TV Broadcasting, Spectrum Administration, Turkmenistan Post, Special Delivery service (Postal), and Training Center. The deputy chairman of the Cabinet of Ministers oversees the work of the ministry and the minister of communications reports directly to him.[25]

The role of the sector minister in controlling the state operator is de facto marginal as the general director of TurkmenTelecom reports directly to the Cabinet of Ministers without referring to the minister. The Internet market is strictly controlled by the Cabinet of Ministers, and receiving an Internet license entails close monitoring of all providers' commercial activities. Each license is for a period of three years, and there are more than 30 different license types in the communications sector. It is anticipated that revisions will be introduced to the Law on Communications (2000), which would provide easier conditions for new technologies to enter the market. President Berdymukhamedov has encouraged some liberalization in the market by allowing alternative Internet operators to apply for licenses. In fact, by law, the state operator does not enjoy exclusive rights. Nonetheless, TurkmenTelecom remains the only ISP in the market with a valid license to operate. The tariffs are set by the operators themselves, while the ministry reviews the tariff proposals when granting the license.

According to existing rules, when an alternative ISP or broadband provider expresses an interest in using an incumbent operator's network, an inspection commission is formed to investigate the operator's proposal. However, as yet, no alternative provider is known to have applied to provide such services.[26]

Although both the old and the new constitutions guarantee freedom of expression and free dissemination of information, the government largely controls all media outlets (television, press, and radio). The Turkmen television is state-owned and provides four channels. Channel One, or ORT, broadcasts of Russian television are restricted to only two hours per day and rarely broadcast live. Any reference related to the Soviet past, erotic topics, prostitution, alcoholism, or drug addiction is removed from movies and soap operas.[27] Foreign television stations and radio are accessible only to the handful of people who have satellite dishes or shortwave radios. The press is controlled by the government, and even the nominally independent newspapers *Adalat* and *Galkynysh* were created by decrees of the former president. Other government-approved newspapers are *Turkmenistan* (published in Turkmen) and *Neutral Turkmenistan* (in Russian).

Publishing houses and photocopying establishments have to receive registration licenses from the government before starting their operations.[28] State media employees cannot establish contacts freely with foreign media.

The lack of mechanisms guaranteeing media freedom, the extensive provisions sanctioning libel and defamation in the Criminal Code, and the broad provisions related to terrorist activities in the Law on Terrorism[29] have imposed total self-censorship on Turkmen society under the former and current governments. Article 132 of the Criminal Code makes libel by way of channels of mass information punishable by fines, up to two years of forced labor, or up to one year in prison. Article 133 of the Criminal Code provides for similar sanctions for certain insults against government agents (who are defined as anyone who permanently or temporarily represents a branch of the government). Article 176 of the Criminal Code seeks to protect the president. Under part 1, any attempts on the life or health of the president are punishable by imprisonment for life or death. Part 2 of this article provides for a prison term of up to five years for libel directed against the president. No specific mention is made of mass media—libel in any form can lead to charges.[30] Libel charges are usually used to arrest journalists, and there is always a danger of false charges being laid for crimes such as embezzlement.

As reported by Radio Free Europe, during the previous regime most of the trials of journalists, government opponents, or any person who was considered a "threat" to the regime were held in secrecy.[31] Under Niyazov, repression of dissenters in Turkmenistan often involved beatings, threats, and arrests.[32] The current president has granted amnesty to many dissidents and journalists who were jailed by the Niyazov regime.[33] However, in spite of the few positive steps taken by President Berdymukhamedov, media groups continue to place Turkmenistan among the "ten worst countries to be a blogger" because of the lack of guarantees for freedom of expression.[34]

Surveillance

In Turkmenistan, few users with access to the Internet are able to read English. Accordingly, only information in Russian disseminated on the Internet might raise serious concerns for the regime. Nonetheless, the preferred method of limiting information on the Internet is simply blocking undesirable content. Such a policy, documented during Niyazov's reign, is still in place.

Reporters Without Borders has declared Turkmenistan, along with Belarus and Uzbekistan, an "Enemy of the Internet," because of a combination of monitoring Internet browsing, filtering Web content, imprisonment, harassment, and the prevention of the posting of political materials.[35]

The Turkmen government maintains tight control on the flow of information through the official mass media. Any dissident criticizing the lack of expression and tight censorship is likely to be included in the government-held blacklist, which can restrict the right to travel abroad.[36] Authorities remain hostile to religious sects, and unregistered religious groups are still not allowed to perform religious activities. The government is also engaged in a long-standing practice of deporting citizens belonging to different religious sects.[37] There has been no stark change in the monitoring and interception of communications over the last two years. Sensitive issues such as discrimination against women, terrorism, religious extremism, and separatism are still censored by the government. Because of the overall restrictive climate, people commit themselves to broad self-censorship.

There are reports that Turkmenistan's security services have put into place a system for Internet surveillance of all ISPs throughout the country.[38] The OpenNet Initiative suspects that an automatic Internet surveillance and filtering system based on deep-packet-inspection technology has been installed on TurkmenTelecom routers. Since all incoming and outgoing information passes through TurkmenTelecom systems, Internet traffic can easily be intercepted. Any traffic can be monitored by authorities, and certain preselected Web sites containing information that could be harmful to the regime are filtered. Other reports confirm that users can be identified if they send encrypted messages and materials containing certain keywords, such as the president's name.[39]

ONI Testing Results

In 2008, OpenNet Initiative testing was conducted in Turkmenistan on a direct land-line connection to TurkmenTelecom. The tests detected substantial filtering of local and regional media and freedom-of-expression Web sites. Significantly, Azeri media sites, including a popular multimedia site with an ".az" extension and an Azeri Web site targeting corrupt officials, were blocked. The ONI revealed targeted filtering on a number of other Web sites including those covering local and international women's rights, human rights, and narcotics, and one Web site containing information about religious beliefs. An environmental site and a P2P site were also blocked. In addition, a number of pornographic and gambling sites were blocked. The ONI also observed reverse filtering of U.S. military domains.[40]

Conclusion

The former Turkmen president exercised strict control over Turkmen society and media, and restricted any information inconsistent with his widely propagandized policies. The current president has pledged to seek a more lenient approach to leading the country, but much still remains to be done. The scope of sensitive issues in Turkmenistan continues to be broad and may involve any criticism of the regime or independent opinion. Few citizens have access to the Internet, and most continue to fear censorship and other unpredictable centralized methods of control. Until liberalization of the Internet market occurs, such measures will continue to be a concern for most Internet users in the country. The few international organizations providing Internet access practice self-censorship in order to protect their staff and their diplomatic position. With so few users of the Internet and the massive risks facing any advocates of freedom of speech, the government continues to hold the future of the Internet in Turkmenistan entirely in its hands.

Notes

1. World Bank, *World Development Indicators 2007*, http://ddp-ext.worldbank.org/ext/ddpreports/ViewSharedReport?&CF=&REPORT_ID=9147&REQUEST_TYPE=VIEWADVANCED.

2. Turkmenistan holds one of the world's largest gas fields. See Energy Information Administration, "Turkmenistan Energy Profile," September 16, 2009, http://tonto.eia.doe.gov/country/country_energy_data.cfm?fips=TX.

3. *BBC News*, "Turkmen Go Back to Old Calendar," April 24, 2008, http://news.bbc.co.uk/2/hi/asia-pacific/7365346.stm.

4. Bruce Pannier, "Turkmenistan: President Reshuffles Government Once Again," Radio Free Europe/Radio Liberty, January 27, 2006, http://www.rferl.org/featuresarticle/2006/1/9C5105E8 -18E7-4F3B-806A-C04A4B981234.html.

5. *BBC News*, "Turkmen Go Back to Old Calendar," April 24, 2008, http://news.bbc.co.uk/2/hi/ asia-pacific/7365346.stm.

6. The BBC concluded that during the last elections no opposition party participated. See Monica Whitlock, "Turkmenistan Poll Turnout 'Low,'" *BBC News*, December 20, 2004, http://news.bbc .co.uk/2/hi/asia-pacific/4110669.stm.

7. *BBC News*, "New Turkmen Leader Is Inaugurated," February 14, 2007, http://news.bbc.co.uk/ 2/hi/asia-pacific/6359569.stm; *BBC News* "Turkmenistan Takes Reformist Step," September 26, 2008, http://news.bbc.co.uk/1/hi/world/asia-pacific/7638102.stm.

8. Embassy of Turkmenistan, Washington, DC, "Government and Politics," http://www .turkmenistanembassy.org/turkmen/gov/gov.html. The official data differ from outside estimations.

9. Amnesty International, "Turkmenistan: The Clampdown on Dissent and Religious Freedom Continues," May 2, 2005, http://web.amnesty.org/library/Index/ENGEUR610032005.

10. The Trans-Asia-Europe fiber-optic line connects Turkmenistan with Uzbekistan and Iran, but the Turkmen-Azerbaijan segment has not yet been constructed. See Business Intelligence Service for the Newly Independent States (BISNIS), "Turkmenistan, Overview of Fiber Optic Telecommunications Network Development," May 22, 2003, http://www.bisnis.doc.gov/bisnis/bisdoc/ 030523txtelecom.htm.

11. U.S. Commercial Service, "Country Commercial Guide," 2000, http://www.buyusainfo.net/ info.cfm?id=93034&keyx=F5F18DBA66F19E220744BD4ECF249FD5&dbf=ccg1&loadnav=no& archived=no&addid=.

12. Foreign companies such as Siemens and Alcatel (Germany), NEC (Japan), and Huawei (China) usually work as subcontractors on government-sponsored projects. See Business Intelligence Service for the Newly Independent States (BISNIS), "Turkmenistan: Overview of the Wireless Communctions Network," March, 2004, http://www.bisnis.doc.gov/bisnis/bisdoc/ 040319TXWrlsComm.htm.

13. Ron Synowitz, "World: Rights Group Lists 'Enemies of the Internet' at UN Summit," Radio Free Europe/Radio Liberty, November 15, 2005, http://www.rferl.org/featuresarticle/2005/11/ 2FDBA63A-153A-4268-AF4B-E6EBCF54E9EF.html.

14. TurkmenTelecom, http://www.online.tm.

15. *Newsru*, "President Turkmenii Reshil Otkyt Dustup k Internetu v Kazhdom Detskom Sadu" [The President of Turkmenistan Decided to Provide Every Kindergarten with Internet Access], April 15, 2008, http://www.newsru.com/world/15apr2008/turkmen.html.

16. *Chrono-tm*, "Paradoksy Razvitiya Interneta v Turkmenistane" [Paradoxical Internet Development in Turkmenistan], June 4, 2008, http://www.chrono-tm.org/?025104416200000000000011000000.

17. *Chrono-tm*, "Internet ne Proshel" [Internet Did Not Come Through], May 11, 2008, http://www.chrono-tm.org/?025104407200000000000001100000.

18. *USA Today*, "A Crack in the Isolation of Turkmenistan: Internet Cafés," February 16, 2007, http://www.usatoday.com/news/world/2007-02-16-turkmenistan_x.htm.

19. Reuters India "Turkmen Leader Sacks Official over Bad Internet," May 20, 2008, http://in.reuters.com/article/technologyNews/idINIndia-33671420080520.

20. The organizations promoting these projects are the Organization for Security and Cooperation in Europe and NATO.

21. Farangis Najibullah, "Turkmenistan: Wireless Internet Hints at End to State Monopoly," EurasiaNet, June 21, 2008, http://www.eurasianet.org/departments/insight/articles/pp062108.

22. International Telecommunication Union (ITU), "Internet Indicators: Subscribers, Users, and Broadband Subscribers," 2008, http://www.itu.int/ITU-D/icteye/Reporting/ShowReportFrame.aspx ?ReportName=/WTI/InformationTechnologyPublic&RP_intYear=2008&RP_intLanguageID=1.

23. *Turkmenistan.ru*, "MTS Podlklychila Turkmenov k Internetu" [MTS Connected Turkmens to the Internet], April 18, 2008, http://www.turkmenistan.ru/?page_id=3&lang_id=ru&elem_id=12590 &type=event&sort=date_desc.

24. Abdulmugamid, "Internet Metamorphoses in Turkmenistan," *NewEurasia*, May 2, 2008, http://www.neweurasia.net/media-and-internet/internet-metamorphoses-in-turkmenistan/.

25. European Bank for Reconstruction and Development, *Comparative Assessment of the Telecommunications Sector in the Transition Countries. Assessment Report Turkmenistan*, December 2008, http://www.ebrd.com/country/sector/law/telecoms/assess/turkmen.pdf.

26. Ibid.

27. *Ferghana.Ru Information Agency*, "Censorship in Turkmenistan: Outright Lunacy," May 18, 2005, http://enews.ferghana.ru/detail.php?id=703673619153.75,823,18180166.

28. U.S. Department of State, "Turkmenistan," http://www.state.gov/g/drl/rls/hrrpt/2005/61681.htm.

29. Unofficial English translation of the Law at http://turkmeniya.tripod.com/turkmenistanlaws/id13.html.

30. Criminal Code of Turkmenistan.

31. Gulnoza Saidazimova, "Central Asia: Rights Group Says Region Suffering after Andijon," Radio Free Europe/Radio Liberty, May 23, 2006, http://www.rferl.org/featuresarticle/2006/5/3CA525C2-D1D1-490B-8985-494F72A25EE5.html.

32. Turkmen dissident writer Rahim Esenov was put in jail in 2004 after refusing to edit his book to Niyazov's liking. Radio Free Europe/Radio Liberty, "RSF: Turkmenistan Should Release RFE/RL Journalists," March 4, 2004, http://www.rferl.org/featuresarticle/2004/3/5C962852-4C09-45C7 -B64C-1340B28704E1.html.

33. Radio Free Europe/Radio Liberty, "Turkmen President Signs Decree on Amnesty," May 25, 2009, http://www.rferl.org/content/Turkmen_President_Signs_Decree_On_Amnesty/1732552.html.

34. Radio Free Europe/Radio Liberty, "Groups Says Iran, Turkmenistan among '10 Worst Countries to Be a Blogger,'" May 1, 2009, http://www.rferl.org/content/Group_Says_Iran_Turkmenistan _Among_10_Worst_Countries_To_Be_A_Blogger/1619910.html.

35. Reporters Without Borders, "First Online Free Expression Day Launched on Reporters Without Borders Website," December 3, 2008, http://www.rsf.org/article.php3?id_article=26086.

36. UNIAN News Agency, "Press Freedom Deteriorated in Europe," May 3, 2006, http://www .unian.net/eng/news/news-153773.html.

37. Felix Corley, "Forum 18," http://www.forum18.org/Archive.php?query=&religion=all&country =32&results=10 and http://www.forum18.org/Archive.php?article_id=1293.

38. Turkmenistan Helsinki Foundation for Human Rights, http://www.tmhelsinki.org/en/ modules/news/article.php?storyid=3310.

39. Ibid.

40. Reverse filtering occurs on the Web server hosting the content, as opposed to at a point along the way of the traffic flow, and is based on restricting requests based on geographical location of the originating Internet Protocol address. Copyright holders who want to restrict access to their content in certain markets often use reverse filtering. Examples include hulu.com, BBC.com, and other sites that syndicate commercial video and audio content that is subject to licensing. The ONI has detected that many U.S. military sites are inaccessible outside the United States. We strongly suspect that this may be as a result of reverse filtering.

Ukraine

Access to Internet content in Ukraine remains largely unfettered, in part as a consequence of the 2005 Orange Revolution in which communication technologies played a significant role. Ukraine possesses relatively liberal legislation governing the Internet and access to information. A number of state initiatives aimed at controlling electronic media have emerged, in-

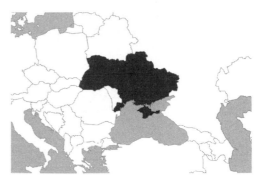

cluding regulations to exercise surveillance over Internet content in order to "protect national security" and limit other forms of "undesirable" content. These regulations embody the potential for expanded formal and informal controls, although they are unlikely to be enacted in the near future.

Background

Among the countries of the CIS, Ukraine is second only to Russia in the size and strength of its IT establishment. Ukraine was the birthplace of Soviet computing and Kyiv remains a major center for IT development. Ukraine is an early adopter of policies aimed at supporting ICT, considered by the government to be a main pillar of national development. The state has demonstrated the political will to undertake vital reforms

RESULTS AT A GLANCE					
Filtering	No Evidence of Filtering	Suspected Filtering	Selective Filtering	Substantial Filtering	Pervasive Filtering
Political	●				
Social	●				
Conflict and security	●				
Internet tools	●				

Other Factors	Low	Medium	High	Not Applicable
Transparency				●
Consistency				●

KEY INDICATORS	
GDP per capita, PPP (constant 2005 international dollars)	6,529
Life expectancy at birth (years)	68
Literacy rate (percent of people age 15+)	100
Human development index (out of 179)	82
Rule of law (out of 211)	152
Voice and accountability (out of 209)	114
Democracy index (out of 167)	53 (Flawed democracy)
Digital opportunity index (out of 181)	90
Internet users (percent of population)	14.6

Source by indicator: World Bank 2009a, World Bank 2009a, World Bank 2009a, UNDP 2008, World Bank 2009b, World Bank 2009b, Economist Intelligence Unit 2008, ITU 2007, Miniwatts Marketing Group 2009.

in the telecommunications sector, although much remains to be done to promote a favorable environment for developing the Internet, fostering e-commerce, and introducing e-governance. In 2008–2009, Ukraine moved up in the global ranking of the Networked Readiness Index to 62nd from 75th place—a notable improvement.[1]

In early 2000, the government invested in developing the country's ICT infrastructure extensively, but more recently the government has deprioritized ICT development. This policy change explains the low position of Ukraine in two separate rankings, both carried out by the World Economic Forum in 2009: "Government Prioritization of ICT" (ranked 110th out of 134 countries) and "Importance of ICT to Government Vision of the Future" (ranked 114th).[2]

The January 2005 Orange Revolution—when opposition groups successfully challenged the outcome of the November 2004 presidential elections that were allegedly unfair—highlighted the latent political power resulting from the "convergence" of information infrastructures (cell phones, Internet, and independent media) and political mobilization. The opposition made full use of these technologies to mobilize and direct supporters in acts of civil disobedience, sit-ins, and general strikes. Although the Internet did not play a determining role in the success of the Orange Revolution, its use by the opposition helped to foster the perception that these technologies served an important strategic role in organizing political opposition (which observers have termed "hyper-democracy").[3] This perception, in turn, prompted neighboring authoritarian governments such as Belarus to crack down on Internet openness.

Following the Orange Revolution, Ukrainian society has become more aware of its power to bring about political changes. Political parties and the government have started using the Internet as an effective tool of political competition while employing techniques such as online political games, unofficial voting, e-meetings, and blogs.

Internet in Ukraine

The partly liberalized Ukrainian telecommunications market is not fully developed. Fixed-line penetration remains low (27.8 percent),[4] and the telephone system requires modernization. The demand for mobile services has expanded rapidly, to reach a penetration of nearly 50 percent. The largest telecom and top-tier ISP, Ukrtelecom, has 92.86 percent state ownership. President Viktor Yushchenko has announced the forthcoming privatization of the state-owned telecom operator Ukrtelecom. The sale of the operator, however, has been delayed a number of times. The government envisages that 50 percent of the shares will be sold for USD 3 billion, though analysts predict a much lower figure. The outdated equipment of Ukrtelecom makes the company less attractive to investors.[5] The state monopolies Ukrtelecom and Utel, the latter controlled by Ukrtelecom, together own 95 percent of the long-distance and international call market.[6]

State-owned Ukrtelecom is the largest ISP in the country, but it does not decisively control the other major ISPs. Ukrtelecom dominates the fixed-line sector[7] and possesses Ukraine's primary network, trunk, and zone telecom lines. Alternative telecommunications providers are dependent on leased lines, because Ukrtelecom owns the majority of the infrastructure and many alternative providers do not have sufficient resources to build their own networks and consequently have to rely on Ukrtelecom's infrastructure. Prices for long-distance and international calls of local operators made over Ukrtelecom lines were regulated by the Order of the Ministry of Communications of November 21, 1996, No. 234, on the basis of revenue sharing (which depends on the number of lines, equipment used, and administrative costs). New interconnection rules were introduced in January 2007, under which interconnection fees are calculated on the basis of traffic volume.

Although ISPs have considerably reduced their access costs (by, for example, leasing outdated or redundant infrastructure from Ukrtelecom) and a few providers offer free access during the night, most Ukrainians cannot afford to use the Internet. Internet penetration increased to 14.6 percent in 2008.[8] With regard to frequency of connecting to the Internet, local sources[9] estimated that in March 2009 almost 8 million Ukrainian users accessed the Internet on at least one occasion over the course of the previous month.[10] There is a significant urban-rural digital divide: As of December 2008, 41 percent of Internet users lived in settlements with more than 50,000 inhabitants. The share of Internet users in rural areas is very low.[11] The majority of users are concentrated in large cities, with Kyiv accounting for nearly 60 percent of Internet users, and the next seven largest cities a further 30 percent of all users.[12] Obstacles impeding expansion include high access costs, poor infrastructure in the regions, high call rates, and low levels of PC ownership.

Men are more frequent users than women (59.3 percent), and most users access the Internet at the office, Internet cafés, or home. Various efforts have been made to boost Internet access at public Internet access places (PIAPs).[13] Pilot projects have also been launched in an effort to improve universal service provision in remote areas. There are more than 3,000 Internet cafés in Ukraine (or one for every 16,000 people in the country).[14] In 2007, 70 percent of all Internet cafés accessed the Internet through a dial-up connection, 20 percent through dedicated lines, and 10 percent through cable TV networks and others.[15]

There are about 400 ISPs in Ukraine according to the State Committee on Communication and Informatization.[16] As of March 2009, there were around 90 ISPs connected to the two Internet traffic exchange points. Ukrtelecom has recently taken steps to encourage massive use of broadband services, and the number of ISPs offering broadband access services has rapidly increased.[17] In March 2005, there were only 10,000 DSL lines in Ukraine.[18] At that time, DSLAMs were installed in 450 cities in Ukraine, and work was under way with Cisco to permit a 1,000 percent increase in DSL subscribers by the second half of 2006. In Ukraine, DSL is used by ISPs as high-speed leased lines. The most widespread technology used for this purpose is HDSL, reaching 2 Mbps data-exchange speeds in both directions.[19] By the end of 2008, there were approximately 1.5 million broadband subscribers (of whom about 500,000 were Ukrtelecom subscribers). Penetration of broadband access in the country exceeded 8 percent.[20]

The government, recognizing the need for attracting foreign investment and stimulating a favorable Internet environment, has also announced plans to provide low-cost access to the Internet in the major cities using WiMAX technology.[21] Indeed, the wireless broadband sector has experienced an increased level of activity as the number of Wi-Fi ISPs has been augmented.

Mobile operators plan to launch fixed-broadband services using frequencies previously used by analog mobile services. Although cable operators have a significant presence throughout the country, the lack of investment has prevented them from offering broadband and digital cable services in most places in Ukraine. A new DTH platform has been launched, and the Ukrainian broadcasting council has allocated Digital Terrestrial TV licenses, opening the way for new services.

There are a number of companies providing Internet access using satellite technologies in Ukraine (these include Ukrsat, Infocom-SK, Spacegate, Adamant, LuckyNet, Ukrnet, and Itelsat). With the exception of Infocom-SK, all these companies are private operators. Ukrchastotnagliad, the Ukrainian frequencies supervisory center, reports that 86 operators have licenses to provide satellite communications services in Ukraine. Despite the large number of operators on the market, however, satellite telecommunications is limited because of its high cost compared to the low average income in the country. The government is nevertheless deploying a digital satellite television and radio broadcasting system, which will also be used for Internet via satellite. In 2007, there were five types of licenses for the provision of direct satellite communications services.

There are currently two industry associations in the Internet sector, the Internet Association of Ukraine,[22] which owns the Ukrainian Internet Exchange (UIE),[23] and the Ukrainian Wireless Association.[24] The Internet Association of Ukraine aims to safeguard the interests of all participants in the Internet market and has successfully ensured a reduction in the price of internal traffic in Ukraine.[25]

Since 2001, the Ukrainian national country code top-level domain (".ua") has been administered by LLC "Hostmaster" founded by representatives of the Ukrainian Internet community.[26] The number of domain names registered under ".ua" is steadily increasing. For example, under ".com.ua," the total number of domain names increased from 31,153 in 2004 to 145,114 in April 2009. The overall number of domain names under ".ua" had increased from 133,907 to 390,197 as of January 1, 2009.[27]

Blogging has also been on the rise. Ukrainian Internet users have opened more than 80,000 blogs on popular portals such as livejournal.com (35,000), liveInternet.ru (27,500), dnevnik.bigmir.net (11,000), drevo.uaportal.com (4,000), diary.ru (2,500), Jeans.com.ua/blogs.php (2,300), and Dnevnik.org.ua (1,200).[28]

The most popular search engines in Ukraine are Ukrainian-based BigMir.net and ukr.net, Russian-based Yandex and Rambler, and Google. The majority (60.3 percent) of online searches in Ukraine are performed through Google, followed by Russian and Ukrainian search engines Yandex (18.3 percent), ukr.net (2.64 percent), Rambler (2.16 percent), and Meta.ua (2.11 percent).[29]

Ukraine's mobile sector is very dynamic. There are six mobile providers in the country: UMS[30] (GSM-900/1800 and NMT-450i), Kyivstar[31] GSM (GSM-900/1800), Astelit[32] (GSM-1800), Ukrainskie Radiosystemy (GSM-1800),[33] and Utel (UMTS/WCDMA).[34]

Legal and Regulatory Frameworks

The Ministry of Transport and Communications (through the State Administration for Communications) is the policymaker in the electronic communications sector. The Law on Communications (2003) established the sector regulator—the National Communication Regulation Commission (NCRC), which was set up two years later. The law of 2003 does not guarantee the independence of the NCRC. Instead, a number of inconsistencies between sector laws have increased the uncertainty about who has the power to appoint the commissioners. The NCRC is responsible for licensing operators, monitoring the market, price regulation, frequency assignment, numbering, ensuring compliance with the legal framework, imposing sanctions, and resolving disputes when interconnection agreements are not reached between operators. The NCRC's work has often been obstructed by claims of unlawful appointments and operation.[35]

Under the Law on Communications, operators are required to have a license before starting activity.[36] License fees vary from around EUR 1.5 million for fixed international telephony down to less than EUR 1,500 for network capacity and 10,000 telephone numbers. A 15-year national license for VoIP costs EUR 150,000.[37] The law specifies that local, intercity, and international telecommunications services, as well as mobile telephone communications and television and radio broadcasting, must be licensed. The term of the license (except for IP-telephony) is determined by the NCRC and cannot be less than five years.[38] With the present government, Internet activity is not subject to licensing or other forms of regulation. Liberalization of the market has also led to a rapid increase in the number of ISPs.

The Law on Communications offers the NCRC a variety of tools to ensure competitive neutrality with regard to building communications infrastructure. According to the current legislation, all telecommunications operators have the right to build telecommunications networks in accordance with a plan that has been approved by the Ministry of Transport and Communications (MTC). Companies must submit their plans to Ukrtelecom or the local government to receive permission to develop telecom networks.

Monopolization by Ukrtelecom, lack of strategy for international telecommunications services market development, and the absence of long-distance and international traffic control mechanisms are major problems for the long-distance and international communications market. Interconnection is governed by Chapter IX of the 2003 Law on Communications and the subsequent NCRC Order on Interconnection and Calculation among Operators. Interconnection is very heavily regulated: the cost of calls from fixed phones to mobile phones is determined by a government decree, and the redistribution of incomes from such calls is based on agreements between Ukrtelecom and the mobile operators. This rate is currently UAH 0.6 per minute. These agreements between Ukrtelecom and mobile operators are signed on a yearly basis. At present, it is difficult to obtain data on interconnection between telephony operators because all parties have an interest in concealing actual conditions of their agreements.[39] There is also no public information available regarding the existence of complaints against interconnection regulation. For fixed-to-mobile interconnection, the termination fee is UAH 0.25 per minute. The price of call termination in the mobile-to-fixed market is decided by commercial agreement between the parties, but the tariff cannot be more than UAH 0.25. Mobile-to-mobile interconnection is negotiated between the parties.

The Law on Communications classifies market players in the telecom sectors as either "operators" or "providers." Under Article 1 of the law, "providers" do not have the right to maintain or operate networks, or to provide channels. Operators are divided into mobile operators, landline operators, and landline wireless operators. Mobile operators need to obtain a license for provision of phone services and for the frequencies they use. Fixed operators are required to have a license for local, national, and international services, while fixed wireless providers need a license for fixed operators as well as for the frequency they operate.

The legal status of VoIP providers has yet to be defined. Within the context of the current definitions, VoIP providers could be considered "operators" and therefore be required to undertake the same licensing procedures as the other categories of operators. Obviously there is a degree of uncertainty in the market. The losses from the illegal termination of voice calls in Ukraine have been calculated. Ukrtelecom offers a termination rate for IP calls of USD 0.75–0.77. It is not known how many (if any) IP telephony companies take advantage of this offer.

The country-code top-level domain (CC TLD) ".ua" is administered by the independent company Hostmaster. In 2008, there were two separate legislative initiatives proposing to establish governmental control over the administrative body. Oleg Shevchuk (Prime Minister of Ukraine, Bloc of Yulia Tymoshenko) suggested that the administration of the CC TLD be performed by a nonprofit NGO representing the IT sector. However, any final appointment decision would be enacted only after approval by a supervisory board, including representatives of the National Communication Regulation Commission (NCRC), the Anti-Monopoly Committee, and other central executive bodies.[40] Another draft law envisioned stricter measures.[41] According to the draft law, the administrator—a noncommercial organization—should be founded by associations of communication providers as well as authorized governmental bodies. The administrator would be approved by the Cabinet of Ministries following a proposal by the State Informatization Committee and the NCRC. Furthermore, the administrator's activity would be organized by a coordination council composed of executive bodies and self-regulated organizations. However, these two proposals were not successful.

At present, there are no controls on Internet access or content. However, this situation may be changing as government figures have made public calls for stricter regulation of the Internet, citing national security concerns.[42] Suggested measures include licensing ISPs, registering Internet resources, and monitoring content related to obscene or harmful material. The threat of Internet censorship was raised in 2005 when the Ministry of Transport and Telecommunications introduced, and subsequently withdrew, a decree regulating registration of Web sites hosted in Ukraine for the purposes of national security.[43] In 2009, the Ukrainian Security Service was instructed to prepare draft legislation that would obligate news Web sites to register as media.[44]

The Law on Protection of Public Morals of November 20, 2003, enacted during the term of the previous government, is still effective. It prohibits the production and circulation of pornography; dissemination of products that propagandize war or spread national and religious intolerance; humiliation or insult to an individual or nation on the grounds of nationality, religion, or ignorance; and the propagation of "drug addition, toxicology, alcoholism, smoking and other bad habits." (Article 161 of the Criminal Code provides for punishment for incitement of national, racial, and religious intolerance, and demeaning of national honor and religious beliefs.)

The National Expert Commission for the Protection of Public Morals (NECPPM) has the authority to monitor and evaluate media materials (including the Internet), issue conclusions on their compliance with the Law on Protection of Public Morals, and propose revocation of operators' licenses in case of violation.[45] The commissioners of the NECPPM are approved by the Cabinet of Ministries. Since 2008, the NECPPM has made several decisions about TV broadcasts, movies, and books that provoked significant controversy in the electronic media community. For example, in November 2008 the commission decided that the Russian-based social network "V kontakte" (vkontakte.ru) contained pornographic materials and instructed the Ministry of Foreign Affairs to address the embassy of the Russian Federation to Ukraine on this issue, in order to prevent further dissemination of such materials by the social network.[46]

Subsequently, on March 20, 2009, the Internet Association of Ukraine and the commission signed the Memorandum on Cooperation about Security Issues in the ".ua" Domain.[47] The association and its members took on the responsibility for monitoring the Ukrainian domain and preventing dissemination of materials violating the Law on Protection of Public Morals.

In September 2005, the Cybercrime Convention of the Council of Europe was ratified by President Yushchenko, with reservations regarding the possession of child pornography and misuse of devices. Ukraine has also signed and ratified the Optional Protocol to the Convention on the Rights of the Child on the Sale of Children, Child Prostitution, and Child Pornography. Prohibition of the importation, production, sale, and distribution of child pornography in Ukraine is detailed in Article 301 of the Ukrainian criminal code. However, there is no prohibition of the possession of such material.

In December 2008, the Ministry of Internal Affairs searched the premises of one of the most popular Ukrainian file-exchange networks (infostore.org) and confiscated servers and other equipment under the pretext that the network was hosting pornographic materials. The owners insisted they provided the required information beforehand and protested against the actions of the law enforcement authorities. Since this incident, infostore.org has been unavailable.[48] The ministry's actions were underpinned by a decision of the National Expert Commission for the Protection of Public Morals.

In October 2008, MP Pavlo Ungurjan (Bloc of Yulia Tymoshenko) submitted a draft law on combating child pornography.[49] He suggested imposing obligations on ISPs to track URLs visited by subscribers and to inform law enforcement about users who attempt to open Web sites containing child pornography. The draft recommends blocking child pornography sites, and envisions criminal liability for ISPs that host such Web sites. The draft law has been widely criticized, but the author has not withdrawn it.[50]

The Supreme Economic Court accepted the 2004 Resolution on Certain Issues Concerning the Resolution of Disputes Related to Copyright and Intellectual Property Rights Protection, which provides procedures for the protection of intellectual property rights—in particular, sales of various computer software programs. Ukrainian legislation has been enhanced and brought into line with the TRIPS requirements by several laws amending Ukrainian Intellectual Property Laws.[51] However, most of the focus in Ukraine in relation to music and software piracy has been on offline infringements, because of the existence of large pirate CD plants in the country. New legislation adopted in May 2005 was intended to resolve legal loopholes with regard to piracy. In subsequent years, further legislation in this field was passed providing legal protection for computer programs, broadcasting and cable retransmission, databases, and resale rights, as well as adequate enforcement measures. According to the Ukrainian Ministry of Justice, around 80–90 percent of legislation in almost all key intellectual-property-rights fields corresponds to the EU *acquis communautaire*.[52]

In February 2007, the Verkhovna Rada adopted amendments to the Criminal Code. Now individuals charged with piracy can face three to six year imprisonment (up from the previous two-year sentence) or a fine that could reach a maximum of UAH 51,000 (USD 10,000).[53] Microsoft Ukraine stated that 80 percent of software used in Ukraine was unlicensed.

In 2004, the Regulation on the Fundamentals of Revealing General Crimes was adopted by Authorities of the Ministry of Internal Affairs. This regulation authorizes the use of the police database for crime-fighting purposes. The police database includes data on the crimes, the persons involved, the items installed, and other relevant investigative data. The regulation does not correspond to the personal data protection provisions of the Council of Europe Data Protection Convention of 1981. There are no national laws on data retention.

Surveillance

The Council of National Security and Defense is the main governmental body responsible for national security and defense. The Council monitors information security and coordinates the work of the other executive bodies in the field. The Security Service of Ukraine is empowered to initiate criminal investigations and use wiretapping devices on communications. Existing legislation has specified neither the circumstances that justify interception of information from communication channels nor the time limits of any such interception. The recently established State Service for Special Communications and Information Protection implements governmental policy on protecting state information and confidential communication, and exercises control over cryptographic and technical information security.[54]

On June 17, 2002, the State Committee on Communications issued Order No. 122, which introduced mechanisms for Internet monitoring. The order required ISPs to install black-box monitoring systems in order to provide access for state organizations. The purpose of this monitoring was to control unsanctioned transmission of data containing state secrets. However, "state secret" is not clearly defined in current regulations, allowing authorities broad discretion in interpretation. The difficulties in separating state from nonstate users also expose the latter to monitoring. By 2006, a significant number of large ISPs installed black boxes, and the Security Service of Ukraine sent out letters to governmental authorities insisting they use their access services.

Under the pressure of public protests and complaints raised by the Internet Association of Ukraine and the Ukrainian Helsinki Human Rights Union, the Ministry of Justice abolished this order in August 2006. Some human rights groups claim the Security Service of Ukraine is keeping intercepted messages and carrying out Internet surveillance on a large scale.[55] Since the revocation of Order No. 122, the service has acted within the limits prescribed by the Law on Operative Investigative Activity. According to estimates from the Internet Association of Ukraine, the service may have the technological capability to do so in 50–60 percent of the cases.[56] The level of surveillance may rise up to 90 percent in regions where it is harder for access providers to oppose the Security Service and other law enforcement bodies.

To compensate for the lack of comprehensive legislative regulation of communication interception and surveillance, the Cabinet of Ministers adopted Order No. 1169 in September 2007. This order decrees that permission must be obtained from a judge or head of the respective Court of Appeals to carry out surveillance. Human rights groups, such as the Internet Association of Ukraine and the Ukrainian Human Rights Ombudswoman, protested against the order, claiming it legalized unlawful infringement upon the right to privacy. Notwithstanding the attacks against it, Order No. 1169 remains active.[57] Statistics also reveal the growing use of interception and surveillance by law enforcement agencies in Ukraine. According to the Supreme Court of Ukraine, the number of applications authorizing the use of monitoring and surveillance tools to the Ukrainian Courts of Appeals initiated by law enforcement bodies grew from 15,000 in 2005 to 19,989 in 2007 and reached 25,086 in 2008. In 2008, the Ministry of Internal Affairs made 14,815 submissions; the Security Service of Ukraine, 8,323; and the tax police, 1,655. It is not known how many submissions were granted, nor is it clear how many were directly related to electronic surveillance.[58]

ONI Testing Results

In 2007 and 2008, the OpenNet Initiative conducted tests in Ukraine from different access points on six main ISPs: Alkar, Intertelecom, Visti Net, Volz, Volia, and UkrTelecom. The ONI concluded that there is no filtering on the backbone in Ukraine. However, the ONI found that a number of U.S. military Web sites as well as one gambling site were subject to reverse blocking and hence inaccessible in Ukraine.[59]

Conclusion

The citizens of Ukraine enjoy unfettered access to the Internet. The country's Internet infrastructure is rapidly developing, and ICTs are beginning to have a more notable influence over the political process. The country possesses an Internet infrastructure that is more oriented toward European ISPs, and this orientation diminishes the influence of any filtering behavior on the part of Russian ISPs. The government has built up an intricate system of bodies and content regulations that can be geared toward surveillance of information carried on telecommunications networks, including the Internet.

Notes

1. The Networked Readiness Framework assesses the extent to which different economies benefit from the latest ICT advances based on three indexes: environment, network readiness, and usage. See World Economic Forum, *The Global Information Technology Report 2008–2009*, http://www.weforum.org/pdf/gitr/2009/gitr09fullreport.pdf.

2. Ibid.

3. Joshua Goldstein, "The Role of Digital Networked Technologies in the Ukrainian Orange Revolution," Berkman Center Research Publication No. 2007-14, December 2007, http://cyber.law.harvard.edu/sites/cyber.law.harvard.edu/files/Goldstein_Ukraine_2007.pdf.

4. Paul Budde Communication Pty., Ltd., "Ukraine—Key Statistics and Telecommunications Market," January 15, 2009.

5. World Dialogue on Regulation for Network Economies, "Ukraine: President Signs Legislation to Privatise Ukrtelekom," January 26, 2007, http://www.regulateonline.org/content/view/918/79/.

6. Andriy Vorobyov, "Ukraine Telecommunications Market Report," BISNIS, 2005, http://www.bisnis.doc.gov/bisnis/bisdoc/0602UkraineTelecomReport.htm.

7. As of April 2005, Ukrtelecom's overall telecommunications network consisted of 78,665 km of lines, of which 17,169 km were fiber-optic communication lines.

8. Miniwatts Marketing Group, "Internet World Statistics: Ukraine," 2009, http://www.internetworldstats.com/europa2.htm#ua.

9. *Delo*, "V Iyule Ukrainskaya Internet-auditoriya Uvelichilas na 3.2%" [Ukrainian Internet Audience Increased by 3.2% in July], March 31, 2009, http://delo.ua/news/after/internet/info-45524.html (accessed May 26, 2009).

10. *Delo*, "V Ukraine Naschitali 8 mln Internet-polsovateley" [8 Million Internet Users Estimated in Ukraine], May 27, 2007, http://delo.ua/news/103981/.

11. *Ekonomichna Pravda*, "Maizhe Polovina Miskih Ukraintsev Koristuetsya Internetom" [Nearly Half of Urban Ukrainians Use the Internet], December 15, 2008, http://www.epravda.com.ua/news/494677832d2cd/.

12. "Globalnaya Statistika Ukrainskogo Internet v Aprele 2008" [Global Statistics of Ukrainian Internet in April 2008], http://www.slideshare.net/segal/2008-398609.

13. For example, the U.S. Embassy gave grants of more than USD 1.4 million (EUR 1.17 million) to provide Internet access in libraries in the period from 2001 to 2004. The UN Development Program and the German International Migration and Development Center have joined forces with local organizations to develop training and support for the creation of PIAPs in Ukrainian schools, the intention being both to boost IT in education and to improve the level of Internet access in schools. See German International Migration and Development Center, http://www.cimonline.de/en/index.asp.

14. "Introducing All-Ukrainian Association of Computer Clubs," http://www.uacc.org.ua/en.

15. Lesya Potapenko, "Copyright Attacks, Part II," *Ukrainska Pravda*, May 4, 2007, http://www.pravda.com.ua/en/news/2007/5/4/7658.htm.

16. *Delo*, "Vo Vtorom Quartale Kolichestvo Abonentov Providerov Internet Uvelichilos na 6.4%" [ISP Subscribers Number Increased by 6.4% in the Second Quarter], July 26, 2007, http://delo.ua/news/after/internet/info-44242.html (accessed May 26, 2009).

17. Light Reading: IP & Convergence, "Ukrtelecom Uses Cisco Routers," News Wire Feed, March 23, 2005, http://www.lightreading.com/document.asp?doc_id=70731; News@Cisco Press Release, "DataGroup to Deliver DWDM Network in Ukraine with Cisco Optical Technology," February 15, 2006, http://newsroom.cisco.com/dlls/2006/prod_021506.html.

18. See Ukrainians Plan IP Explosion, http://www.lightreading.com/document.asp?doc_id=70732.

19. Paul Budde Communication Pty., Ltd., "Ukraine—Internet, Broadband, and Convergence Overview and Statistics," November 9, 2008.

20. State Administration of Communications of Ukraine, "U Sichni 2009 Roku Dohody vid Nadannya Poslug Zvyazku Sklali 3,6 Milliarda Griven" [In January 2009 Communication Revenues were 3.6 Billion Hryvnia], http://www.stc.gov.ua/uk/publish/article/68241.

21. *Ukrainskaya Pravda*, "Ministr Obeshchaet Pokryt' Ukrainu Internetom" [Minister Promises to Cover Ukraine with Internet], January 18, 2006, http://www.pravda.com.ua/ru/news/2006/1/18/36834.htm.

22. Internet Assotsiatsia Ukrainy [Ukraine Internet Association], http://www.inau.org.ua/about.phtml.

23. Ukrainskaya set obmena trafikom (Ukrainian IXP), http://www.ua-ix.net.ua.

24. Wireless Ukraine, http://www.wirelessua.com.

25. For further information about the IA-IX Internet Traffic Exchange, see Ukrainian traffic exchange network at http://ua-ix.net/eng.phtml.

26. Hostmaster Ltd, http://hostmaster.net.ua/.

27. Hostmaster Ltd, "2008 God—Fakty I Kommentarii" [Year 2008 Facts and Comments], http://hostmaster.net.ua/news/?.

28. Makson Pugobskiy, "Ukrainskaya Blogosphere" [Ukrainian Blogosphere], August 16, 2006, *ITC.ua*, http://itc.ua/article.phtml?ID=25235.

29. *Korrespondent.net*, "Opublikovana Globalnaya Statistika Ukrainskogo Internet za Sentyabr" [September Global Ukrainian Internet Statistics have been Published], October 3, 2008, http://korrespondent.net/tech/technews/603860.

30. MTS Subscribers, http://www.mts.com.ua/eng/main.php.

31. Kyivstar, http://www.kyivstar.ua/en/.

32. Life, http://www.life.com.ua/index.php?lng=uk.

33. Beeline, www.beeline.ua/index_ua.wbp.

34. Utel, www.utel.ua.

35. European Bank for Reconstruction and Development (EBRD), "Legal Transition Program: Telecommunications Regulatory Development: Comparative Assessment of the Telecommunications Sector in the Transition Countries: Assessment Report Ukraine," December 2008, http://ebrd.com/country/sector/law/telecoms/assess/ukraine.pdf.

36. Law on Telecommunications of November 18, 2003. The law abolished the provisions of the 1995 Communication Law, including the charges for incoming calls for all kinds of telephone communications.

37. Law on Telecommunications of November 18, 2003. The law abolished the provisions of the 1995 Communication Law, including the charges for incoming calls for all kinds of telephone communications.

38. For each type of telecommunications service, the NCCR is obliged to issue special instructions on the technical and bureaucratic parameters that the enterprise should respect and on the documents needed to confirm that the parameters have been met.

39. The Law on Communications requires operators to provide other operators willing to conclude an interconnection agreement with the information required for negotiation and to offer

interconnection terms that are at least equivalent to those proposed to other operators (Art. 58). The NCCR is authorized to intervene in cases of failure by parties to negotiate (para. 19, Art. 18).

40. Proekt Zakonu pro Vnesennya Zmin do Zakonu Ukrainy "Pro Telekommunikatsii" 3460 [Draft Law No. 3460 Amending the Ukrainian Telecommunications Law], http://gska2.rada.gov .ua/pls/zweb_n/webproc4_1?id=&pf3511=33887.

41. Proekt Zakonu pro Vnesennya Zmin do Zakonu Ukrainy "Pro Telekommunikatsii" 3460–1 [Draft Law # 3460–1 Amending the Ukrainian Telecommunications Law], http://gska2.rada.gov .ua/pls/zweb_n/webproc4_1?id=&pf3511=34117.

42. The director of Ukraine's Security Service, Konstantyn Boyko, pointed out the imminent danger that the Internet may pose to the country, citing "foreign political forces, intelligence departments and extremist organizations, which are able to direct resources and endowments of the Internet to harm our nation." See *Ukrainskaya Pravda*, "SBU Ustroit Totalny Control?" [Security Service to Take Totalitarian Control over Internet?], May 27, 2006, http://www.pravda .com.ua/ru/news/2006/5/27/41096.htm.

43. The decree asked for compulsory registration of Web sites and specified criteria that sites had to respect before being launched. International Press Institute, "2005 World Press Freedom Review, Ukraine."

44. *Sila Naroda*, "Budet li Vveden Control nad SMI Ukrainy?" [Will There Be Control over the Ukrainian Media?], March 2, 2009, http://www.silanaroda.com/index.php?itemid=8317&mode =full.

45. Natsional Expertna Komisiya Ukrainy [Ukrainian National Expert Commission], www.moral .gov.ua.

46. *Telekritika*, "Natskomissiya Pitan Zahistu Suspilnoy Morali Hochet Zaboroni 'V Kontakte'?" [National Commission for Public Morality Wants to Ban 'V Kontakte'?], November 28, 2009, http://www.telekritika.ua/news/2008-11-28/42297.

47. "Natsionalna Ekspertna Komisia Ukraini z Pitan Zahistu Suspilnoy Morali," http://moral.gov .ua/_pidpisano_memorandum_pro_0_0_0_1147_1.html.

48. Alexey Mas, "Syervis Infostore i MVD!" [Service Infostore and MIA!], Alex Mas on the Internet, business and Infostore Blog, December 31, 2009, http://alexeymas.livejournal.com/.

49. Draft law No. 3271 amending the law on child pornography distribution prevention, http:// gska2.rada.gov.ua/pls/zweb_n/webproc4_1?id=&pf3511=33562.

50. Viktoriya Vlasenko, "Pornographicheskiy Zakonproekt" [Pornography Bill], *ProIT*, October 27, 2008, http://proit.com.ua/article/internet/2008/10/27/094219.html.

51. Laws on Several Amendments to Intellectual Property Laws No. 34-IV of July 4, 2002 (devoted to the protection of the copyright on the Internet); No. 850-IV of May 22, 2003; No. 1407-IV of February 2004; and No. 2734-IV of July 6, 2005: "On amendments to the several acts regarding the production and import of discs, recording equipment, and raw materials."

52. In August 2005, the Ukrainian Government introduced restrictions on unsolicited electronic communications, using Article 33 ("Responsibilities of users of telecommunications services") of the 2003 Law on Communications as their legal basis. The rules include obligations for consumers to be able to "opt out" of receiving messages, a prohibition of the falsification of network information, and obligations regarding the provision of a functioning e-mail address and the name of the sender.

53. Lesya Potapenko, "Copyright Attacks, Part II," *Ukrainska Pravda*, May 4, 2007, http://www.pravda.com.ua/en/news/2007/5/4/7658.htm.

54. The agency was established by the Law of February 23, 2006, No. 3475-IV. For excerpts of the law translated into English, see Yaroslav the Wise Institute of Legal Information, "The Law of Ukraine: On the State Service for Special Communications and Information Protection of Ukraine."

55. "Prava Lyudey v Ukraine—2006. V. Pravo na Privatnost" [Human Rights in Ukraine in 2006. V. Privacy Rights], http://www.khpg.org/index.php?id=1186147137.

56. Marina Pekarchuk, "Brigadir Domennogo Tsekha" [Head of the Domain Shop], *Vlast Deneg*, February 2009, http://www.vd.net.ua/rubrics-10/13538/.

57. "Prava lyudey v Ukraine—2007. V. Pravo na privatnost."

58. Information about court hearings on law enforcement investigating by wiretapping. See www.khpg.org/index.php?id=1241091796.

59. Reverse filtering occurs on the Web server hosting the content, as opposed to at a point along the way of the traffic flow, and is based on restricting requests based on geographical location of the originating Internet Protocol address. Copyright holders who want to restrict access to their content in certain markets often use reverse filtering. Examples include hulu.com, BBC.com, and other sites that syndicate commercial video and audio content that is subject to licensing. The ONI has detected that many U.S. military sites are inaccessible outside the United States. We strongly suspect that this may be as a result of reverse filtering.

Uzbekistan

Uzbekistan's tight control of the Internet has resulted in the most pervasive regime of filtering and censorship in the CIS. Filtering is comprehensive and, until 2006, largely undeclared, with the government denying the existence of these practices. At present, the government employs sophisticated multilayered mechanisms to exercise control over the Internet, including adopting restrictive policies, applying technological measures, and compelling self-censorship of the media.

Background

At present, and in spite of the formal separation of powers enshrined in the Constitution of the Republic of Uzbekistan, virtually all power is invested in President Islam Karimov. A former first secretary of the Uzbek Communist Party (UCP) during the Soviet period, Islam Karimov started his current term of office in January 2000. A referendum in January 2002 extended the presidential term of office from five to seven years. The president has almost complete control over the parliament, which supports

RESULTS AT A GLANCE					
Filtering	No Evidence of Filtering	Suspected Filtering	Selective Filtering	Substantial Filtering	Pervasive Filtering
Political					•
Social			•		
Conflict and security			•		
Internet tools			•		

Other Factors	Low	Medium	High	Not Applicable
Transparency	•			
Consistency			•	

KEY INDICATORS	
GDP per capita, PPP (constant 2005 international dollars)	2,290
Life expectancy at birth (years)	67
Literacy rate (percent of people age 15+)	97
Human development index (out of 179)	119
Rule of law (out of 211)	182
Voice and accountability (out of 209)	202
Democracy index (out of 167)	164 (Authoritarian regime)
Digital opportunity index (out of 181)	123
Internet users (percent of population)	8.8

Source by indicator: World Bank 2009a, World Bank 2009a, World Bank 2009a, UNDP 2008, World Bank 2009b, World Bank 2009b, Economist Intelligence Unit 2008, ITU 2007, Miniwatts Marketing Group 2009.

him overwhelmingly. On a few occasions, the government has resorted to the use of force in order to maintain its control over the country. One such occasion were the events in Andijan in 2005 when hundreds of civilians were killed.[1] During the clampdown that followed the public demonstrations, most of the foreign media were expelled from the country. The majority of human rights organizations were ousted and their activities banned.[2]

During his extended authoritarian rule, President Karimov has demonstrated an active commitment to controlling the information environment in the country and constraining the expression of dissident viewpoints. The active opposition has been forced to leave Uzbekistan and has been banned.[3] The Internet often remains the only way for the opposition to communicate with Uzbek society. In 2004, Internews International—a nonprofit organization that supports open media and Internet development worldwide—was banned from Uzbekistan.[4]

In the beginning of October 2008, an unprecedented two-day media seminar in Tashkent focused on freedom of speech in the country. The government did not allow foreign media and independent Uzbek journalists to cover this seminar. The only media admitted were representatives of the state-controlled electronic and print media.

The complex laws and regulations in Uzbekistan have resulted in self-censorship of online publishers, independent journalists, and bloggers. This self-censorship, coupled with a highly sophisticated Internet filtering regime, significantly stifles public discourse on political and human-rights topics.

State control of the Internet stands in stark contrast to the government's official enthusiasm for promoting ICTs. Until 2001, Uzbekistan was a regional leader in the adoption of the Internet and the prioritization of ICT as a mechanism for national development. Uzbekistan was among the first of the post-Soviet republics to establish a national agency responsible for ICT development (UzInfoCom), to contribute state resources to building a sizable academic and research network (UzSCINET), and to launch an ambitious project to provide Internet to the main government institutions (Cabinet of Ministers and presidency). After 2001, Uzbekistan continued to receive sizable foreign support aimed at developing its ICT infrastructure, including a large network of Internet access points in the regions. Uzbek government officials at all levels were sent abroad to study e-government systems and ICT. Until 2001–2002, the Internet remained open and free from filtering, with the exception of some limited filters for pornography that were implemented on UzSCINET.

The turning point in the state's relationship to Internet freedom began following a series of attacks in Tashkent in 2004 blamed on the Hizb-ut-Tahrir (Hit) and the Islamic Movement of Uzbekistan. These attacks have been generally associated with a deepening crackdown on Uzbek society that encompasses all forms and channels of dissent, including the Internet.

Internet in Uzbekistan

Uzbektelecom JSC has retained the status of a legal monopoly on services of access to international telecommunication networks, including the use of VoIP technologies. According to the government resolution, monopoly status will be retained after privatization of Uzbektelecom JSC (at present the state owns 94 percent of Uzbektelecom). As a result, operators and providers are entitled to access international telecommunication networks exclusively through the infrastructure of Uzbektelecom JSC, which facilitates control over Internet content and hinders active competition on the communications market. Uzbektelecom dominates around 90 percent of the fixed market and owns 14 regional and five specialist subsidiaries, which include the national Internet (UzPAK) and a mobile operator.[5]

The legal regime permits competition of the services providing Internet access. The number of ISPs in Uzbekistan has grown considerably: from 25 in 1999 to 539 in 2005. Because of increased legal requirements for operation, the number of ISPs dropped to 430 in 2006 but subsequently increased to 859 as of April 2009.[6] There are seven top-tier ISPs with connections to China, Russia, Italy, Germany, and the Netherlands. Uzbekistan's telecommunications infrastructure supporting Internet access is quite robust compared to neighboring countries. The backbone is connected to the Trans-Asia-Europe Fiber-Optic Communications Line (TAE FOCL), which links China and Europe and has several offshoots. The country also has a network of microwave radio relay lines that provide high-speed data transmission.[7] The sole Internet exchange point, Tas-IX, used by 26 ISPs,[8] is located in Uzbek Central Telegraph's premises.[9]

As of January 2007, the digital communication network in Uzbekistan covered 100 percent of cities, towns, and regional centers.[10] Telecommunication networks (including 89 percent of digital ones) covered 93 percent of rural settlements.[11] The number of Internet users as of 2008 was 2.4 million—approximately 8.8 percent of the country's population.[12] According to local surveys, in contrast to neighboring countries, Uzbek women use the Internet at a rate almost equal to that of their male counterparts, with a difference of 3 percent.[13] About 41.3 percent of Internet users are in the 16 to 20 age range.[14] Uzbek users most commonly access the Internet from their home (42.73 percent) and work (44.60 percent), and over 70 percent of Internet users are in the capital Tashkent. Approximately 30 percent of the Internet users visit Internet cafés.[15] According to official data as of April 2009, there were 873 Internet access centers in Uzbekistan.[16]

Residential Internet services are unaffordable for the majority of the population. The average cost of dial-up services is USD 0.37 per hour, and unlimited access is USD 67.14 per month. The cost of ADSL access is significantly lower: on average, it does not exceed USD 15 per month and offers a speed of 128 Kbps. The quality of Internet access and communication services in Uzbekistan is rapidly improving. The bandwidth capacity of the external channels of Internet access has shown steady growth.[17] As of 2009, it totaled 825 Mbps, up from 44 Mbps in July 2004.[18]

The domain registration of the national ".uz" zone has been decentralized since December 2005 when five operators (now seven)[19] were granted the status of registrars. Created with the support of foreign organizations, the Computerization and Information Technology Developing Center (UzInfoCom) is a NGO that develops computer and information technologies and administers the country-code top-level domain name ".uz."[20] According to UzInfoCom, as of April 2009 the number of domains registered in the ".uz" zone was 8,298.[21]

The most popular language among Uzbek Internet users is Russian (up to 70 percent), followed by Uzbek (25 percent), and English (just about 1 percent). The most visited Web sites in Uzbekistan are media sites and search engines located in the Russian Internet zone (".ru").

According to information published by the State Committee on Radio Frequencies of the Republic of Uzbekistan, the number of cellular phone customers in Uzbekistan has nearly doubled during the last year, and as of November 1, 2008, it had reached the level of 12.5 million.[22] There are five cellular operators currently active on the market of Uzbekistan: MTS-Uzbekistan (GSM), Unitel or Beeline (GSM), Coscom (GSM), Rubicon Wireless Communication–Perfectum Mobile (CDMA), and Uzmobile (CDMA).

Legal and Regulatory Frameworks

The Uzbekistan government has approved the Program for Development of Computerization and Information and Communication Technologies for 2002–2010.[23] This program envisions the establishment of a national segment of the Internet and aims to cover all cities and settlements in the country with ICT services by the end of 2010.

The Internet is legally considered mass media in Uzbekistan. Article 29 of the Uzbek Constitution guarantees freedom of expression, and Article 67 bans censorship. Freedom of information, however, can be legally restricted to protect the moral values of society, national security, and Uzbekistan's spiritual, cultural, and scientific potential. The Central Inspection on Protecting State Secrets in the Press officially censored media until 2002. Since then, the government increasingly imposes self-censorship on online media publishers, bloggers, and opposition leaders.[24] A recent example is the Mass Media Law.[25] Discussions on texts of this law were closed to the public to minimize media criticism against restrictive provisions. The law holds media owners, editors, and staff members responsible for the objectivity of published materials.[26] Independent and foreign media, including online publishers, need to register with the Cabinet of Ministers in Uzbekistan. In addition, the law forbids entities with 30 percent or more foreign participation from establishing their own media outlets in the country. Online versions of newspapers are within the scope of the law and as such are subject to registration if their content differs from the printed publication. In order to gain more control over the Internet, the government has stated that subsequent regulations would specify the type of Web sites that would need to be registered.[27]

Formal regulation of the Internet and electronic mass media commenced with the adoption of Regulation No. 52 by the Cabinet of Ministers of Uzbekistan.[28] In particular, Regulation No. 52 established the National Network of Information Transmission (UzPAK) and ensured its monopoly on international Internet connectivity for purposes of preserving national information security. The government forced ISPs to route their traffic through the state network to access international traffic.[29] Thus, Internet cafés and other clients were subjected to UzPAK's filtering system, and a number of Web sites were temporarily inaccessible. In July 2002, the Communications and Information Agency of Uzbekistan (UzCIA) suspended the work of EastLink, one of the major Uzbekistan-based ISPs, because the ISP had connected to international networks circumventing the national data-transmission network run by UzPAK.[30] Regulation No. 352[31] attempted to abolish UzPAK's monopoly on international connections and foster a decentralization process in the field of Internet providers. However, more than 80 percent of the ISPs still run their connection through UzPAK despite the high tariffs. Only a few ISPs have their own international satellite connections that provide better service than UzPAK, for lower fees.[32] A growing trend among ISPs is using UzPAK's lines to send messages and satellite networks to view or download information. This solution allows the providers to circumvent UzPAK's monitoring network and channels' low capacities.

UzPAK was established within the UzCIA.[33] Under Resolution of the Cabinet of Ministers No. 232 of 2002, UzCIA is responsible for providing information security and regulating providers' activities in the area of communications, including the Internet.[34] The director general of the agency is also the deputy prime minister responsible for telecommunications, and also acts as chairman of the board of Uzbektelecom and as chairman of the State Commission on Radio Frequencies.[35] Since most of the key regulatory functions in the sector are concentrated in the hands of the deputy minister, regulatory independence is practically nonexistent. All ISPs and operators must obtain a license from UzCIA.[36] The licenses are usually very specific, with a typical duration of ten years. Under Order No. 216, Internet providers and operators cannot disseminate information that, inter alia, calls for violent overthrow of the constitutional order of Uzbekistan, instigates war and violence, contains pornography, or degrades and defames human dignity.[37] Uzbektelecom, the national telecommunication operator, has discretionary power to oversee the ISPs' observance of this order.[38] In 2005, the ISPs in Uzbekistan faced another regulatory hindrance to their operation. The new Resolution No. 155 of the Cabinet of Ministers stipulated that only legal entities should be entitled to provide licensed telecommunication services. Individuals have to register as legal entities and obtain new licenses before continuing to provide Internet services.

In 2004, the Cabinet of Ministers adopted Regulation No. 555, establishing the Center for Mass Media Monitoring within UzCIA. The center's key objectives are to analyze the contents of information disseminated online and ensure its consistency with existing laws and regulations.[39] Another regulatory body, the Uzbek Agency for Press and Information (UzPIA), monitors the observance of media law and issues registrations and licenses for media outlets.[40] This agency has the power to suspend media licenses for "systematic" breaches of Uzbekistan's restrictive media and information laws.

The 2002 Law on Principles and Guarantees on Access to Information reserves the government's right to restrict access to information when necessary to protect the individual "from negative informational psychological influence."[41] The government further controls information streams by authorizing the use of political, economic, or other measures when necessary to counteract "threats in the sphere of information security" or "ideas of terrorism and religious extremism."[42]

Surveillance

Internet filtering in Uzbekistan did not begin with the security forces, but rather with the academic and research network, which was funded with foreign development assistance. The first Uzbek ISP to implement a filtering policy was UzSCINET, which used an open-source filtering product (SquidGuard) and a publicly available list of pornographic sites. The network justified its position favoring the filtering of pornography on the basis that it was a provider to schools and universities, as well as the need to conserve bandwidth. However, UzSCINET lacked formal legal status in Uzbekistan and as a result was dependent on UzInfoCom for maintaining its license as a service provider. The formal head of UzSCINET was also the director of UzInfoCom and a deputy director of UzCIA. Simultaneously, he was also acting as an adviser to the presidential Security Council. As a result, pressure was exerted on UzSCINET to cooperate with authorities, and over time the network became a "testing ground" that security forces used to develop a system for selecting and blocking unwanted Web sites. As late as 2005, the system was far from comprehensive, with previous ONI research showing a great deal of divergence among the various ISPs—some comprehensively blocked content, while others allowed unfettered access. The suspicion is that some commercial ISPs had close connections with President Karimov's inner circle and hence were able to withstand pressure to implement filtering, which gave them a commercial advantage (as users who wished to access such content would pay to access the Internet through these ISPs).

Uzbekistan's principal intelligence agency, the National Security Service (SNB), monitors the Uzbek sector of the Internet and "stimulates" ISPs and Internet cafés to practice self-censorship. Soviet-style censorship structures were replaced by "monitoring sections" that work under SNB's guidance. There is no mandatory government prepublication review, but ISPs risk having their licenses revoked if they post "inappropriate" information. Occasionally, the SNB orders ISPs to block access to opposition or religious Web sites.[43] A survey of internet filtering practices among Uzbek ISPs was conducted by ONI in January 2007. Respondents confirmed that they use filtering applications including SquidGuard and FortiGuard. The SNB's censorship is selective and often targets articles on government corruption, violations of human rights, and organized crime. Usually, it affects URL-specific pages instead of top-level domain names. Uzbek ISPs block entire Web sites or individual pages upon SNB's unofficial requests. Accessing a blocked page redirects the user to a search engine or to an error message such as "You are not authorized to view this page." The retransmission of blocked channels is also prohibited.

The SNB regularly exchanges data with Russian intelligence sources and allegedly collaborates with the Russian Foreign Intelligence Academy. The SNB also utilizes a blacklist and keyword approach. The SNB practice of active surveillance contributes to self-censorship among Internet operators and the Internet community as a whole. Most users will not engage in topics that touch on unpopular government policies relating to human rights in the country out of fear of arbitrary prosecution by the authorities.

ONI Testing Results

In 2007 and 2008, the OpenNet Initiative conducted testing on five main ISPs in the country: ArsInform, Buzton, Sharq Telecom, Sarkor Telecom, and Uzbektelecom. The test results show pervasive blocking of different categories of Internet content, including local and international human rights sites (inter alia, content promoting the rights of journalists working in repressive regimes), local and regional media sites, opposition sites (inter alia, content criticizing the president), local NGOs, sites of religious organizations, and terrorist groups. Interestingly, a large number of sites (including forum sites, media sites, and others) remain inaccessible for the user even though they are not blocked outright.

Conclusion

Through investment and legal mechanisms, the government has demonstrated its willingness to promote ICT in Uzbekistan. At the same time, Uzbekistan maintains the most extensive and pervasive filtering system among the CIS countries. Although expressly banned in Uzbek law, filtering is widespread and apparently growing. A large number of sites with political and human rights content sensitive to the government remain inaccessible to Internet users. The security forces in Uzbekistan manually check Internet access at "edge locations" (such as Internet cafés) and monitor users' activities. The regulatory framework is so intricately woven that in most cases ISPs and Internet publishers are unaware of the governing law. To avoid sanctions from the authorities, Internet users frequently commit themselves to self-censorship.

Notes

1. During the most robust of such actions in 2005, hundreds of people were killed. (Government statistics mention 190 people, while unofficial sources suggest that as many as 750 people—the majority of them civilians—lost their lives in the clash with the police forces.)

2. Among those expelled from Uzbekistan in 2006 was the Office of the UN High Commissioner for Refugees, which had helped to relocate refugees from the Andijan events.

3. Two liberal oppositional parties remain banned in the country: Unity (Birlik) and Uzbekistan Liberty Democratic Party (O'zbekistan Erk Demokratik Partiyasi).

4. In 2004, Internews Network Uzbekistan was accused of failing to register a logo and forced on these grounds to suspend its operations, halt its training of media lawyers, close its media resource center in the Ferghana Valley, and take its two highly popular TV news programs off air.

5. European Bank for Reconstruction and Development, *Legal Transition Program: Comparative Assessment of the Telecommunications Sector in the Transition Countries: Assessment Report Uzbekistan*, December 2008, http://ebrd.com/country/sector/law/telecoms/assess/uzbek.pdf.

6. *Infocom.uz*, "Informationno-communicationnie Technologii Uzbekistana" [Information and Communication Technologies of Uzbekistan], April 27, 2009, http://www.infocom.uz/post/?id=4391.

7. Uzbekistan has over 1,900 km of trunk fiber-optic line and over 1,000 km of trunk radio relay line.

8. Tashkent Internet Exchange, http://www.tas-ix.uz/ptspt.php.

9. For more information on the amount of traffic through the IXP, *Infocom.uz*, http://ru.infocom
.uz/.

10. *Infocom.uz*, "Informationno-communicationnie Technologii Uzbekistana" [Information and
Communication Technologies of Uzbekistan], April 27, 2009, http://www.infocom.uz/post/
?id=4391.

11. Ibid.

12. Miniwatts Marketing Group, "Internet World Statistics: Uzbekistan", 2009, http://www
.internetworldstats.com/asia.htm#uz.

13. United Nations Development Program (UNDP) and Communications and Information
Agency of Uzbekistan, *Review of Information and Communication Technology in Uzbekistan, 2005*,
http://ru.ictp.uz/downloads/annual_review_2005eng.pdf.

14. United Nations Development Program (UNDP), *Uzbekistan, Digital Development Initiative*,
2004, http://www.undp.uz/projects/project.php?id=78.

15. The total percentage exceeds 100 percent because respondents provided more than one
answer. UNDP and Communications and Information and Agency of Uzbekistan, *Review of Information and Communications Technology in Uzbekistan*, 2005, http://en.ictp.uz.

16. *Infocom.uz*, "Informationno-communicationnie Technologii Uzbekistana" [Information and
Communication Technologies of Uzbekistan], April 27, 2009, http://www.infocom.uz/post/
?id=4391.

17. According to UzCIA's data, the total modems' capacity in 2006 reached 17,000 Mbps, which
is twice as much as the analogous indicators of 2004.

18. *Infocom.uz*, "Informationno-communicationnie Technologii Uzbekistana" [Information and
Communication Technologies of Uzbekistan], April 27, 2009, http://www.infocom.uz/post/
?id=4391.

19. *Info.nic.ru*, "V Domienie Uzbekstana Uzhe Siem Ofitsialnikh Registratorov" [Uzbekistan Has
Seven Official Domain Registrars], February 10, 2008, http://info.nic.ru/st/25/out_1827.shtml.

20. UzInfoCom, http://www.cctld.uz.

21. *Infocom.uz*, "Informationno-communicationnie Technologii Uzbekistana" [Information and
Communication Technologies of Uzbekistan], April 27, 2009, http://www.infocom.uz/post/
?id=4391.

22. *Gazeta.uz*, "100% Proniknovenie Sotovoy Svyazi Otkladvaytsya" [100% Penetration of Cellular Communication Is Delayed], February 18, 2009, http://www.gazeta.uz/2009/02/18/mobile/.

23. The program was approved by the Resolution of the Cabinet of Ministers of the Republic of
Uzbekistan No. 200 of June 6, 2002.

24. Alisher Taksanov, "Between Scylla and Charybdis: Uzbek Press in Recent Years," in *21st Century Challenges for the Media in Central Asia: Dealing with Libel and Freedom of Information*, (Vienna: Organization for Security and Cooperation in Europe, 2005), 45–86, http://www.osce .org/publications/rfm/2005/07/15670_430_en.pdf.

25. The new Mass Media Law entered into force on January 15, 2007.

26. Institute for War and Peace Reporting, *Internet Hit by Media Law Change*, http://www.iwpr.net/ ?p=buz&s=b&o=328926&apc_state=henh.

27. *ccTLD.uz*, Administration of the "UZ" Domain, "UzNet Websites Will not need a Total Registration" [Totalnaya Registratsiya sitam UzNet ne grozit], January 18, 2007, http://www.cctld.uz/ news/?detail=92.

28. Paragraph 1, Regulation No. 52, On the Establishment of the National Network of Information Transmission and Streamlining the Access to the World Information Networks, adopted on February 5, 1999.

29. David Stubbs, "American Aid Could Worsen Internet Restrictions in Uzbekistan," *EurasiaNet*, March 30, 2002, http://www.eurasianet.org/departments/rights/articles/eav033002.shtml.

30. *Internews Russia*, "EIM Media Report from the CIS," July 2002.

31. Paragraph 1, Regulation No. 352, On the Decentralization of Access to the World Computer Networks, adopted by the Cabinet of Ministers of Uzbekistan on October 10, 2002.

32. Forty satellites are accessible in Uzbekistan, while about 15 of them cover the country. The majority of them belong to INTELSAT, INMARSAT, CCCASIASAT, TURKSAT, and the Russian Federation.

33. UzCIA was established under Regulation No. 215, On the Measures of Improving the Activity of the Uzbek Agency for Communications and Information of 2004.

34. RESEA Republic of Uzbekistan Portal of the State Authority, Communication and Information Agency of Uzbekistan, http://www.gov.uz/en/section.scm?sectionId=2762.

35. European Bank for Reconstruction and Development, *Legal Transition Program: Comparative Assessment of the Telecommunications Sector in the Transition Countries: Assessment Report Uzbekistan*, December 2008, http://ebrd.com/country/sector/law/telecoms/assess/uzbek.pdf.

36. Order No. 285, approved by the Head of the Uzbek Agency for Communications and Information on August 25, 2004.

37. Provision 12, Paragraph 2, Order No. 216, approved by the Head of the Uzbek Agency for Communications and Information on July 23, 2004.

38. Regulation No. 221, adopted by the Cabinet of Ministers of Uzbekistan on October 6, 2005.

39. Paragraph 1, Regulation No. 555, On the Measures of Improving the Organizational Structures in the Sphere of Mass Telecommunications, adopted by the Cabinet of Ministers of Uzbekistan on November 24, 2004.

40. Republic of Uzbekistan Portal of the State Authority, Uzbekistan Agency for Press and Information, http://www.gov.uz/en/section.scm?sectionId=2759.

41. Inera Safargalieva, "Uzbek Media and the Authorities—A Strange Relationship," in *Central Asia—In Defense of the Future: Media in Multi-Cultural and Multi-Lingual Societies*, (Vienna: Organization on Security and Co-operation in Europe, 2003), 259–264, http://www.oscc.org/publications/rfm/2004/02/12243_101_en.pdf.

42. See Article 15, Information Security of the State.

43. Reporters Without Borders, *Internet Under Surveillance 2004—Uzbekistan*, 2004, http://www.unhcr.org/refworld/publisher,RSF,,UZB,46e6919ac,0.html.

Europe

Europe Osa

Europe Overview

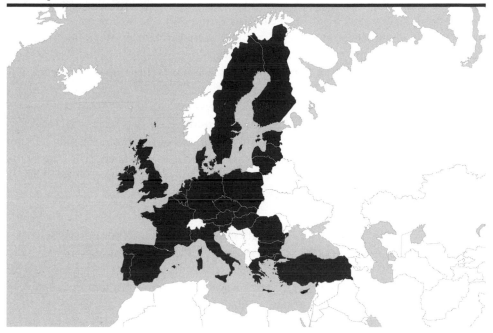

The Internet in Europe is controlled predominantly through a combination of governments and information and communication technology (ICT) companies. Countries, whether members of the 27 member European Union (EU) or otherwise, have all regulated the Internet in some way, with a number of them censoring defamatory speech or monitoring copyright infringement. Meanwhile, ICT firms have taken it upon themselves to censor child pornography and hate speech.

Unlike other parts of the world, however, the Internet in Europe is regulated to a large degree through the coordinated action of states, usually through the processes of the EU. As European governments look to harmonize their cyber-law policies over the coming years, they will increasingly turn to the EU to decide what to regulate and how to regulate the Internet.

Regional Regulation

There is no explicit obligation at the EU level mandating either governments or ICT firms to filter or remove online content, though this position may soon change. In December 2008, the EU approved the next phase of studies of new filtering technologies to fight illegal content. The Safer Internet Program adopted by the EU Council of

Ministers intends to protect minors from illegal and harmful content online, in particular, "child sexual abuse material, grooming and cyber bullying." This program will operate from 2009 to 2013 and cost EUR 55 million.[1] Part of the program involves the development of tracking technologies that will monitor child pornography and help build a Europol database of illegal online behavior.[2]

This program is the latest in a series of related initiatives introduced by the EU. The first EU attempt, "Action Plan for a Safer Internet," aimed at regulating content deemed illegal or harmful by individual states, was passed in 1999 and has been in force since 2002.[3] Illegal content varies between countries; Nazi propaganda, for example, is illegal in France and Germany but not in the United Kingdom. Harmful content is defined more broadly and can include anything that would offend the values and sentiments of races, religious groups, or other minorities. The action plan emphasized the need to take steps in five broad areas in order to curb illegal and harmful content on the Internet:

1. Promoting voluntary industry self-regulation and content monitoring schemes, including the use of hotlines for the public to report illegal or harmful content;
2. Encouraging Internet service provider(s) to provide filtering tools and rating systems that enable parents or teachers to regulate the access of Internet content by children in their care, while allowing adults access to legal content;
3. Raising awareness about services offered by ICT firms to allow users to control access to content;
4. Exploring the legal implications of promoting the safer use of the Internet; and
5. Encouraging international cooperation in the area of regulation.

For the most part, the 2002 action plan left it to individual states to take these steps. The Safer Internet Program, passed in 2005, aims to give the EU broader powers and new tools to achieve these goals itself. Among other things, the 2005 program funded hotlines for citizens to report offending content, sponsored education efforts on consumer and data protection, and authorized new studies into filtering technology for illegal content.[4]

Two European directives may form the basis of expansive legislation regulating the Internet in the coming years. The Electronic Commerce Directive limits the liability of online providers for transferring, caching, and hosting illegal content.[5] The Audiovisual Media Services Directive (AVMSD), meanwhile, aims to extend current EU regulation for broadcast television content to the Internet.[6] The regulations include, among other things, the right of member states to sue content providers living outside their jurisdictions and the responsibility to make harmful content inaccessible to minors. Because the AVMSD was passed only in 2008, it remains unclear whether or not the directive applies to all Internet video content, or just on-demand programming sent over TCP/IP.

Most existing EU regulation regarding filtering overlaps with or supplements the existing policies of individual states. On issues of child pornography, human trafficking, terrorist propaganda, and fraud, there exists a broad consensus to monitor and block offending material. Surprisingly, no such consensus exists on who or what should be held responsible for such material. Most countries have agreed to treat ISPs as mere conduits of information. However, some countries have held these entities responsible for offending material.

The EU maintains a liberal regional policy toward ISPs, limiting their liability under the Electronic Commerce Directive,[7] however, member states have been inconsistent in applying the directive. In July 2007, a Belgian court required an ISP to implement technical measures in order to stop copyright infringements committed by its subscribers through P2P networks.[8] In 2008, the British government warned that, absent ISPs' "voluntary self-regulation," it would hold service providers legally responsible for allowing unlawful file sharing.[9] British ISPs have, by all appearances, already chosen to self-regulate.[10]

Despite the lack of strong EU-level regulation, many member states have taken it upon themselves to filter unwanted content. Many countries, such as the United Kingdom,[11] Sweden,[12] Finland,[13] Denmark,[14] Germany,[15] and Italy,[16] filter child pornography, and some governments (e.g., United Kingdom, France) have pressured ISPs to prevent copyright infringements by filtering.[17] Quite recently, it was reported that a number of Web sites in Belgium were blocked. In contrast to other countries, the Web sites were filtered not because of displaying pornographic content but in order to guarantee the privacy rights of suspects or criminals who committed sexual offenses against children and whose identity was accordingly revealed in the targeted Web sites.[18]

In addition to filtering directed by governments, ISPs and search engines within countries have often taken it upon themselves to monitor and filter controversial content. Often, these companies have decided to self-regulate in order to preempt government regulation.

Copyright

Film studios, record labels, and their associations have all strongly lobbied the EU to require ISPs to block potential copyright infringements and terminate the contracts of subscribers who visit particular Web sites. Yet the EU has been slow to act, authorizing studies but rarely taking action. Generally, however, where the EU has failed to assist the content industries, individual states have been quick to act, enthusiastically prosecuting companies and individuals who violate copyright law, both within and outside their borders.

The EU's policy on intellectual property and illegal file sharing is laid out in three directives. The Electronic Commerce Directive standardizes information and

transparency requirements for ISPs, commercial communications, and electronic contracts.[19] The 2001 Directive on Copyright and Related Rights gives authors, performers,
and film producers the sole right to reproduce and distribute their respective writings,
performances, sound recordings, and films.[20] And the 2004 Directive on the Enforcement of Intellectual Property Rights aims to harmonize intellectual property protection
regimes across the EU and allows member states' judges to issue injunctions against
ongoing or impending intellectual property violations.[21] None of these directives
have mandated the use of filtering technologies to protect intellectual property
regimes. However, where the EU has been slow to respond to the demands of the film
and music industry, individual countries have been more proactive. In 2007, a Danish
court ordered the country's largest ISP to block Allofmp3.com, a Web site offering
illegal music downloads.[22] In March 2007, Bulgarian police arrested the owner of
Arenabg.com, one of Bulgaria's largest BitTorrent trackers, and blocked the Web site
for four days.[23] Most seriously, in June 2008, France established the High Authority
for Copyright Protection and Dissemination of Works on the Internet to monitor
Internet content for illegal file sharing and eventually suspend the Internet connections of repeat file sharers.[24]

European courts have been skeptical of claims to fair use of copyrighted content. In
February 2007, a court in Brussels found that Google, Inc., had violated the copyrights
of Copiepresse, a Belgian newspaper consortium. The court ruled that by taking headlines and short news extracts from Copiepresse's newspapers, Google's news feature
illegally allowed Internet users to read articles without paying proper subscription fees
and without viewing the advertisements on Copiepresse's sites. The court fined Google
GBP 2.4 million and prohibited it from sampling Copiepresse members' articles, pictures, or drawings.[25] The court also required that Google remove, within 24 hours,
any future content that copyright holders said infringed on its rights, or pay a fine of
EUR 1,000 per day.[26] Google had similar fair use problems in France when Agence
France-Presse (AFP) sued the company for USD 17.5 million in 2005. The suit was
dropped in April 2007, following a licensing agreement under which Google could
use stories and photographs from AFP for its news aggregator and for other Google
services. The financial terms of this arrangement have not been publicly disclosed.[27]
Overall, where the EU has hesitated to take aggressive action on intellectual property
regime enforcement, individual states have been eager to step in, enforcing the laws
of their individual regimes on companies both inside and outside their borders.

A controversial Internet piracy bill was adopted by the French Parliament in March
2009. According to the so-called three-strikes bill, the French government will launch a
new agency, HADOPI (High Authority for the Diffusion of Works and the Protection of
Rights on the Internet), that would assess whether a suspect is guilty of having violated
copyright provisions when downloading material online. If it is determined that the
user violated a copyright provision, he or she would receive a warning, followed by a
suspension of Internet access for a maximum of 12 months if he or she did

not comply. Critics of the bill stress that cutting Internet access would require a court order, which is not guaranteed by the law at this stage.

Social Filtering

On issues of child pornography, European nations have worked well together to block offending content, often recruiting private companies to help them in their cause. However, on other social issues, such as gambling, states have been less effective in controlling content, either individually or in coordination with each other.

The landmark model of large-scale voluntary ISP filtering in Europe originated in the United Kingdom. Britain's largest ISP, BT, launched Project Cleanfeed in June 2004,[28] in consultation with the British Home Office. Under the auspices of this program, BT blocks Web sites that the nonprofit Internet Watch Foundation (IWF) declares as hosting images of child abuse. When individuals attempt to access Web sites on IWF's list, they receive an error message.[29] If the Web sites are hosted within the United Kingdom, the ISP is required to take down the offending material. Cleanfeed's success has inspired imitators: in 2008, the ISP Brightview began offering a filtering device, WebMinder, free to other service providers. Today, some 90 percent of broadband subscribers in the United Kingdom have filtering programs of one form or another.[30]

Other countries, such as Norway, Sweden, Denmark, and Italy, have implemented similar programs, though not without controversy.[31] Finland's pilot program received negative attention early on when the Finnish National Bureau of Investigation, which prepares the list of Web sites to be filtered, included lapisporno.info—a Web site discussing the issue of Internet censorship—on the list. A 2005 effort by German search engines to delist harmful content providers came under criticism when the search engines refused to say which Web sites were being removed.[32]

In December 2008, the Romanian Regulatory Authority for Communications and Information Technology on the basis of Law No. 196/2003 ordered ISPs to block access to 40 Web sites containing illegal material. If an ISP does not execute such a blocking order within 48 hours, it may be fined between ROL 100,000 and ROL 500,000,000 (from USD 41,400 to USD 207 million).[33] The block list[34] contained mainly pornographic Web sites, although reportedly a well-known user-generated video-sharing site was also included.[35] The Romanian Regulatory Authority can compel ISPs to block access to any Web site that does not comply with the provisions of the law stating that pornographic Web sites have to be officially authorized, password protected, and charged for at a per-minute rate (determined by the site's operator).[36] The authority is not required by the legislation to give an appropriate waiting period to Web site owners to comply with these legal requirements; instead, it can immediately order ISPs to block access.

Despite criticism, individual countries' efforts at stopping child pornography have met with remarkable success. In 2006, the U.K. Child Exploitation and Online

Protection Center made 13 arrests in a pay-per-view pornography program.[37] In February 2007, Austrian authorities were able to uncover a child-pornography ring involving more than 2,300 people in 77 countries.[38]

As individual countries have moved to filter pornographic content online, they have done so with increasing coordination. Citizens in 19 countries assist in identifying and reporting illegal content—particularly in the area of child pornography—through a network of hotlines established by the EU.[39] Recent reports show that the Save the Children Denmark hotline, financed in part by the European Commission's Safer Internet Plus Program, had nearly 9,000 reports of child abuse images in 2006 alone. In 2004, Spanish police arrested 90 people in the country's largest operation against the distribution of child pornography, also facilitated by the hotlines. At the same time, new regulations at the regional level could force countries to impose stricter filtering regimes within their own countries. The new AVMSD requires member states to take measures to ensure that on-demand audiovisual services that might seriously impair the "physical, mental or moral development of minors" are made inaccessible to minors.[40]

While Europe has been very successful in mobilizing filtering technologies against child pornography, it has been less successful at coordinating efforts against gambling. In 2006, Italy enacted a law that requires ISPs to block the Web sites of gambling operators not licensed nationally. In 2007, however, the European Court of Justice ruled Italy's law in violation of EU standards.[41] In 2002, Swiss politicians attempted a similar block on online gambling. The effort was suspended in 2004, and no further action has been taken since. A 2007 proposal in Norway blocked access to foreign gambling Web sites; Web sites that "desecrate the Flag or Coat of Arms of a foreign nation"; Web sites that promote hatred toward public authorities, contain hate speech, or promote racism; offensive pornography sites; and P2P networks that offer illegal downloads of music, movies, or television shows.[42] To date, no action has been taken on the bill.[43]

Individual countries have been very proactive in instituting filtering and monitoring programs to control child pornography. This enthusiasm has extended to EU-wide regulation. However, no such enthusiasm exists for controlling gambling. Filtering, where it has been instituted, has been done at the country, not the regional, level.

Nationalistic Filtering

European governments have not censored direct political opposition. However, they have on occasion censored content that had the potential to "threaten national identity."

In December 2002, a local Swiss magistrate, Françoise Dessaux, ordered several Swiss ISPs to block access to three Web sites hosted in the United States that were strongly critical of Swiss courts[44] and to modify their DNS servers to block the domain www.appel-au-peuple.org.[45] The Swiss Internet User Group and the Swiss Network Operators Group protested that the blocks could easily be bypassed and that the move was contrary to the Swiss constitution, which guarantees "the right to receive information freely, to gather it from generally accessible sources and to disseminate it" to every person.[46] Nevertheless, the order was enforced, and directors of noncompliant ISPs were asked to appear personally in court, or they would risk facing charges.

On March 7, 2007, Turkey forced ISPs to block YouTube after several videos were posted denigrating Turkey's founding father, Mustafa Kemal Atatürk, and the Turkish flag. In blocking the Web site, Turkish officials invoked Article 301 of the Turkish Penal Code, which criminalizes insults toward Atatürk as well as "Turkishness." Turkey's leading ISP, TurkTelecom, complied with the order but petitioned the court to allow access to the Web site to be restored. The court agreed on the condition that the particular videos be removed. The two-day blocking was heavily criticized both within Turkey and abroad, and likened to "closing a library because of a single book that was found to be improper."[47] Yet YouTube and similar Web sites were again blocked in March 2008 for hosting content insulting to Atatürk.[48]

Hate Speech

Within Europe there is a general consensus in favor of censoring anti-Semitic or Holocaust-denying speech online. Where individual states have more expansive anti-hate regimes, they have enforced those laws, with some success, at the national level. In 2000, a French court ruled that U.S.-based Yahoo! Inc. was liable under French law for allowing the people of France access to auction Web sites that included Nazi memorabilia and demanded that Yahoo block this content in France or face fines.[49] Yahoo brought a suit in a U.S. District Court in San Francisco, claiming that the French court's ruling was unenforceable in the United States. The U.S. court ruled in Yahoo's favor in November 2001,[50] but in 2004 the Ninth U.S. Circuit Court of Appeals overturned that ruling on the grounds that it did not have sufficient jurisdiction over the French parties.[51] After rehearing the case *en banc*, the appeals court dismissed Yahoo's case in January 2006.[52] Though split, the court reasoned that the fact that Yahoo had complied voluntarily and removed the offending content precluded claims as to a possible violation of the right to freedom of expression.[53]

Similarly, the German Federal Court of Justice ruled in December 2000 that material glorifying the Nazis and denying the Holocaust must be censored as per German law, regardless of where it is hosted.[54] In 2002, the Bezirksregierung Düsseldorf (district government) obliged 56 ISPs to restrict access to four foreign Web sites.[55] The attempts to block access have attracted nationwide attention and met fierce opposition from users and service providers.[56] However, neither political demonstrations nor lawsuits have been successful in stopping the blockade. By the end of 2005, 76 Internet service providers had been required to block the named Web sites.[57]

Germany has engaged in other efforts to combat hate speech. According to one study published by the Berkman Center for Internet and Society in 2002, about 91 Web sites were completely or partly excluded by the German sections of the search engine Google.[58] In 2008, about 23 suspects were apprehended by German police in eight German states, and a further 70 suspects had been identified in the investigation because of their illegal sale of right-wing extremist material over the Internet.[59]

Holocaust denial is also legislated at the country level. Fifteen European countries also have laws against Holocaust denial,[60] and others ban material that promotes racial hatred. These have been harmonized in a protocol to the Council of Europe's cyber-crime treaty, which requires that "any written material, any image or any other representation of ideas or theories, which advocates, promotes or incites hatred, discrimination or violence, against any individual or group of individuals, based on race, color, descent or national or ethnic origin, as well as religion if used as pretext for any of these factors" and "material which denies, minimizes, approves of or justifies crimes of genocide or crimes against humanity" must be made illegal by the signatories.[61] As with all illegal content, once it is brought to their attention, ISPs must either take down or block the relevant Web sites (depending on whether they are hosted domestically or abroad).

One issue Europe has yet to resolve with regard to hate speech is whether merely linking to offending content constitutes a crime. A 2000 case, in which French citizens were barred from shopping on Web sites selling Nazi memorabilia,[62] would suggest that Europeans would think it is. Yet, in 2004, the political activist Alvar Freude was accused of linking to right-wing extremist Web sites and was brought to court. A local court found this to be a criminal offense. However, the Stuttgart higher regional court overturned that decision in 2006 and absolved Freude.[63]

Defamation

Two forces are intersecting to shape defamation law in Europe. On the one hand, states are relying on the "effects test" to determine legal jurisdiction; that is, so long as harm is done within the country's borders, the injured party can sue within that country. On the other hand, individual countries are also exercising comparatively harsh anti-defamation laws. Together, these forces mean that more people are being sued outside their home countries, and for more money, than ever before.

Member states of the EU have sought a simplified electronic defamation framework. The traditional principle in cases of defamation concerning the media—that the law of the country where the defamed person lives is applicable—creates a strong incentive for media to gain a potentially impractical degree of knowledge about the privacy and defamation laws of each European country. In Italy, for example, a man in a cross-border custodial battle claimed that his ex-wife, now a resident of Israel, was responsible for posting statements and images on the Internet that were defamatory of him and his ability to care for their two daughters. Italy's highest appellate court, the

Suprema Corte di Cassazione, overturned a prior verdict and held that Italy's laws of libel applied to content on foreign Web sites accessible by Internet users in the country.[64] Italian doctrine thus supports an effects test for choice of law, similar to that used in the United States for personal jurisdiction: if the offending statements, wherever posted, created an effect within the country, they are subject to the Italian law. Other countries are reaching similar conclusions. The German Federal Court of Justice decided in 2000 that the Australian owner of an Australian Web site which denied the Holocaust could be held liable in Germany.[65]

Simultaneously, anti-defamation laws at the domestic level, particularly in Britain, have been criticized for leading to a "Web takedown" culture in which ISPs immediately remove content alleged to be defamatory for fear of lawsuits. A landmark precedent in the United Kingdom led the way for the establishment of a "notice and takedown" system. In *Laurence Godfrey v. Demon Internet Limited*,[66] a defamatory statement was made on a posting to a newsgroup, www.soc.culture.thai, available on a server of Demon Internet Limited. Despite Godfrey's request to remove the post, Demon did not comply. As a result, he claimed damages for libel under section 1 of the Defamation Act of 1996[67] and settled with Demon out of court for over GBP 250,000.[68]

On rare occasions, some countries have attempted to achieve tight Internet regulation by subjecting Web sites to mandatory registration under general media laws or Internet-specific regulations. Such registration directly submits Web site owners and users to civil and/or criminal law liability for content published online, which may arise under provisions sanctioning defamation, dissemination of illegal content, and pornography (among others). In some cases such publication may require preapproval by a state agency. Poland, for instance, shows lack of clarity with regard to the status of online media. A television broadcast segment that criticized the work of a Polish debt collector prompted a series of threatening comments on a forum on the GazetaBytowska.pl (Bytów Newspaper) Web site. Polish police asked the Web site's administrator to give them identifying information for the commentators in question, but he refused. The police then charged the Web site under article 45 of the Press Law Act (PLA) of 1984.[69] A local court determined the Web site to be a daily publication and therefore subject to the PLA, which provides for punishment for editors who publish—even unintentionally—"criminal content," including threats like the ones made in the online forum. The case was appealed to the Regional Court, which ruled in February 2008 that Web sites such as GazetaBytowska.pl must be registered.[70] A ruling of the Polish Supreme Court a year earlier stated that "journals and periodicals do not lose the character of a press release due solely to the fact that they appear in the form of an Internet transmission" and that "the publishing of press in an electronic form, available on the Internet, requires registration." Subsequently, a Supreme Court spokesman emphasized that the ruling was not intended to suggest that all regularly updated Web sites needed to be registered.[71]

Together, these two trends—the increasing use of the effects test and increasingly harsh damages for defamation—have given an incentive for European countries to coordinate anti-defamation laws at the European level.

A 2007 amendment to the Rome II convention attempted to set regional standards for the application of anti-defamation laws. The amendment instructed European courts to obey, with some exceptions, the anti-defamation laws of the country in which the damage occurred.[72]

Surveillance

European countries have worked to coordinate security directives at the regional level, yet these consensus directives have been criticized by outside groups as far too extreme. The 2006 European Data Retention Directive[73] prescribes surveillance on a regional level in the public interest. Because the directive has been transposed into the national legislation of most of the EU member states, ISPs at the local level are required to retain specific data pertaining to electronic communications to assist in tracking down crimes and for future prosecutions. Such data can be collected through users' activities, in particular Internet access, e-mail, and telephony, and can be retained for a minimum period of six months but not exceeding two years.[74] The aim is to bring about a common code of data retention in order to trace illegal content and the source of attacks against information systems, and to identify those who use electronic communications networks for terrorist activities and organized crime. The data to be retained do not concern the content of communications. Yet the directive has inspired controversy within member states and was challenged recently at the German Constitutional Court.[75]

Yet some countries are far exceeding the scope of surveillance allowed by the EU. In March 2007, the Swedish government granted its national defense intelligence agency the power to monitor all cross-border telephone calls and e-mail traffic, even without a warrant. Various critics have raised privacy concerns about the plan, positing that the proposal violates privacy rights and breaches EU law. Notwithstanding the criticism, in January 2009 amendments to the Swedish wiretapping law entered into force, allowing the National Defense Radio Establishment sweeping surveillance powers over online activities. The new law allows special state agencies to monitor telephone calls and Internet traffic, including the content of the traffic itself, which is outside of the scope of the EU Data Retention Directive. In addition, the state agency could develop a plan to search for sensitive keywords in transmitted messages and could even require monitoring content on servers outside the country's borders.[76] A nongovernmental organization has already brought a case against the new law in the European Court of Human Rights.[77] Sweden's own national security police agency called the plan a violation of "personal integrity." Such pervasive policies against online activities have triggered disapproval among big international ICT companies, some of which announced that they would cease making significant investments in the country if the controversial law was not revisited.[78]

A different development of events occurred in Finland, where employers organizations (reportedly including handset giant Nokia)[79] lobbied strongly for introducing legislation that would allow employers to track employees' e-mails to prevent corporate espionage. In March 2009, the Finnish government adopted such a law granting employers access to information about their workers' messages, including the recipients, senders, and the time when e-mails were sent or received, and whether the e-mails contained attachments. The law does not allow the employers to read the content of the messages outright. Nonetheless, employers' otherwise broad rights over employees' electronic communications raise serious privacy concerns.

Germany, too, is taking active steps toward increasing government surveillance online. A new amendment to the national telecommunication law requires that ISPs retain personal data, such as e-mail senders' IP addresses, recipients' IP addresses, date and time of all messages, IP address for each Internet subscriber, and a unique identifier for each client to track online activity.

Germany's federal crime police, the Bundeskriminalamt, have not only monitored e-mails and chat rooms, but also begun performing so-called online raids.[80] The idea is to infect a suspect's personal computer with Trojan horse software to secretly record data entered into the computer. However, this technique remains highly controversial. The federal constitutional court ruled in March 2008 that online raids could only be used in exceptional circumstances.[81]

In 2005, the Italian government authorized increased surveillance of the Internet and telephone networks.[82] The bill requires Internet cafés to keep photocopies of customers' passports and to periodically submit logs of all Web sites visited to the police.[83] The law also increases licensing requirements for telecommunication service operators, making licensing approval dependent upon the existence of satisfactory data-monitoring and retention systems.[84]

In France, two laws have granted increased surveillance powers to the government. The Daily Safety Law (LSQ) was approved almost unanimously by parliament on November 15, 2001, and the Internet Safety Law (LSI) was enacted on February 13, 2003. Together, these laws require that ISPs keep a record of their customers' Internet activity and e-mail traffic for a year and that encryption firms assist authorities in decoding messages involved in criminal trials. Additionally, in June 2008 the French government established the High Authority for Copyright Protection and Dissemination of Works on the Internet, which will monitor all network traffic for possible copyright infringement.

Similar surveillance policies were introduced in Poland, with a February 2003 amendment to the Telecommunications Law. The law requires telecommunication companies to provide the police and other state agencies with access to information sent through telecommunications networks for the purpose of national defense, state security, and public order.[85] The data that may be requested by the police include caller identification, network terminals and/or telecommunication devices used in the connection, data generated during the connection, the circumstances, and the type of connection.[86]

The Polish government has been criticized for conducting a large number of wiretapping operations that may be seen as an invasion of privacy. In early March 2009, the office of the Polish prime minister announced that it had plans to compile a "super database" of information on all Polish citizens. The database would be compiled during the 2011 census and would include information from the ministries of finance, justice, and home affairs, social insurance information, and information gathered from telecommunications suppliers. The plan has met with outrage from Polish Internet users, who claim the database would violate their constitutional rights. The prime minister's office has since released a statement explaining that the database will only include necessary information.[87] It remains to be seen who would then determine what information is necessary and how Internet users' right to privacy would be guaranteed.

The prospect of revenue from online advertising has sometimes driven operators to exercise surveillance over their customers' preferences. Major British operators BT, Talk Talk, and Virgin have all signed up to use Phorm,[88] a Web tracking service, which uses information gathered from a user's browsing history to deliver targeted advertising on members' Web sites. An admission has been made by BT that it ran secret trials of a new advertising platform among 18,000 of its broadband customers in 2006 in order to determine the operational and technical performance of the service. The platform targets advertisements at the operator's customers using their browsing profiles. The EU threatened in April 2009 to pursue legal action against the United Kingdom for breaching Internet privacy laws by allowing operators to use the platform to track their customers' online activities for commercial gain (estimated at GBP 3 billion a year).

Conclusion

Today, Internet content in Europe is controlled by three groups of factors: region-wide organizations (the EU), individual countries, and companies (e.g., ISPs, search engines). While governments have been extremely active in promoting filtering technologies for child pornography and surveillance technologies for copyright infringement, they are increasingly finding that they can achieve their aims through indirect means. Rather than passing explicit regulations, governments have pressured companies to voluntarily self-regulate content, be it pornography, hate speech, or content that infringes upon copyrights. Such pressures show a creeping tendency toward the second- and third-generation controls found elsewhere.

At the EU level, countries are increasingly working to harmonize Internet regulation, especially with regard to defamatory and pornographic content. Given the significant cultural differences between countries and existing regulatory frameworks, creating a common platform for legislation at the regional level is a slow and complex process. Nonetheless, it is increasingly the arena where decisions about Internet filtering and monitoring are made.

Notes

1. European Commission, "Safer Internet Programme 2009–2013." http://ec.europa.eu/ information_society/activities/sip/policy/programme/current_prog/index_en.htm.

2. Web Designers Blog, "EU Share 55 Million to Create Surveillance Technology on the Internet," November 1, 2008, http://web.pdesigner.net/2008/11/01/eu-share-55-million-to-create-surveillance -technology-on-the-internet/.

3. European Commission, "Action Plan for a Safer Internet 1999–2004," January 19, 2007, http:// europa.eu/legislation_summaries/information_society/l24190_en.htm.

4. European Commission, "Safer Internet Programme 2005–2008 (Safer Internet Plus)," January 19, 2007, http://europa.eu/legislation_summaries/information_society/l24190b_en.htm.

5. European Commission, Directive 2000/31/EC of the European Parliament, August 17, 2000, http://eur-lex.europa.eu/LexUriServ/LexUriServ.do?uri=CELEX:32000L0031:EN:HTML.

6. European Commission, "Audiovisual Media Services Directive (AVMSD)," 2007, http://ec .europa.eu/avpolicy/reg/avms/index_en.htm.

7. European Commission, "E-Commerce Directive," May 22, 2000, http://ec.europa.eu/internal _market/e-commerce/directive_en.htm.

8. Brussels Court of First Instance (TGI), *SABAM v. s.a. Scarlet (anciennement Tiscali)*, 04/8975/A, June 29, 2007, http://www.juriscom.net/documents/tpibruxelles20070629.pdf.

9. Francis Elliot, "Internet Users Could Be Banned over Illegal Downloads," *Times Online*, February 12, 2008, http://technology.timesonline.co.uk/tol/news/tech_and_web/the_web/article3353387 .ece.

10. *Cable Forum*, "Virgin Media First UK ISP to Adopt 3-Strikes-and-Out on Illegal Downloads," March 31, 2008, http://www.cableforum.co.uk/article/394/virgin-media-first-uk-isp-to-adopt-3 -strikes-and-out-on-illegal-downloads.

11. Wendy M. Grossman, "IWF Reforms Could Pave Way for UK Net Censorship," *The Register*, December 29, 2006, http://www.theregister.co.uk/2006/12/29/iwf_feature/.

12. *Telenor*, "Telenor and Swedish National Criminal Investigation Department to Introduce Internet Child Porn Filter," May 17, 2005, http://press.telenor.com/PR/200505/994781_5.html.

13. *Helsingin Sanomat*, "Anti-Internet Censorship Website Placed on Police Filter List over Links to Child Porn Sites," February 14, 2008, http://www.hs.fi/english/article/AntiInternet+censorship +website+placed+on+police+filter+list+over+links+to+child+porn+sites/1135234057449.

14. Kristian Hansen, "Danish Filter Catches Romanian Child-Porn Sites," *Computerworld*, June 11, 2008, http://www.computerworld.com/s/article/9097018/Danish_filter_catches_Romanian_child_porn_sites.

15. Lars Vage, "German Search Services Collaborate to Exclude Child Pornography, Right Wing Extremism, and Glorification of Violence," *Pandia*, March 8, 2005, http://www.pandia.com/sw-2005/10-germany.html.

16. Loverock Davidson, "Italy Adopts Microsoft Anti-Child-Porn Technology," *ZDNet*, October 17, 2006, http://talkback.zdnet.com/5208-9588-0.html?forumID=1&threadID=26363&messageID=494518&start=0.

17. Kate Holton, "UK Could Follow France on Internet Piracy Plan," Reuters, February 12, 2008, http://www.reuters.com/article/rbssTechMediaTelecomNews/idUSL1282127820080212.

18. Bart B. Van Bockstaele, "Belgian Government Trying to Censor the Internet," *Digital Journal*, April 22, 2009, http://www.digitaljournal.com/article/271340#tab=featured&sc=0&contribute=&local=.

19. European Commission, "E-Commerce Directive," 2000, http://ec.europa.eu/internal_market/e-commerce/directive_en.htm.

20. European Commission, "Copyright and Related Rights in the Information Society: Harmonisation of Certain Aspects," January 14, 2008, http://europa.eu/legislation_summaries/internal_market/businesses/intellectual_property/l26053_en.htm.

21. European Commission, "Enforcement of Intellectual Property Rights," December 13, 2007, http://europa.eu/legislation_summaries/fight_against_fraud/fight_against_counterfeiting/l26057a_en.htm.

22. City Court of Copenhagen, *IFPI Denmark v. Tele2*, October 25, 2006, Case F1–15124/2006; P2P.net, "IFP vs Tele 2—in English," http://www.p2pnet.net/story/10319.

23. European Digital Rights, "Bulgarian Police Ordered ISPs to Block US-Based Torrent Tracker," April 12, 2007, http://www.edri.org/edrigram/number5.7/bulgarian-block-isp.

24. *Kaldata*, "French Bill Would Ban Internet Use for Illegal Downloaders," June 20, 2008, http://www.kaldata.net/comments.php?catid=3&id=20895.

25. Bruno Waterfield, "Google to Pay £2.4m over 'Copyright Breach,'" *Daily Telegraph*, February 14, 2007, http://www.telegraph.co.uk/news/worldnews/1542549/Google-to-pay-andpound2.4m-over-%27copyright-breach%27.html.

26. European Digital Rights, "Belgium Court Backs Decision against Google," February 14, 2007, http://www.edri.org/edrigram/number5.3/google-belgium.

27. Caroline McCarthy, "Agence France-Presse, Google Settle Copyright Dispute," *CNet*, April 6, 2007, http://news.com.com/2100-1030_3-6174008.html.

28. *BBC News*, "BT Acts against Child Porn Sites," June 8, 2004, http://news.bbc.co.uk/2/hi/technology/3786527.stm.

29. Although BT records the number of access attempts, it does not retain information pertaining to the identity of persons who attempt to access these Web sites. See Michael McDonough, "35,000 Blocks a Day on Internet Child Porn," *Guardian*, February 7, 2006, http://technology .guardian.co.uk/news/story/0,,1704342,00.html.

30. 446 Parl. Deb., H.C. (6th ser.) (2006) 709W.

31. See *Telenor*, "Telenor and Swedish National Criminal Investigation Department to Introduce Internet Child Porn Filter," May 17, 2005, http://press.telenor.com/PR/200505/994781_5.html; *Financial Mirror*, "Filter Blocks Danes from Accessing Child Pornography," November 28, 2005, http://www.financialmirror.com/more_news.php?id=2574; European Digital Rights, "New Italian Law to Block Child Pornography Websites," January 17, 2007, http://www.edri.org/edrigram/ number5.1/italy_blocking.

32. *Heise Online*, "Search Engine Providers Practice Self-Regulation," February 25, 2005, http:// www.heise.de/english/newsticker/news/56817.

33. "Law on the Prevention and Fighting of Pornography," No 196/2003 [Unofficial translation from Romanian], http://www.legi-internet.ro/index.php?id=89&L=2.

34. *Nicu*, "Romanian Censored Sites," December 16, 2008, http://nicubunu.blogspot.com/2008/ 12/romanian-censored-sites-warning-about.html.

35. European Digital Rights, "Romanian Authority Asks ISPs to Block 40 Pornographic Websites," http://www.edri.org/edri-gram/number6.24/anc-blocks-isp-pornography-romania.

36. ANCOM, "ANC cere Blocarea Accesului la 40 de Site uri cu Caracter Pornografic" [ANC Calls for Blocking Access to 40 Pornographic Sites], December 11, 2008, http://www.anrcti.ro/ DesktopDefault.aspx?tabid=3483.

37. *BBC News*, "13 Arrests over Child Sex Images," July 25, 2006, http://news.bbc.co.uk/1/hi/uk/ 5213058.stm.

38. *BBC News*, "Vienna Busts Huge Child Porn Ring," February 7, 2007, http://news.bbc.co.uk/2/ hi/europe/6338125.stm.

39. For the list of countries running hotlines and the organizations involved, see European Commission, "Hotlines," May 5, 2008, http://ec.europa.eu/information_society/apps/projects/ factsheet/index.cfm?project_ref=SIP-2007-HC-121701.

40. European Parliament, "Coordination of Certain of the Member States' Provisions Concerning the Pursuit of Television Broadcasting Activities," December 19, 2007, http://www.europarl .europa.eu/oeil/file.jsp?id=5301252.

41. Eric Pfanner, "Ruling Could Open EU Gambling Market," *New York Times*, March 6, 2007, http://www.nytimes.com/2007/03/06/technology/06iht-gamble.4817616.html?_r=1.

42. Gunnar Hellieson, "The Great Firewall of Norway," *Luni.net*, February 13, 2007, http://luni .net/?p=77.

43. *Libertus.net*, "ISP 'Voluntary'/Mandatory Filtering," February 28, 2008, http://libertus.net/censor/ispfiltering-gl.html#norway.

44. The contested Web sites were http://www.appel-au-peuple.org; http://de.geocities.com/justicecontrol; and http://www.swiss-corruption.com.

45. FITUG e.V., "EDRI-gram," February 12, 2003, http://www.fitug.de/news/newsticker/newsticker120203210053.html.

46. Article 16, sec. 3; unofficial English translation available at http://www.admin.ch/org/polit/00083/index.html?lang=en.

47. European Digital Rights, "YouTube Blocked for 2 Days in Turkey," March 14, 2007, http://www.edri.org/edrigram/number5.5/youtube-turkey.

48. Eric Auchard, "Turkey Blocks Web Site over Insults to Atatürk," Reuters, March 25, 2008, http://www.reuters.com/article/internetNews/idUSN2434354220080325.

49. Center for Democracy and Technology, "Appeals Court Agrees to Reconsider Ruling about French Censorship of U.S. Speech," February 15, 2007, http://www.cdt.org/publications/policyposts/2005/5.

50. *Yahoo! Inc. v. La Ligue Contre le Racisme et l'Antisemitisme*, 169 F.Supp.2d 1181 (N.D. Cal. 2001), *rev'd*, 433 F.3d 1199 (9th Cir. 2006), *cert. denied*, 126 S.Ct. 2332 (2006).

51. *Yahoo! Inc. v. La Ligue Contre le Racisme et l'Antisemitisme*, 379 F.3d 1120 (9th Cir. 2004).

52. *Yahoo! Inc. v. La Ligue Contre le Racisme et l'Antisemitisme*, 433 F.3d 1199 (9th Cir. 2006) (en banc), *cert. denied*, 126 S.Ct. 2332 (2006).

53. *BBC News*, "The Law, Borders, and the Internet," January 24, 2006, http://news.bbc.co.uk/2/hi/technology/4641244.stm.

54. Center for Democracy and Technology, "Foreign Courts' Exercise of Jurisdiction over Web Content Seen in Other Cases," July 11, 2001, http://www.cdt.org/publications/pp_7.06.shtml.

55. *Heise Online*, "Nordrhein-Westfälische Provider Sollen Nazi-Web sites Ausfiltern" [North Rhine-Westphalia Providers Should Filter Nazi Web sites], December 8, 2001, http://www.heise.de/newsticker/Nordrhein-westfaelische-Provider-sollen-Nazi-Websites-ausfiltern–/meldung/21627.

56. *Online-Demonstrations-Plattform für Menschen*, "Declaration for Freedom of Information in the Internet," http://odem.org/informationsfreiheit/en/.

57. *Heise Online*, "Düsseldorfer Bezirksregierung Sieht Sich Erfolgreich im Kampf Gegen Nazi-Websites" [Düsseldorf District Government Sees Itself Successful in the Fight against Nazi Web sites], November 22, 2005, http://www.heise.de/newsticker/Duesseldorfer-Bezirksregierung-sieht-sich-erfolgreich-im-Kampf-gegen-Nazi-Websites–/meldung/66501/.

58. Germar Rudolf, "Censorship of the Internet," 2003, http://www.germarrudolf.com/civil/internet.html.

59. *Lancaster Unity*, "German Police Raid Homes in Far-Right Internet Probe," February 28, 2008, http://lancasteruaf.blogspot.com/2008/02/german-police-raid-homes-in-far-right.html.

60. Wikipedia, "Laws against Holocaust Denial," http://en.wikipedia.org/wiki/Laws_against _Holocaust_denial.

61. Ian Brown, "Internet Censorship: Be Careful What You Ask For," Proceedings of the International Conference on Communication, Mass Media and Culture, Istanbul, October 2006.

62. *CNN.com*, "Yahoo! Loses Nazi Auction Case," November 20, 2000, http://archives.cnn.com/2000/TECH/computing/11/20/france.yahoo.02/.

63. *Heise Online*, "Revisionsverhandlung Gegen Netzaktivisten Steht An" [Revision Negotiation against Net Activists Lines Up], April 19, 2004, http://www.heise.de/newsticker/Revisionsverhandlung-gegen-Netzaktivisten-steht-an–/meldung/72134.

64. Consumer Project on Technology, "CPT's Page on Defamation and Libel Cases," http://www.cptech.org/ecom/jurisdiction/defamation2.html.

65. Florian Rötzer, "Update: Leugnung des Holocaust im Internet Nach Deutschem Recht Strafbar," *Telepolis*, December, 13, 2000, http://www.heise.de/tp/r4/artikel/4/4467/1.html.

66. [1999] 4 All ER 342, [2001] QB 201 (QBD).

67. 1996, c. 36, sec. 1 (Eng.).

68. Yaman Akdeniz, "Case Analysis of *Laurence Godfrey v. Demon Internet Limited*," 1999, http://www.cyber-rights.org/reports/demon.htm; Consumer Project on Technology, "CPT's Page on Defamation and Libel Cases," http://www.cptech.org/ecom/jurisdiction/defamation2.html.

69. The text of the law states, "Anybody who publishes a daily newspaper or a periodical without registration or with registration suspended is subject to a fine penalty or the restriction of liberty." Article 45, Polish Press Law Act of January 26, 1984.

70. Tomasz Rychlicki and Piotr Waglowski, "Polish Courts Say Websites Should Be Registered As Press," *Computer and Telecommunications Law Review*, 2009, 15(1), 9–14, http://prawo.vagla.pl/node/8306.

71. Joanna Kulesza, "Which Legal Standards Should Apply to Web-logs? The present legal position of Internet journals in the European jurisprudence in the light of the European Parliament Committee's on Culture and Education report and Polish Supreme Court decision," *Lex Electronica*, Vol. 13, no. 3 (Winter 2009), http://www.lex-electronica.org/fr/resumes_complets/221.html.

72. European Digital Rights, "MEPs Support Again the Rules on Defamation in Rome II," February, 14, 2007, http://www.edri.org/edrigram/number5.3/romeII.

73. Directive 2006/24/EC of the European Parliament and of the Council of March 15, 2006, on the retention of data generated or processed in connection with the provision of publicly available electronic communications services or of public communications networks and amending Directive 2002/58/EC.

74. European Parliament, "Electronic Communications: Personal Data Protection Rules and Availability of Traffic Data for Anti-terrorism Purposes," March 15, 2006, http://www.europarl.europa.eu/oeil/file.jsp?id=5275032.

75. *Heise Online*, "Data Retention: ISPs Rely on Constitutional Appeals and Exception Rules," January 10, 2008, http://www.heise.de/english/newsticker/news/101624/.

76. European Digital Rights, "Cross-Border Wiretapping Proposed by the Swedish Government," March 14, 2007, http://www.edri.org/edrigram/number5.5/sweden-wiretapping.

77. David Landes, "Norwegian Group Joins Case against Sweden's Wiretapping Law," *The Local*, February 13, 2009, http://www.thelocal.se/17578/20090213/.

78. Paul O'Mahoney, "Google Likens Sweden to Dictatorship," *The Local*, May 30, 2007, http://www.thelocal.se/7452/20070530/.

79. Matti Huuhtanen, "Finnish Parliament Approves e-Mail Tracking Law," *The Age*, March 5, 2009, http://news.theage.com.au/breaking-news-technology/finnish-parliament-approves-email-tracking-law-20090305-8ona.html.

80. Wikipedia, "Online-Durchsuchung," http://de.wikipedia.org/wiki/Online-Durchsuchung#Deutschland.

81. *BBC News*, "The Most Spied Upon People in Europe," February 28, 2008, http://news.bbc.co.uk/2/hi/europe/7265212.stm.

82. *Palomar*, "Decision of the Italian Constitutional Court on the Legitimacy of Immediate Deportation of Aliens for National Security Reasons (Constitutional Court Decision n. 432/2007)," April 2008, http://www.unisi.it/dipec/palomar/italy001_2008.html#6.

83. Sofia Celeste, "Want to Check Your e-Mail in Italy? Bring Your Passport," *Christian Science Monitor*, October 4, 2005, http://www.csmonitor.com/2005/1004/p07s01-woeu.html.

84. Legislation Online, "Italy Adopts New Anti-Terrorism Legislation—2005-08-16," August 16, 2005, http://www.legislationline.org/documents/id/3138.

85. European Digital Rights, "Polish Providers Fight Email Monitoring Obligation," March 27, 2003, http://www.edri.org/edrigram/number5/email.

86. Privacy International, "PHR 2006—Republic of Poland," http://www.privacyinternational.org/article.shtml?cmd[347]=x-347-559594.

87. *PC World*, "GUS chce Przygotować Superbazę Danych o Polakach?" [Does the Chief Statistical Office Want to Prepare a "Superdatabase" of the Poles?], March 17, 2009, http://www.pcworld.pl/news/342115/GUS.chce.przygotowac.superbaze.danych.o.Polakach.html.

88. *BBC News*, "Phorm 'Illegal' Says Policy Group," April 9, 2008, http://news.bbc.co.uk/1/hi/technology/7301379.stm.

France

France continues to promote freedom of the press and speech online by allowing access to most content. France's Internet penetration rate is constantly increasing, and the French government has undertaken numerous measures to protect the rights of Internet users, including the passage of the *Loi pour la Confiance dans l'Économie Numérique* (LCEN, Law for

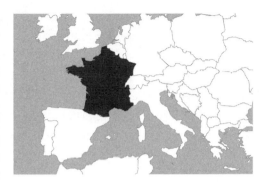

Trust in the Digital Economy) in 2004. However, the passing of a new copyright law threatening to ban users from the Internet upon their third violation has drawn much criticism from privacy advocates as well as the European Union (EU) parliament.

Background

As one of the founding nations of European economic and political integration, France is seen as a key player on the European stage. However, the country sent shockwaves through the EU when its voters rejected the proposed EU constitution in a May 2005 referendum.[1] In May 2007, Nicolas Sarkozy won the presidential election with a 53 percent majority vote.[2] The current government is a center-right administration that

RESULTS AT A GLANCE					
Filtering	No Evidence of Filtering	Suspected Filtering	Selective Filtering	Substantial Filtering	Pervasive Filtering
Political	•				
Social	•				
Conflict and security	•				
Internet tools	•				

Other Factors	Low	Medium	High	Not Applicable
Transparency				•
Consistency				•

KEY INDICATORS	
GDP per capita, PPP (constant 2005 international dollars)	31,625
Life expectancy at birth (years)	81
Literacy rate (percent of people age 15+)	99
Human development index (out of 179)	11
Rule of law (out of 211)	22
Voice and accountability (out of 209)	18
Democracy index (out of 167)	24 (Full democracy)
Digital opportunity index (out of 181)	26
Internet users (percent of population)	51

Source by indicator: World Bank 2009a, World Bank 2009a, World Bank 2009a, UNDP 2008, World Bank 2009b, World Bank 2009b, Economist Intelligence Unit 2008, ITU 2007, ITU 2008.

has sought to reform universities and special pension regimes and to modernize immigration and economic policies.[3]

The French government operates under a traditionally highly centralized decision-making process. Each of France's departments is headed by a prefect appointed by the central government. Although the process of decentralization began in the early 1980s, with regional councils directly elected for the first time in 1986, it has continued at a very slow pace.[4]

As established in the 1789 *Déclaration des Droits de l'Homme et du Citoyen* (Declaration of the Rights of Man and of the Citizen), France adheres to the principle of *laïcité*, or government secularism. Although approximately 85 percent of the French population is Roman Catholic, Europe's largest Muslim and Jewish populations reside in France, comprising 10 and 1 percent of the population, respectively.[5] Notably, as a result of such staunch secularism, France has banned women and girls from wearing the Islamic headscarf in schools, an act which has resulted in criticism from some civil rights groups.[6]

France is a liberal democracy that guarantees freedom of the press and freedom of speech.[7] Article 11 of the 1789 Declaration stipulates that "the free communication of thoughts and of opinions is one of the most precious rights of man: any citizen thus may speak, write, print freely, save [unless it is necessary] to respond to the abuse of this liberty, in the cases determined by the law."[8] In addition, the European Convention on Human Rights, which France signed in 1950, promotes free speech in Article 10.[9]

Freedom of speech is recognized as a constitutional right to be respected by citizens as well as by the government during the process of passing new French legislation. Indeed, a distinctive feature of the French judicial system is that the Constitutional Council protects basic rights against potential violations by new laws, and the Council of State protects basic rights when they might be violated by actions of the state. The

Constitutional Council examines legislation and decides whether it conforms to the constitution. It considers only legislation that is referred to it by parliament, the prime minister, or the president.[10]

If upon examination basic rights are found to be in conflict with each other, the Constitutional Council maintains a balance between freedom of speech and such principles as maintaining law and order, proper administration of justice, and protection of individuals. French law prohibits public speech and writings that incite racial and religious hatred or hatred against people because of their sexual orientation.[11] In addition, amendments have been made to France's 1881 Press Law prohibiting denial of the Holocaust and the Armenian genocide.[12] Those who violate the law face imprisonment and/or a fine of up to EUR 45,000.[13]

Internet in France

The number of Internet users in France increased dramatically from 8.5 million users in 2000[14] to almost 32 million in 2007, with a 51.2 percent Internet penetration rate.[15] Since 2000, France has adopted Internet technology at a furious pace and has had some of the fastest growth rates for Internet usage, PC shipments, and overall information technology spending by businesses, consumers, government, and education throughout Europe.[16] Although global Internet adoption and PC sales have shown some signs of slowing in recent years, France still witnessed significant yearly gains in Internet adoption: in 2005, over 60 percent of adults age 18 or older in France used the Internet regularly, representing more than a 12-point increase from 2004 (when the figure was 48 percent).[17] In addition, the usage of VoIP telephony has risen steadily in recent years, and wireless Internet access by handset/cell phone is expected to continue to grow.[18]

Although the French ISP market has begun to expand since privatization, the market leader remains France Telecom, a publicly traded company that is the main communication access provider in France.[19] Because of the well-developed information and communication technology (ICT) infrastructure, home access is affordable to most of the French population at competitive costs. Since high-speed Internet services were implemented in France in 2001, access has increased significantly, with more than one in five residents having access to high-speed Internet.[20] Public libraries and Internet cafés, prevalent throughout the country, also provide high-speed Internet access.

Studies have shown that, in comparison with other European Internet users, the French spend a considerable amount of time online. A recent ComScore study revealed that French Internet users spent 932 million hours online in February 2009, averaging approximately 27 hours per person.[21] According to one report, the most popular online activities of French Internet users include social networking, watching television, shopping, blogging, and checking the news.

Legal and Regulatory Frameworks

The French media are regulated under the supervision of the *Conseil Supérieur de l'Audiovisuel* (CSA, Higher Audiovisual Council). This independent administrative authority guarantees freedom of communication and checks whether television programs comply with French laws. Special attention is paid to the protection of young audiences, and equal air time is allocated to political candidates during election periods.[22] In response to market pressures on media pluralism, the government established *La Direction du Développement des Médias* (DDM, Department of Media Development) to encourage plurality of the press and to prevent excessive concentrations of ownership.[23]

Illegal content and activity on the Internet are mainly regulated by the LCEN 2004–575 of June 21, 2004, which supersedes European Directive 2000/31/CE.[24] Article 2 of the LCEN relieves ISPs of civil and criminal responsibility if they had "no knowledge of illegal activity or material" or if they "acted promptly to remove or block access to it as soon as they discovered it."[25] Providers are also exempt from civil responsibility if they "have no knowledge of how the illegal activity or material arose." However, once a judicial order has been issued and proper notice given to the hosting Web site, the site is liable for any further reposting of the illegal material. Moreover, a Web site can be held liable for redirecting Internet users to another Web site containing unlawful information.[26] This decision has recently been subject to controversy in France—discussions mainly focus on the definition of "illegal activity or material" and on the need for a clear distinction between editing and hosting activities.[27]

In 2000, a French judge ruled that U.S.-based Yahoo! Inc. had to prevent French users from accessing Web sites auctioning racial hate memorabilia. Yahoo complied by prohibiting users from accessing English-language Web sites selling Nazi memorabilia on its localized French site, yahoo.fr, but claimed that it was technically impossible to ban French users from accessing such content through its U.S. site.[28] In 2001, a U.S. district court ruled that the First Amendment of the Constitution protects content generated in the United States by American companies from being regulated by authorities in countries that have more restrictive laws on freedom of expression.[29]

In 2008, France signed an agreement to block access to child pornography, as well as Web sites promoting racial violence or terrorism.[30]

Surveillance

Although the French Constitution does not expressly include the right to privacy, the French Constitutional Council held in 1995,[31] and confirmed in 1999,[32] that the right to privacy is recognized as a constitutional right implicitly included in Article 2 of the 1789 Declaration.[33] The civil and penal codes expressly recognize the tort of privacy and a penal protection of the right to privacy, respectively.[34] The 1978 Data Protection

Act was amended in 2004 to create the *Commission Nationale de l'Informatique et des Libertés* (CNIL, National Commission for Information and Liberties), an independent administrative authority designed to ensure the protection of privacy and personal data.[35] With a mission of control and investigation, the CNIL can warn and impose financial sanctions in case of Data Protection Act violations. It issues an annual report based on its observations.[36]

Since the September 11, 2001 attacks on the United States, privacy and data protection rights in France have been undermined by two laws: the *Loi sur la Sécurité Quotidienne* (LSQ, Daily Safety Law) that was urgently approved, almost unanimously, by parliament on November 15, 2001, and the *Loi sur la Sécurité Intérieure* (LSI, Internet Safety Law) that was enacted on February 13, 2003.[37] The laws extend to a year the minimum period for which ISPs must keep a record of their customers' Internet activity and e-mail traffic. The LSI authorizes immediate access to the computer data of telecommunications operators, as well as those of almost any public or private institution; it also allows judges to order that "secret methods that cannot be revealed for reasons of national defense" be used to decode encrypted e-mail messages. In addition, authorities can require encryption firms to hand over their codes so that they can read encrypted online messages.[38] These provisions have been considered as a threat to the principle of confidentiality of professional and private communications in France.[39]

As a result of a campaign strongly focused on security issues, closed-circuit television (CCTV) is used in France for surveillance in public places so as to prevent criminal behavior. In 2007, the French Interior Minister announced that the number of CCTV cameras in France would triple by 2009. This policy has been designed and pursued to fight terrorism and street crime.[40]

On May 4, 2008, the French government ordered the creation of biometric passports for its citizens, citing the need to comply with post-9/11 U.S. security demands. French citizens will now be issued biometric passports that will include eight fingerprints and a digital picture; the data are then collected in a national database.[41] On December 11, 2007, the CNIL published an unfavorable opinion concerning this project, fearing serious damage to private life and individual liberties.[42]

On April 9, 2009, the *Projet de loi Favorisant la Diffusion et la Protection de la Création sur Internet* (Bill promoting the dissemination and protection of creation on the Internet), intended to deny Internet access to users who repeatedly downloaded copyrighted content without paying, was rejected by the French National Assembly.[43] The proposed law (widely referred to as HADOPI, an acronym for *Haute Autorité pour la Diffusion des Oeuvres et la Protection des Droits sur Internet* [High Authority for Copyright Protection and Dissemination of Works on the Internet], the agency the bill would create), backed by President Sarkozy and by France's film and record industries, was brought to the National Assembly a second time on May 13, 2009, and approved, pending appeal.[44] The European Parliament, however, voted overwhelmingly to add to a telecoms reform bill a stipulation that agencies such as HADOPI must first obtain permission from French courts before disconnecting violators.[45]

The HADOPI law has faced strong opposition throughout France by various groups, and an employee of French television broadcaster TF1 was even fired for his opposition to the law after a private e-mail sent to his member of parliament was forwarded back to his employer.[46]

ONI Testing Results

The OpenNet Initiative tested two ISPs (Orange and Neuf Cegetel) in France and found no signs of filtering; however, manual testing found one Web site, www.aaargh.com .mx, to be blocked. The Web site, which promotes Holocaust revisionism as well as a boycott of Israel, was blocked by a French court; the court, in turn, has been brought into question for not contacting the Web site's hosts before ordering the filtering.[47]

Conclusion

In France, as in other Western countries, concerns over intellectual property guide online regulatory efforts. However, access to the Internet remains relatively free, apart from limited filtering of child pornography and Web sites that promote terrorism or racial hatred.

Notes

1. *BBC News*, "Country Profile: France," March 3, 2009, http://news.bbc.co.uk/2/hi/europe/country_profiles/998481.stm.

2. *CNN.com*, "Sarkozy: I Have Mandate for Change," May 7, 2007, http://www.cnn.com/2007/WORLD/europe/05/06/france.election/index.html.

3. *Economist.com*, "Country Briefings: France," May 6, 2009, http://www.economist.com/countries/France/profile.cfm?folder=Profile-FactSheet.

4. U.S. Department of State, "Background Note: France," April 2009, http://www.state.gov/r/pa/ei/bgn/3842.htm.

5. Ibid.

6. *BBC News*, "Q&A: Muslim Headscarves," August 31, 2004, http://news.bbc.co.uk/1/hi/world/europe/3328277.stm.

7. Guy Carcassonne, "The Principles of the French Constitution," written for the French Embassy in the U.K., May 2002, http://www.unc.edu/depts/europe/francophone/principles_en.pdf.

8. Encyclopaedia Britannica Online, s.v. "Declaration of the Rights of Man and of the Citizen," http://www.britannica.com/EBchecked/topic/503563/Declaration-of-the-Rights-of-Man-and-of-the -Citizen.

9. Council of Europe, Convention for the Protection of Human Rights and Fundamental Freedoms, Art. 10, http://conventions.coe.int/treaty/en/Treaties/Html/005.htm.

10. U.S. Department of State, "Background Note: France."

11. Law No. 90–615 of July 14, 1990, *Journal Officiel de la République Française* [J.O.] [Official Gazette of France], p. 8333.

12. Press Law of 1881 of July 29, 1881, Duv. & Boc., available at http://www.legifrance.gouv.fr/ affichTexte.do?cidTexte=LEGITEXT000006070722&dateTexte=20090507.

13. Senem Aydin, Sergio Carrera, and Florian Geyer, "France's Draft Law on the Armenian Genocide: Some Legal and Political Implications at the EU Level," Centre for European Policy Studies, October, 2006, http://shop.ceps.eu/downfree.php?item_id=1387.

14. International Telecommunications Union (ITU), "Internet Indicators: Subscribers, Users, and Broadband Subscribers," 2000, http://www.itu.int/ITU-D/icteye/Reporting/ShowReportFrame.aspx ?ReportName=/WTI/InformationTechnologyPublic&RP_intYear=2000&RP_intLanguageID=1.

15. International Telecommunications Union (ITU), "Internet Indicators: Subscribers, Users, and Broadband Subscribers," 2008, http://www.itu.int/ITU-D/icteye/Reporting/ShowReportFrame.aspx ?ReportName=/WTI/InformationTechnologyPublic&RP_intYear=2008&RP_intLanguageID=1.

16. Stephanie Hutchison and Stephen Minton, ".fr," Berkman Center for Internet and Society, Harvard Law School, http://cyber.law.harvard.edu/itg/libpubs/France.pdf.

17. Adam Wright, "Internet Adoption Slowing—But Dependence on It Continues to Grow," *Ipsos News Center*, March 29, 2006, http://www.ipsos-na.com/news/pressrelease.cfm?id=3030.

18. Ibid.

19. *Forbes.com*, "France Telecom Says No Talks on TeliaSonera 'at This Stage,'" April 18, 2008, http://www.forbes.com/feeds/afx/2008/04/18/afx4905996.html.

20. Jennifer L. Schenker, "*Vive la* High-Speed Internet," *BusinessWeek*, July 18, 2007, http:// www.businessweek.com/globalbiz/content/jul2007/gb20070718_387052.htm?chan=globalbiz _europe+index+page_top+stories.

21. Justin Sorkin, "ComScore Releases Its Study on Internet Usage in France," *TopNews*, April 6, 2009, http://topnews.us/content/24758-comscore-releases-its-study-Internet-usage-france.

22. *Conseil Supérieur de l'Audiovisuel*, http://www.csa.fr/multi/introduction/intro.php?l=uk.

23. "Le Ministère d'Aujourd'hui et de Demain: Garantir le Pluralisme des Medias" [The Ministry of Today and Tomorrow: Guarantee of Media Pluralism], http://www.50ans.culture.fr/demain/ missions/pluralisme/1.

24. Law No. 2004–575, June 21, 2004, *Journal Officiel de la République Française* [J.O.] [Official Gazette of France], http://www.legifrance.gouv.fr/affichTexte.do?cidTexte=JORFTEXT000000801164 &dateTexte=.

25. Ibid.

26. European Digital Rights, "France: Linking Can Be Damaging to Your Pockets," April 9, 2008, http://www.edri.org/edrigram/number6.7/linking-decison-france.

27. Jean-Louis Fandiari, "RSS, Hébergeurs 2.0, Liberté d'Expression, Riposte Dégradée: Cinq Dates Clés pour Résumer les Pépites du Mois" [RSS, Hosting 2.0, Freedom of Expression, Damaged Response: 5 Dates to Summarize this Month's Nuggets], *Juriscom.net*, April 20, 2008, http://www .juriscom.net/actu/visu.php?ID=1059.

28. *CNN.com*, "Yahoo! Loses Nazi Auction Case," November 20, 2000, http://archives.cnn.com/ 2000/TECH/computing/11/20/france.yahoo.02/.

29. Richard Salis, "A Look at How U.S. Based Yahoo! Was Condemned by French Law," *Juriscom .net*, January 11, 2001, http://www.juriscom.net/txt/jurisfr/cti/yauctions.htm.

30. "France to Block Child Pornography Websites," Reuters, June 10, 2008, http://www.reuters .com/article/technologyNews/idUSL1077696620080610.

31. Décision 94–352DC du Conseil Constitutionnel du 18 Janvier 1995, http://www.conseil -constitutionnel.fr/decision/1994/94352dc.htm.

32. Décision 99–416DC du Conseil Constitutionnel du 23 juillet 1999, http://www.conseil -constitutionnel.fr/decision/1999/99416/index.htm.

33. Privacy International, "PHR2004—Republic of France," November 16, 2004, http://www .privacyinternational.org/article.shtml?cmd[347]=x-347-83516#_ftn2.

34. Privacy International, "Leading Surveillance Societies in the EU and the World 2007," December 28, 2007, http://www.privacyinternational.org/article.shtml?cmd[347]=x-347-559597.

35. Act No. 78–17 of January 7, 1978, *Journal Officiel de la République Française* [J.O.] [Official Gazette of France], available at http://www.cnil.fr/index.php?id=301.

36. CNIL, *2008 Annual Activity Report*, 2008, http://www.cnil.fr/fileadmin/documents/en/CNIL -AnnualReport-2008.pdf.

37. Privacy International, "Silenced—France," September 21, 2003, http://www.privacy international.org/article.shtml?cmd[347]=x-347-103764.

38. Ibid.

39. Reporters Without Borders, "France: Annual Report 2008," http://www.rsf.org/article.php3 ?id_article=25579.

40. Emma Jane Kirby, "The Most Spied Upon People in Europe," *BBC News*, February 28, 2008, http://news.bbc.co.uk/2/hi/europe/7265212.stm#jkirby.

41. "New Biometric Passports Widely Introduced in France," *Web in France Magazine*, May 6, 2008, http://www.webinfrance.com/biometric-passports-introduced-in-france-506.html.

42. CNIL, "Regulating Biometrics," http://www.cnil.fr/index.php?id=2455.

43. *BBC News*, "French Reject Internet Piracy Law," April 9, 2009, http://news.bbc.co.uk/2/hi/europe/7992262.stm.

44. Robert Andrews, "French Senate Sets Up Three-Strikes Clash with Euro Parliament," *PaidContent: UK*, May 13, 2009, http://www.paidcontent.co.uk/entry/419-french-senate-sets-up -three-strikes-clash-with-euro-parliament/.

45. Nate Anderson, "European Parliament Smacks Down France on Three Strikes Law," *Ars Technica*, May 6, 2009, http://arstechnica.com/tech-policy/news/2009/05/european-parliament-smacks -down-france-on-three-strikes-law.ars.

46. Nate Anderson, "Web Designer Opposes France's '3 Strikes' Law, Loses Job," *Ars Technica*, May 7, 2009, http://arstechnica.com/tech-policy/news/2009/05/web-designer-opposes-frances-3 -strikes-law-loses-job.ars.

47. Legalis.net, "La Cour de Cassation Confirme le Blocage en Référé de l'Accès à un Site Néga-tionniste" [The Court of Cassation Confirms the Blocking of Access to the Denial Site], June 23, 2008, http://www.legalis.net/breves-article.php3?id_article=2340.

Germany

Germany is a country of high Internet penetration, at approximately 76 percent. Occasionally, takedown requests and access restrictions are imposed on ISPs, usually with the justification of protecting minors or in compliance with Germany's objective to suppress hate speech and extremism. In April 2009, the German government signed a bill that would implement large-scale filtering of child pornography Web sites, with the possibility for later expansion. Additionally, the German government recently approved draft legislation to implement data retention.

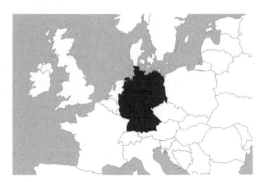

Background

After World War II, Germany was divided into American, British, French, and Russian zones. The Federal Republic of Germany (West Germany), a federal parliamentary republic, was founded in 1949 out of the three Western zones. The German Democratic Republic (East Germany), an authoritarian socialist state, was established in the Russian zone. In both states, continuing to uphold the obligations of Germany's history and preventing a repetition of extremism have been a priority ever since. In

RESULTS AT A GLANCE					
Filtering	No Evidence of Filtering	Suspected Filtering	Selective Filtering	Substantial Filtering	Pervasive Filtering
Political	●				
Social	●				
Conflict and security	●				
Internet tools	●				

Other Factors	Low	Medium	High	Not Applicable
Transparency				●
Consistency				●

KEY INDICATORS	
GDP per capita, PPP (constant 2005 international dollars)	33,181
Life expectancy at birth (years)	80
Literacy rate (percent of people age 15+)	99
Human development index (out of 179)	23
Rule of law (out of 211)	12
Voice and accountability (out of 209)	11
Democracy index (out of 167)	13 (Full democracy)
Digital opportunity index (out of 181)	19
Internet users (percent of population)	76

Source by indicator: World Bank 2009a, World Bank 2009a, World Bank 2009a, UNDP 2008, World Bank 2009b, World Bank 2009b, Economist Intelligence Unit 2008, ITU 2007, ITU 2008.

1990, East Germany joined the Federal Republic of Germany. Since that time, reconciling economic differences has shaped German policy.

In 1949, West Germany adopted its "Basic Law" (*Grundgesetz*)—similar to a constitution—which provides for freedom of expression; however, the Basic Law also restricts expression that is "offensive, injurious, or indecent."[1] Germany maintains a blacklist of books, comic books, magazines, videotapes, and music, the so-called *Index*. The list, originally intended to shield youth from pornographic material, has been expanded to include other items; in particular, materials that make light of Germany's history and those which promote neo-Nazism or deny the Holocaust have been blacklisted.[2] *Volksverhetzung*, defined in Germany as "incitement of hatred against a minority under certain conditions," is also strictly prohibited and punishable with up to five years' imprisonment.[3]

Internet in Germany

The Internet is a central part of the German economy. Over the past ten years, fierce competition has led to low prices and fueled Internet access. In 2008, Internet penetration stood at approximately 76 percent.[4] Germany's primary ISPs are T-Online (47 percent market share), United Internet (15 percent), AOL (12 percent), and Arcor (7 percent).[5]

T-Online is a spin-off of Deutsche Telekom. Deutsche Telekom is the former state-run telecom, hence its high market share. Today, T-Online provides Internet services and software, while Deutsche Telekom maintains the physical connection. Deutsche Telekom still owns the majority of the physical network, including 90 percent of all existing broadband connections.

Broadband access in Germany has increased in recent years, from 200,000 in 2000 to 14.7 million in 2006. Because the service is inexpensive, this number is expected to rise to 21.3 million in 2010.[6] In 2008, T-Online's DSL flat rate was EUR 10 (USD 15) per month.[7] Germany has 16 international Internet exchange points (IXP).[8] The largest one by far is the Deutsche Commercial Internet Exchange DE-CIX in Frankfurt, which is the second-largest IXP in the world with an average throughput of 200 Gbps and a maximum of more than 400 Gbps.[9]

Legal and Regulatory Frameworks

The regulator for the telecommunication sector of the economy is the *Bundesnetzagentur* (Federal Network Agency), which is also responsible for the postal service and energy services.[10] It has been endowed with authority by the *Telekommunikationsgesetz* (TKG, Telecommunications Act) of 2004.[11]

The law that concerns the Internet as a medium is the *Telemediengesetz* (TMG, Telecommunication Media Law) passed by the parliament in January 2007.[12] Section 8 of the TMG explicitly states that providers are not responsible for transmitted information, provided they did not initiate the transmission or modify the transferred data.

The legal foundations for censorship are grounded in Germany's laws prohibiting public incitement of hatred against a minority (*Volksverhetzung*) and Holocaust denial. For example, Section 130(3) of the German Criminal Code notes, "Whoever ... denies or renders harmless an act [of genocide] committed under the rule of National Socialism in a manner capable of disturbing the public peace shall be punished with imprisonment for not more than five years or a fine."[13] Additionally, media considered harmful to minors are regulated by the *Bundesprüfstelle für jugendgefährdende Medien* (BPjM, Federal Department for Media Harmful to Young Persons), which traditionally censored films, print media, and computer games, but has expanded its focus to the Internet.[14]

Because of the federal structure of Germany's political system, Internet censorship can be initiated at the regional level. In 2002, the *Bezirksregierung Düsseldorf* (district government) obliged 56 ISPs to restrict access to four foreign Web sites.[15] Each of these Web sites was based in the United States and contained right-wing extremist material.

The *Bezirksregierung*, which enforces the restrictions on Internet speech in the federal state of North Rhine–Westphalia, offered the ISPs a choice of three ways to implement the blockade: DNS-blockade, IP-blockade, or usage of a proxy server.[16] An online petition condemning these attempts to block access has received more than 26,000 signatures.[17] However, neither political demonstrations nor lawsuits have been successful in stopping the blockade. In the end, the administrative court of Düsseldorf endorsed the blockade in 2005.[18] By now, 76 Internet service providers have been required to block right-wing extremist Web sites.[19]

Furthermore, according to a study published by the Berkman Center for Internet and Society in 2002, a number of Web sites relating to neo-Nazi, white supremacist, or other objectionable materials were completely or partly excluded by the German version of the search engine Google (google.de).[20]

While cases of blocking might occur infrequently, takedown requests, many of which receive a positive response, occur far more often. For example, as a result of the prohibition of Holocaust denial and public incitement of hatred against a minority in Germany, complaints have been filed against companies that host such content. The most prominent example is YouTube. In August 2007, German politicians and the Central Council of Jews in Germany complained about the extremist content that was being hosted on YouTube.[21] A YouTube spokesman promptly promised to improve the system of takedowns to comply with the demands of German law.[22]

A related issue is the political and judicial debate over whether linking to presumably illicit content is illegal. Several instances of this issue have been recorded. For example, in 2004 the political activist Alvar Freude was accused of linking to right-wing extremist Web sites and was brought to court. Freude had documented the censorship by the Düsseldorf district government mentioned previously and had linked to blocked Web sites. The district court found him guilty. However, Stuttgart Regional Court overturned that decision in 2006 and acquitted Freude.[23]

In another case involving prohibited online material, the Federal Court of Justice decided in 2000 that the Australian owner of an Australian Web site denying the Holocaust could be held liable in Germany.[24]

Another reason provided for Internet blocking is the protection of minors. The legal details are regulated in the *Jugendschutzgesetz* (JuSchG, Youth Protection Act)[25] and the *Jugendmedienschutz-Staatsvertrag* (JMStV, Youth Media Protection Treaty).[26] The JuSchG regulates *Trägermedien* (physical media) like books and videos. The JMStV regulates broadcasts and *Telemedien* (transmitted media) like the Internet.

More generally, Section 184(1) of the German Criminal Code states, "Whoever, in relation to pornographic writings ... offers, gives or makes them accessible to a person under eighteen years of age ... shall be punished with imprisonment for not more than one year or a fine."[27] In addition, the dissemination of pornographic performances through electronic media is prohibited if the provider does not ensure by technical or other means that the performance is not accessible to persons under 18 years of age (Section 184d of the German Criminal Code). These laws are taken as a requirement for Web sites with adult content to implement a strict age verification system. For example, Flickr has complied with this perceived requirement by prohibiting German users from accessing photos marked "restricted."[28]

Since the amendment of the JuSchG and JMStV in 2003, the BPjM has maintained a blacklist of Web sites. In order to avoid widespread publicity, this blacklist is not published. One may inquire as to whether an item is on the blacklist by e-mailing liste@bundespruefstelle.de.[29] At the time of writing, the BPjM Web site stated that the number of censored Web sites was 1,948.[30]

In February 2005, Google Germany, Lycos Europe, MSN Germany, AOL Germany, Yahoo, and T-Online agreed to self-regulate their search results under the head of the *Freiwillige Selbstkontrolle Multimedia-Diensteanbieter* (FSM, Voluntary Self-Regulation of Multimedia Service Providers).[31] The FSM is a self-regulatory body for multimedia service providers funded by several Internet companies in 1997. One of the FSM's policies is to exclude Web sites that have been blacklisted by the BPjM from the search indices of its members. The current BPjM blacklist is regularly transferred to a hidden server; the search engines then download the list and automatically remove the relevant entries.

A number of cases have been brought to public attention. One in particular involves bmezine.com, a Web site that "serves to document the activities of the body modification community."[32] In 2005, after BPjM judged the Web site to be a host of content harmful to minors, it required Google.de to remove BMEzine from its search results.[33] A second incident occurred in late 2007, when German adult content providers sued several ISPs in various German states to block several Web sites that contained pornographic content.[34] The pages in question were hosted abroad and thus lacked a strict age verification system. The district court of Frankfurt ordered the respective defendant to block all relevant DNS addresses, while other courts dismissed the actions.[35] In particular, a request to block Google was dismissed.[36] Furthermore, the *Oberlandesgericht Frankfurt* (Higher State Court) confirmed another dismissal of a court of first instance, judging that ISPs could not be held liable for content that they only transmit.[37]

Surveillance

Although Internet access remains mostly unrestricted in Germany, Internet users have recently been subject to state action. Germany's Criminal Procedure Code specifies in Section 100a that "the telecommunication of an individual may be monitored and recorded if:

1. Specific facts substantiate the suspicion that somebody was the perpetrator or participant in a serious crime as listed in paragraph 2 or, in cases where the attempt is liable to persecution, has attempted to commit such crime, or has prepared such crime by means of a criminal offense
2. The alleged crime would weigh heavily even taken individually
3. Investigating the act or determining the suspected person's location by other means would be significantly impeded or futile without surveillance"

Since January 2008, ISPs and online service providers in Germany have been required to retain certain data without initial suspicion of illegal activity (*Vorratsdatenspeicherung*).[38] The parliament passed the relevant law in November 2007,[39] which implements a European Union (EU) directive[40]; prior to its implementation, ISPs were allowed to retain only data required for billing customers. The new law amends the *Telekommunikationsgesetz* (TKG). Section 113a specifies that providers of e-mail services must retain the following data:

- If a message is sent: the sender's e-mail and IP addresses, e-mail addresses of all recipients;
- If a message is received: e-mail address of the sender, e-mail address of the recipient, IP address of the sending server;
- If a client accesses his inbox: his e-mail address and IP address
- For all of the preceding: date, time, and time zone.

Internet service providers, however, must retain the following:

- IP address of the client;
- A unique identifier of the client's landline, allowing the identification of the client;
- Date and time of the beginning and end of the user's Internet access.

The data are then retained for six months. Section 113b establishes that the retained data may be used solely for the following purposes:

1. Prosecuting criminal acts;
2. Preventing substantial dangers to public safety;
3. Fulfilling the lawful obligations of Germany's intelligence offices.

An additional complaint has been filed at Germany's *Bundesverfasssungsgericht* (Federal Constitutional Court) in December 2007, claiming that data retention is unconstitutional. In March 2008, the court issued an injunction to restrict data retention to exceptional cases. A final decision on data retention is still outstanding.

Whatever the final judgment may be, the last several years have displayed a clear trend toward increasing Internet surveillance. Motivating factors behind this development include the impetus to prevent terrorism, to prosecute crimes, and to enforce intellectual property rights.

Finally, the fear of terrorism and right-wing extremism has led not only to the monitoring of e-mails and chat rooms by the *Bundeskriminalamt* (Federal Criminal Police Office), but also to the idea of "online raids."[41] This involves infecting a suspect's personal computer with Trojan software, which records data entered in order to extract the relevant information clandestinely. However, online raids remain highly controversial. The federal constitutional court ruled in March 2008 that online raids may be used only in exceptional circumstances.[42]

ONI Testing Results

In 2007 and 2008, the OpenNet Initiative conducted testing on T-Online, Arcor, and 1&1 and found no evidence of filtering, despite Germany's laws prohibiting certain content. After ONI testing, however, the German government signed an agreement with five leading ISPs for the filtering of child pornography using DNS tampering.[43] Although the filters will initially target a list of approximately 1,000 child pornography sites, the Ministry of Family Affairs has stated that it could be expanded to include other content in the future.

Conclusion

Currently, German users can access the Internet with only mild restrictions. However, the April 2009 filtering bill and the recent legislation on data retention could have a staggering effect on Web site access and Internet surveillance in the future. The decision to implement a large-scale filtering system follows in the footsteps of a number of other European nations, including the United Kingdom and Scandinavian countries, and could prove to be influential for other members of the EU.

Notes

1. Robert Trager and Donna Lee Dickerson, *Freedom of Expression in the 21st Century* (Thousand Oaks: Pine Forge Press, 1999), 8.

2. Ibid., 105.

3. *Strafgesetzbuch* [German Criminal Code], Section 130, http://bundesrecht.juris.de/stgb/__130.html.

4. International Telecommunications Union (ITU), "Internet Indicators: Subscribers, Users, and Broadband Subscribers," 2008, http://www.itu.int/ITU D/icteye/Reporting/ShowReportFrame.aspx ?ReportName=/WTI/InformationTechnologyPublic&RP_intYear=2008&RP_intLanguageID=1.

5. *Rhein-Zeitung Online*, "HanseNet Greift Internetanbieter Deutschlandweit an" [HanseNet Attacks Internet Service Providers throughout Germany], June 30, 2005, http://rhein-zeitung.de/on/05/07/19/service/multimedia/t/rzo163384.html.

6. Bernd W. Wirtz, "Unser Leben im Netz" [Our Life Online], *Deutschland Online*, http://www.studie-deutschland-online.de/do5/sdo_2007_de.pdf.

7. T-Online, "DSL Tarif," http://www.dsl.t-online.de/c/12/42/10/20/12421020.html.

8. European Exchange Points, http://www.ep.net/naps_eu2.html.

9. DE-CIX German Internet Exchange, http://www.de-cix.net/.

10. *Bundesnetzagentur* [Federal Network Agency], http://www.bundesnetzagentur.de/.

11. *Bundesministerium der Justiz* [Federal Ministry of Justice], "Telekommunikationsgesetz" [Telecommunications Act], http://www.gesetze-im-internet.de/tkg_2004/.

12. *Bundesministerium der Justiz* [Federal Ministry of Justice], "Telemediengesetz" [Telecommunication Media Act], http://www.gesetze-im-internet.de/tmg/.

13. German Criminal Code (*Strafgesetzbuch*), Section 130, http://bundesrecht.juris.de/stgb/__130.html.

14. *Bundesprüfstelle für Jugendgefährdende Medien* [Federal Department for Media Harmful to Young Persons], http://www.bundespruefstelle.de/.

15. *Heise Online*, "Nordrhein-westfälische Provider Sollen Nazi-Websites Ausfiltern" [Internet Service Providers in North Rhine–Westphalia are to Filter Nazi Web sites], October 8, 2001, http://www.heise.de/newsticker/Nordrhein-westfaelische-Provider-sollen-Nazi-Websites-ausfiltern--/meldung/21627.

16. *Sperrungsverfügung* [Blocking Order], http://www.odem.org/material/verfuegung/.

17. Internet-Zensur in Deutschland, "Sperrungen Sollen es Ihnen Unmöglich Machen, sich Tausende Internetseiten Anzuschauen" [Blockings Are to Prevent You from Accessing Thousands of Web sites], http://odem.org/informationsfreiheit/en/.

18. *Heise Online*, "Verwaltungsgericht Düsseldorf Bestätigt Sperrungsverfügung in NRW" [Administrative Court of Düsseldorf Confirmed the Blocking Order in North Rhine–Westphalia], http://www.heise.de/newsticker/Verwaltungsgericht-Duesseldorf-bestaetigt-Sperrungsverfuegung-in-NRW--/meldung/60627.

19. *Heise Online*, "Düsseldorfer Bezirksregierung Sieht sich Erfolgreich im Kampf Gegen Nazi-Websites" [Düsseldorf District Government Believes It is Succesful in the Fight against Nazi Web sites], November 22, 2005, http://www.heise.de/newsticker/Duesseldorfer-Bezirksregierung-sieht-sich-erfolgreich-im-Kampf-gegen-Nazi-Website--/meldung/66501/.

20. Jonathan Zittrain and Benjamin Edelman, "Localized Google Search Result Exclusions: Statement of Issues and Call for Data," Berkman Center for Internet and Society, Harvard Law School, October 26, 2002, http://cyber.law.harvard.edu/filtering/google/.

21. *Heise Online*, "Google Intends to Speed Up Removal of Far Right Content from YouTube," August 31, 2007, http://www.heise.de/english/newsticker/news/95230/from/rss09.

22. Rubriken Stern, "YouTube: Nazis Raus!" [YouTube: Get the Nazis Out], August 29, 2007, http://www.stern.de/wirtschaft/news/unternehmen/youtube-nazis-raus-596475.html.

23. *Heise Online*, "Revisionsverhandlung Gegen Netzaktivisten Steht an" [Hearings Ahead in Internet Activist's Appeal], April 19, 2006, http://www.heise.de/newsticker/Revisionsverhandlung-gegen-Netzaktivisten-steht-a--/meldung/72134.

24. Florian Rötzer, "Update: Leugnung des Holocaust im Internet nach Deutschem Recht Strafbar" [Update: Denial of the Holocaust on the Internet Punishable under German Law]," *Heise Online*, December 13, 2000, http://www.heise.de/tp/r4/artikel/4/4467/1.html.

25. *Jugendschutzgesetz* [Youth Protection Act], January 1, 2009, http://www.bmfsfj.de/Kategorien/gesetze,did=5350.html.

26. *Jugendmedienschutz-Staatsvertrag* [Youth Media Protection Treaty], http://www.artikel5.de/gesetze/jmstv.html.

27. *Strafgesetzbuch*, StGB [German Criminal Code], "Section 184 Dissemination of Pornographic Writings," http://www.iuscomp.org/gla/statutes/StGB.htm#184.

28. Flickr, "Content Filters," http://www.flickr.com/help/filters/#249.

29. *Heise Online*, "Betreiber einer Piercing-Site Beklagt Deutsche Zensur," [Owner of Piercing Web site Complains about German Censorship], December 23, 2005, http://www.heise.de/newsticker/Betreiber-einer-Piercing-Site-beklagt-deutsche-Zensur--/meldung/67716.

30. Statistics of the *Bundesprüfstelle für Jugendgefährdende Medien* [Federal Department for Media Harmful to Young Persons], http://www.bundespruefstelle.de/bmfsfj/generator/bpjm/Jugendmedienschutz/statistik.

31. *Heise Online*, "Selbstregulierung der Suchmaschinenanbieter" [Self-regulation of Search Engine Providers], February 24, 2005, http://www.heise.de/newsticker/Selbstregulierung-der-Suchmaschinenanbiete--/meldung/56770.

32. BMEZine, "Warning, Adult Notice, and Charter," http://bmezine.com/why.html.

33. *Heise Online*, "Betreiber einer Piercing-Site Beklagt Deutsche Zensur," [Owner of Piercing Web site Complains about German Censorship], December 23, 2005, http://www.heise.de/newsticker/Betreiber-einer-Piercing-Site-beklagt-deutsche-Zensur--/meldung/67716.

34. *Heise Online*, "Arcor Sperrt Zugriff auf Porno-Seiten" [Arcor Blocks Access to Porn Sites], September 10, 2007, http://www.heise.de/newsticker/Arcor-sperrt-Zugriff-auf-Porno-Seiten--/meldung/95758. Note: among the sites involved were sex.com, YouPorn.com, and privatamateure.com.

35. *Heise Online*, "Arcor Muss YouPorn Sperren [Update]" [Arcor Has to Block YouPorn], October 19, 2007, http://www.heise.de/newsticker/Arcor-muss-YouPorn-sperren-Update--/meldung/97676; *Heise Online*, "Arcor hat Widerspruch Gegen Verfügung zur YouPorn-Sperre Eingelegt" [Arcor Appeals Against Order to Block YouPorn], November 22, 2007, http://www.heise.de/newsticker/Arcor-hat-Widerspruch-gegen-Verfuegung-zur-YouPorn-Sperre-eingelegt--/meldung/99404; *Heise Online*, "Weiterer Antrag auf Sperrung von Pornoseiten Zurückgewiesen" [Further Request to Block Porn Sites Rejected], December 13, 2007, http://www.heise.de/newsticker/Weiterer-Antrag-auf-Sperrung-von-Pornoseiten-zurueckgewiesen--/meldung/100513.

36. *Heise Online*, "Arcor soll Google Sperren" [Arcor Is to Block Google], December 4, 2007, http://www.heise.de/newsticker/Arcor-soll-Google-sperren--/meldung/100035.

37. *Heise Online*, "OLG: Provider Nicht für Netzinhalte Verantwortlich" [Higher State Court: Provider Is Not Responsible for Web Content], January 23, 2008, http://www.heise.de/newsticker/OLG-Provider-nicht-fuer-Netzinhalte-verantwortlich--/meldung/102309.

38. *Stoppt die Vorratsdatenspeicherung*, "5-Minute Overview: German Data Retention Law," http://www.vorratsdatenspeicherung.de/content/view/46/1/lang,en/.

39. The law is called the *Gesetz zur Neuregelung der Telekommunikationsüberwachung und Anderer Verdeckter Ermittlungsmaßnahmen Sowie zur Umsetzung der Richtlinie 2006/24/EG* [Law on the Revision of Telecommunications Surveillance and Other Covert Investigative Measures and to Implement the Directive].

40. "Directive 2006/24/EC of the European Parliament and of the Council of 15 March 2006 on the retention of data generated or processed in connection with the provision of publicly available electronic communications services or of public communications networks and amending Directive 2002/58/EC," http://eur-lex.europa.eu/LexUriServ/LexUriServ.do?uri=CELEX:32006L0024:EN :HTML.

41. Katrin McGauran, "Germany: Permanent State of Pre-emption," *Statewatch Journal*, October–December 2008, http://www.statewatch.org/analyses/no-79-germany-permanent-state-of-preemption .pdf.

42. *BBC News*, "The Most Spied Upon People in Europe," February 28, 2008, http://news.bbc .co.uk/2/hi/europe/7265212.stm.

43. *Metamorphosis*, "German Government Forces ISPs to Put Web Filters," April 27, 2009, http:// www.metamorphosis.org.mk/edri/german-government-forces-isps-to-put-web-filters.html.

Italy

Italy promotes freedom of speech online by allowing access to most content. However, the Italian government has been slow to address many online privacy and freedom-of-information concerns, and Italy lags behind much of Europe in terms of Internet penetration. Italy, like much of the European Union (EU), regulates certain categories of Web sites, including child pornography and gambling. Additionally, a recently proposed law, dubbed the Levi-Prodi law, would impose registration and taxes on anyone creating "editorial content," including bloggers. The law, which has faced significant opposition, has thus far not passed.

Background

Italy has had a multiparty, democratic government since 1946. The 1948 constitution was written to prevent a return to early 20th-century fascism, and powers were spread among the different branches of government to limit the powers of the head of state. During the cold war, the country feared a communist overthrow, and as a result power

RESULTS AT A GLANCE					
Filtering	No Evidence of Filtering	Suspected Filtering	Selective Filtering	Substantial Filtering	Pervasive Filtering
Political	●				
Social			●		
Conflict and security	●				
Internet tools	●				

Other Factors	Low	Medium	High	Not Applicable
Transparency			●	
Consistency	●			

KEY INDICATORS	
GDP per capita, PPP (constant 2005 international dollars)	28,682
Life expectancy at birth (years)	81
Literacy rate (percent of people age 15+)	99
Human development index (out of 179)	19
Rule of law (out of 211)	81
Voice and accountability (out of 209)	28
Democracy index (out of 167)	29 (Full democracy)
Digital opportunity index (out of 181)	28
Internet users (percent of population)	49

Source by indicator: World Bank 2009a, World Bank 2009a, World Bank 2009a, UNDP 2008, World Bank 2009b, World Bank 2009b, Economist Intelligence Unit 2008, ITU 2007, ITU 2008.

was consolidated among centrist parties. This concentration of power led to widespread corruption, and after the fall of communism the judicial branch launched a massive investigation that left no major parties untouched and involved more than one-third of the members of parliament.[1]

Corruption continues to be an issue and has influenced control over the media, particularly television. Prime Minister Silvio Berlusconi, who has held office for three separate terms since 1994, has come under scrutiny multiple times for corruption, including during the passage of a broadcasting law in 2004 that lifted ownership limits for national broadcast channels. Berlusconi now owns three of Italy's seven national television networks and several national newspapers.[2] In April 2006, he violated electoral law three times by exceeding his allotted media time when he broadcast long interviews on his own channels during the parliamentary election campaign.[3]

Internet in Italy

Internet penetration in Italy stood at approximately 49 percent in 2008.[4] According to the first national study of Internet and computer usage, published in 2007, about 33 percent of children under age eleven, 75 percent of adolescents and adult women, and more than 80 percent of adult men access the Internet each month.[5] As of 2006, 47 percent of households had a home computer, and 40 percent of households had Internet access.[6]

The passage of Law No. 58, *Disposizionia per la Riforma del Settore delle Telecomunicazioni* (Rules for the Reform of the Telecommunications Industry), in January 1992 was the beginning of the privatization of Italy's telecommunications industry.[7] Previously, most telecom services had been provided by a collection of companies managed by the *Istituto per la Ricostruzione Industriale/Societa Italiana L Esercizio Telecom* (Institute for Industrial Reconstruction/Italian Telecommunications Society, IRI-STET) group, part of Italy's state holding company. In June 1994, in compliance with Law No. 58, five of these companies merged to form Telecom Italia. Three years later, Telecom Italia merged with *Societa Italiana L Esercizio Telecom* (STET), retaining the Telecom Italia name, to form a privately owned company that is now the country's largest telecommunications service provider.

Telecom Italia currently supplies around 7.7 million customers with broadband connections, accounting for approximately 80 percent of the market.[8] Other major ISPs include Swiss-owned FastWeb, which serves 15 percent of the market,[9] Tiscali, and Wind, owned by Egypt's Orascom.[10] DSL and dial-up access are also available from a number of smaller local and international providers.[11] The country's most widely available type of broadband connection is ADSL, which costs between EUR 19.95 and EUR 40.00 (USD 29.58 to USD 61.78) per month, with speeds ranging from 640 Kbps to 12 Mbps.[12]

Telecom Italia and Tiscali are both tier 2 carriers.[13] Within Italy, four main Internet exchange points operate, in Florence, Milan, Rome, and Turin.[14]

Legal and Regulatory Frameworks

Compared with many of its European counterparts, the Italian government has been slow to come to terms with the digital world, and its attempts to create and apply legislation to the Internet often reflect this fact. In 2000, a group of Internet privacy advocates claimed that while Internet censorship was nonexistent in Italy, the government's lack of understanding of privacy and freedom of information posed significant problems for Internet and computer users.[15] In October 2007, the government proposed a bill, nicknamed the Levi-Prodi law for the lawmakers who proposed it, which would require all "editorial product" owners to register with and pay taxes to the *Registro degli Operatori di Comunicazione*, the regulatory authority that oversees media and broadcasting. The intention of the bill was to simplify Italy's publishing laws. However, the bill was broadly worded enough to be interpreted as applying to bloggers, Web site owners, and possibly even social network users, and drew widespread criticism from these sectors, traditional media sources, and civil rights groups as an example of the government's failure to adapt to modernity.[16] One writer noted that the bill contradicted EU directives and, if enacted, could be challenged before the European Commission and the European Court of Justice.[17] The bill was eventually reworded to apply only to commercial blogs; however, the debate continues, as noncommercial bloggers with advertising would potentially still be included.[18] As of November 2008, the bill had not yet been decided upon.

The government has attempted to regulate the Internet with the same laws that apply to print and broadcast media. These include a press law that holds publishers responsible for the content of their publications. Applied to the Internet, the law holds

Web sites responsible for all content they display, even user-posted content. Web sites with user-generated content, however, are not well suited to this type of supervision. The most visible incident related to this law occurred in November 2006, when prosecutors began an investigation of two representatives of Google after a violent video of four Italian teenagers attacking a disabled student was posted on Google Video.[19] Italian media law restricts the press from publishing anything that might be deemed "counter to morality," a restriction Google allegedly violated by failing to check the content of the video before it was posted.[20]

In 2006, blogger Roberto Mancini was fined EUR 13,500 for criticizing several journalists in northern Italy on his blog. The verdict of the case stated that while the statements were not untrue (they were widely considered to be inappropriate), Mancini was responsible for everything that was posted, including some vulgar reader comments, and that it was his duty to act as an editor and remove any messages that were offensive.[21]

The National Security Committee, established in 2002, handles all Internet-related security concerns. The committee is composed of members from academia, the military, and the legal sector. Some concern has been expressed that nongovernmental civil rights organizations have not been consulted during public hearings held by the committee.[22]

Internet filtering in Italy has come to public attention largely through the government's directives to ISPs. In 2006, Italy enacted a law that requires ISPs to block the Web sites of gambling operators that are not licensed nationally. The law, which affects more than 600 Web sites, isolates the country's EUR 500 million gambling market from all but local operators. Providers that continue to allow users to place bets with banned Web sites after receiving a list of the offending sites from the *Amministrazione Autonoma dei Monopoli di Stato* (AAMS, Autonomous Administration of State Monopolies, a part of the Ministry of Economy and Finances) may be fined anywhere from EUR 30,000 to EUR 180,000 per violation.[23] Internet users who attempt to access the Web sites of foreign bookmakers are shown a message explaining that bets must go through the proper channels, and are directed to the AAMS.[24]

In January 2007, a law was passed requiring ISPs to block Web sites that display child pornography within six hours of receiving a notice from the Ministry of Communications.[25] The *Centro Nazionale per il Contrasto della Pedopornografia* (The National Center against Child Pornography, part of the Ministry of Communications) is in charge of maintaining a list of these Web sites. After receiving an initial list of banned Web sites from the center, ISPs had 60 days to block them at the domain-name level and 120 days to block them at the IP-address level.[26]

The ".it" country code is regulated by the Registro del ccTLD.it Rules Committee, which is made up of representatives of the Ministry of Communications and various Italian Internet associations.[27] Actual registration takes place through private "Maintainers" who register and maintain domain names on behalf of customers. Maintainers must be licensed businesses in Italy and are required to pay an initial fee of EUR 2,500 to the registry. This fee includes start-up costs for the first year and 60 domain names, with invoices for additional domain names sent separately.[28]

Internet Surveillance

A July 2002 EU directive instructs ISPs and telephone companies to temporarily retain all records of user activity and make these available to legal bodies, to the extent that doing so "constitutes a necessary, appropriate and proportionate measure within a democratic society to safeguard national security (i.e., State security), defense, public security, and the prevention, investigation, detection and prosecution of criminal offences or of unauthorized use of the electronic communication system."[29]

As part of a set of antiterrorism measures passed in July 2005, the Italian government authorized Internet and telephone network surveillance.[30] The bill requires Internet cafés to keep photocopies of customers' passports and to submit periodically logs of all Web sites visited to police headquarters.[31] The law also raises licensing requirements for telecommunication service operators, making licensing approval dependent upon the existence of satisfactory data-monitoring and retention systems.[32] In addition, the bill calls for the compilation of a list of all of Italy's cell telephone users.[33]

Public reaction to the bill has come mostly from business owners, who complain that complying with the new regulations is expensive and cumbersome.[34] Several Internet café managers have seen drops in business, primarily from foreign customers who have forgotten their passports or who are unaware of the identification requirement.[35] Most Internet users seem to view the bill as innocuous, perhaps because Internet cafés cater more to tourists than to Italian citizens. A bill requiring ISPs to monitor Internet activity and to store user data for five years, which would have affected all users, failed to pass in 2003 after protests by activists and opposition parties.[36]

ONI Testing Results

The OpenNet Initiative completed testing on four Italian ISPs: iNet,[37] Infostrada,[38] Telecom Italia,[39] and Tiscali,[40] and was able to confirm that one gambling site, partypoker.com, is blocked by Telecom Italia and Tiscali. The ONI was unable to confirm with certainty that the other ISPs have also blocked the Web site.

Conclusion

Although Italy has regulations in place to prohibit access to Web sites within certain categories, access to the Internet remains relatively free apart from limited filtering, particularly of gambling sites. However, the potential passage of the Levi-Prodi law is a cause for concern, as are the government's efforts to increase Internet surveillance.

Notes

1. *Economist.com*, "Italy: History in Brief," May 31, 2007, http://www.economist.com/countries/Italy/profile.cfm?folder=History%20in%20brief.

2. Reporters Without Borders, "Gasparri Law Finally Adopted," April 30, 2004, http://www.rsf.org/article.php3?id_article=8695.

3. Reporters Without Borders, "Italy: Annual Report 2007," http://www.rsf.org/article.php3?id_article=20816.

4. International Telecommunications Union (ITU), "Internet Indicators: Subscribers, Users, and Broadband Subscribers," 2008, http://www.itu.int/ITU-D/icteye/Reporting/ShowReportFrame.aspx?ReportName=/WTI/InformationTechnologyPublic&RP_intYear=2008&RP_intLanguageID=1.

5. Francesco Bricolo, Douglas A. Gentile, Rachel L. Smelser, and Giovanni Serpelloni, "Use of the Computer and Internet among Italian Families: First National Study," *CyberPsychology and Behavior*, December 1, 2007, http://www.liebertonline.com/doi/abs/10.1089/cpb.2007.9952.

6. Organization for Economic Cooperation and Development, "Country Statistical Profiles 2008: Italy," http://stats.oecd.org/wbos/viewhtml.aspx?queryname=469&querytype=view&lang=en.

7. Telecom Italia, "Chronology: 1990s," http://www.telecomitalia.com/cgi-bin/tiportale/TIPortale/ep/contentView.do?tabId=1&pageTypeId=-8661&LANG=EN&channelId=-9751&programId=9434&programPage=/ep/TIgruppo/editorial_cronologia.jsp&contentId=19371&contentType=EDITORIAL.

8. Telecom Italia, "Group: Business," http://www.telecomitalia.com/cgi-bin/tiportale/TIPortale/ep/browse.do?channelId=-8881&LANG=EN&channelPage=%2Fep%2FTIgruppo%2FTIbusiness.jsp&tabId=1&pageTypeId=-8661.

9. Courtney Walsh, "Swisscom Gobbles Up FastWeb," *BusinessWeek*, March 12, 2007, http://www.businessweek.com/globalbiz/content/mar2007/gb20070312_255630.htm; J.D. Power and Associates Reports, "FastWeb Ranks Highest in Customer Satisfaction among Broadband Internet Service Providers in Italy for a Second Consecutive Year," December 17, 2007, http://www.jdpower.com/corporate/news/releases/pressrelease.aspx?ID=2007302.

10. Orascom Telecom, "About Us," http://www.orascomtelecom.com/about/Contents/default.aspx?ID=765.

11. Italy ISPs for Country Code +39, http://www.thelist.com/countrycode/39/.

12. "Broadband: Italy," *SocialText*, http://www.socialtext.net/broadband/index.cgi?italy.

13. *WebUpon*, "Internet Service Provider (ISP) Tiers and Peering," December 21, 2008, http://www.webupon.com/Services/Internet-Service-Provider-isp-Tiers-and-Peering.408773.

14. European Internet Exchange Association, "Euro-IX Member IXPs," https://www.euro-ix.net/member/m/ixp/list.

15. Theta Pavis, "Euros Catching Up with Net," *Wired*, April 7, 2000, http://www.wired.com/politics/law/news/2000/04/35474?currentPage=1.

16. European Digital Rights, "New Italian Draft Law—To Disguise State Censorship," October 24, 2007, http://www.edri.org/edrigram/number5.20/italy-state-censorship; *Out-Law.com*, "Italy Proposes 'Anti-blogger' Law," October 23, 2007, http://www.out-law.com/page-8570; Bernhard Warner, "A Geriatric Assault on Italy's Bloggers," *Times Online*, October 24, 2007, http://technology .timesonline.co.uk/tol/news/tech_and_web/the_web/article2732802.ece.

17. Bernhard Warner, "A Glimmer of Hope for Italian Bloggers?" *Times Online*, October 25, 2007, http://timesonline.typepad.com/technology/2007/10/a-glimmer-of-ho.html.

18. *Il Blog di Daniele Minotti*, "Play It Again, Levi," November 9, 2008, http://www.minotti.net/ 2008/11/09/play-it-again-levi/.

19. Reuters, "Italy Opens Probe into Google over Bullying Video," November 24, 2006, http:// www.reuters.com/article/idUSL2423832220061124.

20. Press Reference, "Italy Press, Media, TV, Radio, Newspapers," http://www.pressreference.com/ Gu-Ku/Italy.html.

21. Reporters Without Borders, "A Blogger Unfairly Convicted of Defamation," June 20, 2006, http://www.rsf.org/article.php3?id_article=18068.

22. Privacy International, "Silenced—Italy," September 21, 2003, http://www.privacyinternational .org/article.shtml?cmd%5B347%5D=x-347-103768.

23. James Rutherford, "Cyber-Fortress Europe," *Ascend Media Gaming Group*, http://web .archive.org/web/20070409094225/http://www.ascendgaming.com/IGWB/magazine_current/ 0306IGWBCoverLead.htm; *Business Today*, "Italian Blockade May Harm SmartCity," March 15, 2006, http://www.businesstoday.com.mt/2006/03/15/opinion.html; European Digital Rights, "Betting Websites Are Blocked in Italy," June 1, 2006, http://www.edri.org/edrigram/number4 .12/italybetting.

24. *ThreadWatch*, "I Know This Is a Trite Title, But . . . It's Not Just China," March 1, 2006, http.// www.threadwatch.org/node/5767.

25. Reuters, "Italy Enacts Law to Block Child Porn Web Sites," January 2, 2007, http://www .reuters.com/article/internetNews/idUSL0227310120070102.

26. Libertus.net, "ISP 'Voluntary'/Mandatory Filtering," http://libertus.net/censor/ispfiltering-gl .html#italy.

27. Registro del ccTLD.it, "Rules Committee: Members," http://www.nic.it/about-us/rules -committee.

28. Registro del ccTLD.it, "Maintainer Contracts," http://www.nic.it/reg-pm/newcontr2009/ FormContrattoMNT.php.

29. Directive 2002/58/EC of the European Parliament and of the Council of 12 July 2002 concerning the processing of personal data and the protection of privacy in the electronic communications sector (Directive on privacy and electronic communications), July 12 2002, http://eur-lex .europa.eu/LexUriServ/LexUriServ.do?uri=CELEX:32002L0058:EN:HTML.

30. Palomar: Osservatoria di diritto costituzionale, "Decision of the Italian Constitutional Court on the legitimacy of immediate deportation of aliens for national Security reasons (Constitutional Court Decision n. 432/2007)," http://www.unisi.it/dipec/palomar/italy001_2008.html#6.

31. Sofia Celeste, "Want to Check Your e-Mail in Italy? Bring Your Passport," *Christian Science Monitor*, October 4, 2005, http://www.csmonitor.com/2005/1004/p07s01-woeu.html.

32. Ibid.

33. *BBC News*, "Italy Approves Anti-terror Steps," July 29, 2005, http://news.bbc.co.uk/2/hi/europe/4728873.stm.

34. Sofia Celeste, "Want to Check Your e-Mail in Italy? Bring Your Passport," *Christian Science Monitor*, October 4, 2005, http://www.csmonitor.com/2005/1004/p07s01-woeu.html.

35. John Hooper, "Passport to Surf," *Guardian Unlimited*, September 29, 2005, http://blogs.guardian.co.uk/news/archives/2005/09/29/passport_to_surf.html.

36. UNHCR, "Internet Under Surveillance 2004—Italy," http://www.unhcr.org/refworld/publisher,RSF,,ITA,46e6918b21,0.html.

37. iNet, http://www.inet.it/en/content/view/94/144/.

38. Infostrada, http://www.infostrada.it/it/adsl/scheda11.phtml.

39. Telecom Italia, http://www.telecomitalia.com/.

40. Tiscali, http://www.tiscali.it/.

Nordic Countries

The five Nordic countries—Denmark, Finland, Norway, Sweden, and Iceland—have become central players in the European battle between file sharers, rights holders, and ISPs. While each country determines its own destiny, the presence of the European Union (EU) is felt in all legal controversies and court cases. The Internet industry extends across borders, and  so do filtering, military surveillance, and the monitoring of users. Privacy issues were formerly a concern of the elite, but with the growth of the information society, the right to privacy is now being discussed more widely in different political contexts. A popular civil rights movement of file sharers and privacy advocates has arisen out of Sweden in response to both national and international trends, and digital rights activism is increasingly directed at the European Parliament. Single-issue political parties concerned with privacy have now also begun to form in countries outside Europe.

Regional ICT Penetration

The World Economic Forum[1] ranks the Nordic countries at the very top of information and communication technology (ICT) use in the world. All five countries were listed in the top ten of a 2008–2009 survey prepared in partnership with the international business school INSEAD.[2]

The Nordic countries each have broadband Internet penetration rates of more than 30 percent of the population. According to a survey by the Organization for Economic Cooperation and Development (OECD) from June 2008, this figure places them in the top eight in comparison with the organization's 25 other member countries:[3]

1. Denmark 36.7 percent (1,996,408 subscriptions)
3. Norway 33.4 percent (1,554,993 subscriptions)
5. Iceland 32.3 percent (98,361 subscriptions)
6. Sweden 32.3 percent (2,933,014 subscriptions)
8. Finland 30.7 percent (1,616,200 subscriptions)

Regional Regulation

Norway and Iceland are the only Nordic countries that are not members of the EU. However, they do form a part of the European Economic Area (EEA) and have officially agreed to enact legislation similar to that passed in the EU in areas such as consumer protection and business law. As a result, laws are integrated in Norway[4] and Iceland[5] differently than in Sweden, Denmark, and Finland.[6]

Directives passed by the EU Commission and the European Parliament form a framework for lawmakers in the 27 member states to implement their own national laws before a certain deadline. Countries may decide to pass tougher laws than required by a directive. A key to understanding the heated European struggle surrounding intellectual property is an antipiracy directive called the International Property Rights Enforcement Directive (IPRED)[7]. This directive gives rights holders wide-ranging freedoms to investigate the identities of suspected file sharers and to obtain court orders to force ISPs to share personal information about customers suspected of digital piracy. The IPRED was introduced in 2004 and was repeatedly revised over the following years after complaints that its criminal-sanctions provisions were too wide ranging. An amended proposal (IPRED2) that may reintroduce some criminal sanctions was still being debated in 2009.[8] However, the Anti-Counterfeiting Trade Agreement (ACTA) being secretly negotiated[9] between the EU, the United States, and other countries seems to have taken over momentum from IPRED2.[10]

Sweden became the first EU country to put IPRED into effect on April 1, 2009. The BBC reported that Internet traffic in Sweden fell by 33 percent when the law was passed.[11] To protect the privacy of their customers following the implementation of IPRED, Swedish ISPs threatened to erase all their IP-number data.[12] Broadband operator AllTele offered their customers "dis-identification" services to hide file sharers from investigators.[13] Another ISP, ePhone, refused to hand over any data to the courts.[14]

In early 2009, such actions were not against Swedish law,[15] but they may be when another EU data-retention (logging) directive[16] is implemented. Swedish lawmakers are working on a proposal for a law that would force ISPs to store data for at least six months.[17]

File sharing is extremely common in Nordic countries. The Swedish newspaper *Svenska Dagbladet* reported that 79 percent of Swedish males aged 15 to 29 are against the IPRED law.[18] Open wireless local area networks (WLANs) have become an issue under IPRED, as innocent subscribers may be liable for illegal downloads by others. An IPRED-resistance movement started in Sweden encouraging people to open their networks and rename them Ipredia to mask actions by individuals.[19]

Copyright

The battles over copyright, private file sharing, and large-scale dissemination of links in the Nordic region are primarily playing out in the courts under the close watch of international organizations like the International Federation of the Phonographic Industry (IFPI). One Swedish court case over a file-sharing site has earned the most notoriety, but there have been several other cases in neighboring countries where copyright disputes ended in Internet filtering.

The Pirate Bay is a Swedish Web site that tracks BitTorrent files.[20] The Web site has an estimated 22 million users and is one of the Internet's largest sources for file sharing. While it is predominantly known for illegal P2P file sharing of music and films, it also handles links to content that can be legally shared. The fate of the Pirate Bay is the subject of a court battle as well as a forceful grassroots Swedish political movement that has resulted in the creation of a new political party called Piratpartiet (The Pirate Party).[21]

In Denmark, any attempt to access the Pirate Bay using a Danish ISP leads to a block page with links to a January 2008 ruling in a Danish civil court that all access to the Web site should be blocked. Rights holders originally filed the case against the Danish ISP Tele2, which today is owned by the Norwegian telecom Telenor. The Danish national court, Østre Landsret, confirmed the decision on November 26, 2008.[22]

In April 2009, the Pirate Bay case[23] was submitted to the Danish Supreme Court. The basic question for the court to consider is whether an ISP can be charged with blocking access to a Web site, and whether the ISP, as the provider of the connection, can be held responsible for any content transmitted. Thus, the case is about the Danish interpretation of the EU Infosoc[24] directive on copyright and related rights, often called the Information Society Directive. Danish and Swedish parliaments and courts disagree on the interpretation of this directive.

This is not the first case of its kind in Denmark. In March 2006, the country's largest ISP, TDC, was forced to block certain IP addresses used for the transmission of copyrighted material by a Supreme Court decision.[25] The court declared that the transmission of copyrighted files was equal to temporary unauthorized copying and thus illegal. Court orders in 2007 forced Danish ISPs to block access to two Russian file-sharing Web sites, Allofmp3[26] and MP3Sparks.

On April 17, 2009, the four founders of the Pirate Bay were sentenced to one year in prison by a Swedish lower court and a combined fine of 30 million Swedish krona (USD 4 million). The Stockholm District Court determined that the defendants worked as a team in the operation and development of the Web site and that they had been aware that copyrighted material was being shared.

The convicted individuals filed a complaint that the presiding judge was biased, as a member of pro-copyright organizations. To the chagrin of the defendants, the court official charged with deciding whether the first judge was biased was also known to have connections to pro-copyright organizations.[27] Furthermore, the judge[28] selected for the appeal case was a member of a pro-copyright group until 2005.

The Norwegian private law firm Simonsen Advokatfirma DA in 2007 obtained permission[29] from the Data Inspectorate (Datatilsynet) to register the IP addresses of users suspected of engaging in illegal file sharing. The firm represents rights holders. After not receiving assistance from the Norwegian police, the law firm attempted to have ISPs hand over the subscriber information associated with these addresses. Simonsen also drafted a cease-and-desist letter, which they requested the ISPs forward to copyright infringing customers. The International Federation of the Phonographic Industry asked Norwegian ISPs to block file-sharing sites, like the Pirate Bay. The ISPs refused to cooperate.

In a May 2009 copyright case regarding the Norwegian movie *Max Manus*, Simonsen sought a court order to get Norway's largest ISP, Telenor, to release the subscriber information of a person suspected of sharing the film illegally. The ruling was made in the lowest court (Stavanger Tingrett) on May 5, 2009, but the verdict was kept secret at the request of the film industry.[30] In fear of Swedish-style IPRED conditions, attempts are being made in Norway to initiate protests against secrecy.[31] The case determined whether private industry (ISPs) or public authorities are the ones responsible for investigating breaches of law on the Internet. Dealing with a basic principle, the case is expected to be pushed into higher courts.

Norwegian telecommunications company and ISP Telenor has said that it is indifferent to preceding Swedish or Danish court decisions. A spokesperson for the ISP said the company would conform exclusively to the rulings of Norwegian courts. At the same time, a spokesperson for the Norwegian activist group FriBit rejected the idea that the *Max Manus* case had any significance, and said, "The Pirate Bay will continue and there are lots of other services like theirs ... the ruling gives no cause to automatically use other means, like censorship, to stop pirates."[32] The fault lines in Norway are similar to the conflicts in other Nordic countries, but the solutions may not be identical.

Filtering

Internet service providers in all Nordic countries deploy filtering to isolate Web sites distributing child pornography. However, other infringements on freedom of expression and privacy have been controversial. Additionally, suspicions that the filters put in place could eventually be used to filter other sites have resulted in protests from many privacy and advocacy groups.

Nordic ISPs participate in the International Association of Internet Hotlines (INHOPE) project with 35 member countries.[33] Suspicious links are reported by organizations and the general public and passed on to relevant authorities for verification.

Partners in Denmark and Finland are Save the Children, and in Iceland, Heimili & Skoli. Financing originates from the EU Safer Internet Plus Program fund.[34] The Swedish nongovernmental child protection organization ECPAT does a similar job. In Norway, there is no official nongovernmental involvement.

Finland has a law to stop distribution of child pornography.[35] According to Section 1, the law was created to protect children and to block access to child pornography sites that are hosted outside of Finland. Finland also has laws against mocking God or religion (Criminal Act, Ch. 17, Sec. 10), but so far no content of this nature has been filtered.

The Finnish National Bureau of Investigation (NBI) compiles a secret list of Web sites containing child pornography and distributes it to ISPs for filtering.[36] In February 2008, the Electronic Frontier Finland (EFF) published an analysis of "Finnish Internet censorship."[37] According to the report, the NBI filtering list contained about 1,700 Web sites in 2008. The EFF stated that a number of nonpornographic Web sites were found on the list.

In early 2009, the Web site Wikileaks,[38] which collects evidence of corporate and government misconduct, published a list of 797 Web sites censored by Finland. These were originally harvested and published by a well-known Finnish "white hat" hacker and activist Matti Nikki.[39] The list included his own Web site lapsiporno.info, where he criticizes secret censorship. Matti Nikki argued that there were several legal Web sites on the blocked list. On February 17, 2008, he stated that "nearly none of the sites on the child porn list seem to contain child porn."[40] On March 23, 2009, all charges in a criminal investigation against him were dropped.

The blacklist operated by the Danish child pornography filtering system (3,863 blocked URLs) was leaked[41] on December 23, 2008, and made available online. Its publication was a protest[42] against secret censorship systems[43] and was supported by an activist group, IT-Politisk Forening. All Danish ISPs filter content based on the list. The head of the Telecommunication Industries Association of Denmark[44] says the list is of Web sites the authorities deem illegal, and that it should be expected to contain not only child pornography, but also racist, offensive, and libelous material. The Danish police IT investigation unit NITEC insists their list consists of illegal pornography sites only.[45] The Danish ISP industry staunchly refuses to filter questionable content (like gambling sites) unless they are contrary to statutory law or unless required to do so by court order. Attempts by politicians have been made in Denmark and other Nordic countries to protect government gambling monopolies from popular online poker.

All Norwegian ISPs operate a voluntary Child Sexual Abuse Anti-Distribution Filter (CSAADF). The filter is a blacklist of DNS addresses maintained and distributed by Kripos, the Norwegian police agency that deals with organized, financial, and other serious crimes. Each ISP implements this blacklist in its DNS servers by redirecting attempts to access blacklisted Web pages to a page with a warning message.[46] The list is generated without judicial or public oversight and is kept secret by the ISPs using it. A list of supposedly blocked addresses was posted to Wikileaks in March 2009, containing 3,518 DNS addresses.[47] According to Wikileaks, many of the sites on the (Norwegian) list had no obvious connection to child pornography. The Norwegian and Danish lists had 1,097 URLs in common. Police in Germany raided the owner of the German Wikileaks domain name (a mirror site) in March 2009[48] because the Web site published copies of Nordic filtering lists.

As a member of the EEA, Norway has enacted legislation in line with the EU directive on electronic commerce,[49] which among other things states that ISPs shall not monitor their subscribers' use of the Internet. However, the general interpretation in Norway of the directive is that ISPs may be responsible for illegal content on their servers (e.g., child pornography, copyrighted material) if the provider, upon obtaining knowledge or awareness that such content is present, does not act expeditiously to remove or disable access to the content.

As a result of this directive, some ISPs have devised user agreements that empower the service provider to remove any controversial content, including content that is not illegal, to protect themselves from being held liable in any controversy surrounding content.

For example, in February 2008 the Norwegian ISP Imbera removed images of the Danish "Muhammad cartoons" from the Web pages of one of their customers, an organization called Human Rights Service, on the grounds that Imbera's user agreement prohibits users from uploading controversial content to Imbera's servers.[50]

In Norway, the police can demand the subscriber information associated with a particular IP address from an ISP without a court order. This authority follows from a Supreme Court decision in 1999, in a case involving an Internet subscriber suspected of distributing child pornography.[51] As a result of the ruling, the police can demand personal information in all types of cases. According to press reports, the refusal of the police to get involved in the *Max Manus* file-sharing case is the reason Simonsen Advokatfirma DA had to go to civil court.

Surveillance

All Nordic countries hold freedom of expression in high regard. Having military intelligence agencies monitor private citizens' telecommunications in detail and without controls has stimulated emotional debate and antisurveillance movements. The two major forces behind the legal changes in the Nordic countries are fear of terrorism and infringements on copyright. Government surveillance and censorship do not sit well with the Nordic notion of being free and democratic societies, and the introduction of new measures has created an unusually emotional debate in the region.

A survey of global surveillance activity by Privacy International in 2007 characterized Denmark as the only Nordic country that is an "extensive surveillance society," while Finland, Sweden, and Norway were listed as exhibiting "systematic failure to uphold safeguards."[52] This classification included areas of privacy outside of digital life like democratic safeguards, visual surveillance, and workplace monitoring. Iceland had "some safeguards but weakened protection." Denmark was placed in the same category as Bangladesh, France, India, Lithuania, the Philippines, and Romania, and was also the only Nordic country facing a "deteriorating situation." Privacy International also publishes critical Country Reports Overviews[53] of current developments (latest dated December 14, 2007) in each country and wide-ranging in-depth analysis[54] (latest December 12, 2007) of each country (except Iceland).

The Danish national police IT-Efterforskningscenteret (NITEC), the center for IT investigations, is in charge of the blacklist for filtering child pornography sites. The unit has reportedly been investigating techniques for monitoring and deciphering conversations on the free online telephony service Skype.[55] The Danish police refuse to discuss their investigation methods. At the EU level, the judicial cooperation unit, EuroJust,[56] has mentioned Skype's desire to cooperate with EU authorities, dating back to 2006.

On September 15, 2007, every Danish Internet user came under a comprehensive surveillance system, covering their history of Web sites visited, incoming and outgoing e-mails, and use of cell phones. The Danish implementation of the EU "data logging directive"[57] forces telecommunications companies, ISPs, hotels, Internet cafés, wireless hotspots, and apartment buildings with private Internet service to log and store information on all personal communication data for at least one year. These logs must be made available to police without a court order. The stated purpose is to fight terrorists. Two former heads of the Danish Security and Intelligence Service (PET)[58] are on record as opposing the expanded monitoring as unnecessary, worrisome, and damaging to the public's basic democratic rights.[59]

In Sweden, no logging law had yet been implemented in mid-2009, but surveillance of cross-border Internet and telecommunications had. Wiretapping and surveillance measures in Sweden have become a divisive issue in recent years. Those advocating the need for increased surveillance point to the threat from international terrorism and organized crime, and claim that additional measures are necessary to keep pace with changing technology. Opponents claim the measures extending the scope of surveillance pose a threat to civil liberties.

Following a prolonged political battle on privacy in the Swedish parliament, a law known as the "FRA-law" narrowly passed in June 2008, giving the Swedish National Defense Radio Establishment (FRA) the right to monitor all cross-border, cabled communication traffic.[60] In practice, all telephone calls, text messages, faxes, and e-mails passing into and out of Sweden became subject to surveillance as of January 1, 2009.

Public outrage over the law led to a significant revision in September 2008, and a number of wide-ranging surveillance permits were repealed.[61] Among the compromises were requirements that court orders be issued before monitoring individuals, that no communications inside Sweden would be logged, and that the FRA could only work on behalf of the government and the military. The FRA thus monitors all "external threats," not just "foreign military threats."

Almost all telecommunication from Finland to the rest of the world passes through Sweden, leading to fear of the FRA-law in Finland. Both Swedish and Norwegian legal organizations have filed petitions at the European Court of Human Rights challenging the Swedish wiretapping law.[62] In neighboring Denmark, citizens scrambled to assess whether they needed to change ISP and telephone companies in order to avoid being monitored. The Danish Federation of Industries, the largest commercial organization in the country, issued an elevated security warning, fearing commercial espionage by Sweden, and published guidelines on how to avoid surveillance of data by foreign governments at the end of 2008.[63]

The law regulating the Norwegian intelligence agency establishes the rules for military Internet surveillance in Norway.[64] It gives the Intelligence Services under the ministry of defense (Forsvarets Etterretningstjeneste, FO/E) a very broad mandate to collect information that "serves the interests of Norway in relation to foreign states, organizations and individuals." They must, however, refrain from collecting information about Norwegian citizens or legal entities, but there seem to be no restrictions as far as foreigners are concerned.[65]

This broad mandate empowers the FO/E to perform electronic surveillance on communications originating from foreign individuals and organizations at the border, in a manner similar to the more explicit Swedish FRA-law. However, it is unknown how the FO/E currently exercises its surveillance mandate.

The legal framework with regard to Internet surveillance by the Norwegian police is the same as for all communications. The existing legal framework[66] for telephone wiretapping has simply been extended. To intercept e-mail or to tap an Internet line requires a court order, and a person under surveillance must be suspected of involvement in a serious crime punishable with ten years or more in prison (e.g., espionage).

Perspectives

All over Europe censorship and surveillance initiatives are promoted, like the French "three strikes" HADOPI law against piracy that introduced online snooping on suspected file sharers.[67] The law, which has already inspired clones in other EU countries, will be challenged because of a recent declaration by the European Parliament that it is illegal for an EU country to sever Internet access from anyone without the approval of a court.[68] In May 2009, the European Parliament went through a new vote on details in a revision of the telecom rules directive.[69] Stemming from a Europewide mass mobilization, the European Parliament, with a large majority, essentially declared Internet access to be a fundamental right in the EU.[70] At the time of writing, conciliation between the European Parliament and the Commission was in progress. Nonetheless, six days later the French National Assembly passed the controversial law limiting these rights, and the following day the French Senate voted and confirmed the HADOPI law.[71]

In April 2008, the Danish parliament's Council on Technology published a report on IT security that said Danish Internet users seem to prefer the government having direct access to their computers in order to control and update their personal software prior to allowing them onto public Web sites.[72] The report stated that users wanted public censorship of undesirable Web sites (e.g., those known for phishing) and preferred government security classification of selected software (like Web browsers). According to the report, there also seemed to be public demand for the introduction of hardware-based "digital identities," somewhat different from the prevailing secure "digital signatures." At the same time, fear of surveillance and registration of individual activities online was strong. The people surveyed also preferred that ISPs filter e-mail automatically rather than having the current opt-in solution.

The independent Danish IT-Political Association argued strongly against this vision of centralized control online. An extremely successful initiative of the association has been Polippix,[73] a Linux-based privacy protection software, distributed widely on CD and online. The Danish IT-Political Association, like its sister organizations in other Nordic countries, is a member of the European digital rights network EDRI, which tracks EU and national attacks on privacy, introduction of surveillance, and limits on Internet freedom. The work of EDRI is considered especially important because most regulation regarding the Internet, copyright, and privacy originate from European institutions or from international institutions with strong influence in Europe. However, the regulations do not prohibit individual countries from passing their own laws in addition to European ones.

A Swedish public opinion poll[74] published on May 18, 2009, showed that 43 percent of the population had no interest in the FRA-law, and among those who were interested, 34 percent were against and 23 percent in favor. The most critical sector of the population belonged to the 15–29 age group. The least worried group was conservatives over 60. The issue of privacy for the online generation has gained significance as a result of the FRA debate and the Pirate Bay file-sharing case. Indeed, a political party by the name Piratpartiet,[75] the Pirate Party, founded in 2006, was Sweden's third-largest party, with more than 48,000 members,[76] immediately before the June 7, 2009, elections. At the time of writing, public opinion polls indicated that Piratpartiet would win representation in the European Parliament and in the national parliament, Riksdagen, in the next general elections (expected in 2010).

Conclusion

Because they are at the forefront of ICT use in the world, the Nordic countries understandably have a lively public debate on copyright and privacy issues. New trends concerning online reality will likely originate here. In these countries, rights holders and the telecommunications industries are lobbying politicians in support of their different interests. Recent developments in Sweden offer hints that the general public, apart from indulging in massive pirating activities, is getting involved at the political level.

Following the FRA-law revision in Sweden, the governing right-wing alliance is deeply shaken by the unexpected and forceful youth movement that draws its energy from new age issues like privacy and file sharing. The Social Democratic Party, the originator of the antiterror surveillance law proposal a few years ago, has with its Green center-left partner announced that the issue of privacy (and the FRA) will be hot during the next Swedish general elections (expected in 2010). They intend to repeal the bill.

The battle over FRA in Sweden was fought with modern communication technology (e.g., Facebook, Twitter, blogs, texting). The use of new methods for political mobilization has reached critical levels, and activists are entering the political mainstream. Issues are crossing borders.

Political scientists Ulf Bjereld and Henrik Oscarsson at the University of Gothenburg in Sweden ask whether the security interests of the nation-state are colliding with the right to free cross-border communication in international networks. In an article published in the leading Swedish daily *Dagens Nyheter* on May 18, 2009, they question whether the Swedish state is struggling to retake control of the globally networked society's most valued raw material, means of influence, and driving force: information. These scholars see the Pirate Party as more than a single-issue platform, rather as a movement of liberal values, individual freedom, and personal integrity, where culture must be set free and patents and private monopolies opposed. Bjereld and Oscarsson believe the party's adherents favor citizen rights and freedoms, and demand clearer regulation and compliance with the social contract between government and citizens. It is a new civil rights movement of the information society.[77]

It is obvious that very strong industrial interests are influencing politicians in the Nordic countries and Europe. The controversial decision by the European Parliament to make access to the Internet a "fundamental right" and the strong response, particularly in Sweden, from the predominantly young digital grassroots may be a forewarning of things to come. The EU and increasingly its individual members are struggling to regulate digital life, while activist users are trying to push back industrial dominance.

The Nordic countries are historically, legally, technically, and culturally very close to one another, and are all in some way associated with the EU. As more countries achieve the high Internet penetration rates of these five countries, we may see similar cultural and political phenomena spilling over to the region, and maybe globally too. Already, "Pirate Parties" have formed or are in the process of being established in 22 other countries.[78] Certainly, the outcome of the legal battles regarding copyright, surveillance, and filtering in the Nordic countries should not be considered as without bearing on the wider region in the near future.

Notes

1. World Economic Forum, "The Global Information Technology Report 2008–2009," March 2009, http://www.weforum.org/en/initiatives/gcp/Global%20Information%20Technology%20Report/GlobalInformationTechnology.

2. INSEAD, "Global Information Technology Report 2008–2009" (interactive version), http://www.insead.edu/v1/gitr/wef/main/home.cfm.

3. OECD Broadband Portal, http://www.oecd.org/sti/ict/broadband.

4. Norwegian Mission to the EU, http://www.eu-norway.org/eu/norway+and+the+eu.htm; Wikipedia on the relationship between Norway and the EU, http://en.wikipedia.org/wiki/Norway_and_the_European_Union.

5. Wikipedia on the relationship between Iceland and the EU, http://en.wikipedia.org/wiki/Iceland_and_the_European_Union.

6. Per Laegreid, Runolfur Smari Steinthorsson, and Baldur Thorhallsson, "Europeanization of Central Government Administration in the Nordic States," *Journal of Common Market Studies*, Vol. 42, No. 2, pp. 347–369, June 2004, http://ssrn.com/abstract=546906.

7. Directive 2004/48/EC of the European Parliament and of the Council of 29 April 2004 on the enforcement of intellectual property rights, http://eur-lex.europa.eu/pri/en/oj/dat/2004/l_195/l_19520040602en00160025.pdf; Amended proposal for a Directive of the European Parliament and of the Council on criminal measures aimed at ensuring the enforcement of intellectual property rights, COM/2006/0168 final—COD 2005/0127, http://eur-lex.europa.eu/LexUriServ/LexUriServ.do?uri=COM:2006:0168:FIN:EN:HTML; Wikipedia on IPRED, Directive on the enforcement of intellectual property rights, http://en.wikipedia.org/wiki/Directive_on_the_enforcement_of_intellectual_property_rights.

8. Detailed Foundation for a Free Information Infrastructure (FFII) documentation of the IPRED2 proposals, http://action.ffii.org/ipred2/#head-35c9f9ab741815ee371ba8a5f6fe95ad3a17b7a3.

9. Foundation for a Free Information Infrastructure, "EU Council Deliberately Obstructs Access to ACTA Documents," January 13, 2009, http://press.ffii.org/Press_releases/EU_Council_deliberately_obstructs_access_to_ACTA_documents?highlight=(ACTA).

10. Ante Wessel, analyst for FFII, in conversation with author, June 4, 2009.

11. *BBC News*, "Piracy Law Cuts Internet Traffic," April 2, 2009, http://news.bbc.co.uk/2/hi/technology/7978853.stm.

12. Mats Lewan, "Swedish ISPs Vow to Erase Users' Traffic Data," *CNET Digital Media*, April 28, 2009, http://news.cnet.com/8301-1023_3-10229618-93.html?tag=mncol;title.

13. Sten Gustafsson, "Bredbandsoperatör Döljer Fildelande" [Broadband Operator Hides File Sharers], *Dagens Nyheter*, May 14, 2009, http://www.dn.se/ekonomi/bredbandsoperator-doljer -fildelande-1.866108.

14. Anders Frelin, "Bevisen i Första Ipred-fallet Ifrågasätts" [Proof of First IPRED Case Questioned], *Dagens Nyheter*, April 23, 2009, http://www.dn.se/dnbok/bevisen-i-forsta-ipred-fallet-ifragasatts -1.850411.

15. Directive 2002/58/EC concerning the processing of personal data and the protection of privacy in the electronic communications sector (Directive on Privacy and Electronic Communications), http://eur-lex.europa.eu/LexUriServ/LexUriServ.do?uri=OJ:L:2002:201:0037:0047:EN:PDF.

16. Directive 2006/24/EC of the European Parliament and of the Council of 15 March 2006 on the retention of data generated or processed in connection with the provision of publicly available electronic communications services or of public communications networks and amending Directive 2002/58/EC, http://eur-lex.europa.eu/LexUriServ/LexUriServ.do?uri=CELEX:32006L0024:EN :HTML.

17. Erika Svantesson, "Lagförslag: IP-adresser Ska Lagras ett Halvår" [Proposal: IP Addresses Must Be Stored for Half a Year], *Dagens Nyheter*, May 15, 2009, http://www.dn.se/nyheter/politik/ lagforslag-ip-adresser-ska-lagras-ett-halvar-1.867054.

18. Tobias Olsson, "Klart Nej till Ny Fildelningslag" [Strong No to File-sharing Law], *Svenska Dagbladet*, March 17, 2009, http://www.svd.se/nyheter/inrikes/artikel_2604781.svd.

19. Ipredia home page, http://ipredia.se/wiki/Huvudsida.

20. BitTorrent P2P file sharing site Pirate Bay, http://thepiratebay.org/.

21. Swedish Pirate Party English home page, http://www.piratpartiet.se/international/english.

22. Danish National Court confirms lower court decision to have ISP Tele2 block access to the Pirate Bay, November 26, 2008, http://issuu.com/comon/docs/kendelsetele2ifpi_261108.

23. Rune Pedersen and Mads Elkær, "Dansk Pirate Bay-sag Skal for Højesteret" [Danish Supreme Court Accepts Pirate Bay Case], *Computerworld*, April 24, 2009, http://www.computerworld.dk/art/ 51238/dansk-pirate-bay-sag-skal-for-hoejesteret?a=fp_3&i=5; Supreme Court date not set, May 25, 2009.

24. EU Infosoc Directive, http://eur-lex.europa.eu/LexUriServ/LexUriServ.do?uri=OJ:L:2001:167 :0010:0019:EN:PDF.

25. Danish Supreme Court decision, February 10, 2006, http://www.it-retsforum.dk/index.php ?module=Pagesetter&type=file&func=get&tid=4&fid=fil&pid=88&download=1.

26. Allofmp3 verdict in Danish—for download, October 25 2006, http://www.dr.dk/NR/ rdonlyres/EF2AAB7A-0E04-4963-963A-463CD7550D72/361965/tele2_... ; "Allofmp3, IT-Pol View,"

Danish IT-Political Association analysis of allofmp3 case, http://itpol.polcast.dk/sager/nyheder/ Allofmp3En.

27. Ossi Carp, "The Pirate Bay: Nya Turer i Jävsfrågan" [Pirate Bay: News on Bias Case], *Dagens Nyheter*, May 20, 2009, http://www.dn.se/kultur-noje/musik/the-pirate-bay-nya-turer-i-javsfragan -1.870677.

28. Jenny Stiernstedt, "Ihrfeldt Ny Pirate Bay-domare" [Ihrfeldt New Pirate Bay Judge], *Dagens Nyheter*, May 19, 2009, http://www.dn.se/kultur-noje/musik/ihrfeldt-ny-pirate-bay-domare-1 .869487.

29. Datatilsynet [Norwegian Data Inspectorate] licensing Simonsen Advokatfirma, December 8, 2006, http://www.datatilsynet.no/templates/article____1640.aspx.

30. Joakim Thorkildsen, "'Max Manus'-kjennelsen Blir Holdt Hemmelig" [*Max Manus* Verdict Kept Secret], *Dagbladet*, May 5, 2009, http://www.dagbladet.no/2009/05/05/kultur/film/max _manus/fildeling/6066821/; Øystein Sættem, "Why the Max Manus Verdict Encompasses So Much More," *FriBit*, May 11, 2009, http://www.fribit.no/2009/05/11/why-the-max-manus-verdict -encompasses-so-much-more/.

31. Marius Jørgenrud, "Aksjonerer mot Hemmelig Kjennelse" [Protests against Secret Judgment], *Digi.no*, May 6, 2009, http://www.digi.no/812555/aksjonerer-mot-hemmelig-kjennelse.

32. Ole Morten Knudsen, "Blir en Nøktern Feiring" [It Will Be a Sober Celebration], *Teknofil.no*, April 17, 2009, http://teknofil.no/wip4/—noektern-feiring/d.epl?id=36355.

33. European Commission, "INHOPE: Association of Internet Hotline Providers in Europe (INHOPE) as European Hotline Co-ordinator," http://ec.europa.eu/information_society/apps/ projects/factsheet/index.cfm?project_ref=SIP-2007-HC-121701.

34. European Commission, "Safer Internet Programme: The Main Framework for European Policy," http://ec.europa.eu/information_society/activities/sip/policy/programme/index_en.htm.

35. Laki Lapsipornografian Levittämisen Estotoimista 1.12.2006/1068 [Law against Spreading Child Pornography], http://www.finlex.fi/fi/laki/ajantasa/2006/20061068.

36. *YLE*, "Police Censor Porn Website," February 13, 2008, http://yle.fi/uutiset/news/2008/02/ police_censor_porn_website_279365.html.

37. Kai Puolamäki, "Finnish Internet Censorship," Electronic Frontier Finland, February 18, 2008, http://www.effi.org/blog/kai-2008-02-18.html.

38. Wikileaks, "797 Domains on Finnish Internet Censorship List, Including Censorship Critic, 2008," January 5, 2009, http://wikileaks.org/wiki/797_domains_on_Finnish_Internet_censorship _list%2C_including_censorship_critic%2C_2008.

39. Lapsiporno.info, "Lapsiporno.info and the Finnish Internet Censorship," http://lapsiporno .info/english-2008-02-15.html.

40. Wikipedia, "Lapsiporno.info," http://en.wikipedia.org/wiki/Lapsiporno.info.

41. Wikileaks, "Denmark: 3863 Sites on Censorship List, Feb 2008," December 23 2008, http://wikileaks.org/wiki/Denmark:_3863_sites_on_censorship_list%2C_Feb_2008; Wikinews, "Wikileaks Tells Wikinews Why They Published Danish Child Porn Censorship List," December 23, 2008, http://en.wikinews.org/wiki/Wikileaks_tells_Wikinews_why_they_published_Danish_child_porn_censorship_list.

42. Mads Bang, "Hvorfor i Alverden vil I Boycotte Red Barnet?" [Why on Earth Do You Want to Boycott Save the Children?], Computerworld, September 18 2008, http://www.computerworld.dk/art/47976.

43. Mads Elkær, "Politiets Børneporno-liste Lækket på Nettet" [Police Child Porn List Leaked Online], Computerworld, December 23, 2008, http://www.computerworld.dk/art/49524.

44. Ib Tolstrup, CEO of The Telecommunication Industries Association of Denmark, personal communications, May 2009.

45. Søren Thomassen, deputy police inspector and head of NITEC, National police IT-investigations center, personal communication, May 2009.

46. The Child Sexual Abuse Anti-Distribution Filter warning Web page from Norwegian ISP Uninett, CSAADF is part of the COSPOL Internet Related Child Abusive Material Project (CIRCAMP) project initiated by the European Chief of Police Task Force, http://csaadf.uninett.no/.

47. Wikileaks, "Norwegian Secret Internet Censorship Blacklist, 3518 Domains, 18 Mar 2009," http://wikileaks.org/wiki/Norwegian_secret_internet_censorship_blacklist%2C_3518_domains%2C_18_Mar_2009.

48. Wikileaks, "Police Raid Home of Wikileaks.de Domain Owner over Censorship Lists," March 24, 2009, http://wikileaks.org/wiki/Police_raid_home_of_Wikileaks.de_domain_owner_over_censorship_lists.

49. "E-Commerce Directive," http://ec.europa.eu/internal_market/e-commerce/directive_en.htm.

50. Ole Morten Knudsen, "Ytringsfriheten Overgår Ikke Alt" [Freedom of Speech Is Not Above Everything], Teknofil.no, February 22, 2008, http://www.teknofil.no/wip4/ytringsfriheten_overgaar_alt/d.epl?id=25769.

51. Norges Høyesterett afgørelse 1999 [Norwegian Supreme Court decision 1999], HR-1999–88-A (not online).

52. Privacy International, "The 2007 International Privacy Ranking," survey of Leading Surveillance Societies around the World, http://www.privacyinternational.org/article.shtml?cmd[347]=x-347-559597&als[theme]=Communications%20surveillance.

53. Privacy International, "PHR2006—Country Reports Overview," December 14, 2007, http://www.privacyinternational.org/article.shtml?cmd[347]=x-347-559061.

54. Privacy International, "Denmark," December 18, 2007, http://www.privacyinternational.org/article.shtml?cmd[347]=x-347-559545; Privacy International, "Norway," December 18, 2007, http://www.privacyinternational.org/article.shtml?cmd[347]=x-347-559510; Privacy International,

"Sweden," December 18, 2007, http://www.privacyinternational.org/article.shtml?cmd[347]=x-347 -559487; Privacy International, "Finland," December 18, 2007, http://www.privacyinternational .org/article.shtml?cmd[347]=x-347-559538.

55. Dan Mygind, "Dansk Skype-aflytning Mørklægges" [Danish Skype-interception Not To Be Discussed], *Computerworld*, August 1, 2008, http://www.computerworld.dk/art/47198?cid=4&q= nitec&sm=search&a=cid&i=4&o=5&pos=6.

56. "Eurojust Will Be Requested to Coordinate Internet Telephony Investigations," Eurojust press release, February 20, 2009, http://www.eurojust.europa.eu/press_releases/2009/25-02-2009.htm.

57. Logningsbekendtgørelsen [Logging Directive in Danish], https://www.retsinformation.dk/ Forms/R0710.aspx?id=2445.

58. The Danish Security and Intelligence Service, PET, http://pet.dk/English.aspx.

59. Rune Pedersen, "Tidl. PET-chef: Logning Fremmer Mistænkeliggørelse" [Former PET-chief: Logging Furthers Suspicion], *Computerworld*, September 24, 2008, http://www.computerworld.dk/ art/41604/tidl-pet-chef-logning-fremmer-mistaenkeliggoerelse; Rasmus Karkov, "Tidligere PET Chef Kritiserer Anti-terror Love" [Former Head of PET Criticizes Anti-terror Laws], *Comon.dk*, December 17, 2008, http://www.comon.dk/news/tidligere.pet.chef.kritiserer.anti-terror.love_39034.html.

60. Economist Intelligence Unit, "Surveillance Sweep: A New Surveillance Law Causes a Rumpus in Sweden," *Economist.com*, July 22, 2008, http://www.economist.com/displayStory.cfm?story_id =11778941.

61. Press release from Sweden's cabinet office: "Alliansen enig om stärkt integritet, tydligare reglering och förbättrad kontroll i kompletteringar till signalspaningslagen" [The alliance agrees on strong integrity, more clear regulation and improved controls in additions of the signals intelligence law], September 25, 2008, http://www.regeringen.se/sb/d/10911/a/112332; Wikipedia analysis of the FRA-law, http://sv.wikipedia.org/wiki/FRA-lagen; Wikipedia on the FRA-law, http:// en.wikipedia.org/wiki/FRA_law.

62. David Landes, "Norwegian Group Joins Case against Sweden's Wiretapping Law," *Thelocal.se*, February 13, 2009, http://www.thelocal.se/17578/20090213/.

63. Rune Pedersen, "DI: Sverige Udgør Forhøjet Sikkerhedstrussel" [Danish Industry: Higher Security Threat from Sweden], *Computerworld*, November 14, 2008, http://www.computerworld.dk/art/ 48926.

64. Lov om Etterretningstjenesten av 1998–03–20 nr. 11[Law on the Intelligence Agency], Norway's legal database, http://www.lovdata.no/all/tl-19980320-011-0.html.

65. Gisle Hannemyr, Department of Informatics, Oslo University, personal communication, May 21, 2009.

66. "Lov om Rettergangsmåten i Straffesaker av 1981-05-22 nr. 25" Kap 16a. Avlytting og Annen Kontroll av Kommunikasjonsanlegg (Kommunikasjonskontroll) [Penal Law Chapter 16a on Control of Communications], http://www.lovdata.no/all/hl-19810522-025.html#map026.

67. Eric Pfanner, "France Approves Crackdown on Internet Piracy," *New York Times*, May 13, 2009, http://www.nytimes.com/2009/05/13/technology/internet/13net.html.

68. European Digital Rights, "European Parliament Votes against the 3 Strikes, Again," May 6, 2009, http://www.edri.org/edri-gram/number7.9/ep-plenary-votes-against-3-strikes.

69. "No Agreement on Reform of Telecom Legislation," press release, European Parliament, May 6, 2009, http://www.europarl.europa.eu/news/expert/infopress_page/058-55086-124-05-19 -909-20090505IPR55085-04-05-2009-2009-true/default_en.htm.

70. Gérald Sédrati-Dinet, "Amendment 138/46 Adopted Again: Internet Is a Fundamental Right in Europe," laquadrature.net, May 6, 2009, http://www.laquadrature.net/en/amendment-138-46 -adopted-again.

71. European Digital Rights, "France: Three Strikes Law Voted for Good," May 20, 2009, http:// www.edri.org/edri-gram/number7.10/france-three-strikes-voted; Ernesto, "France Passes 'Three Strikes' Anti-Piracy Law," TorrentFreak, May 12, 2009, http://torrentfreak.com/france-passes -three-strikes-anti-piracy-law-090512/; Marguerite Reardon, "France Passes Controversial Antipiracy Bill," *ZDNet*, May 13, 2009, http://news.zdnet.co.uk/internet/0,1000000097,39651441,00.htm.

72. "Brugernes It-sikkerhed" [User IT-safety], Teknologirådet [Danish Parliament's Council on Technology—listing of reports], April 22, 2009, http://www.tekno.dk/subpage.php3?page =udgivelser/download.php3&toppic=udgivelser.

73. "Privacy software collection Polippix details," IT-Pol, http://itpol.polcast.dk/sager/polippix/ polippix-den-politisk-cd-privatlivets-fred.

74. Ulf Bjereld and Henrik Oscarsson, "Nästan Varannan Svensk Struntar i FRA-frågan" [Almost Every Second Person Doesn't Care about the FRA-question], op-ed article, *Dagens Nyheter*, May 18, 2009, http://www.dn.se/opinion/debatt/nastan-varannan-svensk-struntar-i-fra-fragan-1.868277.

75. Piratpartiet [Pirate Party's home page], http://www.piratpartiet.se/.

76. Membership listing of Swedish political parties, http://www.piratpartiet.se/medlemsantal.

77. Ulf Bjereld and Henrik Oscarsson, "Nästan Varannan Svensk Struntar i FRA-frågan," *Dagens Nyheter*, May 18 2009, http://www.dn.se/opinion/debatt/nastan-varannan-svensk-struntar-i-fra -fragan-1.868277.

78. List of countries with Pirate Parties: http://www.pp-international.net/.

Turkey

Stretched between Asia and Europe, Turkey amalgamates the cultural, historical, and sociopolitical diversity of two continents. The government has implemented legal and institutional reforms driven by the country's ambitions to become a European Union member state, while at the same time demonstrating its high sensitivity to defamation and other "inappropriate" online content, which has resulted in the closure of a number of local and international Web sites.

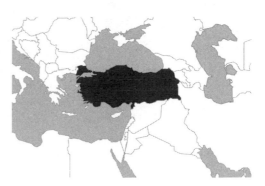

Background

Turkey was established as a secular state in 1923 by Mustafa Kemal Atatürk. The "Father of the Nation" transformed the government from Islamic rule to a secular modern state, with laws based upon the Swiss civil code. The principle of secularity is enshrined in the Constitution[1] to ensure that religious matters do not interfere with state affairs. The Turkish military powers consider themselves to be the guardians of secular democracy and in the past have actively pursued this role, resulting in the forced removal of elected governments on a number of occasions. The Turkish military

RESULTS AT A GLANCE

Filtering	No Evidence of Filtering	Suspected Filtering	Selective Filtering	Substantial Filtering	Pervasive Filtering
Political			•		
Social			•		
Conflict and security	•				
Internet tools			•		

Other Factors	Low	Medium	High	Not Applicable
Transparency		•		
Consistency	•			

KEY INDICATORS	
GDP per capita, PPP (constant 2005 international dollars)	11,825
Life expectancy at birth (years)	72
Literacy rate (percent of people age 15+)	89
Human development index (out of 179)	76
Rule of law (out of 211)	98
Voice and accountability (out of 209)	121
Democracy index (out of 167)	87 (Hybrid regime)
Digital opportunity index (out of 181)	52
Internet users (percent of population)	33.1

Source by indicator: World Bank 2009a, World Bank 2009a, World Bank 2009a, UNDP 2008, World Bank 2009b, World Bank 2009b, Economist Intelligence Unit 2008, ITU 2007, ITU 2008.

has developed a long history of involvement in politics, and as a result the government remains dependent upon it to maintain a balance between religious and secular institutions.

Since Turkey's establishment as a secular republic, the nation has become increasingly integrated with the West through membership in such organizations as the Council of Europe, NATO, the Organization for Economic Cooperation and Development, the Organization for Security and Cooperation in Europe, and the G-20 major economies. Free expression of opinion in Turkey is guaranteed by Article 10 of the European Convention on Human Rights and Fundamental Freedoms, ratified by Turkey in 1954, and by various provisions of the International Covenant on Civil and Political Rights, signed by Turkey in 2000.

Despite Turkey's commitment to free expression and freedom of information, the Penal Code broadly restricts such freedoms by criminalizing speech that insults the Turkish nation, Turkish government institutions, and Turkish ethnicity. A number of other legal acts shape the information available on the Internet by allowing state institutions to apply widely filtering and blocking mechanisms in order to prevent illegal information online.

Internet in Turkey

Turkey's Internet market is growing quickly. Internet penetration was at 7.5 percent in 2004, but increased to 33.1 percent by 2008. The Internet subscribers (i.e., the actual number of dial-up, leased line, and fixed broadband Internet subscribers) were just 7.89 per 100 inhabitants for 2008.[2] Overall, the market witnessed considerable growth propelled by the increase in the number of broadband subscribers during 2006, with ADSL being the predominant broadband access technology.[3]

The telecommunications market has seen a major structural change toward liberalization, after the fixed-telephony network was opened to competition in 2005. Previously a monopoly, Turk Telecom (TT) is still the dominant telecom and broadband Internet operator in the country, preserving a de facto monopoly of the fixed-line services. Before liberalization, Turk Telekomünikasyon A.Ş. (Turk Telecom) was a state company entirely owned by the Undersecretary of the Treasury. After years of national debate and international pressure, the company's privatization was carried out in November 2005 when 55 percent of the shares were bought by private investors.[4] Subsequently, 15 percent of the remaining shares were sold and have recently begun to be traded on the stock market.

There is a growing number of ISPs in the country.[5] Through its wholly owned subsidiary TTNet A.Ş., Turk Telecom focuses on development of broadband services to compensate for the loss of revenue in the liberalized fixed-line voice market. According to a report by the National Telecommunications Authority for the telecoms market in 2007, TTNet had a market share of 95.7 percent in retail ADSL Internet access services, while other operators hold the remaining 4.3 percent.[6] The company has announced plans to invest nearly USD 800 million over the next few years in the sector and increase Internet usage in both urban and rural areas.[7]

Turk Telecom owns international channels for Internet traffic. It operates the Internet backbone network (through TTNet) and leases lines to other providers. Thus, the prices for external and sometimes internal lease of TT's infrastructure affect most of the ISPs.

In July 2008, Turk Telecom began offering VDSL2 (very high speed digital subscriber line 2) service across 73 of 81 provinces. Turk Telecom wholesales this service to ISPs. The VDSL2 service is transmitted over phone lines and increases the Internet connectivity in Turkey eightfold, bringing it into the top third of 23 European countries in terms of fastest connectivity using DSL technology.

The main commercial ISPs in Turkey are TTNet, Superonline, Sabanci Telecom, Kocnet, Smile, Doruknet, DoganOnline, and IsNet. Superonline is owned by the Çukurova Group, which is one of the leading Turkish business conglomerates.[8] Superonline's lines, just like those of other providers, pass through Turk Telecom. Superonline is awaiting approval of a WiMAX license, which would allow it to provide "triple-play" services without being dependent on Turk Telecom's infrastructure.[9]

Some of the other main ISPs are affiliated with banking and media groups, including the Sabanaci Group's turk.net, Is Bank's is.net, and Koc's koc.net. Sabanci Telecom was created through the merger of TTNet, Sabanci Telecom, and AK Internet. The provider offers a range of services (data communications, Internet access, VoIP, and mobile data services in partnership with the mobile operator Telsim).[10] In 2006, Sabanci's investment in the ISP market reached 63 million liras.

Turkey has one official Internet exchange point (IXP), the Turkish Information Exchange, or TIX.[11] Established in 1997 as a private initiative with a large number of members in its first years, TIX languished after it was restructured into a company in 2002.[12] Subsequently, a second IXP was established in June 2003 with the collaboration of a number of leading ISPs. Although this second platform was used extensively for a couple of months, the traffic on this exchange point has also declined, starting at the end of December 2003, as a result of the severe price competition ISPs faced from Turk Telecom.[13]

Following liberalization, Turk Telecom had to transfer its cable assets to a governmental entity (Turksat) responsible for communications satellites as proposed by the Turkish Competition Authority. The largest share of investments in the original cable telecoms company was made by private operators. Government control over the telecom pipelines is expected to be only a temporary solution, but it has caused serious concerns among private operators regarding the certainty of their investments.[14] Of 24 satellite platform operators in the country, Turksat is the main one. The company is also responsible for designing the government portal offering e-government services.

The main mobile operator is the private Turkcell with more than 28.7 million subscribers as of March 31, 2006.[15] The largely private mobile company Telsim is second with 8 million subscribers, followed by Aria with 4 million.[16] Both Turkcell and Telsim have been issued 25-year licenses to operate in the mobile phone sector.

Before initiating operation, VoIP operators need to obtain a license. The "Authorization Regulation on the Telecommunications Services and Infrastructures" of August 26, 2004, states that the general authorization granted to ISPs for performing activities does not include provision of VoIP services (Article 5.1 of Annex A6). Pursuant to Article 4.1. of Annex A9 of the same regulation, the ISPs willing to provide VoIP services would need to obtain a license for long-distance telephony services from the Telecommunications Authority. However, compared to the environment before the market liberalization, VoIP services are more accessible now. There are a number of local VoIP clients providing an alternative to Skype that targets Turkish and even international markets.[17]

Legal and Regulatory Frameworks

Regulatory Framework

The Telecommunications Authority (TA) was established under Law No. 4502 in 2000.[18] Prior to that time, the Ministry of Transportation handled regulatory issues in the field of telecommunications. This ministry still approves the changes in license fees proposed by the telecoms agency. The so-called independent regulatory authorities, including the TA, were recently established in Turkey to regulate and monitor sectors of strategic importance for the state.[19] While these authorities are part of the administrative system and are therefore state agencies, they are organized in a manner that permits a certain level of independence from the executive body (i.e., they do not operate under the traditional administrative hierarchy; their decisions and acts are not subject to the approval or permission of the central administration, nor can their decisions or acts be revoked or amended by the central administration). However, certain legal provisions imply that the central administration, and in particular the government, still maintains considerable control over the Telecommunications Authority. Most notably, pursuant to Article 8 of Law No. 2813, members of the Telecommunications Board (the highest decision-making body of the TA) are appointed by the Council of Ministers. Even the amendments to the law discussed in the following paragraphs do not succeed in safeguarding the independence of the TA from political interference.

The Authorization Regulation of the Telecommunications Services and Infrastructures of 2004 envisions a permissive regime to the ISPs for entering the local market. Providers are required to apply for and obtain a general authorization from the Telecommunications Authority to provide telecommunications services. Internet Law No. 5651, established in 2007, expands the group of regulated providers to include all access and hosting providers.

The Telecommunications Authority Regulation of October 24, 2007, specifies the prerequisites that hosting and access providers need to comply with when applying for an issuance, transfer, renewal, or cancellation of licenses and imposes a number of responsibilities on providers. One of these charges both the access and hosting providers with the duty to remove illegal content from their system upon notification from the Communications Presidency, to the extent that it is technically possible. However, the regulation reaffirms the principle laid out in the Law No. 5651 that neither the access providers nor the hosting providers are under an obligation to ensure the legality of the content they provide.

The licenses granted to hosting providers are valid for five years and are renewable. The licenses issued to access providers are valid for the period during which the relevant provider has been authorized by the Telecommunications Authority to provide telecommunications services.

Legal Framework

Turkey's aspiration to join the EU has been a major influence in driving reform and liberalizing its telecommunications sector.[20] As a candidate to the EU, Turkey is under an obligation to align its national legislation with that of the EU in all 31 areas of the *acquis communautaire*, which includes telecommunications and IT. The EU's telecommunications policies call for liberalization of the sector with a view to making the EU one of the most competitive and dynamic knowledge-based economies by 2010.[21]

In recent years, Turkey has taken substantial steps to reform its telecommunications laws. In this regard, the adoption of Law No. 4502 in 2000, which provides a legal framework for liberalization of the sector and establishes the telecommunications regulatory authority, is particularly noteworthy. Furthermore, the opening of the market to competition by removal of Turk Telecom's monopoly in the sector is another positive development.

Nevertheless, as stated in the "Turkey 2007 Progress Report," prepared by the European Commission, a number of issues still remain to be addressed regarding Turkish harmonization of telecommunications laws. In this regard, the licensing regime and the high communications taxes imposed on operators are considered particularly problematic.[22] The restrictive licensing scheme imposed on access providers by the Telecommunications Authority is out of line with the EU directives. Turkey will need to abolish its licensing regime for electronic communications services and replace it with a clear, predictable, and transparent general authorization process, as proposed by the EU.

A further concern is that Turk Telecom's owners possess a 21-year concession agreement over all equipment, which has to revert to the government at the end of the concession. This provision by itself is inconsistent with the overall character of EU telecommunications law.

Turkey Mass Media Laws Regulating Freedom of Expression

The legal framework that regulates the freedom of expression and freedom of press in Turkey consists of the Press Law[23] and the Law on the Establishment of Radio and Television Enterprises and Their Broadcasts (the RTUK Law).[24] The current Press Law applies only to the print media, while the RTUK Law covers TV and radio broadcasts.

Turkey's 2004 Press Law No. 5187 annuls the former Press Law No. 5680 and its amendments, which was heavily criticized for bringing Internet broadcasting within the ambit of press legislation, thereby subjecting Web sites and ISPs to monitoring standards entirely incompatible with the characteristics of the Internet.[25] After reaffirming the constitutional principle that the press is free, Article 3 of the Press Law goes on to state that "this freedom may be restricted in accordance with the requirements of a democratic society to protect the reputation and rights of others as well as public health and public morality, national security, and public order and public safety; to safeguard the indivisible integrity of its territory; to prevent crime; to withhold information duly classified as state secrets; and to ensure the authority and impartial functioning of the judiciary." In addition, the Press Law sets certain limits on the freedom of press on the following points:

- Compromising the judicial process (Art. 19)
- Encouraging sexual assault, murder, or suicide (Art. 20)
- Illicit disclosure of identities (Art. 21)
- Failure to publish reply and correction (Art. 18)

The RTUK Law's objective is "to prescribe the principles and procedures relating to the regulation of radio and television broadcasts and to the establishment, duties, competence and responsibilities of the Radio and Television Supreme Council." Article 4 of this law provides an extensive list of broadcasting standards that need to be complied with in TV, radio, and data broadcasts, thereby setting the limits on how the TV and radio broadcasting enterprises can exercise their freedom of expression and freedom of press. The list risks burdening the media, as it includes vaguely framed phrases such as "national and moral values of the community," "give rise to feelings of hatred in the community," and "raise the feeling of fear." The Radio and TV Supreme Council is responsible for overseeing the TV and radio stations' adherence to these broadcasting standards and imposing the prescribed sanctions in case a violation occurs. Pursuant to Article 33 of the RTUK Law, the available sanctions are issuance of a warning, fine, suspension, and revocation of broadcasting license permit.

Turkey Internet Laws Regulating Freedom of Expression and Freedom of Information
Until 2005, the Internet in Turkey was a largely free medium. However, in 2005 this situation quickly changed when laws were introduced to restrict Internet content. Widespread use of the Internet and growing concerns about the uncontrolled amount of sensitive content available online pushed authorities to adopt a special law on the Internet. The Law on the Internet (or the Regulation of Broadcasts via Internet and Prevention of Crimes Committed Through such Broadcasts) No. 5651 was passed by the parliament on May 4, 2007, and signed by president Ahmet Necdet Sezer on May 22. This law introduces criminal liability for people who post certain categories of illegal content online. According to this law, if such content is posted it should be taken down immediately either by authorities or by the ISPs themselves.

The law establishes a model that allows a large group of actors, including the government, to petition the court or the Telecommunications Authority to filter certain Internet content. "Sufficient suspicion" that an offense is committed is a sufficient test to meet under the Internet Law to allow block of access. As a result of this law and related legislation, a number of Web sites have been blocked over the past few years in Turkey. This censorship has led to an uproar from large communities within Turkey and abroad, and has placed concerns about filtering of Internet content high on the national agenda.

The most common crime is posting obscene content—that is, content in violation of Article 8, paragraph A (5) of the Internet Law. Statistics provided by a Communications Presidency representative reveal that the posting of obscene content accounts for more than half of the total number of court rulings for blocking Internet access so far—5,629 since November 2007.[26] The remaining rulings banned access to the following types of proscribed content (from most to least common):

1. Crimes against Atatürk (Article 8/b)
2. Prostitution
3. Providing place and opportunity for gambling
4. Sexual abuse of children
5. Encouraging people to commit suicide
6. Supplying drugs that are dangerous for health
7. Facilitation of the abuse of drugs

The second most common reason for shutting down a Web site is posting content insulting Atatürk. A number of such incidents occurred in 2007, as this was the first year in which sites were blocked under direct application of the Internet Law. For the definition of "crimes against Atatürk," the law refers to Turkish Law No. 5816 on Crimes against Atatürk, which criminalizes certain activities against the founder of modern Turkey. As Atatürk is the founder of the secular Turkish state, an insult to him is considered an insult to Turkey's governing system in general and an act of state treason. A closer look at the internal division between secularists and people of faith demonstrates that by insulting Atatürk, one is thought to be insulting the Turkish interpretation of secularism.[27]

The recent Law No. 5728, dated February 2008, introduces a ninth category of crimes in addition to the ones provided in Article 8 of the Law on the Internet. Based on this recent amendment, access to content related to unauthorized online gambling and betting can be banned. These activities were initially prohibited under Law No. 7258 and sanctioned with a fine. Law No. 5728, however, penalizes such conduct as a crime when carried out online. As evident from these laws, activities in Turkey can be criminalized not only in the Criminal Code but in special laws enacted by the Parliament as well.

In addition to the Internet Law, Turkish courts base their access-blocking decisions on violations of other crimes and even some private law rules. Based on statistics from Turk Telecom,[28] banned sites based on norms other than the controversial Article 8 of Internet Law No. 5651 numbered 153 in 2005, 886 in 2006, and 549 in 2007. Turkish authors[29] referring to Turk Telecom's statistics state that access-blocking decisions rendered in violation of norms other than the ones enlisted under Article 8 have been based primarily on the following grounds:

- Downloading of MP3 and movies in violation of copyright laws
- Insults against state organs and private persons
- Crimes related to terrorism
- Violation of trademark regulations
- Unfair trade regulated under the Turkish Commercial Code
- Violation of Articles 24, 25, 26, and 28 of the Constitution (freedoms of religion, expression, thought, and freedom of press)

Under the Internet Law, ISPs become responsible for blocking access to illegal Web content even before the judge rules so. The Telecommunications Authority is tasked with identifying the actor responsible for the offensive content.

The recently created Information Denouncement Center accepts complaints submitted by e-mail or phone that report Web sites that allegedly carry content subsumed in any of the crimes typified in Article 8 of Law No. 5651. A complaint against online content may be submitted to a prosecuting attorney who then must lodge it with the court within 24 hours. In event of an emergency request, the prosecuting attorney may impose a ban on the Web site himself and submit it to a judge within 24 hours. The Internet Law provides for quick procedures and stipulates that once a judge decrees a blocking order, it should be delivered to the relevant ISP for implementation within another 24 hours. Sanctions envisioned for the ISPs or hosts who refuse to block access to offensive content include imprisoning owners or managers for six months to two years.

The law provides that the Telecommunication and Transmission Authority can impose bans on Internet sites without a prior judicial approval if

• the offending Web site hosts the previously mentioned crimes and is hosted outside Turkey, or
• a Web site contains sexual abuse of children or obscenity and its host resides in Turkey.

In this case, the prosecuting attorney may start a criminal action against those responsible for posting the offensive content once they are identified.

In addition to the preceding procedures, anyone may file a formal complaint against posted online content with the Communication Presidency, an entity established under the Internet Act. An individual claim may be sufficient to ban an entire site when the personal rights of the claimant have been violated. The individual can directly request that the content or hosting provider remove the offensive content.

Following the request, the content or hosting provider has to post a response to it within seven days on the Web site where the content is hosted. The provider should begin processing the request within two days. If prolonged, the request is considered rejected. The next recourse to the aggrieved party is to file a complaint with the local Criminal Peace Court within 15 days. The court will then make a decision within three days without a trial, and this decision can be appealed at a higher court. After the court decision, the content or hosting provider must remove or block the content and publish a reply to the claimant within two days. Noncompliance with the court decision is sanctioned with imprisonment. For example, a Google Groups ban was enforced following an individual claim against a blogger who posted a defamatory comment about the claimant on the server.[30]

The Turkish Internet Law provides the opportunity for Web site owners to exercise their right of reply against a content ban. However, this right is usually given after the site has been already blocked. There is no guaranteed right of reply to Web site owners whose content has been banned for a reason other than the ones listed in the Internet Law.

One of the main concerns with court decisions on Internet cases is the lack of proportionality. When the court considers certain content illegal, it orders a complete ban on the Web site hosting the content, instead of only blocking the particular material. Typically, the rulings of the Criminal Peace Court only cite the relevant legal provisions on which they are grounded and the final court order. This procedure does not provide the accused with the rationale behind the decisions, nor does it provide the right to defend against the charges. In addition, the time for submitting the appeal is very short, being only seven days.

Generally, court rulings in Turkey remain hidden from the public eye. The Turkish Attorneys Law does not provide guarantees for publicity of court decisions without regard to the particular type of dispute. Instead, this law restricts the right to make a copy of a court decision, which for privacy concerns remains available only to the party's attorney. Technically, the Attorneys Law allows all attorneys regardless of whether they are representing parties in a particular case to examine court decisions. However, reports from ONI field researchers indicate that attorneys who have made requests to review particular decisions issued in the application of the Internet Law have been denied access by court clerks, because of privacy concerns. This lack of access makes it difficult for Web site owners and their representatives to know how they can fully comply with the law.

Authorities often apply the Internet Law to ban access to online content, as the law provides quick enforcement mechanisms. Since the law does not provide the definitions of the criminalized activities, the court frequently refers to a number of other laws in its rulings, including the Penal Code and the Law on Crimes against Atatürk.

Article 301 was enacted into the Turkish penal code on June 1, 2005, as part of a package of penal-law reform enacted prior to Turkey's proposal for membership into the EU. Between 2005 and 2008, it was used to bring charges in more than 60 cases, many of which were high profile, such as that against internationally renowned novelist Orhan Pamuk.[31] From its inception, Article 301 received significant opposition. Following the 2007 murder of Turkish-Armenian journalist Hrant Dink,[32] such opposition increased significantly, resulting in former deputy prime minister and foreign minister Abdullah Gül declaring that the law was in need of revision.[33] On April 30, 2008, the law was only slightly modified to include lighter sentencing,[34] replacement of "Turkishness" with "Turkish nation" (even though public denigration of the Turks' culture and identity is a crime), and a requirement that the justice minister approve all cases in which Article 301 is to be used.[35] Article 301 has been widely applied by the Criminal Courts of Peace to regulate online activities.

Any proscribed content under Article 301 is immediately removed without first requesting the content provider to remove it. This was the case against YouTube in 2007 and 2008. The media-sharing site was blocked a number of times, primarily because of content that allegedly offended Kemal Atatürk or the so-called "Turkishness." YouTube made an express agreement to take down offensive videos if advised.[36] Despite this agreement, Turkish courts ordered Turkish Telecom to block access to the entire site rather than requesting YouTube to take action.

In addition to Article 301, two other articles broadly limit free speech in Turkey: Article 312 of the Penal Law imposes three-year prison sentences for incitement to commit an offense and incitement to religious or racial hatred,[37] and Article 81 of the Political Parties Law forbids political parties from using languages other than Turkish in written material or at public meetings. The latter affects Turkish Kurds in particular.[38]

Defamation

Defamation is sanctioned under the Turkish criminal law as well as under the civil law. The Penal Code considers defamation an offense against honor. Article 125, entitled "Defamation," contains the following provisions:

1. Any person who acts with the intention to harm the honor, reputation or dignity of another person through concrete performance or giving impression of intent, is sentenced to imprisonment from three months to two years or imposed punitive fine.
2. The offender is subject to above stipulated punishment in case of commission of offense in writing or by use of audio or visual means directed to the aggrieved party.
3. In case of commission of offense with defamatory intent:
a) Against a public officer,
b) Due to disclosure, change or attempt to spread religious, social, philosophical belief, opinion and convictions and to obey the orders and restriction of the one's religion,
c) By mentioning sacred values in view of the religion with which a person is connected, the minimum limit of punishment may not be less than one year.
4. The punishment is increased by one sixth in case of performance of defamation act openly; if the offense is committed through press and use of any one of publication organs, then the punishment is increased up to one third.

By providing that defamation can be committed by use of audio or other visual means, the second paragraph of Article 125 brings defamatory acts committed on the Internet within the ambit of criminal law, with the consequence that the persons who commit this offense may face imprisonment or fines.[39]

Numerous civil law defamation claims have been brought before courts in the recent years. The legal basis for civil law defamation claims in Turkish law is Article 41 and Article 49 of the Code of Obligations.

Article 41 contains the following stipulations:

A person who wrongfully harms another either intentionally, negligently or imprudently, is under an obligation to compensate the other party for this harm.

A person who knowingly harms another through an immoral act is also under an obligation to compensate the other party for this harm.

Article 49, entitled "Harm to Personal Interests," states the following:

A person whose personal rights have been unlawfully violated is entitled to bring a claim for monetary compensation for the nonpecuniary damages he has incurred.

The Turkish Code of Obligations provides for a civil law claim for defamation whereby the claimant can ask for monetary compensation instead of blocking access to content. However, most claimants prefer to turn to the Internet Law's protection when such is provided. One of the reasons for this preference is that the Turkish Code of Obligations bans excessive enrichment through compensation while the Internet Law provisions allow claimants to apply for a direct access ban.

Reports indicate that the Telecommunications Authority has announced plans to bring defamation carried out online and hacking under the scope of Article 8 of Law No. 5651, thereby providing people whose personal rights have been violated by online content with an alternative mechanism that would allow them to seek an access-banning remedy instead of monetary damages under the Law of Obligations or fines under criminal law.[40] As the procedure for obtaining a remedy under Internet Law is more expedient than in civil and criminal law cases, this amendment equips the aggrieved party with a much easier and quicker mechanism against online defamatory content.

Surveillance

The National Security Bill, or the "Draft Act on National Information Security Agency and Its Tasks," does not include a provision on the Internet. The bill envisages the establishment of a national information security agency as a public body. It requires the public bodies and agencies as well as private entities (companies, etc.) to provide "national information" necessary to ensure national information security to the security agency when requested to do so. "National information," however, is vaguely defined in the bill's present version. The bill, if enacted, may be used by the government to compel ISPs to supply the state with information on users' communications and activities at any time.

At present, the Telecommunications Authority Regulation of 2007 introduces state monitoring over access and hosting providers and their activities. Article 15-c of the regulation stipulates that access providers that cease their operations are obliged to submit all records of traffic logs pertaining to their last year of operation, as well as their user IDs, to the Telecommunications Authority.

ONI Testing Results

Turkey has one main commercial backbone connection, owned and controlled by Turk Telecom and the educational network, UlakNet. Most of the filtering of international traffic takes place on the Turk Telecom network, which links to other commercial ISPs within the country. Testing by the OpenNet Initiative shows that the academic network does not currently engage in filtering. UlakNet primarily provides Internet access to academic centers and some government institutions, including the military.

The ONI testing found a number of sites blocked on Turk Telecom in a variety of categories. Sites containing information on Turkish Kurds, including www.pajk-online.com, hpg-online.com, and the official Web site of the Kurdistan Workers' Party, or PKK were blocked. Interestingly, two sites belonging to well-known Muslim creationist Adnan Oktar (adnanoktar.wordpress.com and yahyaharun.com) were blocked, as was 19.org, the site of Oktar's rival Edip Yuksel. According to some reports, Oktar is responsible for the bans on Yuksel's sites and Wordpress, as well as the 2008 blocking of evolutionist Richard Dawkins' site in Turkey.[41] Other blocked sites included P2P sites such as the Pirate Bay (thepiratebay.org) and myp2p.eu. Gambling sites were also blocked.

Since the Internet Law came into effect, the number of blocked sites has drastically increased. The most high-profile filtering has been of the popular video-sharing site YouTube.com. YouTube access has been blocked a number of times in 2007 and 2008, in response to complaints about specific videos, most of which were considered to "insult Turkishness." Access has been restored following the takedown of each video. Wordpress and all blogs on the Wordpress domain, as well as popular blogging platform Blogspot, have been blocked and unblocked a number of times as well.

Conclusion

Turkey has implemented a series of reforms in its telecommunications and Internet sectors, showing its firm determination to stay on the membership path to the European Union. Nonetheless, further reforms are needed to terminate the de facto monopoly of the main telecoms and Internet service provider Turk Telecom. All Internet traffic passes through Turk Telecom's infrastructure, thereby allowing centralized control over online content and facilitating the implementation of shutdown decisions. Unless the government rethinks its current Internet policy and abandons blocking

Web sites as a method for combating illegal content, freedom of expression in Turkey will remain compromised.

Notes

1. The Constitution of the Republic of Turkey, Article 2.

2. International Telecommunication Union (ITU), "Internet Indicators: Subscribers, Users, and Broadband Subscribers," 2008, September 2008, http://www.itu.int/ITU-D/icteye/Reporting/ShowReportFrame.aspx?ReportName=/WTI/InformationTechnologyPublic&RP_intYear=2008&RP_intLanguageID=1.

3. Paul Budde Communication, Pty., Ltd., "Turkey," 2007.

4. Oger Telekomünikasyon A.Ş. (a Consortium led by Saudi Oger and Telecom Italia).

5. Some authors claim that the number of active ISPs is as high as 250. See Aytac Mestci, "Turkie Internet Raporu 2007" [Turkey Internet Report 2007], InternetPazarlama.net, http://ab.org.tr/ab08/bildiri/17.pdf; Turk Telecom reports that Internet operators are no more than 95. See Turk Telecom, "Yetkilendrime ve Hizmet Turlerine goie Isletmeci Sayilari" [Number of Operators According to Types of Authorization and Services], http://www.tk.gov.tr/doc/lisans/isletmeci_sayilari.htm.

6. Turkiye Telekomunikasyon Sektorundeki Gelismeler ve Egilimler, 2007 Yili Raporu, Telekomunikasyon Kurumu Sektorel Arastirma ve Stratejiler Dairesi Baskanligi, Subat 2008.

7. Turk Telecom announced that the number of ADSL subscribers reached 5 million by the end of 2007. Turk Telecom, http://www.turk.internet.com/haber/yazigoster.php3?yaziid=20773.

8. Cukorova Group holds investments in top-notch companies—currently 143—in various industries ranging from automotive, paper, chemicals, textiles, telecommunications, construction, banking, insurance, media, and services to maritime transportation and information technology services. Cukorva Group, http://www.cukurovaholding.com.tr/index2.htm.

9. In addition, however, Superonline has signed a "local loop unbundling" agreement with Turk Telecom to install its own equipment inside the Telecom switches and accessing the telephone lines of the end-user directly "last-mile," which would allow to service directly to consumer.

10. Paul Budde Communication, Pty., Ltd., "Turkey."

11. The TIX Web site (http://www.tix.net) is currently not active.

12. Packet Clearing House, "Internet Exchange Directory: Turkish Internet Exchange," http://www.pch.net/ixpdir/Detail.pl?exchange_point_id=247.

13. *Turk.Internet*, "LINX 10 Yasina Basti ... Ya Turkiye' de Neler Oldu" [LINX Turns Ten ... but What has Happened in Turkey?], http://turk.internet.com/haber/yazigoster.php3?yaziid=11420.

14. James B. Burnham, "Telecommunications Policy in Turkey: Dismantling Barriers to Growth, *Telecommunications Policy*, 31 (2007).

15. Turkcell, "Turkcell Iletisim Hizmetleri AS," http://www.turkcell.com.tr/en/AboutTurkcell/corporateInfo/companyHistory.

16. Anima Investment Network, "Country Perspectives—Turkey: Telecom & Internet," http://www.animaweb.org/en/pays_turquie_telecominternet_en.php.

17. For a list of VoIP providers in Turkey, see VoIP Providers List, "VoIP Providers Turkey," http://www.voipproviderslist.com/country/voip-turkey/voip-providers-turkey.

18. Law No: 4502 of January 29, 2000, http://www.oib.gov.tr/telekom/telekom_law_4502.htm.

19. Some other examples of independent regulatory authorities in Turkey are the Competition Authority, Energy Market Regulatory Authority, and Capital Markets Board.

20. James B. Burnham, "Telecommunications Policy in Turkey: Dismantling Barriers to Growth, *Telecommunications Policy*, 31 (2007).

21. Presidency conclusions, Lisbon European Council, March 23 and 24, 2000.

22. Commission of the European Communities, "Turkey 2007 Progress Report," ec.europa.eu/enlargement/pdf/key_documents/2007/nov/turkey_progress_reports_en.pdf.

23. Law No: 5187 of June 26, 2004, http://www.tbmm.gov.tr/kanunlar/k5187.html.

24. Law No. 3984 of April 20, 1994, http://www.rtuk.org.tr/sayfalar/IcerikGoster.aspx?icerik_id=b41eac9a-bc39-4213-91f3-0d39931c1f1d.

25. Asli Tunc, "Creating an Internet Culture in Turkey: Historical and Contemporary Problem Analyses," in *New Media in Southeast Europe*, ed. Orlin Spassov and Christo Todorov (Sofia: SOEMZ, 2003), http://soemz.euv-frankfurt-o.de/media-see/newmedia/main/articles/a_tunc.htm.

26. *Turk.Internet*, "TİB : Katalog Suçlar Sanal Kumar ve Bahis Konularının Eklenmesiyle 9'a Çıktı 5" [Telecommunications Directorate: The Number of "Checklist" Crimes Increases to 9 with the Addition of Online Gambling and Bribery], April 25, 2008, http://turk.internet.com/haber/yazigoster.php3?yaziid=20755.

27. Sarah Rainsford, "Turkey Awaits AKP's Next Step," *BBC News*, July 23, 2007, http://news.bbc.co.uk/1/hi/world/europe/6912052.stm; Stephanie Irvine, "Defending the Secular Faith," *BBC News*, April 28, 2007, http://news.bbc.co.uk/1/hi/world/europe/6603141.stm.

28. *Turk.Internet*, "5651 Disi Site Erisim Kapatmalarinda Sorun Var" [Problems in Blocking Access to Websites not Covered Under Law #5651], May 1, 2008, http://turk.internet.com/haber/yazigoster.php3?yaziid=20850.

29. Ibid.

30. *Monsters and Critics*, "Turkey Bans Biologist Richard Dawkins' Website," September 16, 2008, http://www.monstersandcritics.com/science/news/article_1431422.php/Turkey_bans_biologist_Richard_Dawkins_website.

31. English PEN, "The Case of Orhan Pamuk," *New York Review of Books*, December 15, 2008, http://www.nybooks.com/articles/18574.

32. Human Rights Watch, "Turkey: Outspoken Turkish-Armenian Journalist Murdered," January 19, 2007, http://www.hrw.org/en/news/2007/01/19/turkey-outspoken-turkish-armenian-journalist-murdered.

33. *BBC News*, "Turkey Reforms Controversial Law," April 30, 2008, http://news.bbc.co.uk/1/hi/world/europe/7374665.stm.

34. Ibid.

35. *Today's Zaman*, "EU Welcomes 301 Amendment but Calls for More," May 1, 2008, http://www.todayszaman.com/tz-web/detaylar.do?load=detay&link=140606.

36. Nico Hines, "YouTube Banned in Turkey after Video Insults," *Times Online*, March 7, 2007, http://www.timesonline.co.uk/tol/news/world/europe/article1483840.ece.

37. Yonah Alexander, Edgar H. Brenner, and Serhat Tutuncuoglu Krause, *Turkey: Terrorism, Civil Rights and the European Union* (New York: Routledge, 2008), 275.

38. Christopher Panico, *Turkey: Violations of Free Expression in Turkey* (New York: Human Rights Watch, 1999), 102.

39. English text is available at http://www.legislationline.org/legislation.php?tid=1&lid=7480.

40. *Zaman.com*, "Internette Hakaret Artik Siteyi Kapatma Sebei" [From Now on, Defamation Is Grounds for Website Shutdown], July 9, 2008, http://www.zaman.com.tr/haber.do?haberno=711846.

41. Andrew Higgins, "An Islamic Creationist Stirs a New Kind of Darwinian Struggle," *Wall Street Journal*, March 17, 2009, http://online.wsj.com/article/SB123724852205449221.html.

United Kingdom

The United Kingdom (U.K.) has a notable libertarian tradition, manifested by, among other things, solid guarantees of freedom of expression, freedom of information, and protection of privacy. Nonetheless, over the last few years the country has witnessed a quick shift toward increased surveillance and police measures in both online and physical space. Combating terrorism and preventing child abuse have been widely used by state agencies and private commercial actors (e.g., Internet service providers) to justify the implementation of interception of communications and direct filtering measures in the country, which have drawn growing criticism.

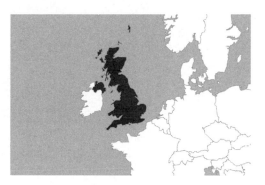

Background

The U.K., consisting of England, Wales, Scotland, and Northern Ireland, is a constitutional monarchy currently headed by Queen Elizabeth II.[1] Previously a colonial power, the U.K. emerged from the World Wars as a leading global financial center and Western democracy.[2] As the country is a member of the European Union (EU), the bloc's law takes precedence over national law, with U.K. courts required to recognize the jurisdiction of the European Court of Justice (ECJ) in matters of EU law.

RESULTS AT A GLANCE					
Filtering	No Evidence of Filtering	Suspected Filtering	Selective Filtering	Substantial Filtering	Pervasive Filtering
Political	•				
Social	•				
Conflict and security	•				
Internet tools	•				

Other Factors	Low	Medium	High	Not Applicable
Transparency				•
Consistency				•

KEY INDICATORS	
GDP per capita, PPP (constant 2005 international dollars)	33,717
Life expectancy at birth (years)	79
Literacy rate (percent of people age 15+)	99
Human development index (out of 179)	21
Rule of law (out of 211)	15
Voice and accountability (out of 209)	13
Democracy index (out of 167)	21 (Full democracy)
Digital opportunity index (out of 181)	10
Internet users (percent of population)	79.6

Source by indicator: World Bank 2009a, World Bank 2009a, World Bank 2009a, UNDP 2008, World Bank 2009b, World Bank 2009b, Economist Intelligence Unit 2008, ITU 2007, ITU 2008.

The U.K. has a vast media network, led by the British Broadcasting Corporation (BBC), a publicly funded institution,[3] with a mandate to remain independent.[4] Other media institutions in the U.K. also enjoy journalistic freedom and represent a broad spectrum of political ideas.[5] Despite the officially recognized journalistic freedom, there have been reports of journalists being jailed or detained for divulging state secrets.[6] The U.K. is a strong supporter of fundamental human rights and freedoms, including freedom of expression.[7] However, recent developments in U.K. antiterrorism laws, in particular the Terrorism Act (2000) and subsequent legislation in 2005 and 2006, have drawn harsh criticism. Advocacy groups claim that new provisions focused on expanding police powers and allowing communication providers to retain personal data for the purpose of "protecting national security or preventing or detecting crime that relates to national security"[8] are contrary to basic human rights principles.[9]

Internet in the United Kingdom

Residents of the U.K. currently form the fifth-largest broadband subscriber population in the world.[10] In the U.K., 61 percent of households had Internet access in 2007, with 84 percent of those having a broadband connection.[11] The sector regulator reports that broadband technology is available for practically every U.K. citizen to connect to the Internet.[12] In 2006, 63 percent of adults in the U.K. were estimated to have accessed the Internet within a three-month period.[13] Internet usage is more widespread among the younger generations, with over 90 percent of people aged 16 to 24 accessing the Internet in a three-month period, and only 24 percent of those aged over 65 accessing it during the same period.[14] Most of the users access the Internet from their home location (87 percent).[15] As a result of affordability and enhanced market competition, mobile penetration is very high.[16] However, the percentage of people accessing the Internet with their handsets is surprisingly small (only 3 percent in 2007).[17]

In 2007, there were around 700 Internet service providers (ISPs) in the U.K.[18] Of the broadband providers, however, Virgin Media and BT (formerly British Telecom) provided services for half of the market;[19] along with the three next largest providers, they comprise 84 percent of the market.[20] Broadband service has expanded so significantly in the last four years that it is now more affordable than dial-up service.[21] Currently, no restrictions exist on the amount of information a user can send and receive when subscribing to broadband service, but it is recognized that network management might be required in the future.[22]

In December 2008, the majority of ISPs in the U.K. agreed to better inform their customers about Internet connection speeds. This scheme, which would benefit approximately 95 percent of the U.K.'s Internet users, was adopted in response to consumer confusion about advertisements that promised broadband speeds that were largely unattainable.[23]

Legal and Regulatory Frameworks

The telecommunications industries are regulated by the Office of Communications (Ofcom).[24] Ofcom's mandate includes, among other duties, the protection of audiences against harmful material, unfairness, and infringements of privacy.[25] Broadcasting in the U.K. is regulated by the Department for Culture, Media, and Sport (DCMS).[26]

As a member state of the European Union, the U.K. has integrated the bloc's communication directives into its national law. The European Parliament has recently voted on the new proposals by the European Commission (EC) to reform the telecommunications regulations with the idea of promoting competition on a pan-European level and taking further steps to preserve information security, including controlling spam, spyware, and other malicious software.[27] Updated regulations are expected to be integrated into national legislation starting in 2010.

In 2000, the EU adopted a proposal concerning, inter alia, the dissemination of child pornography on the Internet.[28] The notes to the proposal explicitly state that service providers normally will not be held liable for any dissemination, caching, or hosting of child pornography, though they are held liable if they commit illegal acts that benefit the service provider.[29] This is consistent with broader EU law which states that ISPs acting as "mere conduits" of information are not liable for any illegal information transmitted.[30] European Union law specifically provides that ISPs are under no obligation to monitor the information they transmit, but they must be able to provide information on its transmission given an appropriate request from the government.[31]

Though U.K. authorities do not oblige ISPs to monitor the information being transmitted, at least one major ISP, BT, filters child pornography materials.[32] However, BT stresses that they do not affirmatively search for sites to block, but rather act only upon reports by users and information provided by the Internet Watch Foundation

(IWF).[33] The implementation of this filtering practice is known as "CleanFeed."[34] The IWF, a nonprofit organization based in the U.K. that works with the U.K. government, compiles a list of Web sites it deems illegal and transmits this information to BT and other ISPs.[35] The list compiled by the IWF usually contains 800–1,200 unique and live URLs.[36] In addition to filtering content for child sexual abuse, the IWF also detects and attempts to take down Web sites hosted in the U.K. that promote racial hatred,[37] which are illegal under the Public Order Act 1986.[38]

In 2006, Home Office Minister Vernon Croaker announced that from 2008 onward he expected that all ISPs would block access to child pornography using a "CleanFeed" style system.[39] The announcement also suggested that if the filtering was not done by ISPs on a voluntary basis, Parliament would consider legislative enforcement.[40] At that time, the largest ISPs in Britain, which together provided over 90 percent of all broadband access, all used some sort of filtering system.[41]

The U.K. commissioned a report on child safety on the Internet that was released in March 2008 (the Byron Report).[42] This report recognized that it would not be possible to remove fully all obscene material from the Internet and that any effective control would have to be adopted voluntarily by ISPs.[43] It stated that there was a strong case to block illegal material such as child pornography, though it also recommended that no attempts be made to filter illegal material at the network level.[44] The U.K. government has agreed to implement all the recommendations contained in the Byron Report.[45]

In December 2008, a number of British ISPs blocked a Wikipedia page displaying an image of an album cover from 1976 that portrayed a naked teenage girl. The ISPs made the decision after receiving a warning from the IWF claiming the image may be illegal. Wikipedia users complained that the ISPs blocked not only the image but the entire article; they also noted that the ISPs did not apply the block systematically, as access to commercial sites, such as Amazon.com, that sold the album and displayed its cover image, was still available.[46] Furthermore, the block temporarily prevented users on the affected ISPs from editing Wikipedia.[47] Several days after the block was imposed, the IWF reviewed the case and decided to remove the article from their list of offensive sites, citing the negative effects of the block and the wide availability of the image on other sites.[48]

United Kingdom law requires that information that glorifies or incites terrorism be censored.[49] According to section 3 of the Terrorism Act (2006), once provided with a notice that a Web site may contain terrorism-related content, an ISP may be liable for the content if it does not take every reasonably expected step to block access to the content.[50]

Filtering technologies such as the "CleanFeed" system are criticized for not publicizing the list of filtered Web sites, which could lead to abuses.[51] In addition, because

ISPs and the IWF are not public institutions, they are not subject to judicial review.[52] Instead, the IWF offers an internal appeal procedure.[53]

Internet Surveillance

The U.K., together with the United States, was ranked as one of the worst offenders against individual privacy rights in the democratic world by Privacy International for 2007.[54]

Among areas of great concern are the estimated 4 million CCTV cameras installed in practically every corner of Britons' social life.[55] Based on the EU Data Retention Directive but at times exceeding its scope, the data retention scheme in the U.K. took a significant step forward. There are "hundreds of thousands" of requests from state agencies to communications providers for traffic data.[56]

In the U.K., the Information Commissioner's Office (ICO) is an independent authority with the goal of promoting access to official information and protecting personal information. It is also responsible for enforcing the Data Protection Act 1998 (DPA).[57] The commissioner has a broad mandate but only minimal enforcement powers.[58] A new act has been proposed to amend the DPA and give the ICO the authority to impose fines for deliberate data protection breaches.[59] The ICO reports to Parliament and is sponsored by the Ministry of Justice.[60] Recently, concerns have arisen over ISPs tracking user activity to customize viewed ads.[61] The commissioner himself warned in 2004 that the U.K. was in danger of becoming a "surveillance society." This concern was reiterated in the House of Lords' February 2009 report entitled "Surveillance: Citizens and the State."[62] However, after a review of the situation the ICO noted that as long as users are "informed when a cookie is placed on their computer, given clear and comprehensive information about the purpose of the storage and given the ability to refuse it being placed on the system ... there does not appear to be any detriment to users," and that the developing companies are not in violation of the Data Protection Act 1998.[63]

The U.K. government's power to collect communications data is primarily addressed in the Regulation of Investigatory Powers Act 2000 (RIPA).[64] Warrants to approve the collection of communication content are issued by the Secretary of State upon proof that the intrusion is necessary and proportionate when balanced with individuals' privacy interests.[65] The Secretary of State has broad powers that are loosely regulated.[66] The collection of noncontent data, including subscriber information, traffic, and location data, can be authorized without a warrant by various public officials.[67]

As for other electronic surveillance, the Foundation for Information Policy Research notes that even before the events of September 11, 2001, the U.K. was utilizing sophisticated systems for electronic surveillance against crime. The foundation warns that further "safeguards and democratic oversight" are needed.[68] On May 21, 2008, *The Guardian* warned of the possibility of a database that records every telephone call, e-mail, and Web site visit made in Britain.[69] On June 9, 2008, the ICO released a statement recognizing the necessity to consider the impact of the development of such tools on individuals' privacy and the need to minimize unnecessary intrusion. It further recommends that "every possible step ... be taken to ensure public trust in the way that personal information is collected and stored."[70] Although plans for the database to collect all user information were canceled, the Home Secretary has requested that communications firms record contact between customers, including e-mails, phone calls, and Internet use, as well as visits to social networking sites.[71]

In a different area, expectations of commercial gain due to online advertising have led some of the most important operators in the country (BT, Talk Talk, and Virgin) to use different applications to track the browsing history of their customers. In April 2009, the EU expressed its intent to commence legal actions against the U.K. for allowing this Web-tracking practice, which, according to the EU, would violate privacy laws.

ONI Testing Results

The OpenNet Initiative comprehensively tested three ISPs in the United Kingdom: Easynet,[72] Be,[73] and BT,[74] and did not find any evidence of filtering; however, the U.K. openly blocks child pornography Web sites (which ONI does not test) and has allegedly blocked other sites containing "illegal material."[75]

Conclusion

Protecting freedom of expression and encouraging tolerance to diverse viewpoints, the U.K. is one of the pioneers in nurturing politically sensitive debates and promoting the use of new technology. Freedom of expression and protection of privacy over the Internet is guaranteed in the law. Nevertheless, motivated by national security concerns, the state has provided for vast surveillance measures over online communications. Moreover, certain filtering and tracking practices do take place. Such practices are sometimes encouraged by the state but most often voluntarily implemented by private operators. The U.K. government, however, has to ensure that blocking practices do not lead to abuse in the absence of external and independent control.

Notes

1. *BBC News*, "Country Profile: United Kingdom," http://news.bbc.co.uk/2/hi/europe/country _profiles/1038758.stm.

2. Central Intelligence Agency, "The World Factbook: United Kingdom," https://www.cia.gov/library/publications/the-world-factbook/geos/uk.html.

3. BBC, "About the BBC: How the BBC Is Run," http://www.bbc.co.uk/info/running/.

4. BBC Trust, "About the Trust," http://www.bbc.co.uk/bbctrust/about/index.html.

5. *BBC News*, "Country Profile: United Kingdom," http://news.bbc.co.uk/2/hi/europe/country_profiles/1038758.stm.

6. Reporters Without Borders, "United Kingdom," http://www.rsf.org/article.php3?id_article=25478&Valider=OK.

7. Amnesty International, "UK—Amnesty International Report 2008," http://www.amnesty.org/en/region/uk/report-2008.

8. Privacy International, "United Kingdom of Great Britain and Northern Ireland," 2007, http://www.privacyinternational.org/article.shtml?cmd[347]=x-347-559479.

9. Ibid.

10. Om Malik, "Broadband Subscribers, 300 Million Strong," *GigaOm*, June 22, 2007, http://gigaom.com/2007/06/22/broadband-subscribers-300-million-strong/.

11. National Statistics Online, "Internet Access: 65% of Households Had Access in 2008," August 26, 2008, http://www.statistics.gov.uk/cci/nugget.asp?id=8.

12. Ofcom, "The Consumer Experience—Research Report 07," http://www.ofcom.org.uk/research/tce/ce07/.

13. National Statistics, "Internet Access 2007: Households and Individuals," http://www.statistics.gov.uk/pdfdir/inta0807.pdf.

14. Ibid.

15. Ibid.

16. Central Intelligence Agency, "The World Factbook: United Kingdom," https://www.cia.gov/library/publications/the-world-factbook/geos/uk.html.

17. National Statistics, "Internet Access 2007: Households and Individuals," http://www.statistics.gov.uk/pdfdir/inta0807.pdf.

18. Ofcom, "The Consumer Experience—Research Report 07," http://www.ofcom.org.uk/research/tce/ce07/.

19. Ibid.

20. Ibid.

21. Ibid.

22. Ibid.

23. *BBC News*, "Net Speed Rules Come into Force," December 4, 2008, http://news.bbc.co.uk/2/hi/technology/7764489.stm.

24. Ofcom, "Statutory Duties and Regulatory Principles," http://www.ofcom.org.uk/about/sdrp/.

25. Ibid.

26. BBC, "About the BBC: How the BBC Is Run," http://www.bbc.co.uk/info/running/.

27. European Commission, "eCommunications: Reforming the Current Telecom Rules," http://ec.europa.eu/information_society/policy/ecomm/tomorrow/index_en.htm.

28. Activities of the European Union, Summaries of Legislation, "Combating Trafficking in Human Beings, the Sexual Exploitation of Children and Child Pornography," December 20, 2006, http://europa.eu/legislation_summaries/employment_and_social_policy/equality_between_men_and_women/l33089b_en.htm.

29. Ibid.

30. Council Directive 2000/31, art. 12, 2000 O.J. (L 178) 1 (EC).

31. Ibid. at art. 15.

32. *Fronterra*, "Facing Up to ... Extreme Abuse of the Internet," May 2004, http://www.btplc.com/Societyandenvironment/Ourapproach/CSRresources/Hottopics/Abuseoftheinternet/Abuseoftheinternet.pdf; BT, "The Historical Development of BT," http://www.btplc.com/Thegroup/BTsHistory/History.htm.

33. *Fronterra*, "Facing Up to ... Extreme Abuse of the Internet," May 2004, http://www.btplc.com/Societyandenvironment/Ourapproach/CSRresources/Hottopics/Abuseoftheinternet/Abuseoftheinternet.pdf.

34. IWF/BT Project CleanFeed, "Extreme Pornography Websites," http://www.iwf.org.uk/government/page.101.220.htm.

35. Internet Watch Foundation (IWF), http://www.iwf.org.uk/.

36. Internet Watch Foundation, "IWF URL list," http://www.iwf.org.uk/public/page.148.htm.

37. Internet Watch Foundation, "Role and Remit," http://www.iwf.org.uk/public/page.35.htm.

38. Public Order Act, chapter 64, section 4, Fear or Provocation of Violence.

39. 446 Parl. Deb., H.C. (6th ser.) (2006) 709W.

40. Ibid.

41. Ibid.

42. Tanya Byron, "Safer Children in a Digital World: The Report of the Byron Review," March 2008, http://www.dcsf.gov.uk/byronreview/pdfs/Final%20Report%20Bookmarked.pdf.

43. Ibid.

44. Ibid.

45. Press Release, Department for Culture, Media, and Sport and Department for Children, Schools, and Families [U.K.], "Government Commits to Delivering Byron Recommendations," March 27, 2008, http://www.culture.gov.uk/reference_library/media_releases/5061.aspx/.

46. *BBC News*, "Wikipedia Child Image Censored," December 8, 2008, http://news.bbc.co.uk/2/hi/uk_news/7770456.stm.

47. Barry Collins, "Brits Blocked from Wikipedia over Child Porn Photo," *PC Pro*, December 8, 2008, http://www.pcpro.co.uk/news/241440/brits-blocked-from-wikipedia-over-child-porn-photo.html.

48. ISPreview, "Internet Watch Foundation U-Turns on Wikipedia Block," December 10, 2008, http://www.ispreview.co.uk/news/EkkllAlVuVbKzPsVgN.html.

49. Terrorism Act, 2006, c. 11 (U.K.).

50. Ibid. at sec. 3.

51. Lillian Edwards, "From Child Porn to China, in One Cleanfeed," *SCRIPT-ed*, vol. 3, no. 3, 174 (2006), http://www.law.ed.ac.uk/ahrc/script-ed/vol3-3/editorial.pdf.

52. Ibid.

53. Internet Watch Foundation, "Complaints, Appeals and Correction Procedures," http://www.iwf.org.uk/public/page.148.341.htm.

54. Privacy International, "The 2007 International Privacy Ranking," http://www.privacyinternational.org/article.shtml?cmd[347]=x-347-559597.

55. *BBC News*, "Warning over 'Surveillance State,'" February 6, 2009, http://news.bbc.co.uk/1/hi/uk_politics/7872425.stm.

56. Privacy International, "The 2007 International Privacy Ranking."

57. Data Protection Act 1998, http://www.opsi.gov.uk/Acts/Acts1998/ukpga_19980029_en_1.

58. The Information Commissioner is appointed by Her Majesty by Letters Patent; House of Lords report, "Surveillance: Citizens and the State," February 6, 2009, http://www.publications.parliament.uk/pa/ld200809/ldselect/ldconst/18/18.pdf.

59. Section 55A was inserted into the DPA by Section 144 of the Criminal Justice and Immigration Act (CJIA) 2008, not yet in force. As reported in "Response to the Data Sharing Review Report," http://www.justice.gov.uk/docs/response-data-sharing-review.pdf.

60. Information Commissioner's Office, "About the ICO," http://www.ico.gov.uk/about_us.aspx.

61. Cahal Milmo, "Internet's Founder Attacks Scheme to Monitor Web Usage," *The Independent*, March 18, 2008, http://www.independent.co.uk/life-style/gadgets-and-tech/news/internets-founder-attacks-scheme-to-monitor-web-usage-797133.html.

62. House of Lords report, "Surveillance: Citizens and the State," February 6, 2009, http://www
.publications.parliament.uk/pa/ld200809/ldselect/ldconst/18/18.pdf.

63. Information Commissioner's Office, "Phorm—Website and Open Internet Exchange,"
April 18, 2008, http://www.whatdotheyknow.com/request/10456/response/30346/attach/2/Phorm
%20the%20ICO%20view%2018%20April%2008%20v1.3.doc.doc.

64. Regulation of Investigatory Powers Act 2000, Chapter 23, http://www.opsi.gov.uk/acts/
acts2000/ukpga_20000023_en_1; for ECHR compliance, see "Editorial," Crim. L.R. 2000, Nov,
877–878, http://www.homeoffice.gov.uk/documents/cons-2003-access-comms-data. Part II covers
surveillance, differentiating "directive" from "intrusive" surveillance.

65. Regulation of Investigatory Powers Act 2000, Chapter 23.

66. Ibid.

67. Various offices, ranks, or positions within the public authorities are "persons designated" by
the Secretary of State in Part I Chapter II of RIPA.

68. Foundation for Information Policy Research, http://www.fipr.org.

69. Bobbie Johnson, "Plan to Record All Calls and Emails Alarms Watchdogs," *The Guardian*,
May   21,   2008,   http://www.guardian.co.uk/technology/2008/may/21/freedomofinformation
.civilliberties.

70. ICO, "Statement on Home Affairs Committee," June 9, 2008, http://www.ico.gov.uk/upload/
documents/pressreleases/2008/statement_home_affairs_committee.pdf.

71. Dominic Casciani, "Plan to Monitor All Internet Use," *BBC News*, April 27, 2009, http://news
.bbc.co.uk/2/hi/uk_news/politics/8020039.stm.

72. Easynet, http://www.easynet.com/gb/en/.

73. Be, https://www.bethere.co.uk/.

74. BT UK, http://www.bt.com/.

75. Internet Watch Foundation, "IWF Facilitation of the Blocking Initiative," http://www.iwf.org
.uk/public/page.148.htm.

North America

United States and Canada Overview

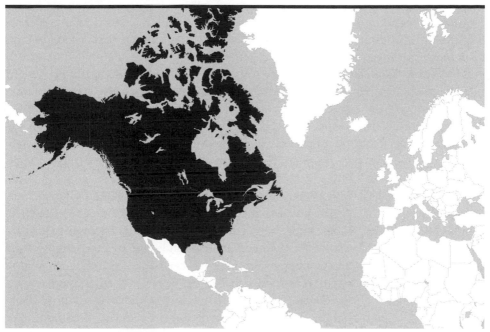

The Internet in the United States and Canada is highly regulated, supported by a complex set of legally binding and privately mediated mechanisms. Technical filtering plays a minor role in this regulation. The first wave of regulatory actions in the 1990s in the United States came about in response to the profusion of sexually explicit material on the Internet within easy reach of minors. Since that time, several legislative attempts at creating a mandatory system of content controls in the United States have failed to produce a comprehensive solution for those pushing for tighter controls. At the same time, the legislative attempts to control the distribution of socially objectionable material on the Internet in the United States have given rise to a robust system that limits liability over content for Internet intermediaries such as Internet service providers (ISPs) and content hosting companies. Proponents of protecting intellectual property online in the United States have been much more successful, producing a system to remove infringing materials that many feel errs on the side of inhibiting legally protected speech. National security concerns have spurred on efforts to expand surveillance of digital communications and fueled proposals for making Internet communication more traceable.

After a decade and half of ongoing contentious debate over content regulation in the United States, the country is still very far from reaching political consensus on the acceptable limits of free speech and the best means of protecting minors and policing illegal activity on the Internet. Gambling, cyber security, and dangers to children who frequent social networking sites—real and perceived—are important ongoing debates.

Canadian legislators have been less aggressive than their U.S. counterparts in proposing specific legislative remedies for problems arising from Internet use. Canadians have been more inclined to employ existing regimes developed for regulating offline speech and less apt to propose broad solutions. Canadians do not currently pursue copyright infringement online with the same zeal as their U.S. counterparts. Neither does Canadian law provide the same formal protection for intermediaries. Unlike the United States, publishing of hate speech is restricted in Canada. Under section 320.1 of the Canadian Criminal Code, a judge can issue a warrant authorizing the deletion of (publicly available) online hate propaganda from computer systems located within the jurisdiction of the court.

Public dialogue, legislative debate, and judicial review have produced filtering strategies in the United States and Canada that are different from those described elsewhere in this volume. In the United States, many government-mandated attempts to regulate content have been barred on First Amendment grounds, often after lengthy legal battles.[1] However, the United States government has been able to exert pressure indirectly where it cannot directly censor. In Canada, the focus has been on government-facilitated industry self-regulation. With the exception of child pornography, Canadian and U.S. content restrictions tend to rely more on the removal of content than blocking; most often these controls rely upon the involvement of private parties, backed by state encouragement or the threat of legal action.[2] In contrast to much of the world, where ISPs are subject to state mandates, most content regulation in the United States and Canada occurs at the private level.

The United States and Canada both have relatively high Internet penetration rates. In each country, nearly three-quarters of the population has access to the Internet.[3] Despite such high Internet penetration rates, the two countries have relatively low broadband subscription rates, with the United States at 23 percent and Canada at 28 percent. Internet subscription rates on the whole are only slightly higher: the United States has a 24 percent subscription rate, while Canada's rests at 31 percent.[4] The broadband stimulus push of President Barack Obama's administration in early 2009 may improve these rates in the United States.

These high rates of Internet usage increase the ability of citizens to publish and widely distribute dissenting points of view. At the same time, Internet users engage in a large number of other online activities, such as accessing pornography, that test a society's dedication to free expression and privacy.

Regulating Obscene and Explicit Content

The United States Congress passed the Communications Decency Act (CDA) as part of the Telecommunications Act of 1996. Signed into law by President Bill Clinton in

February 1996, the CDA was designed to criminalize the transmission of "indecent" material to persons under 18 and the display to minors of "patently offensive" content and communications.[5] The CDA took aim not only at the authors of "indecent" material but also at their Internet service providers, although it offered them each safe harbor if they imposed technical barriers to minors' access.[6]

Prior to taking effect, the CDA was challenged in federal court by a group of civil liberties and public interest organizations and publishers who argued their speech would be chilled by fear of the CDA's enforcement. The three-judge district court panel concluded that the terms "indecent" and "patently offensive" were sufficiently vague such that enforcement of either prohibition would violate the First Amendment.[7] "As the most participatory form of mass speech yet developed," Judge Stewart Dalzell wrote in a concurring opinion, "the Internet deserves the highest protection from governmental intrusion."[8] The U.S. Supreme Court affirmed this holding in 1997, invalidating the CDA's "indecency" and "patently offensive" content prohibitions.[9] In the landmark case *Reno v. ACLU*, the Court held that CDA was not the "least restrictive alternative" by which to protect children from harm. Rather, parent-imposed filtering could effectively block children's access to indecent material without preventing adults from speaking and receiving this lawful speech.[10] Other sections of the CDA continue to remain in force, including Section 230, which provides immunity to ISPs for content that third-party users place online.[11] Section 230 has had an undeniably powerful impact in promoting free speech in the United States. A growing body of case law suggests that it is being used by ISPs to settle or quickly dismiss claims that are brought against them.[12] Many question whether the sweeping protections offered by Section 230 offer in fact too much protection for online speech and excessively limit the ability of victims and the state to suppress harmful speech.[13]

Lawmakers responded to the Supreme Court's decision in *Reno v. ACLU* by enacting the Child Online Protection Act (COPA)—a second attempt at speaker-based content regulation. In COPA, the U.S. Congress directed its regulation at commercial distributors of materials "harmful to minors."[14] The slightly narrower focus of COPA did not solve the constitutional problems that doomed the CDA. The district court enjoined COPA on First Amendment grounds.[15] After a few trips to the Supreme Court and back for fact-finding, the district court issued its ruling in March 2007, finding COPA void for vagueness and not narrowly tailored to the government's interest in protecting minors. Once again, the court held that criminal liability for speakers and service providers was not the "least restrictive means" to accomplish the government's purpose because the private use of filtering technologies could more effectively keep harmful materials from children. The Third U.S. Circuit Court of Appeals later affirmed this decision, and, in January 2009, the Supreme Court put the legislation to rest—at least for now—by refusing to hear the case.

Plaintiffs successfully argued that CDA and COPA would chill the provision and transmission of lawful Internet content in the United States. Faced with the impossible task of accurately identifying "indecent" material and preemptively blocking its diffusion, ISPs would have been prompted to filter arbitrarily and extensively in order to avoid the threat of criminal liability, while writers and publishers would feel compelled to self-censor.

Stymied at restricting the publication of explicit material, congressional leaders changed their focus to regulating what someone might hear, rather than what they say. The Children's Internet Protection Act (CIPA) of 2000 forced public schools and libraries to use Internet filtering technology as a condition of receiving federal E-Rate funding. A school or library seeking to receive or retain federal funds for Internet access must certify to the FCC that it has installed or will install technology that filters or blocks material deemed to be obscene, child pornography, or material "harmful to minors."[16] The Supreme Court rejected First Amendment challenges to CIPA, holding that speakers had no right of access to libraries and that patrons could request unblocking.[17] In response, some libraries and schools have rejected E-Rate funding,[18] but most have felt financially compelled to install the filters.

In the aftermath of CDA, COPA, and CIPA, Internet filtering in the United States is carried out largely by private manufacturers. These companies compete for market share in a lucrative business area. Schools, businesses, parents, and other parties wishing to block access to certain content have a broad range of software packages available to them.[19] While some programs filter heavily, permitting access only to a "white list" of preapproved sites (for example, those appropriate for young children), others generate blacklists of blocked sites through a combination of automated screenings of the Web, staff members who "rate" sites on appropriateness, and user complaints.

Although CIPA mandates the presence of filtering technology in schools and libraries receiving subsidized Internet access, it effectively delegates blocking discretion to the developers and operators of that technology. The criteria "obscene," "child pornography," and "harmful to minors" are defined by CIPA and other existing legislation, but strict adherence to these rather vague legal definitions is beyond the capacity of filters and inherently subject to the normative and technological choices made during the software design process. Moreover, while CIPA permits the disabling of filters for adults and, in some instances, minors "for bona fide research or other lawful purposes,"[20] it entrusts school and library administrators with deactivating the filters, giving them considerable power over access to online content. Once FCC certification requirements have been met, it is these individuals who shoulder the burden of ensuring access to constitutionally protected material.[21]

Attempts to filter Internet content in the United States have also reached the state level. In 2004, Pennsylvania authorized the state attorney general's office to force ISPs to block Pennsylvania residents' access to sites that the attorney general's office identified as child pornography.[22] A district court struck down this regulation as unconstitutional where this state law in effect was regulating activity occurring wholly outside the state's borders, but did not strike down the act due to over-breadth.[23] The court noted that "there is an abundance of evidence that implementation of the Act has resulted in massive suppression of speech protected by the First Amendment."[24]

The complexities of government-led efforts to restrict online speech have given rise to quasi-voluntary initiatives supported by the force of law. Since possession and distribution of child pornography are criminal acts in the United States, service providers respond to removal requests and report any requests to the National Center for Missing and Exploited Children. In June 2008, the New York state attorney general signed an agreement with Comcast, AT&T, Inc., AOL, Verizon Communications, Inc., Time Warner Cable, and Sprint to purge their servers of child pornography identified by the National Center for Missing and Exploited Children.[25] The agreement attempts to curtail access to child pornography by implementing a new system to rapidly identify child pornography images as well as responding to user complaints about child pornography. In addition, several ISPs agreed to stop supporting access to Usenet newsgroups, identified by the attorney general's office as a source of child pornography.

The desire to protect children from harm online continues to drive efforts at content-based restrictions on the Internet. Law enforcement agencies use pressure to convince private companies to take on voluntary Internet regulatory initiatives. Concerns over child safety online have focused attention on the potential risks associated with time spent on social network sites such as Facebook and MySpace, where children may come into contact with sexual predators and be subject to cyberbullying by their peers. Law enforcement officials in the United States have been vocal in promoting age and identity verification systems in order to better police online sites frequented by minors.[26] The Internet Safety Technical Task Force, a group of technology companies, Internet businesses, nongovernmental organizations, and academics, was brought together by agreement with 49 U.S. state attorneys general to study the use of technologies by industry and end users to promote Internet safety for minors. The task force report of January 2009 recommended a model of collaboration among industry groups, law enforcement, and others rather than implementation of a series of mandatory technical controls to protect children online.

Another U.S. legislative attempt to control online speech, the Megan Meier Cyberbullying Prevention Act, would criminalize "severe, repeated and hostile" speech online.[27] This proposed legislation, named after a girl who committed suicide thought to be induced by online harassment, has been harshly criticized as unnecessary, given the existing off-line remedies for harassment, and for its potential impact on protected online speech, as it could be applied to many incidents of online speech far beyond the cyberbullying targeted by the legislation.[28] Seventeen of the 50 states have passed laws against cyberbullying.[29]

While legislators in the United States have pursued broader definitions of offenses and mandates on Internet filtering, Canada has tended to act conservatively in response to online obscenity. In its response to online sexually explicit material, Canada has made only de minimis amendments to preexisting law.[30] Legislators have simply revised existing obscenity provisions to encompass online offenses. For example, the passage of the Criminal Law Amendment Act of 2001 established online acts of distributing and accessing child pornography and luring a child as crimes.[31] The Criminal Code mandates a system for judicial review of material (including online material) alleged to be child pornography. It does not, however, require ISPs to judge the legality of content posted on their servers or to take corrective action prior to a judicial determination.[32] If a judge determines that the material in question is illegal, ISPs may be required to take it down and help the court identify and locate the person who posted it.[33]

There have been instances in Canada of ISPs attempting to filter content hosted outside of Canada despite regulatory uncertainty in the area. For three days in July 2005, the Canadian ISP Telus blocked access to a Web site run by members of the Telecommunication Workers Union during a labor dispute containing what Telus argued was proprietary information and photographs that threatened the security and privacy of its employees.[34] This unilateral action by Telus deviated from the general practice of Canadian ISPs to pass on any and all information without regard for content in exchange for immunity from liability over content.[35] This action also conflicted with Section 36 of the Canadian Telecommunications Act, which states that, without the approval of the Canadian Radio-Television and Telecommunications Commission (CRTC), a "Canadian carrier shall not control the content or influence the meaning or purpose of telecommunications carried by it for the public."[36] Telus's blocking also affected the customers of other ISPs that connect via Telus.[37] The matter was resolved when Telus was able to obtain court orders from Alberta and British Columbia requiring the Web site operator, who lives and works in Canada, to remove the offending materials (the site was hosted in the United States).[38]

In August 2006, Canadian human rights lawyer Richard Warman filed an application with the CRTC to authorize Canadian ISPs to block access to two hate speech sites hosted outside of Canada.[39] The CRTC denied the application, but the decision recognized that although the CRTC cannot require Canadian ISPs to block content, it could authorize them to do so. However, the CRTC noted that the "scope of this power has yet to be explored."[40] In a 2009 decision by an Ontario court, Richard Warman was successful at getting an order for a Web site to disclose the identities of eight of its anonymous contributors.[41] The decision has been appealed by the defendants.[42] The rules that the court relied on were general duty of disclosure rules in Ontario civil procedure that were not written with the intent of applying to this situation. The state of court involvement in online speech therefore remains uncertain.

In November 2006, Canada's largest ISPs launched Project Cleanfeed Canada in partnership with Cybertip.ca, the nation's child sexual exploitation tipline. The project, modeled after a similar initiative in the United Kingdom, is intended to protect ISP customers "from inadvertently visiting foreign Web sites that contain images of children being sexually abused and that are beyond the jurisdiction of Canadian legal authorities."[43] Acting on complaints from Canadians about images found online, Cybertip.ca analysts assess the reported information and forward potentially illegal material to the appropriate foreign jurisdiction. If a URL is approved for blocking by two analysts, it may be added to the Cleanfeed distribution list. Each of the participating ISPs voluntarily blocks this list without knowledge of the sites it contains, precluding ISP involvement in the evaluation of URLs. Blocked sites fail to load, but attempts to access them are not monitored and users are not tracked.[44]

Since Project Cleanfeed Canada is a voluntary program, the blocking mechanism is up to the discretion of the ISPs. Sasktel, Bell Canada, and Telus all claim to block only specific URLs, not IP addresses, in an attempt to avoid overblocking.[45] Beside the significant public outcry that would most likely occur, overblocking itself may be illegal under the Telecommunications Act mentioned previously.

Under Section 163 of the Canadian Criminal Code, accessing child pornography—as well as making it accessible—is unlawful.[46] Therefore, the filtering of such content does not infringe on rights of access or speech afforded by the Canadian Charter of Rights and Freedoms within Canada's constitution. Moreover, because ISP participation in Project Cleanfeed is voluntary, the blocking of sites through the project cannot be said to be state sponsored. However, the project remains controversial for other reasons. First, Project Cleanfeed has not yet sought or received authorization from the CRTC. Second, the blacklist maintained by Cybertip.ca remains secret, as publishing a "directory" of child pornography would itself be illegal. This lack of transparency inevitably generates distrust of the list and the process by which it is compiled. Third, the procedure for appealing the blocking of a site may have implications for anonymity.[47] A content owner or ISP customer may complain to the ISP or directly to Cybertip.ca, which will reassess the site and, if necessary, obtain an independent and binding judgment from the National Child Exploitation Coordination Centre. It is unclear whether this process might expose the complainant's identity and create a potential for abuse of that individual's rights by the ISP or perhaps even by authorities.

Canada's response to online obscenity and its voluntary filtering initiative are minimal in contrast to the more vigorous regulatory efforts of the United States.

Regulation of Online Gambling

In 2006, the United States House of Representatives passed legislation designed to limit online gambling by prohibiting the transfer of funds to gambling sites. The Unlawful

Internet Gambling and Enforcement Act (UIGEA), which was slipped into the SAFE Port Act,[48] banned gambling, prohibited online poker sites and other betting companies from "knowingly accepting" money from United States–based customers, and encouraged financial institutions to deny Internet gambling transactions. Since the act's inception, its legality has been in question.[49]

Two states in the United States have attempted to further limit gambling online. In October 2008, a circuit court judge in the state of Kentucky granted a request by the governor to have 141 Web sites used by online gaming operations transferred to state control.[50] In January 2009, following a petition filed by members of the Center for Democracy and Technology, the Electronic Frontier Foundation, and the American Civil Liberties Union of Kentucky,[51] a Kentucky appeals court overturned the judge's request.[52] In May 2009, John Willems, director of the Alcohol and Gambling Enforcement Division (AGED) of Minnesota's Department of Public Safety (DPS), filed an order requiring that 11 ISPs, including Comcast, Charter, and Verizon Wireless, prevent state residents from reaching approximately 200 gambling sites.[53] iMEGA (Interactive Media, Entertainment, and Gaming Association) had filed a lawsuit against Willems seeking an injunction to block implementation of the AGED order,[54] which was later dropped when the Minnesota DPS reached a settlement with iMEGA. ISPs are no longer required to block state residents' access to gambling sites.[55]

In 2008, Representative Barney Frank (Democrat, Massachusetts) again announced plans to introduce legislation aimed at overturning the UIGEA.[56] He had failed a previous attempt in 2007 in the form of an act entitled the Internet Gambling Regulation and Enforcement Act.[57]

The legality of online gambling in Canada is unclear, as few gaming cases exist to provide guidelines, although persons running online gaming operations can be subject to criminal liability.[58] As a result, offshore gambling sites are currently legal to use in Canada.[59] Advertising of such services is generally held to be illegal in Canada.

Defamation

As in other countries, the potential for legal liability for civil violations, including defamation and copyright, constrains the publishers of Internet content and certain service providers in the United States and Canada. These pressures can have a "chilling effect" on lawful online content and conduct, and can threaten the anonymity of users. The content and court adjudication of such laws constitute state action, even when the lawsuits and threats are brought by private individuals or entities.

One crucial factor in determining liability for defamation is the provider's relation to the content—whether the provider functioned as a carrier, distributor, or publisher of the defamatory content. In the United States the common law has been overridden by a federal statute, a holdover portion of the CDA, 47 U.S.C. 230. A key part of the CDA survived judicial scrutiny. Section 230 immunizes ISPs for many of their users' actions including defamation (copyright and criminal activity is excluded): "No provider or user of an interactive computer service shall be treated as the publisher or speaker of any information provided by another information content provider."[60] Moreover, the First Amendment shields speakers from liability for much speech about public figures.[61]

Canada has no statutory equivalent to the statutory protection for ISPs under CDA 230. However, Canadian case law suggests that ISPs are entitled to a certain degree of immunity: in June 2004, the Supreme Court of Canada unanimously held that ISPs cannot be held liable for violations of Canadian copyright law committed by their subscribers.[62] The decision ruled that the act of caching content by an ISP would not make it liable and that an ISP's knowledge of potential infringements by subscribers is not necessarily sufficient to create liability either.[63] In Canada, ISPs are therefore able to escape liability if they prove that they are merely acting as "conduits."[64] They may, however, face liability as publishers if they exercise editorial control over material. This situation stands in contrast to the United States, where CDA 230 provides publisher immunity to ISPs, limited only where the provider or host has acted as an "information content provider" and actually created some or all of the content.[65] An important caveat to the U.S. immunity is that it does not apply to intellectual property law—while the Canadian situation exemplified in the case described earlier does provide immunity to ISPs regarding intellectual property matters such as copyright.[66] Overall, both Canadian and U.S. service providers receive legal protections that favor the protection of free speech online. Canadian ISPs, however, lack the clearly set out statutory protection that exists in the United States and may feel compelled to take down allegedly defamatory content (e.g., postings to message boards) when threatened with the possibility of costly lawsuits.

Copyright

U.S. copyright law has evolved more quickly than Canadian law both in addressing the issue of ISP liability and in encouraging removal of infringing material. The Online Copyright Limitations of Liability Act, a part of the Digital Millennium Copyright Act (DMCA) of 1998,[67] gives service providers a "safe harbor" from liability for their users' copyright infringement provided they implement copyright policies and provides the legal basis for a notice-and-takedown regime. Where a service provider unknowingly transmits, caches, retains, or furnishes a link to infringing material by means of an automatic technical process, it is protected from liability so long as it promptly removes or blocks access to the material upon notice of a claimed infringement.[68] Section 512 (c) of the DMCA[69] provides that "a service provider shall not be liable for monetary relief, . . . , for injunctive or other equitable relief, for infringement of copyright by reason

of the storage at the direction of a user of material that resides on a system or network
. . . if the service provider

• does not have actual knowledge that the material or an activity using the material on
the system or network is infringing;
• in the absence of such actual knowledge, is not aware of facts or circumstances from
which infringing activity is apparent; or
• upon obtaining such knowledge or awareness, acts expeditiously to remove, or disable access to, the material;
• does not receive a financial benefit directly attributable to the infringing activity, in a
case in which the service provider has the right and ability to control such activity; and
• upon notification, . . . responds expeditiously to remove, or disable access to, the material that is claimed to be infringing or to be the subject of infringing activity."

The notice-and-takedown provisions of the DMCA have been put to broad use and
have proven to be an effective instrument for combating copyright infringement online. This has also been seen as giving copyright owners—potentially anyone who has
fixed an "original work of authorship"—unwarranted leverage over service providers
and their subscribers. When a provider is notified of an alleged infringement, risk aver-
sion encourages it to remove or disable access to the specified material, probably without first informing the subscriber. The subscriber may file a counternotice and have the
content restored if the copyright owner does not file a claim in court, but such challenges are rare.[70] Subscribers, like the providers hosting their Web sites, are more likely
to concede to takedown pressures, even when an infringement may not actually be
occurring. If a subscriber is sued, his or her identity may be subpoenaed, as in cases of
defamation, and with similarly little judicial scrutiny.[71] Major search engines such as
Google comply with hundreds of removal requests a month, even though it is not
even clear that provision of a hyperlink would incur copyright liability.[72]

When Canada began to consider amending its copyright laws, it appeared to be following in the footsteps of the United States. In 2004, the House of Commons Standing
Committee on Canadian Heritage retabled its Interim Report on Copyright Reform,
which proposed a "notice and takedown" policy similar to that of the DMCA, under
which Canadian service providers would be compelled to remove content immediately
upon receiving notice of an alleged infringement from a professed copyright holder.
The report came under fire from the Canadian Internet Policy and Public Interest
Clinic (CIPPIC), Digital Copyright Canada, and the Public Interest Advocacy Centre
(PIAC); numerous petitions and critiques followed, calling for balance between the
rights of content creators and fair public use.[73] The "Canadian DMCA" has since been
proposed, in the form of Bill C-61 in 2008, which appears to be even more restrictive
that the U.S. DMCA.[74] The consensus on this bill is that it is unlikely to pass, although
it continues to be a priority of the Conservative government.[75]

With no legislation yet enacted, Canadian ISPs have implemented a "notice and notice" policy for handling copyright infringement. This policy would be continued under Bill C-61.[76] "Notice and notice" was a concept originally proposed in the now-defunct Bill C-60, which was dropped from the legislative agenda in 2005 with the collapse of the Liberal government.[77] Under this policy, copyright owners send notices to ISPs regarding possible copyright infringement by subscribers. Providers then forward these notices to their subscribers—instead of being obligated themselves to remove the content.[78] Even though the notices do not mean that immediate legal action will follow if infringing activities do not cease, they have been successful in getting significant portions of infringing subscribers to remove their materials.[79]

Legal protections against defamation and copyright infringement afforded under U.S. and Canadian law are in tension with the rights of service providers and Internet users. This often gives rise to the censoring and self-censoring of material. Canadian service providers erring on the side of caution may remove content from subscribers' sites, as U.S. providers do when informed of alleged copyright violations. User material is therefore subject to censorship based on unsubstantiated claims. Moreover, because subpoenas offer plaintiffs an avenue for ascertaining subscribers' identities without scrutiny, the potential for misuse of these subpoenas can instill a fear of improper discovery in subscribers that leads to self-censorship. These chilling effects have been well documented,[80] and while they are indirect rather than direct state-mandated filtering, they constitute real censorship of online speech.[81]

Computer Security

Security concerns drive many of the state-mandated limitations on the speech and privacy interests of citizens. These security concerns in the United States and Canada take two forms: national security and computer security.

Computer security has led to certain content restrictions in the United States and Canada. Concerns about unwanted messages reaching computers, in various flavors of spam, have prompted content-based restrictions such as the CAN-SPAM Act of 2003 in the United States. In Canada, a National Task Force on Spam was convened in 2005 to study the spam problem.[82] While some laws, such as the Personal Information Protection and Electronic Documents Act, were found to at least tangentially apply to spam, the task force found a need for legislation directly limiting spam that originates in Canada.[83] The "Anti-Spam Bill" was finally tabled by the Canadian Government on April 24, 2009, as the Electronic Commerce Protection Act (Bill C-27) and is headed for committee review.[84] Government materials accompanying the release of Canada's ECPA point to plans to establish a Spam Reporting Centre similar to the U.S. FTC reporting mechanism.[85] The U.S. Congress has considered a range of options for limiting the free flow of bits across the Internet to address the problem of malicious software infecting computers, though most of the efforts to filter information based upon content deemed to be computing security risks are carried out by private firms or individuals on a voluntary basis.[86] Calls are also being made to promote greater responsibility among ISPs for malicious software spread over their networks in order to contain the worst of "zombie" computers sending spam and distributing malware, in the interest of preserving network safety for other connected PCs. In sum, there is still an active, ongoing discussion about how and why regulation of the flow of obviously malicious code over the Internet might take place.[87]

Network Neutrality

As a new Federal Communications Commission begins its work in the Obama Administration, network neutrality and the problem of bandwidth throttling are near the top of the list of issues it must tackle. One common mode of filtering Internet traffic is for ISPs to discriminate based upon the type or amount of data sent or requested through the network. Many people have had the experience of seeking to send an e-mail to a colleague with a large attachment, such as a photo or a video, only to have the e-mail bounce back with a note stating that an e-mail server along the way had rejected the message because of its size. Writ large, this same issue arises for ISPs and their users. Providers practice various forms of network management, where they decide to favor some data packets over others, often to combat network scourges like spam and malware. Some ISPs, for instance, allow users only a certain amount of bandwidth for certain activities. In August 2008, the FCC ruled that Comcast, a large ISP, had violated federal network neutrality rules when it practiced bandwidth throttling to prevent usage of the BitTorrent service.[88] The Comcast decision—a vote of 3–2 by the commission—marked the first such intervention by the FCC, but by no means resolved the issue of what kind of reasonable network management ISPs are permitted to practice. The new Obama administration FCC will likely be called upon to consider new legislation by Congress, new regulatory systems, and new allegations of infractions of the sort carried out by Comcast.

Surveillance

Concerns related to national security in the United States have contributed to the development of an extensive and technologically sophisticated online surveillance system. The U.S. surveillance system was expanded significantly under the Bush administration following the attacks of September 11, 2001. Government wiretaps are reported to have included taps on major Internet interconnect points and data mining of Internet communications.[89] Tapping these interconnect points would give the government the ability to intercept every overseas communication and many domestic ones. The U.S. government has moved to dismiss lawsuits filed against it and against AT&T by asserting the state secrets privilege; district courts in California and Michigan have refused to dismiss the lawsuits. If the allegations prove to be true, they show that the United States maintains the world's most sophisticated Internet surveillance regime. The Bush administration also pushed to expand the Communications Assistance to Law Enforcement Act (CALEA) to force providers to give law enforcement wiretap access to electronic communications networks. The attorney general under the Bush administration, Alberto Gonzales, called for data retention laws to force ISPs to keep and potentially produce data that could link Internet subscribers to their otherwise anonymous communications.[90] During Barack Obama's election campaign, he criticized both the Bush administration's use of warrantless surveillance and its reliance on the state secrets privilege, yet in January 2009 defended congressional legislation immunizing telecommunications companies from lawsuits regarding their participation in the Bush administration's surveillance programs.[91]

The U.S. government is required to produce annual reports on the number of wire-taps it conducts under Title III of the Omnibus Safe Streets and Crime Control Act of 1968 (the "Wiretap Act"), as well as communication interceptions conducted under the Foreign Intelligence Surveillance Act (FISA) and the Pen Register and Trap and Trace statute (Pen/Trap statute).[92] No reports have been provided under the Pen/Trap statute since 1998.[93]

In Canada, Part VI of the Criminal Code governs the powers of law enforcement to engage in electronic surveillance of private communications when conducting criminal investigations. The Criminal Code requires the production of annual reports on the details of the interceptions that occur.[94] Canadian electronic surveillance for foreign intelligence is primarily undertaken by the National Defense's secretive Communications Security Establishment (CSE), which operates in close cooperation with its U.S. counterpart and other allied intelligence networks. A commissioner is appointed to review the actions of the CSE and produce annual reports commenting on the adherence of the agency to its legislative mandate in the National Defense Act.[95] The commissioner's annual reports, while providing some oversight, provide little additional transparency, as no statistics on the number of communications interceptions are reported.

Conclusion

While there is little technical filtering in either country, the Internet is subject to substantial state regulation in the United States and Canada. With respect to surveillance, the United States is believed to be among the most aggressive countries in the world in terms of listening to online conversations.

Legislators in both countries have imposed Internet-specific regulation that limits their citizens' access to Internet content. In addition, lawmakers have empowered private entities to press Internet intermediaries, including ISPs, for content removal or to carry out filtering. Although the laws are subject to legislative and judicial debate, these private actions may be less transparent. Governments in both countries, however, have experienced significant resistance to their content restriction policies, and, as a result, the extreme measures carried out in some of the more repressive countries of the world have not taken hold in North America.

Notes

1. Derek E. Bambauer, "Cybersieves," *Duke Law Journal*, vol. 59 (2009), http://papers.ssrn.com/sol3/papers.cfm?abstract_id=1143582&rec=1&srcabs=1026597#.

2. John Palfrey and Robert Rogoyski, "The Move to the Middle: The Enduring Threat of Harmful Speech to the End-to-End Principle," *Washington University Journal of Law and Policy*, vol. 21 (2006): 31–65.

3. International Telecommunication Union (ITU), "Internet Indicators: Subscribers, Users, and Broadband Subscribers," 2007, http://www.itu.int/ITU-D/icteye/Reporting/ShowReportFrame.aspx ?ReportName=/WTI/InformationTechnologyPublic&RP_intYear=2007&RP_intLanguageID=1.

4. Ibid.

5. 47 U.S.C.A. §§223(a), §223(d) (Supp. 1997).

6. Solveig Bernstein, "Beyond the Communications Decency Act: Constitutional Lessons of the Internet," Cato Institute, Cato Policy Analysis No. 262, November 4, 1996, http://www.cato.org/pubs/pas/pa-262.html.

7. *ACLU v. Reno*, 929 F. Supp. (E.D. Pa. 1996) at 854–865.

8. *ACLU v. Reno*, 929 F. Supp. (E.D. Pa. 1996) at 883.

9. *Reno v. ACLU*, 521 U.S. 844 (1997).

10. Ibid.

11. 47 U.S.C. §230.

12. Citizen Media Law Project, "Section 230 of the Communications Decency Act," http://www.citmedialaw.org/section-230.

13. Adam Thierer and John Palfrey, "Dialogue: The Future of Online Obscenity and Social Networks," *ArsTechnica*, March 5, 2009, http://arstechnica.com/tech-policy/news/2009/03/a-friendly -exchange-about-the-future-of-online-liability.ars.

14. 47 U.S.C. §231.

15. *ACLU v. Reno*, No. 98–5551 (February 1, 1999).

16. Federal Communications Commission, "Children's Internet Protection Act," http://www.fcc.gov/cgb/consumerfacts/cipa.html.

17. *United States v. American Library Association*, 539 U.S. 194 (2003).

18. Federal Communications Commission, "E-Rate," http://www.fcc.gov/learnnet/.

19. Electronic Frontiers Australia, "Internet Content Filtering and Blocking: Reviews of Internet Filtering Software," http://www.efa.org.au/Issues/Censor/cens2.html#reviews.

20. 20 U.S.C. §6777(c); 20 U.S.C. §9134(f)(3); 47 U.S.C. §254(h)(6)(D).

21. Marjorie Heins, Christina Cho, and Ariel Feldman, "Internet Filters: A Public Policy Report," Brennan Center for Justice at NYU Law School (2006), 4–7, http://www.brennancenter.org/dynamic/subpages/download_file_36644.pdf.

22. Jim Hu, "Court Strikes Down Pennsylvania Porn Law," *CNet News*, September 10, 2004, http://news.cnet.com/Court-strikes-down-Pennsylvania-porn-law/2100-1028_3-5361999.html.

23. *Harvard Law Review*, "The First Amendment Overbreadth Doctrine," vol. 83, no. 4 (1970): 844–927, http://www.jstor.org/pss/1339842; *Broadrick v. Oklahoma* 413 U.S. 601 (1973); *CDT v. Pappert*, 337 (E.D. Penn. 2004) http://www.cdt.org/speech/pennwebblock/20040910memorandum.pdf.

24. *CDT v. Pappert*, 337 F.Supp.2d 606 (E.D. Penn. 2004). For an extensive analysis, see Jonathan Zittrain, "Internet Points of Control," *Boston College Law Review*, 44 (2003): 653.

25. David Kravets, "Communications Decency Act Tipping under Cuomo Kid-Porn Accord," *Wired Threat Level*, June 10, 2008, http://www.wired.com/threatlevel/2008/06/analysis-commun/.

26. Brad Stone, "Online Age Verification for Children Brings Privacy Worries," *New York Times*, November 15, 2008, http://www.nytimes.com/2008/11/16/business/16ping.html?scp=1&sq=protecting%20children%20online&st=cse.

27. See *Megan Meier Cyberbullying Prevention Act*, http://www.govtrack.us/congress/bill.xpd?bill=h111-1966.

28. Euguene Volokh, "Federal Felony to Use Blogs, the Web, Etc. to Cause Substantial Emotional Distress through 'Severe, Repeated, and Hostile' Speech?" April 30, 2009, http://volokh.com/posts/1241122059.shtml.

29. See the First Amendment Center's overview of state cyberbullying laws, at http://www.firstamendmentcenter.org/PDF/cyberbullying_policies.pdf.

30. This approach was first recommended in a 1997 study commissioned by Industry Canada.

31. Passed as Bill C-15a, 1st Session, 37th Parl., 2001; R.S. 1985, c. C-46, §§163.1(3), 163.1(4.1), 172.1.

32. Project Cleanfeed Canada, "Frequently Asked Questions," http://www.cybertip.ca/en/ cybertip/cf_faq; R.S., 1985, c. C-46, section IV, http://www.canlii.org/en/ca/laws/stat/rsc-1985-c -c-46/latest/rsc-1985-c-c-46.html.

33. R.S., 1985, c. C-46, §164.1, http://laws.justice.gc.ca/en/showdoc/cs/C-46/bo-ga:l_V//en #anchorbo-ga:l....

34. Michael Geist, "Telus Breaks ISPs' Cardinal Rule," *Toronto Star*, August 1, 2005, http://www .michaelgeist.ca/index.php?option=content&task=view&id=919.

35. Ibid.

36. Telecommunications Act, R.S.C., ch. 38, §§27(2), 36, http://www.crtc.gc.ca/eng/LEGAL/ TELECOM.HTM.

37. OpenNet Initiative, "Telus Blocks Consumer Access to Labour Union Web Site and Filters an Additional 766 Unrelated Sites," August 2, 2005, http://opennet.net/bulletins/010.

38. See "TELUS Removes Blocking from VFC Website," July, 28, 2005, http://www.voices-for -change.ca/news/archive.asp?PagePosition=2 (accessed November 10, 2006).

39. Canadian Radio-Television and Telecommunications Commission, "Papazian Heisey Myers for Richard Warman—Application for Interim Approval to Permit Canadian Carriers to Block the Content of Certain Hate Websites and Additional Follow-up Relief, " August 22, 2006, http://www .crtc.gc.ca/PartVII/eng/2006/8646/p49_200610510.htm.

40. Ibid.

41. Michael Geist, "Ontario Court Orders Website to Disclose Identity of Anonymous Posters," March 24, 2009, http://www.michaelgeist.ca/content/view/3777/125/.

42. SteynOnline, "Anonymous Commenter Sues Anonymous Commenters," April 1, 2009, http://www.steynonline.com/content/view/1939/128/.

43. Project Cleanfeed Canada, "ISPs and Tipline Set Up Battle against Internet Child Exploitation," November 24, 2006, http://www.cybertip.ca/en/cybertip/cleanfeed_canada (accessed November 10, 2006).

44. Project Cleanfeed Canada, "Frequently Asked Questions," http://www.cybertip.ca/app/en/ media_faq.

45. *Slashdot*, "Cleanfeed Canada: What Would It Accomplish?" December 15, 2006, http://yro .slashdot.org/article.pl?sid=06/12/15/1624215.

46. Criminal Code of Canada (R.S., 1985, c. C-46) §163.

47. Project Cleanfeed Canada, "Appeal Process," http://www.cybertip.ca/app/en/cleanfeed_p1 #anchor_menu.

48. SAFE Port Act, http://www.gpo.gov/fdsys/pkg/PLAW-109publ347/content-detail.html.

49. Bob Dart, "Poker Players Push for a New Deal on Internet," *Denver Post*, October 25, 2007, http://www.denverpost.com/headlines/ci_7271902.

50. Brian Krebs, "Kentucky Tests State's Reach against Online Gambling," *Washington Post*, October 8, 2008, http://www.washingtonpost.com/wp-dyn/content/article/2008/10/08/AR2008100802870.html.

51. Grant Gross, "Groups Ask Kentucky Court to Reverse Domain Seizures," *PC World*, November 14, 2008, http://www.pcworld.com/businesscenter/article/153930/groups_ask_kentucky_court_to_reverse_domain_seizures.html.

52. Jaikumar Vijayan, "Domain Names Can't Be Appropriated, Court Says," *PC World*, January 22, 2009, http://www.pcworld.com/businesscenter/article/158169/domain_names_cant_be_appropriated_court_says.html.

53. Wendy Davis, "Minnesota Faces Tough Odds in Limiting Online Gambling," *MediaPost*, May 4, 2009, http://www.mediapost.com/publications/?fa=Articles.showArticle&art_aid=105194.

54. Pokerstrategy.com, "IMEGA Files Lawsuit against Minnesota," May 9, 2009, http://www.pokerstrategy.com/news/world-of-poker/IMEGA-Files-Lawsuit-Against-Minnesota_19471.

55. iMEGA, "Minnesota Drops 'Black List' Blocking Order in Settlement with iMEGA," June 8, 2009, http://www.imega.org/2009/06/09/minnesota-drops-black-list-blocking-order-in-settlement-with-imega/.

56. Eric Pfanner, "A New Chance for Online Gambling in the U.S.," *New York Times*, April 26, 2009, http://www.nytimes.com/2009/04/27/technology/internet/27iht-gamble.html?_r=1&ref=globalhome.

57. Tom Somach, "Gambling ... Gold Rush?" *San Francisco Chronicle*, June 2, 2007, http://www.sfgate.com/cgi-bin/article.cgi?f=/c/a/2007/07/02/BUG5LQO5P11.DTL.

58. Javad Heydary, "Advertising for Online Gambling—Is It Legal?" *E-Commerce Times*, April 28, 2005, http://www.heydary.com/publications/online-gambling-laws.html.

59. Tim Naumetz, "Senate Saves the Day for Online Gambling," *Law Times*, December 10, 2007, http://www.lawtimesnews.com/200712103704/Headline-News/Senate-saves-the-day-for-online-gambling.

60. 47 U.S.C. §230(c)(1).

61. *New York Times Co. v. Sullivan*, 376 U.S. 254 (1964).

62. *Society of Composers, Authors and Music Publishers of Canada v. Canadian Assn. of Internet Providers*, [2004] 2 S.C.R. 427 [hereinafter *CAIP v. SOCAN*]: http://scc.lexum.umontreal.ca/en/2004/2004scc45/2004scc45.html.

63. Javad Heydary, "Guidelines Evolving on ISP Liability for Users' Misdeeds," *Tech News World*, August 12, 2004, http://www.technewsworld.com/story/35750.html.

64. Ibid.

65. 47 U.S.C. §230 .

66. 47 U.S.C. §230(e)(2).

67. Public Law No. 105–304, 112 Stat. 2860 (1998).

68. 17 U.S.C. §§512(a)–(d).

69. 17 U.S.C. §512(c) (2007).

70. 17 U.S.C. §512(g).

71. 17 U.S.C. §512(h).

72. See Chilling Effects, "DMCA Safe Harbor," http://www.chillingeffects.org/dmca512/.

73. Department of Canadian Heritage: Copyright Policy Branch, http://www.pch.gc.ca/pc-ch/org/sectr/ac-ca/pda-cpb/index-eng.cfm.

74. Michael Geist, "The Canadian DMCA: Check the Fine Print," June 12, 2008, http://www.michaelgeist.ca/content/view/3025/125; Bill C-61, http://www2.parl.gc.ca/HousePublications/Publication.aspx?Docid=3570473&file=4.

75. Michael Geist, "Entertainment Software Association Lobbies for Reintroduction of C-61," http://www.michaelgeist.ca/content/view/3883/196/.

76. Michael Geist, "Why Notice-and-Notice Should Be Part of the Canadian DMCA," June 6, 2008, http://www.michaelgeist.ca/content/view/3009/125/; see Bill C-61, s.41.26, http://www2.parl.gc.ca/HousePublications/Publication.aspx?Docid=3570473&file=4.

77. Online Rights Canada, "What Are Copyright Reform and Bill C-60?" December 7, 2005, http://www.onlinerights.ca/learn/what_is_c-60/.

78. Michael Geist, "The Effectiveness of Notice and Notice," February 15, 2007, http://www.michaelgeist.ca/content/view/1705/125/.

79. *CBC News*, "E-Mail Warnings Deter Canadians from Illegal File Sharing," February 15, 2007, http://www.cbc.ca/consumer/story/2007/02/14/software-warnings.html.

80. See the work of Chilling Effects Clearinghouse, www.chillingeffects.org.

81. The Electronic Frontier Foundation, "Unsafe Harbors: Abusive DMCA Subpoenas and Takedown Demands," September 2003, http://www.eff.org/IP/P2P/20030926_unsafe_harbors.php#_edn3.

82. Industry Canada, "Stopping Spam: Creating a Stronger, Safer Internet," May 2005, http://www.ic.gc.ca/epic/site/ecic-ceac.nsf/en/h_gv00317e.html.

83. Michael Geist, "Spam Plans," March 15, 2007, http://www.michaelgeist.ca/content/view/1805/125/.

84. Michael Geist, "Canada Introduces Electronic Commerce Protection Act," April 24, 2009, http://www.michaelgeist.ca/content/view/3891/125/; Bill C-27 itself: http://www2.parl.gc

.ca/HousePublications/Publication.aspx?DocId=3832885&Language=e&Mode=1; Michael Geist, "Electronic Commerce Protection Act Headed to Committee Following Odd Debate," May 12, 2009, http://www.michaelgeist.ca/content/view/3956/125/.

85. Michael Geist, "The Electronic Commerce Protection Act—The Enforcement Prohibitions," April 28, 2009, http://www.michaelgeist.ca/content/view/3902/125/.

86. Consider, for instance, the interstitial pages that search giant Google places between search results and certain pages on the Internet deemed to host malware that might harm an end user's computer. See StopBadware.org, http://stopbadware.org.

87. Jonathan Zittrain, *The Future of the Internet and How to Stop It* (New Haven, CT: Yale University Press, 2008), 153–199.

88. Declan McCullagh, "FCC Formally Rules Comcast's Throttling of BitTorrent Was Illegal," *CNet News*, August 1, 2008, at http://news.cnet.com/8301-13578_3-10004508-38.html.

89. James Risen and Eric Lichtblau, "Spy Agency Mined Vast Data Trove, Officials Report," *New York Times*, December 24, 2005, http://www.nytimes.com/2005/12/24/politics/24spy.html.

90. Declan McCullagh, "Gonzales Pressures ISPs on Data Retention," *CNet News*, May 27, 2006, http://news.zdnet.com/2100-1009_22-148226.html.

91. David Kravets, "Obama Sides with Bush in Spy Case," *Wired.com*, January 22, 2009, http://www.wired.com/threatlevel/2009/01/obama-sides-wit/.

92. Respectively: 18 U.S.C. §§ 2510–22; 50 U.S.C. §§1801–11; 18 U.S.C. §§3121–7.

93. Electronic Privacy Information Center, "FBI Reporting Concerning Pen Register/Trap and Trace Statistics," April 29, 2009, http://epic.org/privacy/wiretap/ltr_pen_trap_leahy_final.pdf.

94. Criminal Code (R.S., 1985, c. C-46), s.195, http://laws.justice.gc.ca/en/C-46/; Public Safety Canada, *Annual Report on the use of Electronic Surveillance 2007*, 2008, http://www.publicsafety.gc.ca/abt/dpr/le/elecsur-07-eng.aspx.

95. Office of the Communications Security Establishment Commissioner, "Annual Reports," http://ocsec-bccst.gc.ca/ann-rpt/index_e.php; *National Defense Act* (R.S., 1985, c. N-5) Part V.1, s.273.63, http://laws.justice.gc.ca/en/N-5/section-273.63.html.

Australia and New Zealand

Australia and New Zealand Overview

Australia maintains some of the most restrictive Internet policies of any Western country and over the past two years has taken steps toward a nationwide mandatory Internet filtering scheme. Its neighbor, New Zealand, regulates the Internet considerably less rigorously. Australia's constitution does not explicitly give the right to free speech,[1] and in fact contains a clause giving the Australian government "communications power," allowing it to regulate "postal, telegraphic, telephonic, and other like services," including the Internet.[2] A number of state and territorial governments in Australia have passed legislation making the distribution of offensive material a criminal offense, as the constitution does not afford that power to the national government.[3]

The Australian government has for some time promoted and financed an "opt-in" filtering program, in which users voluntarily accept filtering software that blocks offensive content hosted outside the country. In 2008, the government announced plans for a layered filtering scheme, proposing a mandatory filter to block pornographic and illegal content, as well as an opt-out filter that would block even more content. The filter, which faces considerable opposition from Australian and international anti-censorship groups and, in some cases, the ISPs themselves, will first be tested by six ISPs before going live.[4]

In contrast, New Zealand has less strict Internet regulations. The government maintains a more limited definition of offensive content that can be investigated by a designated government entity, although—unlike in Australia—the definition includes hate speech (despite its being illegal in both countries). Furthermore, the government of New Zealand has not passed legislation to allow issuance of takedown notices for such content, and its enforcement of Internet content regulation by prosecution almost solely focuses on child pornography. New Zealand has not yet formalized its copyright laws and has rejected multiple proposals to do so, most recently scrapping proposed Section 92A of the Copyright Amendment (New Technologies) Act.[5] The country's defamation and surveillance laws are similar to those of Australia. Overall, Australian Internet regulations are significantly stricter than those of New Zealand and much of the Western world.

Offensive Content

Australia's and New Zealand's approaches to offensive content on the Internet both rely on government-run content-classification systems. However, their approaches differ in terms of what is considered offensive and what is done about the offending content.

Australian laws relating to the censorship of offensive content are based on the powers delineated in and protections omitted from the Australian constitution. Section 51(v) of the document gives Parliament power to "make laws for the peace, order, and good government of the Commonwealth with respect to: (v) postal, telegraphic, telephonic, and other like services."[6] With no explicit protection of free speech in the constitution, the Australian government has invoked its "communications power" to institute a restrictive regime of Internet content regulation.

The Broadcasting Services Amendment (Online Services) Bill 1999, an amendment to the Broadcasting Services Act 1992, establishes the authority of the Australian Communications and Media Authority (ACMA)[7] to regulate Internet content. The ACMA is empowered to look into complaints from Australians about offensive content on the Internet and issue takedown notices. The ACMA is not mandated to scour the Internet for potentially prohibited content, but it is allowed to begin investigations without an outside complaint.[8]

Web content that is hosted in Australia may be subject to a takedown request from the ACMA if the Office of Film and Literature Classification finds that it falls within certain categories as defined by the Commonwealth Classification (Publications, Films and Computer Games) Act 1995, a cooperative classification system agreed to by the national, state, and territorial governments.

The levels and definitions of prohibited content are as follows:

1. R18: Contains material that is likely to be disturbing to those under 18. This content is not prohibited on domestic hosting sites if there is an age-verification system certified by the ACMA in place.
2. X18: Contains nonviolent sexually explicit content between consenting adults. This content may be subject to ACMA takedown provisions if hosted on domestic servers.
3. RC: Contains content that is Refused Classification (child pornography, fetish, detailed instruction on crime, etc.) and is prohibited on Australian-hosted Web sites.[9]

The classification system chosen for Internet content is the more restrictive standard used for films, rather than the publications classification. As a result, some content allowable offline is banned when brought online.[10]

Once the determination has been made that content hosted within Australia is prohibited, the ACMA issues a takedown notice to the Internet content provider (ICP). It is not illegal for the ICP to host prohibited content, but legal action could be taken against it by the government if it does not comply with the takedown notice.

For offensive content hosted outside of Australia, the ACMA itself determines whether content is prohibited and notifies a list of certified Web-filter manufacturers to include the prohibited Web sites in their filters.[11] To obtain certification, these certified "Family Friendly Filters" must agree to keep lists of prohibited sites confidential.[12] Providers are then required to offer a Family Friendly Filter to all their customers, though customers are not required to accept them.[13] As a result, content taken down in Australia could be posted outside the country and still be accessible to the majority of Australian Internet users. Electronic Frontiers Australia, a nonprofit group dedicated to protecting online freedoms, reports that at least one Web site taken down has moved to the United States, even keeping its URL under the ".au" domain. It is not known how many Web sites have moved overseas in this fashion.[14]

States and territories in Australia have instituted a variety of laws that criminalize the downloading of illegal content and the distribution of content that is "objectionable" or "unsuitable for minors."[15] The state of Victoria, for example, in Section 57 of its Classification (Publication, Films and Computer Games) (Enforcement) Act 1995, makes it illegal to "use an on-line information service to publish or transmit, or make available for transmission, objectionable material."[16] There is no uniformity between the states, however. In Western Australia, for example, it is not illegal to distribute R18 and X18 to adults online (though the ACMA can still issue takedown notices), but the possession of any RC content (not just child pornography, as is the case in other states) is illegal.[17]

In March 2007, all mainland states in Australia banned access to YouTube over school networks because of an uploaded video depicting a 17-year-old Australian girl being abused, beaten, and humiliated by a group of young people. Eight youths have been charged in connection with the assault.[18] School blocking of YouTube has faced opposition, notably from Google executive Vint Cerf, who noted his belief that "many young people have those skills that may be well beyond those of their parents and their teachers and will find ways of accessing information."[19]

The Commonwealth is also implementing new Internet filtering initiatives. In June 2006, the Australian government announced an AUD 116.6 million initiative, "Protecting Australian Families Online." The initiative included AUD 93.3 million to be spent over three years to provide all families with free Web filters. The government also announced that it would test an ISP-level blocking system in Tasmania. At the time, Helen Coonan, the minister for communications, information technology, and the arts, opposed implementing this system on a countrywide basis.[20]

However, in December 2007, Telecommunications Minister Stephen Conroy announced a strengthened "clean feed" policy, under which all Australian ISPs are required to provide Internet filtering services that prevent child pornography and other "inappropriate" material from reaching schools and houses.[21] Those who link to banned sites from their own sites will be fined AUD 11,000 per day.[22] Instead of opting in to the program, as users did under the 2006 initiative, users who wish to see adult material must opt out (there is no opt-out for illegal content). In conjunction with the new policy, the ACMA released a set of updated regulations entitled the Restricted Access System Declaration of 2007,[23] requiring content service providers to implement age-verification systems on all Web sites containing mature or adult content.[24] As of April 2009, ACMA was still conducting trials for ISP-level content filtering; eight ISPs had agreed to participate.[25]

The plan was initially kept under wraps. In October 2008, a policy advisor in Conroy's office sent an e-mail to the Internet Industry Association (IIA) instructing the IIA to inform ISPs that they must keep quiet about the country's filtering scheme.[26] The incident was widely reported by the Australian press, and several heads of ISPs spoke out against what they considered to be an attempt at censorship.[27]

One concern of those opposed to the scheme is the potential for nonillegal Web sites to be banned, a fear that has turned out not to be unfounded. In March 2009, ACMA added pages from the whistle-blowing site Wikileaks to its blacklist of banned URLs after the site published a secret Internet censorship list for Denmark.[28] In doing so, Australia became one of only three countries in the world to censor the site—the other two are China and the United Arab Emirates. In retaliation, a group of anonymous activists published ACMA's confidential blacklist on Wikileaks.[29]

Although New Zealand has not yet instituted a filtering scheme like that which Australia is working to implement, a vaguely worded page on the Department of Internal Affairs' (DIA) special censorship page entitled "Censorship and the Internet" states that the department "takes a proactive role in prosecuting New Zealanders who trade objectionable material via the Internet. If a publication is categorised as 'objectionable' it is automatically banned by the Films, Videos, and Publications Classification Act 1993."[30] Electronic Frontiers Australia has stated that this act likely covers Internet materials as well.[31] Under the act, any material that "describes, depicts, expresses, or otherwise deals with matters such as sex, horror, crime, cruelty, or violence in such a manner that the availability of the publication is likely to be injurious to the public good" is considered objectionable and is illegal to distribute or possess.[32] Specifically, any material that promotes or supports "the exploitation of children, or young persons, or both, for sexual purposes; or the use of violence or coercion to compel any person to participate in, or submit to, sexual conduct; or sexual conduct with or upon the body of a dead person; or the use of urine or excrement in association with degrading or dehumanizing conduct or sexual conduct; or Bestiality; or acts of torture or the infliction of extreme violence or extreme cruelty" is banned.[33] There is also a decision procedure described in the act for any content that might be objectionable but does not fall within this specific list, including discriminatory and hateful material.[34] This law has formed the basis of the DIA's enforcement of Internet censorship in the country.

Like Australia's ACMA, the DIA "proactively" investigates potentially banned material[35] and submits any such material not already classified to the Office of Film and Literature Classification for a ruling.[36] This office then classifies the material as "unrestricted" or "objectionable," except in certain circumstances of restricted access or for "educational, professional, scientific, literary, artistic, or technical purposes."[37]

There is, however, no explicit legal mechanism for the takedown of objectionable material. Instead, the nonprofit InternetNZ is in the process of establishing an industry-wide code of conduct that would require its signatories to agree not to host illegal content.[38] As a result, the government focuses its efforts on prosecuting the distributors or possessors. The Films, Videos, and Publications Classifications Amendment Act 2005 sets the penalty for distributing objectionable material at a maximum of ten years in prison (up from a maximum of one year) and for knowingly possessing objectionable materials at a maximum of five years in prison or a NZD 50,000 fine.[39] According to various sources, the DIA has almost completely focused its enforcement of Internet censorship on child pornography.[40]

Hate Speech

Both Australia and New Zealand have legislation addressing hate speech generally, and both have applied this legislation to the Internet through different means. New Zealand, however, has an institutionalized investigation system, while Australia does not.

Australia addresses hate speech through the Racial Discrimination Act 1975, which makes it "unlawful for a person to do an act, otherwise than in private, if: the act is reasonably likely, in all the circumstances, to offend, insult, humiliate or intimidate another person or a group of people; and the act is done because of the race, colour or national or ethnic origin of the other person, or of some or all of the people in the group."[41]

Australian courts applied this law to the Internet for the first time in October 2002 in the *Jones v. Töben* case. Jeremy Jones and the Executive Council of Australian Jewry brought a lawsuit against Frederick Töben, the director of the Adelaide Institute, because of material on Töben's Web site (www.adelaideinstitute.org) that denied the Holocaust. The Federal Court, ruling that publication on the Internet without password protection is a "public act," found that posting this material online was in direct violation of Section 18C of the Racial Discrimination Act 1975 (quoted earlier) and called for the material to be removed from the Internet.[42]

Australia does not, however, give the ACMA authority to investigate complaints or issue takedown notices for hateful or racist materials online, even if they would be illegal under the Racial Discrimination Act 1975.[43] Schedule 5 of the Broadcast Services Act 1992 gives the ACMA authority only over materials deemed "offensive" within the classification scheme described earlier. As a result, there appears to be no venue other than the courts in which to pursue complaints about hateful or racist materials online. However, Chilling Effects reports that Google received notice on May 5, 2006, of a site in its search results that "allegedly violates section 18C of the Racial Discrimination Act 1975" and removed it from the Google Australia site (www.google.com.au).[44] This action may be indicative of a new notice-based system taking form.

New Zealand, in contrast, has both explicit prohibition of discrimination based on race, religion, age, disability, and sexual orientation in Section 21(1) of the Human Rights Act 1993[45] and explicit prohibition of the publication of material that "represents (whether directly or by implication) that members of any particular class of the public are inherently inferior to other members of the public by reason of any characteristic of members of that class, being a characteristic that is a prohibited ground of discrimination specified in Section 21(1) of the Human Rights Act 1993"[46] in Section 3e of the Films, Videos, and Publication Classifications Act 1993. The DIA uses these statutes to pursue investigations into potentially discriminatory material.

Copyright

Australia's copyright laws underwent a significant overhaul following the acceptance of the Australia–United States Free Trade Agreement in 2004. Pursuant to that agreement, Australia was required to bring its copyright laws closer in line with those of the United States.[47] Some of the relevant requirements included the following:

1. Agreeing to World Intellectual Property Organization (WIPO) Internet treaties.
2. Implementing an "expeditious" takedown system of copyright-infringing materials.

3. Strengthening control over copyright protection technology circumvention.

4. Agreeing to copyright protection standards.

5. Increasing the length of copyright to life plus seventy years from its previous level of life plus fifty years.[48]

Most of these provisions were implemented in the U.S. Free Trade Agreement Implementation Act 2004, though new regulations in response to requirement 3 were recently implemented in the Copyrights Amendment Act 2006.[49]

After implementing a system of copyright more consistent with that of the United States, the Australian government decided to pursue another overhaul of its copyright laws in 2006, as *ABC Science Online* reports, to "keep up with the rapidly changing digital landscape."[50] The proposed amendments to the Copyright Act 1968 were worrisome to many. Google argued that certain provisions would allow copyright owners to pursue legal action against it and other search engines for caching material without obtaining express permission from each Web site. These provisions would "condemn the Australian public to the pre-Internet era," Google argued.[51] Other critics contended that the proposed amendments would make possession of an iPod or other music-listening device designed to play MP3 files illegal, and uploading a video of oneself singing along to a pop song a crime.[52]

Although these two final concerns have been remedied in the resulting Copyrights Amendment Act 2006 (it is still legal to own an iPod and it is allowable to post a lip-synching video),[53] the caching issue still appears to be unresolved. There is an exception in the act that allows computer networks of educational institutions to cache copyright-protected online material "to facilitate efficient later access to the works and other subject-matter by users of the system."[54] However, this provision does not appear to offer the exception that Google sought.

Overall, though, the amendments allow for a greater number of exceptions to the copyright laws to establish more realistic fair use of copyrighted material, such as "time-shifting, format-shifting and space-shifting" (recording a television show to watch later, scanning a book to view it electronically, and transferring material from CDs to iPods, respectively), and greater protection of parody and satire.[55]

The Australian judiciary has been active in copyright enforcement online as well. In a landmark decision in December 2006, the Federal Court upheld a lower court ruling that found the Web site operator of mp3s4free.net, Stephen Cooper, and the hosting ISP, E-Talk, liable for copyright infringement. Cooper's site did not itself host any copyright-protected material, but rather served as a search engine through which users could find and download copyright-protected music for free. In its ruling, the court found that merely linking to copyright-protected material was grounds for infringement. In addition, the court found that ISP E-Talk was also liable for copyright infringement because it posted advertisements on the site and was unwilling to take the site down.[56] Interestingly, Dale Clapperton, of Electronic Frontiers Australia, has argued that this decision could be used against search engines such as Google. In an article in the *Sydney Morning Herald*, he stated that "what Cooper was doing is basically the exact same thing that Google does, except Google acts as a search engine for every type of file, while this site only acts as a search engine for MP3 files."[57]

In New Zealand, recent attempts to regulate copyright law to include digital provisions have been rejected by the national government.[58] Therefore, New Zealand's current law is contained within the Copyright Act 1994. The term of a copyright is set at life plus fifty years.[59]

The Copyright (New Technologies and Performers' Rights) Amendment Bill currently being considered in New Zealand, however, would dramatically change the digital copyright landscape into one that more closely mirrors the Digital Millennium Copyright Act (DMCA) of the United States. If passed, the bill would allow for format shifting and space shifting of music,[60] criminalize the distribution of the means to subvert technological protection measures protecting copyrighted content, and establish a system in which ISPs are required to remove copyright-infringing content and notify the poster if the ISP "obtains knowledge or becomes aware that the material is infringing."[61] This removal system is somewhat different from the U.S. system of notice and takedown in that it requires knowledge of infringement and not simply notification.[62]

Defamation

Through a variety of court cases, both Australia and New Zealand have applied their respective defamation laws to the Internet, and both countries, with New Zealand courts following the Australian courts' example, have controversially expanded their jurisdiction in defamation suits to online materials hosted outside their borders.

Defamation in Australia, except for a small range of cases, is handled through state and territorial law;[63] until December 2005, states and territories maintained largely nonuniform codes of defamation.[64] After what amounted to a threat that the Commonwealth would act if states and territories did not, the states and territories finally decided to enact uniform laws in December 2005.[65] Since defamation laws are applied where material is seen, read, or experienced, nonuniform laws meant that writers and publishers had to be wary of different sets of laws all over the country under which they might be sued under various definitions of defamation.[66] Now the laws are uniform, so this liability risk has been mitigated. No legislation specifically targets defamation on the Internet, and, therefore, its regulation is essentially the same as that for all other publications.[67]

The judiciary has played an important role in setting online defamation policy because of jurisdictional issues. In a major decision in December 2002, the Australian

High Court ruled that a party within Australia can sue a foreign party in Australian court for defamation resulting from an online article hosted on a foreign server. The specific case involved a lawsuit pitting Joseph Gutnick, an Australian businessman, against Dow Jones over a defamatory article written about him in Barron's Online in October 2000. Dow Jones argued that since its servers (and therefore the article) were in the United States, the defamation case should have been tried in the United States. A decision allowing the case to be tried in Australia, they argued, would restrict free speech around the world because it would require authors and publishers to take into account the laws of foreign countries under which they could be sued when publishing material online.[68]

The court countered, however, that the "spectre of 'global liability' should not be exaggerated. Apart from anything else, the costs and practicalities of bringing proceedings against a foreign publisher will usually be a sufficient impediment to discourage even the most intrepid of litigants. Further, in many cases of this kind, where the publisher is said to have no presence or assets in the jurisdiction, it may choose simply to ignore the proceedings. It may save its contest to the courts of its own jurisdiction until an attempt is later made to enforce there the judgment obtained in the foreign trial. It may do this especially if that judgment was secured by the application of laws, the enforcement of which would be regarded as unconstitutional or otherwise offensive to a different legal culture."[69] The parties eventually settled for AUD 180,000 in damages and AUD 400,000 in legal fees."[70]

New Zealand defamation law was first found to apply to online material in a district court decision, *O'Brien v. Brown*, in late 2001. In the case, Patrick O'Brien, chief executive officer of the New Zealand domain manager Domainz, sued Alan Brown, the head of a Manawatu ISP, for Brown's posting of harsh criticisms and calls for fraud investigation into Domainz on a publicly available Internet Society of New Zealand bulletin board.[71] The judge in the case found that the Internet afforded no additional freedom of expression to the defendant than any other medium and, further, that publication on the Internet required a greater award of damages than through another medium because of the ease with which Domainz's potential customers and clients could access the defamatory material.[72]

In addition, the New Zealand courts have followed Australia's example in determining the jurisdiction for defamation suits over online content hosted in a foreign country. Ironically, the relevant suit involved an Australian defendant. In 2004, the Wellington High Court found that the University of Newlands (based in New Zealand) could sue Nationwide News, Ltd. (based in Australia) in New Zealand court for Nationwide's inclusion of the plaintiff in a list of "Wannabe Unis" and "degree mills" in its online newspaper, *The Australian*. This ruling more closely aligned New Zealand defamation policy with Australia.[73]

Surveillance

Both Australia and New Zealand have taken steps toward greater Internet security, passing laws to give government agencies greater authority to investigate illegal activities online.

Australia's Internet surveillance regime is primarily based on two laws. The first is the Telecommunications (Interception and Access) Act 1979. This act, amended in June 2006, prohibits intercepting telecommunications or accessing, without first notifying both the sender and the receiver, stored telecommunications by any person or entity, except in cases such as the installation or maintenance of telecommunications equipment.[74] It also establishes two warrant systems, controlled by the attorney general, by which law enforcement may gain access to these communications: "telecommunications service warrants" (for real-time interception) and "stored communications warrants" (for access to stored communications without a requirement to notify the communicants).[75]

The second relevant law is the Surveillance Devices Act 2004, which significantly increases the authority of law enforcement to install surveillance devices such as keystroke recorders under newly created "surveillance device warrants."[76] Electronic Frontiers Australia has expressed worry that these warrants will be used by law enforcement to avoid applying for a telecommunications service warrant, essentially allowing them to intercept communications where a telecommunications service warrant would not have been authorized.[77]

Further, in 2003, the Australian Internet Industry Association (IIA) attempted to establish a code of practice requiring ISP signatories to retain user information for six or twelve months and provide it to law enforcement upon official request. Specifically, personal data—such as name, address, and credit card details—were to be retained by ISPs for six months after a customer ends service with that ISP or twelve months after the record is created, whichever is longer. Operational data, such as proxy logs and e-mail information, were to be kept for six months after creation of the data.[78] Law enforcement could request this information using the certificate system set up in the Telecommunications Act 1997,[79] which allows private information to be disclosed if "an authorized officer of a criminal law-enforcement agency has certified that the disclosure is reasonably necessary for the enforcement of the criminal law."[80]

In New Zealand, the most relevant piece of legislation to Internet security is Supplemental Order Paper 85 to the Crimes Amendment Bill No. 6, passed in 2003. The act essentially makes it illegal to hack or intercept electronic communications, but exempts the police, the Security Intelligence Service, and the Government Communications Security Bureau acting under interception warrants as described by the Crimes Act 1961. As noted on the Web site of the Green Party, however, these warrants could be "quite broad in their application and cover a class of people."[81]

Conclusion

Australian laws and policies toward the Internet are aligned with those of many Western countries, while New Zealand's are less stringent. The Australian government has instituted a strict takedown regime for offensive content, and various states and territories have made distribution of such content a criminal offense. The government is pursuing voluntary programs to increase home filtration of the Internet, and Australia's evolving hate speech, copyright, defamation, and security policies offer further justification for restricting Internet content. A countrywide ISP-level filtering scheme is currently being tested.

New Zealand, in contrast, has instituted a more limited classification system—though it does include hate speech—with no takedown notices and has not yet formally adopted copyright legislation that applies to the Internet. Its broad defamation and security policies, however, are more reminiscent of Australia.

Overall, however, Australia's Internet censorship regime is strikingly severe relative to both its neighbor and similar Western states, and it is helping to push the normative boundaries of filtering for an industrialized democratic state. It is not, however, at the level of the most repressive regimes that the OpenNet Initiative has studied.

Notes

1. Roy Jordan, "Free Speech and the Constitution," Parliamentary Library, June 4, 2002, http://www.aph.gov.au/LIBRARY/Pubs/RN/2001-02/02rn42.htm.

2. Geraldine Chin, "Technological Change and the Australian Constitution," *Melbourne University Law Review*, 25 (2000), http://www.austlii.edu.au/au/journals/MULR/2000/25.html.

3. Electronic Frontiers Australia, "Internet Censorship Laws in Australia," March 31, 2006, http://www.efa.org.au/Issues/Censor/cens1.html.

4. Fran Foo, "Green Light for ISP Filtering Trials," *Australian IT*, February 11, 2009, http://www.australianit.news.com.au/story/0,24897,25040645-15306,00.html.

5. Chris Keall, "Section 92A to Be Scrapped," *National Business Review*, March 23, 2009, http://www.nbr.co.nz/article/section-92a-be-scrapped-89121.

6. Geraldine Chin, "Technological Change and the Australian Constitution," *Melbourne University Law Review*, 25 (2000), http://www.austlii.edu.au/au/journals/MULR/2000/25.html.

7. The Australian Communications and Media Authority was formed in July 2005, merging the Australian Broadcasting Authority and the Australian Communications Authority. See Australian Communications and Media Authority, "The ACMA Overview," http://www.acma.gov.au/WEB/STANDARD//pc=ACMA_ORG_OVIEW.

8. Electronic Frontiers Australia, "Internet Censorship Laws in Australia," March 31, 2006, http://www.efa.org.au/Issues/Censor/cens1.html.

9. Ibid.; Office of Film and Literature Classification, "Guidelines for the Classification of Films and Computer Games," 2005, http://www.ag.gov.au/www/agd/rwpattach.nsf/VAP/ (CFD7369FCAE9B8F32F341DBE097801FF)~60000PB+-+Guidelines+for+the+Classification+of+ Computer+Games+(Amendments+No+1)+(GN+~+Superceded+InstrumentsAMENDNO1GN22.pdf/ $file/60000PB+-+Guidelines+for+the+Classification+of+Computer+Games+(Amendments+No+1)+ (GN+~+Superceded+InstrumentsAMENDNO1GN22.pdf.

10. Electronic Frontiers Australia, "Internet Censorship Laws in Australia," March 31, 2006, http://www.efa.org.au/Issues/Censor/cens1.html.

11. Australian Communications and Media Authority, "Online Regulation," February 2007, http:// www.acma.gov.au/web/STANDARD//pc%3DPC_90169.

12. Schedule 1, "Codes for Industry Co-regulation in Areas of Internet and Mobile Content (Pursuant to the Requirements of the Broadcasting Services Act 1992)," May 2005, http://www.acma .gov.au/acmainterwr/aba/contentreg/codes/internet/documents/iia_code.pdf.

13. Internet Industry Association, "IIA Guide for ISPs," March 23, 2006, http://www.iia.net.au/ index.php?option=com_content&task=view&id=121&Itemid=33.

14. Electronic Frontiers Australia, "Internet Censorship Laws in Australia," March 31, 2006, http://www.efa.org.au/Issues/Censor/cens1.html.

15. Ibid.

16. Classification (Publications, Films and Computer Games) (Enforcement) Act 1995, §57, http:// www.austlii.edu.au/au/legis/vic/consol_act/cfacga1995596/s57.html.

17. Electronic Frontiers Australia, "Internet Censorship Laws in Australia," March 31, 2006, http://www.efa.org.au/Issues/Censor/cens1.html.

18. Stephen Hutcheon, "YouTube Bans Don't Work: Internet Founder," March 8, 2007, *Sydney Morning Herald*, http://www.smh.com.au/articles/2007/03/08/1173166844770.html.

19. Ibid.

20. Stephen Deare, "ISP Level Porn Filtering Won't Work, Says Coonan," *CNet Australia*, June 15, 2006, http://www.cnet.com.au/broadband/0,239036008,240063710,00.htm.

21. *ABC News*, "Conroy Announces Mandatory Internet Filters to Protect Children," December 31, 2007, http://www.abc.net.au/news/stories/2007/12/31/2129471.htm.

22. Asher Moses, "Banned Hyperlinks Could Cost You $11,000 a Day," *The Age*, March 17, 2009, http://www.theage.com.au/news/home/technology/banned-hyperlinks-could-cost-you-11000-a-day/ 2009/03/17/1237054787635.html?page=fullpage#contentSwap1&page=-1/.

23. ACMA, "Restricted Access System Declaration 2007," http://www.acma.gov.au/WEB/ STANDARD/pc=PC_310905.

24. Tom Corelis, "Australia Approves Mandatory Age Verification for Internet Content," *Daily Tech*, December 26, 2007, http://www.dailytech.com/Australia+Approves+Mandatory+Age+ Verification+for+Internet+Content/article10137.htm.

25. "Optus Joins ISP Net Filter Trials," *ITNews*, April 22, 2009, http://www.itnews.com.au/News/101538,optus-joins-isp-net-filter-trials.aspx.

26. Asher Moses, "Filtering Out the Fury: How Government Tried to Gag Web Censor Critics," *Sydney Morning Herald*, October 24, 2008, http://www.smh.com.au/news/technology/biztech/government-gags-web-censor-critics/2008/10/23/1224351430987.html?page=2.

27. Andrew Hendry and Darren Pauli, "'Appalled' Opposition Hits Back at Conroy's Internet Censorship," *ComputerWorld*, October 24, 2008, http://www.computerworld.com.au/article/264974/appalled_opposition_hits_back_conroy_internet_censorship?pp=3&fp=4194304&fpid=1.

28. Wikileaks, "Australia Secretly Censors Wikileaks Press Release and Danish Internet Censorship List," March 16, 2009, http://www.wikileaks.org/wiki/Australia_secretly_censors_Wikileaks_press_release_and_Danish_Internet_censorship_list,_16_Mar_2009/.

29. Liam Tung, "Wikileaks Spills ACMA Blacklist," *ZDNet*, March 19, 2009, http://www.zdnet.com.au/news/security/soa/Wikileaks-spills-ACMA-blacklist/0,130061744,339295538,00.htm?omnRef=http://www.google.com/search?q=ACMA%20trial%20australia&ie=utf-8&oe=utf-8&aq=t&rls=org.mozilla:en-US:official&client=firefox-a.

30. Department of Internal Affairs: Censorship Compliance, "Censorship and the Internet," http://www.censorship.dia.govt.nz/diawebsite.nsf/wpg_URL/Services-Censorship-Compliance-Censorship-and-the-Internet?OpenDocument.

31. Electronic Frontiers Australia, "Internet Censorship: Law and Policy around the World," March 28, 2002, http://www.efa.org.au/Issues/Censor/cens3.html#nz.

32. Films, Videos, and Publications Act 1993, §3, http://rangi.knowledge-basket.co.nz/gpacts/reprint/text/2005/se/042se3.html.

33. Ibid.

34. Ibid.

35. Department of Internal Affairs: Censorship Compliance, "Censorship and the Internet," http://www.censorship.dia.govt.nz/diawebsite.nsf/wpg_URL/Services-Censorship-Compliance-Censorship-and-the-Internet?OpenDocument.

36. Department of Internal Affairs, "Censorship Compliance," December 2006, http://www.dia.govt.nz/diawebsite.nsf/wpg_URL/Services-Censorship-Compliance-Index?OpenDocument.

37. Films, Videos, and Publications Act 1993, §23, http://rangi.knowledge-basket.co.nz/gpacts/public/text/1993/se/094se23.html.

38. InternetNZ, "ICOP," May 2006, http://www.internetnz.net.nz/proceedings/tf/archive/icop05_wp_index.htm.

39. Department of Internal Affairs, Amendment Act 2005, April 2005, http://www.dia.govt.nz/diawebsite.nsf/wpg_URL/Services-Censorship-Compliance-Amendment-Act-2005?OpenDocument.

40. Keith Manch and David Wilson, "Objectionable Material on the Internet: Developments in Enforcement," Department of Internal Affairs, 2003, http://www.netsafe.org.nz/Doc_Library/

netsafepapers_manchwilson_objectionable.pdf; Electronic Frontiers Australia, "Internet Censorship: Law and Policy around the World," March 28, 2002, http://www.efa.org.au/Issues/Censor/cens3.html#nz.

41. Racial Discrimination Act 1975, §18C, http://austlii.law.uts.edu.au/au/legis/cth/consol_act/rda1975202/s18c.html.

42. Galexia, "Article: *Jones v Töben*: Racial Discrimination on the Internet," October 2002, http://www.galexia.com/public/research/articles/research_articles-art22.html#fn357.

43. Australian Department of Communications, Information Technology and the Arts, "Racism and the Internet," November 2002, http://www.archive.dbcde.gov.au/__data/.../Racism_and_the_Internet.doc.

44. Chilling Effects, "Google Removal Complaint: Section 18C of Australia's Racial Discrimination Act of 1975," May 5, 2006, http://www.chillingeffects.org/international/notice.cgi?NoticeID=4266.

45. Human Rights Act 1993, §21(1), http://www.legislation.govt.nz/act/public/1993/0082/latest/DLM304475.html.

46. Films, Videos, and Publication Act 1993, §3e, http://rangi.knowledge-basket.co.nz/gpacts/reprint/text/2005/se/042se3.html.

47. Austrade, "The Australian–United States Free Trade Agreement," http://www.austrade.gov.au/AUSFTA8310/default.aspx.

48. Australian Department of Foreign Affairs and Trade, "Intellectual Property," http://www.dfat.gov.au/trade/negotiations/us_fta/outcomes/08_intellectual_property.html; Australian Department of Foreign Affairs and Trade, "A Guide to the Agreement: Intellectual Property," http://www.dfat.gov.au/trade/negotiations/us_fta/guide/17.html.

49. Australian Department of Foreign Affairs and Trade, "Intellectual Property," http://www.dfat.gov.au/trade/negotiations/us_fta/outcomes/08_intellectual_property.html.

50. Judy Skatssoon, "Google Warns Aust Copyright Laws Could Cripple the Internet," *ABC Science Online*, November 7, 2006, http://www.abc.net.au/news/newsitems/200611/s1782921.htm.

51. Ibid.

52. Jeff Garnet, "Australian Law Could Spell Trouble for iPod Users," iPod Observer, November 21, 2006, http://www.ipodobserver.com/ipo/article/Australian_Law_Could_Spell_Trouble_for_iPod_Owners/.

53. Attorney General, "Copyright Amendment Act 2006," December 2006, http://www.ag.gov.au/www/agd/agd.nsf/Page/Copyright_IssuesandReviews_CopyrightAmendmentAct2006.

54. Ibid.

55. Australian Copyright Council, Copyright Amendment Act 2006, January 2007, http://www.copyright.org.au/g096.pdf.

56. Asher Moses, "Copyright Ruling Puts Hyperlinking on Notice," *Sydney Morning Herald*, December 19, 2006, http://www.smh.com.au/news/web/copyright-ruling-puts-linking-on-notice/2006/12/19/1166290520771.html.

57. Ibid.

58. Allan Swann, "Entire Copyright Act to Be Scrapped," *National Business Review*, May 1, 2009, http://www.nbr.co.nz/article/entire-copyright-act-be-scrapped-101820.

59. Ministry of Economic Development, "Copyright Protection in New Zealand," November 29, 2005, http://www.med.govt.nz/templates/Page____7290.aspx.

60. Copyright (New Technologies and Performers' Rights) Amendment, §44, http://www.parliament.nz/NR/rdonlyres/5A88D15B-C4A1-42C2-AE75-9200DD87F738/51071/DBHOH_BILL_7735_40199.pdf.

61. Judith Tizard, "Digital Copyright Bill: Questions and Answers," Official Web site of New Zealand government, December 21, 2006, http://www.beehive.govt.nz/ViewDocument.aspx?DocumentID=28179.

62. Ibid.

63. Electronic Frontiers Australia, "Defamation Laws and the Internet," January 14, 2006, http://www.efa.org.au/Issues/Censor/defamation.html#2006.

64. Australian Government, Attorney General's Department, "Defamation Law Reform," http://www.ag.gov.au/www/agd/agd.nsf/Page/Defamationlawreform_Defamationlawreform.

65. Ibid.

66. Rhonda Breit, "Uniform Defamation Laws: A Fresh Start or the Same Chilling Problems?" *Australian Policy Online*, May 11, 2006, http://search.arrow.edu.au/main/redirect_to_title?identifier=oai%3Aarrow.nla.gov.au%3A120883974282815.

67. Electronic Frontiers Australia, "Defamation Laws and the Internet," January 14, 2006, http://www.efa.org.au/Issues/Censor/defamation.html.

68. *Out-Law*, "Australia Rules on Where to Sue for Internet Defamation," December 10, 2002, http://www.out-law.com/page-3184.

69. *Dow Jones and Company Inc. v. Gutnick*, December 10, 2002, http://www.austlii.edu.au/au/cases/cth/high_ct/2002/56.html.

70. Jack Goldsmith and Tim Wu, *Who Controls the Internet? Illusions of a Borderless World* (New York: Oxford University Press, 2006), 148.

71. Caslon Analytics, "Brown, O'Brien, and Domainz," http://www.caslon.com.au/defamationprofile10.htm#brown; Simpson Grierson, "Say No Evil: Defamation in Cyberspace," FindLaw, http://www.findlaw.com/12international/countries/nz/articles/852.html.

72. Simpson Grierson, "Say No Evil: Defamation in Cyberspace," FindLaw, http://www.findlaw.com/12international/countries/nz/articles/852.html.

73. *The University of Newlands and Anor v. Nationwide News Pty. Ltd.* [2006] N.Z.S.C. 16 SC.

74. Telecommunications (Interceptions and Access) Act 1979, §7 and §108, http://www.austlii .edu.au/au/legis/cth/consol_act/taaa1979410/.

75. Electronic Frontiers Australia, "Telecommunications Privacy Laws," October 19, 2006, http:// www.efa.org.au/Issues/Privacy/privacy-telec.html.

76. Ibid.

77. Electronic Frontiers Australia, "Comments on the Surveillance Devices Bill 2004," May 18, 2004, http://www.aph.gov.au/senate/committee/legcon_ctte/completed_inquiries/2002-04/surveillance/ submissions/sub8.pdf.

78. Internet Industry Association, Cybercrime Code of Practice, §7, September 2003, http://www .iia.net.au/cybercrime_code_v2.doc (accessed March 16, 2007).

79. Internet Industry Association, Cybercrime Code of Practice, §8, September 2003, http://www .iia.net.au/cybercrime_code_v2.doc (accessed March 16, 2007).

80. Telecommunications Act 1997, §282 (3), http://www.austlii.edu.au/au/legis/cth/num_reg_es/ tar200232002n297457.html.

81. Green Party of Aotearoa New Zealand, "Fact Sheet on Government Plans for E-mail Snooping and Computer Hacking on the Public," March 31, 2001, http://www.votegreen.org.nz/searchdocs/ other4819.html.

Asia

Asie

Asia Overview

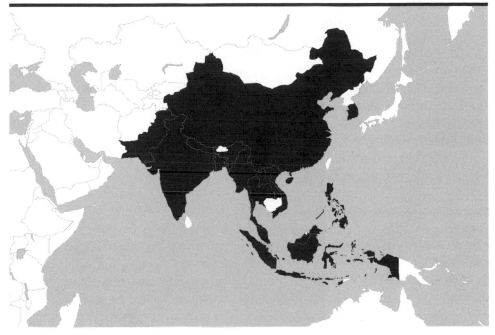

The dynamism and creativity driving the development of networked spheres in Asia showed no signs of abating through the early months of 2009. As more citizens began to utilize Internet tools for disseminating and producing information, online expression, activism, and networking have begun to permeate the national political and cultural fabric across the spectrum of Asian countries.

In 2007–2008, the OpenNet Initiative conducted in-country testing in Bangladesh, China, India, Indonesia, Laos, South Korea, Malaysia, Burma, Nepal, Pakistan, the Philippines, Singapore, Vietnam, and Thailand. Testing results found filtering practices to be largely consistent with 2006 results.

China, Burma, and Vietnam continued to rely on pervasive filtering practices to shape public knowledge and expression by targeting primarily content specific to politically sensitive topics in their own countries, especially Web sites in local languages. China, Burma, and Vietnam also continued to block with the greatest breadth and depth, spanning human rights issues, reform and opposition activities, independent media and news, and discrimination against ethnic and religious minorities. On the opposite end of the spectrum, Singapore continued to block a nominal amount of adult content and pornographic Web sites.

South Korea increased its filtering across content categories to include a selective number of the Korean-language pornography Web sites, but otherwise remained consistent with its 2006 filtering practices, specifically targeting Web sites containing North Korean propaganda or promoting the reunification of North and South Korea, as well as a handful of gambling Web sites. In contrast to 2006, ONI in 2007–2008 found no evidence of filtering of pornography and religious conversion sites in Pakistan. Otherwise, Pakistan continued to engage in security and conflict filtering as well as social filtering of Web sites containing "blasphemous" content.

The ONI found no evidence of national filtering in Indonesia, Laos, Nepal, or the Philippines. During ONI testing periods, Bangladesh, Indonesia, and Malaysia were not filtering the Internet, but media reported that these countries also began blocking selectively for brief periods in 2007–2008.

Internet in Asia

Asia continues to be home to some of the most and least connected countries in the world, while a large middle tier of countries are witnessing rapid and steady growth. In 2008, Thailand and Vietnam each reached penetration rates of a quarter of their populations.[1] China trailed at 22.6 percent,[2] though in 2008 it became the country with the most Internet users in the world, at 298 million.[3] China, where the number of Internet users increased 42 percent from 2007,[4] also saw remarkable growth in broadband usage. Over 90 percent of Internet users in China had broadband access by the end of 2008, a spike of over 100 million.[5] In contrast, concerns about a saturated market were prominent in South Korea, which by early 2008 had become the most penetrated broadband market in the world at 90 percent of households.[6] While Malaysia, with a penetration rate of 61 percent, trailed behind only Singapore in Southeast Asia and has strongly encouraged adoption of broadband Internet throughout the country,[7] broadband penetration only surpassed 17 percent in the third quarter of 2008, from 7 percent in 2005.[8]

On the opposite end of the spectrum, countries with less than a 10 percent Internet penetration rate including India, Nepal, and the Philippines have been actively promoting and investing in infrastructure and access, particularly in rural areas that have been affected most profoundly by the digital divide. About 80 percent of Bangladesh's fixed-line connections are installed in or around its four largest cities, yet about 80 percent of all Bangladeshis live outside these cities.[9] In Nepal, with an Internet penetration rate of only 1.4 percent,[10] the Nepal Wireless Project wirelessly connected 22 remote mountain villages to the Internet in five years, allowing villagers to exchange information about commodity prices, local goods, and markets, and implemented telemedicine facilities.[11]

The exception to the general embrace of information and communication technology (ICT) development has consistently been Burma. The country's largest ICT development at Yadanabon City, supported by foreign investment and set to serve as the national backbone connecting to China, India, and Thailand, is currently under construction near Mandalay.[12] However, the military government under the State Peace and Development Council (SPDC) was responsible for one of the most severe crackdowns on the Internet documented. On September 29, 2007, in order to cut off the stream of footage and images of its violent response to stopping protests led by monks and civilians, the SPDC made use of its comprehensive control over the country's Internet gateways to completely shut down Internet access (with intermittent periods of connectivity) for approximately two weeks.[13] The government also restricts upload speeds to half the download speeds for Internet subscribers and frequently implements slowdowns in Internet access speeds, which many critics claim are attempts to restrict Internet usage and enhance monitoring capabilities.[14]

The increasing popularity of interactive Web sites and social media platforms such as video-sharing sites, Web portals, discussion forums, and blogs has enabled them to have a resounding impact in Asia. By facilitating the easy production and sharing of user-generated content, online social media have served as important vehicles for news dissemination and independent expression, especially in countries where mainstream media are state controlled or closely aligned with ruling interests. For example, bloggers have been named the "fifth estate" in Asian countries such as Vietnam, Thailand, and China, whose governments maintain strict control over most news and media outlets. In Malaysia, independent news sites and blogs were credited with providing opposition parties with a platform to mobilize during the March 2008 general elections, in which the ruling Barisan Nasional (BN) coalition had its worst showing ever and five bloggers were elected to seats for opposition parties.[15] Though Internet penetration lags in rural areas (representing 15 percent of households with Internet access),[16] alternative messages and information available only online reached beyond young, middle class, and urban voters through short-message-service (SMS) messages, video compact discs (VCDs) of online television programming, and printed fliers.[17] The only media organization to provide live coverage of election results, Malaysiakini.com, has reportedly become the country's most popular alternative news source and was one of about ten of the first online news sites granted media accreditation in July 2008.[18]

In November 2007, President Pervez Musharraf of Pakistan declared a state of emergency and shut down the country's independent broadcast media, including news, sports, and entertainment television stations.[19] In response, these stations went online and offered free broadcasts on their Web sites, while YouTube became the vehicle for lawyers, journalists, and activists to post footage of protests and other news.[20]

Perhaps the most dramatic demonstration of citizens utilizing online tools to circumvent their governments' control over information occurred during the so-called Saffron Revolution in Burma. On August 19, 2007, leaders of the 88 Generation student movement organized a rally to protest a sudden sharp increase in fuel prices in Rangoon,[21] and over the next month, leadership of the protests passed to Buddhist monks, with participation swelling to an estimated crowd of 150,000 protesters on September 23.[22] Throughout these extraordinary demonstrations and the first days of the junta's violent crackdown on monks, students, and others, citizen video journalists and bloggers fed raw, graphic footage and eyewitness accounts to the outside world over the Internet and through trusted networks. This vital information was posted by overseas Burmese news organizations and international media, and fed back into the country by satellite television and radio, thus achieving a bidirectional flow of information only fully cut off when the government implemented a complete shutdown of the Internet beginning on September 29.[23] Despite the Burmese government's continuous efforts to restrict Internet access and online expression, the use of blogs and social media sites for the independent gathering and dissemination of information appears to have taken hold: in the aftermath of Cyclone Nargis in May 2008, which devastated much of the Irrawaddy river delta and left more than 138,000 dead or missing and millions in need of food, water, shelter, and medical care,[24] citizens nevertheless set out to record the damage as well as the government's response.[25]

In Asia, citizens' application of the array of Internet tools available to them has often tested societal and cultural boundaries for acceptable behavior. In 2005, a girl in South Korea who allowed her dog to defecate on the subway was filmed, tracked down, publicly exposed, and ultimately quit her university in humiliation.[26] As "dog poop girl," she became emblematic of an online vigilantism that would drive the implementation of real-name registration requirements in South Korea. Known in China as "human flesh search engines," this phenomenon can thrive across borders. For example, in April 2008, as groups around the world organized actions around the crackdown on unrest in Tibet, a Chinese student was filmed attempting to referee between two opposing groups of protesters at Duke University.[27] After the video was posted on YouTube and other Web sites, the online reaction was swift: she was lambasted in Chinese-language discussion forums and portals, and her parents living in China went into hiding after threats were painted on their apartment.[28]

Since 2006, many Asian governments have quickly realized the potential benefits of exploiting opportunities for conducting propaganda or public relations strategies over the Internet, even while cracking down on independent and critical voices thriving in these online spaces—an example of the evolution toward third-generation controls. The Chinese government has carefully orchestrated symbolic engagements with its online citizens as well as mass strategies to boost public relations. On June 20, 2008, President Hu Jintao participated in his first online chat on the People's Daily Online's

"Strong China" (*qiangguo*) discussion forum,[29] while the so-called *Fifty Cent Party*, in reference to an estimated 280,000 Web commentators nationwide who zealously support the Chinese Communist Party and were initially rumored to net 50 cents per post, are directly organized by the government to "guide" online public opinion.[30] In South Korea, with its credibility badly damaged by protests over the decision to end the ban on imports of American beef that were largely fueled by Internet debate, President Lee Myung-bak's administration ordered government ministries and organizations to begin blogging in order to inform the public of news and events.[31] It took these steps amid attempts to legislate further restrictions on what it saw to be a proliferation of slanderous and malicious commentary online. After Malaysia's general election in March 2008,[32] Prime Minister Abdullah Ahmad Badawi said that his Barisan Nasional (BN) coalition's "biggest mistake" in the elections was in believing that the "cyberwar" was unimportant.[33] Even the Burmese government, which has taken the most draconian measures to keep its citizens off-line, reportedly launched its Web portal www.khitlunge.org.mm, run by the government-aligned Union Solidarity and Development Association, to "spread government propaganda and counter media attacks by exiled Burmese media groups."[34]

Legal and Regulatory Frameworks

In 2007–2008, the leadership of many Asian governments facing political threats or crises took measures to further restrict certain forms of expression on the Internet. These measures, which especially targeted acts of cyber defamation and independent news reporting and criticism on social media platforms such as YouTube, reflected the growing relevance and impact of the Internet as a source of information from independent and diverse sources.

In Thailand, ongoing political turmoil between "red-shirt" and "yellow-shirt" factions, organized around their support of or opposition to former Prime Minister Thaksin Shinawatra and the constituencies he championed, led Thai Prime Minister Samak Sundaravej to declare a state of emergency on September 2, 2008. Upon his declaration, the Ministry of Information and Communications Technology ordered ISPs to immediately shut down around 400 Web sites and block 1,200 more, all alleged to disturb social order or endanger national security.[35] Although these Web sites were reportedly detected between March and August 2008, the blocking order and simultaneous requests for court orders required by law were instituted as the Thai government faced challenges by protesters occupying government buildings and accusations that it committed electoral fraud by buying votes in the December 2007 election.[36]

Providing an indication of the types of activities that will be targeted under the Computer Crimes Act, in March 2009 police arrested the director and moderator of the political news site www.prachatai.com for reportedly allowing a comment referencing the royal family to remain on the site for 20 days.[37] Chiranuch Premchaiporn was arrested under Section 15 of the Computer Crimes Act, which extends the liability for illegal activities to service providers that intentionally support or consent to them.[38] Illegal activities defined in the framework for regulating Internet content include inputting obscene data; forged or false data likely to cause injury to another person, the public, or national security; and data that constitute a criminal offense relating to national security or terrorism.[39] Individuals who either input these illegal data, which include online messages and information, into computer systems or publish or forward them with the knowledge of these offenses, are subject to a maximum sentence of five years imprisonment and a THB 100,000 fine.[40]

In the race to curb the "harmful" effects of social media, user-generated content, and the unabated growth of online commentary, Asian governments have enacted cyber crimes laws that purport to deter acts of online defamation and vigilantism, but could also potentially be applied to stifle citizen journalism. The Thai cyber crimes law creates civil and criminal liability for individuals who publicly post photographs of others that are "likely to" impair their reputation or expose them to shame, public hatred, or contempt.[41] In Pakistan, a cyber crimes ordinance taking effect September 2008 made "cyber stalking"—which requires "intent to coerce, intimidate, or harass any person" using computers or networks—a crime punishable by up to seven years' imprisonment.[42]

In April 2008, South Korean President Lee Myung-bak's administration agreed to resume imports of American beef after a five-year ban,[43] sparking about a hundred days of candlelight vigils and some of the largest street protests in 20 years.[44] A television program that aired on April 29 claiming that "Koreans are 94 percent more likely to contract a human form of mad cow disease" also contributed to stoking online debate, especially on the Agora forum of Korea's second-largest portal Daum (which saw its daily page view count spike from 40 million to 200 million).[45] These demonstrations also went interactive: protesters uploaded images to the Internet, sent messages on protest meet-ups and warnings on arrests via SMS, and threw themselves into online debate.[46] Ultimately, his entire cabinet resigned and President Lee was forced to call for a "new beginning" for his government.[47]

In the following months, President Lee's administration introduced legislation that would attempt to address the increase in reported online defamation, "false rumors," and "malicious postings." The regulatory body for policing online content, the Korean Communications Standards Commission, would be authorized to force Internet portals and P2P Web sites to delete content or suspend publishing for a minimum of 30 days upon receiving a complaint of articles accused of being "fraudulent" or "slanderous," during which the commission would determine whether disputed articles should be removed permanently.[48] Internet portals that fail to temporarily block online postings containing defamatory information would be subject to a fine of up to KRW 30 million or could be forced to shut down,[49] while portals or individuals involved in improperly manipulating Internet search results should be subject to imprisonment of up to one year and a fine up to KRW 10 million.[50] The proposed addition of the crime of "cyber defamation" would punish those who openly insult others through the Internet with up to two years' imprisonment or a KRW 10 million fine.[51]

The South Korean government also pursued an approach similar to its regulation of other emergent forms of harmful or illegal content—by deputizing private actors such as portals, bulletin boards, and other Internet content providers (ICPs) to actively police slanderous content. While legislation would compel them to set up constant in-house monitoring functions,[52] many of Korea's Internet portals also implemented their own measures to curb postings considered to violate privacy. For example, Naver created a simplified process for users to immediately block "groundless rumors or postings."[53]

In China, where it is common for dissidents and activists to be charged with subversion and other crimes involving national security for criticizing government officials online,[54] authorities have also begun levying criminal defamation charges against those who accuse them of corruption. A few cases of alleged online defamation publicized in Spring 2009 implicated not only the freedom of expression, but also people's right to criticize and make suggestions to any state organ, rights both guaranteed in the constitution.[55] After petitions and other attempts to protect concerned farmers' legal rights had failed, Wu Baoquan and Wang Shuai were detained for their online criticism of land seizures for commercial development pushed through by local government officials, in which farmers were inadequately compensated after being forced off their land.[56] Wu Baoquan was tried twice for criminal defamation and ultimately had his sentence increased to two years, although the same court that affirmed his conviction decided to review his case in April 2009.[57] Wang Shuai was detained on March 6, 2009, and released on bail only after signing a written confession.[58]

Since 2007, when its bloggers (now over a million strong) reportedly began discussing sensitive topics ranging from government corruption and foreign relations to HIV/AIDS,[59] Vietnam has steadily been refining its legal framework for online activity to bring social media firmly under control.

Article 12 of the Law on Information Technology defines illegal content by proxy, by prohibiting the use of digital information for the purposes of opposing the state or undermining the "all-peoples unity bloc"; inciting violence, propagating wars of aggression, sowing hatred among nations and peoples or obscenity, depravation, crime, social evils or superstition; undermining the nation's fine traditions and customs; revealing state secrets or other secrets provided for by law; distorting, slandering, or offending the prestige of organizations or the honor, dignity, or prestige of citizens; and advertising for or propagating goods or services banned by law.[60] Implementing regulations added "sowing hatred and conflict between ethnic groups and nations" to the list of prohibited acts.[61]

Internet users and organizations involved in Internet activity in Vietnam are legally responsible for the content they create, upload, store, and transmit on the Internet.[62] Bloggers are additionally responsible for ensuring that even hyperlinks do not contain illegal content.[63] However, Vietnam does offer a "safe harbor" of sorts for organizations and individuals who transmit or temporarily or automatically store information created by others. Third-party hosts and providers are generally not responsible for this content unless they initiate the transmission, choose recipients for the information, or select or modify the contents of transmitted information.[64] However, they are expressly responsible for taking "necessary measures" to stop the illegal access to or illegal deletion of information upon government request.[65] All online social services providers, including blog service providers, must be prepared to give ad hoc as well as formal, biannual reports on their services, including data on blogs that violate terms-of-service rules.[66]

Singapore, whose political elite have a long history of pursuing their opponents and critics with costly and frequent defamation suits, strengthened its penal code with amendments (effective in 2008) to include crimes committed by electronic means.[67] For example, abetting a crime now includes acts done outside of Singapore, as long as the crime was committed in Singapore.[68] In May 2008, blogger Gopalan Nair, a U.S. citizen living in Fremont, California, had returned to Singapore to support Dr. Chee Soon Juan in defamation proceedings.[69] On May 29, Nair posted his observations of the trial and called High Court judge Belinda Ang a "stooge" who was "prostituting herself" as an employee of Prime Minister Lee Hsien Loong and his father, Mentor Minister Prime Minister Lee Kuan Yew.[70] Nair was also accused of insulting another judge in an e-mail from 2006, and ultimately convicted of "intentional insult or interruption to a public servant sitting in any stage of a judicial proceeding"[71] and sentenced to three months' imprisonment on September 17, 2008.[72]

Critics of Malaysia's ruling party also continued to be targeted through the use of existing punitive legal mechanisms, as reflected in the bevy of sedition, defamation, and even national security charges levied against blogger Raja Petra Kamarudin for his online writings. On April 25, 2008, Kamarudin had published an article on his influential political Web site, Malaysia Today, linking Deputy Prime Minister Najib Razak (sworn in as Prime Minister in April 2009) and his wife to the October 2006 murder of a Mongolian translator.[73] Kamarudin was charged with sedition in May 2008[74] and faces three criminal defamation charges in a related case.[75] From September 12 to November 7, 2008, Kamarudin, who had been released on bail in May, was detained under Malaysia's notorious Internal Security Act of 1960 (ISA), which authorizes the preventive detention of individuals for up to two years (renewable indefinitely) without trial or any judicial review.[76] Kamarudin was accused of creating a national security threat by causing potential tension in Malaysia's multiracial and multifaith society through his online activities.[77]

In Pakistan, President Musharraf's crackdown on the broadcast media after declaring a state of emergency in November 2007 resulted in an actual increase in online dissemination of news and synchronicity between online and off-line citizen activism. The Pakistan Electronic Media Regulatory Authority (PEMRA) was established when Musharraf allowed for the creation of privately owned, independent broadcast media in 2002. As conditions for obtaining a broadcast license, media outlets were required to prevent content containing violence, terrorism, discrimination, extremism, sectarianism, pornography, and obscenity from receiving coverage in programming and advertising.[78] Media were also directly prohibited from broadcasting any content that is obscene, disturbs public order, endangers national security, or is "against the ideology of Pakistan."[79]

Upon declaring the state of emergency in 2007, Musharraf further amended PEMRA's charter to prohibit programming that "defames or brings into ridicule the head of state, or members of the armed forces, or executive, legislative or judicial organ of the state."[80] Video footage of suicide bombers, other terrorists, and their victims was banned,[81] and PEMRA was empowered to close any broadcast service in a "situation of emergency" and seize equipment or seal the premises of licensees "in the public interest."[82] All privately owned radio and television stations were shut down, some by force,[83] and cable operators were banned from broadcasting any national or international news channels.[84] Because Musharraf did not take such an assiduous approach toward restricting online content during the emergency, privately owned television stations taken off the air took advantage of the relative openness of the Internet and sent text messages announcing the live streaming of their programming online.[85]

Since 2007, offended citizens and groups in India have demanded that social net working Web sites be scrubbed of what they believe to be defamatory or obscene content online. Google's Orkut is the most popular social networking Web site in India and the second-most-visited portal nationally. As a result of citizens filing complaints with the police, several individuals have been arrested for violating Article 67 of the IT Act, which punishes the online publication or transmission of obscene content.[86] In February, Chandigarh IT professional Jatinder Singh Marok was alleged to have created an obscene profile on Orkut of a girl, including her personal identification and photos.[87] In another high-profile case, Rahul Krishnakumar Vaid, a 22-year-old IT consultant, was accused of posting obscene and derogatory comments about Sonia Gandhi on an Orkut forum. According to an official account, police obtained Vaid's identity by asking Google to disclose his IP address, as well as the identification information in his Gmail account.[88]

With the enactment of its cyber crimes law in June 2007, Thailand became one of the few countries in Asia to require its government to obtain court authorization to block Internet content.[89] Vietnam and South Korea are also notable in Asia for expressly mandating filtering as a preventive mechanism against "harmful" content.

Vietnam imposes a positive responsibility upon the state, society, and schools to protect children from the negative impacts of information that is either obscene or incites violence, which includes authorizing state agencies to build and disseminate content filters.[90] All providers must refuse or suspend services to individuals engaged in prohibited online activities, implement a reporting regime, and submit to inspection and examination by competent state agencies. However, online social service providers must also "block and remove illegal content upon detection or at the request of competent state agencies."[91]

South Korea authorizes regulation of Internet content through the Korea Communications Standards Commission (KCSC), whose authority extends to ordering the blocking of Web sites, the deletion of a particular message identified as an improper communication, a Web site's closure, or the suspension of the particular user ID of the individual who posted the improper writing.[92] The KCSC was originally empowered to develop general principles or codes of telecommunications ethics, conduct deliberation of and request the "correction" of information declared illegal by presidential decree, and operate reporting centers against unhealthy telecom activities.[93] Thus, its filtering mandate is part of its power to make determinations on information "harmful" to youth,[94] as well as recommend action against Web sites containing illegal content, including pornography, information for cyber criminals, gambling services, and Web sites that express support for communism or for the government of North Korea.[95]

Filtering

Asia, with its diversity, is home to several organically grown models for Internet filtering. Singapore, along with China, began experimenting with Internet filtering as early as 1996. Beginning September 15, 1996, users were forced to access the Internet through proxy servers that filtered sites banned by the Media Development Authority or MDA (then called the Singapore Broadcasting Authority, or SBA).[96] These servers reportedly contained a database of frequently accessed "approved" material, and also refused access according to an SBA list of banned Web sites.[97] At the time, the SBA targeted primarily pornography, with plans to also restrict "unacceptable political and religious discussion, defamation, and racist writings."[98] However, by 2002, these ambitions had been scaled back to the "ceremonial" filtering of a modest number of Web sites, a policy the government reaffirmed in March 2007.[99]

Singapore has refined a "dual regulation approach" to content regulation,[100] where mainstream media are state controlled or heavily regulated while alternative media such as independent Web sites and blogs are relatively free to publish. At the core of this "light touch" regulatory framework for online content is a class license scheme that requires all ISPs and those ICPs determined to be political parties or persons "engaged in the propagation, promotion or discussion of political or religious issues relating to Singapore" to register with the Media Development Authority.[101] Thus, individuals, groups, and other organizations engaged solely in the discussion of these issues online must register for a license.[102] However, the class license scheme has been rarely enforced, achieving greater efficacy in cultivating what its critics call a "culture of silence" through self-censorship.[103] In April 2007, the Singaporean government created an advisory council to study and make recommendations on its regulatory regime for "interactive digital media."[104] The Advisory Council on the Impact of New Media (AIMS) report, issued on December 8, 2008, praised the long-standing "light touch" approach to regulation of new media, while proposing some incremental changes. For example, AIMS recommended that the registration requirement for political parties be eliminated, but also argued for the class license scheme to be preserved.[105]

Like Singapore, China promoted the development of Internet infrastructure and services while strictly regulating media outlets and other forms of speech. While China has never formalized its filtering policy, it diverged from Singapore in developing aggressive filtering practices in concert with a robust internal market for Internet services and content, resulting in the emergence of public-private localized filtering.[106] In addition to the broad range of content filtered at the international gateways and through the blocking of keywords, domestic providers wishing to remain in regulatory compliance are required to install internal filtering mechanisms and devote staff resources to monitor content on their Web sites or face civil and criminal liability. For example, in April 2009 an employee of China's leading search engine, Baidu.com, leaked a folder containing the tools of internal censorship.[107] These included lists of topics, keywords, and URLs to be blocked, lists of banned forums, employee guidelines for monitoring work, censorship guidelines for the popular Baidu discussion forums called post bars, and guidelines for how to search for information that needs to be banned.[108] As a result, China has cultivated a model that buttresses a broad filtering regime with strict regulation of its own content providers, allowing it to maintain more optimal levels of control over its expansive domestic market.

For governments, the surge in user-generated content and multimedia files through online social media sites has made the implementation of filtering policies more complex.[109] In February 2008, Pakistan provided one of the most severe examples of a clumsy technical approach to restricting social media, when the government's attempt to block YouTube in Pakistan made the entire Web site inaccessible to most Internet users around the world for up to two hours.[110] On February 22, the Pakistan Telecommunication Authority (PTA) issued an order to block access to a single video on YouTube—the film *Fitna* by the Dutch parliamentarian Geert Wilders that purportedly mocked the Prophet Muhammad—while listing three IP addresses.[111] In response, the Pakistan Telecommunications Company, Ltd., the telecom that implements blocking orders, redirected requests for YouTube videos to its own network. This rerouting was advertised to the Internet at large and was picked up by the Hong Kong–based ISP PCCW, which then broadcast the redirect to ISPs around the world.[112] YouTube staff worked with PCCW to restore access within two hours.[113] Access to YouTube was restored in Pakistan after the video listed in the PTA blocking order was removed. Indonesia followed suit, ordering ISPs to block YouTube in April 2008 over the same film after Google reportedly did not respond to the government's request to remove the video from the Web site.[114]

Authorities in Bangladesh, a country with an Internet penetration rate of less than 1 percent,[115] nevertheless chose to block YouTube for a few days in March 2009 in order to protect the "national interest." The disputed video covered a partial audio recording of a meeting between the prime minister and military officials, who were angry at the government's handling of a mutiny by border guards in Dhaka that left more than 70 people dead.[116] The Bengali language blogging platform Sachalayatan was also reported to be inaccessible beginning on July 15, 2008, and was forced to migrate to a new IP address.[117] Although its blocking was not officially confirmed, Sachalayatan was likely Bangladesh's inaugural filtering event.

Even China, which has developed domestic content-control mechanisms for its Internet market that help to shield it from the difficult choices facing other countries, can be vulnerable to the reverberations of social media. Google confirmed that YouTube was blocked in China beginning on March 23, 2009,[118] which media reported could have been prompted by a graphic video released by Tibetan exiles in which Chinese troops beat a group of Tibetans.[119] Multiple users also reported that YouTube was blocked in China around March 4, 2009, coinciding with the one-year anniversary of the crackdown on protests in Tibetan regions as well as the 50th anniversary of the Tibetan uprising of 1959.[120]

As the proliferation of borderless social media reduces the effectiveness of the blacklist-and-block model, governments are increasingly looking to technology companies to act as gatekeepers for facilitating transnational public-private filtering.[121] In Asia, Thailand may present an example of an alternative to the approaches taken by China and Singapore. Thailand also blocked YouTube in April 2007 for hosting a number of videos that insulted King Bhumibol Adulyadej or his family, which constitutes a crime of lèse majesté under Thai law punishable by up to 15 years imprisonment.[122] By May 2007, YouTube agreed to remove a number of the specified videos for violating its terms of service, and the block on the YouTube domain was lifted in August 2007 upon Google's creation of a program of geolocational filtering for blocking access to specified videos for users in Thailand.[123] In 2008, investigations by a project of the MIT Free Culture group appeared to have uncovered the code for a technical mechanism that YouTube uses to allow certain videos to be seen everywhere except in those locations specified in a media restriction tag.[124] Although Thailand's filtering of the Internet has been ramped up in recent years, Thai law also requires court authorization to block a

Web site. Thus, Thailand has secured the cooperation of the world's dominant video aggregator site in implementing selective geolocational filtering on its behalf, without having to resort to a formal or transparent legal process. Its experience could also signal further public-private transnational cooperation between governments and private technology companies that result in selective filtering: a Vietnamese information ministry official stated in 2008 that the government would ask transnational gatekeepers such as Google and Yahoo to help regulate the Vietnamese blogosphere.[125]

Ultimately, there continues to be no single or uniform approach to filtering in Asia. In August 2008, in contravention of its own policy, Malaysia joined the growing collection of countries that filter the Internet. On August 27, media reported Malaysia Today blocked by order of the Malaysian Communications and Multimedia Commission (MCMC) for violating Articles 211 and 233(1) of the Communications and Multimedia Act of 1998 (CMA).[126] Malaysia Today was alleged to have published offensive, false, and indecent content, especially "comments relating to Islam and how Muslims practice it."[127] The blocking order was labeled a preventative action under Section 263 of the CMA, requiring the cooperation of licensees such as ISPs to cooperate in enforcing the laws of Malaysia.[128] Former Prime Minister Mahathir Mohamad criticized this "reneging of a promise" not to censor the Internet as loss of credibility and the public's respect.[129] Although a government official later clarified that MCMC did not receive a direct order to block Malaysia Today but had exercised its discretion under the CMA, Communications Minister Datuk Shaziman Abu Mansor disclosed that over 100 Web sites and blogs, including Malaysia Today, were blocked for violating various sections of the CMA.[130] On September 11, the Malaysian cabinet ordered the MCMC to unblock all Web sites, stating that existing laws would be used to prosecute blogs and Web sites in violation of the CMA, which would be monitored by an MCMC committee comprising police officials, officials from the Attorney General's Chambers, and the Home Ministry.[131]

Conclusion

Filtering conducted by Asian governments followed the same broad trajectories in 2007–2008 as it had previously with some incremental changes, and continues to be most clearly demarcated along national lines and by local language and content rather than according to any regional or categorical formula. Increased scrutiny of filtering practices worldwide has contributed to greater awareness about escalated filtering taking place during political events like elections and political emergencies, with at least six Asian countries reported to have blocked YouTube between 2007 and early 2009. Most of the governments in Asia where the OpenNet Initiative conducted in-country testing are expanding their legal mandate and authority to filter and regulate content, especially in targeting online defamation. As social media platforms such as video aggregator Web sites, Web portals, and online discussion forums gain in size and relevance, legal regulation of the Internet is also converging on data-retention requirements, delegated liability for ISPs and ICPs, increased criminal penalties for content producers, and other mechanisms that could create a dragnet around the individuals operating in these increasingly networked public spheres. These measures fall in line with emerging second-generation controls.

Notes

1. Paul Budde Communication Pty., Ltd., "Thailand—Key Statistics, Telecom Market Overview and Forecasts," February 11, 2009; Paul Budde Communication Pty., Ltd., "Vietnam—Key Statistics, Telecom Market Overview and Forecasts," April 11, 2009.

2. China Internet Network Information Center, "Statistical Survey Report on the Internet Development in China," March 23, 2009, http://www.cnnic.net.cn/uploadfiles/pdf/2009/3/23/131303.pdf.

3. Ibid.

4. Ibid.

5. Ibid.

6. Paul Budde Communications Pty., Ltd., "South Korea Broadband Market—Overview and Statistics," September 6, 2008, p. 1.

7. Lee Min Keong, "Malaysia Lowers Broadband Targets," *ZDNet Asia*, September 11, 2007, http://www.zdnetasia.com/news/communications/0,39044192,62032069,00.htm.

8. Malaysian Communications and Multimedia Commission, "Communications and Multimedia: Selected Facts and Figures," Q3 2008, p. 28, http://www.skmm.gov.my/facts_figures/stats/index.asp; Lee Min Keong, "Malaysia Lowers Broadband Targets," *ZDNet Asia*, September 11, 2007, http://www.zdnetasia.com/news/communications/0,39044192,62032069,00.htm; Paul Budde Communication Pty., Ltd., "Malaysia—Internet Services," February 7, 2009.

9. Paul Budde Communication Pty., Ltd., "Bangladesh—Key Statistics, Telecom Market Overview and Forecasts," December 28, 2008.

10. Miniwatts Marketing Group, "Asia Internet Usage Stats and Population Statistics," 2009, http://www.internetworldstats.com/asia.htm.

11. *Nepali Times*, "Web Pioneer—Mahabir Pun Put Nepal on the Information Technology Map Not by Complaining about How the Poor Didn't Have Access to Computers, but Actually Doing Something about It," August 3, 2007, http://www.nepalitimes.com.np/issue/360/Nation/13821.

12. Yadanabon Cyber City, http://www.yadanaboncybercity.com/.

13. OpenNet Initiative Bulletin, "Pulling the Plug: A Technical Review of the Internet Shutdown in Burma," November 2007, http://opennet.net/research/bulletins/013/.

14. Interview with public access center operator; OpenNet Initiative Blog, "Doubts Surface over Announced Internet Maintenance in Burma," March 24, 2009, http://opennet.net/blog/2009/03/doubts-surface-over-announced-internet-maintenance-burma; Lawi Weng, "Internet Slowdown to Continue at Least One More Day," *The Irrawaddy*, April 2, 2009, http://irrawaddy.org/article.php?art_id=15429; Reporters Without Borders, "Growing Restrictions on Free Flow of Information," May 15, 2009, http://www.rsf.org/Growing-restrictions-on-free-flow.html.

15. Kalinga Seneviratne, "Bloggers Sit on Opposition Benches," Inter Press Service, March 13, 2008.

16. Malaysian Communications and Multimedia Commission, "Communications and Multimedia".

17. Jeremy Au Yong, "The Next Frontier; Media Experts and Top Malaysian Bloggers Attracted Attention for the Role They Played in Malaysia's Recent General Election," *The Straits Times*, April 12, 2008.

18. Carolyn Hong, "KL Hands Out Press Passes for Online Media; Coming of Age for Internet Journalists, Who Now Can Cover Gov't Events," *The Straits Times*, July 9, 2008.

19. *Financial Express*, "Blacked Out Pakistani TV Channels Turn to Internet," November 7, 2007, http://www.financialexpress.com/news/blacked-out-pakistani-tv-channels-turn-to-internet/237012/.

20. Huma Yusuf, "Old and New Media: Converging During the Pakistan Emergency (March 2007-February 2008)," Center for Future Civic Media (MIT), January 12, 2009, http://civic.mit.edu/watchlistenlearn/old-and-new-media-converging-during-the-pakistan-emergency-march-2007-february-2008?page=0%2C0.

21. Seth Mydans, "Steep Rise in Fuel Costs Prompts Rare Public Protest in Myanmar," *New York Times*, August 22, 2007, http://www.nytimes.com/2007/08/23/world/asia/23myanmar.html.

22. Human Rights Watch, "Crackdown: Repression of the 2007 Popular Protests in Burma," December 2007, http://www.hrw.org/sites/default/files/reports/burma1207web.pdf.

23. OpenNet Initiative Bulletin, "Pulling the Plug: A Technical Review of the Internet Shutdown in Burma," November 2007, http://opennet.net/research/bulletins/013/.

24. Seth Mydans, "Myanmar Rulers Still Impeding Access," *New York Times*, June 3, 2008, http://www.nytimes.com/2008/06/03/world/asia/03myanmar.html.

25. Juliana Rincón Parra, "Myanmar: Citizen Videos in Cyclone Nargis' Aftermath," Global Voices Online, May 16, 2008, http://globalvoicesonline.org/2008/05/16/video-burmamyanmar-in-cyclone-nargis-aftermath/.

26. Jonathan Krim, "Subway Fracas Escalates into Test of the Internet's Power to Shame," *Washington Post*, July 7, 2005, http://www.washingtonpost.com/wp-dyn/content/article/2005/07/06/AR2005070601953.html.

27. The video footage is available on YouTube, http://www.youtube.com/watch?v=zomgZuZoDoM.

28. Grace Wang, "Caught in the Middle, Called a Traitor," *Washington Post*, April 20, 2008, http://www.washingtonpost.com/wp-dyn/content/article/2008/04/18/AR2008041802635.html; National Public Radio, "Duke Student Targeted for Mediating Tibet Protest," April 21, 2008, http://www.npr.org/templates/story/story.php?storyId=89803198.

29. *People's Daily Online*, "Hu Jintao Talks to Netizens via People's Daily Online," June 20, 2008, http://english.peopledaily.com.cn/90001/90776/90785/6433952.html.

30. David Bandurski, "China's Guerrilla War for the Web," *Far Eastern Economic Review*, July 2008, http://www.feer.com/essays/2008/august/chinas-guerrilla-war-for-the-web.

31. Brian Lee, "Blue House Tries to Plug the Holes in PR Machine," *JoongAng Daily*, May 6, 2009, http://joongangdaily.joins.com/article/view.asp?aid=2904455.

32. Kalinga Seneviratne, "Bloggers Sit on Opposition Benches," Inter Press Service, March 13, 2008.

33. Agence France Presse, "Malaysia PM Says 'Big Mistake' to Ignore Cyber-Campaign," March 25, 2008.

34. Min Lwin, "Junta Approves Investment in Cyber City," *The Irrawaddy*, July 30, 2008, http://www.irrawaddy.org/article.php?art_id=13614&Submit=Submit; Brian McCartan, "Myanmar on the Cyber-Offensive," *Asia Times Online*, October 1, 2008, http://www.atimes.com/atimes/Southeast_Asia/JJ01Ae01.html.

35. Oliver Luft, "Thai Government Tries to Shut Down 400 Websites," *Guardian*, September 3, 2008, http://www.guardian.co.uk/media/2008/sep/03/digitalmedia.thailand.

36. CNN.com, "Constitution Protests Continue in Thailand," June 2, 2008, http://www.cnn.com/2008/WORLD/asiapcf/06/02/thailand.protests/index.html.

37. Marwaan Macan-Markar, "MEDIA-THAILAND: Police Target Websites Unflattering to Royalty," *IPS*, March 8, 2009, http://www.ipsnews.net/news.asp?idnews=46023; Jonathan Head, "Police Arrest Thai Website Editor," *BBC News*, March 6, 2009, http://news.bbc.co.uk/mobile/i/bbc_news/asia_pacific/792/79281/story7928159.shtl.

38. Marwaan Macan-Markar, "MEDIA-THAILAND: Police Target Websites Unflattering to Royalty," *IPS*, March 8, 2009, http://www.ipsnews.net/news.asp?idnews=46023.

39. Act on Computer Crime B.E. 2550 (2007), http://advocacy.globalvoicesonline.org/wp-content/plugins/download-monitor/download.php?id=2.

40. Ibid.

41. Ibid., Section 16.

42. Article 13, Prevention of Electronic Crimes Ordinance, 2008 (Ordinance No. IV of 2008).

43. Choe Sang-hun, "Korean Leader Considers Ways to Rework Government," *New York Times*, June 11, 2008, http://www.nytimes.com/2008/06/11/world/asia/11korea.html.

44. *The Dong-a Ilbo*, "Anti-US Beef Protests: One Year Later," April 29, 2009, http://english.donga .com/srv/service.php3?biid=2009042903068.

45. Ibid.; Jon Herskovitz and Rhee So-eui, "South Korean Internet Catches 'Mad Cow Madness,'" Reuters, June 13, 2008, http://in.reuters.com/article/internetNews/idINSEO30506420080613?sp= true.

46. Jon Herskovitz and Rhee So-eui, "South Korean Internet Catches 'Mad Cow Madness,'" Reuters, June 13, 2008, http://in.reuters.com/article/internetNews/idINSEO30506420080613?sp=true.

47. Choe Sang-hun, "Korean Leader Considers Ways to Rework Government," *New York Times*, June 11, 2008, http://www.nytimes.com/2008/06/11/world/asia/11korea.html.

48. Michael Fitzpatrick, "South Korea Wants to Gag the Noisy Internet Rabble," *Guardian*, October 8, 2008, http://www.guardian.co.uk/technology/2008/oct/09/news.internet; Kim Tong-hyung, "Cabinet Backs Crackdown on Cyber-Bullying," *Korea Times*, July 22, 2008, http://www .koreatimes.co.kr/www/news/biz/2008/07/123_28003.html.

49. Kim Hyung-eun, "Do New Internet Regulations Curb Free Speech?" *JoongAng Daily*, August 13, 2008, http://joongangdaily.joins.com/article/view.asp?aid=2893577.

50. Lee Sang-bok, "New Regulations Proposed for Internet Postings," *JoongAng Daily*, August 21, 2008, http://joongangdaily.joins.com/article/view.asp?aid=2893939.

51. Ser Myo-ja, "GNP Files Bills To Alter The Nation's Media Landscape," *JoongAng Daily*, December 4, 2008, http://joongangdaily.joins.com/article/view.asp?aid=2898166.

52. Kim Hyung-eun, "Do New Internet Regulations Curb Free Speech?" *JoongAng Daily*, August 13, 2008, http://joongangdaily.joins.com/article/view.asp?aid=2893577.

53. Sung So-young, "Portals Beef Up Measures against Malicious Postings," *JoongAng Daily*, October 23, 2008, http://joongangdaily.joins.com/article/view.asp?aid=2896433.

54. See, for example, the case of Hu Jia, Amnesty International, "Hua Jia Jailed for Three and a Half Years," April 4, 2008, http://www.amnesty.org/en/news-and-updates/news/chinese-activist -gets-jail-sentence-20080403.

55. Article 41, Constitution of the People's Republic of China, http://english.peopledaily.com.cn/ constitution/constitution.html.

56. Joshua Rosenzweig, "China's Battle over the Right to Criticize," *Far Eastern Economic Review*, May 1, 2009, http://www.feer.com/essays/2009/may/chinas-battle-over-the-right-to-criticize.

57. Siweiluozi's Blog, "Update: Review Underway in Wu Baoquan's Case," April 22, 2009, http:// siweiluozi.blogspot.com/2009/04/update-review-underway-in-wu-baoquans.html; Siweiluozi's Blog, "Updated Update: Ordos Law Enforcement Officials 'Clearing Their Thoughts' Regarding Wu Baoquan," April 27, 2009, http://siweiluozi.blogspot.com/search/label/Wang%20Shuai.

58. Joshua Rosenzweig, "China's Battle over the Right to Criticize," *Far Eastern Economic Review*, May 1, 2009, http://www.feer.com/essays/2009/may/chinas-battle-over-the-right-to-criticize.

59. Geoffrey Cain, "Bloggers the New Rebels in Vietnam," *San Francisco Chronicle*, December 14, 2008, http://www.sfgate.com/cgi-bin/article.cgi?f=/c/a/2008/12/14/MNJ814GR9H.DTL&type= printable.

60. Law on Information Technology (No.67/2006/QH11), http://vbqppl4.moj.gov.vn/law/en/ 2001_to_2010/2006/200606/200606290015_en/lawdocument_view.

61. Article 6(1), Decree No. 97/2008/ND-CP of August 28, 2008, on the Management, Provision and Use of Internet Services and Electronic Information on the Internet, http://www.mic.gov.vn/ lawfiles/31236373.PDF (accessed May 25, 2009).

62. Article 9, Law on Information Technology; Article 12(2)(c), Decree on the Management, Provision and Use of Internet Services.

63. Articles 3.1, 4, Circular No. 07/2008/TT-BTTTT of December 2008, guiding a number of contents of the Government's Decree No. 97/2008/ ND-CF of August 28, 2008, on the Management, Provision and Use of Internet Services and Information on the Internet regarding the supply of information on blogs, http://www.mic.gov.vn/lawfiles/23434370.pdf (accessed May 25, 2009).

64. Article 16(4), Law on Information Technology.

65. Article 16(3), Law on Information Technology.

66. Article 6, Circular No. 07/2008/TT-BTTTT of December 2008.

67. For example, on October 13, 2008, Singapore Democratic Party (SDP) leader Chee Soon Juan and his sister were ordered to pay more than SGD 600,000 in damages for defaming Mentor Minister Prime Minister Lee Kuan Yew and his son, Prime Minister Lee Hsien Loong, in a 2006 SDP newsletter likening the conduct of government officials to another corruption scandal involving the National Kidney Foundation. Zakir Hussain, "PM, MM Get $950k Damages; Amount Determined in Part by 'Egregious' Conduct of the Chees," *The Straits Times*, October 14, 2008.

68. Article 108B, Penal Code (Amendment) Act 2007, http://statutes.agc.gov.sg/non_version/ html/homepage.html.

69. Inter Press Service, "Singapore: State Sues Blogger for Criticizing High Court Judge," June 7, 2008.

70. Urban Rant Blog, "Singapore Courts Grant Arrest Warrant Without Bail For Insulting a Judge," June 2, 2008, http://singaporedissident.blogspot.com/2008/05/singapore-judge-belinda -angs-kangaroo.html.

71. Article 228, Penal Code (Amendment) Act 2007, http://statutes.agc.gov.sg/non_version/html/ homepage.html.

72. Zakir Hussain, "Gopalan Nair Jailed 3 Mths," *The Straits Times*, September 17, 2008, http:// www.asiamedia.ucla.edu/article-southeastasia.asp?parentid=97420.

73. Lee Glendinning, "Malaysian Blogger Raja Petra Kamarudin Goes on Trial over Sedition Charges," *Guardian*, October 6, 2008, http://www.guardian.co.uk/world/2008/oct/06/malaysia .pressandpublishing.

74. *New York Times*, "Malaysian Blogger Charged with Sedition," May 6, 2008, http://www.nytimes.com/2008/05/06/world/asia/06iht-malay.1.12610343.html.

75. Kamarudin allegedly defamed Razak's wife, Datin Rosmah Mansor, Lieutenant Colonel Abdul Aziz Buyong, and Lieutenant Colonel Norhayati Hassan in a public court declaration in June 2008. Sushma Veera, "Second Arrest Warrant Out for Raja Petra," *New Straits Times*, May 26, 2009, http://www.nst.com.my/Current_News/NST/Wednesday/National/2567087/Article/index.html.

76. Human Rights Watch, "Detained Without Trial: Abuse of Internal Security Act Detainees in Malaysia," September 26, 2005, http://www.hrw.org/en/reports/2005/09/26/detained-without-trial-0.

77. Pertubuhan Berita Nasional Malaysia, "Detained Raja Petra's Actions Threat to National Security—Deputy IGP," September 12, 2008.

78. Article 20, Pakistan Electronic Media Regulatory Ordinance 2002, http://www.pemra.gov.pk/pdf/ordinance1.pdf.

79. Article 27, Pakistan Electronic Media Regulatory Ordinance 2002, http://www.pemra.gov.pk/pdf/ordinance1.pdf.

80. Article 20(m), Pakistan Electronic Media Regulatory Ordinance, 2007 (LXV of 2007), http://www.pemra.gov.pk/pdf/ord031107.pdf.

81. Article 20(j), Pakistan Electronic Media Regulatory Ordinance, 2007 (LXV of 2007), http://www.pemra.gov.pk/pdf/ord031107.pdf.

82. Article 30(4), Pakistan Electronic Media Regulatory Ordinance, 2007 (LXV of 2007), http://www.pemra.gov.pk/pdf/ord031107.pdf.

83. CNN.com, "Pakistani Police Storm Television Station," November 3, 2007, http://www.cnn.com/2007/WORLD/asiapcf/11/03/pakistan.media/.

84. Muhammad Najeeb, "Pakistani Media Gagged, Even Internet Not Spared," *Hindustan Times*, November 4, 2007, http://www.hindustantimes.com/StoryPage/StoryPage.aspx?id=460572ab-dea2-4703-93e4-280a1763bbf4&&Headline=Pakistani+media+gagged%2c+even+Internet+not+spared.

85. *Financial Express*, "Blacked Out Pakistani TV Channels Turn to Internet," November 7, 2007, http://www.financialexpress.com/news/blacked-out-pakistani-tv-channels-turn-to-internet/237012/.

86. Information Technology Act, Article 67, 2000. Under the act, anyone who publishes "any material which is lascivious or appeals to the prurient interest or if its effect is such as to tend to deprave and corrupt ..." is subject to a fine and up to five years in prison. See http://www.sarai.net/journal/pdf/133-135%20(bill).pdf (accessed May 25, 2009).

87. Press Trust of India, "IT Professional Held for Creating Girl's Obscene Orkut Profile," February 21, 2008, http://www.expressindia.com/latest-news/IT-professional-held-for-creating-obscene-Orkut-profile/275541/.

88. *Times of India*, "One Held for Posting Obscene Orkut Message on Sonia," May 18, 2008, http:// timesofindia.indiatimes.com/Pune/One_held_for_posting_obscene_Orkut_message_on_Sonia/ articleshow/3049971.cms.

89. Article 20, Act on Computer Crime B.E. 2550 (2007), English translation at http://advocacy .globalvoicesonline.org/wp-content/plugins/download-monitor/download.php?id=2.

90. Article 73, Law on Information Technology (No.67/2006/QH11), http://vbqppl4.moj.gov.vn/ law/en/2001_to_2010/2006/200606/200606290015_en/lawdocument_view.

91. Article 11(c), Decree No. 97/2008/ND-CP of August 28, 2008, on the Management, Provision and Use of Internet Services and Electronic Information on the Internet, http://www.mic.gov.vn/ lawfiles/31236373.PDF (accessed May 25, 2009).

92. See Decisions of the Korean Constitutional Court, Opinion 14–1 KCCR 616, 99Hun-Ma480, June 27, 2002, http://www.ccourt.go.kr/home/english/decision_etc/decision2003.htm.

93. Article 53–2, Telecommunications Business Act (1995), Law 4903, January 5, 1995, http:// www.itu.int/ITU-D/treg/Legislation/Korea/BusinessAct.htm.

94. KCSC, "Operation Committees," http://www.icec.or.kr/eng/02_Operation/Committees.php.

95. KCSC, "Subject of Report," http://www.singo.or.kr/eng/02_report/Subject_Report.php; Reporters Without Borders, "South Korea—2004 Annual Report," http://www.rsf.org/en-rapport59 -id_rubrique416-South_Korea.html.

96. *The Economist*, "NetNanny States China and Singapore Restrict Citizens' Access to World Wide Web," September 14, 1996, http://www.highbeam.com/doc/1G1-18675318.html.

97. Robert Uhlig, "Singapore to Censor Net Porn, Violence," *Daily Telegraph*, September 3, 1996.

98. United Press International, "Singapore Begins to Block Internet," September 14, 1996.

99. Ministry of Information, Communications, and the Arts, "Censorship Review Committee Report of 2003," http://www.mda.gov.sg/wms.file/mobj/mobj.316.Censorship_Review_2003.pdf; Agence France Presse, "Singapore Vigilant on Sedition, 'Ceremonial' on Porn Censorship," March 22 2007.

100. Cherian George, "One Country, Two Systems: For How Long?" Singapore: New Media, Politics & the Law, March 10, 2007, http://singaporemedia.blogspot.com/2007_03_01_archive.html; Tor Ching Li, "The Dangers of Dual Media Regulation," Channel News Asia, January 12, 2007, http://www.channelnewsasia.com/stories/singaporelocalnews/view/252084/1/.html.

101. Broadcasting (Class License) Notification 2001, July 15, 1996, http://www.mda.gov.sg/ wms.file/mobj/mobj.487.ClassLicense.pdf (accessed January 1, 2007).

102. See Media Development Authority (MDA), "Internet," http://www.mda.gov.sg/wms.www/ devnpolicies.aspx?sid=161.

103. "Proposals for Internet Freedom in Singapore," April 21, 2008, http://www.yawningbread .org/ybsamplerfiles/bloggerssub.pdf.

104. The Online Citizen, "AIMS Seeks Feedback On New Media," September 17, 2008, http://theonlinecitizen.com/2008/09/aims-seeks-feedback-on-new-media/.

105. IFACCA, "Engaging New Media, Challenging Old Assumptions, A Report by the Advisory Council on the Impact of New Media on Society," pp. 74–76, December 2008, http://www.ifacca.org/national_agency_news/2009/01/09/engaging-new-media-challenging-old-assumptions/.

106. Robert Faris, Stephanie Wang, and John Palfrey, "Censorship 2.0," *Innovations: Technology/Governance/Globalization* (MIT Press), Winter 2008.

107. Xiao Qiang, "Baidu's Internal Monitoring and Censorship Document Leaked," *China Digital Times*, April 30, 2009, http://chinadigitaltimes.net/2009/04/baidus-internal-monitoring-and-censorship-document-leaked/.

108. Ibid.

109. Robert Faris, Stephanie Wang, and John Palfrey, "Censorship 2.0," *Innovations: Technology/Governance/Globalization* (MIT Press), Winter 2008.

110. OpenNet Initiative Blog, "Pakistan's Internet Has a Bad Weekend," February 25, 2008, http://opennet.net/blog/2008/02/pakistan%E2%80%99s-internet-has-a-bad-weekend; Martin A. Brown, "Pakistan Hijacks YouTube," Renesys Blog, February 24, 2008, http://www.renesys.com/blog/2008/02/pakistan_hijacks_youtube_1.shtml.

111. "Corrigendum—Most Urgent: Subject: Blocking of Offensive Website," Pakistan Telecommunication Authority, February 22, 2008, http://www.renesys.com/blog/pakistan_blocking_order.pdf.

112. Declan McCullagh, "How Pakistan Knocked YouTube Offline (and How to Make Sure It Never Happens Again)," *CNet News*, February 25, 2008, http://www.news.com/8301-10784_3-9878655-7.html.

113. Martin A. Brown, "Pakistan Hijacks YouTube," Renesys Blog, February 24, 2008, http://www.renesys.com/blog/2008/02/pakistan_hijacks_youtube_1.shtml.

114. CNN.com, "Indonesia Blocks YouTube to Protest Islam Film," April 8, 2008, http://www.cnn.com/2008/WORLD/asiapcf/04/08/indonesia.youtube/index.html.

115. Paul Budde Communication Pty., Ltd., "Bangladesh, Key Statistics, Telecom Market Overview and Forecasts," December 28, 2008.

116. *BBC News*, "Bangladesh Imposes YouTube Block," March 9, 2009, http://news.bbc.co.uk/2/hi/south_asia/7932659.stm.

117. Aparna Ray, "Bangladesh Gets a 'Blog-Ban' Scare," Global Voices Online, July 28, 2008, http://globalvoicesonline.org/2008/07/28/bangladesh-gets-a-blog-ban-scare/.

118. OpenNet Initiative Blog, "Google Confirms YouTube Blocked in China," March 24, 2009, http://opennet.net/blog/2009/03/google-confirms-youtube-blocked-china.

119. Jane Macartney, "Film of Tibet Violence May Have Prompted China to Block YouTube," *The Times*, March 26, 2009, http://www.timesonline.co.uk/tol/news/world/asia/article5975252.ece.

120. See Herdict, http://www.herdict.org.

121. Robert Faris, Stephanie Wang, and John Palfrey, "Censorship 2.0," *Innovations: Technology/Governance/Globalization* (MIT Press), Winter 2008, p. 175.

122. *The Nation*, "Ban on YouTube Lifted after Deal: Website to Block Clips Offensive to Thais or That Break Thai Law," August 31, 2007, http://www.nationmultimedia.com/2007/08/31/headlines/headlines_30047192.php.

123. Ibid.; *Sydney Morning Herald*, "YouTube Removes Clips Mocking Thai King," May 12, 2007, http://www.smh.com.au/news/World/YouTube-removes-clips-mocking-Thai-king/2007/05/12/1178899145725.html.

124. OpenNet Initiative Blog, "YouTube and the Rise of Geolocational Filtering," March 13, 2008, http://opennet.net/blog/2008/03/youtube-and-rise-geolocational-filtering.

125. Geoffrey Cain, "Bloggers the New Rebels in Vietnam," *San Francisco Chronicle*, December 14, 2008, http://www.sfgate.com/cgi-bin/article.cgi?f=/c/a/2008/12/14/MNJ814GR9H.DTL&type=printable.

126. See Malaysia Today, "Move to Block Blog 'Not Govt Directive,'" August 30, 2008, https://mt.m2day.org/2008/content/view/11968/84/. Article 211(1) makes it illegal to provide content which is indecent, obscene, false, menacing, or offensive in character with intent to annoy, abuse, threaten, or harass any person. According to Article 233, it is illegal for any person to make any comment, request, suggestion, or other communication transmitting the same types of illegal content over networks. Articles 211(1), 233, Malaysian Communications and Multimedia Act of 1998, http://www.skmm.gov.my/the_law/NewAct/Act%20588/Act%20588/a0588s0211.htm.

127. *The Edge Malaysia*, "Net Value: CMA Provides for Prohibition of Offensive Content," September 8, 2008.

128. Ibid.

129. *The Straits Times*, "Mahathir Slams Blocking of Malaysia Today Portal," August 30, 2008.

130. *The Star Online*, "SKMM Not Ordered to Block Access to Website," August 30, 2008, http://thestar.com.my/news/story.asp?file=/2008/8/30/nation/22210685&sec=nation.

131. Sim Leoi Leoi and Florence A. Sam, "MCMC Told to Unblock Malaysia Today (Update 2)," *The Star Online*, September 11, 2008, http://thestar.com.my/news/story.asp?file=/2008/9/11/nation/20080911145128&sec=nation.

Burma

Despite very low connectivity, Internet users in Burma have managed to communicate valuable information to the outside world during explosive political events. The Burmese military government continues to enforce stringent overall access restrictions, the most extreme of which occurred during the complete shutdown of the Internet in Burma in September and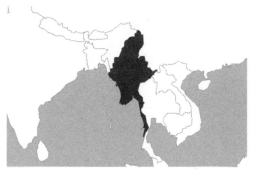
October 2007. On top of these barriers to access, the government also polices Internet content through one of the most severe regimes of information control in the world.

Background

The State Peace and Development Council (SPDC), the military government that rules the Union of Myanmar, maintained its stranglehold on economic and political developments in Burma through several major crises in 2007 and 2008.

On August 19, 2007, precipitating what would become known as the Saffron Revolution, leaders of the 88 Generation student movement organized a rally to protest a sudden sharp increase in fuel prices in Rangoon (Yangon).[1] Burmese spend up to

RESULTS AT A GLANCE					
Filtering	No Evidence of Filtering	Suspected Filtering	Selective Filtering	Substantial Filtering	Pervasive Filtering
Political					•
Social				•	
Conflict and security				•	
Internet tools				•	

Other Factors	Low	Medium	High	Not Applicable
Transparency		•		
Consistency		•		

KEY INDICATORS	
GDP per capita, PPP (constant 2005 international dollars)	854
Life expectancy at birth (years)	62
Literacy rate (percent of people age 15+)	90
Human development index (out of 179)	135
Rule of law (out of 211)	199
Voice and accountability (out of 209)	208
Democracy index (out of 167)	163 (Authoritarian regime)
Digital opportunity index (out of 181)	179
Internet users (percent of population)	0.1

Source by indicator: World Bank 2005, World Bank 2009a, World Bank 2009a, UNDP 2008, World Bank 2009b, World Bank 2009b, Economist Intelligence Unit 2008, ITU 2007, ITU 2008.

70 percent of their monthly income on food alone,[2] making the fuel price hikes amid chronic inflation—which reached 30 percent in 2006 and 2007—untenable.[3] Over the next month, leadership of the protests passed from the former student leaders and a number of female activists to Buddhist monks, with participation swelling to an estimated crowd of 150,000 protesters on September 23.[4] Throughout the crisis, citizen journalists and bloggers continued to feed raw, graphic footage and eyewitness accounts to the outside world over the Internet. The violent crackdown that began on September 26 ultimately left up to 200 dead,[5] including a Japanese journalist whose shooting was caught on video.[6] Burmese security forces raided monasteries, detaining and disrobing thousands of monks, and despite claims in official state media that only 91 people remained in detention as of December 2007, Human Rights Watch claimed the number to be in the hundreds.[7]

On May 2 and 3, 2008, Cyclone Nargis hit lower Burma and devastated Rangoon and much of the Irrawaddy River delta, with more than 138,000 dead or missing and millions in need of food, water, shelter, and medical care.[8] After initially blocking aid for two critical weeks, the junta accepted relief efforts coordinated through the Tripartite Core Group—the military junta, the United Nations (UN), and the Association of Southeast Asian Nations (ASEAN)—and has been cautiously credited with exhibiting greater openness since.[9] However, a year later, half a million people were still living in temporary shelters, over 200,000 lacked local supplies of drinking water, and villagers were still coping with chronic food shortages and the slow resumption of farming and fishing.[10] A recovery program requiring USD 690 million through 2011 had raised only USD 466 million in commitments at the end of 2008.[11]

On the heels of the release of Burma's longest-serving political prisoner, Win Tin, a 79-year-old journalist freed as part of an amnesty granted to 9,000 inmates,[12] around 300 individuals were sentenced to harsh prison terms for political crimes between October and December 2008.[13] Most were tried by police prosecutors and convicted by judges operating from prison courts, including the notorious Insein prison.[14] During the week of November 10, 2008, alone, more than 80 individuals were convicted, including 14 democracy activists who were sentenced to 65 years' imprisonment for leading protests in the summer of 2007, Buddhist monks, poets, musicians, and student leaders.[15] According to the UN Special Rapporteur on the situation of human rights in Myanmar, 16 journalists and bloggers were in prison in March 2009.[16] Not surprisingly, given the crackdown that followed, the Committee to Protect Journalists has labeled Burma the worst place in the world to be a blogger.[17]

On May 14, 2009, Nobel laureate and democracy leader Aung San Suu Kyi was taken from her home to Insein prison to stand charges of violating the terms of her house arrest by affording temporary shelter to an American man who had swum across a lake to her residence.[18] Aung San Suu Kyi, facing five years' imprisonment under these charges, had lived under house arrest for 13 of the past 19 years, and she was arrested only weeks before her current six-year term was set to expire.[19]

Internet in Burma

Unlike the rest of Asia, a combination of government restrictions, connection speeds, and prohibitive costs has kept Internet access rates relatively stagnant in Burma. The International Telecommunications Union estimates the number of Internet users at a low 45,000 for 2008,[20] representing a steep drop from recent figures of up to 300,000 users.[21] Burma's fixed-line, cell phone, and Internet penetration rates remain below 1 percent.[22] Connection speeds are slow, and steep costs significantly limit access. For example, initial costs for broadband range from USD 900 on Myanmar Teleport (MMT) to USD 2,300 on Myanmar Post and Telecommunication (MPT), with wireless access on MMT starting at USD 1,500.[23] As a result, broadband is available only to an estimated 2,000 subscribers, primarily government and businesses and used mostly for Internet telephony by VoIP.[24] Assuming that there are about ten to 15 users per subscription, media have calculated that there are more than 300,000 users of MMT (formerly Bagan Cybertech) and MPT, the two state-owned ISPs. Costs limit access significantly: even households that can afford a personal computer and long-distance connection fees outside the capital Rangoon and Mandalay cannot pay USD 20 per month and upward for a dial-up or broadband account.[25]

According to news reports, an entity called Information Technology Central Services (ITCS) was launched in 2007, to be run by the government-aligned Union Solidarity and Development Association.[26] Though ITCS is not an ISP, it provides telecommunication services such as voice mail, mail to SMS (short message service, or text message), and an information portal (www.khitlunge.org.mm).

However, the arrival of a new ISP, predicted to become the largest in Burma, presented the most convincing evidence that the government intended to expand

Internet access while maintaining strict control over online activity. The new ISP, Hanthawaddy National Gateway, which was reportedly launched in July 2008, will serve the entire country with the exception of Rangoon.[27] In the case of Hanthawaddy, which officials state will operate to "international standards," Internet security will be achieved largely through filtering. According to an MPT official, "The main advantages of having this ISP is that the Internet connection will be fast-moving, and good security will be available because of the website filtering system."[28] The Irrawaddy, an overseas news site, reported that Hanthawaddy "received technical assistance from China's Alcatel Shanghai Bell Company."[29]

As a signatory to the e-ASEAN Framework Agreement initiated in 2000, Burma has formed the e-National Task Force to support IT development.[30] Yadanabon Cyber City (in Pyin Oo Lwin), set to become Burma's largest IT development, is also part of an information and communications technology (ICT) development master plan under the Initiative for ASEAN Integration (IAI).[31]

Although the government initially cited a preference for investment from local companies or foreign companies that are cooperating with local companies, rather than solely foreign-owned enterprise, three foreign companies—Russian-owned CBOSS, Maxinet of Australia, and Global Technology (believed to be based in either Thailand or the U.K.)—were among the 12 technology companies approved to invest USD 22 million in the site, which is somewhat isolated by being 30 miles from Mandalay.[32] However, Shin Satellite of Thailand, Alcatel Shanghai Bell of China, and Malaysia's IP Tel Sdn Bh were reportedly rejected as investment partners.[33] The Irrawaddy quoted sources from computer universities as stating that Yadanabon's objective was to tighten control over Internet connections as well as prevent users from gaining access to or distributing information critical of the regime.[34]

Both MPT and MMT are currently connected to the Hanthawaddy Gateway backbone (a move announced in September 2008 but only recently executed),[35] but Yadanabon will ultimately serve as the national backbone (with a bandwidth of 600+ Mbps according to some sources), connected to China and eventually India and Thailand through overhead optical fiber (STM 1 or higher), underground optical fiber (STM 1 or higher), satellite communication systems, and the SMW-3 undersea cable system.[36]

To counterbalance price and access controls, most users access the Internet in Internet cafés (between USD 0.30 and USD 0.50 per hour).[37] Officially, there are 433 public access centers (PACs) nationwide, and the government plans to achieve full coverage of PACs in every township in the country.[38] In reality, the number of PACs and Internet cafés has increased rapidly in Rangoon, Mandalay, and other major towns and cities across the country, with more than 1,000 PACs operating without licenses in Rangoon alone.[39] Some PACs are owned by Union Solidarity and Development Association (USDA) and run Internet café services in their local offices in townships. Some

PACs provide VoIP services such as Skype, Pfingo, MediaRingTalk, and others. Centers are prevented from installing bypass software on their computers, but generally allow customers to use laptops. According to one PAC operator, 60 percent of users use dial-up connections or prepaid access kits while the rest use broadband connections such as ADSL or WiMAX, as well as satellite connections provided by the state-controlled MMT and MPT.

Despite the limitations imposed on connectivity in Burma, throughout the days of escalating protests in September 2007 and the first glimpses of a violent crackdown, a small band of citizen bloggers and journalists fed graphic footage and eyewitness accounts to the outside world through the Internet and their personal networks.[40] Vital information, including photographs and videos taken with cell phones and digital cameras and not obtainable through traditional means, was uploaded to the Internet, broadcast over television and radio, and spread in communities throughout the country. Although described invariably as tech-savvy university students and youth, these citizen journalists helped multiple generations of Burmese to find linkages to each other through blogs and other social media.[41]

On September 29, 2007, the SPDC made use of its comprehensive control over the country's Internet gateways to completely shut down Internet access, with intermittent periods of connectivity, for approximately two weeks.[42] A small group of netizens had vividly demonstrated that the tools of information technology can have a strong impact on the global coverage of events as they are unfolding. The Internet shutdown was the government's most direct and drastic option to cut off this bidirectional flow of information, so that the picture of reality for people on both sides of the Burmese border would remain distorted.

In April 2008, the overseas news organization Mizzima News reported that the government had formulated a sector-based Internet shutdown strategy to deal with the constitutional referendum scheduled for May 10.[43] As soon as information leaks began, Internet cafés and PACs would be cut off, followed by the commercial sector if information continued to flow out, and presumably by the hospitality and tourism sector. Authorities planned both shutdowns of access and significant slowdowns in connection speeds,[44] a strategy that was made moot in the wake of Cyclone Nargis.

Slowdowns in Internet access speeds are not infrequent in Burma. For example, a prolonged slowdown on MMT began on March 22, 2009, and continued until April 21.[45] MMT had announced that the submarine cable SE-ME-WE 3 (South East Asia Middle West Europe 3) would be undergoing maintenance from March 21 to March 25, but both MMT and MPT shut down their service for several hours on the afternoon of March 22. For end users, the announced network maintenance resulted in frustration with delays (in addition to those caused by the use of circumvention tools) in accessing popular online services, including Gmail, Google Talk, Skype,

Pfingo, and VZOChat, while many Internet cafés were closed while waiting for the resumption of normal Internet access speeds.

Slow upload speeds are an indication not just of capacity in Burma, but also of intentional design. Even after connectivity was largely resumed after the Internet shutdown, Internet speeds controlled with proxy caching servers were slowed to 256 Kbps in a likely attempt to prevent or diminish the uploading of videos and photos.[46] Although broadband subscribers can choose to pay according to access speeds (512 kbps, 256 kbps, or 128 kbps), they must also accept upload speeds that are half the download speeds in each subscription.[47]

Legal and Regulatory Frameworks

Despite ongoing and grave human rights violations committed by the SPDC, equal protection under the law (Art. 347), freedom of expression and peaceful assembly (Art. 354), the right to education (Art. 366), freedom of religion (Art. 36), and other fundamental rights are guaranteed in the amended constitution adopted in May 2008.[48] Although the SPDC has stated that 380 domestic laws are being reviewed for compliance with constitutional human rights provisions,[49] it continues to apply broad laws and regulations to punish citizens harshly for any activity deemed detrimental to national interests or its continued grip on power.

All domestic radio and television stations, as well as daily newspapers, are state owned and controlled.[50] While more than 100 print publications are now privately owned,[51] the Ministry of Information limits licensing to media outlets that agree to print only approved material and to submit to vigorous advanced censorship by its Press Scrutiny and Registration Division.[52] For example, in the wake of Cyclone Nargis, media were prohibited from publishing stories depicting the devastation and human suffering.[53] Publishing license regulations issued by the Ministry of Information in 2005 are prodigious in scope, banning negative news and commentary about ASEAN, any "nonconstructive" criticism of government departments, coverage of national disasters and poverty that affect the public interest, and the citation of foreign news sources that are detrimental to the state.[54] In effect since 1962, the Printers and Publishers Registration Law applies to all "printed published matter" and requires the registration of all printing presses, printers, and publishers, as well as the submission of all books and newspapers as they are published.[55] Similar restrictions apply in the Video and Television Law, which provides for three years' imprisonment for "copying, distributing, hiring or exhibiting videotape" that has not received the prior approval of the Video Censor Board.[56]

Online access and content are stringently controlled through legal, regulatory, and economic constraints. As in other areas, however, the state's policies are difficult to assess because they are rarely published or explained.

According to the 1996 Computer Science Development Law (CSDL), network-ready computers must be registered (for a fee) with the MPT; failure to do so can result in fines and prison sentences of seven to 15 years.[57] In the Electronic Transactions Law (2004), anyone who uses "electronic transactions" technology to receive or send information relating to state secrets or state security or to commit any act harming state security, community peace and tranquility, or national solidarity, economy, or culture can be sentenced to between seven and 15 years' imprisonment.[58] Terms-of-service rules for MPT users issued in 2000 provide a warning that online content will be subject to the same kind of strict filtering that the Press Scrutiny and Registration Division carries out: users must obtain MPT permission before creating Web pages, and they cannot post anything "detrimental" to the government or simply related to politics.[59] Furthermore, sharing registered Internet connections is also punishable by revocation of access and the threat of "legal action,"[60] the equivalent to which can be found in the CSDL, which punishes unauthorized computer networks or links with seven to 15 years' imprisonment.[61] The MPT can also "amend and change regulations on the use of the Internet without prior notice."[62]

The threat to the junta posed by Burmese activists and other dissenting voices using online tools to communicate with and transmit information to the outside world became evident in the rash of draconian sentences handed down in November 2008 against 88 Generation's leaders, bloggers, and others. Closed courts, mostly operating out of Insein prison, applied the Electronic Transactions Law and the Television and Video Law to deliver sentences of up to 65 years. On November 11, fourteen 88 Generation activists were sentenced to 65 years' imprisonment, a staggering term consisting of 15 years for each of four counts of illegally using electronic media[63]; formation of an illegal organization added five years to that sentence.[64] Nay Phone Latt, a blogger and owner of several Internet cafés, was arrested in January 2008 and sentenced in November to 20 years' imprisonment by a special court in Insein prison, 15 of those years for violating Articles 33(a) and 38 of the Electronic Transactions Law and over three years of the sentence for violating Article 32(b) and 36 of the Television and Video Law.[65]

The Electronic Transactions Law also constituted part of the 59-year sentence handed down to comedian, film director, and blogger Maung Thura (who uses the stage name Zarganar), convicted for circulating his footage of relief work after Cyclone Nargis on DVD and the Internet, as well as for giving interviews critical of government aid efforts to overseas media.[66] Both Nay Phone Latt and Zarganar had their sentences reduced, to 12 and 35 years, respectively, in February 2009.[67]

As for Internet cafés, the government has been urging business owners to become licensed as PACs under the management of Myanmar Info-Tech, a state-owned company.[68] The general manager of Myanmar Info-Tech claimed that more than 1,000 Internet cafés were operating in Rangoon without PAC licenses, and café owners reportedly have informal bribe-paying arrangements with government employees that allow them to operate and offer proxy tools and other services that are technically forbidden.[69] In addition to requirements that screenshots be taken every five minutes and that records of Internet usage be sent to Myanmar Info-Tech every two weeks, café owners are told to arrange computer monitors for easy public viewing and to ensure that only state-run e-mail providers are used.[70] Operators of PACs must also record the names, identification numbers, and addresses of their customers.[71] However, it is widely reported that, despite regular crackdowns, most PAC owners largely ignore these regulations and provide customers with proxy servers and alternative means of accessing blocked Web sites.[72]

Surveillance

In Burma, the fear of surveillance is pervasive and embedded in daily life.[73] Offline, the state can effectively monitor its citizens through a dragnet that functions with the assistance of various civilian organizations it directly controls. These overlapping organizations include mass organizations such as the USDA, which imposes mandatory membership on citizens in specific professions and is being cultivated as a "future military-controlled civilian government in Burma," with President Gen Than Shwe as a primary patron.[74] State and local Peace and Development Councils (PDCs) are also effective tools of social control. For example, all households must provide their local ward PDCs with a list and photographs of all persons residing in the household and register any overnight guests before dark, a policy that is reinforced by regular mid-night checks of homes.[75] Another mass-based organization, known as the Swan Arr Shin, pays its members to conduct routine neighborhood surveillance and police as-sistance, delegating others to engage in violence against opposition figures for higher remuneration.[76] During the Fall 2007 protests, intelligence officials videotaped and photographed protesters, and security forces relied on the information to enlist PDCs, the USDA, and local law enforcement authorities in identifying individuals in order to immediately begin making arrests in the ensuing crackdown.[77]

Until it was disbanded in 2004, the Defense Services Computer Directorate (DSCD) had become focused on information warfare operations such as monitoring telephone calls, faxes, and e-mails focused on military communications, while the computer center of the intelligence agency Directorate of Defense Services Intelligence (DDSI) under the Ministry of Defense monitored opposition groups.[78] After the DSCD was reformed as the Military Affairs Security (MAS), it presumably took over information warfare duties.[79]

While the government's aptitude at conducting online surveillance is not entirely clear, it certainly appears to be pursuing a combination of methods to monitor the small proportion of its citizens that access the Internet. Despite the reported wide-spread lack of compliance, at the most popular Internet access point—Internet cafés—owners and operators, as mentioned earlier, are required to record users' personal identification, take screenshots every five minutes, arrange computer monitors for easy public viewing, allow the use of only state-run e-mail providers, and forbid the use of circumvention tools.[80] A new service in 2009, Mtalk, offers an instant messaging application and private e-mail and is a rare joint venture between MPT and a private company, Myanmar Technology Gateway.[81] Mtalk's MPT-hosted server can access GTalk with a single login, causing Internet users to worry about potential surveillance and the exposure of their contact lists.[82]

The military government's stringent filtering regime fosters fear and self-censorship. For example, according to ONI sources the banning of certain political blogs in mid-2007 sparked rumors that more would be banned if this trend continued, spurring many local bloggers to self-monitor their postings in the hope that their blogs would not be added to the blacklist.[83] Government e-mail services, theoretically boosted by the blocking of many free Web-based e-mail services, are widely believed to be under surveillance, with delays of up to several days between the sending and receipt of e-mails, or with messages appearing with attachments deleted.[84] Blogger Nay Phone Latt was allegedly convicted in part for storing a cartoon of General Than Shwe in his e-mail account.[85] Internet slowdowns fuel speculation of enhanced online monitoring, especially where users are required to click through pages equipped with network visibility applications (such as Bluecoat) that allow for monitoring of network activity and behavior in order to access the Internet.[86]

Surveillance methods are more effective when there are fewer targets, and a possible strategy of the Burmese regime may be to keep more people offline. During the October 2007 Internet shutdown, surveillance, or at least perceived surveillance, was attributed as a rationale for various government responses, including the government's policy of originally limiting Internet access to the curfew hours between 9:00 p.m. and 5:00 a.m.[87] Not only would the late hours significantly reduce the number of users (as most Burmese users do not have access to the Internet at home), but it would also make the task of identifying targeted users easier for a government without much experience in tracking and investigating Internet usage.

In 2008, persistent and severe distributed denial of service (DDoS) attacks hit the Democratic Voice of Burma (DVB) and Mizzima News in July, the community forums Mystery Zillion and Planet Myanmar in August, and The Irrawaddy, DVB, and the New Era Journal in September.[88] In all these attacks, these Web sites, mostly overseas news organizations, were effectively inaccessible after being flooded with data in short amounts of time and thus becoming overloaded with information requests.[89]

ONI Testing Results

In verifying the parameters of the Internet shutdown in September 2007, researchers from the OpenNet Initiative were able to determine the outage periods using router paths advertised by the Autonomous Systems (AS) corresponding to these ISPs, recorded by Border Gateway Protocol (BGP) monitors of the RIPE project.[90] The outage on MPT, the main government ISP, can be divided in two phases. Phase One of the outage was a complete shutdown from September 29 to October 4.[91] The sole exception was one brief period of connectivity on October 1 for six hours starting at 6:35 p.m. Phase Two consisted of a regulated outage lasting all day except during the period between approximately 10:00 p.m. and 4:00 a.m. each night from October 4 through October 12. On October 7, MPT had one extra period of connectivity from 9:40 a.m. to 3:37 p.m. In addition to Internet connectivity coinciding approximately with the curfew period,[92] there is evidence that the Internet was also available from around noon (starting anywhere between 11:00 a.m. and 1:00 p.m.) until approximately 4:00 p.m. from October 9 to October 12. As of noon on October 13, MPT appears to have resumed operation as a stable network with few changes in routing paths.

The outage on BaganNet follows a similar pattern, with Phase One comprising a complete shutdown from 7:00 p.m. on September 29 until 10:24 p.m. on the evening of October 4, also with one exception. Phase Two comprises a regulated shutdown all day from October 4 until October 9, except during the curfew period from 10:00 p.m. to 4:00 a.m. As BaganNet's Internet connectivity is established through MPT, it was also up from October 9 through October 12 during the approximate curfew period as well as for a period starting between 12:00 p.m. and 1:30 p.m. for a few hours daily. Two long periods of connectivity thereafter, the first from 10:00 p.m. on October 12 to 4:04 a.m. on October 13 and the second from 12:05 p.m. on October 13 to 10:40 p.m. on October 15, were followed by one long outage, from 10:40 p.m. on October 15 to 9:00 a.m. on October 16. Throughout the outage, a small collection of pre-approved Web sites on the country's Intranet, known as the Myanmar Wide Web, was unaffected.

Testing was conducted on MMT and MPT at various periods in 2008 and early 2009. Both MMT and MPT continued to filter extensively and focused overwhelmingly on independent media, political reform, human rights, and pornography sites relating to Myanmar, as well as free Web-based e-mail services and circumvention tools. While MMT blocks entire root domains, MPT is slightly more selective and only blocks specific pages of sensitive Web sites—MPT treated Blogspot and the Asia Observer this way, blocking a number of URLs but not the root domain.

Both ISPs blocked approximately the same number of circumvention tools, including Proxify, Proxyweb, Guardster, and Proxyweb.net. Psiphon was inconsistently blocked: it was filtered at one time during testing but was accessible at others.

In June 2006, Gmail and Google Talk were made inaccessible and Skype was banned[93]—reportedly an attempt not only to censor communications but also to preserve the government's monopoly over telephone and e-mail services as MPT's revenues dipped.[94] Testing by ONI confirmed filtering practices consistent with 2007 findings: search engines as well as the suite of additional services (e.g., Google Groups, Picasa, Google Docs, Google News, and Google Translate) offered by Google, Yahoo, and MSN were all accessible, with the exception of Google Video and google.at (Austrian Google), which were blocked by MPT. However, free e-mail services continued to be filtered, with Yahoo! Mail, Gmail, Hushmail, and mail2web blocked by both ISPs. In addition, MPT took the precaution of blocking additional e-mail sites including hotmail.msn.com (though not www.hotmail.com). While MMT and MPT blocked the Web site www.skype.com, once Skype is accessed and downloaded using circumvention tools, it is possible to use the Skype VoIP service on both ISPs.

Testing in 2008–2009 revealed that MMT targeted social media sites more than MPT. Only MMT blocked Flickr, YouTube (although MPT blocked Google Video), Geocities, and Blogspot. Blocking of the entire Blogspot/Blogger domain by MMT rendered many of the blogs that were the most active in disseminating images and information relating to the Saffron Revolution inaccessible. However, while MPT kept the Blogspot domain open, it blocked the individual blogs of at least four prominent bloggers featured by international media during the Saffron Revolution: ko-htike.blogspot.com and niknayman.blogspot.com, two blogs reported blocked in September 2007,[95] as well as moemaka.blogspot.com and myochitmyanmar.blogspot.com. To avoid being casualties of the blocking of popular domains such as Blogspot and Wordpress, bloggers sought their own personal domain, such as blog.mghla.com, with its content hosted by Blogspot.

International news agencies filtered by both ISPs included Radio Free Asia (www.rfa.org), the Voice of America Burmese and English Web sites, and the BBC Burmese service. Only MPT blocked the main BBC Web site and *BBC News*, while MMT filtered CNN and the *Financial Times*. Both MMT and MPT blocked many major independent news sites reporting on Myanmar, including overseas regional publications such as *The Irawaddy*, *Mizzima News*, *Democratic Voice of Burma* (www.dvb.no), and *BurmaNet News*, as well as Web sites exclusively in the national language (www.burmatoday.net). While both ISPs blocked some regional publications, such as Thailand's *The Nation* newspaper, the *Asia Times* (www.atimes.com), and the *Asian Tribune*, MMT targeted regional news sites slightly more than MPT.

Web sites containing content on human rights advocacy and democratic reform continued to be a priority for blocking. A substantial number of nongovernmental organization Web sites with different levels of involvement in Myanmar human rights issues were blocked on both ISPs, from international rights organizations such as Human Rights Watch, the Open Society Institute, and Amnesty International, to a wide range of Burma-focused groups (e.g., Burma Watch; www.burmacampaign.org.uk). Within this group were Web sites documenting the persecution of ethnic minorities and the personal Web site of Aung San Suu Kyi. Other continuities in blocking between 2006 and 2007 and 2008–2009 included coalitions for democratic change in Myanmar, such as the Web site of the coalition government of the Union of Burma (www.ncgub.net), opposition movements (www.chinforum.org), and rights groups (www.womenofburma.org).

There continue to be indications that the military government does not take an entirely systematic approach to filtering. For example, MPT appeared to have reduced filtering of certain content from previous testing periods, particularly of pornographic or adult content sites. Based on testing conducted in 2008 and 2009, it now appears that MMT has overtaken MPT in blocking pornography.

In addition, as was the case in 2006–2007, testing done in 2008–2009 found significant differences in filtering between the two ISPs. Of the sites blocked, less than a third were filtered on both ISPs. The remaining blocked Web sites were blocked on one ISP or the other, but not both. MMT blocked a greater number of Web sites dealing with domestic issues, where the term "Burma" or "Myanmar" in the URL was one of the common threads among the filtered list. Thus, groups critical of the government (the Burma Lawyer's Council) as well as peripheral personal Web sites (such as those with photographs of Myanmar) were blocked. On the other hand, MPT chose to filter some additional Web sites of international organizations, including the UN's Human Rights page (www.un.org/rights) and the Center for Constitutional Rights, and particularly those with projects related to Burma listed on their home pages, including Earth-Rights International (www.earthrights.org) and the International Confederation of Free Trade Unions.

Conclusion

The Burmese military government has demonstrated that it is willing to take extreme steps to maintain its control over the flow of information within and outside its borders, including shutting down Internet access entirely. Despite the ability of a small group of Internet users to continue to disseminate information online, access to connectivity as well as actual content are severely hampered by extensive filtering, stringent laws and regulations, and heightened surveillance, all factors contributing to a pervasive climate of fear.

Notes

1. Seth Mydans, "Steep Rise in Fuel Costs Prompts Rare Public Protest in Myanmar," *New York Times*, August 22, 2007, http://www.nytimes.com/2007/08/23/world/asia/23myanmar.html?scp =1&sq=myanmar%20fuel%20price%20hike%20protest&st=cse.

2. Washington Post Foreign Service, "In Broken Economy, Burmese Improvise or Flee," *Washington Post*, August 16, 2008, http://www.washingtonpost.com/wp-dyn/content/article/2008/08/15/ AR2008081503655.html.

3. Asian Development Bank, "Asian Development Outlook 2009: Myanmar," http://www.adb.org/Documents/Books/ADO/2009/MYA.pdf.

4. Human Rights Watch, "Crackdown: Repression of the 2007 Popular Protests in Burma," December 2007, 8, http://www.hrw.org/sites/default/files/reports/burma1207web.pdf.

5. Justin McCurry, Jonathan Watts, and Alex Duval Smith, "How Junta Stemmed a Saffron Tide," *Guardian*, September 30, 2007, http://www.guardian.co.uk/world/2007/sep/30/burma.justinmccurry.

6. Mark Tran, Ian MacKinnon, David Batty, and agencies, "Burma Video Shows Shooting of Japanese Journalist," *Guardian*, September 28, 2007, http://www.guardian.co.uk/world/2007/sep/28/burma.marktran1.

7. Human Rights Watch, "Crackdown: Repression of the 2007 Popular Protests in Burma," December 2007, 8, http://www.hrw.org/sites/default/files/reports/burma1207web.pdf.

8. Seth Mydans, "Myanmar Rulers Still Impeding Access," *New York Times*, June 3, 2008, http://www.nytimes.com/2008/06/03/world/asia/03myanmar.html.

9. *New York Times*, "A Year after Storm, Subtle Changes in Myanmar," April 29, 2009, http://www.nytimes.com/2009/04/30/world/asia/30myanmar.html?ref=asia&pagewanted=all.

10. Associated Press, "Villagers Still Struggle Year after Storm," *The Irrawaddy*, April 29, 2009, http://irrawaddy.org/article.php?art_id=15552.

11. Asian Development Bank, "Asian Development Outlook 2009: Myanmar," http://www.adb.org/Documents/Books/ADO/2009/MYA.pdf.

12. Kenneth Denby, "Burmese Junta Releases Win Tin from Jail in 'Amnesty' of 9,002 Prisoners," *The Times* September 24, 2008, http://www.timesonline.co.uk/tol/news/world/asia/article4810939.ece.

13. UN Economic and Social Council, "Situation of Human Rights in Myanmar: Report of the Special Rapporteur, Tomás Ojea Quintana," A/HRC/10/19, March 11, 2009, http://daccess-ods.un.org/access.nsf/Get?Open&DS=A/HRC/10/19&Lang=E.

14. Ibid.

15. Sharon Otterman, "Myanmar Gives Comedian 45-Year Sentence for Cyclone Comments," *New York Times*, November 21, 2008, http://www.nytimes.com/2008/11/22/world/asia/22myanmar.html?ref=world; *New York Times*, "Prison Terms for Activists in Myanmar," November 11, 2008, http://www.nytimes.com/2008/11/12/world/asia/12myanmar.html; Saw Yan Naing, "Rangoon Trials Continue—At Least 19 Condemned Today," *The Irrawaddy*, November 13, 2008, http://irrawaddy.org/article.php?art id=14628.

16. UN Economic and Social Council, "Situation of Human Rights in Myanmar: Report of the Special Rapporteur, Tomás Ojea Quintana," A/HRC/10/19, March 11, 2009, http://daccess-ods.un.org/access.nsf/Get?Open&DS=A/HRC/10/19&Lang=E.

17. Committee to Protect Journalists, "10 Worst Countries to Be a Blogger," April 10, 2009, http://cpj.org/reports/2009/04/10-worst-countries-to-be-a-blogger.php.

18. Seth Mydans and Mark Macdonald, "Pro-Democracy Leader Goes on Trial in Myanmar," *New York Times*, May 18, 2009, http://www.nytimes.com/2009/05/19/world/asia/19myanmar.html.

19. Carol Huang, "The American Mystery Man Behind Aung San Suu Kyi's Latest Troubles," Christian Science Monitor Global News blog, May 28, 2009, http://features.csmonitor.com/globalnews/2009/05/28/the-american-mystery-man-behind-aung-san-suu-kyis-latest-troubles/.

20. Paul Budde Communication Pty., Ltd., "Myanmar (Burma)—Telecoms Market Overview and Statistics," January 3, 2009; Xinhua News Agency, "Internet Users in Myanmar Number Nearly 300,000," November 8, 2006; International Telecommunication Union, "ITU Internet Indicators, 2006," http://www.itu.int/ITU-D/icteye/Reporting/ShowReportFrame.aspx?ReportName=/WTI/InformationTechnologyPublic&RP_intYear=2006&RP_intLanguageID=1.

21. Paul Budde Communication Pty., Ltd., "Myanmar (Burma)—Telecoms Market Overview and Statistics".

22. Ibid.

23. See Redlink ISP, http://www.redlink.net.mm/; one foreign exchange certificate (FEC) is officially equal to USD 1. BaganNet, "Access Services," http://www.bagan.net.mm/products/access/broadband_ADSL.asp.

24. Paul Budde Communication Pty., Ltd., "Myanmar (Burma)—Telecoms Market Overview and Statistics".

25. BaganNet, "Access Services," http://www.bagan.net.mm/products/access/broadband_ADSL.asp.

26. Min Lwin, "Junta Approves Investment in Cyber City," *The Irrawaddy*, July 30, 2008, http://www.irrawaddy.org/article.php?art_id=13614.

27. Kyaw Zin Htun, "New ISP Set for May Launch Date," *Myanmar Times*, May 19–25, 2008, http://www.mmtimes.com/no419/n019.htm.

28. Paul Budde Communication Pty., Ltd., "Myanmar (Burma)—Telecoms Market Overview and Statistics".

29. Min Lwin, "Web Sites Back Online, but Fears of Further Attacks Remain," *The Irrawaddy*, September 23, 2008, http://www.irrawaddy.org/article.php?art_id=14294.

30. The Association of Southeast Asian Nations e-ASEAN Initiative, "The Challenge of ICT Revolution," http://www.aseansec.org/7659.htm.

31. Min Lwin, "Junta Approves Investment in Cyber City," *The Irrawaddy*, July 29, 2008, http://www.irrawaddy.org/article.php?art_id=13614; Xinhua News Agency, "Companies from 4 Countries to Invest in Myanmar Cyber City Project," September 12, 2007, http://news.xinhuanet.com/english/2007-09/12/content_6708999.htm.

32. Yadanabon Cyber City, http://www.yadanaboncybercity.com/; Min Lwin, "Junta Approves Investment in Cyber City," *The Irrawaddy*, July 29, 2008, http://www.irrawaddy.org/article.php?art_id=13614.

33. Min Lwin, "Junta Approves Investment in Cyber City," *The Irrawaddy*, July 29, 2008, http://www.irrawaddy.org/article.php?art_id=13614.

34. Ibid.

35. Arkar Moe, "Internet Users Face More Restrictions," *The Irrawaddy*, May 12, 2009, http://www.irrawaddy.org/article.php?art_id=15620.

36. Yadanabon Cyber City, http://www.yadanaboncybercity.com/.

37. Soe Myint, "Bloggers in Burma Write at Great Risk," CPJ Blog, May 1, 2009, http://cpj.org/blog/2009/05/bloggers-in-burma-write-at-great-risk.php.

38. *Xinhua News Agency*, "Myanmar to Allow Opening of More Public Access Centers," April 22, 2009, http://english.cri.cn/6966/2009/04/22/2001s477563.htm.

39. Violet Cho, "Burma to Enforce Licensing for All Internet Cafes," *The Irrawaddy*, March 14, 2008.

40. OpenNet Initiative Bulletin, "Pulling the Plug: A Technical Review of the Internet Shutdown in Burma," November 2007, http://opennet.net/research/bulletins/013/.

41. Ibid.

42. Ibid.

43. *Mizzima News*, "Burma Authorities Planning Internet Cut-off," April 28, 2008.

44. Ibid.

45. OpenNet Initiative Blog, "Doubts Surface over Announced Internet Maintenance in Burma," March 24, 2009, http://opennet.net/blog/2009/03/doubts-surface-over-announced-internet-maintenance-burma; Lawi Weng, "Internet Slowdown to Continue at Least One More Day," April 2, 2009, *The Irrawaddy*, http://irrawaddy.org/article.php?art_id=15429.

46. OpenNet Initiative Bulletin, "Pulling the Plug: A Technical Review of the Internet Shutdown in Burma," November 2007, http://opennet.net/research/bulletins/013/.

47. ONI interview with PAC operator.

48. Constitution of the Republic of the Union of Myanmar (2008), http://www.scribd.com/doc/14252154/Myanmar-Constitution-English.

49. UN Economic and Social Council, "Situation of Human Rights in Myanmar: Report of the Special Rapporteur, Tomás Ojea Quintana," A/HRC/10/19, March 11, 2009, http://daccess-ods.un.org/access.nsf/Get?Open&DS=A/HRC/10/19&Lang=E.

50. Freedom House, "Burma (Myanmar) Country Report 2008," http://www.freedomhouse.org/template.cfm?page=22&year=2008&country=7363.

51. Roy Greenslade, "How Burma Quashes Press Freedom," Guardian Greenslade Blog, September 26, 2007, http://www.guardian.co.uk/media/greenslade/2007/sep/26/howburmaquashespressfreedo.

52. Saw Yan Naing, "Suppressed," *The Irrawaddy*, February 2009, http://www.irrawaddy.org/article.php?art_id=15004. See also http://www.myanmar.gov.mm/ministry/home/secrutiny.htm.

53. Article 19 Press Release, "Burma: Crackdown on Opposition and Media," May 22, 2008.

54. *People's Daily Online*, "More Publications Granted in Myanmar," June 6, 2006, http://english.peopledaily.com.cn/200606/06/eng20060606_271309.html.

55. Printers and Publishers Registration Act (1962), http://www.burmalibrary.org/docs6/Printers_and_Publishers_Registation_Act.pdf.

56. Article 32, Television and Video Law (The State Law and Order Restoration Council Law No. 8/96), July 26, 1996, http://www.blc-burma.org/html/Myanmar%20Law/lr_e_ml96_08.html.

57. Articles 27, 28, 32, Computer Science Development Law, September 20, 1996, http://www.blc-burma.org/HTML/Myanmar%20Law/lr_e_ml96_10.html.

58. Article 33, The Electronic Transactions Law (2004), http://www.burmalibrary.org/docs/Electronic-transactions.htm.

59. MPT terms of service, January 31, 2000, http://web.archive.org/web/20010220220441/http://dfn.org/voices/burma/webregulations.htm.

60. Ibid.

61. Article 33, Computer Science Development Law.

62. MPT terms of service, January 31, 2000, http://web.archive.org/web/20010220220441/http://dfn.org/voices/burma/webregulations.htm.

63. Jonathan Head, "Harsh Sentences for Burma Rebels," *BBC News*, November 11, 2008, http://news.bbc.co.uk/2/hi/asia-pacific/7721589.stm.

64. Ibid.

65. *BBC News*, "Burma Blogger Jailed for 20 Years," November 11, 2008, http://news.bbc.co.uk/2/hi/asia-pacific/7721271.stm. Other sources report that Latt was sentenced for offenses under the Computer Science Development Law. See, Min Lwin, "Regime Tightens Reins on the Internet," *The Irrawaddy*, November 13, 2008, http://irrawaddy.org/article.php?art_id=14627.

66. International Freedom of Expression Exchange, "Comedian and Blogger 'Zarganar' Sentenced to 45 Years in Prison; Sports Journalist Zaw Thet Htwe gets 15 Years," November 21, 2008, http://www.ifex.org/en/content/view/full/98774; Than Htike Oo, "Total Prison Term for Zarganar Climbs to 59 Years," *Mizzima News*, November 28, 2008, http://www.mizzima.com/news/inside-burma/1377-total-prison-term-for-zarganar-climbs-to-59-years-.html.

67. *The Irrawaddy*, "Popular Burmese Blogger's Jail Term Reduced," February 20, 2009, http://www.irrawaddy.org/article.php?art_id=15160.

68. Khin Hninn Phyu, "Myanmar Times via BBC: Burma Enforces Licensing of Internet Cafés," *Myanmar Times*, March 20, 2006, http://www.burmanet.org/news/2006/03/31/myanmar-times-via-bbc-burma-enforces-licensing-of-internet-cafes/.

69. Violet Cho, "Burma to Enforce Licensing for All Internet Cafes," *The Irrawaddy*, March 14, 2008.

70. OpenNet Initiative Blog, "Burmese Regulations for Cybercafés Stringent as Expected," July 2, 2008, http://opennet.net/blog/2008/07/burmese-regulations-cybercafes-stringent-expected.

71. Ibid.

72. Daniel Pepper, "Aftermath of a Revolt: Myanmar's Lost Year," *New York Times*, October 4, 2008, http://www.nytimes.com/2008/10/05/weekinreview/05pepper.html?scp=2&sq=myanmar saffron revolution&st=cse.

73. Tyler Chapman, "In Burma, Fear and Suspicion Prevail," Radio Free Asia, April 19, 2009, http://www.rfa.org/english/blog/burma_diary/rangoon-04172009150342.html.

74. Human Rights Watch, "Crackdown: Repression of the 2007 Popular Protests in Burma," December 2007, 8, http://www.hrw.org/sites/default/files/reports/burma1207web.pdf.

75. Ibid., 106.

76. Ibid.

77. Ibid.

78. Brian McCartan, "Myanmar on the Cyber-Offensive," *Asia Times*, October 1, 2008, http://www.atimes.com/atimes/Southeast_Asia/JJ01Ae01.html.

79. Ibid.

80. OpenNet Initiative Blog, "Burmese Regulations for Cybercafés Stringent As Expected," July 2, 2008, http://opennet.net/blog/2008/07/burmese-regulations-cybercafes-stringent-expected.

81. MTalk Search Engine, http://www.mtalk.net.mm/.

82. Interview with IT professional in Burma, May 2009.

83. OpenNet Initiative Bulletin, "Pulling the Plug: A Technical Review of the Internet Shutdown in Burma," November 2007, http://opennet.net/research/bulletins/013/.

84. Ibid.; U.S. State Department Bureau of Democracy, Human Rights, and Labor, "2008 Country Reports on Human Rights Practices: Burma," February 25, 2009, http://www.state.gov/g/drl/rls/hrrpt/2008/eap/119035.htm.

85. Saw Yan Naing, "Young Burmese Blogger Sentenced to More Than 20 Years in Jail," *The Irrawaddy*, November 10, 2008, http://www.irrawaddy.org/article.php?art_id=14604.

86. OpenNet Initiative Blog, "Doubts Surface over Announced Internet Maintenance in Burma."

87. OpenNet Initiative Bulletin, "Pulling the Plug: A Technical Review of the Internet Shutdown in Burma," November 2007, http://opennet.net/research/bulletins/013/.

88. Zarni, "Websites of Three Burmese News Agencies in Exile under Attack," *Mizzima News*, September 17, 2008, http://www.mizzima.com/news/regional/1052-websites-of-three-burmese-news-agencies-in-exile-under-attack.html.

89. Information Warfare Monitor, "Burmese News Agencies under DOS Attack," May 28, 2009, http://128.100.171.10/modules.php?op=modload&name=News&file=article&sid=1907.

90. OpenNet Initiative Bulletin, "Pulling the Plug: A Technical Review of the Internet Shutdown in Burma," November 2007, http://opennet.net/research/bulletins/013/.

91. The times reported here are in local Burma time.

92. On September 26, 2007, the Burmese government imposed a 60-day curfew from 21:00 to 5:00. This curfew was reduced on October 13, 2007, to the period between 23:00 and 3:00. See Associated Press, "Burma Eases Curfews," October 14, 2007, http://www.thestar.com/article/266690; ABC News, "Burma Sets Curfew Amid Mass Protests," September 26, 2007, "http://www.abc.net.au/news/stories/2007/09/26/2043355.htm.

93. *Hindustan Times*, "Google, Gmail Banned in Myanmar: Surfers," June 30, 2006, http://www.highbeam.com/doc/1P3-1069831001.html.

94. Reporters Without Borders, "Internet Increasingly Resembles an Intranet as Foreign Services Blocked," July 4, 2006, http://www.rsf.org/article.php3?id_article=18202; *The Irrawaddy*, "Junta Blocks Google and Gmail," June 30, 2006, http://www.irrawaddy.org/article.php?art_id=5924.

95. Nam Davies, "Junta Blocks Popular Blogs," *Mizzima News*, September 27, 2007, http://www.bnionline.net/media-alert/2606-junta-blocks-popular-blogs.html.

China

China has devoted extensive resources to building one of the largest and most sophisticated filtering systems in the world. As the Internet records extraordinary growth in services as well as numbers of users, the Chinese government has undertaken to limit access to any content that might potentially undermine the state's control or social stability by pursuing strict supervision of domestic media, delegated liability for online content providers, and, increasingly, a propaganda approach to online debate and discussion.

Background

The convening of the Seventeenth Chinese Communist Party (CCP) Congress in October 2007, at which China's top echelon of government leaders chose their eventual successors, was the beginning of a momentous year for China, and consequently for domestic and international news media. On March 10, 2008, hundreds of monks in the Tibetan autonomous region led a series of protests to demand loosening of restrictions on religious practices and even independence for Tibet.[1] Chinese authorities

RESULTS AT A GLANCE					
Filtering	No Evidence of Filtering	Suspected Filtering	Selective Filtering	Substantial Filtering	Pervasive Filtering
Political					•
Social				•	
Conflict and security					•
Internet tools				•	

Other Factors	Low	Medium	High	Not Applicable
Transparency	•			
Consistency			•	

KEY INDICATORS	
GDP per capita, PPP (constant 2005 international dollars)	5,084
Life expectancy at birth (years)	73
Literacy rate (percent of people age 15+)	93
Human development index (out of 179)	94
Rule of law (out of 211)	121
Voice and accountability (out of 209)	196
Democracy index (out of 167)	136 (Authoritarian regime)
Digital opportunity index (out of 181)	77
Internet users (percent of population)	22.6

Source by indicator: World Bank 2009a, World Bank 2009a, World Bank 2009a, UNDP 2008, World Bank 2009b, World Bank 2009b, Economist Intelligence Unit 2008, ITU 2007, ITU 2008.

rapidly responded with arrests and a violent crackdown against thousands of monks and rioting Tibetans.[2] A corresponding clampdown on reporting from the region and other Tibetan-populated areas in western China left media with a dearth of reliable information; official accounts and dispatches released by Tibetan exile organizations put issues like the actual death toll in question. The crackdown in Tibet galvanized protests both in support of and opposed to China's policies toward its religious and ethnic minorities, especially as symbolized in the Olympic torch making its way in an elaborate tour around the world. The conflicts that erupted in cities as distant as Paris[3] and Seoul in March and April contributed to a so-called transnational Chinese backlash against Western media portrayals of China, culminating in an "anti-CNN" movement and a call for a boycott against the French supermarket chain Carrefour.[4]

On May 12, 2008, a 7.9-magnitude earthquake, with its epicenter in Wenchuan county, Sichuan province, killed around 90,000 people and injured hundreds of thousands, leveling more than 5 million buildings and leaving millions homeless.[5] During the massive relief efforts and national mobilization of volunteers and monetary contributions immediately following the quake, media were allowed to operate with unprecedented openness, with official state outlets such as China Central Television winning notice and praise for presenting timely and uncanned news. However, within a few weeks authorities began to encircle and regulate the story—for example, by issuing more bans on coverage of certain topics and requiring registration of reporters. It took authorities repeated efforts to quash coverage of one of the most potent and enduring controversies: the tragic deaths of thousands of schoolchildren and teachers attributed to shoddy school construction, along with the implication that government officials were responsible.[6] Authorities did not release an official statistic of the number of schoolchildren who died until almost a year after the quake, and some claimed that the official figure of 5,335 was too low, compared to Reuters' estimate of 9,000 deaths, calculated from reports by the state news agency and local media.[7] This accusation led one commentator to state, "Chinese news reports on this major story unfolded in a complicated environment, and it is impossible to render a simple verdict about media coverage."[8]

With more than USD 40 billion spent on hosting the 2008 Olympic Games in Beijing, the Chinese government acted to assert control over this global event while presenting an open and welcoming environment for athletes, media, foreign dignitaries, and visitors.[9] As part of these overtures, the government issued regulations in January 2007 allowing journalists to travel across the country without registering with local authorities and to interview subjects without official consent.[10] While the unblocking of Web sites and improved access to officials at Olympics venues marked some improvement in openness and transparency, the government also stepped up surveillance around Beijing and prevented activists from petitioning to use legally sanctioned protest zones.

After a news conference held by the U.S. men's volleyball team, in which several Chinese reporters had their notebooks (and at least one tape recorder) confiscated, Beijing Olympics spokesman Sun Weide denied knowledge of this differential treatment of Chinese reporters: "I am not very clear about the situation you raised," he said. "For Chinese journalists, they very much enjoy the rights to cover the Beijing Olympic Games.... the rights are protected by the constitution in China."[11] Yet China's "open-door" policy for journalists as a result of the Olympics had a marginal impact on Olympics coverage by domestic media. The government persisted in its clampdown on local Chinese media,[12] and the Foreign Correspondents' Club of China confirmed 63 cases of reporting interference during the Olympics, out of a total of 178 in 2008, including ten incidents of police roughing up reporters and breaking their cameras.[13] While the relaxed rules for foreign journalists were made permanent in October 2008,[14] new rules issued in February 2009 required reporters based in Hong Kong and Macao to apply for a permit prior to every reporting trip to mainland China.[15]

A month after the Olympics concluded, a scandal erupted over tainted milk products that killed six infants and sickened nearly 300,000 others.[16] Information soon emerged indicating that provincial governments and central government agencies, as well as officials from the Sanlu group, China's leading seller of milk powder, had either suppressed earlier reports or failed to act, likely at the cost of human lives.[17] Although it had been receiving complaints about its infant milk powder since December 2007, the Sanlu group only informed its board in August 2008, prompting its joint venture partner Fonterra to inform the New Zealand government.[18] A reporter for the newspaper *Southern Weekend*, known for its investigative reports, wrote in a blog post that he and several other journalists were prevented in July from publishing findings about how milk powder was making children sick because of pressure from Sanlu officials as well as an overall Olympics-related clampdown on negative news coverage.[19] In January 2009, 21 defendants were convicted for their roles in the production and sale of melamine-tainted products, including two melamine producers, who received death sentences, and the former Sanlu chairwoman, who was sentenced to life imprisonment.[20]

As 2008 progressed, the Chinese government demonstrated a perceptible shift in its media-control policies in order to better manage the handling of negative news reports, which continued to spread with incredible speed and intensity on the Internet. This approach involves the government responding more actively and rapidly to fast-breaking news events, primarily by attempting to set the agenda for coverage rather than suppress it.[21] With lessons learned about the upsides of transparency and timeliness from the early Sichuan earthquake coverage and other emergencies, the central government reportedly began allowing local governments to disclose information about unrest and protests in an apparent attempt to "control the news by publicizing the news."[22] However, despite gestures toward broader openness with the media, the government clearly did not intend to relinquish control.[23] This tactic often resulted in the same delivery of "authoritative" facts, with state news agencies such as Xinhua and the *People's Daily* benefiting over commercial media from this selectively enhanced coverage.[24] In February 2009, the official China News Service announced that it would create a blacklist of journalists engaged in "unhealthy professional conduct," and those found breaking rules would be prohibited from engaging in news reporting and editing work.[25]

Coming off of these perceived triumphs and devastating crises, the Chinese government warned that extra vigilance was needed in 2009. The potential for increased social instability triggered by the global financial crisis increased anxieties in a year already punctuated by powerful anniversaries of events tainting the legacy of the CCP, which will also commemorate 60 years since the founding of the People's Republic of China: 20 years since the June 4, 1989, Tiananmen Square crackdown; 50 years since the Tibetan uprising that led to the Dalai Lama's exile; and ten years since the Falun Gong spiritual movement was banned quickly after their 10,000-strong flash protest in front of Zhongnanhai, the compound of the Chinese central leadership. Thus, officials repeatedly issued reminders that "stability preservation work"[26] would be a top priority. At a media forum in January, an official in China's Internet affairs bureau said, "You have to check the channels one by one, the programs one by one, the pages one by one.... You must not miss any step. You must not leave any unchecked corners."[27] Efforts to enforce stability preservation have resulted in predictable crackdowns on media reporting; for example, in March 2009, reporters were detained, turned back, or had their recordings confiscated when trying to visit Tibetan areas in three provinces ahead of the first anniversary of the unrest in Tibet.[28]

Internet in China

China leads the world with 298 million Internet users, an increase of 42 percent from 2007 to the end of 2008.[29] More astoundingly, in this same time period more than 90 percent of these users had broadband access, a spike of over 100 million.[30] China also has the world's biggest cell phone market, with some 583.5 million subscribers.[31] The rural-urban divide that influences many gaps in the informatization of the national economy is closing, but it remains substantial. Rural areas and the poorer western provinces are beginning to gain ground, against a national Internet penetration rate of 22.6 percent.[32] At the end of 2008, rural Internet users made up almost a third of the entire online population, a jump of over 60 percent.[33] While many of the poorer and western provinces such as Yunnan, Gansu, and Guizhou continue to have penetration rates of less than 10 percent, they also have considerable growth rates, upward of 50 percent.[34] Driven by the policy goal that "every village has access to the telephone and every township has access to the Internet" by 2010, infrastructure development has expanded broadband Internet access to 92 percent of townships.[35] Gender is also an important demographic factor in the urban-rural divide, with rural male users outnumbering women by 15 percent. Internet users between the ages of 10 and 19 gained ground in 2008, increasing to 35 percent of all users and overtaking the 20–29 age group to become the leading demographic using the Internet.[36]

Web sites registered in China are another exponential growth area, increasing by 91.4 percent since 2007.[37] Social media platforms continue to take hold: 210 million Internet users in China have visited video-sharing sites, 54 percent have blogs (although only 35 percent of those update them at least once every six months), almost a third participate in online discussion forums, and 19 percent belong to social networking sites.[38] Chinese netizens have access to a wide variety of well-developed Internet platforms for the domestic market, which have typically outpaced foreign services, such as search engines (Baidu's market share is at 63 percent compared to Google's 28 percent), online portals (the top four portals—Sohu, Sina, Tencent, and Netease—claim 73 percent of sector revenue), bulletin board services (BBS) and discussion forums, online video sites, blogs, social networking (the service Kaixin has an estimated 30 million daily users), and booming business-to-customer e-commerce.[39] Since 2006, when only China Netcom and China Telecom were permitted to offer pilot commercial VoIP services in selected cities,[40] the number of VoIP service providers has reached 3,000, mainly in Beijing and Shanghai, with the number of users reaching 80 million.[41]

In 2008, China's telecom regulator, the Ministry of Information Industry (MII), was dissolved and its functions absorbed into the new Ministry of Industry and Information Technology (MIIT).[42] In addition to the MII mandate to regulate telecommunications, Internet, broadband, electronics, computing, and software, the MIIT's enhanced authority includes supervision of IT development, formerly held by the National Development and Reform Commission.[43] Physical access to the Internet is controlled by the MIIT and is provided by eight state-licensed Internet access providers (ISPs), each of which has at least one connection to a foreign Internet backbone.[44] China's international outlet bandwidth reached 640 Gbps in 2008, an increase of 73.6 percent, but China Telecom (ChinaNET) maintained more than 50 percent of that bandwidth.[45] China Netcom (now China Unicom) joined China's second-largest ISP, China169, after China Telecom split off in 2003.[46]

In an effort to boost the fixed-line phone industry's competitiveness in the mobile market, in 2008 numerous ministries jointly decided to merge the assets of the nation's six state-owned telecommunication companies and form three groups, announcing a plan to issue licenses for high-speed 3G cell phone services after the restructuring.[47] As part of the reorganization, China Netcom was fully incorporated into China Unicom in October 2008, reportedly completing the biggest merger in Chinese history.[48] In January 2009, the MIIT issued three 3G licenses, with China Unicom and China Telecom receiving licenses for established 3G services and China Mobile authorized to carry a Chinese TD-SCDMA service, so far unproven, that has been a priority of research and development for the government.[49]

By sheer scope and range of topics—from online novels to video satires[50]—the Internet "cannot be ignored as a battleground for spreading public opinion" and sentiment.[51] Frequently, incidents that go viral (gaining widespread popularity by virtue of being shared on the Internet) are then catapulted into national prominence, frequently leading to calls for government action and response. According to Hu Yong, a journalism professor, dedicated coverage by online portals, extensive commentary on discussion forms, and the potency of Internet rumors that reverberate back into traditional media are driving convergence in the communications industry—especially in spawning "new media events" that often result in consequences for the officials, businesspeople, or celebrities involved.[52] In an unpublished investigative report obtained by David Bandurski of the China Media Project, the vice president of People's Daily Online said that of the numerous secret internal reports sent up to the Central Party Committee each year, two-thirds of the few hundred reports given priority and action by top leaders are from the Internet Office of the State Council Information Office.[53]

The rising prominence of collective efforts over the Internet to target and expose personal data,[54] known as "human flesh search engines," appear to serve a voracious appetite within the Chinese online community for personal accountability. According to Xinhua, the phenomenon had its origins in 2001, when a man posted a picture of a woman he claimed to be his girlfriend on the portal Mop.com, and other Internet users identified her as a model for Microsoft, proving him a liar.[55] They can initiate investigations as straightforward as looking for missing relatives, but sometimes stray into questionable acts of vigilantism involving threats and harassment. In the years since, the human flesh search engines have scored a series of successes in identifying corrupt officials who have acted shamefully or abused their office (and are often subsequently punished), as well as attacking private individuals engaging in perceived distasteful behavior.[56] These loosely networked efforts are capable of launching campaigns against people like Grace Wang, a Chinese student at Duke University who was filmed in April 2008 attempting to referee between two opposing groups of protesters at a "Free Tibet" action on campus.[57] After the video was posted on YouTube and other Web sites, the online reaction was swift: she was lambasted in Chinese-language discussion forums and portals for being "brainwashed" and a "race traitor," among other things, and her parents living in China went into hiding after threats were painted on their apartment.[58]

At times, online activity has tested this relationship between citizens and government on a range of sensitive issues. Signed by more than 300 Chinese activists, scholars, lawyers, and others, Charter 08 was issued online on December 9, 2008, as a manifesto inspired by the founding of Charter 77 in Czechoslovakia in 1977.[59] It called for the protection of human rights, an independent judiciary, a republican system of "one person, one vote," and other comprehensive reforms.[60] Charter 08 provoked a clear response from authorities, who questioned or detained more than 100 of the original signatories, including Liu Xiaobo, a well-known dissident who was detained without process on December 8 and continued (as of May 13, 2009) to be held at an unknown location.[61] However, through circulation by e-mail and other means, Charter 08 had garnered more than 7,000 signatures by early 2009.[62]

Beyond the hot-button incidents that carry news cycles,[63] the interaction between top-down media supervisory structures and a more porous and unpredictable online sphere have also contributed to the rise of a number of phenomena unique to the Chinese cybersphere. The so-called *Fifty Cent Party*, a term referring to an estimated 280,000 Web commentators nationwide who zealously support the CCP and were initially rumored to net 50 cents per post, are directly organized by the government to "guide" online public opinion.[64] It had its origins at Nanjing University in 2005, where students were recruited with work-study funds to advocate the party line on an online student forum, and it has been institutionalized to the extent that the Ministry of Culture developed Web commentator trainings (complete with exams and job certification) and major Web sites are required to have in-house teams of these government-trained commentators.[65] Thus, while the government continues to aggressively intervene in news media coverage, these Fifty Cent Party members are proliferating because the CCP also has come to recognize the potential benefits of a public relations approach to online discourse.

Legal and Regulatory Frameworks

Although China's constitution formally guarantees freedom of expression and publication[66] and the protection of human rights,[67] legal and administrative regulations
ensure that the Chinese Communist Party will be supported in its attempt at strict supervision of all forms of online content. The Internet has been targeted for monitoring
since before it was even commercially available,[68] and the government seems intent on
keeping regulatory pace with its growth and development.

Underlying all regulation of the Internet is a pantheon of proscribed content.
Citizens are prohibited from disseminating between nine and eleven categories of
content that appear consistently in most regulations[69]; all can be considered subversive and trigger fines, content removal, and criminal liability.[70] Illegal content,
although broadly and vaguely defined, provides a blueprint of topics the government
considers sensitive, including endangering national security and contradicting officially accepted political theory, conducting activities in the name of an illegal civil
organization, and inciting illegal assemblies or gatherings that disturb social order.[71]

Campaigns directed at cracking down on the perceived harmful societal effects of
Internet development have been both publicly mobilized and opaquely implemented,
but the latter are no less of a reality. The severity of Internet content control also fluc-
tuates during different time periods, especially those buffering politically sensitive
events. For example, an official announcement from the General Administration of
Press and Publications stating that "a healthy and harmonious environment for a
successful Seventeenth Party Congress" would be encouraged by stamping out "illegal
news coverage" and "false news" precipitated a crackdown on political news reporting,
commentary, and Internet discussion through the close of the Party Congress in October.[72] In those sensitive months, authorities closed 18,401 "illegal" Web sites and targeted Internet data centers, the physical computers that private firms rent to offer
online interactive features.[73]

On January 5, 2009, seven ministries (including the Ministry of Public Security and
the Ministry of Culture) were convened by the State Council Information Office (SCIO)
to discuss selected activities for repairing the flood of "vulgar" (*disu*) content on the
Internet that harms the minds and bodies of youth.[74] The crackdown was soon
extended to include cell phone messages, online games and novels, videos, and radio
programs; by January 23, the China Internet Illegal Information Reporting Center
(CIIRC) had received nearly 19,000 reports of harmful content, leading authorities to
shut down 1,250 illegal Web sites and to delete more than 3 million items.[75] The targeting of vulgar and pornographic content also netted some political casualties, notably the blog service provider Bullog.cn (*Niubo*), founded in 2006 by blogger Luo
Yonghao. Bullog, which had become an important platform for liberal-leaning intel-
lectuals and political bloggers, was shut down on January 9, 2009, for "picking up

harmful information on political and current affairs."[76] Its closure was linked to its status as the leading domestic circulator of Charter 08,[77] as it had already survived a suspension in October 2007 during the Seventeenth Communist Party Congress and the purging of multiple high-profile blogs.[78] By April 2009, Luo had migrated the site as Bulloger.com to a server overseas, which was accessible only by proxy server and "unlikely ever to be allowed to exist in China."[79]

In addition to campaigns dedicated to "strict supervision" of online providers in order to curb various types of "harmful" information,[80] the government has managed to develop a relatively comprehensive strategy for managing online media. Since 2004, when essays and articles posted online began to be restricted more systematically, government supervision has evolved to rely largely on informal controls within official structures and stringent formal regulation. Nevertheless, it has been a challenge for the Chinese government to establish the same level of control over the Internet and online media as it has over the traditional media, because of factors including the relative decentralization of government supervision, the scale and viral possibilities of content available online, and the greater number of nonstate actors.

A major development in Chinese cyberspace since 2005 has been the flourishing of online news media, which now rank among the top online activities and reached 234 million Internet users in 2008.[81] Not only do Chinese users cite the Internet as their most important source for information, more important than television and newspapers, but also the national information clearinghouse on information technology, the China Internet Network Information Center, acknowledges that "the report[ing] of major events, such as the Olympics, has enabled network[ed] media to stand on a par with mainstream media."[82] Supervision of the media, previously executed primarily by the Propaganda Department of the CCP, has been split with the SCIO, whose local branches have supervisory responsibility over Internet content.[83] As a result, most major online content providers and portals are registered in Beijing and are managed by the Beijing Internet Information Administration Bureau under the Beijing Information Office. Web sites and content providers have been reported to operate with greater or lesser levels of freedom depending on where they are registered.[84]

Any organization transmitting content electronically about current politics, economic issues, and other public affairs must abide by the 2005 Provisions on the Administration of Internet News Information Services ("Internet News Regulations").[85] These regulations introduced a complex regulatory scheme with the result that only news originating from state-supervised news outlets could be posted online. Government-licensed and authorized news agencies are limited to covering specific subjects approved by the state,[86] but at least are allowed to conduct original reporting on "current events news information," defined as "reporting and commentary relating to politics, economics, military affairs, foreign affairs, and social and public affairs, as well as reporting and commentary relating to fast-breaking social events."[87] All Web sites that are nongovernmental entities, or otherwise not licensed news agencies, are restricted from performing any journalistic function, limiting them to reprinting content from central news outlets or media under the direct control of provincial governments.[88] In practice, major portals are not permitted to repost many articles published by print media online.

To discipline media, government ministries and Communist Party organs use both formal controls, such as policies and instructions and defamation liability, and informal mechanisms, including editorial responsibility for content, economic incentives, intimidation, and other forms of pressure.[89] Generally, authorities prefer to issue instructions advising on topics to be censored informally by means of short message service (SMS), chat, or e-mail, or at regular meetings with editors. Coverage of politically sensitive events is zealously managed at every stage in order to reduce the risk of exposure to the smallest possible degree.[90] This management includes prior bans on publication and time limits for obeying instructions, as well as "guidance" that serves a more propagandistic function, including instructions on whether to place news, when to place news, where to place it, and in what form it should be publicized. When "mass incidents" or major events such as the 2008 Olympic Games reach their conclusion, the grasp loosens over time, but it remains an unrelenting presence.

Despite the challenges and intense resources required to effectively police online media, many of these formal and informal controls have nevertheless been extended to Chinese cyberspace. China's legal framework for Internet access and usage is achieved by the participation of state and nonstate actors at all institutional levels.[91] Control over Internet expression and content is multilayered and achieved by distributing criminal and financial liability, licensing and registration requirements, and self-monitoring instructions to nonstate actors at every stage of access, from the ISP to the content provider and the end user. Some of these blunt and frequently applied methods include job dismissals; the closure of Web sites, often by their Web hosting service, for a broad array of infractions[92]; and the detention of journalists, writers, and activists. In 2008, 49 individuals were known to be imprisoned for online activities,[93] including several (such as Huang Qi and Du Daobin) serving their second period of detention for Internet-related crimes.[94] Internet users have also been targeted for posting photographs and other multimedia online.[95] For example, journalist Qi Chonghuai was questioned by police about an article he cowrote about a corrupt local official and photographs of a luxurious government office building on the anti-corruption online forum of the Xinhua News Agency, before being sentenced to four years imprisonment on fraud and extortion charges.[96] Schoolteacher Liu Shaokun was detained on June 25, 2008, and sentenced to one year of "reeducation through labor" for posting pictures of school buildings that collapsed in the Sichuan earthquake.[97]

Internet content providers, such as BBS and other user-generated sites, are directly responsible for what is published on their services.[98] All services providing Internet users with information that fail sufficiently to monitor their Web sites and report violations, or that produce, publish, or distribute harmful information, face fines and other serious consequences, including shutdown, criminal liability, and license revocation.[99] The government has used this approach to bring social media like video-sharing sites in line with the larger governing framework for Internet content regulation. The Provisions on the Management of Internet Audio and Video Programming Services ("Video Regulations"), effective January 1, 2008, were a further refinement of the government's attempt to create a sustainable "walled garden" of self-policed local-language content for the Chinese cybersphere.[100] Jointly issued by the broadcast media regulator the State Administration of Radio, Film, and Television (SARFT) and the MII, the regulations require video service providers that produce their own content to obtain both a broadcast production license and rarely issued Internet news information services licenses, which are regulated by the MII,[101] thus carrying forward the model introduced in the Internet News Regulations. Just as unlicensed service providers may not upload or transmit content for anyone, they are also prohibited from allowing any individuals to upload content pertaining to "current events" news.[102]

In addition to the types of illegal content routinely proscribed in Internet regulations, SARFT issued a notice on March 30, 2009, detailing 21 unusually specific and wide-ranging additional content categories that online video providers should edit or delete.[103] These include distortions of Chinese culture and history; disparaging depictions of revolutionary leaders, heroes, police, army, or judiciary; depictions of torture; mocking depictions of catastrophe, including major natural disasters; excessively frightening images and sound effects; and "sexually suggestive or provocative content that leads to sexual thoughts."[104] The notice also mandates providers to improve their content administration systems by hiring personnel to review and filter content, especially online music videos and other video entertainment, original content, and even netizen reporters (*paike*).[105]

For the first time, individuals are singled out in the Video Regulations, so that "primary investors" and "managers" can be fined up to RMB 20,000 or barred from engaging in similar services for five years for violations such as not sufficiently policing content or changing shareholders without going through specified procedures.[106]

Implementation of these regulations has been uneven, a trademark of many laws in China. A significant degree of uncertainty was also created by the inaugural requirement that online video service providers be either wholly state owned (as defined in Article 65 of the 2005 Company Law) or entities where the state holds the controlling interest, until the government clarified in February 2008 that this provision did not apply to already established Web sites.[107] Initially, 25 video-sharing portals were shut down (including 56.com), and another 32 video-sharing Web sites including

Tudou.com—China's largest video-sharing portal—were warned for hosting improper material in March 2008.[108] The third-largest Chinese video-sharing site, 56.com, went off-line mysteriously in June 2008 for more than a month,[109] and Youku.com received a license from SARFT in July 2008.[110]

Technical filtering associated with the so-called Great Firewall of China is only one tool of informal control applied in China. For example, to manage the explosion of the Chinese blogosphere, which reached 162 million blogs at the end of 2008,[111] blog service providers must not only install filters that do not allow the posting of potentially thousands of keyword combinations, but also flag certain posts for review. Comment sections, forums, and other interactive features that pose a higher risk of containing sensitive content can be shut off, while posts can be deleted or concealed by the provider so that only the author can see them.[112] Bloggers who are considered to have written too many troublesome posts can have their accounts canceled at will.

The unfolding of one mass incident presents a crucial case study on the range of online and media strategies to gather and communicate information, as well as government attempts to manage them. On June 22, 2008, the body of middle school student Li Shufen was found in the Ximen River in Weng'an county, Guizhou province.[113] Although authorities declared her death to be caused by accidental drowning, her family believed that she was a victim of a crime and pressed for an investigation. Rumors circulated that relatives of the country party secretary and police chief were among the people Li was with on the night of her death, one of whom said she jumped suddenly while he was doing push-ups.[114] In less than a week, the furor had grown so much that a group of hundreds of marchers heading toward government offices morphed into a crowd of up to 30,000 rioters, who surrounded a police headquarters and set fire to buildings and police vehicles.[115] For a week, local officials were silent, and only one piece of news was released by the official Xinhua News Agency, describing protesters as "some people who did not know about the exact context of what had happened."[116] In contrast to the silence of state-run media, numerous photos and video clips of the rioting appeared immediately on blogs and various online forums such as Tianya and the People's Daily Strong China forum, while unconfirmed and conflicting stories about the girl's death were circulated on the Internet.[117] Angry netizens and Web site moderators dueled vigorously, with users posting in increasingly oblique and creative ways and Web sites aggressively deleting and blocking information about the incident.[118] Furthermore, although hundreds of video clips appeared on YouTube, Chinese users could not access certain videos about the incident, and none appeared on two of biggest China's domestic video-sharing sites, Tudou.com and Uume.com.[119] Soon after, state-run media began increasingly to report news and official announcements regarding the Weng'an riot on Chinese news sites, but without allowing Internet users to leave comments. Other media attempting to cover the story were compelled to apply for special press passes in order to secure interviews, which were then attended by local officials.[120] By early July, state media were providing updates on the girl's cause of death and confirming that four officials had been fired as a result of the incident.[121]

At the same time, because these compulsory control mechanisms are actually implemented through informal processes, provider-based content control is neither narrow nor entirely predictable. A study of Chinese blog service providers demonstrated that there is substantial variation in censorship methods, the amount of content censored, and providers' transparency about deleting or depublishing content.[122] Similar findings were reached in a Citizen Lab study of four popular search engines in China, which found significant variations in the level of transparency about filtering, actual content censored, and methods used, suggesting that there is not a comprehensive system for determining censored content.[123] While Google and Microsoft, which are hosted outside China, actually delisted certain search results, the two search engines hosted inside China, Yahoo and Baidu, ran their Web crawlers behind China's filtering system, and therefore did not index Web sites already blocked by the Chinese government. Although Google censored considerably less than the other search engines, it also has a practice of prioritizing authorized local content, which researcher Nart Villeneuve found amplified the significance of the censored Web sites, as they were the only ones to offer differing viewpoints.[124] Indeed, the complexity of these informal control mechanisms was further revealed in April 2009, when an employee of China's leading search engine, Baidu, leaked a folder containing the substance and flow of internal censorship.[125] These included lists of topics, keywords, and URLs to be blocked, lists of banned forums, employee guidelines for monitoring work, censorship guidelines for the popular Baidu post bars, and guidelines of how to search for information that needed to be banned.[126]

The government's filtering practices can cause considerable anger among China's Internet users, especially when entire platforms or tools such as RSS feed sites or Twitter are blocked.[127] The uses of social media form the building blocks for what blogger Isaac Mao calls sharism, where the "co-computing of people, networks, and machines" forms a networked pipeline system to spread information in the face of Internet crackdowns.[128]

Because of a wide range of factors—from economic incentives and demographic factors of the online community to the dragnet of legal liability—the impact of self-censorship is likely enormous and increasingly public, if difficult to measure. Furthermore, the efforts of industry organizations at self-discipline are not entirely removed from government oversight. In promoting "Internet cooperation," officials place self-discipline hand-in-hand with admonitions to abide by Chinese laws.[129] The CIIRC encourages the reporting of "illegal" or "harmful" information and is sponsored by the Internet Society of China, formally registered as a civil society organization.[130] Yet the CIIRC cited Baidu and Google's Web and image search engines for returning a large number of obscene and pornographic links as part of an announced official crackdown on obscene and pornographic content in January 2009. Google and Baidu were among a total of 19 Web sites singled out for harmful, vulgar content available to minors, including Sina.com, Sohu.com, Wangyi, and Tianya.[131]

The Chinese constitution protects people's right to criticize and make suggestions to any state organ.[132] However, a few cases of alleged online defamation publicized in Spring 2009 exemplify how the Internet is illuminating some of the complexities of influence and power in the relationships between media, different levels of government, and citizens seeking justice.

Land requisitions for commercial development by local governments in China, where farmers are often inadequately compensated for land and suffer significant losses in income, are a common problem of poor governance and an inadequate legal system.[133] After petitions and other attempts to protect concerned farmers' legal rights had failed, Wu Baoquan and Wang Shuai were detained for their online criticism of local government land seizures.[134] In 2007, Wu Baoquan had posted information and conducted his own investigation about a land requisition in Ordos, Inner Mongolia, where officials forced residents off their land in order to sell it to developers, earning exorbitant profits while paying compensation well below market rates to the farmers.[135] Wu was tried twice for criminal defamation and ultimately his sentence was increased to two years, although the same court that affirmed his conviction decided to review his case in April 2009.[136]

Wang Shuai was the author of a satirical blog post suggesting officials from his hometown, Lingbao city in Henan province, had misappropriated funds for combating drought by carrying out policies that actually encouraged drought in order to drive down land values and justify paying farmers less compensation for requisitioning their land.[137] He was detained in Shanghai by Lingbao officials on March 6, 2009, and released on bail only after he signed a written confession and his family agreed to cut down their fruit trees, reducing the compensation they would receive for their land.[138] As is often the case, it took media attention, this time through a story in a national newspaper, the *China Youth Daily*, to spark the online public scrutiny that would influence the outcome of Wu's case. In this instance, higher party officials issued an apology (from the Henan province chief of public security), compensated Wang for his eight days in detention, and fired the local party secretary and punished three others responsible for the unauthorized land requisition as well as demolishing crops and buildings before compensation was paid.[139]

Neither Wang nor Wu was a journalist using a professional platform to disseminate information, but media were in large part responsible for exponentially expanding public awareness and discourse on their detention and the problems underpinning their cases.

The first litigation to be launched over human flesh search engines also tested how Internet libel would be dealt with under Chinese law. A Beijing woman named Jiang Yan had committed suicide in December 2007, months after learning about her husband Wang Fei's infidelity.[140] According to her instructions, posts from the blog diary she left recounting her ordeal were published posthumously by major Web portals, and Wang's anonymous human flesh search engine critics went to work publishing her husband's name, address, and other personal details.[141] In March 2008, after he was publicly condemned, harassed, and fired from his job, Wang sued the classmate of his wife who had posted her blog on his Web site and the portals Daqi.com and Tianya. In December, after convening a rare panel of 54 judges, a Beijing court ruled in Wang's favor, finding that the classmate and Daqi violated Wang's rights of privacy and reputation, ordering them to pay a total of almost USD 1,200 in damages for emotional distress, remove the posts, and apologize.[142] However, since Wang admitted to his infidelity, the court did not find that Wang had been slandered. It also exonerated Tianya, which had acted "appropriately" by deleting a user post containing Wang's personal information upon his request.[143] Interestingly, after issuing its judgment the Beijing district court held a press conference to recommend that the MIIT use technology to monitor Internet speech and prevent similar infringements.[144]

While one legal scholar argued that the Chinese legal system "weighs privacy pretty heavily against free speech, even when the speech is truthful,"[145] the relatively low fine may not act as quite as strong a deterrent as plaintiffs like Wang may desire. However, the legal system has become increasingly responsive to those who feel victimized by the human flesh search engines, especially corrupt officials. In March 2009, the Standing Committee of the National People's Congress approved an amendment to the Criminal Law that would punish government and corporate employees with access to personal data who illegally obtain, sell, or leak such information, while Xuzhou city in Jiangsu province became the first jurisdiction to prohibit the dissemination of others' personal information on the Internet.[146]

Surveillance

The government has continued to refine Internet surveillance mechanisms to closely track individuals' online activities.[147] In November 2006, the Ministry of Public Security announced the completion of the essential tasks of constructing the first stage of its "Golden Shield" project, which is a digital national surveillance network with almost complete coverage across public security units nationwide.[148] Despite the vagueness of public pronouncements on the implementation of the Golden Shield, the surveillance efforts of local governments, as well as organizations delegated responsibility for surveillance such as schools and ICPs, are clearly becoming more sophisticated. Since

2006, local governments have been developing "Safe City" surveillance and communications networks that connect police stations, through IP video surveillance, security cameras, and back-end data management facilities, to specific locations including Internet cafés, financial centers, and entertainment areas.[149] Private firms known as "censorship entrepreneurs" have also jumped into the fray, providing advanced text-mining solutions to enable censors to monitor, forecast, and "manage" online public opinion, thereby avoiding scandalous and damaging revelations such as the Internet post in June 2007 that exposed how children were kidnapped and forced into slave labor at illegal brick kilns in Shanxi province.[150] One company featured by international media, TRS Information Technology, claims to be the "leading search and content management technology and software provider in China," serving over 90 percent of the State Council ministries, 50 percent of newspaper press groups, and 300 universities and colleges.[151] Although TRS disclosed that its high-end surveillance systems had been generally adopted by police—specifically that the company had installed data-mining systems at eight Shanghai police stations so that one Internet police officer could now do the work of ten—TRS does not list the Ministry of Public Security as one of its customers.[152]

Chinese law offers few viable protections for individual privacy, although clauses in most Internet laws and regulations technically provide for the confidentiality of user information. The exceptions, however, are more important. For example, regulations on the management of e-mail services provide that e-mail service providers are duty-bound to keep personal information and e-mail addresses of users confidential, and may not disclose them except with user consent or when authorized for national security reasons or criminal investigations according to procedures stipulated by law.[153] Most Internet regulations allow for disclosure of user information when required by law, for reasons involving national security, and for criminal investigations, but do not specify what formal procedures are required or what evidentiary standards must be met for the disclosure of information. In practice, as has been demonstrated in a number of cases,[154] all ISPs and ICPs not only must capitulate to Chinese government demands for censoring content, but also are required to assist the government in monitoring Internet users and recording their online activities. Requests to turn over personal data are often informal or provide little detail, and providers have no discretion to refuse turning over information to public security officials.[155]

Real-Name Registration

Registration requirements are often the first step to monitoring citizens' online activities. Although this rule is not enforced, new subscribers to ISPs have been expected to register with their local police bureaus since 1996.[156] In March 2005, as part of a CCP campaign to exercise tighter control over culture, education, and media, all university BBSs were ordered to block off-campus users and require users to reregister with their personal identifying information when going online, eliminating online anonymity.[157] The city of Hangzhou was slated to become the first in China to require real-name Web registration for users to participate in local chat rooms or online forums, but these regulations were put on hold in May 2009.[158] The momentum for real-name systems might be stronger with cell phones, however. In January 2009, Beijing Mobile announced that it would begin requiring customers to show identification when purchasing its Easyown prepaid SIM cards (which amount to 70 percent of the customers on China Mobile, the nation's largest carrier) and limit purchases to three per person.[159]

Data Retention

In China, ISPs and ICPs must fulfill data retention obligations. Internet service providers are required to record important data (such as identification, URLs visited, length of visit, and activities) about all of their users for at least 60 days and to ensure that no illegal content is being hosted on their servers.[160] While 78 percent of users in China connect from home, 42 percent of users also use Internet cafés as a main access location.[161] However, since 2002, Internet cafés have been heavily regulated: all cafés are required to install filtering software, ban minors from entering, monitor the activities of their users, and record every user's identity and complete session logs for up to 60 days.[162] In many cities, they are also connected by live video feed to local police stations. The providers of electronic bulletin services, including bulletin board services, online discussion forums, chat rooms, and so on, are required to monitor the contents of information released in their service system, time of release, and URL or domain name, and to keep it for 60 days.[163]

Owned by Tencent, QQ is China's most popular instant messenger. This service was found to have installed a keyword-blocking program in its client software to monitor and record users' online communication, offering it to the police if required.[164]

Filtering and surveillance are often complementary processes, especially when ISPs and ICPs that are liable for the activities of their users delegate human monitors to monitor and flag content for further review or deletion. Online communications by e-mail and instant messaging (such as QQ and Skype) are also examined and monitored by the government.[165] In October 2008, a joint report by the Information Warfare Monitor and ONI Asia provided a chilling example of the possibilities for surveillance conducted by nonstate actors on a massive scale.[166] The Chinese-marketed TOM-Skype, a version of the VoIP and chatting software Skype, kept more than a million user records in seven types of log files, including IP addresses, user names, and time and date stamps in all the log files that could be decrypted. All these log files, along with the information required to decrypt them, were kept on publicly accessible servers. For call information logs dating from August 2007, the user name and phone number of the recipient were also logged, while content filter logs dating from August

2008 also contained full texts of chat messages (which themselves contained sensitive information such as e-mail addresses, passwords, and bank card numbers). Of the eight TOM-Skype surveillance servers traced by Nart Villeneuve, one server hosted a special version designed for use in Internet cafés and contained log files and the censored keyword list, while another contained logs for TOM Online's wireless services.

The TOM-Skype surveillance system was triggered when a TOM-Skype user sent or received messages containing a banned keyword listed in a key file, and those messages were then stored in log files on a TOM-Skype server. Within the content of these messages stored in the file logs, when filtered out to eliminate English language obscenities, almost 16 percent contained the word "communist," 7 percent the word "Falun," and 2.5 percent "Taiwan independence." However, the logged messages also made reference to other content outside the range of these long-sensitive topics, such as earthquakes and milk powder.[167]

Furthermore, the data also contained personal information of Skype users that interacted with TOM-Skype users. Users who attempt to access www.skype.com from China are redirected to skype.tom.com. While Skype claimed that TOM fixed the security breaches within 24 hours of the report's publication,[168] the report issued a warning for "groups engaging in political activism or promoting the use of censorship circumvention technology accessed through services provided by companies that have compromised on human rights." From the information contained in the log files, it would be possible to conduct politically motivated surveillance by using simple social networking tools to identify the relationships between users.

Like all other ICPs, most bulletin boards and chat rooms assign personnel to monitor the content of messages.[169] Messages submitted by users are censored by human censors and filtering systems before appearing online.[170] In order to enhance the surveillance on bulletin board systems, since 2005 the users of campus bulletin boards have been mandated to reregister with their real identifying information before posting messages online.[171]

In recent years, serious concerns have been raised about the ability of the Chinese government to spy on the country's 624 million cell phone subscribers: in 2008, one Chinese state-run cell phone company revealed that it had unlimited access to the personal data of their customers and hands the data over to Chinese security officials upon request.[172] Since 2004, the Chinese government has been drafting legislation to regulate personal mobile phone communication, which would require all cell phone subscribers to register for mobile phone service with their real name and identification card.[173] In addition, Chinese police have installed filtering and surveillance systems for mobile and SMS providers to block and monitor "harmful" short-message communications.[174] Anyone who distributes "harmful" messages or rumors using SMS on mobile phones can be arrested and convicted.[175]

Cyber Attacks

In 2008, organizations advocating for human rights in Tibet and China experienced escalated cyber attacks during politically explosive events, such as the crackdown on Tibetan protesters in March, and in the lead-up to the Olympic Games in August. The preferred method of these attackers was reportedly e-mail viruses, which are more likely to be undetected by commercial antivirus software because they are hand-crafted.[176] From field research conducted at the offices of the Tibetan Government in exile in Dharamsala and several Tibetan missions abroad, researchers at the SecDev Group and the Citizen Lab at the University of Toronto discovered an extensive malware-based cyber-espionage network that also used "contextually relevant e-mails" to gain "complete, real-time" control of at least 1,295 infected computers in 103 countries.[177] This network, which they called GhostNet, sent e-mails to specific targets containing a Trojan called Gh0st RAT, which in taking full control of infected computers allowed GhostNet to search and download specific files and covertly operate attached devices such as microphones and Web cameras. Among the high-value infections, comprising close to 30 percent of the computers affected, were many foreign affairs ministries, embassies, regional organizations (such as the ASEAN Secretariat), and news organizations. Although the complicity or awareness of Chinese authorities could not be conclusively established, researchers tracked the instances of Gh0st RAT to commercial Internet access accounts located on the island of Hainan in China.

ONI Testing Results

The "Great Firewall of China" uses a variety of overlapping techniques for blocking content containing a wide range of material considered politically sensitive by the Chinese government. While China employs filtering techniques used by many other countries, including domain name system (DNS) tampering and Internet protocol (IP) blocking, it is unique in the world for its system of filtration, targeting Internet connections when triggered by a list of banned keywords. Known as a TCP reset, this content filtering by keyword targets content regardless of where it is hosted.

Reset filtering using TCP is based on inspecting the content of IP packets for keywords that would trigger blocking, either in the header or the content of the message. When a router in the Great Firewall identifies a bad keyword, it sends reset packets to both the source and destination IP addresses in the packet, breaking the connection.

China employs targeted yet extensive filtering of information that could have a potential impact on the Communist Party's control over social stability, and is therefore predominantly focused on Chinese-language content relating to China-specific issues. For the government, information constituting a threat to public order extends well beyond well-publicized sensitive topics, such as the June 1989 military crackdown, the Tibetan rights movement, and the Falun Gong spiritual organization (all of which are methodically blocked), and includes independent media and dissenting voices, as well as content on human rights, political reform, sovereignty issues, and circumvention tools.

Filtering during the 2008 Olympic Games

The OpenNet Initiative monitored a short list of prominent blogs, Chinese-language and international news sites, advocacy organizations, and social media platforms continuously from late July to mid-September 2008. This period generally marked one of the most significant openings in access to information since ONI began monitoring Internet filtering in China in 2004, but the foundations of censorship based on control over domestic media and civil society remained.

In 2001, China issued this decree in its official bid for the 2008 Olympic Games: "There will be no restrictions on journalists in reporting on the Olympic Games."[178] This promise was significantly compromised, not only in China's purported long-term attempt to build a more open and transparent media system,[179] but also in the lack of transparency over its policy on access to online information.

At a press conference on July 28, the media director of the Beijing Olympic Committee responded to a *Wall Street Journal* reporter who physically displayed the filtering of certain Web sites on his laptop by denying anything was amiss.[180] This time, a Chinese Foreign Ministry spokesperson laid part of the blame with the Web sites themselves, claiming they have problems making them "not easy to view in China."[181] Yet, three days later, on July 31, the IOC admitted to accepting a deal with the Chinese government in which sensitive Web sites that were "not considered Games-related" would be blocked.[182]

During the Olympics, access was partitioned between the Olympics Main Press Center (MPC) in the Olympic Green and the Beijing International Media Center, the main press venue for non-IOC-accredited journalists.[183] The ONI compared data from the Olympics MPC to that from other locations in Beijing, compiling a snapshot of Internet filtering in China leading up to the Olympics. Testing conducted by the ONI at the Olympics MPC confirmed that filtering of Internet content continued even for members of the foreign press through TCP reset keyword blocking and IP address blocking, the latter accounting for the vast majority of filtering at the MPC. For each test at the MPC, the ONI tested at other locations in Beijing with broadband Internet access provided by China Netcom. Throughout this time period, filtering was nearly identical between the MPC and consumer-level access on China Netcom and China Telecom, indicating that the incrementally increased openness was implemented nationally.

Many sites that are routinely blocked by the Chinese government for containing politically sensitive content remained accessible from August 1 to at least mid-September 2008, including the Web sites of human rights organizations and foreign-hosted

Chinese-language news sites. Overseas news organizations such as the World Journal and the BBC News Chinese Web site were the main beneficiaries of China's Olympic guarantees.

Even though the IOC acknowledged on July 31 that filtering would continue to take place, a number of Web sites blocked at the MPC on July 25 were accessible a week later, including Amnesty International, Chinese-language Wikipedia (zh.wikipedia.org), and an increased swath of independent media including Taiwan's *Liberty Times*, the Hong Kong–based *Apple Daily* newspaper, Voice of America news, and Radio Free Asia (www.rfa.org) and its Chinese Web site.

However, RFA's Tibetan- and Uyghur-language Web sites became inaccessible again around August 20. Although Flickr remained accessible throughout the testing period, two of its photo servers were filtered until mid-August. Most of the sites unblocked for the Olympics remained accessible until at least mid-September 2008 on China Netcom, although a few (including Amnesty International) were again blocked on China Telecom by September 15.

At the same time, the ONI found that the sites being filtered frequently address tumultuous and controversial changes wrought in preparation for the games, from crackdowns on civil society to the transformation of a capital city and other social upheavals. Thus, the majority of advocacy sites and politically "sensitive" organizations remained blocked, sweeping across a broad range of issues from citizen journalism (www.zuola.com) to the Three Gorges Probe, as well as nearly all of the Tibetan exile advocacy groups. Groups staunchly critical of Chinese government policy, including the press freedom groups Reporters Without Borders and Freedom House, continued to be blocked. The status of certain news sites, including the China Digital Times Internet news and information clearinghouse and Boxun.com, a dissident news Web site that Chinese government officials reportedly look to as a source of internal news, remained unchanged. Furthermore, the accessibility of any Web site does not guarantee that content on that site will be available, as China's practice of filtering keywords through a TCP reset appears as robust as ever.

On December 19, 2008, the Web site of the *New York Times* was reported blocked even as restrictions were lifted on the Chinese-language Web sites of the BBC, Voice of America, and Asiaweek, which had been blocked earlier that week.[184]

In addition to testing during the Olympics period, the ONI also conducted testing in late 2008 on two backbone providers, the state-owned telecoms China Unicom (CU), formerly China Netcom, and China Telecom (CT), which between them provide coverage nationwide. Because both control access to an international gateway, URL filtering and domain name system (DNS) tampering implemented by CU and CT affect all users of the network regardless of ISP.

Nearly all the DNS tampering was executed by CU, while CT blocked a number of human rights organizations, pornographic sites, and one Hong Kong–based publisher (mirrorbooks.com) using this method. China Unicom also used IP blocking to filter nearly 400 IP addresses. These correlated closely with sites blocked on CT through a method obscured to analysis, in which users were presented with an error page informing the user that a network error occurred while accessing the Web site. While the error page can appear in the case of legitimate network errors, the repeated appearance of the error page indicates blocking is taking place. China Telecom also used a squid proxy to block a handful of Web sites, including several Flickr photo servers. While the two backbone providers showed less overlap in filtering methods when compared with 2006–2007, there continued to be almost complete correlation in blocking between CU and CT.

At time of testing, most international social media platforms were accessible, including Flickr, Blogspot, Wordpress, Facebook, and Twitter. In contrast to 2006–2007, when all individual Blogspot blogs tested were accessible on China Netcom and blocked or inaccessible on China Telecom, in 2008 CU and CT blocked nearly all of the same individual Blogspot blogs tested. Technorati continued to be blocked.

In late 2008, China had resumed blocking many Web sites that were blocked in 2006–2007 and made accessible during at least part of the Olympics period. These included the independent overseas news sites (*The Liberty Times*) and Radio Free Asia's main Web site and its Mandarin-, Uyghur-, and Tibetan-language sites. However, in contrast to 2006–2007, some of these Web sites were unreliably or intermittently accessible during December 2008 testing, possibly as a result of the TCP reset filtering method used. Sites blocked using the TCP reset included YouTube, Chinese-language Wikipedia, and BBC News.

A few sites that were accessible in 2006–2007 had been blocked by 2008 testing, most notably Wikipedia (en.wikipedia.org). The site Wikileaks (www.wikileaks.org) was also blocked by both ISPs in 2008 testing.

The greatest variations in filtering patterns between 2006–2007 and 2008 occurred with Chinese-language news media Web sites, likely in continuity from the Olympics. As in 2006–2007, few international news organizations were filtered, and some formerly blocked (e.g., Voice of America news) were accessible. Notably, some prominent Chinese-language media blocked in 2006–2007 were accessible in 2008, including the World Journal, www.singtao.com, and the *Apple Daily*. However, a significant number of independent media representing different points on the political spectrum continued to be filtered.

In 2006–2007 and 2008, China filtered a significant portion of content specific to its own human rights record and practices. As such, only a few global human rights sites with a global scope continued to be filtered, including Human Rights and Freedom House. Article 19 and Human Rights First were no longer blocked in 2008, and filtering on Amnesty International was renewed after a hiatus during the Olympics period. A typical example of this targeting of China-related content is the differential treatment of two related organizations: while the Web site for the writers' association PEN American Center hosted content on the jailed dissident and Charter 08 coauthor Liu Xiaobo, it was accessible (www.pen.org) at the same time that the Chinese PEN Center (www.chinesepen.org), a site with both English and Chinese content, was blocked by both ISPs. The sites of watchdogs on Chinese rights defenders and labor rights continued to be blocked, as did a substantial number of rights organizations based in Hong Kong.

Certain targets for blocking continued to cut across political and social lines of conflict in 2008. The consistent filtering of Web sites supporting greater autonomy and rights protection for the Uyghur (www.uyghurcongress.org), Tibetan, and Mongolian (www.innermongolia.org) ethnic minorities is not surprising, as these issues have already been excluded from official discourse inside China. Nearly all the overseas Tibetan organizations, which conduct activities ranging from news broadcasting for the Tibetan community to the Tibetan Youth Congress, which lobbies for full independence for Tibet, have been blocked. China also continued to block a substantial number of sites on religion, including the International Coalition for Religious Freedom, Catholic organizations, and sites on Islam in Arabic, including those presenting extremist viewpoints (www.alumah.com).

In 2008, China continued to filter a significant number of sites presenting alternative or additional perspectives on its policies toward Taiwan and North Korea. For example, the Democratic Progressive Party (DPP) of Taiwan (www.dpp.org.tw) is continually filtered. However, a number of sites with no political content but ending with the domain ".tw" were blocked, and Greenpeace Taiwan was the only country Web site of the organization blocked by both ISPs.

As in 2006–2007, the major exceptions to the focus on politically sensitive topics specific to China in 2008 were circumvention tools and pornography. A portion, though not a majority, of proxy tools and anonymizers in both the Chinese (gardennetworks.com) and English (www.peacefire.org) languages were blocked. The circumvention tool Psiphon was also blocked, along with the Web sites of the Citizen Lab at the University of Toronto and the Information Warfare Monitor, sister institutions engaging in research on circumvention and surveillance. Both ISPs also blocked a substantial amount of pornographic content.

Although the scope of Internet filtering in China extends far beyond the highly sensitive issues known as the "three Ts: Tibet, Tiananmen, and Taiwan," the continued potency of these subjects evidently prompted the Chinese government to step up filtering of leading international Web sites and social media platforms in 2009. On March 24, 2009, Google officially confirmed that YouTube was blocked in China; traffic dropped steeply on the evening of March 23 to "near zero" by March 24.[185] The Web site www.herdict.org also captured accounts providing evidence of a previous reported block of YouTube beginning on March 4, coinciding with the one-year anniversary of the crackdown on protests in Tibetan regions (during which YouTube was also reported blocked in March 2008) as well as the 50th anniversary of the Tibetan uprising of 1959. Blogspot became inaccessible around May 9,[186] and on June 2, two days before the 20th anniversary of the June 4 military crackdown, Flickr, Twitter, live.com, and Hotmail were blocked in rapid succession.[187]

In May 2009, the Ministry of Industry and Information Technology in China sent a notification to computer manufacturers of its intention to require all new PCs sold in China after July 1 to have filtering software preinstalled.[188] The notice, jointly issued by the MIIT, the Civilization Office of the Central Communist Party Committee, and the Ministry of Finance, according to the PRC Government Procurement Law, mandates the procurement of all rights and services related to a designated software called "Green Dam Youth Escort" to be made available for free public use. Green Dam is a product of the Jinhui Computer System Engineering Company, which reportedly received RMB 40 million from the government for a year-long contract.[189]

The purported intent of the Green Dam software is to filter harmful online text and image content in order to prevent this information from affecting youth and promote a healthy and harmonious Internet environment.[190] However, researchers at the OpenNet Initiative and the Stop Badware Project conducting an initial technical assessment of the software found that Green Dam's filtering not only is ineffective at blocking pornographic content as a whole, but also includes unpredictable and disruptive blocking of political and religious content normally associated with the Great Firewall of China.[191]

As a computing tool, Green Dam is far more powerful than the centralized filtering system China currently implements, as it actively monitors individual computer behavior to the extent that its "language processing" tool can institute extremely intrusive "kill" action on sites if the content algorithm detects "inappropriate" sensitive political or religious speech.[192] These actions include the sudden termination of Web browser tabs, whole browsers, and a wide range of programs including word processing and e-mail. The program installs components deep into the kernel of the computer operating system in order to enable this application layer monitoring. Researchers also found that the killing of sites upon inappropriate keywords or URLs like http:// falundafa.org extends to killing single letters that autocomplete in location boxes and autocomplete lists in browsers. For example, if a user enters "epochtimes.com" into the location, the user will see the page briefly, see the warning box briefly, and then have the whole browser terminated. But after the user restarts the browser, epochtimes.com will be in the browser history and therefore in the autocomplete list, so that the user may only have to type "e" into the location box to trigger the appearance of epochtimes.com in the autocomplete list and cause Green Dam to terminate the whole browser.[193]

The monopoly status granted to Jinhui is unprecedented, representing the first instance where a government mandated a specific filtering software product for use at a national level instead of performance standards that encourage consumer choice, security, and product quality. The mandated procurement and preinstallation of Green Dam also adds a new and powerful control mechanism to the existing filtering system, in addition to blocking already done at the international backbones and by individual online content providers. Distributing control mechanisms to end users at the periphery allows the government to partially offload the burden of monitoring and blocking content to individual machines on the network, amounting to a "huge distributed super computer dedicated to controlling online content."[194]

In addition to interfering with the performance of personal computers in an unpredictable way, the poor design of Green Dam also presents security risks that allow any Web site the user visits to take control of the user's computer, with the potential for malicious sites to steal private data and commit other illegal acts, or even turn every Chinese computer running Green Dam into a member of a botnet.[195] The Stop Badware Project at the Berkman Center for Internet and Society confirmed that the application violates its Badware guidelines for software, as it does not disclose the filtering of political speech or the unexpected behavior of completely killing processes that contain such speech.[196]

Conclusion

The Chinese government has maintained a strict and vigorous approach toward Internet censorship, interfering with public knowledge and discourse through pervasive filtering practices and a multitude of nontechnical methods. In 2008, China led the world with 300 million Internet users, and the sheer scale and expanding scope of online content presented a significant challenge for a government intent on maintaining social stability and order in China's networked spheres. China continues to fine-tune its system of information control, including attempts to promote a public relations approach to online commentary and news reporting. The foundation of China's information-control framework continues to be built on ensuring that domestic providers are responsible for filtering and monitoring hosted content. The government has also taken measures to distribute control mechanisms to end users through the procurement of filtering software on home computers. The 2008 Olympic Games held in Beijing had a net positive impact on access to information, but this has abated without continued international pressure for greater openness and transparency.

Notes

1. Jim Yardley, "Monk Protests in Tibet Draw Chinese Security," *New York Times*, March 14, 2008, http://www.nytimes.com/2008/03/14/world/asia/14china.html.

2. Jim Yardley, "Tibetans Clash with Chinese Police in Second City," *New York Times*, March 16, 2008, http://www.nytimes.com/2008/03/16/world/asia/16tibet.html?ref=asia.

3. Roland Soong, "The Olympic Torch Tour as Public Relations Disaster," EastSouthWestNorth blog, April 10, 2008, http://zonaeuropa.com/20080410_1.htm.

4. Dune Lawrence and Lee Spears, "China Rejects CNN Apology, Demands 'Sincere' Response," Bloomberg, April 17, 2008, http://www.bloomberg.com/apps/news?pid=20601204&sid=aVIfJJeTKWMc; Xinhua News Agency, "Chinese Netizens Urge Carrefour Boycott after Torch Relay Incident," April 16, 2008, http://news.xinhuanet.com/english/2008-04/16/content_7989807.htm.

5. *BBC News*, "China Earthquake Toll Jumps Again," May 23, 2008, http://news.bbc.co.uk/2/hi/asia-pacific/7416035.stm.

6. Qian Gang, "Looking Back on Chinese Media Reporting of School Collapses," China Media Project, May 7, 2009, http://cmp.hku.hk/2009/05/07/1599/; Edward Wong, "Year after China Quake, New Births, Old Wounds," *New York Times*, May 6, 2009, http://www.nytimes.com/2009/05/06/world/asia/06quake.html.

7. Tania Branigan, "China Releases Earthquake Death Toll of Children," *Guardian*, May 7, 2009, http://www.guardian.co.uk/world/2009/may/07/china-earthquake-anniversary-death-toll.

8. Qian Gang, "Looking Back on Chinese Media Reporting of School Collapses," China Media Project, May 7, 2009, http://cmp.hku.hk/2009/05/07/1599/.

9. Michael Bristow, "Big Olympic Spend, but Little Debate," *BBC News*, July 31, 2008, http://news.bbc.co.uk/2/hi/asia-pacific/7523235.stm.

10. Xinhua News Agency, "Regulations on Reporting Activities in China by Foreign Journalists during the Beijing Olympic Games and the Preparatory Period," January 8, 2007, http://www.chinese-embassy.org.uk/eng/lsyw/Journalist/t287657.htm.

11. Jacquelin Magnay, "China's Media Censored over Stabbing," *The Age*, August 12, 2008, http://www.theage.com.au/world/chinas-media-censored-over-stabbing-20080811-3tmf.html.

12. OpenNet Initiative Blog, "The Catch-22 of Protests and Surveillance," August 19, 2008, http://opennet.net/blog/2008/08/the-catch-22-protests-and-surveillance.

13. Foreign Correspondents' Club of China, "Reporting Interference Tally Update," December 3, 2008, http://www.fccchina.org/2008/12/03/reporting-interference-tally-update/; Foreign Correspondents' Club of China, "China Fails to Make Olympic Podium on Media Freedom," August 23, 2008, http://www.fccchina.org/2008/08/23/china-fails-to-make-olympic-podium-on-media-freedom/#more-35.

14. *BBC News*, "China's Press Freedoms Extended," October 18, 2008, http://news.bbc.co.uk/2/hi/asia-pacific/7675306.stm.

15. Foreign Correspondents' Club of China, "FCCC Urges Withdrawal of Restrictions on HK Journalists," February 13, 2009, http://www.fccchina.org/2009/02/13/fccc-urges-withdrawal-of-restrictions-on-hk-journalists/.

16. Xinhua News Agency, "60 Arrested over Melamine-Tainted Sanlu Milk Powder," January 11, 2009, http://www2.chinadaily.com.cn/china/2009-01/11/content_7385532.htm.

17. *The Australian*, "China Accused of Olympic Milk Cover-up," October 1, 2008, http://www.theaustralian.news.com.au/story/0,25197,24430439-2703,00.html.

18. Jim Yardley and David Barboza, "Despite Warnings, China's Regulators Failed to Stop Tainted Milk," *New York Times*, September 27, 2008, http://www.nytimes.com/2008/09/27/world/asia/27milk.html?pagewanted=print.

19. Ibid.

20. Zhu Zhe and Cui Xiaohuo, "Sanlu Ex-Boss Gets Life for Milk Scandal," *China Daily*, January 22, 2009, http://www.chinadaily.com.cn/china/2009-01/22/content_7422297.htm.

21. David Bandurski, "Taxi Strikes in China Highlight Changing Press Controls," China Media Project, November 12, 2008, http://cmp.hku.hk/2008/11/12/1344/.

22. Tania Branigan, "China Tells State Media to Report Bad News," *Guardian*, November 20, 2008, http://www.guardian.co.uk/media/2008/nov/20/china-media-freedom.

23. Maureen Fan, "In China, Media Make Small Strides," *Washington Post*, December 28, 2008, http://www.washingtonpost.com/wp-dyn/content/article/2008/12/27/AR2008122701218.html.

24. David Bandurski, "The Longnan Riots and the CCP's Global Spin Campaign," China Media Project, November 20, 2008, http://cmp.hku.hk/2008/11/20/1368/.

25. Reuters, "China to Introduce Journalist 'Black List,'" February 13, 2009, http://in.reuters.com/article/worldNews/idINIndia-37996920090213?sp=true.

26. David Bandurski, "In Today's Headlines, an Absence Speaks a Thousand Words," China Media Project, May 27, 2009, http://cmp.hku.hk/2009/05/27/1647/.

27. Andrew Jacobs and Jonathan Ansfield, "Chinese Learn Limits of Online Freedom as the Filter Tightens," *New York Times*, February 5, 2009, http://www.nytimes.com/2009/02/05/world/asia/05beijing.html.

28. Foreign Correspondents' Club of China, "China Should Allow Access to Tibetan Areas," March 9, 2009, http://www.fccchina.org/2009/03/09/china-should-allow-access-to-tibetan-areas/.

29. China Internet Network Information Center, "Statistical Survey Report on the Internet Development in China," March 23, 2009, http://www.cnnic.net.cn/uploadfiles/pdf/2009/3/23/131303.pdf.

30. Ibid.

31. Janet Ong, "China to Merge Telecom Companies, Issue 3G Licenses," Bloomberg, May 24, 2008, http://www.bloomberg.com/apps/news?pid=20601087&sid=an0_Sig7jjE0&refer=home.

32. China Internet Network Information Center, "Statistical Survey Report on the Internet Development in China," March 23, 2009, http://www.cnnic.net.cn/uploadfiles/pdf/2009/3/23/131303.pdf.

33. Ibid.

34. Ibid.

35. Zhao Zhiguo, "Development and Administration of the Internet in China," China.org.cn, November 7, 2008, http://www.china.org.cn/china/internetForum/2008-11/06/content_16719106 .htm.

36. China Internet Network Information Center, "Statistical Survey Report on the Internet Development in China," March 23, 2009, http://www.cnnic.net.cn/uploadfiles/pdf/2009/3/23/131303 .pdf.

37. Ibid.

38. Ibid.

39. Paul Budde Communication Pty., Ltd., "China—New Internet Economy," April 24, 2009.

40. SinoCast China IT Watch, "China to Issue Its First VoIP License," March 13, 2006.

41. CC Time, "Analysis of Recent Developments and Forecasts for China's VOIP Industry," March 19, 2008, http://www.cctime.com/html/2008-3-19/20083191040597146.htm.

42. See Ministry of Industry and Information Technology of the People's Republic of China, http://www.miit.gov.cn/n11293472/index.html.

43. *People's Daily Online*, "Highlights of China's Institutional Restructuring Plan," March 16, 2008, http://english.peopledaily.com.cn/90001/90776/90785/6374104.html.

44. China Internet Network Information Center, "Statistical Survey Report on the Internet Development in China," March 23, 2009, http://www.cnnic.net.cn/uploadfiles/pdf/2009/3/23/131303 .pdf.

45. Ibid.

46. Paul Budde Communication Pty., Ltd., "China—Telecommunications Infrastructure," April 24, 2009.

47. Ibid.

48. Xinhua News Agency, "China Netcom, China Unicom Merger Completed, Biggest in Country's History," October 15, 2008, http://news.xinhuanet.com/english/2008-10/15/content _10200183.htm.

49. Sumner Lemon, "After Years of Delays, China Finally Issues 3G Licenses," *PCWorld*, January 7, 2009, http://www.pcworld.com/businesscenter/article/156612/after_years_of_delays_china_finally _issues_3g_licenses.html.

50. *"Nnali you hexie, nali you caonima,"* or, "Where there are river crabs, there are grass-mud horses," is based on plays on characters and meaning, forming a "law of Chinese cyberpolitics": online censorship always meets resistance. See China Digital Times, "Grass Mud Horse," http:// chinadigitaltimes.net/china/grass-mud-horse/.

51. China Internet Network Information Center, "Statistical Survey Report on the Internet Development in China," March 23, 2009, http://www.cnnic.net.cn/uploadfiles/pdf/2009/3/23/131303.pdf.

52. Alice Xin Liu, "Hu Yong Interview: The Digital Age, Orwell's 'Newspeak' and Chinese Media," Danwei, April 16, 2009, http://www.danwei.org/media/hu_yong_interview.php.

53. David Bandurski, "China's Guerrilla War for the Web," *Far Eastern Economic Review*, July 2008, http://www.feer.com/essays/2008/august/chinas-guerrilla-war-for-the-web.

54. Dave Lyons, "Day 2 4.1: Chen Lu, Human Flesh Search," Global Voices, One World blog, May 28, 2009, http://www.lokman.org/2009/05/28/day-2-41-chen-lu-human-flesh-search/.

55. Bai Xu and Ji Shaoting, "'Human Flesh Search Engine': An Internet Lynching?" Xinhua News Service, July 4, 2008, http://news.xinhuanet.com/english/2008-07/04/content_8491087.htm.

56. Ryan McLaughlin, "Human Flesh Search Engines—Crowd-Sourcing 'Justice'," CNet Asia Blogs, January 28, 2009, http://asia.cnet.com/blogs/thetechdynasty/post.htm?id=63008617.

57. The video footage is available on YouTube, http://www.youtube.com/watch?v=zomgZuZoDoM.

58. National Public Radio, "Duke Student Targeted for Mediating Tibet Protest," April 21, 2008, http://www.npr.org/templates/story/story.php?storyId=89803198.

59. *New York Review of Books*, "China's Charter 08" [unofficial translation by Perry Link], January 15, 2009, http://www.nybooks.com/articles/22210.

60. Ibid.

61. China Human Rights Defenders, "Over One Hundred Signatories Harassed since Launch of Charter 08," January 8, 2009, http://crd-net.org/Article/Class9/Class98/200901/20090108141140_12945.html.

62. John Garnaut, "Late-Night Visit from Police as Charter 08 Support Grows," *Sydney Morning Herald*, January 13, 2009, http://www.smh.com.au/articles/2009/01/12/1231608616941.html.

63. Roland Soong, "A Review of the Chinese Internet in 2008," EastSouthWestNorth blog, January 24, 2009, http://www.zonaeuropa.com/20090124_1.htm.

64. David Bandurski, "China's Guerrilla War for the Web," *Far Eastern Economic Review*, July 2008, http://www.feer.com/essays/2008/august/chinas-guerrilla-war-for-the-web.

65. Ibid.

66. Article 34, Constitution of the People's Republic of China, amended March 14, 2004, by the 10th NPC at its 2nd Session, http://english.peopledaily.com.cn/constitution/constitution.html.

67. Ibid.

68. See State Council, *Zhonghua Renmin Gongheguo Jisuanji Xitong Anquan Baohu Tiaoli* [The Regulations of the People's Republic of China for the Safety Protection of Computer Information Systems], February 18, 1994.

69. The nine types of content that have been illegal to produce or disseminate since the earliest Internet Regulations are (1) violating the basic principles as they are confirmed in the Constitution; (2) endangering state security, divulging state secrets, subverting the national regime, or jeopardizing the integrity of national unity; (3) harming national honor or interests; (4) inciting hatred against peoples, racism against peoples, or disrupting the solidarity of peoples; (5) disrupting national policies on religion, propagating evil cults and feudal superstitions; (6) spreading rumors, disturbing social order, or disrupting social stability; (7) spreading obscenity, pornography, gambling, violence, or terror, or abetting the commission of a crime; (8) insulting or defaming third parties, infringing on legal rights and interests of third parties; and (9) other content prohibited by law and administrative regulations. Two categories of prohibited content were added in Article 19 of the Provisions on the Administration of Internet News Information Services (Internet News Information Services Regulations) (*hulianwang xinwen xinxi fuwu guanli guiding*), promulgated by the State Council Information Office and the Ministry of Information Industry on September 25, 2005. These two additional categories are (1) inciting illegal assemblies, associations, marches, demonstrations, or gatherings that disturb social order; and (2) conducting activities in the name of an illegal civil organization. Unofficial English translation is available at Congressional Executive Commission on China Virtual Academy, "Provisions on the Administration of Internet News Information Services," September 25, 2005, http://www.cecc.gov/pages/virtualAcad/index.phpd ?showsingle=24396.

70. See NPC Standing Committee, *Quanguo renda changweihui guanyu weihu hulianwang anquan de guiding* [Rules of the NPC standing committee on safeguarding Internet security], December 28, 2000.

71. Ministry of Information Industry and the State Council Information Office, *hulianwang xinwen xinxi fuwu guanli guiding* [Provisions on the administration of news information services], September 25, 2005, http://www.isc.org.cn/20020417/ca315779.htm; Congressional Executive Commission on China Virtual Academy, "Provisions on the Administration of Internet News Information Services."

72. Human Rights Watch, "China: Media Chokehold Tightens before Party Congress," August 17, 2007, http://china.hrw.org/press/news_release/china_media_chokehold_tightens_before_party _congress; Michael Bristow, "China Tightens Grip Ahead of Congress," BBC News, September 14, 2007, http://news.bbc.co.uk/2/hi/asia-pacific/6992946.stm.

73. Peter Ford, "Why China Shut Down 18,401 Websites," *Christian Science Monitor*, September 25, 2007, http://www.csmonitor.com/2007/0925/p01s06-woap.html?page=1.

74. Xinhua News Agency, "*qi bumen kaizhan zhengzhi hulianwang disu zhifeng xingdong*" [Seven departments launch operation for fixing the spread of vulgarity on the Internet], January 5, 2009, http://www.gov.cn/jrzg/2009-01/05/content_1196447.htm.

75. Xinhua News Agency, "Porn Crackdown to Shield China's Youth during Holiday," China .org.cn, January 23, 2008, http://www.china.org.cn/china/news/2009-01/23/content_17178010 .htm.

76. Vivian Wu, "Popular Blog Service Provider Shut Down," *South China Morning Post*, January 10, 2009.

77. John Garnaut, "Nervous China Tightens Grip on Internet," *Sydney Morning Herald*, January 12, 2009.

78. *China Digital Times*, "Bullog Shut Down," January 9, 2009, http://chinadigitaltimes.net/2009/01/bullog-shut-down/.

79. Radio Free Asia, "China Closes 'Porn' Sites," April 1, 2009, http://www.rfa.org/english/news/china/internet-04012009101155.html.

80. For example, in June 2006, the Information Office under the State Council and the MII embarked on a period of "strict supervision" of search engines, chat rooms, and blog service providers to curb the circulation of "harmful" information online. See Howard W. French, "Chinese Discuss Plan to Tighten Restrictions on Cyberspace," *New York Times*, July 4, 2006, http://www.nytimes.com/2006/07/04/world/asia/04internet.html.

81. China Internet Network Information Center, "Statistical Survey Report on the Internet Development in China," March 23, 2009, http://www.cnnic.net.cn/uploadfiles/pdf/2009/3/23/131303.pdf.

82. Ibid.

83. David Shambaugh, "China's Propaganda System: Institutions, Processes, and Efficacy," *China Journal*, No. 57 (January 2007): 25–58.

84. Rebecca MacKinnon, "China's Censorship 2.0: How Companies Censor Bloggers," *First Monday*, 14, No. 2 (2009), http://www.uic.edu/htbin/cgiwrap/bin/ojs/index.php/fm/article/view/2378/2089.

85. Ministry of Information Industry and the State Council Information Office, *hulianwang xinwen xinxi fuwu guanli guiding* [Provisions on the administration of news information services], September 25, 2005, http://www.isc.org.cn/20020417/ca315779.htm; Congressional Executive Commission on China Virtual Academy, "Provisions on the Administration of Internet News Information Services."

86. Ibid.

87. Ibid.

88. Ibid.

89. Benjamin Liebman, "Watchdog or Demagogue? The Media in the Chinese Legal System," *Columbia Law Review*, 105, No. 1 (January 2005): 41.

90. Stephanie Wang and Robert Faris, "Welcome to the Machine," *Index on Censorship*, 37, No. 2, (May 2008): 106–113.

91. Anne S.Y. Cheung, "The Business of Governance: China's Legislation on Content Regulation in Cyberspace," *New York University Journal of International Law and Politics*, 28 (Fall 2005–Winter 2006): 1–37

92. Chinese Human Rights Defenders, "Tug of War over China's Cyberspace: A Sequel to Journey to the Heart of Censorship (Part II)," March 19, 2009, http://crd-net.org/Article/Class9/Class11/200903/20090319000543_14370.html.

93. Reporters Without Borders, "2009 Annual Report: China," http://www.rsf.org/en-rapport57-China.html.

94. Chinese Human Rights Defenders, "Tug of War over China's Cyberspace: A Sequel to Journey to the Heart of Censorship (Part II)," March 19, 2009, http://crd-net.org/Article/Class9/Class11/200903/20090319000543_14370.html.

95. Chinese Human Rights Defenders, *Zhongguo Wangluo Jiankong Yu Fanjiankong Niandu Baogao*" [Annual Report on Chinese Internet Surveillance 2007], July 10, 2008, http://www.crd-net.org/Article/Class1/200807/20080710165332_9340.html.

96. Reporters Without Borders, "Journalist Gets Four Years for Exposing Communist Party Corruption in Shandong," May 15, 2008, http://www.rsf.org/article.php3?id_article=27034.

97. Human Rights in China, "Family Visits Still Denied to Sichuan School Teacher Punished after Quake-Zone Visit," July 29, 2008, http://www.hrichina.org/public/contents/press?revision_id=66556&item_id=66524.

98. Ministry of Information Industry, Article 13, *Hulianwang dianzi gonggao fuwu guanli guiding* [Rules on the management of Internet electronic bulletin services], October 7, 2000.

99. State Council, Article 20, *Hulianwang xinxi fuwu guanli banfa* [Measures for managing Internet information services], September 25, 2000.

100. OpenNet Initiative Blog, "China Incentivizes Self-Censorship in Regulation of Online Video," January 4, 2008, http://opennet.net/blog/2008/01/china-incentivizes-self-censorship-regulation-online-video.

101. State Administration of Radio, Film, and Television (SARFT) and the Ministry of Information Industry of the People's Republic of China, Article 9, Provisions on the Management of Internet Audio and Video Programming Services, December 20, 2007. Unofficial translation available at OpenNet Initiative, http://opennet.net/news/china-provisions.

102. Ministry of Information Industry and the State Council Information Office, *hulianwang xinwen xinxi fuwu guanli guiding* [Provisions on the administration of news information services], September 25, 2005, http://www.isc.org.cn/20020417/ca315779.htm; Congressional Executive Commission on China Virtual Academy, "Provisions on the Administration of Internet News Information Services."

103. State Administration of Radio, Film and Television (SARFT), *Guangdian zongju guanyu jiaqiang hulianwang shiting jiemu neirong guanli de tongzhi* [Notice for strengthening the administration of Internet audio and video programming content], March 30, 2009, http://www.sarft.gov.cn/articles/2009/03/30/20090330171107690049.html; Danwei, "New Rules Imposed on Internet Video Content," April 1, 2009, http://www.danwei.org/media_regulation/new_rules_imposed_on_internet.php.

104. State Administration of Radio, Film and Television (SARFT), *Guangdian zongju guanyu jiaqiang hulianwang shiting jiemu neirong guanli de tongzhi*, Section 2 (1–21).

105. Ibid., Section 3.

106. State Administration of Radio, Film, and Television (SARFT) and the Ministry of Information Industry of the People's Republic of China, Article 23, Provisions on the Management of Internet Audio and Video Programming Services.

107. Paul Budde Communication Pty., Ltd., "China—New Internet Economy," April 24, 2009.

108. Interactive Investor, "China Orders 8 More Online Video-Sharing Web Sites to Shut Down," May 21, 2008, http://www.iii.co.uk/news/?type=afxnews&articleid=6721662&action=article.

109. Jonathan Richards, "'Chinese YouTube' Shut Down amid Censor Fears," *Times Online*, June 20, 2008, http://technology.timesonline.co.uk/tol/news/tech_and_web/article4179103.ece; Loretta Chao, "Closure of Chinese Online-Video Site Sparks Concern," *Wall Street Journal*, June 20, 2008, http://online.wsj.com/article/SB121390202591089267.html?mod=2_1567_leftbox; Reuters, "Vobile Announces Commercial Deployment with Leading Video Sharing Website 56.com," March 23, 2009, http://www.reuters.com/article/pressRelease/idUS95209+23-Mar-2009+PRN20090323.

110. Steven Schwankert, "China Approves Video Site Youku's License," July 10, 2008, *PCWorld*, http://pcworld.about.com/od/internet/China-Approves-Video-Site-Youk.htm.

111. China Internet Network Information Center, "Twenty-third Statistical Survey Report on the Internet Development in China."

112. Stephanie Wang and Robert Faris, "Welcome to the Machine," *Index on Censorship*, 37, No. 2, (May 2008): 106–113.

113. Roland Soong, "The Weng'an Mass Incident," EastSouthWestNorth blog, July 1, 2008, http://www.zonaeuropa.com/20080701_1.htm.

114. Bob Chen, "China: Let's Do Push-up!," Global Voices Online, July 7, 2008, http://globalvoicesonline.org/2008/07/07/china-lets-do-push-up/.

115. Roland Soong, "The Weng'an Mass Incident," EastSouthWestNorth blog, July 1, 2008, http://www.zonaeuropa.com/20080701_1.htm.

116. Xinhua News Agency, "Police Station Assaulted, Torched by Local People in Southwest China County," June 20, 2009, http://news.xinhuanet.com/english/2008-06/29/content_8456602.htm.

117. OpenNet Initiative Blog, "China's Net Nannies in Full Force after Riot in Southern China," July 2, 2008, http://opennet.net/blog/2008/07/china%E2%80%99s-net-nannies-full-force-after-riot-southern-china.

118. Jonathan Ansfield, "Guizhou Riots: How Much Steam Can the Machine Filter?" Newsweek blog, July 2, 2008, http://blog.newsweek.com/blogs/beijing/archive/2008/07/02/can-the

-propaganda-machine-filter-the-steam.aspx; OpenNet Initiative Blog, "China's Net Nannies in Full Force After Riot in Southern China," July 2, 2008, http://opennet.net/blog/2008/07/china %E2%80%99s-net-nannies-full-force-after-riot-southern-china.

119. OpenNet Initiative Blog, "China's Net Nannies in Full Force after Riot in Southern China," July 2, 2008, http://opennet.net/blog/2008/07/china%E2%80%99s-net-nannies-full-force-after -riot-southern-china.

120. Roland Soong, "The Weng'an Mass Incident," EastSouthWestNorth blog, July 1, 2008, http://www.zonaeuropa.com/20080701_1.htm.

121. Xinhua News Agency, "Final Autopsy Shows Girl in Southwest China Protest Drowned," July 10, 2008, http://news.xinhuanet.com/english/2008-07/10/content_8519852.htm.

122. Rebecca MacKinnon, "China's Censorship 2.0: How Companies Censor Bloggers," *First Monday*, 14, No. 2 (2009), http://www.uic.edu/htbin/cgiwrap/bin/ojs/index.php/fm/article/view/ 2378/2089.

123. Nart Villeneuve, "Search Monitor Project: Toward a Measure of Transparency" (Working paper, Citizen Lab, University of Toronto, June 2008), http://www.citizenlab.org/papers/ searchmonitor.pdf.

124. Ibid.

125. China Digital Times, "Baidu's Internal Monitoring and Censorship Document Leaked (1) (Updated)," April 30, 2009, http://chinadigitaltimes.net/2009/04/baidus-internal-monitoring-and -censorship-document-leaked/.

126. Xiao Qiang, "Baidu's Internal Monitoring And Censorship Document Leaked (2)," *China Digital Times*, April 29, 2009, http://chinadigitaltimes.net/2009/04/baidus-internal-monitoring -and-censorship-document-leaked-2/.

127. Xiao Qiang, "Chinese Censors Cut Off Twitter, Hotmail and Flickr," *China Digital Times*, June 2, 2009, http://chinadigitaltimes.net/2009/06/chinese-censors-cut-off-twitter-hotmail-and-flickr/.

128. isaacmao.com, "Great Firewall vs. Social Media," March 3, 2009, http://www.isaacmao.com/ meta/2009/03/great-firewall-vs-social-media.html.

129. Consulate-General of the People's Republic of China in Chicago, "Foreign Ministry Spokes-person Liu Jianchao's Regular Press Conference on December 16, 2008," December 17, 2008, http://www.chinaconsulatechicago.org/eng/fyrth/t526582.htm.

130. See China Internet Illegal Information Reporting Center, http://ciirc.china.cn/.

131. Xinhua News Agency, *"qi bumen kaizhan zhengzhi hulianwang disu zhifeng xingdong"* [Seven departments launch operation for fixing the spread of vulgarity on the internet], January 5, 2009, http://www.gov.cn/jrzg/2009-01/05/content_1196447.htm.

132. Article 41, Constitution of the People's Republic of China, http://english.peopledaily.com .cn/constitution/constitution.html.

133. See Paulina Hartono, "China's Emerging Land Rights Movement," December 22, 2007, *China Digital Times*, http://chinadigitaltimes.net/2007/12/chinas-emerging-land-rights-movement/.

134. Joshua Rosenzweig, "China's Battle over the Right to Criticize," *Far Eastern Economic Review*, May 1, 2009, http://www.feer.com/essays/2009/may/chinas-battle-over-the-right-to-criticize.

135. Cai Ke, "Wrongly Jailed Blogger Fights for Justice," *China Daily*, May 20, 2009, http://www .chinadaily.com.cn/china/2009-05/20/content_7793902.htm.

136. Siwciluozi's Blog, "Update: Review Underway in Wu Baoquan's Case," April 22, 2009, http:// siweiluozi.blogspot.com/2009/04/update-review-underway-in-wu-baoquans.html; Siweiluozi's Blog, "Updated Update: Ordos Law Enforcement Officials 'Clearing Their Thoughts' Regarding Wu Bao-quan," April 27, 2009, http://siweiluozi.blogspot.com/search/label/Wang%20Shuai.

137. Joshua Rosenzweig, "China's Battle over the Right to Criticize," *Far Eastern Economic Review*, May 1, 2009, http://www.feer.com/essays/2009/may/chinas-battle-over-the-right-to-criticize.

138. Ibid.

139. Jane Chen, "Officials Punished over Land Scandal," *Shanghai Daily*, April 29, 2009, http:// www.shanghaidaily.com/sp/article/2009/200904/20090429/article_399326.htm.

140. Chen Wangying, "The First 'Human Flesh Search' Trial," EastSouthWestNorth blog, August 2, 2008, http://www.zonaeuropa.com/20080802_1.htm.

141. Ibid.

142. Reuters, "Man Wins Case vs 'Human Flesh Search Engine,'" December 19, 2008, http:// www.reuters.com/article/technologyNews/idUSTRE4BI1I620081219.

143. *Wall Street Journal*: China Journal blog, "A Verdict in the Case of the 'Human Flesh Search Engine,'" December 19, 2008, http://blogs.wsj.com/chinajournal/2008/12/19/a-verdict-in-the -case-of-the-human-flesh-search-engine/.

144. Caijing.com, "Webmasters Found Guilty of Online Harassment," December 22, 2008, http:// english.caijing.com.cn/2008-12-22/110041383.html.

145. Chinese Law Prof Blog, "Court Decision in 'Human Flesh Search Engine' Case" January 13, 2009, http://lawprofessors.typepad.com/china_law_prof_blog/2009/01/court-decision.html.

146. Xinhua News Agency, "Law Amendments Adopted to Protect Personal Information, Punish Bribe-Taking Relatives of Officials," February 28, 2009, http://news.xinhuanet.com/english/2009 -02/28/content_10916168.htm; Li Xinran, "Xuzhou Shuts Down 'Human Flesh Search Engine,'" *Shanghai Daily*, January 20, 2009, http://www.shanghaidaily.com/sp/article/2009/200901/ 20090120/article_388687.htm.

147. Rebecca Ruiz, "Who Will Be Watching You in Beijing?" Forbes.com, July 8, 2008, http://www.forbes.com/travel/2008/07/08/olympics-security-privacy-forbeslife-olympics08-cx_rr _0708security.html.

148. Ministry of Public Security, *Guojia fazgaiwei zhuchi zhaokai dahui tongguo "jindun gongcheng" jianshe xiangmu guojia yanshou* [National development and reform commission issues national approval for the "Golden Shield" construction project at management conference], November 17, 2006, http://www.mps.gov.cn/cenweb/brjlCenweb/jsp/common/article.jsp?infoid= ABC00000000000035645 (accessed May 25, 2009); Greg Walton, "China's Golden Shield: Corporations and the Development of Surveillance Technology in the People's Republic of China," International Center for Human Rights and Democratic Development, October 2001, http://www.dd-rd.ca/site/publications/index.php?id=1266&subsection=catalogue.

149. *China Tech News*, "Safe-City Project Home for New Chinese IP Video Surveillance Technology," March 11, 2008, http://www.chinatechnews.com/2008/03/11/6475-safe-city-project-home-for-new-chinese-ip-video-surveillance-technology/; Reuters, "China Security and Surveillance Announces Additional Safe City Project Win in Yinchuan," July 30, 2008, http://www.reuters.com/article/pressRelease/idUS125704+30-Jun-2008+PRN20080630.

150. Kathrin Hille, "China Bolsters Internet Censors' Scrutiny," *Financial Times*, January 5, 2009, http://www.ft.com/cms/s/0/f858f9aa-dac8-11dd-8c28-000077b07658,dwp_uuid=9c33700c-4c86-11da-89df-0000779e2340.html.

151. TRS Information Technology, "About TRS," 2008, http://www.trs.com.cn/en/TRS/about/.

152. Ibid.

153. Ministry of Information Industry, Article 3, *Huliangwang dianzi youjian fuwu guanli banfa* [Measures for the management of e-mail services], November 7, 2005.

154. Chinese cyber dissidents and activists, such as the journalist Shi Tao, have been convicted in part because of some e-mail service providers' disclosure of their users' personal information to the Chinese police. See Reporters Without Borders, "Cyber-Dissident Convicted on Yahoo! Information Is Freed after Four Years," November 9, 2006, http://www.rsf.org/article.php3?id_article =8453; Human Rights in China, "Case Highlight, Shi Tao and Yahoo," 2005, http://hrichina.org/public/highlight/index.html.

155. Dui Hua News blog, "Police Document Sheds Additional Light on Shi Tao Case," July 25, 2007, http://www.duihua.org/2007/07/police-document-sheds-additional-light.html.

156. Human Rights Watch, "Freedom of Expression and the Internet in China," August 1, 2001, http://www.hrw.org/backgrounder/asia/china-bck-0701.htm; Alfred Hermida, "Behind China's Internet Red Firewall," BBC News, September 3, 2002, http://news.bbc.co.uk/1/low/technology/2234154.stm.

157. Phillip Pan, "Chinese Crack Down on Student Web Sites," *Washington Post*, March 24, 2005, http://www.washingtonpost.com/wp-dyn/articles/A61334-2005Mar23.html.

158. Xinhua News Agency, "Internet Real-Name Registration System: Why So Difficult to Implement? An Investigation into the Implementation of the Hangzhou Regulations for Network Security Protection," May 19, 2009, http://news.xinhuanet.com/newscenter/2009-05/19/content _11399392.htm; David Bandurski, "Xinhua: Hangzhou's 'Real-Name Web Registration System' Is 'on the Shelf,'" China Media Project, May 20, 2009, http://cmp.hku.hk/2009/05/20/1632/.

159. *China Digital Times*, "Beijing Mobile's Plan for Real Name Registration of Easyown Cell Phone Numbers," January 24, 2008, http://chinadigitaltimes.net/2008/01/beijing-mobiles-plan-for-real-name-registration-for-easyown-cell-phone-numbers/.

160. State Council, Article 14, *Hulianwang xinxi fuwu guanli banfa* [Measures for managing Internet information services], September 25, 2000.

161. China Internet Network Information Center, "Statistical Survey Report on the Internet Development in China," March 23, 2009, http://www.cnnic.net.cn/uploadfiles/pdf/2009/3/23/131303.pdf.

162. State Council, Articles 19, 21, 23, *Hulianwang shangwang fuwu guanye changsuo guanli tiaolie* [Regulations on the administration of business sites providing Internet services], September 29, 2002.

163. Ministry of Information Industry, Article 14, *Hulianwang dianzi gonggao fuwu guanli guiding* [Rules on the management of Internet electronic bulletin services], October 7, 2000.

164. Chinese Human Rights Defenders, *"zhengfu ruhe jiankong women de dianzi wangluo tongxu"* [How does government monitor our online communication?], http://crd-net.org/Article/Class1/200803/20080324093843_8168.html.

165. Ibid.

166. Nart Villeneuve, "Breaching Trust: An Analysis of Surveillance and Security Practices on China's TOM-Skype Platform," Information Warfare Monitor/ONI Asia, October 1, 2008, http://www.nartv.org/mirror/breachingtrust.pdf.

167. John Markoff, "Surveillance of Skype Messages Found in China," *New York Times*, October 1, 2008, http://www.nytimes.com/2008/10/02/technology/internet/02skype.html?pagewanted=all.

168. Sky Canaves, "Skype Responds to China Surveillance Report," *Wall Street Journal* Blogs: China Journal, October 2, 2008, http://blogs.wsj.com/chinajournal/2008/10/02/skype-response-on-china-surveillance-report/?mod=googlenews_wsj.

169. Sumner Lemon, "China Tightens Surveillance of Internet Forums," *The Standard*, March, 2005, http://archive.thestandard.com/internetnews/002807.php.

170. Reporters Without Borders, "'Living Dangerously on the Net,'" May 12, 2003, http://www.rsf.org/article.php3?id_article=6793.

171. Phillip Pan, "Chinese Crack Down on Student Web Sites," *Washington Post*, March 24, 2005, http://www.washingtonpost.com/wp-dyn/articles/A61334-2005Mar23.html.

172. Australia Broadcasting Corporation, "China's Mobile Network: A Big Brother Surveillance Tool?" January 28, 2008, http://www.abc.net.au/news/stories/2008/01/28/2147712.htm.

173. *China Business Daily*, *"tongxin duanxiaoxi fuwu guanli guiding jijiang chutai"* [Regulation on the management of short message service will soon come into being], March 27, 2008, http://www.txxxb.com/news/article.php?id=7544; Australia Broadcasting Corporation, "China's Mobile

Network."; Chinese Human Rights Defenders, *"zhengfu ruhe jiankong women de dianzi wangluo tongxu"* [How does government monitor our online communication?], http://crd-net.org/Article/Class1/200803/20080324093843_8168.html.

174. Australia Broadcasting Corporation, "China's Mobile Network: A Big Brother Surveillance Tool?" January 28, 2008, http://www.abc.net.au/news/stories/2008/01/28/2147712.htm.

175. Ibid.

176. Brian Krebs, "Cyber Attacks Target Pro-Tibet Groups," *Washington Post*, March 21, 2008, http://www.washingtonpost.com/wp-dyn/content/article/2008/03/21/AR2008032102605.html.

177. Information Warfare Monitor, "Tracking GhostNet: Investigating a Cyber Espionage Network" (Citizen Lab/the SecDev Group), March 29, 2009, http://www.tracking-ghost.net.

178. Human Rights Watch, "In the Words of Chinese Officials," June 13, 2008, http://china.hrw.org/in_the_words_of_chinese_officials.

179. Xinhua News Agency, "Openness to Foreign Media to Remain after Games," July 30, 2008, http://www.chinadaily.com.cn/china/2008-07/30/content_6890786.htm.

180. Jacquelin Magnay, "Fury Vented at Great Firewall of China," *Sydney Morning Herald*, July 28, 2008, http://www.smh.com.au/news/beijing2008/reporters-vent-fury-at-great-firewall-of-china/2008/07/27/1217097058479.html.

181. Katie Thomas, "Officials Investigate Reports of Censorship at Olympic Press Center," *New York Times*, Jul 29, 2008, http://olympics.blogs.nytimes.com/2008/07/29/officials-investigate-reports-of-censorship-at-olympic-press-center/?hp.

182. Nick Mulvenney, "Update 1—Olympics—IOC Admits to Deal with China on Censorship," Reuters, July 30, 2008, http://www.reuters.com/article/olympicsNews/idUSPEK15086520080730?sp=true.

183. Xinhua News Agency, "Beijing Olympic Press Centers Open," July 8, 2008, http://news.xinhuanet.com/english/2008-07/08/content_8509880.htm

184. Keith Bradsher, "China Blocks Access to the Times's Web Site," *New York Times*, December 19, 2008, http://www.nytimes.com/2008/12/20/world/asia/20china.html.

185. Miguel Helft, "YouTube Blocked in China, Google Says," *New York Times*, March 24, 2009, http://www.nytimes.com/2009/03/25/technology/internet/25youtube.html?_r=1&hp.

186. See Herdict Web Site Report, "www.blogger.com in China," as of May 25, 2009, http://www.herdict.org/web/explore/detail/id/CN/2488.

187. Tania Branigan, "China Blocks Twitter, Flickr and Hotmail Ahead of Tiananmen Anniversary," *Guardian*, June 2, 2009, http://www.guardian.co.uk/technology/2009/jun/02/twitter-china.

188. See Rebecca MacKinnon, "Original Government Document Ordering 'Green Dam' Software Installation," RConversation Blog, June 8, 2009, http://rconversation.blogs.com/rconversation/2009/06/original-government-document-ordering-green-dam-software-installation.html.

189. Ministry of Industry and Information Technology, *guanyu jisuanji yuzhuang luse shangwang guolu ranjian de tongzhi* [Notice regarding the pre-installation of "green" online filtering software on computers], May 19, 2009, http://tech.sina.com.cn/it/2009-06-09/17073163327.shtml; Human Rights in China, "Chinese Government Orders Computer Manufacturers to Pre-install Filtering Software," June 8, 2009, http://www.hrichina.org/public/contents/press?revision_id=169834&item_id=169820; Xinhua News Agency, "Anti-porn Filter Software Stirs Up Disputes in China," June 11, 2009, http://news.xinhuanet.com/english/2009-06/11/content_11522822.htm.

190. Ministry of Industry and Information Technology, *guanyu jisuanji yuzhuang luse shangwang guolu ranjian de tongzhi* [Notice regarding the pre-installation of "green" online filtering software on computers], May 19, 2009, http://tech.sina.com.cn/it/2009-06-09/17073163327.shtml.

191. OpenNet Initiative, "China's Green Dam: The Implications of Government Control Encroaching on the Home PC," June 12, 2009, http://opennet.net/chinas-green-dam-the-implications-government-control-encroaching-home-pc.

192. Ibid.

193. Ibid.

194. Ibid.

195. Scott Wolchok, Randy Yao, and J. Alex Halderman, "Analysis of the Green Dam Censorware System," Computer Science and Engineering Division, University of Michigan, June 11, 2009, http://www.cse.umich.edu/~jhalderm/pub/gd/.

196. OpenNet Initiative, "China's Green Dam: The Implications of Government Control Encroaching on the Home PC," June 12, 2009, http://opennet.net/chinas-green-dam-the-implications-government-control-encroaching-home-pc.

Pakistan

In 2007–2008, political turmoil and campaigns to curb media coverage in Pakistan took place against a relatively stable backdrop of Internet filtering directed at content determined to be blasphemous, secessionist, anti-state, or anti-military. One of the most widely reported instances of filtering occurred in February 2008, when a government order to prevent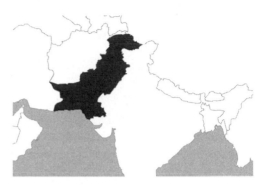
access to a YouTube video mocking the Prophet Muhammad resulted in a near-global block of the entire YouTube Web site for around two hours.

Background

During General Pervez Musharraf's first term as president, military control was applied over the judiciary and the ruling party in Parliament, and print and electronic media were censored where the content was deemed to be anti-government or anti-Islam. Government repression of media has been particularly acute with regard to Balochi and Sindhi political autonomy, content considered blasphemous, and other anti-state or anti-religious content.

RESULTS AT A GLANCE					
Filtering	No Evidence of Filtering	Suspected Filtering	Selective Filtering	Substantial Filtering	Pervasive Filtering
Political		•			
Social				•	
Conflict and security				•	
Internet tools			•		

Other Factors	Low	Medium	High	Not Applicable
Transparency		•		
Consistency	•			

KEY INDICATORS	
GDP per capita, PPP (constant 2005 international dollars)	2,357
Life expectancy at birth (years)	65
Literacy rate (percent of people age 15+)	54
Human development index (out of 179)	139
Rule of law (out of 211)	169
Voice and accountability (out of 209)	169
Democracy index (out of 167)	108 (Hybrid regime)
Digital opportunity index (out of 181)	127
Internet users (percent of population)	10

Source by indicator: World Bank 2009a, World Bank 2009a, World Bank 2009a, UNDP 2008, World Bank 2009b, World Bank 2009b, Economist Intelligence Unit 2008, ITU 2007, ITU 2008.

In October 2007, Musharraf won an indirect, widely boycotted presidential election held while his two major political opponents were in exile. Leading the court challenge over Musharraf's eligibility to run while still serving as army chief was Chief Justice Ifthikar Muhammad Chaudhry, who had himself been suspended by Musharraf in March 2007 and reinstated in July 2007, after a "Lawyer's Movement" instigated court boycotts and massive rallies around the country.[1] Musharraf responded by suspending the constitution and placing the country under a state of emergency on November 3, the second since his bloodless coup in 1999.[2] While waiting for the court's decision, Musharraf's government shut down all privately owned television stations and other independent media outlets, arrested lawyers and about 60 senior judges, and jammed cell phone and Internet connections.[3]

Under growing international pressure, Musharraf resigned from his army position in late November and was sworn in for his second term as president, finally lifting the emergency on December 15. However, in August 2008 the two main governing parties agreed to launch impeachment proceedings, and Musharraf resigned under pressure.[4] In September 2008, Asif Ali Zardari, the husband of assassinated Pakistan Peoples Party (PPP) leader Benazir Bhutto, was elected Pakistan's new president by legislators.[5]

A vibrant civil society movement working against Internet censorship continues to operate in Pakistan and monitors developments in filtering.[6] International human rights groups have reported on the persecution of journalists at the hands of the Pakistani military intelligence agency and extremist groups, while advocacy groups such as the Pakistan Federal Union of Journalists continue to call for investigations into attacks against journalists, which are often unresolved.[7] According to the Committee to Protect Journalists, at least five journalists were killed in connection with their work in 2008, several of them in the conflict-torn regions of Northwest Frontier Province and Swat.[8] Six journalists and media workers were killed in 2007.[9]

Internet in Pakistan

With 3.7 million Internet subscribers, an estimated 22 million Pakistanis were online in 2008, constituting a penetration rate of around 10 percent.[10] Pakistan has experienced considerable growth in its information and communication technology (ICT) sector; in 2003, the government deregulated its telecom market, opening itself up to corporate competition in telephone, cellular, and Internet services.[11] Internet access is widely available at Internet cafés, which accommodate many lower-income and casual users. Rates for usage range between PKR 15 and PKR 40 per hour (USD 0.25–0.60 per hour), depending on location and amenities. Internet café managers are expected to monitor the activities in their establishments, but based on user experience these cafés appear to be mostly unregulated by the regular police.

Since deregulation, the market has become highly competitive, and there are currently approximately 50 ISPs in Pakistan of varying size and quality of service.[12] The largest ISPs in the country include Cybernet, Comsats, Brainnet, Gonet, and Paknet (a subsidiary of the Pakistan Telecommunications Company Limited, or PTCL). Although the estimated penetration rate for broadband Internet is just over 1 percent and demand has historically been low, Pakistan is ranked fourth globally in broadband Internet growth, with a growth rate of over 180 percent in metropolitan areas.[13]

All Internet traffic in and out of Pakistan is routed by the PTCL, which controls the IT infrastructure of the country through its subsidiary, the Pakistan Internet Exchange (PIE), with three international gateways at Islamabad/Rawalpindi, Lahore, and Karachi, and small/medium points of presence (POPs) in six other cities.[14] Domestic Internet traffic is peered at the PIE gateways within the country. In 2007, the PTCL's Karachi exchange reportedly processed at least 95 percent of Pakistan's Internet traffic.[15] In February 2008, the construction of a fifth undersea cable system that would link India and France (I-ME-WE) was announced, to be available for service by the end of 2009 and serving nine telecoms, including the PTCL.[16] The company invested USD 50 million into I-ME-WE, expected to have a capacity of 3.84 terabits per second.[17]

The Internet, as a tool for dissemination of information and mobilization of civil society, has been increasingly integrated into the political life of Pakistan. Bloggers across Pakistan objected to the intermittent block on the Blogspot platform and the temporary blocking of Wikipedia in 2006, and initiated a virtual civil society movement to repeal the orders.[18] In the movement against Musharraf's declaration of emergency in November 2007, with lawyers leading mass protests and acts of civil disobedience against the suspension of judges and the constitution,[19] a convergence between new and old media became evident.[20] According to one contributor to the Emergency Times blog (pakistanmartiallaw.blogspot.com), created to keep people informed about news and protests, "the real resistance to the emergency was built on the Internet."[21]

In the face of stringent media regulation, individual journalists, lawyers, and viewers uploaded news broadcasts from banned television stations to YouTube, while stations offered free streaming on their own Web sites.[22] Millions signed online petitions, while students, youth, and others created blogs (such as the Emergency Times) and dynamically utilized an array of tools, including SMS2Blog, Facebook, and video and photos uploaded to social media sites such as Flickr, to plan flash protests and document their resistance in the face of a media blackout.[23]

Legal and Regulatory Frameworks

Internet filtering in Pakistan is regulated by the Pakistan Telecommunication Authority (PTA),[24] under the directive of the government, the Supreme Court of Pakistan, and the Ministry of Information Technology (MoIT), formerly the Ministry of Information Technology and Telecommunications (MITT). The PTA implements its censorship regulations through directives handed down to the PTCL,[25] of which the Emirates Telecommunications Corporation (Etisalat) took majority control in 2006.[26]

In December 2007, the government passed a cyber crimes ordinance, followed by the Prevention of Electronic Crimes Ordinance (PECO) enacted less than a year later and taking effect on September 29, 2008.[27] Cyber crimes are investigated under the jurisdiction of the Federal Investigation Agency (FIA),[28] with the support of the National Response Centre for Cyber Crime (NRCCC), which provides technical assistance and a reporting center, and leads awareness campaigns.[29] In addition to laying out offenses for electronic forgery, fraud, criminal data access, and the use of malicious code, the ordinance made "cyber stalking"—which requires "intent to coerce, intimidate, or harass any person" using computers or networks—a crime punishable by up to seven years' imprisonment.[30] Media rights advocates expressed concern that the prohibition against taking or distributing photographs of a person without consent made one of the major components of citizen journalism illegal.[31] The ordinance also makes "cyberterrorism," defined as the access or utilization of a computer network or electronic system or device by a person or group with "terroristic intent," an offense punishable by life imprisonment or death.[32]

In the absence of a specific legal framework, Pakistan's filtering practices have evolved largely out of executive action taken by various government organs. Blocking orders have been issued through an opaque process that invites speculation as to the political motivations behind them, with authorizing agencies alternating between the MoIT, the PTA, the courts, and law enforcement. For example, in August 2008 the civil society organization Pakistan ICT Policy Monitors Network announced that six URLs were blocked upon the request of retired Admiral Afzal Tahir, accused in a number of YouTube videos of abusing his office in a personal land dispute.[33] In October 2008, the government announced that the terrorism wing of the country's FIA would be tasked with hunting down the "antidemocratic" forces that were circulating YouTube videos and text messages aimed at discrediting the ruling party's politicians.[34]

On September 2, 2006, the MoIT announced the creation of a committee to monitor the content of offensive Web sites. Composed of representatives from the MoIT, the PTA, the Ministry of the Interior, and the cabinet, as well as members of security agencies, and presided over by the Secretary of the MoIT, the Inter-Ministerial Committee for the Evaluation of Websites (IMC) was tasked with examining and blocking Web sites containing blasphemous, pornographic, or anti-state material.[35] To address the grievances of Internet users with this censorship body, the government set up the Deregulation Facilitation Unit to deal with users' complaints.[36]

Much of the episodic filtering in Pakistan has been ordered in reaction to "blasphemous" content. On February 28, 2006, the PTCL issued a blocking directive banning a dozen URLs posting controversial Danish cartoons depicting images of the Prophet Muhammad.[37] Within two weeks in March, in a series of escalating instructions, the Supreme Court directed the government to block all Web sites displaying the cartoons, to explain why they had not been blocked earlier, to block all blasphemous content, and to determine how access to such content could be denied on the Internet worldwide.[38] The Supreme Court also ordered police to register cases of publishing or posting the blasphemous images under Article 295-C of the Pakistan Penal Code, where blasphemy or defamation of the Prophet Muhammad is punishable by death.[39]

President Musharraf's crackdowns on the media included content prohibitions and enhanced government discretion as to licensing requirements in order to cultivate self-censorship. The Pakistan Electronic Media Regulatory Authority (PEMRA) was established when Musharraf allowed for the creation of privately owned, independent broadcast media in 2002. One of its first acts was to lay out the regulatory framework that would ultimately support Musharraf's drive to control and restrict independent journalism. This framework instructed that in order to obtain a broadcast license, media outlets were required to preserve the sovereignty, security, integrity, values, and constitutional principles of public policy of Pakistan.[40] Article 27 of the 2002 ordinance also directly prohibited the broadcast or distribution of any content "against the ideology of Pakistan," as well as programming that "is likely to create hatred among the people, is prejudicial to the maintenance of law and order, is likely to disturb public peace and tranquility, endangers national security or is pornographic, obscene or vulgar or is offensive to the commonly accepted standards of decency."[41]

Upon declaring a state of emergency in 2007, Musharraf further amended PEMRA's charter to prohibit programming that "defames or brings into ridicule the head of state, or members of the armed forces, or executive, legislative or judicial organ of the state,"[42] as well as content "against the ideology, sovereignty, integrity or security of

Pakistan."[43] Video footage of suicide bombers, terrorists, and their victims was banned.[44] PEMRA was now empowered to close any broadcast service in a "situation of emergency" and to seize equipment or seal the premises of licensees "in the public interest,"[45] with penalties expanded to include three years' imprisonment and the maximum fine increased from PKR 1 million to PKR 10 million.[46] For print media, the Press, Newspapers, News Agencies and Books Registration Ordinance, 2002 (XCIII of 2002) was amended to reflect the same content prohibitions and grant the government the same emergency authority to shutter any publication for up to 30 days.[47] In April 2008, the MoIT introduced a bill to repeal these amended provisions, reduce the maximum fine to PKR 1 million, and abolish the provision banning broadcasts "against the ideology of Pakistan."[48]

Musharraf did not take such an assiduous approach toward restricting online content during the emergency, although telephone and Internet access were intermittently cut. However, all privately owned radio and television stations were shut down, some by force,[49] and cable operators were banned from broadcasting any national or international news channels.[50] The Code of Conduct created after the emergency was characterized as voluntary,[51] but most of these stations were allowed to resume broadcasting in December only after agreeing to abide by the Code of Conduct.[52] In December 2008, the Pakistan Broadcasters Association (PBA) announced that it would formulate its code of conduct and self-regulate among its members.[53]

Internet Surveillance

The Prevention of Electronic Crimes Ordinance requires ISPs to retain all traffic data for at least 90 days and to provide it to the government upon request, or face fines and up to six months' imprisonment.[54] Providers may also be required to cooperate in the collection of real-time data (including traffic data) and to keep their involvement confidential.[55] The bill ostensibly focuses on the use of the Internet to commit acts of terrorism, but its scope is broad enough that Pakistani bloggers and Reporters Without Borders expressed concern over the impact on Internet freedom.[56]

Pakistani media have reported that the PIE, which controls the international gateways, monitors all incoming and outgoing Internet traffic in Pakistan. This capability, in addition to filtering, allows it to monitor and store all e-mails for a certain period of time.[57] There are no reported cases of people imprisoned for their online activities, and most Pakistani bloggers view government surveillance as more clumsy than frightening. At the same time, political events that generate unusual amounts of online chatter and debate, including the suspension of Chief Justice Chaudry in March 2007, cause bloggers and other users to worry about being censored or targeted.[58] After the imposition of de facto martial law in November 2007, several bloggers made arrangements to have their blogs published outside of Pakistan.[59]

ONI Testing Results

Episodic filtering, in addition to routine blocking of Web sites considered blasphemous or threatening Pakistan's internal security, continued through the end of Musharraf's term as president and into the tenure of the new civilian government. In December 2007, the enactment of the cyber crimes ordinance was followed shortly by the reported blocking of several hundred anti-government blogs.[60] In late December 2008, upon the recommendation of the IMC, the PTA issued an order to block six URLs: three from dictatorshipwatch.com, a Web site created after Musharraf declared a state of emergency; one from makepakistanbetter.com, a social and political discussion forum; one from friendskorner.com, another discussion forum; and one from buzzvines.com.[61] The common thread among the Web pages appeared to be information about Punjab Governor Salman Taseer,[62] rather than any type of content under the authorized purview of the IMC.

OpenNet Initiative testing was conducted on Cybernet, LINKdotNET, the PTCL, and Micronet in May through July 2008. There is no uniform method of blocking among the four ISPs tested. Cybernet blocks by setting a DNS lookup failure; both LINKdotNET and Micronet employ block pages—LINKdotNET by means of Squid Proxy and Micronet using both proxy server and Squid Proxy. The PTCL had appeared to rely on DNS poisoning by redirecting to an IP address they own containing no content, but during later rounds of testing switched to a block page using a proxy server.

A comparison of ONI testing results from 2006–2007 and 2008 indicates that despite high-profile filtering incidents, ISPs may actually be blocking less content. For example, in contrast to testing results from 2006 to 2007, where the PTCL implemented a limited block on pornography and religious conversion sites, 2008 testing found no evidence of filtering in these categories.

A form of collateral filtering, the blocking of additional content that is unintended and caused by imprecise filtering methods,[63] has long been a feature of Internet censorship in Pakistan. For example, in March 2007, in an attempt to comply with a Supreme Court order to filter blasphemous content "at all costs," the PTCL implemented a blanket IP address block at their Karachi PIE exchange that lasted for four days and impacted the Akamai servers, leading to disruptions in accessing Google, Yahoo, BBC, CNN, ESPN, and several other major Web sites.[64] In January 2008, several bloggers reported the blocking of the Blogspot.com and Wordpress.com domains.[65]

One of the most severe examples of collateral filtering took place in February 2008, when a government attempt to block YouTube in Pakistan made the entire Web site inaccessible to most Internet users around the world for up to two hours.[66] On February 22, the PTA issued an order to block access to a single video, while listing three IP addresses.[67] The film *Fitna* by the Dutch parliamentarian Geert Wilders, which contained "blasphemous" content considered offensive to Islam, was the official cause of the block, but others claim that the government could have been trying to suppress a video depicting a woman engaging in election fraud in Karachi.[68] In response, the PTCL redirected requests for YouTube videos to its own network. This rerouting was advertised to the Internet at large and was picked up by the Hong Kong–based ISP PCCW, which then broadcast the redirect to ISPs around the world.[69] YouTube staff worked with PCCW to restore access within two hours.[70] Access to YouTube was restored in Pakistan after the video listed in the PTA blocking order was removed.

The Web sites blocked by all four ISPs provide a representative snapshot of 2008 filtering practices, consisting entirely of Balochi news, independence, and culture Web sites, with the exception of two: the anti-Islamist jihadwatch.org and themoviefitna .com, a Web site dedicated to coverage of Geert Wilders and his film *Fitna*.

The filtering of material considered blasphemous or anti-Islamic has long been a purported objective in Pakistan. In 2006–2007, most material relating to the Danish cartoon incident that led to a block on the entire Blogspot.com domain was blocked by ISPs; 2008 testing showed that many of these have since been hacked or unblocked. Cybernet, LINKdotNET, and the PTCL blocked a right-wing American Web site containing the cartoons (zombietime.com), while leaving only Cybernet to block one other relevant Web site, mohammeddrawings.com.

By April 2006, the PTA extended their blocking to anti-state Web sites as well as those promoting Balochi human rights and political autonomy.[71] Testing done by the ONI in 2006–2007 confirmed that internal security conflicts had become a strong focus for filtering, including Web sites relating to Balochi independence movements, Sindhi human rights, and political autonomy movements. Among these categories, Web sites addressing Balochi political independence were the most comprehensively blocked.

Filtering of content in 2008 continued to target these categories of Web sites, albeit a smaller number and with even greater inconsistency. All four ISPs blocked Web sites tested relating to human rights, news, and justice (e.g., www.balochistaninfo.com) in the province of Balochistan. However, a number of Balochistan-related Web sites blocked by all four ISPs have been closed, including www.balochfront.com and baloch2000.org. Other Web sites were blocked by a combination, but not all, of the ISPs, including the Balochistan Legal Fund (www.bso-na.org) by Cybernet, LINKdotNET, and the PTCL; the Balochi independence Web site balochestan.com by Cybernet and LINKdotNET; and www.balochtawar.net by Cybernet and Micronet. A limited selection of Balochi-related blogs were also blocked, with all four ISPs filtering www.rahimjaandehvari.blogfa.com.

A selected number of the Sindhi sites tested continued to be blocked in 2008, such as www.worldsindhi.org, which was blocked by the PTCL, Micronet, and LINKdotNET. Unlike in 2006–2007, none were blocked by all four ISPs. However, in contrast to

2006–2007, when the few existing Web sites pertaining to Pashtun secessionism were fully accessible, Micronet blocked the Pashtun discussion board www.kitabtoon.com.

The blocking of a selective number of blogs and Web sites containing purported anti-Islamic and anti-Pakistani content was one continuity between 2006–2007 and 2008 testing, such as the Indian militant extremist sites www.hinduunity.com that was blocked by Cybernet and LINKdotNET and anti-Islamic Web sites (www.plusultrablog .com by Cybernet; www.nordish.net blocked by Cybernet, LINKdotNET, and the PTCL). However, there was also less filtering of blogs in 2008. A limited number of Web sites not directed at Pakistani issues were filtered by some, but not all, ISPs. For example, the blog of Michelle Malkin, a popular conservative American blogger, was inaccessible on all ISPs in 2006–2007; in 2008, only Cybernet filtered michellemalkin .com. A free online radio site, Live365.com, was filtered by Cybernet, LINKdotNET, and the PTCL.

Since the last round of testing, it appears that more responsibility for implementing filtering is being shifted down to the ISP level. The most recent round of testing also showed that filtering across ISPs is less consistent than in 2006–2007, when all but a handful of filtered Web sites were blocked by all the ISPs. In 2008, Cybernet blocked the greatest number of Web sites tested, filtering twice as much as the nearest ISP; Cybernet was followed by LINKdotNET, PakNet, and Micronet (in descending order). Between ISPs, the greatest overlap in filtering occurred between Cybernet and LINKdotNET.

The ONI testing in 2008 showed that in continuity with 2006–2007 results, the vast majority of newspapers and independent media, social media such as YouTube and Blogspot.com, circumvention tools, international human rights groups, VoIP services, civil society groups, minority religious Web sites, Indian and Hindu human rights groups, Pakistani political parties, and sexual content (including pornography and gay and lesbian content) were accessible on all four ISPs.

Conclusion

Pakistanis currently have unimpeded access to most sexual, political, social, and religious content on the Internet. Although the Pakistani government does not currently employ a sophisticated blocking system, a limitation which has led to collateral blocks on entire domains such as Blogspot.com and YouTube.com, it continues to block Web sites containing content it considers to be blasphemous, anti-Islamic, or threatening to internal security.

Online civil society activism that began in order to protect free expression and blogging rights has expanded as citizens utilize new media to disseminate information and organize in the face of media blackouts and other political crises.

Notes

1. James Traub, "The Lawyers' Crusade," *New York Times Magazine*, June 1, 2008, http://www .nytimes.com/2008/06/01/magazine/01PAKISTAN-t.html.

2. Kamal Siddiqi, "Emergency in Pakistan: Musharraf's Second Coup," *Hindustan Times*, November 3, 2007, http://www.hindustantimes.com/StoryPage/StoryPage.aspx?sectionName=&id=68bca3c7 -30a8-4be9-a446-e7ed77f79cb9&Headline=Musharraf+declares+state+of+Emergency+in+Pak.

3. Neha Viswanathan, "Pakistan: Emergency Declared—No News, No Internet," Global Voices Online, November 3, 2007, http://www.globalvoicesonline.org/2007/11/03/pakistan-emergency -declared-no-news-no-internet/.

4. Reza Sayah and Saeed Ahmed, "Musharraf's Resignation Accepted," CNN, August 18, 2008, http://www.cnn.com/2008/WORLD/asiapcf/08/18/musharraf.address/.

5. *BBC News*, "Timeline: Pakistan," August 19, 2009, http://news.bbc.co.uk/2/hi/south_asia/ country_profiles/1156716.stm.

6. Don't Block the Blog campaign, http://dbtb.org/; Pakistan 451, http://pakistan451.wordpress .com/; http://pakistanictpolicy.bytesforall.net/.

7. Reporters Without Borders, "Pakistan: Annual Report 2008," http://www.rsf.org/article.php3 ?id_article=25678.

8. Committee to Protect Journalists, "Attacks on the Press in 2008: Pakistan," http://cpj.org/2009/ 02/attacks-on-the-press-in-2008-pakistan.php.

9. Pakistan Press International, "Murder of Journalist in Pakistan Must Be Investigated Promptly: IFJ," February 11, 2008.

10. Pakistan Telecommunication Authority (PTA), "Value Added Services," accessed May 16, 2009, http://www.pta.gov.pk/index.php?option=com_content&task=view&id=651&Itemid=604. Paul Budde Communication Pty., Ltd., "Pakistan—Internet Market," January 2, 2009.

11. PTA, "Deregulation Changes Telecom Scenario," http://www.pta.gov.pk/index.php?cur_t= vtext&option=com_content&task=view&id=522&Itemid=1&catid=95.

12. ISP Association of Pakistan, http://www.ispak.com.pk/.

13. PTA, "Growth of Broadband in Pakistan and Current Situation," June 2008, http://www.ispak .com.pk/Downloads/Growth_of_broadband-PTA.pdf.

14. Interview with Convener of Internet Service Provider Association of Pakistan (ISPAK).

15. Naveed Ahmad, "PTCL Blocks Vital Internet Sites to Comply with SC Order," *The News*, March 3, 2007, http://www.thenews.com.pk/top_story_detail.asp?Id=6254.

16. *Asia Pulse*, "Bharti to Set Up Undersea Cable Linking India, France," February 7, 2008.

17. *The Nation*, "PTCL Invests $50 Million in Submarine Cable Project," February 7, 2008.

18. Don't Block the Blog campaign, http://dbtb.org/; Help Pakistan.com, "Don't Block the Blog," http://help-pakistan.com/main/dont-block-the-blog/.

19. David Rohde and Jane Perlez, "Ousted Chief Justice in Pakistan Urges Defiance," *New York Times*, November 7, 2007, http://www.nytimes.com/2007/11/07/world/asia/07pakistan.html; Jane Perlez, "Lawyer Says Pakistan Heading toward 'Rigged' Vote," *New York Times*, December 1, 2007, http://www.nytimes.com/2007/12/01/world/asia/01pakistan.html.

20. Huma Yusuf, "Old and New Media: Converging during the Pakistan Emergency (March 2007–February 2008)," Center for Future Civic Media (MIT), January 12, 2009, http://civic.mit.edu/watchlistenlearn/old-and-new-media-converging-during-the-pakistan-emergency-march-2007-february-2008?page=0%2C0.

21. Samad Khurram, "Dawn," Pakistan Online, February 17, 2009, http://www.asiamedia.ucla.edu/print.asp?parentid=104858.

22. Huma Yusuf, "Old and New Media: Converging during the Pakistan Emergency (March 2007–February 2008)," Center for Future Civic Media (MIT), January 12, 2009, http://civic.mit.edu/watchlistenlearn/old-and-new-media-converging-during-the-pakistan-emergency-march-2007-february-2008?page=0%2C0.

23. Agence France Presse, "Facebookers, Bloggers Fight Pakistan Emergency," November 17, 2007, http://afp.google.com/article/ALeqM5i64vTXHkRTFOIpXrpl843N6QpPtw. See also Huma Yusuf, "Old and New Media: Converging during the Pakistan Emergency (March 2007–February 2008)," Center for Future Civic Media (MIT), January 12, 2009, http://civic.mit.edu/watchlistenlearn/old-and-new-media-converging-during-the-pakistan-emergency-march-2007-february-2008?page=0%2C0.

24. Pakistan Telecommunication Authority, http://www.pta.gov.pk/.

25. Ibid.

26. "Deal Signed to Give Etisalat PTCL Control," DAWN, March 13, 2006, http://www.dawn.com/2006/03/13/top5.htm.

27. Prevention of Electronic Crimes Ordinance (Ordinance No. IV of 2008), http://www.na.gov.pk/ordinances/prevention_electronic_crimes2008_200808.pdf.

28. Federal Investigation Agency, http://www.fia.gov.pk/.

29. Federal Investigation Agency, http://www.fia.gov.pk/prj_about_nr3c.htm; *Business Recorder*, "FIA Taking Steps to Curb Cyber Crime," February 25, 2009.

30. Prevention of Electronic Crimes Ordinance (Ordinance No. IV of 2008), Article 13.

31. Reporters Without Borders, "Government Urged to Clarify New Law on Cyber-Crime," January 16, 2008, http://www.rsf.org/article.php3?id_article=25053&var_mode=calcul.

32. Prevention of Electronic Crimes Ordinance (Ordinance No. IV of 2008), Article 17.

33. Pakistan ICT Policy Monitors Network, "Internet Censorship in Pakistan—Naval Chief Misusing his Powers," August 18, 2008, http://pakistanictpolicy.bytesforall.net/?q=node/145.

34. Fatima Bhutto, "Online Crimes," *Guardian*, February 11, 2009, http://www.guardian.co.uk/commentisfree/2009/feb/10/pakistan-cyber-terrorism-law.

35. Nasir Iqbal, "Body Set Up to Block Websites," DAWN, September 3, 2006, http://www.dawn.com/2006/09/03/nat3.htm.

36. Ibid.; Ministry of Information Technology, "De-Regulation Policy for the Telecommunication Sector," July 2003, http://www.pta.gov.pk/media/telecom25092003.pdf.

37. *BBC News*, "Pakistan Blocks Blogs on Cartoons," March 3, 2006, http://news.bbc.co.uk/2/hi/south_asia/4771846.stm.

38. Mohammad Kamran, "SC Seeks Legal Avenues to Ban Blasphemous Cartoons Worldwide," *Daily Times*, March 14, 2006, http://www.dailytimes.com.pk/default.asp?page=2006%5C03%5C14%5Cstory_14-3-2006_pg1_7.

39. Mohammad Kamran, "Gov't Directed to Block 'Blasphemous' Websites," *Daily Times*, March 3, 2006, http://www.dailytimes.com.pk/default.asp?page=2006%5C03%5C03%5Cstory_3-3-2006_pg7_27; Akbar S. Ahmed, "Pakistan's Blasphemy Laws: Words Fail Me," *Washington Post*, May 19, 2002, http://www.washingtonpost.com/ac2/wp-dyn?pagename=article&node=&contentId=A36108-2002May17&notFound=true.

40. Pakistan Electronic Media Regulatory Ordinance 2002, Article 20, http://www.pemra.gov.pk/pdf/ordinance1.pdf.

41. Pakistan Electronic Media Regulatory Ordinance 2002, Article 27.

42. Pakistan Electronic Media Regulatory Ordinance, 2007 (LXV of 2007), Article 20(m), http://www.pemra.gov.pk/pdf/ord031107.pdf.

43. Pakistan Electronic Media Regulatory Ordinance, 2007 (LXV of 2007), Article 20(k).

44. Pakistan Electronic Media Regulatory Ordinance, 2007 (LXV of 2007), Article 20(j).

45. Pakistan Electronic Media Regulatory Ordinance, 2007 (LXV of 2007), Article 30(4).

46. Pakistan Electronic Media Regulatory Ordinance, 2007 (LXV of 2007), Article 33.

47. *Daily Times*, "Text of Press Ordinance," November 4, 2007, http://www.dailytimes.com.pk/default.asp?page=2007\11\04\story_4-11-2007_pg7_25.

48. Raja Aqeel, "Bill to Abolish PEMRA Ordinance Curbs Introduced in National Assembly," *Business Recorder*, April 12, 2008.

49. CNN, "Pakistani Police Storm Television Station," November 3, 2007, http://www.cnn.com/2007/WORLD/asiapcf/11/03/pakistan.media/.

50. Muhammad Najeeb, "Pakistani Media Gagged, Even Internet Not Spared," *Hindustan Times*, November 4, 2007, http://www.hindustantimes.com/StoryPage/StoryPage.aspx?id=460572ab-dea2-4703-93e4-280a1763bbf4&&Headline=Pakistani+media+gagged%2c+even+Internet+not+spared.

51. Human Rights Watch, "Pakistan: Media Restrictions Undermine Election," February 18, 2008, http://www.hrw.org/en/news/2008/02/15/pakistan-media-restrictions-undermine-election.

52. Salman Masood and David Rohde, "Pakistan's News Media No Longer Silent, but Musharraf Has Muted His Critics," *New York Times*, December 11, 2007, http://www.nytimes.com/2007/12/11/world/asia/11pmedia.html. However, according to Human Rights Watch, TV stations were "effectively coerced" into adopting the restrictions as conditions for remaining open. Human Rights Watch, "Pakistan: Media Restrictions Undermine Election," February 18, 2008, http://www.hrw.org/en/news/2008/02/15/pakistan-media-restrictions-undermine-election.

53. *Business Recorder*, "PBA to Formulate Code of Conduct," December 26, 2008.

54. Prevention of Electronic Crimes Ordinance (Ordinance No. IX of 2008), Article 28.

55. Prevention of Electronic Crimes Ordinance (Ordinance No. IX of 2008), Article 27.

56. Society against Internet Censorship in Pakistan, "Cyber Crime Ordinance Promulgated by President," January 8, 2008, http://groups.google.com/group/AGABBIP/browse_thread/thread/95fa5fccb314369e.

57. Cecil J. Chen, "Bloggers Brace for Blackouts over CJ," *Daily Times*, March 17, 2007, http://www.dailytimes.com.pk/default.asp?page=2007\03\17\story_17-3-2007_pg12_9.

58. Ibid.

59. Society against Internet Censorship in Pakistan, "Urgent Message to All Bloggers in Pakistan," November 3, 2007, http://groups.google.com/group/AGABBIP/browse_thread/thread/e56dbff06e869763#.

60. Voice of South, "Pakistan Blocks Anti-establishment Blogs," January 15, 2008, http://voiceofsouth.org/2008/01/15/pakistan_blogs/.

61. Jillian York, "Pakistan Communication Authority Issues Directive to Block Web Sites," OpenNet Initiative Blog, http://opennet.net/blog/2009/01/pakistan-communication-authority-issues-directives-block-web-sites.

62. Urooj Zia, "PTA Orders Blockade of Political Webpages, Discussion Forums," *The News*, January 2, 2009, http://www.thenews.com.pk/daily_detail.asp?id=155004.

63. Nart Villeneuve, "The Filtering Matrix: Integrated Mechanisms of Information Control and the Demarcation of Borders in Cyberspace," *First Monday*, Vol. 11, No. 1 (January 2006), http://firstmonday.org/issues/issue11_1/villeneuve/index.html.

64. Naveed Ahmad, "PTCL Blocks Vital Internet Sites to Comply with SC Order," *The News*, March 3, 2007, http://www.thenews.com.pk/top_story_detail.asp?Id=6254; Pakistaniat, "Google, Yahoo, BBC, CNN and Others Websites Blocked in Pakistan as PTCL Fumbles a Censorship Extravaganza," March 7, 2007, http://pakistaniat.com/2007/03/07/pakistan-blog-ban-block-ptcl-yahoo-google-cnn-websites-censorship-internet/.

65. Voice of South, "Pakistan Blocks Anti-establishment Blogs," January 15, 2008, http://voiceofsouth.org/2008/01/15/pakistan_blogs/.

66. OpenNet Initiative Blog, "Pakistan's Internet Has a Bad Weekend," February 25, 2008, http:// opennet.net/blog/2008/02/pakistan%E2%80%99s-internet-has-a-bad-weekend; Martin A. Brown "Pakistan Hijacks YouTube," Renesys Blog, February 24, 2008, http://www.renesys.com/blog/ 2008/02/pakistan_hijacks_youtube_1.shtml.

67. Pakistan Telecommunication Authority, Blocking Order NWFP-33–16 (BW)/06/PTA, February 22, 2008, http://www.renesys.com/blog/pakistan_blocking_order.pdf.

68. Agence France Presse, "Pakistan Blocks YouTube for 'Blasphemous' Content: Officials," February 24, 2008, http://afp.google.com/article/ALeqM5io-SE_bmENEzM46rwdVuDt9iK5zg; Huma Yusuf, "Old and New Media: Converging during the Pakistan Emergency (March 2007–February 2008)," Center for Future Civic Media (MIT), January 12, 2009, http://civic.mit.edu/watchlistenlearn/old -and-new-media-converging-during-the-pakistan-emergency-march-2007-february-2008?page=0%2C0.

69. Declan McCullagh, "How Pakistan Knocked YouTube Offline (and How to Make Sure It Never Happens Again)," *CNet*, February 25, 2008, http://www.news.com/8301-10784_3-9878655-7.html.

70. Martin A. Brown "Pakistan Hijacks YouTube," Renesys Blog, February 24, 2008, http://www .renesys.com/blog/2008/02/pakistan_hijacks_youtube_1.shtml.

71. Pakistan Telecommunication Authority, blocking order No.PTA-LH/F.10–6/49, http://www .nartv.org/blogimages/PTA_-_Blocking_of_website_25-4-06.pdf.

South Korea

Over the years, the growing sophistication and dynamism of the Internet in South Korea have also raised concerns of its power to spread harmful slander and information. In response, the South Korean government is authorized through an expansive regulatory framework to exercise significant discretion over "illegal" Internet content and "harmful" material for  youth. In addition to rigorously regulating providers, government agencies also enforce real-name registration requirements for participation in Internet services and closely monitor election-related online activities.

Background

The Republic of Korea (also known as South Korea) was established in 1948 and spent most of its first four decades under authoritarian rule. In 1987, after a massive protest movement, the government enacted a democratic constitution that has endured to this day. Overall, South Korea's human rights record has steadily and markedly improved since the 1990s. Since that time, South Korea has become one of the most

RESULTS AT A GLANCE					
Filtering	No Evidence of Filtering	Suspected Filtering	Selective Filtering	Substantial Filtering	Pervasive Filtering
Political	•				
Social				•	
Conflict and security					•
Internet tools	•				

Other Factors	Low	Medium	High	Not Applicable
Transparency			•	
Consistency			•	

KEY INDICATORS	
GDP per capita, PPP (constant 2005 international dollars)	23,399
Life expectancy at birth (years)	79
Literacy rate (percent of people age 15+)	99
Human development index (out of 179)	25
Rule of law (out of 211)	53
Voice and accountability (out of 209)	69
Democracy index (out of 167)	28 (Full democracy)
Digital opportunity index (out of 181)	1
Internet users (percent of population)	77.8

Source by indicator: World Bank 2009a, World Bank 2009a, World Bank 2009a, UNDP 2008, World Bank 2009b, World Bank 2009b, Economist Intelligence Unit 2008, ITU 2007, ITU 2008.

vibrant democracies in Asia. Its citizens enjoy universal suffrage and broad constitutional freedoms, and they choose their leaders in free and fair multiparty elections.

South Korean foreign relations remain dominated by the state's relationship with the Democratic People's Republic of Korea (or North Korea), with which South Korea has technically been at war since the two sides fought to a stalemate in 1953. Since that time, the South Korean government has often been intolerant of dissident views and those espousing communism or supporting North Korea; publicly praising North Korea has been, and remains, illegal. Human rights groups charge that, since its enactment in 1948, thousands of South Koreans have been arrested under the state's anticommunist National Security Law (NSL). Those arrested over the years have included students, publishers, trade unionists, political activists, professors, and Internet users, many peacefully expressing their political views.[1] While prosecutions under the NSL have decreased significantly since the transition to democracy, there have been a few recent high-profile investigations using the NSL.[2] As of 2004, Amnesty International reported that 14 people were in prison under the law.[3]

Internet in South Korea

South Korea is one of the most connected countries in the world, with over 77 percent of South Koreans age six and older using the Internet.[4] South Korea has also become the most penetrated broadband market in the world: by early 2008, 90 percent of households used broadband.[5] Following heavy investment in broadband infrastructure after the Asian financial crisis in the late 1990s, South Korea now provides its citizens with a national network that carries data at speeds for the average broadband user of 50–100 Mbps.[6] Over three-quarters of South Korean Internet users use the Internet more than once per day.[7]

By 2008, Korea's 114 Internet service providers (ISPs) were connecting at six Internet exchanges (IX) providing a total of 1,450 Gbps capacity to South Korean Internet users.[8] However, three South Korean ISPs (KT, formerly known as Korea Telecom, Hanaro Telecom, and Korea Thrunet) control nearly 85 percent of the broadband market. The largest broadband supplier, KorNet, provides about half the ADSL lines in the country, making it the largest ADSL supplier in the world.[9]

Dedicated blog service providers, video sites, and online news sites saw the biggest growth in 2008.[10] Over 50 percent of Korean Internet users have created user-generated content (UGC), with over 30 percent producing content at least once a month.[11] Most UGC is centered around Web portals and is text based, though over 50 percent is in video and flash-generated formats.[12] The government has acknowledged that UGC has powered social and political transformation: whereas political dialogue tends to be limited to that between politicians and major media, high-speed Internet infrastructure and social media tools have allowed users anywhere to engage in real-time dialogue.[13] Of the 67 percent of Korean Internet users who read news online, almost 90 percent rely on news services provided by portals, followed by 60 percent viewership of Web sites of print publications.[14]

Thus, it is not surprising that citizens of South Korea, one of the world's most networked countries, have come to influence and in some cases transform the political and social fabric through their online participation. In April 2008, as part of trade negotiations with the United States, President Lee Myung-bak's administration agreed to resume imports of American beef after a five-year ban.[15] On April 29, 2008, a television program called *PD Notebook* on the network MBC claimed that "Koreans are 94 percent more likely to contract a human form of mad cow disease," sparking a flood of online debate, especially on the Agora forum of Korea's second-largest portal, Daum (which saw a daily page-view count spike from 40 million to 200 million).[16] A group called the People's Association for Measures against Mad Cow Disease, led by organizations such as the Korean Confederation of Trade Unions and the Korean Teachers' and Educational Workers' Union, led about 100 days of protests and demanded the resignation of the Lee Myung-bak administration.[17] These protests were coupled with online action, as protesters uploaded images to the Internet, sent messages on protest meet-ups and warnings on arrests via text messaging, and engaged in online debate.[18] Ultimately, his entire cabinet resigned and Lee was forced to call for a "new beginning" for his government.[19]

The power of the Korean cyberspace was also chillingly demonstrated in the suicides of at least four celebrities in 2007 and 2008.[20] Korea's online community was blamed for spreading malicious rumors and attacks on actress Choi Jin Sil's character that were alleged to have driven her to commit suicide in October 2008.[21] In hundreds of thousands of posts, Internet users circulated rumors that Choi was a loan shark who had pressured the actor Ahn Jae Hwan to repay a USD 2 million loan, and ultimately kill himself.[22] After Choi's suicide, the Cyber Terror Response Center of the National Police Agency launched a one-month probe into "false rumors and malicious postings" on the Internet, mobilizing its 900 investigators to crack down on "malpractice" conducted over the Internet as well as cell phones.[23] The police reported more than 10,000 cases of online libel in 2007.[24]

Legal and Regulatory Frameworks

Despite Korea's democratic credentials, its free speech protections are weak relative to many other democracies. Article 21 of the Korean constitution guarantees that "all citizens shall enjoy freedom of speech and the press," but also contains the qualification that "neither speech nor the press shall violate the honor or rights of other persons nor undermine public morals or social ethics."[25] This caveat empowers the government to impose restrictions on a broad range of expression.

Laying the foundation for all digital and analog content regulation, Article 53(1) of the Telecommunications Business Act (1991) states "a person in use of telecommunications shall not make communications with contents that harm the public peace and order or social morals and good customs."[26] Harmful communications were to be determined by presidential decree,[27] and under the original formulation constituted contents that "aim at or abet a criminal act, aim at committing antistate activities, and impede good customs and other social orders."[28] Further, harmful communications could be refused, suspended, or restricted by order of the minister of the Ministry of Information and Communication (MIC), which delegated this authority to the Information and Communication Ethics Committee (ICEC).[29] The ICEC was established under an amended Telecommunications Business Act (1995) to regulate the content of communications and inform state policy aimed at suppressing subversive communications and "promoting active and healthy information."[30]

In June 2002, the Supreme Court struck down the provisions of the Telecommunications Business Act defining "harmful" content and granting the government unlimited authority to regulate it.[31] It held Article 53(1) to be insufficiently specific and clear, and Article 53(2) to violate the rule against blanket delegation.[32] A student at Hankook Aviation University had posted a message in June 1999 entitled, "Exchange of Gunfire in the West Sea, Sloppy Kim Dae-jung!" on the "urgent message board" of the online community Chanwoomul, which a systems administrator deleted before suspending the student's use of the service for one month in accordance with an order from the MIC.[33] In August 1999, the student filed a constitutional complaint, arguing that the provisions infringed on his freedoms of expression, science, and arts, and violated due process and the principle against excessive restriction. However, the Supreme Court found that MIC orders to refuse, suspend, or restrict communications violated neither the principle of proportionality nor due process of law, and did not infringe on the freedom of expression. It cautioned that under the Administrative Procedures Act, users are to be given advance notice of administrative agency decisions, should be given opportunities to submit opinions, and have the right to participate at formal or public hearings.[34]

In December 2002, the National Assembly amended Article 53 to prohibit content that is "illegal" rather than "harmful," while upholding the executive powers of the MIC and the delegated regulatory authority of the ICEC.[35] This provision was ultimately repealed with the 2007 amendment of the Act on Promotion of Information and Communications Network Utilization and Information Protection (Information Act),[36] although this definition remains in place at least functionally.[37] Illegal information included in types of information to be reported continues to be described as that which infringes upon public interests and social order, specifically obscenity, defamation, violence or cruelty, incitement to gambling, and public order.[38]

Specific laws to protect youth, national security, and other national priorities have informed the scope of content regulated by the government-delegated bodies responsible for filtering. For example, the NSL provides "up to seven years in prison for those who praise, encourage, disseminate or cooperate with antistate groups, members or those under their control."[39] The NSL has been used to criminalize advocacy of communism[40] and groups suspected of alignment with North Korea,[41] although arrests under the NSL have become much less frequent in recent years. Nevertheless, the law continues to have a chilling effect on public discussion of North Korea[42] and provides a justification for censorship of Web sites related to North Korea and communism.

Similarly, the directive to protect the country's youth from "harmful" Internet content, broadly described as "immoral, violent, obscene, speculative and antisocial information,"[43] has been one of the central planks in the development of South Korea's filtering policy. The standard of harm in the Enforcement Decree of the Juvenile Protection Act (JPA) was developed from criteria for deliberation of media materials harmful to juveniles, which include provocative, obscene, antisocial, violent, or unethical materials that may harmfully affect their mental and physical health.[44] In accordance with the JPA, ISPs are responsible, as "protectors of juveniles," for making inappropriate content inaccessible on their networks.[45] Web sites carrying adult content must warn visitors and require identification verification for access, measures meant to prevent minors under 19 from accessing pornographic material.[46]

In February 2008, the Korea Communications Commission (KCC) was created to consolidate the MIC and the Korean Broadcasting Commission (KBC). Under South Korea's current legal framework, regulation of Internet content is conducted primarily by two government agencies: the Korean Communications Standards Commission (KCSC)[47] (formerly KISCOM) and the National Election Commission (NEC).

The KCSC integrated the functions of the KBC and KISCOM in February 2008.[48] KISCOM's mandate was originally established through the creation of the ICEC in

1995.[49] Accordingly, the two KCSC subcommissions deal separately with broadcasting and telecommunications standards.[50]

At its inception, the ICEC was empowered to develop general principles or codes of telecommunications ethics, conduct deliberation on and request the "correction" of information declared "harmful" by presidential decree, and operate reporting centers against unhealthy telecommunications activities.[51] The KCSC telecom subcommission continues to make determinations on "requests for correction" with respect to ISPs and Internet content providers (ICPs).[52] Thus, the KCSC is empowered to make determinations on information "harmful" to youth under the Juvenile Protection Act,[53] as well as recommend action against Web sites containing "illegal" content, including pornography, information for cyber criminals, gambling services, and Web sites that express support for communism or for the government of North Korea.[54] The scope of its authority extends to ordering the blocking of Web sites, the deletion of a particular message identified as an improper communication, a Web site's closure, or the suspension of the particular user identification of the individual who posted the improper writing.[55] In addition to special advisory committees, the KCSC also mediates disputes over online defamation. The KCSC said it received 156,000 complaints in 2006 about Internet postings considered inaccurate, and 216,000 in 2007.[56]

With President Lee's full support, government ministries proposed a battery of legislation beginning in July 2008 that would create a framework for addressing defamation, "false rumors," and "malicious postings." In July 2008, the KCC introduced the Comprehensive Measures on Internet Information Protection, which would institute 50 changes to communications and Internet regulation.[57] In amendments to the Information Act, the South Korean government further expanded the already significant regulatory authority of the KCC by adding to online providers' liability for the acts of their users. The KCSC would be authorized to force Internet portals and peer-to-peer Web sites to delete content or suspend publishing for a minimum of 30 days upon receiving a complaint of articles accused of being "fraudulent" or "slanderous," during which the commission would determine whether disputed articles should be removed permanently.[58] Internet portals that failed to temporarily block online postings containing defamatory information would be subject to a fine of up to KRW 30 million or could be forced to shut down,[59] while portals or individuals involved in improperly manipulating Internet search results could be subject to imprisonment for up to one year and a fine up to KRW 10 million.[60] Upon a leak of personal information, the portal must inform the victim of the privacy breach and report the matter to the KCC.

Following an approach taken with other emergent forms of harmful or illegal content, portals, bulletin boards, and other Internet content providers have increasingly taken on responsibility for policing slanderous content. While they would be legally compelled to set up constant in-house monitoring functions,[61] Korea's two largest

Internet portals also implemented their own measures to curb postings considered to violate privacy; for example, Naver created a simplified process for users to quickly block "groundless rumors or postings" and Daum required users to click on a different box if they want to read other users' comments.[62]

In July 2008, Minister of Justice Kim Kyung-hwan announced the introduction of the crime of "cyber defamation," which would punish those who openly insult others through the Internet with up to two years imprisonment or a KRW 10 million fine.[63] Under this rubric, criminal law would apply to defamation and threats, while penalties for cyber defamation and "cyberstalking" would be pursued under information and communication laws.[64]

Although the Lee administration denied that it had orchestrated the crackdown, government prosecutors also pursued blogger Park Dae-sung on charges of "spreading false data in public with harmful intent," punishable by as many as five years in prison or fines of up to KRW 50 million.[65] Using the pen name Minerva, blogger Park Dae-sung had posted nearly 300 entries on Daum's Agora Internet forum between March 2008 and January 2009.[66] His accurate predictions of financial events such as the fall of Lehman Brothers and the crash of the won gained him prophetic status, but also drew allegations that he cost the government billions of dollars by undermining financial markets.[67] Park was arrested in January 2009 but acquitted in April; prosecutors announced that they would appeal the ruling.[68]

On April 1, 2009, the National Assembly adopted a "three-strikes" approach to copyright infringement, particularly file sharing and downloading movie content.[69] In an amendment to Article 133 of the Copyright Law dealing with the "Collection, Abandonment, and Deletion of Illegal Reproductions," the Minister of Culture, Sports, and Tourism would be authorized to shut down message boards that refuse to comply with more than three warnings to remove copyrighted content,[70] while users who upload such content may also have their accounts canceled.[71] These punitive measures could be taken regardless of whether a takedown request by a copyright holder has been issued.[72]

Social media sites whose "main purpose is to enable different people to interactively transmit works, etc., among themselves" are treated as "special types of online service providers" under Article 104 of the Copyright Law.[73] Article 104 providers are obliged to take "necessary measures" to intercept the illegal interactive transmission of copyrighted works upon the request of rights holders. Article 142(1) lays out fines for these special providers who fail to take necessary measures at a maximum of KRW 30 million, while other providers who "seriously damage" the enforcement of copyright as a result of their failure to take down reproductions or "interactive transmissions" are also subject to fines of up to KRW 10 million.[74] Under the amended legislation, Article 104 providers who have been fined under Article 142(1) twice and have failed to take necessary measures can be blocked upon the issuance of a third fine.[75]

South Korea's elections framework allows significant limits to be placed on political speech prior to and during elections, in order to prevent corruption, promote equal opportunity, and minimize the social economic losses and "side effect[s]" that "unlimited free campaigns" might cause.[76] Elections are restricted by numerous detailed prohibitions on campaign-related activities that would be standard practice in many other democracies, including endorsing a candidate if you are an elected official,[77] conducting a public opinion poll within the six days before an election,[78] and setting limits on campaign locations, the posting of campaign paraphernalia, and so on.

The Election Law also extends these restrictions to campaign activities conducted on information and communication networks. As the prohibition with the greatest impact on Internet speech, Article 93 of the Public Official Election Law ("Election Law") makes it illegal for noncandidates to distribute information supporting, recommending, or opposing any political party or candidate.[79] Election commissions that discover information posted online that violates the Election Law may demand that the Web site or hosting service delete, restrict, or suspend the relevant information; the service provider must promptly comply or raise an objection.[80]

The NEC is responsible for controlling all aspects of Korean elections, from counting votes to monitoring the media and tracing campaign contributions.[81] The NEC monitors and censors domestic online media platforms in order to maintain the country's restrictions on election-related political speech,[82] especially its ban on public advocacy of candidates prior to an election period. It has used this power to remove more than 100,000 election-related articles, comments, and blog entries from the Internet,[83] as well as more than 65,000 movies posted to video-sharing Web sites.[84] The NEC began censoring the Internet in the early 2000s, partly in reaction to the significant role the Internet played in the 2002 presidential election. It currently has two divisions that are devoted to Internet regulation and censorship: the Internet Election News Deliberation Commission (IENDC), which handles newspaper Web sites and other online media sources (or "Internet press"),[85] and the Cyber Censorship Team (CCT), which monitors personal blogs, videos, message board comments, and other Web sites.[86]

The IENDC's mission is to ensure that newspaper Web sites, online news agencies, and other semiofficial online news sources are impartial in their campaign coverage and do not violate election laws.[87] The IENDC has a great deal of discretion to decide what constitutes a violation of these rules and to censor the Internet press accordingly. Generally, it does so by contacting the relevant Internet press organizations and telling them to change their content or to issue a correction.

Started in 2002, the CCT has the formidable task of policing everything else on the Internet, including blogs, personal Web sites, video postings, and message boards.[88] The CCT has three main tasks: first, to prevent people from making damaging and untrue statements about the candidates in an election; second, to maintain the prohibition against campaigning at any time other than the officially sanctioned two- to three-week election period; third, to ensure that all message board users only make comments during the election using their full, real names. All three tasks are usually executed by requesting the Web site's hosting service to delete or change offending content, and if the hosting service refuses to delete it, the CCT will open an investigation and press charges. Monitoring is carried out by about 1,000 part-time workers, who are hired nationwide 120 days before every election to run a search program to find and flag suspicious content.[89]

Violation of the law against advocating a candidate prior to the election period can be punished with a fine of up to KRW 4 million or two years in prison.[90] Offending acts include posting long opinions on Web portals and Web sites of political parties, posting comments on online news articles, or any similar acts on personal Web sites or blogs.[91] However, the NEC has stated that "there is small chance that citizens will face legal charges for posting their opinion as they will be viewed flexibly in actual crackdowns."[92]

The line between campaigning and normal discussion is extremely vague, and the decision to censor is made at the discretion of the CCT's officers. This vagueness has had a chilling effect on online political discourse, especially at video-sharing sites, whose election-related content has been reduced to little more than videos produced by the campaigns themselves.[93] Between the 2004 and 2007 presidential elections, the total number of deletion requests for early campaigning skyrocketed, from 2,425 to 76,277. Media have also reported that from June 2006 to May 2007, up to 19,000 online election-related messages were deleted, while legal punishment was pursued against 13 messages containing false rumors about candidates.[94]

Surveillance

The South Korean constitution guarantees that the privacy (Article 17) and the privacy of correspondence (Article 18) of citizens shall not be violated.[95] While most scholars believe that Article 17 forms the basis of a right to privacy,[96] the Supreme Court has also held that together with Article 10, guaranteeing human dignity and the right to pursue happiness, "these constitutional provisions not only guarantee the right to be let alone, which protects personal activity from invasion by others and public exposure, but also an active right to self-control over his or her personal information in a highly informatized modern society."[97]

Internet service providers are generally directed to gather the minimum amount of information necessary and are restricted from disclosing personal information beyond the scope of notification or from collecting certain personal information, such as "political ideology, religion, and medical records," that would likely infringe the user's privacy without consent.[98] However, these protections do not apply where special provisions apply or other laws specify otherwise.

Real-name registration requirements have been a part of the South Korean Internet landscape since 2003, when the MIC sought the cooperation of four major Web portals (Yahoo Korea, Daum Communications, NHN, and NeoWiz) in developing real-name systems for their users.[99] While implicating deeper privacy concerns, the purported goal of these real-name measures is to reduce abusive behavior on the Internet, and a number of prominent cases (such as the suicides of a number of actresses) have made this a major issue for the Korean public.[100]

In 2004, election laws began requiring individuals who post comments on Web sites and message boards in support of, or opposition to, a candidate to disclose their real names.[101] In 2005, the government implemented a rule that requires anyone who creates an account with an e-mail or online chat service to provide detailed information that includes name, address, profession, and identification number.[102] This policy was tightened further by the MIC on July 27, 2007, when users were required to register their real names and resident identification numbers with Web sites before posting comments or uploading video or audio clips on bulletin boards.[103] In December 2008, the KCC extended its reach to require all forum and chat room users to make verifiable real-name registrations.[104] Furthermore, in April 2009 an amendment to the Information Act took effect, requiring Korea-domain Web sites with at least 100,000 visitors daily to confirm personal identities through real names and resident registration numbers.[105] Previously, real-name registration was required for news Web sites with more than 200,000 visitors a day or portals and user-generated content sites with over 300,000 daily visitors.[106] On April 9, reportedly citing freedom of expression as "the most important value to uphold on the Internet" as justification, Google disabled the features on its Korean language YouTube site (kr.youtube.com) for uploading videos and comments.[107]

Amendments to the Protection of Communications Secrets Act put forward in 2007 would establish extensive data retention requirements and also expand the government's surveillance capabilities. First, it would require telecommunications companies and ISPs to retain access records and log files (online transactions conducted; Web sites visited; time of access; and files downloaded, edited, read, and uploaded) for at least three months, along with date and time stamps, telephone numbers of callers and receivers, and GPS location information for 12 months.[108]

The National Human Rights Commission of Korea (NHRCK) recommended that a number of proposed amendments be removed, including the inclusion of GPS information to locate users.[109] It also questioned the need for additional penalties for telecommunication service providers that refuse to comply with requests to provide communications records, despite existing provisions allowing investigators to obtain evidence by search and seizure in ordinary investigations.[110] In 2008, three years after a scandal over the illegal wiretapping of the cell phones of influential political figures forced them to destroy their equipment, the National Intelligence Service asked for permission to resume the practice.[111] E-mails (after submission and receipt) are already considered by law enforcement authorities to be "objects," subject to ordinary search and seizure requirements, rather than "means of communications" requiring wiretapping warrants and notification to parties within 30 days.[112]

ONI Testing Results

OpenNet Initiative testing conducted in 2007 and 2008 confirmed that South Korea filters political and social content, specifically targeting Web sites containing North Korean propaganda or promoting the reunification of North and South Korea, as well as a handful of Web sites devoted to gambling. These findings are consistent with 2006–2007 analysis, with one exception: in 2007 and 2008, Korean ISPs were also shown to selectively filter the Korean-language pornography Web sites tested.

Testing was conducted on three of the largest South Korean ISPs—KT's KorNet, LG Dacom, and Hanaro Telecom's Hananet—from May to August 2008 and in November 2008. On each ISP, ONI detected DNS tampering, which prevents Internet domain names from resolving to their proper IP addresses. All Web sites blocked resolved to a block page jointly hosted by the police and the KCSC.

The ONI determined that a significant number of pro–North Korea or pro-unification Web sites on ONI's testing list were blocked, along with a selected number of gambling-related Web sites. The blocking was extremely consistent across the three ISPs tested, although KorNet and LG Dacom blocked more of the same Web sites as compared to Hananet.

The ONI testing suggests that the extent of filtering in South Korea is still not commensurate with other measures the government has taken to cleanse the Korean Web of illegal or harmful social content. At the same time, the relatively low rate of filtering is consistent with the government's approach to regulating content, which is far more reliant on ordering content and Web-hosting providers to police their own content directly through deletions, suspensions, and takedowns.

Conclusion

Although South Korea is a world leader in Internet and broadband penetration, its citizens do not have access to a free and unfiltered Internet. South Korea's government maintains a wide-ranging approach toward the regulation of specific online content and imposes a substantial level of censorship on elections-related discourse and on a large number of Web sites that the government deems subversive or socially harmful.

Notes

1. Amnesty International, "South Korea: Time to Reform the National Security Law," February 1, 1999, http://web.amnesty.org/library/Index/ENGASA250031999?open&of=ENG-KOR.

2. Cho Chung-un, "Korea: Kang Case Rekindles Debate on National Security Law," The *Korea Herald*, October 17, 2005, http://www.asiamedia.ucla.edu/article.asp?parentid=31651; *The Hankoryeh*, "3 Arrested for Allegedly Meeting N.K. Agent in China," October 27, 2006 http://english.hani.co.kr/arti/english_edition/e_national/167694.html.

3. Reporters Without Borders, "Two Draft Laws: One Good, One Bad for Press Freedom," November 4, 2004, http://www.rsf.org/article.php3?id_article=11781.

4. National Internet Development Agency of Korea, "Survey on the Computer and Internet Usage," September 2008, http://isis.nida.or.kr.

5. Paul Budde Communications Pty., Ltd., "South Korea Broadband Market—Overview and Statistics."

6. National Internet Development Agency of Korea, "Korea Internet White Paper," May 2008, http://isis.nida.or.kr/eng/ebook/ebook.html.

7. National Internet Development Agency of Korea, "Survey on the Computer and Internet Usage," September 2008, http://isis.nida.or.kr.

8. National Internet Development Agency of Korea, "Korea Internet White Paper," May 2008, http://isis.nida.or.kr/eng/ebook/ebook.html.

9. Paul Budde Communications Pty., Ltd., "South Korea Broadband Market—Overview and Statistics," May 27, 2008, 5–6.

10. National Internet Development Agency of Korea, "Korea Internet White Paper," May 2008, http://isis.nida.or.kr/eng/ebook/ebook.html.

11. Ibid., 21.

12. Ibid.

13. Ibid., 23.

14. Ibid., 69.

15. Choe Sang-hun, "Korean Leader Considers Ways to Rework Government," *New York Times*, June 11, 2008, http://www.nytimes.com/2008/06/11/world/asia/11korea.html.

16. *The Dong-a Ilbo*, "Anti-US Beef Protests: One Year Later," April 29, 2009, http://english.donga.com/srv/service.php3?biid=2009042903068; Jon Herskovitz and Rhee So-eui, "South Korean Internet Catches 'Mad Cow Madness,'" Reuters, June 13, 2008, http://in.reuters.com/article/internetNews/idINSEO30506420080613?sp=true.

17. *The Dong-a Ilbo*, "Anti-US Beef Protests: One Year Later," April 29, 2009, http://english.donga.com/srv/service.php3?biid=2009042903068.

18. Jon Herskovitz and Rhee So-eui, "South Korean Internet Catches 'Mad Cow Madness,'" Reuters, June 13, 2008, http://in.reuters.com/article/internetNews/idINSEO30506420080613?sp=true.

19. Choe Sang-hun, "Korean Leader Considers Ways to Rework Government," *New York Times*, June 11, 2008, http://www.nytimes.com/2008/06/11/world/asia/11korea.html.

20. Justin McCurry, "Storm in South Korea over Jang Ja-yeon's Suicide," *Guardian*, April 1, 2009, http://www.guardian.co.uk/world/2009/apr/01/south-korea-entertaiment-jang-jayeon.

21. Choe Sang-Hun, "Web Rumors Tied to Korean Actress's Suicide," *New York Times*, October 2, 2008, http://www.nytimes.com/2008/10/03/world/asia/03actress.html.

22. Jennifer Veale, "South Koreans Are Shaken by a Celebrity Suicide," *Time*, October 6, 2008, http://www.time.com/time/world/article/0,8599,1847437,00.html.

23. *The Hankyoreh*, "KCC's Childish Threat to Google,"April 17, 2009, http://english.hani.co.kr/arti/english_edition/e_editorial/350258.html; Lee Sang-eon and Chun In-sung, "Cyber Terror Sleuths Planning Internet Crackdown," *JoongAng Daily*, October 06, 2008, http://joongangdaily.joins.com/article/view.asp?aid=2895724.

24. Choe Sang-Hun, "Korean Star's Suicide Reignites Debate on Web Regulation," *New York Times*, October 12, 2008, http://www.nytimes.com/2008/10/13/technology/internet/13suicide.html.

25. Constitution of the Republic of South Korea, Articles 21(1), 21(4), http://www.ccourt.go.kr/home/english/welcome/republic.jsp.

26. Telecommunications Business Act (wholly amended by Act No. 4394 on August 10, 1991), Article 53(1), Decisions of the Korean Constitutional Court, Opinion 14–1 KCCR 616, 99Hun-Ma480, June 27, 2002, http://www.ccourt.go.kr/home/english/decision_etc/decision2003.htm.

27. Ibid., Article 53(2).

28. Enforcement Decree of Telecommunications Business Act (wholly amended by Presidential Decree No. 13558 on December 31, 1991), Article 16, Decisions of the Korean Constitutional Court, Opinion 14–1 KCCR 616, 99Hun-Ma480, June 27, 2002, http://www.ccourt.go.kr/home/english/decision_etc/decision2003.htm.

29. Telecommunications Business Act (wholly amended by Act No. 4394 on August 10, 1991), Article 53(3), Decisions of the Korean Constitutional Court, Opinion 14–1 KCCR 616, 99Hun-Ma480, June 27, 2002, http://www.ccourt.go.kr/home/english/decision_etc/decision2003.htm.

30. Article 53–2, Telecommunications Business Act (1995), Law 4903, January 5, 1995, http://www.itu.int/ITU-D/treg/Legislation/Korea/BusinessAct.htm.

31. Decisions of the Korean Constitutional Court, Opinion 14–1 KCCR 616, 99Hun-Ma480, June 27, 2002, http://www.ccourt.go.kr/home/english/decision_etc/decision2003.htm.

32. Ibid.

33. Ibid.

34. Ibid.

35. Act on Promotion of Information and Communications Network Utilization and Information Protection, Law No. 8289, January 16, 2007, http://eng.kcc.go.kr/download.do?fileNm=TELECOMMUNICATIONS_BUSINESS_ACT.pdf; Privacy International and the GreenNet Educational Trust, "Silenced: An International Report on Censorship and Control of the Internet," September 2003, www.privacyinternational.org/survey/censorship/Silenced.pdf.

36. Ibid.

37. On its Web site, the Korean Communications Standards Commission defines illegal information as "all sorts of information against the positive law of the Republic of Korea, that is, information infringed upon the public interests and social orders." Korean Communications Standards Commission, "Subject of Report," http://www.singo.or.kr/eng/02_report/Subject_Report.php.

38. Korean Communications Standards Commission, "Subject of Report," http://www.singo.or.kr/eng/02_report/Subject_Report.php.

39. National Security Law, Article 7(1) (unofficial translation provided by the Korea Web Weekly), http://www.kimsoft.com/Korea/nsl-en.htm.

40. Ser Myo-ja, "Security Law Marks 60 Years of Strife," *JoongAng Daily*, September 1, 2008, http://joongangdaily.joins.com/article/view.asp?aid=2894346.

41. Human Rights Watch, "Retreat from Reform: Labor Rights and Freedom of Expression in South Korea," November 1, 1990, http://www.hrw.org/en/reports/1990/11/01/retreat-reform; Brad Adams, "South Korea Should Act Like it Knows," Human Rights Watch, April 13, 2006, http://www.hrw.org/en/news/2006/04/12/south-korea-should-act-it-knows.

42. Brad Adams, "South Korea: Defend Human Rights," Human Rights Watch, January 15, 2008, http://www.hrw.org/en/news/2008/01/22/south-korea-defend-human-rights.

43. Korean Communications Standards Commission, "Subject of Report," http://www.singo.or.kr/eng/02_report/Subject_Report.php.

44. Juvenile Protection Act, Article 10, Decisions of the Korean Constitutional Court, Opinion 14–1 KCCR 616, 99Hun-Ma480, June 27, 2002, http://www.ccourt.go.kr/home/english/decision_etc/decision2003.htm.

45. See Youth Protection Committee Web site, http://youth.go.kr/.

46. Act on Promotion of Information and Communication Network Utilization and Information Protection (2001), Article 42; *Korea Herald*, "45 Websites Violate Youth Law," March 31, 2009.

47. Korean Communications Standards Commission, http://www.singo.or.kr/eng/01_introduction/introduction.php.

48. Korean Communications Standards Commission, "Chronology," http://www.icec.or.kr/eng/01_About/Chronology.php.

49. Telecommunications Business Act (1995), Law 4903, Article 53–2, January 5, 1995, http://www.itu.int/ITU-D/treg/Legislation/Korea/BusinessAct.htm.

50. Korean Communications Standards Commission, "Committees," http://www.icec.or.kr/eng/02_Operation/Committees.php.

51. Telecommunications Business Act (1995), Law 4903, Article 53–2, January 5, 1995, http://www.itu.int/ITU-D/treg/Legislation/Korea/BusinessAct.htm.

52. For an explanation of the reporting process of suspected illegal content, see Korean Communications Standards Commission, "Report Process," http://www.singo.or.kr/eng/02_report/Process.php.

53. Korean Communications Standards Commission, "Committees," http://www.icec.or.kr/eng/02_Operation/Committees.php.

54. Korean Communications Standards Commission, "Subject of Report," http://www.singo.or.kr/eng/02_report/Subject_Report.php; Reporters without Borders, "South Korea—2004 Annual Report," http://www.rsf.org/en-rapport59-id_rubrique416-South_Korea.html.

55. Decisions of the Korean Constitutional Court, Opinion 14–1 KCCR 616, 99Hun-Ma480, June 27, 2002, http://www.ccourt.go.kr/home/english/decision_etc/decision2003.htm.

56. Kim Hyung-eun, "Do New Internet Regulations Curb Free Speech?" *JoongAng Daily*, August 13, 2008, http://joongangdaily.joins.com/article/view.asp?aid=2893577.

57. Jung Ha-won, "Internet to Be Stripped of Anonymity," *JoongAng Daily*, July 23, 2008, http://joongangdaily.joins.com/article/view.asp?aid=2892691.

58. Michael Fitzpatrick, "South Korea Wants to Gag the Noisy Internet Rabble," *Guardian*, October 8, 2008, http://www.guardian.co.uk/technology/2008/oct/09/news.internet; Kim Tong-hyung, "Cabinet Backs Crackdown on Cyber-bullying," *Korea Times*, July 22, 2008, http://www.koreatimes.co.kr/www/news/biz/2008/07/123_28003.html.

59. Kim Hyung-eun, "Do New Internet Regulations Curb Free Speech?" *JoongAng Daily*, August 13, 2008, http://joongangdaily.joins.com/article/view.asp?aid=2893577.

60. Lee Sang-bok, "New Regulations Proposed for Internet Postings," *JoongAng Daily*, August 21, 2008, http://joongangdaily.joins.com/article/view.asp?aid=2893939.

61. Kim Hyung-eun, "Do New Internet Regulations Curb Free Speech?" *JoongAng Daily*, August 13, 2008, http://joongangdaily.joins.com/article/view.asp?aid=2893577.

62. Sung So-young, "Portals Beef Up Measures against Malicious Postings," *JoongAng Daily*, October 23, 2008, http://joongangdaily.joins.com/article/view.asp?aid=2896433.

63. Ser Myo-ja, "GNP Files Bills to Alter the Nation's Media Landscape," *JoongAng Daily*, December 4, 2008, http://joongangdaily.joins.com/article/view.asp?aid=2898166.

64. Lee Sang-eon and Chun In-sung, "Cyber Terror Sleuths Planning Internet Crackdown," *JoongAng Daily*, October 6, 2008, http://joongangdaily.joins.com/article/view.asp?aid=2895724.

65. Choe Sang-Hun, "South Korea Frees Blogger Who Angered Government," *New York Times*, April 20, 2009, http://www.nytimes.com/2009/04/21/world/asia/21blogger.html; Oh Byung-sang, "After Minerva: Gaining Balance," *JoongAng Daily*, April 24, 2009, http://joongangdaily.joins.com/article/view.asp?aid=2903946.

66. Ser Myo-ja, "Prognosticator 'Minerva' Is Acquitted by a Seoul Court," *JoongAng Daily*, April 21, 2009, http://joongangdaily.joins.com/article/view.asp?aid=2903837.

67. Choe Sang-Hun, "South Korea Frees Blogger Who Angered Government," *New York Times*, April 20, 2009, http://www.nytimes.com/2009/04/21/world/asia/21blogger.html.

68. John M. Glionna and Ju-min Park, "South Korea: Blogger 'Minerva' Found Not Guilty," *Los Angeles Times*, April 21, 2009, http://www.latimes.com/news/nationworld/world/la-fg-minerva21 -2009apr21,0,850967.story.

69. IP World, "South Korea Passes Three-Strikes Internet Piracy Law," April 15, 2009, http://www .ipworld.com/ipwo/doc/view.htm?id=217097&searchCode=H. http://news.softpedia.com/news/File -Sharers-Cornered-Again-84010.shtml.

70. Proposed Amendment to Copyright Law of Korea (July 2008), Article 133–2(3), http://ipleft .or.kr/bbs/view.php?board=ipleft_5&id=488&page=1&category1=3.

71. Ibid.

72. Nate Anderson, "South Korea Fits Itself for a '3 Strikes' Jackboot," Ars Technica, April 15, 2009, http://arstechnica.com/tech-policy/news/2009/04/korea-fits-itself-for-a-3-strikes-jackboot.ars.

73. Copyright Law of Korea, Article 104, http://eng.copyright.or.kr/law_01_01.html.

74. Ibid., Article 142(1).

75. Proposed Amendment to Copyright Law of Korea (July 2008), Article 133–2(4)(1) (unofficial English translation), http://ipleft.or.kr/bbs/view.php?board=ipleft_5&id=488&page=1&category1 =3, accessed May 15, 2009.

76. National Election Commission, "Features of Korean Election," http://www.nec.go.kr/english/ features/20041223/1_280.html (accessed March 1, 2008). The English-language version of the National Election Commission's Web site explains these restrictions: "To prevent corruption due to money power/government authority/slanderous propaganda, and to minimize the social economic loss and side effect of the unlimited free campaign might cause, to prevent inequality in campaign opportunity due to candidates' disparity in wealth, to reflect public opinion without distortion, there is need to limit the freedom of campaign, so more emphasis put on the fair competition than on freedom in election campaign, thereby we have limit on freedom in campaigning for the harmony of two constitutional idea, freedom in campaigning and equal opportunity in election campaign."

77. Public Official Election Law, Act No. 8879, Article 86, February 29, 2008, http://www.nec .go.kr/english/NEC/Public_Official_Election.zip. Former President Roh Moo-hyun was charged by the NEC and impeached for violating this law. He was later reinstated as president. See *BBC News*, "Obituary: Roh Moo-hyun," May 23, 2009, http://news.bbc.co.uk/2/hi/asia-pacific/2535143.stm.

78. Public Official Election Law, Article 108.

79. Ibid., Article 93.

80. Ibid., Articles 82–4(3–5).

81. ONI interview with an official from the IENDC.

82. Public Official Election Law, Article 8–5.

83. National Election Commission, "The Overview of Cyber Crackdown Service Related to the 18th National Election."

84. Bruce Wallace, "Emotions Don't Reach S. Korea Voters," *Los Angeles Times*, December 15, 2007, http://articles.latimes.com/2007/dec/15/world/fg-korea15.

85. National Election Commission Web site, "About IENDC," http://www.nec.go.kr/english/NEC/nec_IENDC01.html.

86. ONI interview with an official from the Cyber Censorship Team.

87. Public Official Election Law, Article 8–5(1). According to the NEC, IENDC bans the Internet media from doing the following: (1) Reporting on public opinion polls during the 2- to 3-week election period, or reporting on polls during any other period in a way the IENDC considers biased or inaccurate; (2) using headlines that "reduce, overstate or distort" election-related news; (3) reporting "distorted or false" news by "overstating, highlighting, cutting or hiding important facts that may have substantial impacts on the decisions of voters"; (4) falsely attributing any statements or other actions to candidates or political parties; (5) misinforming voters with reports on election results estimated without any reasonable basis; (6) failing to draw a sharp line between facts and opinions; (7) failing to equally represent different points of view when asking candidates or other people for their opinions; (8) modifying pictures or videos to create a negative portrayal of a candidate; (9) allowing opinion advertisements that support or oppose a particular party or candidate. National Election Commission Web site, "Internet Election News Deliberation Commission Regulation No. 1," Articles 1 through 18.

88. ONI interview with an official from the Cyber Censorship Team.

89. ONI interview with IENDC official.

90. Shin Hae-in, "Korea: Controversy Mounts over Ban on Internet Election," *Korea Herald*, June 25, 2007, http://www.asiamedia.ucla.edu/print.asp?parentid=72445.

91. Ibid.

92. Ibid.

93. Bruce Wallace, "Emotions Don't Reach S. Korea Voters," *Los Angeles Times*, December 15, 2007, http://articles.latimes.com/2007/dec/15/world/fg-korea15.

94. Shin Hae-in, "Korea: Controversy Mounts over Ban on Internet Election," *Korea Herald*, June 25, 2007, http://www.asiamedia.ucla.edu/print.asp?parentid=72445.

95. Constitution of the Republic of Korea, Articles 17–18, http://www.ccourt.go.kr/home/english/welcome/republic.jsp.

96. Soon Chul Huh, "Invasion of Privacy v. Commercial Speech: Regulation of Spam with a Comparative Constitutional Point of View," *Albany Law Review*, 2006, 70, 181.

97. 96 Da 42789 (S. Korea 1998).

98. Act on Promotion of Information and Communications Network Utilization and Information Protection, Article 22–24.

99. Winston Chai, "Real User IDs on Chat Groups: Korean Govt," ZDNet Asia, May 23, 2003, http://www.zdnetasia.com/news/hardware/0,39042972,39133165,00.htm.

100. Choe Sang-Hun, "Web Rumors Tied to Korean Actress's Suicide," *New York Times*, October 2, 2008, http://www.nytimes.com/2008/10/03/world/asia/03actress.html.

101. Public Official Election Law, Article 82–6.

102. Xinhua News Agency, "Internet Real-Name System Boosts Cyber Security in S Korea," April 24, 2008. http://news.xinhuanet.com/english/2008-04/24/content_8039953.htm.

103. *Korea Herald*, "Web Identification System Not Effective," July 3, 2007.

104. Brian Lee, "Blue House tries to Plug the Hole in PR Machine," *JoongAng Daily*, May 6, 2009, http://joongangdaily.joins.com/article/view.asp?aid=2904455; Michael Fitzpatrick, "South Korea Wants to Gag the Noisy Internet Rabble," *Guardian*, October 8, 2008, http://www.guardian.co.uk/technology/2008/oct/09/news.internet.

105. Antone Gonsalves, "Google Scales Back YouTube Korea," *InformationWeek*, April 13, 2009, http://www.informationweek.com/news/internet/google/showArticle.jhtml?articleID=216500489; Martyn Williams, "Google Disables Uploads, Comments On YouTube Korea," *The Industry Standard*, April 12, 2009, http://www.thestandard.com/news/2009/04/13/google-disables-uploads-comments-youtube-korea.

106. Kim Hyung-eun, "Do New Internet Regulations Curb Free Speech?" *JoongAng Daily*, August 13, 2008, http://joongangdaily.joins.com/article/view.asp?aid=2893577.

107. Antone Gonsalves, "Google Scales Back YouTube Korea," *InformationWeek*, April 13, 2009, http://www.informationweek.com/news/internet/google/showArticle.jhtml?articleID=216500489.

108. Association for Progressive Communications, "South Korea: Opposition to Draft Legislation on 'Communication Data Retention,'" April 19, 2007, http://www.apc.org/en/news/security/asiapacific/south-korea-opposition-draft-legislation-communica.

109. National Human Rights Commission of Korea, "NHRCK Announces Opinion on Proposed Amendments to the Protection of Communications Secrets Act," January 30, 2008, http://www.humanrights.go.kr/english/activities/view_01.jsp?seqid=713&board_id=Press%20Releases.

110. Ibid.

111. Brian Lee, "What Happens When Intelligence Fails," *JoongAng Daily*, September 28, 2008, http://joongangdaily.joins.com/article/view.asp?aid=2895216; *People's Daily*, "S. Korean Spy Agency Admits Conducting Illegal Wiretapping," August 5, 2005, http://english.people.com.cn/200508/05/eng20050805_200519.html.

112. *The Hankyoreh*, "Prosecutors Have Indiscriminate Access to Personal Email Communications," April 24, 2009, http://english.hani.co.kr/arti/english_edition/e_national/351496.html.

Middle East and North Africa

MENA Overview

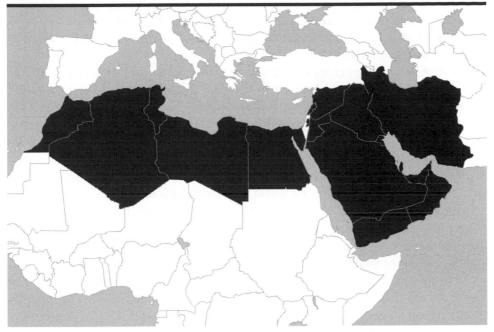

Introduction

Countries in the Middle East and North Africa continue to invest in information technology infrastructure and media projects as part of their strategies to develop local
economies and create employment. Among the major examples is Jordan's plan to
establish a free IT zone in Amman, which will give sales and income tax breaks to the
software companies and business development firms based in the zone. The zone is
part of a strategy designed to increase the number of Internet users from 26 percent to
50 percent of the population. It aims to increase employment in the IT sector and to
boost the sector's revenues from USD 2.2 billion in 2009 to USD 3 billion by the end
of 2011.[1]

In addition to existing regional hubs Dubai Media City and Dubai Internet City, the
United Arab Emirates (UAE) launched a new content-creation zone to support media
content creators in the Middle East and North Africa. The new Abu Dhabi–based zone
aims to employ Arab media professionals in film, broadcast, digital, and publishing.
Among the partners of the zone are CNN, the BBC, the *Financial Times*, the Thomson
Reuters Foundation, and the Thomson Foundation.[2]

At the same time, some countries have initiated efforts to develop Arabic Web content. In this regard, Microsoft is working on translation technology that would make the Arabic language more accessible to Internet users, as part of Qatar's Supreme Council for Information and Communication Technology's initiative to develop more Web sites with Arabic content.[3]

The number of Internet users is likely to continue to rise, especially with the introduction of technologies that overcome poor information and communication technology (ICT) infrastructure that hinders Internet access in the region. WiMAX, for example, was commercially available by the end of March 2009 in Algeria, Bahrain, Jordan, Kuwait, Saudi Arabia, and Tunisia, while operators in other parts of the region have started testing the service.[4] Additionally, broadband markets are growing fast in Algeria, Egypt, Morocco, and Tunisia, and commercial 3G mobile services have been launched in Egypt, Libya, Morocco, Sudan, Syria, and Tunisia.[5]

Demographic factors are also expected to contribute to the growth of the Internet population. *Arab Media Outlook, 2008–2012* states, "Digital media will thrive in the Arab market because the market has a large, technologically accomplished demographic group—its youth—who are comfortable with it and will customize it to their own requirements." The report also revealed that "over 50% of the population in Yemen, Oman, Saudi Arabia, Jordan, Morocco and Egypt are estimated to be currently less than 25 years old, while in the rest of the countries the under-25, 'net generation' makes up around 35% to 47% of total population."[6]

Liberalization of telecommunications markets has already taken place in several Arab countries. Most of the incumbent telecom companies in North Africa are already in private hands, with the exception of Algérie Télécom, the privatization of which has been postponed because of the global economic crisis.[7] However, experts say telecom liberalization in the Middle East and North Africa still lags behind the rest of the world in terms of cost and efficiency, a matter which does not encourage direct foreign investment.[8]

The Media Environment

The Middle East and North Africa is one of the most heavily censored regions in the world. Human rights watchdogs and free speech advocacy groups continue to criticize the media restrictions and repressive legal regimes, and over the past few years, a great number of bloggers and cyber dissidents have been jailed.

In April 2009, the International Federation of Journalists called for a radical overhaul of media laws in the Middle East, stating that the laws in most of the region's countries still permit the jailing of journalists for undermining the reputation of the state, the president, the monarch, or religion. Such laws have often been used to suppress reporting of corruption or scrutiny of government actions.[9] This media environment created by authorities has been hostile to bloggers and online activism, resulting in a number of arrests across the region. In a list created by the Committee to Protect Journalists of the ten worst countries to be a blogger, five countries (Egypt, Syria, Iran, Tunisia, and Saudi Arabia) were from the region.[10]

Internet and Media Regulations: The Debate

The last few years have witnessed an increase in debates over media and Internet censorship in the region. Rifts between censors and local and regional advocates of freedom of speech have intensified, and more voices continue to express concern about media regulations in the region.

Interestingly, while advocates in the region criticize the regimes for repressive regulations, which limit freedom of speech online, some governments claim they arrest bloggers and online activists because they exploit what the regimes call "media freedom." In Egypt, for example, the authorities arrested a blogger in May 2009 under the accusation of "exploitation of the democratic climate prevailing in the country to overthrow the regime." The Cairo-based Arab Network for Human Rights Information deplored the charges and described them as a black comedy.[11]

Another example of such a rift is from the Gulf countries, where the head of the Doha Center for Media Freedom criticized Dubai Police for allegedly asking Google to censor YouTube. The head of the center was later criticized by Qatar officials as well as some journalists and was accused of endorsing pornography,[12] which is a sensitive topic in many Middle East and North African societies.

While it is common for Internet groups and online activists in the region to organize online campaigns to condemn online censorship and arrests of bloggers and online writers, other online campaigns that call for and support social censorship—mostly online pornography—have emerged in the past few years. For instance, an Arabic Web site called Ehjeb (Arabic for the verb "to block") is becoming increasingly popular, particularly among users of Web forums. The Web site offers to facilitate the blocking of Web sites by sending user-submitted URLs of questionable content to censors in some of the region's countries. Also, some Internet users in North African countries where there is no social filtering have organized online campaigns to demand filtering of sexually explicit content.[13]

Pro-censorship advocates and anti-censorship activists have also used the court system in their attempts to implement or remove censorship. For example, a judge in Egypt filed a lawsuit requesting the banning of 51 Web sites considered offensive. The court rejected the lawsuit in December 2007 and emphasized support for freedom of expression as long as the Web sites do not harm religious beliefs or public order.[14]

However, in May 2009 a Cairo court ruled in favor of an Egyptian lawyer and ordered the Egyptian government to ban access to pornographic Web sites because they are deemed offensive to the values of religion and society.[15]

In Tunisia, however, a blogger challenged the Web-filtering regime in the country by filing a legal suit against the Tunisian Internet Agency (ATI) for censoring the social networking site Facebook after it was briefly blocked in August 2008. The court dismissed the case in November 2008 without providing any explanation.[16] These examples and cases illustrate how the fight over access controls is taking different and often more subtle shapes and forms, and also indicate that different players will continue the debate and challenge each other.

Access Control

Access controls in the Middle East and North Africa are multilayered; governments and authorities use first- and second-generation measures to regulate Internet access and online activities. These measures include laws and regulations, technical filtering, physical restrictions, surveillance and monitoring, and harassment and arrests. Among the laws and regulations used to control access in the region are the press and publication laws, penal codes, emergency laws, antiterrorism laws, Internet-specific laws, ISPs' terms and conditions, and telecommunications decrees.

Press and Publication Laws, Penal Codes, Emergency Laws, and Antiterrorism Bills

Many countries in the region use restrictive press laws to regulate online publishing and traditional journalism. For example, censorship of online media and print journalism in Bahrain is exerted using the 2002 Press Law.[17] Kuwait's 2006 press law allows the imprisonment of journalists for making references to Islam that are deemed insulting[18] or for articles seen as "against national interests."[19] Oman's 1984 Press and Publication Law authorizes the government to censor publications deemed politically, culturally, or sexually offensive.[20] Syria's 2001 Press Law sets out sweeping controls over publications printed in Syria.[21] Journalists in Tunisia have been prosecuted by Tunisia's press code, which bans offending the president, disturbing order, and publishing what the government perceives as false news.[22] Yemen's 1990 Press and Publications Law subjects publications and broadcast media to broad prohibitions and harsh penalties.[23] The press law in Morocco has been used to suppress outspoken online writers.[24]

In addition to press codes, some countries often use penal codes to suppress journalists and online writers. Yemen's Ministry of Information declared in April 2008 that the penal code will be used to prosecute writers who publish content on the Internet that "incites hatred" or "harms national interests."[25] Syria's penal code criminalizes spreading news abroad.[26] Though the Bahraini government in May 2008 introduced amendments to the 2002 press law that eliminate prison sentences for journalists and prior censorship on publications, journalists can still be charged and jailed using the penal code and antiterrorism law.[27]

In addition to the use of penal and press codes, two countries—Egypt and Syria—both of which have been under emergency law for some time, have taken advantage of this status to punish individuals deemed threatening. Egypt's emergency law, in force since the declaration of the state of emergency in 1981, grants the government powers to search, arrest, and detain individuals without the supervision of judicial bodies. Rights groups say that the uninterrupted application of the emergency law since 1981 has led to the emergence of a parallel legal system unchecked by ordinary judicial bodies.[28] Similarly, Syria uses the ongoing state of emergency (which began in 1963) to arrest media workers.[29]

Morocco uses its antiterrorism bill, passed following suicide bombings in Casablanca in 2003, to punish journalists. The bill grants the government sweeping legal power to arrest journalists for publishing content deemed to "disrupt public order by intimidation, force, violence, fear or terror."[30]

Internet-Specific Laws

Few countries in the region have introduced Internet-specific laws to regulate Internet activities; among them are the UAE and Saudi Arabia. The UAE's 2007 federal cyber law criminalizes hacking, abusing holy shrines or religious rituals, opposing the Islamic religion, transcending family principles and values, setting up a Web site for groups promoting programs in breach of public decency and order, and setting up a Web site or publishing information for a terrorist group under fake names with intent to facilitate contacts with their leadership, or to promote their ideologies and finance their activities, or to publish information on how to make explosives or any other substances to be used in terrorist attacks.[31]

In January 2008, Saudi Arabia implemented 16 articles of a new law on the use of technology. The law includes penalties of ten years in prison and a fine for Web site operators who advocate or support terrorism; three years and a fine for financial fraud or invasion of privacy; and five years and a fine for those guilty of distributing pornography or other materials that violate public law, religious values, and social standards of the kingdom. Accomplices of the guilty parties and even those who are proven to have only intended to engage in unlawful IT acts can receive up to half of the maximum punishments.[32]

Terms and Conditions of ISPs

Terms and conditions imposed on users by ISPs are also used to control access in some countries. In Oman, for example, Internet use is regulated by the ISP Omantel's terms and conditions, which mandate that users "not carry out any unlawful activities which contradict the social, cultural, political, religious or economical values of the Sultanate of Oman or could cause harm to any third party," as any abuse and misuse of the Internet services will "result in the termination of the subscription and/or in the proceedings of Criminal or Civil lawsuits against the Customer."[33]

Another example is Yemen, where the terms and conditions set by the ISP TeleYemen (or Y.Net) prohibits "sending any message which is offensive on moral, religious, communal, or political grounds." TeleYemen reserves the right to control access "and data stored in the Y.Net system in any manner deemed appropriate by TeleYemen." Section 6.3.3 cautions subscribers that TeleYemen will report "any use or attempted use of the Y.Net service which contravenes any applicable Law of the Republic of Yemen."[34]

Telecommunications Laws

Telecommunications laws are used to control what ISPs can and cannot host. In Algeria, for example, article 14 of a 1998 telecommunications decree makes ISPs responsible for the Web sites they host and requires them to take "all necessary steps to ensure constant surveillance" of content to prevent access to "material contrary to public order and morality."[35] Bahrain's Telecommunications Law of 2002 contains penalties for illicit use of the Internet, including the transmission of messages that are offensive to public policy or morals.[36] In Tunisia, the 1998 post and telecommunications law enables the authorities to intercept and check the content of e-mail messages.[37] Electronic surveillance such as filtering of e-mail messages of government opponents has been reported in Tunisia.[38]

Surveillance and Monitoring

Measures to monitor Internet activities, particularly in Internet cafés, have been introduced in many Arab countries. In Algeria, security forces started raiding Internet cafés and checking the browsing history of Internet users after terrorist attacks hit the country in April 2007. In April 2008, the security forces increased their monitoring and surveillance efforts of Internet cafés, and cafés were required to collect names and identification numbers of their customers and report this information, together with any suspicious activities, to the police.[39]

Similarly, in March 2008 Jordan began to increase restrictions on the country's Internet cafés. Cameras were installed in Internet cafés to monitor users, and owners were required to register the IP number of the café, their users' personal data, the time of use, and the data of Web sites explored.[40]

Additionally, Saudi Arabia's Ministry of Interior in April 2009 ordered Internet cafés to install hidden cameras and provide a record of names and identities of their customers.[41] In Kuwait, Internet café owners also were required to maintain a record of customers' names and identifications, which they must submit to the Ministry of Communications upon request.[42]

Some Internet café operators in Lebanon admit that they use computer surveillance software that enables them to monitor the desktops and browsing habits of their clients under the pretext of protecting the security of their computer networks or to stop their clients from accessing pornography.[43] However, there is no evidence that the government orders these measures.

In March 2008, the Syrian authorities ordered Internet café users to provide their names, identification cards, and the times they use the Internet café to café owners, who will consequently present them to the authorities.[44]

In October 2007, police in Yemen ordered some Internet cafés to close at midnight and demanded that users show their identification cards to the café operator.[45] Some owners use surveillance software to monitor the online activities of their customers and refuse access to clients who access pornography.[46]

In August 2008, Egyptian authorities imposed new monitoring measures by demanding that Internet café clients must provide their names, e-mail addresses, and telephone numbers before they can use the Internet. Once the data are provided, clients will receive a text message on their cell phones and a PIN number that they can use to access the Internet.[47]

In addition to the preceding measures, some countries impose physical restrictions on Internet cafés as part of their monitoring efforts. For example, Yemen[48] and Oman[49] require that computer screens in Internet cafés must be visible to the floor supervisor. No closed rooms or curtains that might obstruct the view of the monitors are allowed.

Technical Filtering

The OpenNet Initiative conducted tests for technical Internet filtering in all the countries in the Middle East and North Africa between 2008 and 2009. Test results prove that the governments and ISPs censor content deemed politically sensitive; critical of governments, leaders, or ruling families; morally offensive; or in violation of public ethics and order.

Testing also revealed that political filtering continues to be the common denominator across the region. Many states in the Middle East and North Africa prevent their citizens from accessing political content or have blocked such content in the past. For example, Bahrain, Qatar, Jordan, Iran, United Arab Emirates, Syria, Saudi Arabia, Morocco, Libya, and Tunisia have censored Web sites containing content critical of governments and leaders, Web sites that claim human rights violations, and/or Web sites of opposition groups. Mauritania briefly blocked the news Web site Taqadoumy, and Egypt at one point blocked the Web site of the Islamic opposition group Muslim Brotherhood, as well as the Web site of the Labor Party's newspaper.

To one degree or another, the Gulf countries, Sudan, Tunisia, Gaza, Yemen, and Iran censor pornography, nudity, gay and lesbian content, escort and dating services, and Web sites displaying provocative attire. Also censored by most of these countries are Web sites that present critical reviews of Islam and/or attempt to convert Muslims to other religions. Some of these countries also filter Web sites related to alcohol, gambling, and drugs.

Generally, the countries that implement political or social filtering also target to various degrees proxies and circumvention tools to prevent users from bypassing filters. Some of these countries also block online translation services and privacy tools, apparently because they can also be used to access blocked content.

Testing by ONI revealed no evidence of technical filtering in Algeria, Iraq, Lebanon, and the West Bank between 2008 and 2009.

Regional Trends in Access Control

Internet censorship in the Middle East and North Africa is on the rise, and the scope and depth of filtering are increasing. Previous ONI tests revealed that political filtering was limited in some countries, but 2008–2009 results indicate that political censorship is targeting more content and is becoming more consistent. For example, previous tests found that Yemen temporarily blocked political Web sites in the run-up to the 2006 presidential elections, and Bahrain did the same ahead of parliamentary elections. However, 2008–2009 testing revealed that filtering in these two countries has been consistently extended to include several Web sites run by opposition groups or news Web sites and forums that espouse oppositional political views.

In the meantime, countries that have been filtering political content continue to add more Web sites to their political blacklists. For example, filtering in Syria was expanded to include popular Web sites such as YouTube, Facebook, and Amazon, as well as more Web sites affiliated with the Muslim Brotherhood and Kurdish opposition groups. Another example is Tunisia, which added more political and oppositional content as well as other apolitical Web sites such as the OpenNet Initiative and Global Voices Online.

Social filtering is also increasing and is catching up with the continuously growing social Web. Testing revealed that most of the Arab countries have begun blocking Arabic-language explicit content that was previously accessible. Interestingly, filtering of Arabic-language explicit Web content in the Middle East and North Africa is usually not as fast as that of other languages. The ONI investigation revealed that the U.S.-based commercial filtering software used by most of the ISPs in the region (e.g., Smart-Filter, Websense, and Bluecoat) do not pick up Arabic content as comprehensively as content in other languages.

Increases in filtering are the norm in the Middle East and North Africa, and lifting blocks is the exception. Among the few examples of the unblocking of Web sites are

Syria's restoration of access to Wikipedia Arabic, Morocco's lifting of a ban on a few pro-Western-Sahara-independence Web sites, and Libya's allowing access to some previously banned political Web sites. Sudan's filtering of gay and lesbian, dating, provocative attire, and health-related Web sites was also more limited compared to previous test results.

Another regional trend toward second-generation controls is that more Arab countries are introducing regulations to make Web publishing subject to press and publication laws, and are requiring local Web sites to register with the authorities before they can go live. In Jordan in September 2007, for example, the country's Legislation Bureau in the Prime Minister's Office issued a decision that Web sites and electronic press must comply with the provisions of the publications and publishing law and fall under the oversight of the Publications and Publishing Department, which announced that it would exercise immediate supervision and censorship.

Another example is Saudi Arabia, which announced in May 2009 plans to enact legislation for newspapers and Web sites that will require Saudi-based Web sites to get official licenses from a special agency under the purview of the Ministry of Information.

Bahrain already has a similar system that requires local Web sites to register with the Ministry of Information.

Among the new trends in controlling access through second-generation methods is the increase in incidents of hacking of opposition and dissident Web sites and blogs. Such incidents have been reported in Tunisia and Yemen. On the other hand, sectarian cyber attacks among different religious groups in the region, namely Shiite and Sunni groups, have occurred in the past few years. The cyber attacks managed to deface the Web sites of significant Shiite and Sunni organizations and individuals, and in some cases the attackers managed to remove content from some of these Web sites. Additionally, Israeli, Palestinian, and Lebanese Web sites run by Hezbollah have been targets of attacks, especially during conflicts.

Conclusion

Governments in the Middle East and North Africa continue to invest in media and IT projects, and at the same time are continuing to invest in censorship technologies to prevent their citizens from accessing a wide range of objectionable content. Also, while Western companies build ICT infrastructure necessary for development in the region, other Western companies provide the censors with technologies and data used to filter the Internet.

First- and second-generation access controls are evident throughout the Middle East and North Africa. Censors in the region attempt to control political content using technical filtering, laws and regulations, surveillance and monitoring, physical restrictions, and extralegal harassment and arrests. Filtering of content deemed offensive for religious, moral, and cultural reasons is pervasive in many countries, and is growing.

Though many governments acknowledge social filtering, most continue to disguise their political filtering practices by attempting to confuse users with various error messages.

The absence of technical filtering in some countries in the region by no means indicates free online environments in those countries; surveillance and monitoring practices and extralegal harassment from security agencies create a climate of fear used to silence online dissidents and conform to second-generation controls found elsewhere in the world.

Many ISPs block popular politically neutral online services such as online translation services and privacy tools, fearing that they can be used to bypass the filtering regimes. The censors also overblock Web sites and services such as social networking sites and photo and video sharing sites because of the potential for content considered objectionable.

More users in the Middle East and North Africa are using the Internet for political campaigning and social activism; however, states continue to introduce more restrictive legal, technical, and monitoring measures, amid growing local and regional calls to ease restrictions and remove barriers to the free flow of information.

Notes

1. Mohammad Ghazal, "Jordan, UAE Firms in Talks over Free IT Zone," *Jordan Times*, May 16, 2009, http://www.jordantimes.com/?news=16742.

2. Keach Hagey, "Capital Launches Media Zone to Nurture Young Arab Talent," *The National*, October 13, 2008, http://www.thenational.ae/article/20081012/BUSINESS/13341341/1119/NEWS.

3. Chris V. Panganiban, "Technology to Promote Arabic Online," *The Peninsula*, April 19, 2009, http://www.thepeninsulaqatar.com/Display_news.asp?section=local_news&month=april2009&file=local_news2009041913642.xml.

4. Arab Advisors Group, "Has the Age of Fixed Wireless Broadband Services Arrived in the Arab World? By End of March 2009, Six Arab Countries Had Eleven Commercially Launched," April 16, 2009, http://www.arabadvisors.com/Pressers/presser-160409.htm.

5. ChinaCCM, "2008 Africa—Telecoms, Mobile and Broadband in Northern Region," December 2008, http://www.chinaccm.com/4S/4S16/4S1607/news/20081205/111435.asp.

6. PricewaterhouseCoopers, "Arab Media Outlook, 2008–2012," http://www.pwc.com/extweb/pwcpublications.nsf/docid/14D97CB491E2A59B85257334000B8AAB.

7. ChinaCCM, "2008 Africa—Telecoms, Mobile and Broadband in Northern Region," December 2008, http://www.chinaccm.com/4S/4S16/4S1607/news/20081205/111435.asp.

8. Dana Halawi, "MENA Telecoms Need Liberalization—Hasbani," *Daily Star*, April 17, 2009, http://www.dailystar.com.lb/article.asp?edition_id=1&categ_id=3&article_id=101067#.

9. International Federation of Journalists, "IFJ Demands Overhaul of Repressive Media Laws in the Middle East," April 29, 2009, http://www.ifj.org/en/articles/ifj-demands-overhaul-of-repressive-media-laws-in-the-middle-east.

10. Committee to Protect Journalists, "10 Worst Countries to be a Blogger," April 30, 2009, http://cpj.org/reports/2009/04/10-worst-countries-to-be-a-blogger.php.

11. Arabic Network for Human Rights Information, "Egypt: New Comic Crimes Written by the State Security: Blogger in Custody, on Charges of Exploitation of the Democratic Climate," May 14, 2009, http://anhri.net/en/reports/2009/pr0514-2.shtml.

12. *The Economist*, "The Limits to Liberalisation," May 14, 2009, http://www.economist.com/world/mideast-africa/displaystory.cfm?story_id=13649580.

13. OpenNet Initiative Blog "Users' Initiative to Block Web Sites," October 24, 2008, http://opennet.net/blog/2008/10/users-initiatives-block-web-sites.

14. Arabic Network for Human Rights Information, "Weekly Update for the Arabic Network for Human Rights Information #192," December 28, 2007, http://www.anhri.net/en/newsletter/2008/newsletter1003.shtml.

15. Agence France Presse, "Cairo Court Rules to Block Porn Sites," May 12, 2009, http://newsx.com/story/52677.

16. Lina Ben Mhenni, "Tunisia: Facebook Case Thrown Out of Court," Global Voices Online, November 29, 2008, http://globalvoicesonline.org/2008/11/29/as-usual-the-tunisian-legal-system-has-been-faithful-to-the-values-of-fair-trial/.

17. Bahrain Center for Human Rights, "Website Accused of Violating Press Code, BCHR Concerned That Move Is Aimed at Silencing Critical Voices," September 2008, http://www.bahrainrights.org/en/node/2446.

18. *BBC News*, "Country Profile: Kuwait," August 10, 2009, http://news.bbc.co.uk/2/hi/middle_east/country_profiles/791053.stm.

19. Reporters Without Borders, "Kuwait—Annual Report 2007," http://www.rsf.org/article.php3?id_article=20767.

20. United Nations Development Program, "Program on Governance in the Arab Region (UNDP-POGAR): Oman," http://www.pogar.org/countries/civil.asp?cid=13.

21. Freedom House, "Map of Press Freedom 2008," 2008, http://www.freedomhouse.org/template.cfm?page=251&year=2008.

22. Joel Campagna, "Tunisia Report: The Smiling Oppressor," Committee to Protect Journalists, September 23, 2008, http://cpj.org/reports/2008/09/tunisia-oppression.php.

23. Yemen News Agency (Saba), Press and Publications Law, http://www.sabanews.net/en/news44000.htm.

24. Reporters Without Borders, "Appeal Court Overturns Blogger's Conviction," September 18, 2008, http://www.rsf.org/article.php3?id_article=28603.

25. Saba News, "al-Lawzi: ma yunshar fi sahafat alinternet lan yakoun baeedan 'an almusa'lah bimawjeb alqanoon" [al-Lawzi: Online journalism content will be subject to the penal code], April 1, 2008, http://www.sabanews.net/ar/news150790.htm.

26. Freedom House, "Map of Press Freedom 2008," 2008, http://www.freedomhouse.org/template.cfm?page=251&year=2008.

27. International Federation of Journalists, "Despite Advances, Journalists Still Face Possible Jail Terms under Prevailing Laws, Warns IFJ," June 12, 2008, http://www.ifex.org/en/content/view/full/94435/.

28. Sarah Carr, "Journalists Challenge Egypt's Exceptional Laws at Seminar," *Daily News Egypt*, August 1, 2008, http://dailystaregypt.com/article.aspx?ArticleID=15464.

29. Reporters Without Borders, "Syria—Annual Report 2007," http://www.rsf.org/article.php3?id_article=20777.

30. Human Rights Watch, "Background: The State of Human Rights in Morocco," November 2005, http://hrw.org/reports/2005/morocco1105/4.htm.

31. *Gulf News*, "UAE Cyber Crimes Law," November 2, 2007, http://archive.gulfnews.com/uae/uaessentials/more_stories/10018507.html.

32. David Westley, "Saudi Tightens Grip on Internet Use," *Arabian Business*, January 26, 2008, http://www.arabianbusiness.com/509226-saudi-tightens-grip-on-internet-useoni.

33. Omantel, "Omantel Terms and Conditions," http://www.omantel.net.om/policy/terms.asp.

34. Y.Net, "Terms and Conditions for Y.Net Service," http://www.y.net.ye/support/rules.htm.

35. Reporters Without Borders, "Internet under Surveillance 2004—Algeria," 2004, http://www.rsf.org/spip.php?page=article&id_article=10806.

36. Telecommunication Regulatory Authority (TRA)—Kingdom of Bahrain, "Legislative Decree No. 48 of 2002 promulgating the Telecommunications Law," http://www.tra.org.bh/en/home.asp?dfltlng=1.

37. Reporters Without Borders, "A Textbook Case in Press Censorship for the Past 20 Years," November 5, 2007, http://www.rsf.org/article.php3?id_article=24264.

38. Reporters Without Borders, "Repression Continues as Ben Ali Marks 21st Anniversary as President," November 7, 2008, http://www.rsf.org/article.php3?id_article=29208.

39. Fathiya Borowinah, "*al-Jazaer: Ajhizat alamn tolin al-harb ala magahi alinternet liihbat masharee' khalaya irhabiya naemah*" [Algeria: Security apparatus declares war on cyber cafes to abort potential

terrorist activities of sleeping cells], *Al-Riyadh*, May 1, 2007, http://www.alriyadh.com/2007/05/01/article246175.html.

40. Arabic Network for Human Rights Information, "Jordan: New Restrictions on Internet Cafes and Violating Privacy of Users," March 11, 2008, http://anhri.net/en/reports/2008/pr0311.shtml.

41. OpenNet Initiative Blog, "Restriction on Internet Use in the Middle East on the Rise: Internet Cafés in Saudi Must Install Hidden Cameras," April 16, 2009, http://opennet.net/blog/2009/04/restriction-internet-use-middle-east-rise-internet-caf%C3%A9s-saudi-must-install-hidden-came.

42. U.S. Department of State, "Country Reports on Human Rights Practices—2007," released by the Bureau of Democracy, Human Rights, and Labor, March 11, 2008, http://www.state.gov/g/drl/rls/hrrpt/2007/100599.htm.

43. *Dar al-Hayat*, *"Baramij Malomatiya tadbut elaqat al-Jumhur bemaqahi al-Internet lima' aljins waltajasos wasirqat albareed aleliqtoroni"* [Information software to control the relationship between the public and Internet cafés and to prevent access to sex, spying, and stealing e-mails], June 24, 2007.

44. Khaled Yacoub Oweis, "Syria Expands 'Iron Censorship' over Internet," Reuters, March 13, 2008, http://uk.reuters.com/article/internetNews/idUKL138353620080313?sp=true.

45. *Mareb Press*, "Internet Cafés Closed after Midnight," February 20, 2008, http://marebpress.net/news_details.php?sid=10305.

46. Moneer Al-Omari, "Search for Pornographic Material on Rise; Children Are Most Vulnerable," *Yemen Post*, January 12, 2009, http://www.yemenpost.net/63/Reports/20084.htm.

47. Agence France Presse, "Egypt Demanding Data from Cyber Cafés Users: NGO," August 9, 2008, http://afp.google.com/article/ALeqM5hN_tktRSmeojLOOn65lVULB4lj8A.

48. Moneer Al-Omari, "Search for Pornographic Material on Rise; Children Are Most Vulnerable," *Yemen Post*, January 12, 2009, http://www.yemenpost.net/63/Reports/20084.htm.

49. Oman Telecommunications Company, "Procedures for Internet Cyber Café Pre-Approval," http://www.omantel.net.om/services/business/internet/preapprovaleng.pdf.

Egypt

There is no evidence of Internet filtering in Egypt, although a small group of politically sensitive Web sites have been blocked in the past. The authorities have increased their crackdown on online writers and bloggers and have harassed and detained them for their online activities. Surveillance efforts have also increased. Similar to second-generation controls found else-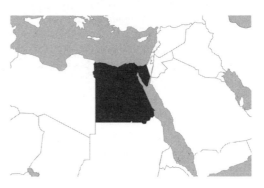where in the world, Egypt has used broad national security laws to justify restrictions on new media services, such as satellite television and cellular phones.

Background

Egypt has amended its constitution to allow opposition parties to contest presidential polls, but potential candidates face restrictive criteria for participation. Political reform activists have become more outspoken and have organized street protests in defiance of an emergency law in force since 1981.[1]

The emergency laws grant the government the power to search, arrest, and detain individuals without the supervision of judicial bodies. Rights groups state that the

RESULTS AT A GLANCE					
Filtering	No Evidence of Filtering	Suspected Filtering	Selective Filtering	Substantial Filtering	Pervasive Filtering
Political	•				
Social	•				
Conflict and security	•				
Internet tools	•				

Other Factors	Low	Medium	High	Not Applicable
Transparency				•
Consistency				•

KEY INDICATORS	
GDP per capita, PPP (constant 2005 international dollars)	5,052
Life expectancy at birth (years)	71
Literacy rate (percent of people age 15+)	66
Human development index (out of 179)	116
Rule of law (out of 211)	101
Voice and accountability (out of 209)	184
Democracy index (out of 167)	119 (Authoritarian regime)
Digital opportunity index (out of 181)	91
Internet users (percent of population)	15.4

Source by indicator: World Bank 2009a, World Bank 2009a, World Bank 2009a, UNDP 2008, World Bank 2009b, World Bank 2009b, Economist Intelligence Unit 2008, ITU 2007, ITU 2008.

uninterrupted application of emergency laws has led to the emergence of a parallel legal system, one that is unchecked by ordinary judicial bodies.[2] Despite this, journalists now openly criticize the regime's policies, and both private and opposition media have started to break taboos despite judicial, bureaucratic, and economic pressure against them.[3]

Egypt was listed by the Committee to Protect Journalists as one of the top ten worst countries to be a blogger, because the authorities monitor Internet activity on a regular basis and have detained a large number of active bloggers (more than 100 in 2008 alone) for open-ended periods.[4] Nevertheless, Egyptian bloggers and online activists have managed to utilize the power of the Internet to organize street protests and to expose human rights violations in Egypt. For example, two government officials were arrested and imprisoned in November 2007 for torturing prisoners after video clips of their actions were posted on the Internet by online activists.[5]

Internet in Egypt

Egypt has become a leading Internet market in Africa in terms of users, international bandwidth, and services offered. Also, unlike in many Arab countries, the international bandwidth market and VoIP telephony have been liberalized, and more than 200 Internet and data service providers operate in Egypt, making ADSL services among the least expensive in Africa.[6] The ICT sector continues to grow—Egypt's spending on information and communication technology (ICT) reached USD 9.8 billion in 2008 and is expected to rise to USD 13.5 billion by 2011.[7]

As part of the Egyptian government's ambitious program to expand access to ICT, an agreement to spread personal computers to every home was signed in August 2008 among the Ministry of Communications and Information Technology (MCIT), the National Telecommunications Regulatory Authority (NTRA), the Egyptian National

Post Organization (ENPO), and the Computer and Software Department at the Federation of Egyptian Chambers of Commerce. The agreement is the second phase of a 2002 initiative and is part of the MCIT's strategy of spreading the practice and utilization of IT tools and the Internet to all social segments in Egypt, focusing on remote areas and limited-income families. The initiative will include offering integrated packages of personal computers and 512 Kbps ADSL subscriptions for three years for monthly installments.[8]

Furthermore, telecommunications companies continue to enable users to access Internet content. For example, Egypt's telecommunications giant Vodafone, which has 15 million subscribers, announced in August 2008 its intention to buy a majority stake in content provider Sarmady Communications (Sarcom) in an attempt to boost its Internet service by providing content to its customers, which is also part of a strategy to dominate the Internet market.[9]

Egypt's monopoly fixed-line telephone company, Telecom Egypt, owns a 45 percent stake in Vodafone Egypt and had 11.3 million fixed-line subscribers at the end of June 2008. Other Egyptian mobile operators pay Telecom Egypt for use of its network for mobile to fixed-line calls and for international calls. Egypt's plans to sell a second fixed-line license in September 2008 would end Telecom Egypt's monopoly.[10]

Almost a million Egyptian households have access to broadband, thanks to sharing of ADSL lines. In fact, 63.4 percent of Egyptian households share connections with their neighbors. In 81.9 percent of households that share lines, the connection is shared with more than three other households. Egypt had 427,085 ADSL lines by the end of 2007. It is estimated that 75 percent of those are residential ADSL lines. Among Egyptian Internet users, 81.2 percent state a preference for browsing Arabic-language Web sites. Internet cafés remain an important source of connectivity for Egyptians, with 27.8 percent of Internet users reporting they use Internet café services.[11]

The number of blogs in Egypt has risen from just 40 in 2004 to an estimated 160,000 in July 2008, according to a report released by the Egyptian Cabinet's Information and Decision Support Center (IDSC). Of these Egyptian bloggers, 76.8 percent write in Arabic, 20.8 percent in mixed Arabic and English, and 9.6 percent solely in English. Egyptian blogs account for more than 30 percent of all Arabic blogs. Most of the bloggers are young men in their 20s, 27 percent are female, and over half of all bloggers are between the ages of 20 and 30.[12]

Legal and Regulatory Frameworks

The government continues to stifle freedom of the press and restricts the flow of information. For example, it proposed a draft bill on audiovisual media that critics say is aimed at cracking down on dissent and opposition voices on television and the Internet across the region.[13] The bill requires journalists and broadcasters to avoid damaging "social peace," "national unity," "public order," and "public values." Violators of the rules face imprisonment, cancellation of broadcasting licenses, confiscation of equipment, and fines.[14] The bill will create a National Agency for Regulation of Audio and Visual Broadcast to enforce the implementation of the proposed rules. The agency will be composed of representatives from national security and military intelligence entities. This draft bill coincides with an increase in the closure of television channels by the government.[15]

The Egyptian government enforced media licensing laws to punish an Egyptian satellite company for broadcasting protest footage of antigovernment demonstrations in April 2008.[16] The company was later shut down. This incident came a few weeks after three other satellite channels were dropped by Egypt's state-controlled Nilesat satellite.[17]

As the Egyptian blogosphere continues to grow, so too does the government's crackdown on bloggers and Internet users. For example, blogger Abdel Kareem Nabil Suleiman Amer ("Kareem Amer") was sentenced to four years in prison in February 2007 for "incitement to hatred of Islam" on his blog and for insulting Egyptian President Hosni Mubarak. He became a symbol of online repression for the country's bloggers.[18] Other Egyptian bloggers have been arrested for their online activities and some were sentenced to prison. One of the most recent examples is blogger Mohamed Refaat, editor of the blog Matabbat (matabbat.blogspot.com), who was arrested in August 2008 under the state emergency law.[19] He was accused of "offending the state institutions, destabilizing public security, and inciting others to demonstrate and strike via the Internet."[20]

The Egyptian authorities have also taken measures to restrict the potential use of cell phones for activism. Under the pretext of protecting public security, the Egyptian government asked cell phone companies to block service to anonymous subscribers in May 2008.[21] Reuters reported that "the move comes as Egypt tries to combat a wave of public discontent over rising prices and low wages that have sparked a series of labor and anti-government strikes, organized largely by mobile phone and over the Internet."[22]

In a landmark legal case, an administrative court in December 2007 rejected a lawsuit brought by a judge calling for the banning of 51 Web sites in Egypt. The court emphasized its support for freedom of expression as long as such Web sites did not harm fundamental beliefs or public order.[23] However, in May 2009, a Cairo court ruled that the Egyptian government must ban access to pornographic Web sites because they are deemed offensive to religion and society's values.[24] The suit was filed by a lawyer who claimed that a recent case of an Egyptian couple who were sentenced to prison for starting a swingers club over the Internet highlighted what he called "the dangers posed by such offensive Web sites."[25] It remains to be seen whether the authorities will enforce this court order.

Surveillance

Despite the government's initiatives to encourage Internet use, the Egyptian authorities continue to place restrictions on how Egyptians use the Internet. In February
2005, for example, Egypt's Ministry of Interior ordered Internet café managers and
owners to record their customers' names and identification numbers and threatened
to close the cafés if they refused to implement the order. This kind of action was condemned by a Cairo-based human rights group, which described it as "a gross violation
to the right to privacy."[26]

In August 2008, the Egyptian authorities imposed new measures that increased the
extent of censorship on Internet users by demanding that Internet café customers be
required to provide their names, e-mail addresses, and telephone numbers before they
could use the Internet. Once the data were provided, customers would then receive a
text message on their cell phones with a personal identification number (PIN) that
they could use to access the Internet. A Cairo-based human rights group, the Arabic
Network for Human Rights Information, considered these requirements to be censorship procedures.[27]

Egypt has witnessed an increase in the use of Facebook for social activism, which
alerted the government to the potential force of the social networking site.[28] As a
result, there were rumors that it might be blocked, especially after a group of activists
managed to recruit supporters using Facebook for a general strike that took place on
April 6, 2008, protesting against rising food prices and President Mubarak's government.[29] Another opinion suggested that the authorities would rather leave Facebook
accessible so that they could trace back suspect online activities to the individuals
responsible and punish them.[30] Because of the increasing use of Facebook for political
activism in Egypt, activists have reported that the government has started to monitor
the social networking site for the organization of any possible activities similar to that
of April 6, 2008. The vice chairman of Egypt's El Ghad opposition party, Wael Nawara,
said, "The word is that there is even a special division called the State Security Investigation Police for Facebook."[31]

In addition to monitoring online activism, a constitutional reform approved by parliament in March 2007 gave authorities the power to spy on the correspondence of
suspected terrorists and to tap their telephones without a court order.[32] In fact, Vodafone's global head of content standards, Annie Mullins, revealed in February 2009 that
Vodafone handed over communications data to the Egyptian authorities in response to
government demands. This data may have been used to help identify rioters who were
protesting over the bread crisis, which erupted in the Egyptian town of Mahallah el-
Hubra in April 2008. During the demonstrations, many protesters carried cell phones,
using them to call friends and send text messages. On December 22, individuals were
convicted in connection with the food riots.[33]

Interestingly, Egypt's minister of telecommunications and information technology publicly admitted that he allowed the security offices to monitor, record, and tap fixed lines and cell phones. A member of parliament considered this access unconstitutional and a violation of human rights.[34]

Egyptian telecommunications law mandates that telecom operators and providers shall provide, at their own expense, equipment and software that enable the armed forces and national security entities to exercise their powers within the law.[35]

ONI Testing Results

OpenNet Initiative in-country tests in 2008–2009 were conducted using the ISPs Link Egypt and TEData. As in previous testing, ONI found no evidence of Internet filtering in Egypt.

In 2005, most ISPs blocked the official Web site of the Muslim Brotherhood (www.ikhwanonline.com), Egypt's largest opposition movement. At one time, the popular ISP LINKdotNET blocked www.alshaab.com, the Web site of the Labor Party's biweekly newsletter; it no longer does so.[36]

A number of ISPs offer optional filters to block pornography. The ISP TEData, for example, offers Internet services with "content control," which eliminates "all of the Internet's indecent content that might affect your children."[37]

Conclusion

Egypt has become a leading Internet market in Africa, and Internet users enjoy unfiltered access to the Internet. However, the May 2009 court order to block access to pornography online might result in a shift in filtering policy. The government monitors online activities and has increased its surveillance efforts. Egyptian bloggers continue to use the Internet for online activism, which continues to result in government harassment, arrests, and intimidation. Current legislation allows jail terms for journalists, editors, and online writers, including bloggers.

Notes

1. *BBC News*, "Country Profile: Egypt," March 10, 2009, http://news.bbc.co.uk/1/hi/world/middle _east/country_profiles/737642.stm.

2. Sarah Carr, "Journalists Challenge Egypt's Exceptional Laws at Seminar," *Daily News Egypt*, August 1, 2008, http://dailystaregypt.com/article.aspx?ArticleID=15464.

3. Reporters Without Borders, "Egypt: Annual Report 2008," 2008, http://arabia.reporters-sans -frontieres.org/article.php3?id_article=25429.

4. Committee to Protect Journalists, "10 Worst Countries to Be a Blogger," April 30, 2009, http://www.cpj.org/reports/2009/04/10-worst-countries-to-be-a-blogger.php.

5. Reporters Without Borders, "Egypt: Annual Report 2008," 2008, http://arabia.reporters-sans-frontieres.org/article.php3?id_article=25429.

6. Paul Budde Communication Pty., Ltd., "Egypt—Convergence Broadband and Internet Markets," March 2009, http://www.researchandmarkets.com/research/64a7a1/egypt_convergenc.

7. *Daily News Egypt*, "Egypt ICT Spending to Reach $13.5 Billion, Says Report," September 8, 2008, http://dailystaregypt.com/article.aspx?ArticleID=16314.

8. Ministry of Communications and Information Technology, "Dr. Kamel Witnesses Agreement Signing to Spread PC for Every Home Initiative Nationwide," August 25, 2008, http://www.mcit.gov.eg/PressreleaseDetailes.aspx?id=hSXOldo18K4=.

9. Theodore May, "Vodafone Egypt Clinches Sarcom Content to Boost Internet Service," *Daily News Egypt*, August 21, 2008, http://dailystaregypt.com/article.aspx?ArticleID=15900.

10. Will Rasmussen, "Update: 2-Telecom Egypt Says Q2 Profit Jumps on Mobile Revenue," Reuters, August 14, 2008, http://www.reuters.com/article/rbssTechMediaTelecomNews/idUSLE69056820080814?sp=true.

11. *ITP*, "Nearly One Million Egyptian Households Have Broadband," April 28, 2008, http://www.itp.net/news/517740-nearly-one-million-egyptian-households-have-broadband.

12. Meghan Michael, "Blogging on the Rise in Egypt Despite Security Risks, Threats, Says Report," *Daily News Egypt*, July 31, 2008, http://www.thedailynewsegypt.com/article.aspx?ArticleID=15427.

13. David Stanford, "Egypt Faces New Media Censorship," *Aljazeera*, August 7, 2008, http://english.aljazeera.net/focus/2008/08/20088791952617974.html.

14. Ibid.

15. Ibid.

16. Human Rights Watch, "Government-Shuttered Company, Its Owner Face Continuing Harassment over Broadcasts of Anti-government Protests," May 28, 2008, http://www.ifex.org/en/content/view/full/94083.

17. Ibid.

18. Reporters Without Borders, "Two Years for a Blog: That's Enough! Reporters Without Borders Calls for Release of Blogger Kareem Amer," November 5, 2008, http://www.rsf.org/article.php3?id_article=29192.

19. Arabic Network for Human Rights Information, "Blogger Arrested, Faces Charges under State of Emergency Law," August 26, 2008, http://www.ifex.org/en/content/view/full/96460/.

20. Ibid.

21. Cynthia Johnston, "Egypt Asks Mobile Firms to Bar Anonymous Users," Reuters, May 5, 2008, http://ca.reuters.com/article/technologyNews/idCAL056268520080505?sp=true.

22. Ibid.

23. Arabic Network for Human Rights Information, "Weekly Update for the Arabic Network for Human Rights Information #192," December 28, 2007, http://www.anhri.net/en/newsletter/2008/newsletter1003.shtml.

24. Agence France Presse, "Cairo Court Rules to Block Porn Sites," May 12, 2009, http://newsx.com/story/52677.

25. Ibid.

26. Arabic Network for Human Rights Information, "Egypt: Increasing Curb over Internet Usage Harassments against Net Cafés Should Immediately End," February 23, 2005, http://www.anhri.net/en/reports/2005/pr0223.shtml.

27. Agence France Presse, "Egypt Demanding Data from Cyber Cafés Users: NGO," August 9, 2008, http://afp.google.com/article/ALeqM5hN_tktRSmeojLOOn65lVULB4lj8A.

28. Arab Press Network, "Rumors of a Facebook Block Persist in Egypt," *Menassat*, August 29, 2008, http://www.menassat.com/?q=en/news-articles/4508-rumors-facebook-block-persist-egypt.

29. Noam Cohen, "In Egypt, a Thirst for Technology and Progress," *New York Times*, July 21, 2008, http://www.nytimes.com/2008/07/21/business/media/21link.html.

30. Arab Press Network, "Rumors of a Facebook Block Persist in Egypt," *Menassat*, August 29, 2008, http://www.menassat.com/?q=en/news-articles/4508-rumors-facebook-block-persist-egypt.

31. Ibid.

32. Reporters Without Borders, "Egypt: Annual Report 2008," 2008, http://arabia.reporters-sans-frontieres.org/article.php3?id_article=25429.

33. OpenNet Initiative Blog, "Can They Hear Me Now? (On ICT Regulations, Governments, and Transparency)," February 24, 2009, http://opennet.net/blog/2009/02/can-they-hear-me-now-on-ict-regulations-governments-and-transparency.

34. Mohammed al-Mutasem, *"Naeb parlamani yutalib bimuhasabat wazir alittisalat"* [A parliament member calls for holding Minister of Telecommunication responsible], *al-Arabiya*.net, December 29, 2008, http://www.alarabiya.net/articles/2008/12/29/63061.html.

35. National Telecom Regulatory Authority, Egypt Telecommunication Regulation Law, Law No. 10 of 2003, Article 64, http://www.tra.gov.eg/uploads/law/law_en.pdf.

36. Human Rights Watch, "False Freedom: Online Censorship in the Middle East and North Africa: Egypt," November 2005, http://hrw.org/reports/2005/mena1105/4.htm.

37. See Family Internet service provided by TE Data, http://www.familyinternet.net/Default.aspx?SecId=1.

Iran

The Islamic Republic of Iran continues to expand and consolidate its technical filtering system, which is among the most extensive in the world. A centralized system for Internet filtering has been implemented that augments the filtering conducted at the Internet service provider (ISP) level. Iran now employs domestically produced technology for identifying and blocking 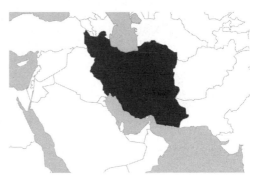 objectionable Web sites, reducing its reliance on Western filtering technologies. The regulatory agencies in Iran charged with policing the Internet continue to expand. The Revolutionary Guard has begun to play an active role in enforcing Internet content standards. In conjunction with expansive surveillance, this increase in regulatory attention exacerbates an online atmosphere that promotes self-censorship and discourages dissenting views. The blocking of political Web sites during the 2009 presidential elections energized opposition to Internet censorship within Iran and has brought fresh attention to the issue of press controls.

Background

Speech in the Islamic Republic of Iran is heavily regulated. The limits on freedom of expression in Iran are grounded in the constitution, and speech restrictions extend

RESULTS AT A GLANCE					
Filtering	No Evidence of Filtering	Suspected Filtering	Selective Filtering	Substantial Filtering	Pervasive Filtering
Political					•
Social					•
Conflict and security				•	
Internet tools					•

Other Factors	Low	Medium	High	Not Applicable
Transparency		•		
Consistency			•	

KEY INDICATORS	
GDP per capita, PPP (constant 2005 international dollars)	10,346
Life expectancy at birth (years)	71
Literacy rate (percent of people age 15+)	82
Human development index (out of 179)	84
Rule of law (out of 211)	165
Voice and accountability (out of 209)	191
Democracy index (out of 167)	145 (Authoritarian regime)
Digital opportunity index (out of 181)	105
Internet users (percent of population)	31.3

Source by indicator: World Bank 2009a, World Bank 2009a, World Bank 2009a, UNDP 2008, World Bank 2009b, World Bank 2009b, Economist Intelligence Unit 2008, ITU 2007, ITU 2008.

over a broad range of topics, including religion, immorality, social harmony, and politics. In comparison to the well-developed state controls over print media, radio, and television, the Internet initially offered a relatively unfettered medium for communication in Iran, allowing independent media and opposition voices to flourish.[1] The Internet also has provided Iranian expatriates a platform for publishing opinions in opposition to the government, such as pro-secular and reformist political viewpoints, outside the reach of standard offline strategies for enforcing speech restrictions. The growing popularity of the Internet has led to increasing government scrutiny. Dissenting voices online, including human rights activists, bloggers, and online media outlets, have became the target of government regulatory action and are subject to arrest, imprisonment, and torture.[2] Internet control mechanisms have continued to grow in scope and scale to address this digital challenge to information control in Iran. Regulators have invested in more sophisticated technical control mechanisms, and new regulatory agencies have been created to identify and block expression deemed offensive. The presidential elections in 2009 led to an increase in online political organizing, which provided a further impetus for increasingly contentious controls on the Web sites used by legitimate opposition contenders.

Efforts to control online speech by the Iranian government have relied primarily on large-scale Internet filtering and the threat of targeted legal action. The declaration of a spokesman from the Revolutionary Guard to launch 10,000 blogs written by members of the Basij, a volunteer Iranian paramilitary force under the authority of the Iranian Revolutionary Guards, hints at the adoption of a different strategy for shaping online information: a government-backed war of words on the Internet.[3] This is similar conceptually to the government information dissemination strategies seen in just a small number of countries—for example, the *Fifty Cent Party* in China, where workers are reportedly paid for producing progovernment content, and in Russia, where pro-Kremlin bloggers are suspected of receiving government support.[4]

Internet in Iran

Internet usage in Iran continues to increase at a sharp rate. Over the past eight years, the number of Internet users in Iran has growth at an average annual rate of approximately 48 percent, increasing from under 1 million Internet users in 2000[5] to around 23 million in 2008.[6] This rate of growth is higher than any other country in the Middle East. Internet users now account for approximately 31.3 percent of the population of Iran. This Internet penetration rate is considerably higher than the Middle East average of 23 percent.[7]

The Persian blogosphere has been heralded as one of the largest and most active in the world. The number of active Persian blogs is estimated to be approximately 60,000—a formidable number of independent voices for a country accustomed to tightly controlling the press.[8]

Iranian Internet policies reflect a strong tension between the regulatory urge to reign in free speech and the promotion of innovation and economic growth supported by expanding access to information and communication technologies (ICT). Bolstered by the strong growth in Internet penetration in Iran, Iran's Fourth Five-Year Development Plan called for enhanced broadband penetration, with 1.5 million high-speed Internet connections nationwide.[9] However, in October 2006, the Ministry of Information and Communications Technology (MICT) issued an order that appears to have been designed to thwart household access to broadband Internet, forbidding ISPs from providing Internet connectivity to households and public Internet access points at speeds greater than 128 Kbps. This policy, which restricts the ability of Internet users to download multimedia content, is likely intended to inhibit online alternative media sources that might compete with the tightly controlled radio and television media in Iran and to hinder access to alternative media sources.[10]

At the time of this order, approximately 250,000 users had access to high-speed Internet service, with demand continuing to grow.[11] Over the prior two years, 11 companies had been licensed to provide such high-speed services and had invested significant capital in importing the required machinery and setting up the required infrastructure. These regulations on Internet access speed were met with intense opposition, including a campaign to overturn the policy by members of parliament.[12] Reports at the time suggested that the restrictions would be lifted once more effective content control mechanisms were put into place. However, the ban on high-speed service for households and public access points remains in place, although universities and private businesses are able to obtain high-speed broadband service. Before this policy was enacted, fiber-optic networks had been expanding rapidly in Iran, more than doubling from 2005 to 2007.[13] The growth of fiber-optic networks in Iran has since dropped off precipitously.[14] Mohammad Soleimani, Minister of Information and Communications, publicly defended the ceiling on access speeds and indicated that slower speeds are adequate and that there is no demand for higher speeds.[15] Iran is the only country in the world to have instituted an explicit cap on Internet access speed for households.

Efforts to gain control over the Internet were already under way in 2001, when the government of Iran asserted control over all Internet access points coming into the country.[16] Commercial ISPs in Iran that offer Internet connectivity to the public are required to connect through the state-controlled Telecommunication Company of Iran (TCI).[17] OpenNet Initiative research corroborates that ISPs offering Internet service to the public all connect through TCI. The other international connections to the Internet are associated with research and academic organizations. Designing the Internet infrastructure around a government-managed gateway—rare for a country with this many Internet users—offers a central point of control that facilitates the implementation of Internet filtering and monitoring of Internet use.

Legal and Regulatory Frameworks

Speech regulation in Iran is rooted in its constitution, which declares that "the media should be used as a forum for healthy encounter of different ideas, but they must strictly refrain from diffusion and propagation of destructive and anti-Islamic practices."[18] Applying these principles to the Internet has proven to be difficult. A number of government regulatory initiatives have been launched over the past decade to assert control over online communications, although the legal status of Web sites and blogs continues to be contested.

The legal and institutional basis for the technical filtering system in Iran grew out of a series of decrees passed down by the Supreme Council of the Cultural Revolution (SCRC) in December 2001 that required ISPs to employ filtering systems.[19] An interagency committee, the Committee in Charge of Determining Unauthorized Sites (CCDUS), was set up a year later to set criteria for identifying unauthorized Web sites to be blocked.[20] This committee also decides on the blocking of specific domains. The SCRC issues guidelines to this committee and oversees committee members, who include representatives of MICT, the Ministry of Culture and Islamic Guidance (MCIG), the Ministry of Intelligence and National Security, and the Tehran Prosecutor General.[21]

The implementation of the filtering decisions is charged to a filtering division within the Information Technology Company of Iran (ITC), an agency under MICT.[22] Another agency, the Communication Infrastructure Company, has been given the task of unifying filtering across Iran.[23]

Iran has promoted the development of domestic tools and technical capacity to carry out Internet filtering in order to reduce its reliance on Western technologies. Prior ONI research reported the use of SmartFilter, a product of the U.S.–based firm Secure Computing, for filtering Internet content.[24] Secure Computing denied any knowledge of the use of their products in Iran.[25] The use of Western technology was problematic for both the companies involved and the Iranian government. For the companies, involvement in Internet censorship in Iran was a public relations liability, as they were viewed as contributing to the suppression of legitimate speech, if not breaking U.S. law by violating trade sanctions against Iran. For the Iranian government, the reliance on Western technologies was seen as a source of weakness and a potential vulnerability for the integrity of the Iranian Internet. Some within Iran were concerned that Western software might include a "backdoor" that would give outsiders access to key infrastructure.[26]

Several Iranian technology companies are now producing hardware and software products for use in the Iranian filtering system.[27] Domestically produced technology is currently used for filtering. Iranian technology is also used for searching the Internet for objectionable content and tracking keywords and links to banned Web sites, which are used by filtering authorities to make blocking decisions.[28] With the emergence of this domestic technical capacity, Iran joins China as the only countries that aggressively filter the Internet using their own technology.

The legal structures for enforcing speech restrictions in Iran are ambitious in their reach and offer authorities several alternatives for targeting objectionable speech and implementing the wide mandate to curtail a broad range of impermissible speech in Iran. Significant ambiguity in the statutes and directives used to regulate speech in Iran leaves the agencies charged with executing these laws with broad discretionary powers.

The Press Law of 1986 is the principal instrument for regulating media in Iran and frames the boundaries of permissible speech by media. This legislation is unusual in that it not only describes restricted speech but also lays out normative objectives for the press, who are required to "propagate and promote genuine Islamic culture and sound ethical principles."[29] The Press Law outlines broad restrictions on speech, including prohibitions on "promoting subjects that might damage the foundation of the Islamic Republic ... offending the Leader of the Revolution ... or quoting articles from the deviant press, parties or groups that oppose Islam (inside and outside the country) in such a manner as to propagate such ideas ... or encouraging and instigating individuals and groups to act against the security, dignity and interests of the Islamic Republic of Iran."[30] Other provisions prohibit insulting Islam or senior religious authorities.[31]

The application of this law to Web sites and blogs in Iran has been contested. An amendment to the Press Law in 2000 appears to have brought electronic publications under the aegis of the law.[32] In April 2009, another amendment to the Press Law was passed by the Iranian parliament that could facilitate the application of Press Law to online sources of content. The 2009 amendment stipulates that "the rules stated in this Press Law apply to domestic news sites and domestic websites and set out their rights, responsibilities, legal protection, crimes, punishments, judicial authority and procedure for hearings."[33] This article, which was rejected a year earlier when proposed to the previous parliament, was reportedly passed this time with strong pressure from the government of President Mahmoud Ahmadinejad.[34] Given the ambiguous wording of the April 2009 amendment to the Press Law, critics say that personal Web sites and blogs may also fall within the new definition, allowing greater scope for inhibiting freedom of expression on the Internet. The government claims that the law now applies to all "Internet publications."[35]

As applied to Web sites and blogs, the Press Law would not only subject online content to the comprehensive set of speech restrictions in the law, but also require Web sites to obtain a license prior to publication. Bloggers and online media sources would also be subject to the regulatory authority of the Press Supervisory Board under the Ministry of Islamic Culture and Guidance (MICG), which has the power to revoke licenses, ban publications, and refer complaints to a special Press Court.[36]

Internet "publications" that do not obtain a license under the Press Law, however, are subject to the stricter general laws of the Penal Code and come under the jurisdiction of the general courts. The Penal Code incorporates content-based crimes such as propaganda against the state and allows for the death penalty or imprisonment of up to five years for speech deemed to be an "insult to religion."[37] Additional punishable offenses include creating "anxiety and unease in the public's mind," spreading "false rumors," or writing about "acts which are not true." Another provision criminalizes criticism of state officials. Cases heard in the general courts do not have the benefit of a jury trial, which is used only in the Press Courts, increasing the risk for those that opt not to register their Web site or blog.

Both supporters and critics of the 2009 amendment to the Press Law agree that implementing these new provisions is beyond the capacity of current regulatory agencies. Critics suspect that the proximity of the law's approval to the 2009 elections was linked to the incumbent president's desire to limit the influence of reformist candidates in cyberspace.[38]

Authorities in Iran have struggled for many years with the challenges of regulating speech on the Internet, complicated by the relative ease of anonymous speech online and access to content hosted outside the country. Internet service providers and subscribers are subject to prohibitions on 20 types of activities, where insulting Islam and religious leaders and institutions, as well as fomenting national discord and promoting drug use or obscenity and immoral behaviors, are prominent.[39] In 2006, a directive of the SCRC declared Web sites and blogs that did not obtain a license from the MICG to be illegal.[40] The MICG issued a notice in January 2007 requiring registration by March 1, 2007. A Telecommunications Ministry official, however, indicated that enforcement was not feasible.[41] The number of blogs that have registered with the state is thought to be very low.[42]

Another key piece of legislation for regulating online content in Iran is the Bill of Cyber Crimes' Sanctions (Cyber Crimes Bill) ratified into law in November 2008. This bill was still under review by the Guardian Council at the time of writing.[43] The bill requires ISPs to ensure that "forbidden" content is not displayed on their servers, that they immediately inform law enforcement agencies of violations, that they retain the content as evidence, and that they restrict access to the prohibited content.[44] Under the Cyber Crimes Bill, ISPs that do not abide by government regulations (including filtering regulations) will be fined, and with subsequent offenses temporarily or permanently suspended.[45] The bill also includes provisions for the protection and disclosure of confidential data and information as well as the publishing of obscene content.[46] A prior draft of the legislation included provisions that made ISPs criminally liable for content transmitted over their networks. These provisions have been removed from the latest draft of the Cyber Crimes Bill.

The role of different government agencies in deciding on blocking, and the legality of doing so, has been a point of contention. The Internet Bureau of the Judiciary has issued mandates to ISPs to block Web sites through court orders, which are considered a form of lawful punishment imposed on legal entities.[47] Tehran Prosecutor General Saeed Mortazavi, who has led harsh crackdowns on media and has also been implicated in cases of torture of detainees, including 21 bloggers arrested in 2004, has also ordered that certain sites be censored.[48]

The legality of Iran's filtering regime was brought into question following the blocking of the conservative online journal Baztab (formerly baztab.com) in February 2007. Baztab was made accessible inside Iran again after the Supreme Court of Iran ruled against the filtering of the Web site.[49] This incident sparked a debate within Iranian legal and media circles over the authority of the CCDUS and whether as an executive body of government it was improperly involved in making legislative or judicial decisions.[50] This debate did not forestall the eventual closing of the offices of Baztab.[51]

Surveillance

Iran is reportedly investing in improving its technical capacity to extensively monitor the behavior of its citizens on the Internet. The routing of Internet traffic through proxy servers offers the potential for monitoring and logging essentially all unencrypted Web traffic, including e-mail, instant messaging, and browsing. The architecture of the Iranian Internet is particularly conducive to widespread surveillance, as all traffic from the dozens of ISPs serving households is routed through the state-controlled telecommunications infrastructure of TCI. The MICT, when announcing the creation of a centralized filtering system, indicated that they would keep a record of Web sites visited by users. A later statement denied that this infrastructure would be used for tracking browsing habits and identifying users.[52]

In 2008, two European companies reportedly sold a sophisticated electronic surveillance system capable of monitoring Internet use that could be utilized for tracking and monitoring the online activities of human rights organizations and political dissidents. The Telecommunication Company of Iran is said to have received the equipment from Nokia Siemens Networks, a joint venture between the Finnish cell phone maker and the German company Siemens.[53] Women's rights activists reported that they were shown transcripts of instant messaging sessions by authorities after their arrest, which, if true, would support the existence of an advanced surveillance program.[54]

ONI Testing Results

The OpenNet Initiative conducted testing in 2008 and 2009 on five ISPs in Iran: ITC, Gostar, Parsonline, Datak, and Sepanta. The testing results confirm that Iran has continued to consolidate its position as one of the most extensive filterers of the Internet. Iran consistently filters a broad range of Web sites that are offensive to the moral standards of Iran's religious leadership. Internet censors in Iran have moved decisively against a number of political targets over the past two years, including women's rights groups, human rights organizations, and political opposition parties.

Filtering in Iran is implemented by routing all public Internet traffic through proxy servers. This allows the employment of filtering software to target specific Web pages as well as the blocking of keywords. The blocking of Web sites is carried out in a transparent manner in Iran; a block page is displayed to users who attempt to access a blocked site with a warning that they are not permitted to access a particular Web site. The block pages, which vary by ISP, generally include a contact e-mail address for users who might wish to contact the filtering administrators to question or contest the blocking of a Web site.

A noteworthy recent development in Iran's filtering regime is the implementation of a centralized filtering regime. Historically, there has been substantial variation in blocking across different ISPs, with several ISPs filtering fewer Web sites than TCI and thereby offering a more permissive view of the Internet.[55] This variation in access to Web sites was the result of differences in the implementation of government filtering instructions by ISPs. This differential filtering practice has now been effectively replaced by a uniform filtering pattern with the implementation of the supplementary centralized filtering system. The vestiges of the ISP-based system, however, are still apparent: the source of filtering is made evident by the block page that appears, which in some cases comes from the respective ISPs and in other cases from a standard block page issued by TCI. It is unclear what the long-term structure of the filtering system will be. Options include continuing with the current dual-location filtering system or switching to either a system in which all filtering is carried out at a central point or to a distributed but centrally coordinated filtering system. Regardless of the method chosen for implementation, it appears that Iran is firmly on the path toward a centralized filtering system under the control of the government, as carried out in Saudi Arabia, for example.

The Iranian filtering system continues to strengthen and deepen. In addition to targeting "immoral" content on the Internet, independent and dissenting voices are filtered across a range of issues, including political reform, criticism of the government, reporting on human rights issues, and minority and women's rights. A notable change in the scope of filtering in Iran over the past several years has been an expansion of political filtering and blocking of human rights organizations, particularly targeting the women's rights movement in Iran. Blocking orders issued by CCDUS in May 2008 added many new Web sites to the blocking lists. These included numerous Web sites and blogs of women's rights and human rights activists in addition to several well-known journalists, including www.roozmaregiha2.blogfa.com and pargas1.blogfa.com. Women's rights Web sites in Farsi, such as www.we-change.org and feministschool .com, are consistently blocked in Iran.

A prominent example of targeted political filtering is the blocking in February 2009 of www.yaarinews.ir, a Web site created for the planned election campaign of former president Mohammad Khatami. A Web site of the reformist coalition, www .baharestaniran.com, was blocked in March 2008. The blocking of Facebook in May 2009 has proven to be particularly controversial in Iran. Many believe that supporters of President Mahmoud Ahmadinejad were behind the blocking orders, as a reformist candidate for president, MirHossein Mousavi, had been using Facebook for political organizing.[56] Ahmadinejad has since denied any involvement in the decision to block Facebook.[57] The blocking of the popular social network Web site was reversed several days later after strong popular opposition to the blocking in Iran.[58] Facebook had been blocked in the past: ONI testing showed that it was blocked in Fall 2008, with access to the Web site allowed again in February 2009.[59]

The role of speech restrictions in the political realm are also evident in the guidelines passed down from SCRC to CCDUS in April 2009 that defined allowable speech during the 2009 presidential elections for Web sites and ISPs. These guidelines outlined 20 categories of prohibited speech, including "disrupting national unity" and "creating negative feelings toward the Islamic government."[60]

Independent media Web sites offered only in English are inconsistently blocked, though a number of prominent Western news Web sites have been blocked in Iran. The Huffington Post and the Web site for Al-Arabiya (alarabiya.net) are blocked in Iran. The *New York Times*, available in May 2009, has been blocked on several occasions in the past. Global Voices, an international blog aggregator, was blocked in May 2009.

The Web sites of numerous international free-speech organizations are blocked, including rsf.org, epic.org, citizenlab.org, and eff.org. The Web sites of Amnesty International and the OpenNet Initiative were not blocked in May 2009.

A higher proportion of independent media Web sites in Farsi are blocked than are sites with English-language content. The BBC's Persian service (www.bbc.co.uk/persian) was blocked soon after its launch in January 2009. The introduction of this new broadcast station was condemned by the Iranian government and declared to be illegal.[61] In addition, Iranian.com, roozonline.com, and radiozamaneh.com are among the independent sources of news and opinion that are blocked in Iran.

A popular Farsi social networking and independent news Web site, Balatarin.com, was blocked in 2007, reportedly for a user-contributed post with a link to a Web site that included a rumor of the death of Supreme Leader Ali Hoseyni Khamenei. Strident objections by users to the blocking of Balatarin were not successful in reversing the blocking decision, and Balatarin continues to be blocked.

The Web sites of several ethnic and religious minorities are blocked in Iran, including those associated with the Baha'i faith and Kurdish movements. Web sites that are critical of Islam are widely blocked. A higher proportion of Web sites in Farsi related to religious and minority rights are blocked than those in English.

The blocking of blogs in Iran is focused primarily on individual blogs. However, several blog-hosting services are blocked in their entirely, including www.livejournal.com and www.xanga.com. Also, technorati.com and boingboing.com are blocked.

In fall 2008, the ONI tested a sample of approximately 8,800 blogs, drawing the sample from the blogs in the Farsi blogosphere that had the highest number of links to one another.[62] Of these, approximately 9 percent were found to be blocked by TCI. A majority of the blogs that were blocked are associated with secular politics and reformist viewpoints. However, blogs from the conservative and religious segments of the blogosphere were blocked as well, several of which apparently included content deemed to be too extreme. Further ONI analysis carried out over a sample of filtered and unfiltered blogs displays a systematic targeting of blogs with oppositional views but with substantial inconsistency; many blogs with solidly dissident views remain unblocked, while other blogs without controversial content are blocked.

Several popular social networking Web sites are blocked in Iran, including MySpace.com and Orkut.com. Prior to being blocked, Orkut was highly popular in Iran. Among the more prominent social media Web sites, Flickr.com, www.bebo.com, www.metacafe.com, www.photobucket.com, and delicious.com are all blocked. After several episodes of blocking in the past, YouTube, one of the most popular destinations for Iranian Internet users, was available in May 2009.

Consistent with one of the stated objectives of Iran's filtering policy, pornographic content is heavily filtered. Iran is highly successful in blocking pornography, blocking a vast majority of the Web sites tested by ONI. Sites that include photographs depicting provocative attire are also consistently blocked. Esmail Radkani, of Iran's quasi-official Information Technology Company, claimed in an interview in September 2006 that 10 million Web sites were filtered at that time, 90 percent of which contained "immoral" content.[63] Another official was quoted in November 2008 saying that 5 million Web sites were blocked in Iran.[64] Given the large number of Web sites with sexual content blocked in Iran, neither of these estimates is implausible.

The filtering of material related to sexuality extends as well to Web sites offering content related to sexual education. Approximately half of the dating Web sites tested by ONI were found to be blocked in Iran. OpenNet Initiative testing also found significant blocking of content related to homosexuality, particularly if it had any connection to Iran. A number of Web sites related to drugs, alcohol, and gambling are blocked in Iran, although many remain unblocked.

Web sites that offer tools and techniques for circumventing filters are also heavily filtered. Just as new Web sites with options for circumventing Internet filters are regularly offered by Internet users around the world, blocking lists in Iran are frequently updated to include these new Web sites. A great majority of Web sites offering information about and access to circumvention tools tested by ONI were blocked.

The proxy server filtering strategy also permits filtering by keyword. Web searches that include the keyword "women" are still blocked in Iran. The word "sex" and a broad range of words related to sexual activity both in English and Farsi are blocked. The Farsi word for "photograph" is also blocked.

Conclusion

Iran continues to strengthen the legal, administrative, and technical aspects of its Internet filtering systems. The Internet censorship system in Iran is one of the most comprehensive and sophisticated in the world. Advances in domestic technical capacity have contributed to the implementation of a centralized filtering strategy and a reduced reliance on Western technologies. Despite the deeply held commitment to regulating Internet content, authorities continue to be challenged in their attempts to control online speech. Political filtering related to the 2009 presidential campaign, including the blocking of Facebook and several opposition party Web sites, brought renewed attention to the role of filtering in Iran and shows a clear inclination toward second-generation controls.

Notes

1. Peter Feuilherade, "Iran's Banned Press Turns to the Net," BBC News, August 9, 2002, http://news.bbc.co.uk/1/hi/not_in_website/syndication/monitoring/media_reports/2183573.stm.

2. Human Rights Watch Report, "False Freedom: Online Censorship in the Middle East and North Africa: Iran," November 2005, http://hrw.org/reports/2005/mena1105/5.htm#_Toc119125727;

Clark Boyd, "The Price Paid For Blogging Iran," BBC News, http://news.bbc.co.uk/2/hi/technology/4283231.stm.

3. *BBC Persian, "basij haba 10 hazar habalagh mi aind"* [Basij start up 10,000 blogs], November 19, 2008, http://www.bbc.co.uk/persian/iran/2008/11/081119_mg_basij_filtering.shtml.

4. David Bandurski, "China's Guerilla War for the Web," *Far Eastern Economic Review*, July 2008, http://www.feer.com/essays/2008/august/chinas-guerrilla-war-for-the-web?searched=Bandurski&highlight=ajaxSearch_highlight+ajaxSearch_highlight1.

5. International Telecommunications Union (ITU), "Internet Indicators: Subscribers, Users, and Broadband Subscribers," 2000, http://www.itu.int/ITU-D/icteye/Reporting/ShowReportFrame.aspx?ReportName=/WTI/InformationTechnologyPublic&RP_intYear=2000&RP_intLanguageID=1.

6. International Telecommunications Union (ITU), "Internet Indicators: Subscribers, Users, and Broadband Subscribers," 2008, http://www.itu.int/ITU-D/icteye/Reporting/ShowReportFrame.aspx?ReportName=/WTI/InformationTechnologyPublic&RP_intYear=2008&RP_intLanguageID=1.

7. Miniwatts Marketing Group, "Middle East Internet Usage and Population Statistics," 2009, http://www.internetworldstats.com/stats5.htm.

8. John Kelly and Bruce Etling, "Mapping Iran's Online Public: Politics and Culture in the Persian Blogosphere," Berkman Center for Internet and Society, April 5, 2008, http://cyber.law.harvard.edu/publications/2008/Mapping_Irans_Online_Public.

9. Atieh Bahar Consulting, "Iran Telecom Brief," October 20, 2008, http://www.atiehbahar.com/Resource.aspx?n=1000014.

10. *BBC Persian, "kulhash seer 'at braee internet perserat dir Iran"* [Speed reduced for high speed Internet in Iran] October 20, 2006.

11. Ibid.

12. Robert Tait, "Iran Bans Fast Internet to Cut West's Influence," *Guardian*, October 18, 2006, http://www.guardian.co.uk/technology/2006/oct/18/news.iran.

13. Telecommunication Company of Iran, "Performance Report," September 2008, http://irantelecom.ir/pdfs/amar/SEP_2008.pdf.

14. Ibid.

15. Mehr News, *"naqd azhar at wazeer artbatat dir moord seer 'at internet"* [Criticism of the minister of communications' statement in regard to Internet speed], May 25, 2008, http://www.mehrnews.ir/NewsPrint.aspx?NewsID=689151.

16. Iran CSOs Training and Research Center, "A Report on the Status of the Internet in Iran," November 8, 2005, http://www.genderit.org/upload/ad6d215b74e2a8613f0cf5416c9f3865/A_Report_on_Internet_Access_in_Iran_2_.pdf.

17. See Ministry of Information and Communications Technology, http://www.itc.ir/Portal/Home/ShowPage.aspx?Object=GENERALTEXT&CategoryID=b518fb25-587d-4c16-9520-9d3f1d3a24ae&LayoutID=372f2627-7ccb-40fa-b30a-7a128ef777a5.

18. Constitution of the Islamic Republic of Iran, translation at http://www.servat.unibe.ch/icl/ir00000_.html.

19. Iran CSOs Training and Research Center, "A Report on the Status of the Internet in Iran," November 8, 2005, http://www.genderit.org/upload/ad6d215b74e2a8613f0cf5416c9f3865/A_Report _on_Internet_Access_in_Iran_2_.pdf.

20. Ibid.

21. Ibid.

22. Information Technology Company, *"mahmtreen rakhdadhalee huza internet wa fanawree atla'alt dir sal 1387"* [The most important events in the field of Information and Communication Technology in 1387], March 25, 2009, http://www.itc.ir/Portal/Home/ShowPage.aspx?Object=News& ID=52d93a02-e5ce-4353-9ba6-50c4eb97eb34&LayoutID=db2099c4-7b41-414c-a965-1b4cc4da6584 &CategoryID=8e9c4343-3ea3-41f0-a025-0cca398f147f.

23. ITNA, *"tadween mazham jama'a hamahanag filtering az deeta bat zeersajat saprada shid"* [Development of a comprehensive system of filtering data to coordinate with infrastructure was buried], May 30, 2008, http://www.itna.ir/archives/news/009919.php.

24. OpenNet Initiative, "Internet Filtering in Iran in 2004–2005: A Country Study," http://opennet.net/studies/iran.

25. Ibid.

26. Iran ICT News, "Study of Some of the Shortcomings of the Filtering System," April 7, 2006, http://backdoor.iranictnews.ir/T_34469%D8%A8%D8%B1%D8%AE%DB%8C%D9%86%D9%88 %D8%A7%D9%82%D8%B5%D8%B3%DB%8C%D8%B3%D8%AA%D9%85%D9%81%DB%8C %D9%84%D8%A8%D8%B1%DB%8C%D9%86%DA%AF%D8%B4%D8%B1%DA%A9%D8%AA %D9%81%D9%86%D8%A7%D9%88%D8%B1%DB%8C%D8%A7%D8%B7%D9%84%D8%A7 %D8%B9%D8%A7%D8%AA.htm (accessed June 10, 2009).

27. *Akhbar Rooz,* *"sharkat hae bazrag censor kanandat e internet dir Iran"* [Corporations censor the Internet in Iran], September 4, 2008, http://www.akhbar-rooz.com/news.jsp?essayId=16978.

28. Ibid.

29. Article 19, "Memorandum on Regulation of the Media in the Islamic Republic of Iran," March 2, 2006, http://www.unhcr.org/refworld/country,,ART19,,IRN,,475e4e270,0.html.

30. Press Law of the Islamic Republic of Iran, Article 6, http://www.parstimes.com/law/press _law.html.

31. Ibid., Articles 26 and 27.

32. Note 2 of Article 1 of Iran's Press Law (as amended in on April 18, 2000) defines electronic publications as "publications regularly published under a permanent name, specific date and serial number ... on different subjects such as news, commentary, as well as social, political, economic, agricultural, cultural, religious, scientific, technical, military, sports, artistic matters, etc,

via electronic vehicles." Publications must also have obtained "publication licenses from the Press Supervisory Board in the Ministry of Cultural and Islamic Guidance"; otherwise they "fall out of the scope of the Press law and become subject to General Laws."

33. *Deutsche Welle, "Tasveeb-e Layeheye Janjaali-e Eslaah-e Ghaanoon-e Matboo'aat dar Majles"* [The passage of the controversial bill of reforming the press law in Majlis], April 15, 2009, http://www .dw-world.de/dw/article/0,,4178392,00.html.

34. *Ghalam News,* "The New Decision for the Internet Media by the Parliament," April 15, 2009, http://www.ghalamnews.ir/news-6261.aspx (accessed June 10, 2009).

35. Ibid.

36. Article 19, "Memorandum on Regulation of the Media in the Islamic Republic of Iran," March 2, 2006, http://www.unhcr.org/refworld/country,,ART19,,IRN,,475e4e270,0.html.

37. Islamic Penal Code of Iran, May 22, 1996, Article 500 states that "anyone who undertakes any form of propaganda against the state . . . will be sentenced to between three months and one year in prison"; unofficial translation at http://mehr.org/index_islam.htm.

38. *Ghalam News,* "The New Decision for the Internet Media by the Parliament," April 15, 2009, http://www.ghalamnews.ir/news-6261.aspx (accessed June 10, 2009).

39. Human Rights Watch Report, "False Freedom: Online Censorship in the Middle East and North Africa: Iran," November 2005, http://hrw.org/reports/2005/mena1105/5.htm.

40. BBC Monitoring International Reports, citing text of report by E'temad-e Melli, "Iran Press Iranian Activists Oppose Regulation of Websites, Weblogs," January 2, 2007. See also Omid Memarian, "Bloggers Rebel at New Censorship," Inter Press Service News Agency, January 10, 2007, http://www.ipsnews.net/news.asp?idnews=36123, reporting that prohibited content includes criticism of religious figures, sexual matters, content considered offensive to the Ayatollah Khomeini, or content slanderous of Islamic law.

41. BBC Monitoring International Reports, "Iran Press Iranian Activists Oppose Regulation of Websites, Weblogs," January 2, 2007.

42. One report puts the number of blog registrations at 850.

43. The status of draft legislation is reported in Farsi at http://tarh.majlis.ir/?Report&RegId=121.

44. Cybercrimes Bill, Chapter 6, Article 23, http://tarh.majlis.ir/?Download&Id=2288.

45. Ibid., Chapter 6, Article 21.

46. Ibid., Chapter 3: Articles 3 and 4.

47. Information Technology News Agency, "Report of an ISP Closure by Judicial System Agents," http://www.itna.ir/archives/article/000665.php; Human Rights Watch, "Iran: Prosecute Torturers, Not Bloggers," December 12, 2006, http://hrw.org/english/docs/2006/12/12/iran14824.htm; Human Rights Watch, "'Like the Dead in Their Coffins': Torture, Detention, and the Crushing of Dissent in Iran," June 7, 2004, http://www.hrw.org/campaigns/torture/iran/.

48. Information Technology News Agency, "Report of an ISP Closure by Judicial System Agents," http://www.itna.ir/archives/article/000665.php.

49. *The Age*, "Iran Lifts Ban on Conservative Web Site," March 20, 2007, http://www.theage.com.au/news/Technology/Iran-lifts-ban-on-conservative-website/2007/03/20/1174153008276.html.

50. Iranian Student News Agency (ISNA), Interview with Head of Iran Law Society, February 16, 2007, http://www.isna.ir/Main/NewsView.aspx?ID=News-877388.

51. "Offices of Website Closed," International Freedom of Expression Exchange, September 24, 2007, http://www.ifex.org/iran/2007/09/24/offices_of_website_closed/.

52. Bill Samii, "Iran: Government Strengthens Its Control of the Internet," Radio Free Europe/Radio Liberty, September 29, 2006, http://www.rferl.org/content/article/1071706.html.

53. Eli Lake, "Fed Contractor, Cell Phone Maker Sold Spy System to Iran," *Washington Times*, April 13, 2009, http://www.washingtontimes.com/news/2009/apr/13/europe39s-telecoms-aid-with-spy-tech/print/.

54. Ibid.

55. OpenNet Initiative, "Country Profile: Iran," May 9, 2007, http://opennet.net/research/profiles/iran.

56. Najmeh Bozorgmehr, "Facebook Sets Tone in Iran's Electoral Contest," *Financial Times*, May 13, 2009, http://www.ft.com/cms/s/0/da46ad4e-3f19-11de-ae4f-00144feabdc0.html?nclick_check=1.

57. CNN, "Ahmadinejad Denies Calling for Facebook Ban," May 25, 2009, http://www.cnn.com/2009/WORLD/meast/05/25/iran.ahmadinejad.facebook/.

58. *Ghalam News*, "Facebook Unblocked," May 26, 2009, http://www.ghalamnews.ir/news.aspx?id=16014 (accessed June 10, 2009).

59. Golnaz Esfandiari, "Why Did Iran Unblock Facebook?" Radio Free Europe/Radio Liberty, March 14, 2009, http://www.rferl.org/content/Why_Did_Iran_Unblock_Facebook/1510005.html.

60. Aftab, "Sending the 'Not to Do List' to News," April 7, 2009, http://www.aftab.ir/news/2009/apr/07/c1c1239084884_politics_iran_election.php (accessed June 10, 2009).

61. *BBC News*, "Iran Blocks BBC Persian Website," January 24, 2006, http://news.bbc.co.uk/2/hi/middle_east/4644398.stm.

62. For a description of the Persian blogosphere, see John Kelly and Bruce Etling, "Mapping Iran's Online Public: Politics and Culture in the Persian Blogosphere," Berkman Center for Internet and Society, April 5, 2008, http://cyber.law.harvard.edu/publications/2008/Mapping_Irans_Online_Public.

63. Interview with Esma'il Radkani, Iranian Communication and Information Technology News Agency, September 11, 2006, http://citna.ir/435.html.

64. Reporters Without Borders, "Two Cyber-Dissidents Jailed, 5 Million Websites Censored," November 20, 2008, http://www.rsf.org/article.php3?id_article=29366.

Saudi Arabia

Saudi Arabia filters Web sites related to opposition political groups, human rights issues, and religious content deemed offensive to Muslims. Pornography and Web sites containing LGBT content are pervasively filtered, as are circumvention and online privacy tools. Bloggers have been arrested and blogs and Web sites run by online activists have been blocked.

Background

Saudi Arabia is the birthplace of the Prophet Muhammad and the cradle of Islam. It embraces a strict interpretation of Sunni Islam and has a strong religious self-identity. Political parties are banned, and activists who publicly call for reform risk being jailed.[1] Journalism is strictly controlled, and journalists must exercise self-censorship in order to avoid government scrutiny and dismissal.[2]

Despite substantial Saudi investment in pan-Arab satellite television such as the Dubai-based MBC channels and the Bahrain-based Orbit Satellite Network, the media environment within Saudi Arabia is one of the most tightly controlled in the region.

RESULTS AT A GLANCE					
Filtering	No Evidence of Filtering	Suspected Filtering	Selective Filtering	Substantial Filtering	Pervasive Filtering
Political				•	
Social					•
Conflict and security			•		
Internet tools					•

Other Factors	Low	Medium	High	Not Applicable
Transparency			•	
Consistency			•	

KEY INDICATORS	
GDP per capita, PPP (constant 2005 international dollars)	21,659
Life expectancy at birth (years)	73
Literacy rate (percent of people age 15+)	85
Human development index (out of 179)	55
Rule of law (out of 211)	87
Voice and accountability (out of 209)	193
Democracy index (out of 167)	161 (Authoritarian regime)
Digital opportunity index (out of 181)	75
Internet users (percent of population)	30.5

Source by indicator: World Bank 2009a, World Bank 2009a, World Bank 2009a, UNDP 2008, World Bank 2009b, World Bank 2009b, Economist Intelligence Unit 2008, ITU 2007, ITU 2008.

The kingdom's four television networks—including news channel Al-Ikhbaria—and its radio stations are operated by the state-owned Broadcasting Service of the Kingdom of Saudi Arabia (BSKSA), which is chaired by the Saudi minister of culture and information.[3] Private television and radio stations are prohibited on Saudi soil.[4] However, the minister of culture and information said in May 2009 that an official committee had been formed to study the draft privatization project of Saudi television and the Saudi News Agency, and that the Ministry of Culture and Information was considering granting a number of radio licenses.[5]

Blogging has grown as a medium for expression in Saudi Arabia, with an estimated 2,000 bloggers in 2006, half of whom are women.[6] In 2005, the government tried to ban Blogger, the platform most often used by Saudi bloggers.[7] However, after a few days the ban was lifted, with the censors choosing to block specific content hosted on the platform instead.[8]

In November 2008, Saudi activists launched for the first time a daring move to support a human rights campaign online and called for a two-day public hunger strike to protest the detention without charges of human rights activists. The campaign was highly publicized and received coverage from international media.[9]

In early 2009, Saudi Arabia was ranked by the Committee to Protect Journalists as one of the ten worst countries in which to be a blogger, citing the widespread self-censorship and local calls by influential clerics for harsh punishment for online writers who post content deemed heretical.[10]

Internet in Saudi Arabia

Since its creation in 1998, the state-run Saudi Telecom Company (STC) had been the sole provider of telecom services. However, in an effort to join the World Trade Organization (WTO), the government opened the telecommunication sector to competition in 2002.[11] To enhance the information and communication technology (ICT) infrastructure in the kingdom, STC started installation of IP-VPN service at various speeds of up to 2.5 Gbps.[12]

The telecom sector continues to grow with relative consistency. Service revenues have been climbing steadily at an annual average rate of nearly 15 percent since 2001. Despite high mobile revenues, the kingdom's broadband penetration rate of about 1 percent remains well below the world average of 5 percent and the 20 percent benchmark of developed countries.[13] This situation, however, is likely to change as advanced ICT projects are introduced. These projects include STC's launch of a home fiber-optic service providing Internet speed reaching 100 Mbps for its clients in the kingdom.[14]

The government's Internet Services Unit (ISU), a department of the King Abdulaziz City for Science and Technology (KACST), has been responsible for overseeing Internet services in Saudi Arabia and for implementing government censorship.[15] As its Web site explains, 25 licensed ISPs connect users to the national network.[16] In accordance with a Council of Ministers decision, the Saudi Communications Commission was renamed the Communications and Information Technology Commission and took charge of licensing and filtering processes previously managed by KACST.[17]

Because of numerous restrictions on the public interaction of unrelated men and women and the limited roles of women in open society, the Internet has emerged not only as a popular means of socialization but also as one that is dominated by women. Reports estimate that two-thirds of Saudi Internet users are women.[18] Some Saudis believe that cyberspace has encouraged people to lead "double lives," conducting themselves in a more conservative manner in the public eye while engaging in far more liberal behavior online.[19]

Legal and Regulatory Framework

Saudi newspapers are established by decree. Although pan-Arab newspapers are available, they are subject to censorship and tend to conform to the state's standards when contemplating the publication of sensitive content.[20] Public criticism of the Saudi leadership and the questioning of Islamic beliefs are not generally tolerated, but in the post-9/11 era and amid instances of internal militancy, a bolder and more candid approach has brought about at least some press and television coverage of more controversial topics.[21] This approach remains limited, however. For example, in January 2008 the Ministry of Culture and Information imposed a nationwide ban on all live broadcasts from Saudi public television channels two days after disgruntled viewers phoned in to the Al-Ikhbariya news channel and made critical remarks targeting senior Saudi officials. The ban compelled Reporters Without Borders to call for a reversal of the government's action and the reinstatement of the network's director, who had been fired after the incident.[22]

The Saudi government openly admits to filtering and explains its policy in a section of the ISU Web site.[23] According to this Web site, KACST is directly responsible for filtering pornographic content, while other Web sites are blocked upon request from "government security bodies." The Web site also has forms that enable Internet users to request that certain Web sites be blocked or unblocked. According to a KACST official, "The majority of blocked Web sites contain pornographic content, and over 90 percent of Internet users have tried to access a blocked Web site."[24] The censors rely on citizens, who send in roughly 1,200 requests a day to have Web sites blocked.[25]

In January 2008, Saudi Arabia implemented 16 articles of a new law on the use of technology. Its provisions include penalties of ten years in prison and a fine for Web site operators that advocate or support terrorism; three years and a fine for financial fraud or invasion of privacy; and five years and a fine for those guilty of distributing pornography or other materials that violate public law, religious values, and social standards of the kingdom. Accomplices of the guilty parties and even those who are proven to have only intended to engage in unlawful IT acts can receive up to half of maximum punishments.[26]

Providers and distributors of Internet equipment can also be held liable under the new law, including Internet café managers whose facilities are used to post content that infringes upon the "values" of the kingdom.[27]

The new law was implemented amid global scrutiny of the landmark imprisonment of Saudi blogger Ahmad Fouad Al-Farhan, who was arrested by the Saudi government for violating "nonsecurity regulations." Al-Farhan is reported to have stated that he was arrested because he "wrote about political prisoners in Saudi Arabia."[28] Al-Farhan was freed after more than four months in prison.[29]

The new law has also been applied in nonpolitical cases. For example, a court fined a young man 50,000 Saudi riyals (approximately USD 13,000) and sentenced him to 22 months in jail and 200 lashes after he was found guilty of breaking into a woman's e-mail account and stealing photos of her. The man threatened to post the photos of the woman on the Internet if she did not agree to have an affair with him.[30]

In July 2008, the Saudi authorities reportedly refused to renew the residence permit of an Egyptian national who had lived in Saudi Arabia for 44 years for writing articles in newspapers and on the Internet that were critical of the Egyptian regime.[31] The Arabic Network for Human Rights Information claimed that the writer's activities "only amount to writings about his concerns and opinions about Egypt and do not include any Saudi related matters."[32]

In an unprecedented move, Saudi Arabia's National Human Rights Society announced attempts to have Web sites of Arab and international human rights organizations unblocked by the Saudi authorities.[33] The chairman of the society said that they are aware of the blocking of Web sites of Human Rights Watch, Reporters Without Borders, and the Arabic Network for Human Rights Information inside Saudi

Arabia. He added that "blocking these sites is tantamount to depriving Saudi Arabia of its rights as a member of the UN Human Rights Council" and that "blocking those websites violates clause 19 of the International Human Rights Declaration, which deals with freedom of expression and clause 23 of the Arab Human Rights Charter."[34]

In May 2009, 13 female Saudi journalists filed complaints with the Ministry of Interior accusing the local online newspaper *Kul Al-Watan* (All of the Homeland) of "defaming and distorting the image of the Saudi media." The journalists said the on-line newspaper published an offensive report entitled "Saudi Women in Red Nights," in which it alleged that prostitution, alcohol, and drugs have become widespread in Saudi society and that female journalists rely on illicit relationships with newspaper bosses to get support and fame. One of the female journalists accused the writer of taking advantage of an absence of censorship in online publishing in Saudi Arabia.[35] Shortly thereafter, the minister of culture and information announced that Saudi Arabia intends to enact laws, regulation, and legislation for newspapers and Internet Web sites. This regulation will require Saudi-based Web sites to get official licenses from a special agency under the purview of the Ministry. The minister said the pro-posed regulation aims to deter "dangerous" writing in newspapers and on Web sites.[36]

Surveillance

Like many countries in the Middle East, the Saudi authorities monitor Internet activ-ities. In March 2009, Internet cafés were ordered by the Ministry of Interior to install hidden cameras and provide a record of names and identities of their customers.[37]

The Saudi religious police have also expressed an interest in practicing online surveil-lance. Members of the religious police (the Commission for Promotion of Virtue and Prevention of Vice) asked the chairman of the Saudi Shura (Consultative) Council to enable them to have access to blocked Web sites, "to monitor immoral practices by visitors of these sites."[38] The religious police have argued that some young people "get involved in negative practices away from the eyes of the Saudi authorities" on these blocked Web sites, and are therefore striving to put a stop to the "immoral practices" online.[39] The chairman of the Shura Council, however, questioned the legit-imacy of the request and stated, "These justifications must be supported by clear evi-dence, otherwise there is no need for it."[40]

ONI Testing Results

The OpenNet Initiative conducted in-country testing on three ISPs: STC, National Engineering Services and Marketing (Nesma), and Arabian Internet and Communica-tions Services (Awalnet). The three providers blocked the same Web sites, as expected given the centrally administered filtering system.

Using Secure Computing's SmartFilter software for technical implementation and to identify Web sites for blocking, the Saudi censors have increased the number of targeted Saudi political reformists and opposition groups. In addition to the previously blocked Web sites such as the Web sites of the Islah movement (www.islah.tv and islah.info) and the Tajdeed movement (tajdeed.net), the authorities have added more opposition Web sites to the block list. Examples include www.alumah.com and www.alhijazonline .com. Testing in 2008–2009 also revealed that the censors now target user-generated oppositional content such as the forum New Arabia (www.newarabia.org).

The ONI monitored in-country access to the blog of Saudi blogger Ahmad Fouad Al-Farhan, who was jailed for more than four months. His blog was found to be blocked during his arrest and continued to be blocked even after he was released from prison. Also, the ONI verified that the Web site of the Voice of Saudi Women (www.saudiwomen.net), now defunct, was indeed blocked in October 2008. The Web site, according to Reporters Without Borders, published a number of analytical reports about the status of women in Saudi society and has denounced impediments to women becoming effective actors in Saudi society.[41]

The ONI also found that the blog Saudi Christian (christforsaudi.blogspot.com) was blocked in Saudi Arabia in January 2009, after reports that Saudi blogger Hamoud Bin Saleh declared on his blog that he converted from Islam to Christianity. The ONI monitored the blog and found that it was removed in March 2009 for unknown reasons.

In keeping with the Saudi government's emphasis on protecting the "sanctity of Islam" and the legitimacy of the regime, a number of Web sites opposing each are also blocked. These include Web sites relating to minority Shia groups (www.yahosein .com), a Bahai site (www.bahai.com), and sites that espouse alternative views of Islam, such as the Web site of the Institution for the Secularization of Islamic Society (www.secularislam.org). Web sites that present critical reviews of the religion of Islam and try to convert Muslims to other religions were also censored (answering-islam.org, www.islamreview.com).

The Web pages of a few global free speech advocates, such as Article19 (www .article19.org) and the Free Speech Coalition (www.freespeechcoalition.com), are blocked. However, filtering of human rights content primarily targets Saudi or regional organizations. All Web pages of the Saudi Human Rights Center (www.saudihr.org) are blocked.

The human rights Web site www.humum.net was found blocked in 2008–2009 testing, whereas only the page related to Saudi Arabia was found to be blocked in the previous phase of testing. The Web site receives complaints on human rights violations from Arab citizens and is run by the Cairo-based Arab Human Rights Information Network.

Most global media Web sites tested, including Israel-based news outlets such as the daily *Haaretz* (www.haaretz.com), were accessible. However, Web sites of certain prominent Arabic newspapers and news portals were blocked, including the Arab-language newspaper *Al-Quds Al Arabi* (www.alquds.co.uk) and the news portal Elaph (www.elaph.com). Access to Elaph was restored several months after testing.

"Immoral" social content continues to be a priority target for Saudi censors. The vast majority of pornographic Web sites that were tested were blocked, as were most of those featuring provocative attire or gambling. The 2008–2009 testing also showed that censorship has expanded to block Arabic-language Web sites containing explicit content.

Also blocked were numerous Web sites containing content relating to alcohol and drugs, gay and lesbian issues, and sex education and family planning. A substantial number of Internet tools, including anonymizers and translators, were filtered.

Conclusion

Saudi Arabia publicly acknowledges censoring morally inappropriate and religiously sensitive material, but the authorities also filter political opposition Web sites and resources on human rights issues. In addition, the state has introduced new surveillance measures at Internet cafés and announced plans to start a system that will require local Web sites to register with the authorities.

Saudi citizens have started to use the Internet for online activism, but the authorities have arrested several online writers and blocked their content. A local human rights group expressed interest in legally challenging the government's censorship of human rights Web sites.

Generally, Internet filtering in Saudi Arabia mirrors broader attempts by the state to repress opposition and promote a single religious creed.

Notes

1. *BBC News*, "Country Profile: Saudi Arabia," August 20, 2009, http://news.bbc.co.uk/1/hi/world/middle_east/country_profiles/791936.stm.

2. Reporters Without Borders, "Saudi Arabia: Annual Report 2007," http://www.rsf.org/article.php3?id_article=20775&Valider=OK.

3. *BBC News*, "Country Profile: Saudi Arabia," August 20, 2009, http://news.bbc.co.uk/1/hi/world/middle_east/country_profiles/791936.stm.

4. Reporters Without Borders, "Saudi Arabia: Annual Report 2007," http://www.rsf.org/article.php3?id_article=20775&Valider=OK.

5. Khaled al Oweigan, "Saudi Arabia to Regulate Kingdom-Based Websites," *Asharq Alawsat*, May 13, 2009, http://aawsat.com/english/news.asp?section=5&id=16714.

6. Faiza Saleh Ambah, "New Clicks in the Arab World," *Washington Post*, November 12, 2006, http://www.washingtonpost.com/wp-dyn/content/article/2006/11/11/AR2006111100886.html.

7. Reporters Without Borders, "Saudi Arabia: Annual Report 2007," http://www.rsf.org/article .php3?id_article=20775&Valider=OK.

8. Ibid.

9. Internet and Democracy Blog, "Saudi Activists Launch a Daring and Bold Move to Support Human Rights," November 3, 2008, http://blogs.law.harvard.edu/idblog/2008/11/03/saudi-activists -launch-a-daring-and-bold-move-to-support-human-rights/.

10. Committee to Protect Journalists, "10 Worst Countries to Be a Blogger," April 30, 2009, http:// www.cpj.org/reports/2009/04/10-worst-countries-to-be-a-blogger.php.

11. *Khaleej Times Online*, "Saudi Arabia's Telecom Sector Growing Rapidly," March 24, 2008, http://www.khaleejtimes.com/DisplayArticleNew.asp?xfile=data/business/2008/March/business _March715.xml&section=business&col=.

12. *Arab News*, "STC to Continue Free Installation of IP-VPN Service," June 1, 2008, http://www .arabnews.com/?page=6&section=0&article=110452&d=1&m=6&y=2008.

13. *Khaleej Times Online*, "Saudi Arabia's Telecom Sector Growing Rapidly," March 24, 2008, http://www.khaleejtimes.com/DisplayArticleNew.asp?xfile=data/business/2008/March/business _March715.xml&section=business&col=.

14. *Saudi Gazette*, "STC Starts Fiber Optic Network for Homes," http://www.saudigazette.com.sa/ index.cfm?method=home.regcon&contentID=2008122825183.

15. Internet Services Unit, King Abdul Aziz City for Science and Technology, http://www.isu.net .sa/.

16. Ibid.

17. Communications and Information Technology Commission, http://www.citc.gov.sa/.

18. Reporters Without Borders, "Saudi Arabia: Annual Report 2007," http://www.rsf.org/article .php3?id_article=20775&Valider=OK.

19. *Arab News*, "Online Campaigns to Protect Girls from Scandals," April 4, 2008, http://www .arabnews.com/?page=1&section=0&article=108566&d=4&m=4&y=2008&pix=kingdom.jpg& category=Kingdom.

20. *BBC News*, "Country Profile: Saudi Arabia," August 20, 2009, http://news.bbc.co.uk/1/hi/ world/middle_east/country_profiles/791936.stm.

21. Ibid.

22. Reporters Without Borders, "Information Minister Bans Live Programmes on State Television," February 1, 2008, http://www.rsf.org/article.php3?id_article=25340.

23. Internet Services Unit, "Introduction to Content Filtering," http://www.isu.net.sa/saudi-internet/contenet-filtring/filtring.htm.

24. Raid Qusti, "Most of Kingdom's Internet Users Aim for the Forbidden," *Arab News*, October 2, 2005, http://www.arabnews.com/?page=1&section=0&article=71012&d=2&m=10&y=2005.

25. Peter Burrows, "Internet Censorship, Saudi Style," *BusinessWeek*, November 13, 2008, http://www.businessweek.com/magazine/content/08_47/b4109068380136.htm?chan=magazine+channel_in+depth.

26. David Westley, "Saudi Tightens Grip on Internet Use," *Arabian Business*, January 26, 2008, http://www.arabianbusiness.com/509226-saudi-tightens-grip-on-internet-useoni.

27. Reporters Without Borders, "Blogger Fouad al Farhan Freed after More Than Four Months in Prison," April 28, 2008, http://www.rsf.org/article.php3?id_article=26746.

28. David Westley, "Saudi Tightens Grip on Internet Use," *Arabian Business*, January 26, 2008, http://www.arabianbusiness.com/509226-saudi-tightens-grip-on-internet-useoni.

29. Reporters Without Borders, "Blogger Fouad al Farhan Freed after More Than Four Months in Prison," April 28, 2008, http://www.rsf.org/article.php3?id_article=26746.

30. *Arab News*, "Ahsa Youth Sentenced under Cyber Crime Law," December 3, 2008, http://www.arabnews.com/?page=1&section=0&article=116942&d=3&m=12&y=2008&pix=kingdom.jpg&category=Kingdom.

31. Arabic Network for Human Rights Information, "The Arabic Network Calls on the Saudi Authorities to Annul the Decision to Expel Egyptian Resident Abdullah Al Khyat," July 26, 2008, http://anhri.net/en/reports/2008/pr0726.shtml.

32. Ibid.

33. Mariam Al Hakeem, "Rights Group Seeks to Unblock Access to Websites," *Gulf News*, April 1, 2008, http://www.gulfnews.com/News/Gulf/saudi_arabia/10202016.html.

34. Ibid.

35. Najah Alosaimi, "Web Newspaper Charged with Defamation," *Arab News*, May 2, 2009, http://www.arabnews.com/?page=1&section=0&article=122106&d=2&m=5&y=2009&pix=kingdom.jpg&category=Kingdom.

36. Khaled al Oweigan, "Saudi Arabia to Regulate Kingdom-Based Websites," *Asharq Alawsat*, May 13, 2009, http://aawsat.com/english/news.asp?section=5&id=16714.

37. OpenNet Initiative Blog, "Restriction on Internet Use in the Middle East on the Rise: Internet Cafés in Saudi Must Install Hidden Cameras," April 16, 2009, http://opennet.net/blog/2009/04/restriction-internet-use-middle-east-rise-internet-caf%C3%A9s-saudi-must-install-hidden-came.

38. Mariam Al Hakeem, "Religious Police Demand Access to Blocked Websites," *Gulf News*, August 28, 2008, http://archive.gulfnews.com/news/gulf/saudi_arabia/10240886.html.

39. Ibid.

40. Ibid.

41. Reporters Without Borders, "Saudi Arabia: Authorities Block Women's Rights Website," October 30, 2008, http://www.rsf.org/fil_en.php3?id_rubrique=682&mois=10 (accessed July 30 2009).

Syria

The Syrian government has expanded the range of Web content it filters, continues to detain citizens for expressing their opinions online, and monitors Internet use closely. Broadly worded laws, characteristic of second-generation controls, invite government harassment and have prompted Internet users to engage in self-censorship and self-monitoring in order to avoid the state's ambiguous grounds for arrest.

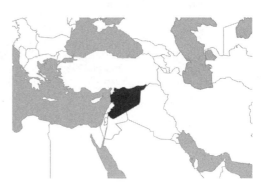

Background

In Syria, the media are primarily owned and controlled by the government and the ruling Baath party. Criticism of the president and his family is not allowed, journalists practice self-censorship, and foreign reporters rarely receive accreditation.[1] Though there have been improvements in Syrian press freedom since Bashar al-Assad became president in 2000,[2] the state continues to use the ongoing state of emergency to arrest media workers.[3] Journalists and political activists constantly risk arrest for virtually any reason and are "up against a whimsical and vengeful state apparatus which continually adds to the list of things banned or forbidden to be mentioned."[4] Syrian journalists

RESULTS AT A GLANCE					
Filtering	No Evidence of Filtering	Suspected Filtering	Selective Filtering	Substantial Filtering	Pervasive Filtering
Political					•
Social			•		
Conflict and security				•	
Internet tools					•

Other Factors	Low	Medium	High	Not Applicable
Transparency	•			
Consistency			•	

KEY INDICATORS	
GDP per capita, PPP (constant 2005 international dollars)	4,260
Life expectancy at birth (years)	74
Literacy rate (percent of people age 15+)	83
Human development index (out of 179)	105
Rule of law (out of 211)	133
Voice and accountability (out of 209)	198
Democracy index (out of 167)	156 (Authoritarian regime)
Digital opportunity index (out of 181)	104
Internet users (percent of population)	16.7

Source by indicator: World Bank 2009a, World Bank 2009a, World Bank 2009a, UNDP 2008, World Bank 2009b, World Bank 2009b, Economist Intelligence Unit 2008, ITU 2007, ITU 2008.

have been arrested for interviewing exiled regime opponents, participating in conferences abroad, and criticizing government policies.[5] In 2006, Reporters Without Borders ranked Syria among the 13 "enemies of the Internet,"[6] and in 2007 described Syria as the biggest prison for cyber dissidents in the Middle East because of the number of arrests and the frequency of mistreatment of online activists.[7] In 2009, the Committee to Protect Journalists ranked Syria third in a list of the ten worst countries in which to be a blogger, given the arrests, harassment, and restrictions that online writers in Syria have faced.[8]

The government admits to censoring "pro-Israel and hyper-Islamist" Web sites, such as those run by the illegal Muslim Brotherhood and those calling for autonomy for Syrian Kurds.[9] In defense of these practices, former Minister of Technology and Communications Amr Salem has said that "Syria is currently under attack ... and if somebody writes, or publishes or whatever, something that supports the attack, they will be tried."[10]

Internet in Syria

The telecommunications market in Syria is the most regulated in the Middle East and is among the least developed. State-owned Syrian Telecom (STE) owns all telecommunications infrastructure and has made some substantial investment to bring services to rural areas, but limited competition exists with private ISPs competing with STE in the Internet provision market.[11]

A government body that is part of the Ministry of Telecommunications and Technology, STE is also the regulator of telecommunications in Syria; in addition to being an ISP, it enjoys a monopoly over wired and wireless services provided anywhere in Syria.[12] Telecom providers in Syria include Syriatel,[13] MTN,[14] Aya,[15] and SCS-Net, which is the ISP arm of the Syrian Computer Society.[16] Additionally, MTN and Syriatel now offer 3G mobile broadband in four major cities, as well as EDGE and GPRS connectivity (WAP) across the country.[17] However, 3G is prohibitively expensive for most Syrians at nearly USD 50 per month.

The Internet was introduced to the general public in Syria in 2000 as part of the modernization reforms of President al-Assad. In the subsequent seven years, Internet use soared by 4,900 percent, far exceeding the global growth rate of 249 percent. The vast majority of Syrian users get online service at Syria's ubiquitous Internet cafés and from houses using dial-up connections over landlines.[18] Syrian users continue to access blocked Web sites using proxies and circumvention tools, and prefer to use Internet cafés to browse banned content because they believe the government can monitor Web surfing through home Internet connections.[19]

Legal and Regulatory Frameworks

The constitution of Syria provides for freedom of speech and of the press, but the Syrian government restricts press freedom with repressive laws such as the Emergency Law, which was put in place in December 1962 and broadly mandates the censorship of various forms of communication; the 2001 Press Law which sets out sweeping controls over publications printed in Syria; articles 286 and 287 of the penal code, which criminalize spreading news abroad; and Decree No. 6 of 1965, which criminalizes "publishing news aimed at shaking the people's confidence in the revolution."[20]

The Syrian authorities extended their censorship of Internet activities and monitoring of Internet users in March 2008 by ordering Internet café users to provide users' names, identification cards, and times they use their services.[21] The head of the Syrian Media Center told Reuters, "These steps are designed to terrorize Internet users and spread fear and self-censorship in violation of the right to privacy and free expression."[22] Government officials said these measures were necessary to guard against what they described as attempts to spread sectarian divisions and "penetration by Israel."[23]

In addition, an increasing number of Syrians have faced trial or been jailed for their online writings, and the Syrian authorities continue judicial persecution of cyber dissidents. For example, Habib Saleh was tried in December 2008 for publishing articles calling for democracy in Syria on the Web site Elaph.com, which is censored in Syria, and was given a three-year prison sentence in March 2009. Saleh was convicted under article 285 of the criminal code for "weakening national sentiment" (a charge that is applicable only in wartime, said his lawyer).[24] Similarly, blogger Tariq Biasi received a three-year sentence for "weakening national sentiment" as well as "publishing false information" on a blog.[25]

In addition, owners of opposition Web sites face harassment by the authorities. For example, lawyer and Web site editor Abdallah Souleiman Ali was detained for 12 days for "persisting in publishing legal and political articles criticizing the role of the government" on his Web site Al Nazaha (alnazaha.org) in July 2008.[26]

Access to the social networking site Facebook was blocked in November 2007 as part of a crackdown on political activism on the Internet. According to a women's rights advocate, this action was taken because Facebook helped Syrian civil society form civic groups outside government control.[27] However, the government claimed that Facebook was blocked because it could become a conduit for Israeli penetration of Syrian youth.[28] The advocacy group Syrian Media Center claims that at least 153 Web sites have been blocked, among which are Blogger (owned by Google), the Arabic blogging host service Maktoob, YouTube, and Web sites of opposition parties, Lebanese newspapers, and Lebanese groups opposed to "Syrian interference in Lebanon."[29] In September 2008, the Public Institution for Telecommunication ordered the blocking of the entire Web site of the Cairo-based Arabic Network for Human Rights Information (ANHRI) as well as their blogs (www.katib.org). Prior to that, only one page on ANHRI's site containing information about human rights violations in Syria was blocked. The organization believes that this blocking was ordered by the security forces, "which have a louder voice than the law and the Constitution in Syria."[30]

Internet cafés in Syria are subject to tough measures that make opening one very difficult. To start an Internet café, one needs to get a license from the Syrian Telecommunications Institution, as well as a security license from the Interior Ministry, which sets security instructions that require each café visitor to provide his or her name, identification, and the names of his or her mother and father.[31] The café owner must also show visitors which religious and political Web sites they are banned from using.[32] Failure to follow the rules can result in closure of the café, large fines, and, in extreme cases, jail time.[33]

Surveillance

On its Web site, STE states that the telecommunications it provides remain private and shall not be shared except by law and regulations at an official request.[34]

However, café operators have reported that the authorities ask them to spy on their customers and that they believe everything is monitored.[35] A young cyber dissident who was arrested at an Internet café in Damascus in late 2006 for his critical online writings said security services often request café owners to spy on clients, and they provide them with software programs for the task.[36] In addition, as mentioned earlier, Internet café operators must keep a record of their clients' names and identification to present to the authorities on request.

Furthermore, Syria-based Web sites were ordered by the government in 2007 to reveal the identity and name of those behind any article or comment they published.[37]

The use of cell phones is also subject to surveillance. The Interior Ministry and the Syrian Telecommunications Institution have banned the sale of cell phones that have GPS and have WAP services that are not being properly monitored by the service providers.[38]

Technical censorship in Syria is implemented using software from a Canadian company called Platinum, Inc.[39] The company uses the ThunderCache solution for URL filtering, which is a system capable of monitoring and controlling a user's dynamic Web-based activities as well as conducting deep packet inspection.[40]

ONI Testing Results

OpenNet Initiative testing was conducted on two ISPs in Syria: formally SCS-Net (also known as Aloola) and Aya.

The testing results for 2008–2009 indicate that Syria's Internet filtering regime has increased the scope and depth of targeted content. Censorship has been extended to include high-profile Web sites such as the video-sharing site YouTube, the social networking site Facebook, and the online shop Amazon.

Political filtering continues to be pervasive. For example, Web sites of the Syrian branch of the Muslim Brotherhood such as ikhwansyria.com and jimsyr.com (now defunct) were blocked. Unlike results from 2006 to 2007, more Web sites affiliated with the Muslim Brotherhood, including that of the Egyptian branch, were blocked. Examples include www.ikhwanonline.com, www.ikhwanweb.com, and www.ikhwan.net.

Results from 2006 to 2007 testing indicated that only two Kurdish Web sites were blocked, but results from 2008 to 2009 testing show that several Kurdish Web sites have been added to the block list. These include www.kurdnas.com, amude.net, www.kurdistanabinxete.com, www.pajk-online.com, www.kurdmedya.com, and www .kurdax.net.

Also blocked were the Web site of the United States Committee for a Free Lebanon (freelebanon.org), which campaigns for an end to Syrian influence in Lebanese politics; the Web site of the Lebanese Forces (www.lebanese-forces.org); and some Lebanese newspapers such as www.annahar.com.

Several political Web sites were also filtered. Among them are the Web site of the Reform Party of Syria (www.reformsyria.org), a Web site of a communist party in Syria (www.syriaalaan.com), the Web site of the Hizb al-Tahrir or Liberation Party (www .hizb-ut-tahrir.org)—an Islamist group that seeks to restore the Caliphate—and various news and oppositional Web sites such as www.thisissyria.net, www.free-syria.com, and www.syriatruth.org.

The tests conducted by ONI revealed that a number of Syrian blogs hosted on Google's popular blogging engine Blogger (blogspot.com) continue to be blocked, a finding which strongly suggests that ISPs have blocked access to all blogs hosted on this service, including many apolitical blogs. Interestingly, Blogger.com (the site from which users of the service write posts) is not blocked, meaning Syrian users can blog but cannot read blogs (including their own). Also blocked was freesyria.wordpress.com, a blog created to campaign for the release of Michel Kilo, a prominent Syrian journalist imprisoned for his writings.

Results for 2008–2009 confirmed that Syria has unblocked access to the popular e-mail service Hotmail as well as the small Web-based e-mail sites address.com and netaddress.com. All three were found to be blocked in previous rounds of testing. None of the Arabic-language e-mail sites ONI tested were blocked, though the Arabic-language hosting site www.khayma.com was. Among the few Web sites found unblocked since 2006–2007 testing were the localized Arabic version of Wikipedia and the Web site of the Lebanese Free Patriotic Movement (www.tayyar.org).

Though most foreign news Web sites were accessible, those of some prominent Arabic newspapers and news portals were found to be blocked. Examples include the pan-Arab, London-based, Arabic-language newspapers *Al-Quds al-Arabi* (www.alquds .co.uk/) and *Al-Sharq al-Awsat* (www.asharqalawsat.com), the news portal elaph.com, the Kuwaiti newspaper *Al Seyassah* (www.alseyassah.com), the U.S.-based Web site of the *Arab Times* (www.arabtimes.com), and the Islam-oriented news and information portal Islam Online (islamonline.net). These publications frequently run articles critical of the Syrian government.

Web sites of human rights organizations were generally available. Those associated with the London-based Syrian Human Rights Committee (SHRC) and the Web site of the Syrian Observatory Human Rights (www.syriahr.com) were notable exceptions. As indicated previously, some blogs that criticize the human rights record of Syria were also blocked.

Several Israeli Web sites were tested to confirm whether or not Syria blocks the entire ".il" domain. All tested Web sites within the domain were blocked, suggesting that the entire domain is indeed blocked. In addition, URLs containing the keyword "Israel" were found to be blocked.

Nearly one-third of the anonymizer Web sites tested were blocked, indicating some measure of effort to preempt circumvention. None of the Web sites containing pornographic content were found to be blocked, including the select few found blocked in 2006–2007 testing. Additionally, as in the 2006–2007 rounds of testing, Web sites that focus on LGBT issues were generally available.

Syrian ISPs offer an optional filtering system to block content deemed immoral and violent, as well as chat Web sites. The ONI did not test the scope and depth of these optional systems.

Filtering continues to lack transparency; there is no explicit block page, and the ISPs and telecom regulators do not publish clear information about what they filter.

Conclusion

In addition to high-profile Web sites such as YouTube, Amazon, and Facebook, the Web sites blocked in Syria span a range of categories, with the most substantial filtering being of Web sites that criticize government policies and actions or espouse oppositional political views. Repressive legislation and the imprisonment of journalists and bloggers for their activities online have led many Syrians to engage in self-censorship, which conforms to second-generation controls found in other parts of the world. Meanwhile, the government continues to promote the growth of the Internet throughout the country.

Notes

1. *BBC News*, "Country Profile: Syria," July 29, 2009, http://news.bbc.co.uk/1/hi/world/middle_east/country_profiles/801669.stm.

2. Ibid.

3. Reporters Without Borders, "Syria—Annual Report 2007," http://www.rsf.org/article.php3?id_article=20777.

4. Ibid.

5. Ibid.

6. Reporters Without Borders, "List of the 13 Internet Enemies," November 7, 2006, http://www,rsf.org/spip.php?page=article&id_article=19603.

7. Reporters Without Borders, "Syria—Annual Report 2007," http://www.rsf.org/article.php3?id_article=20777.

8. Committee to Protect Journalists, "10 Worst Countries to be a Blogger," April 30, 2009, http://www.cpj.org/reports/2009/04/10-worst-countries-to-be-a-blogger.php.

9. Guy Taylor, "After the Damascus Spring: Syrians Search for Freedom Online," Reason Online: Free Minds and Free Markets, February 2007, http://www.reason.com/news/show/118380.html.

10. Ibid.

11. Paul Budde Communication Pty., Ltd., "Syria—Telecoms, Mobile and Broadband," http://www.budde.com.au/buddereports/1168/Syria_-_Telecoms_Market_Overview__Statistics.aspx?r=51.

12. Syrian Telecom, http://www.ste.gov.sy.

13. Syriatel, http://www.syriatel.sy.

14. MTN, http://www.mtnsyria.com.

15. Aya, http://aya.sy/.

16. SCS-Net/Aloola Web site, http://www.scs-net.org/.

17. Zawya.com, "Syria: MTN and Syriatel Both Launch 3G Services," January 21, 2009, http://ae.zawya.com/countries/sy/macrowatch.cfm?eiusection=MTN%20AND%20SYRIATEL%20BOTH%20LAUNCH%203G%20SERVICES&pass=1.

18. Phil Sands, "Syria Tightens Control over Internet," *The National*, September 30, 2008, http://www.thenational.ae/article/20080930/FOREIGN/664681062/1135.

19. International Relations and Security Network, "Syrian Youth Break through Internet Blocks," June 3, 2008, http://www.isn.ethz.ch/isn/Current-Affairs/Security-Watch/Detail/?ots591=4888CAA0-B3DB-1461-98B9-E20E7B9C13D4&lng=en&id=88422.

20. Freedom House, "Map of Press Freedom 2008," http://www.freedomhouse.org/template.cfm?page=251&year=2008.

21. Khaled Yacoub Oweis, "Syria Expands 'Iron Censorship' over Internet," Reuters, March 13, 2008, http://uk.reuters.com/article/internetNews/idUKL138353620080313?sp=true.

22. Ibid.

23. Ibid.

24. Reporters Without Borders, "Cyber-Dissident Habib Saleh Sentenced to Three Years in Jail," March 16, 2009, http://www.rsf.org/article.php3?id_article=30591.

25. Gideon Spitzer, "Dissident Watch: Tariq Biasi," *Middle East Quarterly*, Vol. 16, No. 1 (2009): 96, http://www.meforum.org/2098/dissident-watch-tariq-biasi#_ftn2.

26. Reporters Without Borders, "Lawyer Held for 12 Days Is Latest Victim of Government Harassment of Opposition Websites," August 18, 2008, http://www.rsf.org/article.php3?id_article=28190.

27. Khaled Yacoub Oweis, "Syria Blocks Facebook in Internet Crackdown," Reuters, November, 23, 2007, http://www.reuters.com/article/worldNews/idUSOWE37285020071123.

28. Ibid.

29. Khaled Yacoub Oweis, "Syria Expands 'Iron Censorship' over Internet," Reuters, March 13, 2008, http://uk.reuters.com/article/internetNews/idUKL138353620080313?sp=true.

30. Arabic Network for Human Rights Information, "Arabic Network for Human Rights Information's Website Is Entirely Blocked in Syria," September 29, 2008, http://www.anhri.net/en/reports/2008/pr0929.shtml.

31. Omar Abdelatif, "Opening Up an Internet Café in Syria? Good Luck," *Menassat*, June 13, 2008, http://www.menassat.com/?q=en/news-articles/3943-opening-internet-caf-syria-good-luck.

32. Ibid.

33. Ibid.

34. Syrian Telecom, http://www.ste.gov.sy.

35. Omar Abdelatif, "Opening Up an Internet Café in Syria? Good Luck," *Menassat*, June 13, 2008, http://www.menassat.com/?q=en/news-articles/3943-opening-internet-caf-syria-good-luck.

36. Zeina Karam, "Syria Tightens Controls on Internet Users," *New York Times*, March 25, 2008, http://www.nytimes.com/2008/03/25/technology/25iht-media.4.11415911.html?_r=1.

37. Khaled Yacoub Oweis, "Syria Expands 'Iron Censorship' over Internet," Reuters, March 13, 2008, http://uk.reuters.com/article/internetNews/idUKL138353620080313?sp=true.

38. Omar Abdelatif, "Opening Up an Internet Café in Syria? Good Luck," *Menassat*, June 13, 2008, http://www.menassat.com/?q=en/news-articles/3943-opening-internet-caf-syria-good-luck.

39. Syrian Observatory Human Rights, *Taqrir al-Markez al-Suri lile'lam wahuriyat altabir 'an halat 'a'elam walhuriyat alsahafiyah* [Syrian Center for Media and Freedom of Expression's report on media and press freedom in Syria], May 3, 2009, http://www.syriahr.com/3-5-2009-syrian %20observatory6.htm.

40. Platinum, Inc., http://platinum.sy/index.php?m=90; ThunderCache, http://www.thundercache .com/pages/filtering.html.

Tunisia

Although Tunisia has actively sought to develop its information and communication technology (ICT) infrastructure, the government continues to pervasively block a range of Web content and has used nontechnical means, characteristic of second-generation Internet controls, to impede journalists and human rights activists from doing their work. The

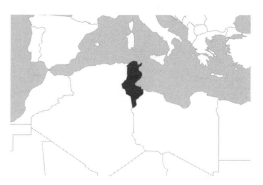

filtering of political content and restrictions on online activity have prompted frequent criticism from foreign governments and human rights organizations, as well as online protest campaigns from Tunisian Internet users.

Background

The Tunisian constitution guarantees freedom of the press under "conditions laid down by law," but the government closely controls the media. Additionally, the Press Law criminalizes defamation, and those who violate it can be imprisoned and fined.[1] Tunisia is considered by media watchdog Reporters Without Borders to be "the region's most authoritarian regime" in regard to civil liberties. Journalists and human rights activists have been banned from leaving the country and are subject to arrest and

RESULTS AT A GLANCE					
Filtering	No Evidence of Filtering	Suspected Filtering	Selective Filtering	Substantial Filtering	Pervasive Filtering
Political					•
Social					•
Conflict and security			•		
Internet tools					•

Other Factors	Low	Medium	High	Not Applicable
Transparency	•			
Consistency		•		

KEY INDICATORS	
GDP per capita, PPP (constant 2005 international dollars)	7,102
Life expectancy at birth (years)	74
Literacy rate (percent of people age 15+)	78
Human development index (out of 179)	95
Rule of law (out of 211)	84
Voice and accountability (out of 209)	181
Democracy index (out of 167)	141 (Authoritarian regime)
Digital opportunity index (out of 181)	87
Internet users (percent of population)	27.5

Source by indicator: World Bank 2009a, World Bank 2009a, World Bank 2009a, UNDP 2008, World Bank 2009b, World Bank 2009b, Economist Intelligence Unit 2008, ITU 2007, ITU 2008.

imprisonment. The majority of the country's newspapers conform to the official line of the government, and opposition newspapers have been seized.[2] The Internet is also heavily regulated and perceived as a potential threat to the stability and security of the country.[3] There are also instances of banning foreign publications for publishing content that is deemed prejudicial to Islam.[4]

Internet in Tunisia

Tunisia has one of the most developed telecommunications infrastructures in North Africa, with a high mobile penetration rate and one of the lowest broadband prices in Africa.[5] As of October 2008, the number of GSM subscribers had reached 9 million, while the number of Internet users was 1.7 million, 114,000 of whom have broadband subscriptions.[6] Out of a population of 10.2 million, nine out of ten Tunisians own a cell phone.[7] Of the Internet users, 84 percent access the Internet at home, 75.8 percent use it at work, and 24 percent use Internet cafés.[8]

The Tunisian Ministry of Communications established the Tunisian Internet Agency (ATI) to regulate the country's Internet and DNS services, which had formerly fallen under the purview of the Regional Institute for Computer Sciences and Telecommunications (IRSIT).[9] The ATI is also the gateway from which all of Tunisia's 11 ISPs lease their bandwidth.[10] Six of these ISPs are public (ATI, INBMI, CCK, CIMSP, IRESA, and Defense's ISP); the other five—Planet Tunisie, 3S Global Net, HEXABYTE, TopNet, and TUNET—are private.[11]

The government has made concentrated efforts to spread Internet access. The ATI reports connectivity of 100 percent for the education sector (universities, research laboratories, secondary schools, and primary schools).[12] Government-brokered "free Internet" programs that provide Web access for the price of a local telephone call and increased competition among ISPs have significantly reduced the economic barriers to

Internet access. Tunisians for whom personal computers remain prohibitively expensive may access the Internet from more than 300 Internet cafés set up by the authorities.[13]

Legal and Regulatory Frameworks

In addition to filtering Web content, the government of Tunisia utilizes laws, regulations, and surveillance to achieve strict control over the Internet.

For example, journalists have been prosecuted by Tunisia's press code, which bans offending the president, disturbing order, and publishing what the government perceives as false news.[14] The government also restricts the media by controlling the registration of print media and licensing of broadcasters, refusing permission to critical outlets, and controlling the distribution of public sector advertisement.[15] Journalists are also charged in court with vague violations of the penal code.[16]

Online dissidents face severe punishment. For example, human rights lawyer Mohamed Abbou was sentenced to three and a half years in prison in 2005 for publishing on a banned Web site a report in which he accused the government of torturing Tunisian prisoners.[17]

In a landmark legal case that challenged the Web-filtering regime in the country, journalist and blogger Ziad El Heni filed a legal suit against the ATI for censoring the social networking site Facebook.[18] The Tunisian Union of Free Radio Stations and the Unionist Freedoms and Rights Observatory joined El Heni in the lawsuit and called for Tunisian President Zine El Abidine Ben Ali to testify.[19] Facebook was blocked on August 18, 2008, and then unblocked on September 2 at the Tunisian president's request.[20] The Third District Court of Tunisia, however, dismissed the case in November 2008 without providing any explanation.[21]

In addition to being blocked in Tunisia, many opposition and dissident Web sites and blogs have been targets of hacking attempts and, in some cases, successful content removal and shutting down of servers.[22] Although it is not clear who is behind these cyber attacks, many Tunisian opposition leaders believe the government is responsible.[23] For example, the independent news site Kalima (www.kalimatunisie.com) was hacked into and shut down in October 2008. The eight-year Arabic and French archives were completely destroyed. The Web site has been blocked since it was launched in 2000. Its administrator accused the government of being responsible for the attack because, as she told the Committee to Protect Journalists, "The only ones who benefit from this attack are the authorities."[24] She also stated, "I would not rule out the possibility that this act was committed by the secret services, with the aid of hackers or pirates based in Tunisia or abroad." The Web-based newsletter Tunis News (www.tunisnews.net) and a blog run by a judge (tunisiawatch.rsfblog.org) have been subject to similar attacks.[25]

Tunisia does not have specific laws that regulate online broadcasting. As a result, a group of journalists exploited the lack of legal obstacles to broadcast on the Internet and on December 10, 2007, launched Tunisia's first Internet radio station, Radio 6, to mark the 59th anniversary of the World Declaration of Human Rights.[26]

Web filtering in Tunisia is achieved through the use of a commercial software program, SmartFilter, sold by the U.S.-based company Secure Computing. Since all fixed-line Internet traffic passes through facilities controlled by ATI, the government is able to load the software onto its servers and filter content consistently across Tunisia's 11 ISPs. Tunisia purposefully hides its filtering from Internet users. SmartFilter is designed to display a 403 error message when a user attempts to access a blocked Web site; the Tunisian government has replaced this message with a standard 404 error message, which gives no hint that the requested Web site is actively blocked.[27]

Surveillance

The Tunisian authorities practice various forms of Internet surveillance and request that service providers such as Internet cafés become partners in controlling Internet use. For example, the authorities monitor Internet cafés, instruct Internet users to show identification before they can use the Internet in some regions, and hold Internet café operators responsible by law for their clients' online activities.

There is also technical surveillance, whereby downloading or adding attachments to an e-mail must go through a central server. Under the pretext of protecting public order and national security, a 1998 post and telecommunications law enables the authorities to intercept and check the content of e-mail messages;[28] in fact, electronic surveillance such as the filtering of e-mail messages of government opponents has been reported.[29] Global Voices Advocacy director and Tunisian activist Sami Ben Gharbia conducted a test from the Netherlands with two Tunisia-based activists, and confirmed by logging on to their e-mail accounts from the Netherlands that what he saw was not what the bloggers saw when they logged on from Tunisia, and that the bloggers could not access some of the messages they received.[30]

ONI Testing Results

The OpenNet Initiative carried out tests in Tunisia using the ISPs Planet Tunisie and TopNet. Similar to 2006–2007 test results, 2008–2009 testing revealed pervasive filtering of Web sites of political opposition groups such as the Democratic Forum for Labor and Liberty (www.fdtl.org), Al-Nadha Movement (www.nahdha.info), Tunisian Workers' Communist Party (www.albadil.org), and Democratic Progressive Party (pdpinfo.org).

Also blocked were Web sites run by opposition figures such as activist Moncef Marzouki (www.moncefmarzouki.net) and Web sites that contain oppositional news and politics such as www.nawaat.org, www.perspectivestunisiennes.net, www.tunisnews.com, and www.tunezine.com.

Web sites that publish oppositional articles by Tunisian journalists were also blocked. For example, ONI verified the blocking of the French daily *Libération* in February 2007 because articles by Tunisian journalist Taoufik Ben Brik critical of President Zine el-Abidine Ben Ali appeared on its Web site.[31]

Also blocked are Web sites that criticize Tunisia's human rights record. These include the Web sites of Amnesty International (www.amnesty.org), Freedom House (www.freedomhouse.org), Reporters Without Borders (www.rsf.org and www.rsf.fr), the International Freedom of Expression eXchange (www.ifex.org), the Islamic Human Rights Commission (www.ihrc.org), and the Arabic Network for Human Rights Information (www.hrinfo.org). Although the home page of Human Rights Watch (HRW) was accessible, the Arabic- and French-language versions of an HRW report on Internet repression in Tunisia were blocked.

The prominent video sharing sites YouTube (www.youtube.com) and Dailymotion (www.dailymotion.com) were found blocked, apparently because Tunisian activists used them to disseminate content critical of the regime's human rights practices. Interestingly, the Web site of ONI (opennet.net) was blocked. Also blocked was the Web site of Global Voices (www.globalvoicesonline.org), a nonprofit global citizens' media project. Most of the tested Web sites in the anonymizers and circumvention tools category were blocked. These include Psiphon (psiphon.civisec.org), TOR (tor.eff.org), Anonymizer (www.anonymizer.com), e-mail privacy service provider Stealth Message (www.stealthmessage.com), Guardster (www.guardster.com), and JAP (anon.inf.tu-dresden.de).

The filtering regime pervasively filters pornographic content, several gay and lesbian information or dating pages, provocative attire, and several online translation services. Also blocked were a few Web sites that criticize the Quran (www.thequran.com) and Islam (www.islameyat.com). Although the small number of such sites indicates that there is limited filtering of religious content in Tunisia.

Conclusion

Tunisia's government continues to suppress critical speech and oppositional activity, both in real space and in cyberspace. Unlike other states that employ filtering software, Tunisia endeavors to conceal instances of filtering by supplying a fake error page when a blocked Web site is requested. This technique makes filtering more opaque and clouds users' understanding of the boundaries of permissible content.

Tunisia maintains a focused, effective system of Internet control that blends content filtering with harsh laws to censor objectionable and politically threatening information characteristic of second-generation controls.

Notes

1. Freedom House, "Map of Press Freedom 2007," http://www.freedomhouse.org/template.cfm ?page=251&country=7290&year=2007.

2. Reporters Without Borders, "Repression Continues as Ben Ali Marks 21st Anniversary as President," November 7, 2008, http://www.rsf.org/article.php3?id_article=29208.

3. Ibid.

4. *Menassat*, "Morocco: French Magazine *L'Express* Banned over Religious Issue," November 3, 2008, http://www.menassat.com/?q=en/alerts/5053-morocco-french-magazine-lexpress-banned -over-religion-issue.

5. Paul Budde Communication Pty., Ltd., "Tunisia—Telecoms Market Overview and Statistics," March 2009, http://www.researchandmarkets.com/research/b46cf3/tunisia%5ftelecoms.

6. Tunisia Online News, "Tunisia Has 9 Million GSM Subscribers and 1.7 Million Internet Users," October 2008, http://www.tunisiaonlinenews.com/2008/10/03/tunisia-has-9-million-gsm-subscribers -and-17-million-internet-users/.

7. Ibid.

8. Arab Advisors Group, "Tunisia's Internet Users Spent Over US$ 132.7 Million in B2C E-commerce during the Past 12 Months," August 27, 2008, http://www.arabadvisors.com/Pressers/ presser-082708.htm.

9. Tunisia Online, "Internet in Tunisia: History," June 25, 2002, http://www.tunisiaonline.com/ internet/history.html.

10. Tunisian Internet Agency, "The National Internet Service Provider in Tunisia," http://www .ati.tn/.

11. Ibid.

12. Ibid.

13. Reporters Without Borders, "Tunisia: Annual Report 2008," http://www.rsf.org/article.php3 ?id_article=25442&Valider=OK.

14. Committee to Protect Journalists, "Tunisia Report: The Smiling Oppressor," September 23, 2008, http://cpj.org/reports/2008/09/tunisia-oppression.php.

15. Ibid.

16. Freedom House, "Freedom in the World—Tunisia (2008)," http://www.freedomhouse.org/ inc/content/pubs/fiw/inc_country_detail.cfm?year=2008&country=7507&pf.

17. Freedom House, "Map of Press Freedom 2007," http://www.freedomhouse.org/template.cfm ?page=251&country=7290&year=2007.

18. Jamel Arfaoui,"Surprises Force Delay in Lawsuit against Tunisian Internet," *Magharebia*, November 5, 2008, http://www.magharebia.com/cocoon/awi/xhtml1/en_GB/features/awi/features/ 2008/11/05/feature-01.

19. Ibid.

20. Ibid.

21. Lina Ben Mhenni, "Tunisia: Facebook Case Thrown Out of Court," Global Voices Online, November 29, 2008, http://globalvoicesonline.org/2008/11/29/as-usual-the-tunisian-legal-system -has-been-faithful-to-the-values-of-fair-trial/.

22. Sami Ben Gharbia, "Silencing Online Speech in Tunisia," Global Voices Advocacy, August 20, 2008, http://advocacy.globalvoicesonline.org/2008/08/20/silencing-online-speech-in-tunisia/.

23. Ibid.

24. Committee to Protect Journalists, "Independent News Site Destroyed," October 14, 2008, http://cpj.org/2008/10/independent-news-site-destroyed.php.

25. IFEX, "IFEX Member Websites in Tunisia and Burma Under Attack," October 15, 2008. http:// www.ifex.org/en/content/view/full/97628/.

26. Jamel Arfaoui,"Tunisia Welcomes First Internet Radio Station," *Magharebia*, December 17, 2007, http://www.magharebia.com/cocoon/awi/xhtml1/en_GB/features/awi/features/2007/12/17/ feature-01.

27. Nart Villeneuve, "Tunisia. Internet Filtering," Internet Censorship Explorer, June 2005, http:// www.nartv.org/2005/06/07/tunisia-internet-filtering/

28. Reporters Without Borders, "A Textbook Case in Press Censorship for the Past 20 Years," November 5, 2007, http://www.rsf.org/article.php3?id_article=24264.

29. Reporters Without Borders, "Repression Continues as Ben Ali Marks 21st Anniversary as President," November 7, 2008, http://www.rsf.org/article.php3?id_article=29208.

30. Sami Ben Gharbia, "Silencing Online Speech in Tunisia," Global Voices Advocacy, August 20, 2008, http://advocacy.globalvoicesonline.org/2008/08/20/silencing-online-speech-in-tunisia/.

31. Reporters Without Borders, "Internet Enemies 2008: Tunisia," http://www.rsf.org/article.php3 ?id_article=26158.

United Arab Emirates

The government of the United Arab Emirates (UAE) censors political and religious content and pervasively filters Web sites that contain pornography or relate to alcohol and drug use, LGBT issues, or online dating or gambling. Online privacy and circumvention tools, as well as some Web sites belonging to Nazis or historical revisionists, are also blocked. Addi-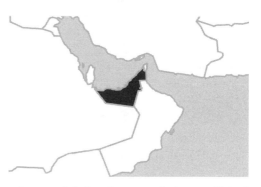
tionally, legal controls limit free expression and behavior, restricting political discourse and dissent online.

Background

The UAE is a federation of seven emirates formed in 1971 after independence from Britain. Each emirate maintains a large degree of independence, and the UAE is governed by the Supreme Council of Rulers of the seven emirs of the emirates. Though the UAE is one of the most liberal countries in the Gulf, it was until December 2006 the only state in the region not to have elected bodies.[1]

The UAE's economy continues to grow, but civil society remains stagnant, and human rights progress has been slow. Authorities have exerted censorship on a wide

RESULTS AT A GLANCE					
Filtering	No Evidence of Filtering	Suspected Filtering	Selective Filtering	Substantial Filtering	Pervasive Filtering
Political				•	
Social					•
Conflict and security			•		
Internet tools					•

Other Factors	Low	Medium	High	Not Applicable
Transparency		•		
Consistency		•		

KEY INDICATORS	
GDP per capita, PPP (constant 2005 international dollars)	51,586
Life expectancy at birth (years)	79
Literacy rate (percent of people age 15+)	90
Human development index (out of 179)	31
Rule of law (out of 211)	64
Voice and accountability (out of 209)	160
Democracy index (out of 167)	147 (Authoritarian regime)
Digital opportunity index (out of 181)	37
Internet users (percent of population)	65.2

Source by indicator: World Bank 2009a, World Bank 2009a, World Bank 2009a, UNDP 2008, World Bank 2009b, World Bank 2009b, Economist Intelligence Unit 2008, ITU 2007, ITU 2008.

range of activists, impeding the kind of vigorous monitoring and reporting that can draw attention to and help curb human rights abuses.[2] Although the prime minister decreed in 2007 that journalists should not face prison for "for reasons related to their work," current media laws allow for the imprisonment of journalists and suspension of publication for publishing "materials that cause confusion among the public." The government monitors press content, and journalists routinely exercise self-censorship.[3]

Though the emirate of Dubai has established itself as a regional and international hub for media in which there is a media zone authority that allows 100 percent foreign ownership and offers tax breaks, the Internet is filtered in this hub, as ONI test results show, and there are reports of other forms of censorship.[4] For example, Dubai authorities interrupted the broadcast of two Pakistani television stations, Geo News and Ary One World, in November 2007. Geo News said the decision resulted from constant pressure by Pervez Musharraf, then president of Pakistan, who had at the time implemented a state of emergency in Pakistan.[5] Dubai later allowed the two stations to resume broadcasting following negotiations with the Pakistani government and Dubai Media City.[6]

Internet in the UAE

According to a World Economic Forum report, the UAE continues to lead the Arab world in the adoption of information and communication technology (ICT)[7] and is expected to spend about USD 3.3 billion on ICT hardware for schools, hospitals, and other civil projects for the period 2008–2011.[8]

According to the Internet Telecommunication Union, Internet penetration in the UAE has increased from 36 percent in 2006 to an estimated 65.2 percent in 2008.[9] The Arab Advisors Group states account penetration to be at approximately 25 percent.

By the end of 2008, 11 percent of the total population had ADSL/broadband accounts. By the end of October 2008, the ISP Etisalat's ADSL accounts constituted around 36 percent of the operator's total fixed lines.[10]

Etisalat remains the dominant telecom provider, but in the interests of competition the UAE's Telecommunications Regulatory Authority (TRA) facilitated the launch of the Emirates Integrated Telecommunications Company, named Du. Established in 2007, Du is an integrated telecommunications provider that offers voice, data, and entertainment on mobile networks and converged broadband, television, and landline services.[11]

Competition in the broadband Internet market is limited because the two ISPs still do not share each other's networks, and Du is unable to offer broadband Internet or landline telephone services outside of a handful of property developments in Dubai where it owns the physical telephone network.[12] Because Etisalat has been the sole telecom company for 30 years, it owns the national telephone network, based on both copper-wire and new fiber-optic cables.[13]

Legal and Regulatory Framework

A new draft media law is expected to be issued in 2009. The highest regulatory media organization in the UAE, the National Media Council (NMC), claims the draft law provides unprecedented provisions that protect and promote freedom of expression in the country. It also states that the draft law, "provides journalists freedom from coercion to reveal sources, reflecting the government's commitment to the journalistic right to protect sources; in this particular regard, the pending law's protection exceeds that of many advanced democracies, including the United States."[14]

The pending law, passed by the Federal National Council in January 2009, was rejected by the UAE Journalists Association because, according to the association's chairman, "It has nothing to do with the concept of media; it contains 45 articles which don't provide a proper description of the media's duties and rights. Similarly, there are 10 articles which talk about penalties and punishments."[15]

International advocacy groups have also expressed concerns over the draft law. Human Rights Watch argues that the pending draft law unlawfully restricts free expression and will unduly interfere with the media's ability to report on sensitive subjects, and that it includes provisions that would grant the government virtually complete control in deciding who is allowed to work as a journalist, as well as which media organizations are allowed to operate in the country. Human Rights Watch further states that while the new law contains some improvements over the draconian media law currently in effect, it will continue to punish journalists for such infractions as "disparaging" government officials or publishing "misleading" news that "harms the country's economy."[16]

The Committee to Protect Journalists has also expressed concern over the draft law in a letter they sent to the president of the UAE urging him to reject the law in its current form because, if passed, "it will negatively impact the state of press freedom in the UAE."[17]

The telecommunication services in the UAE are regulated by the TRA, which was established in 2003 by a federal law and is tasked with ensuring adequacy of telecommunications services throughout the UAE and establishing and implementing a regulatory and policy framework.[18] The TRA is responsible for producing the Internet Access Management (IAM) policy, which outlines prohibited online content categories for ISPs. These categories include Internet tools for accessing blocked content, content providing information on criminal skills and illegal drugs, content containing pornography and nudity, gambling sites, Web sites for hacking and malicious codes, content offensive to religions, phishing Internet sites, Internet content that downloads spyware, Web sites providing unlicensed VoIP service, terrorism content, and prohibited top-level domain,[19] apparently a reference to the top-level domain of Israel (".il"), which is blocked in the UAE.

The UAE government has issued a federal law on combating cyber crimes. Cyber-Crime Law No. 2 of 2006 considers any intentional act that abolishes, destroys, or reveals secrets or that results in the republishing of personal or official information to be a crime. Individuals may be imprisoned for using the Internet to defame Islamic places of worship and traditions, insult any recognized religion, or promote "sinful acts." Anyone convicted of "transcending family principles and values" or setting up a Web site for groups "calling for, facilitating, and promoting ideas in breach of the general order and public decency" may be jailed.[20]

In August 2007, a court in the Emirate of Ras al-Khaimah sentenced the creator of Web site majan.net to one year in prison and a fine for defaming a local official. The court also ordered the site to be shut down. In September, the same individual received a five-month prison sentence and a fine in a second defamation case involving another local official, but was released on bail at the end of September 2007. Two months later, his two prison sentences were overturned by an appeals court after defamation complaints were withdrawn by the officials. In the end, he received a one-year suspended prison sentence after being convicted in a third defamation case.[21]

In April 2009, the chief of Dubai's police force denied allegations that Dubai Police had asked UAE's Telecommunication Regulatory Authority to censor Web sites. In earlier reports, the head of the Doha Media Freedom Center claimed that the Dubai Police had developed a list of 500 keywords, by which access to certain Web sites would be blocked.[22] The police chief stated that the government did not attempt to censor Web sites critical of the UAE, that the 500 search terms were designed to shield UAE Internet users against pornographic content, and that they were proposed by the telecommunication regulators themselves, not the Dubai Police.[23] This denial came shortly after Dubai's police chief called for the blocking of the video-sharing site YouTube because, he said, it contained religiously inappropriate content.[24] YouTube and Google have denied that they are engaged in plans to censor online content in the UAE.[25]

Although Etisalat and Du conform to the TRA policies by automatically blocking Web sites that offer free VoIP services, individuals—including Internet café owners—have found ways of getting around the ban by using the Internet to make cheap international calls. Violators have been prosecuted. For example, a police officer in the emirate of Ras Al Khaimah warned several Internet café owners against the use of "illegal calling cards" for making inexpensive international telephone calls. Several violating cafés were referred to the police for investigation.[26]

Surveillance

The authorities have established committees and electronic surveillance departments to monitor objectionable Internet activities. For example, a government committee was established in March 2009 to monitor Internet cafés in order to ensure that Internet connections in these cafés do not bypass filtering regimes set up by the two national ISPs, as per the regulations of the TRA. This move was in response to speculation that some Internet cafés provided unfiltered Internet connections using virtual private networks (VPNs).[27]

In addition, an online surveillance team was set up by Dubai Police to carry out around-the-clock checks on the Internet. The team, known as e-police, investigated a total of 222 cases in 2008. The cases include 87 involving fraud and other financial crimes, 38 cases of illegal hacking, and 92 cases of defamation and extortion. The electronic patrol team has set up special forums and used assumed names in an attempt to collect information about potential criminal activity.[28] This online surveillance department announced in April 2009 that it managed to track down and later arrest women who promoted their sexual services online and publicized their Dubai phone numbers on Web sites. In addition, the surveillance team announced that it managed to track down individuals who offered inexpensive illegal VoIP services from their apartments.[29]

ONI Testing Results

OpenNet Initiative testing in 2008–2009 revealed that the UAE's censors have increased the scope and depth of Internet filtering.

One of the significant policy shifts that occurred during 2008–2009 testing is the implementation of TRA-mandated filtering by the ISP Du, which used to offer unfettered access to the Internet in the Dubai free zones, including Dubai Media City, Dubai Internet City, and the residential areas affiliated with the free zones. Du began filtering on April 14, 2008; 2008–2009 test results show that its filtering is almost as extensive as that of the other national ISP, Etisalat, which has the lion's share of the market.

The two ISPs were found to block Web sites that express alternative political or religious views. For example, in addition to blocking UAE prison (uaeprison.com), a Web site hosting testimonials of former prisoners and critiques of the government's human rights practices, and the Web site of the U.S.-based Arab Times (arabtimes .com), the ONI found that the censors blocked the Web site "Save Zack Shahin" (www.savezackshahin.com), an online campaign calling for the release of U.S. citizen Zack Shahin from a UAE prison. The Web site encourages Americans to help him by sending letters to members of Congress. Shahin is a former chief executive of a Dubai property developer who in April 2009, together with a former UAE minister, was charged with seizing public money and harming state interests.[30]

Another example is the blocking of the Web site UAE Torture (uaetorture.com), which posted video clips that allegedly show a member of the UAE royal family torturing an Afghan businessman. The story drew the attention of international media such as ABC[31] and human rights advocates such as Human Rights Watch.[32] Blocking of this Web site has been inconsistent, however: it has been found to be accessible and inaccessible at different times.

The UAE's censors are also apparently sensitive to content that is critical of the state of the local economy or society. For example, censors blocked access to the Arabic UAE blog Mujarad Ensan (mujarad-ensan.maktoobblog.com) in October 2008, a few days after the anonymous blogger published a post sarcastically entitled, "Laugh with Me and Say: Our Economy Is in a Good Condition." In the text of the blog post, he accused the UAE government of lacking transparency when dealing with the U.S. financial crisis and the local papers of lying about the real status of the local economy. The writer also accused government-owned real estate companies of publishing exaggerated information about business deals to create the impression that the local economy had not been negatively affected by the U.S. financial crisis. The ONI monitored access to the blog and found that it became accessible a few days later for unknown reasons.

Another example is the blocking of the blog Secret Dubai Diary (secretdubai .blogspot.com), which was also found blocked in 2006–2007 testing. Apparently, this blog was blocked because it offers a critical review of social life in the UAE.

Similar to 2006–2007 testing results, several Web sites presenting unorthodox perspectives on Islam (thequran.com, islamreview.com, secularislam.org) were blocked, along with a handful of Web sites promoting minority faiths (albrhan.org, ansarweb .net). Among the few Web sites considered "extremist" that are filtered in the UAE are hinduunity.org, which advocates Hindu solidarity and resistance to Islam, and kahanetzadak.com, a Web site devoted to the founder of the militant Jewish Defense League.

Testing conducted in 2008–2009 showed that censors have expanded filtering in these categories to include previously accessible Web sites such as the presumably UAE-based atheist blogs Ben Kerishan (benkerishan.blogspot.com), The Land of

Sands (thelandofsands.com), and Ben Short (benshort.blogspot.com). Also blocked are Wikipedia pages that contain information about religiously sensitive content such as *Fitna*, a film produced by Dutch politician Geert Wilders and considered by many to be offensive to Islam, and the Wikipedia page about the Islamic prophet Muhammad, possibly because the page displays drawings of the Prophet.

In March 2009, censors blocked access to the Web site Ahmed and Salim (ahmedandsalim.com), an Israeli Web site that posted video episodes considered offensive to Arabs and Muslims.[33] The UAE also blocked access to the YouTube links where the video clips appeared. The UAE's TRA ordered the blocking of the Web site and the YouTube links only a few days after the content appeared online, apparently because, in addition to the content perceived as offensive to Islam, one of the characters was dressed in traditional Gulf attire and the UAE flag appeared in several scenes.[34]

Interestingly, several Web sites on Nazism, Holocaust denial, and historical revisionism were blocked. These include the Web site hitler.org and that of the Institute for Historical Review's publishing arm (www.noontidepress.com). Also blocked was the Web site vdare.com, which is often described as carrying anti-Semitic content. Meanwhile, the state continues to deny access to all Web sites on the Israeli country code top-level domain ".il."

Testing done in 2008–2009 also revealed that UAE filters still target social networking sites, video- and photo-sharing sites, bookmarking services, and blogging services. However, filtering of these Web sites has not been consistent. For example, Livejournal.com, a free service for blogging, was blocked in the UAE in June 2008, apparently because it was categorized as a dating site in the database of Secure Computing, a commercial filtering product. The UAE uses SmartFilter, a product of Secure Computing, to block access to various content categories including dating, pornography, sex, and gambling.[35] Access was restored a few weeks later.

Similar to 2006–2007 testing results, 2008–2009 testing revealed pervasive filtering of pornographic and LGBT content. The 2008–2009 results also revealed blocking of previously accessible Arabic forums, which are commonly used to facilitate the exchange of Arabic sexually explicit content.

Compared to 2006–2007 testing, fewer Web sites relating to sexual health education were found to be blocked. For example, previously filtered Web sites such as circumcision.org and sexualhealth.com were found accessible, though others in the same categories are still blocked. Some Web sites containing provocative attire (lingerie.com) were still filtered. Web sites promoting alcohol and drug use or facilitating online gambling or dating were also blocked in large numbers, and many Arabic-language dating sites or Web sites that target Arabic users (e.g., www.arablounge.com, www.gaymiddleeast.com/country/uaemirates.htm) have been added to the blacklist. Nudity, even if in an artistic context and nonerotic, is censored (an example is the Arabic magazine www.jasadmag.com).

Internet tools, including those which facilitate hacking (e.g., thesecretlist.com), anonymizers (e.g., anonymizer.com), and translation tools (Google Web site translator, not the text translator), remain substantially filtered. Similarly, numerous VoIP sites (Skype.com, www.pc2call.com) were still blocked in accordance with the national ban on such applications.

In October 2006, the UAE unblocked access to social networking and multimedia sharing sites, including YouTube.com, Flickr.com, Metacafe.com, and MySpace.com. However, sections of these Web sites containing objectionable material remain unavailable. The photo-sharing site Flickr (Flickr.com) was later blocked entirely.

Conclusion

The UAE continues to prevent its citizens from accessing a significant amount of Internet content spanning a variety of topics. Though the vast majority of Web sites filtered are those deemed obscene in some way, a select few political Web sites are blocked, as are some pertaining to Nazis, Holocaust denial, and historical revisionism. The entire ".il" top-level domain continues to be blocked as well, which is more indicative of the UAE's opposition to the state of Israel than to the content.

Additionally, the state has extended its filtering scheme to the Dubai free zones, which previously enjoyed unfettered Internet access, and has increased the depth of technical filtering, blocking more Web sites across broader categories.

The UAE employs SmartFilter software to block content related to nudity, sex, dating, gambling, the occult, religious conversion, and drugs. Web sites pertaining to anonymizer tools, hacking, translation tools (as these have been used as proxies), and VoIP applications are also filtered in this manner.

Lastly, there are government efforts to monitor Internet activities in public Internet cafés to ensure that connections provided there do not bypass national filtering. Electronic surveillance to monitor objectionable online activities is publically acknowledged by the authorities.

Notes

1. *BBC News*, "Country Profile: United Arab Emirates," August 3, 2009, http://news.bbc.co.uk/2/hi/middle_east/country_profiles/737620.stm.

2. Human Rights Watch, "United Arab Emirates: Events of 2007," http://hrw.org/englishwr2k8/docs/2008/01/31/uae17622.htm.

3. Ibid.

4. *BBC News*, "Country Profile: United Arab Emirates," August 3, 2009, http://news.bbc.co.uk/2/hi/middle_east/country_profiles/737620.stm.

5. Reporters Without Borders, "Dubai Urged to Reverse Decision, Taken under Pressure from Musharraf, to Suspend Broadcasting by Two Pakistani TV Stations," November 17, 2007, http://www.rsf.org/article.php3?id_article=24415.

6. Lynne Roberts, "Pakistan TV to Resume Dubai Broadcasts," *Arabian Business*, November 19, 2007, http://www.arabianbusiness.com/504302-pakistan-tv-to-resume-dubai-broadcasts.

7. Tom Gara, "UAE Leads Region in IT, Says Report," *The National*, April 16, 2009, http://www.thenational.ae/article/20090416/BUSINESS/448045865/-1/ART.

8. *Khaleej Times*, "UAE Will Spend $3.3b in IT and Communications," March 19, 2009, http://www.khaleejtimes.com/DisplayArticleNew.asp?col=&section=business&xfile=data/business/2009/March/business_March818.xml.

9. International Telecommunication Union (ITU), "Internet Indicators: Subscribers, Users, and Broadband Subscribers," 2008, http://www.itu.int/ITU-D/icteye/Reporting/ShowReportFrame.aspx?ReportName=/WTI/InformationTechnologyPublic&RP_intYear=2008&RP_intLanguageID=1.

10. Arab Advisors Group, "Cementing Its Stance as the Arab World's Internet Leader, the UAE's ADSL Penetration Reached around 11% by End of 2008," March 16, 2009, http://www.arabadvisors.com/Pressers/presser-160309.htm-1.

11. UAE Interact, "United Arab Emirates Yearbook 2007: Infrastructure," http://www.uaeinteract.com/uaeint_misc/pdf_2008/English_2008/eyb6.pdf.

12. Tom Gara, "Du Relies on Network Sharing to Compete," *The National*, April 24, 2009, http://www.thenational.ae/article/20090425/BUSINESS/704249787/1005.

13. Ibid.

14. *Gulf News*, "UAE National Media Council Welcomes All Debates on Draft Media Law," April 13, 2009, http://www.gulfnews.com/nation/Media/10303708.html.

15. Alia Al Theeb, "Draft Media Law: Journalists 'Will Insist on Changes,'" *Gulf News*, April 28, 2009, http://www.gulfnews.com/nation/Media/10308566.html.

16. Human Rights Watch, "UAE: Media Law Undermines Free Expression," April 13, 2009, http://www.hrw.org/en/news/2009/04/13/uae-media-law-undermines-free-expression.

17. Committee to Protect Journalists, "CPJ Concerned about UAE Draft Media Law," March 9, 2009, http://cpj.org/2009/03/cpj-concerned-about-uae-draft-media-law.php.

18. Telecommunications Regulatory Authority (TRA), http://www.tra.org.ae.

19. Internet Access Management (IAM) policy, http://www.ctisalat.ae/assets/document/blockcontent.pdf.

20. *Gulf News*, "UAE Cyber Crimes Law," November 2, 2007, http://archive.gulfnews.com/uae/uaessentials/more_stories/10018507.html; Cyber-Crime Law No. 2 of 2006, Articles 15, 16, and 20.

21. Amnesty International, "UAE—Amnesty International Report 2008," http://www.amnesty.org/en/region/uae/report-2008.

22. *Gulf News*, "Dahi Dismisses Web Policing Allegations," April 23, 2009, http://archive.gulf-news.com/articles/09/04/24/10307260.html.

23. Ahmed Shaaban, "Police 'Play No Role' in Censorship: Tamim," *Khaleej Times*, April 25, 2009, http://www.khaleejtimes.com/DisplayArticle08.asp?xfile=/data/theuae/2009/April/theuae_April599.xml&section=theuae.

24. *Khaleej Times*, "Call to Blank Out YouTube in Emirates Too," March 10, 2009, http://www.khaleejtimes.com/DisplayArticleNew.asp?col=&section=theuae&xfile=data/theuae/2009/March/theuae_March239.xml.

25. Ahmed Shaaban, "Police 'Play No Role' in Censorship: Tamim," *Khaleej Times*, April 25, 2009, http://www.khaleejtimes.com/DisplayArticle08.asp?xfile=/data/theuae/2009/April/theuae_April599.xml&section=theuae.

26. Asma Ali Zain and Sebugwaawo Ismail, "Cyber Cafes Work around the Ban to Provide VoIP Services," *Khaleej Times*, April 2, 2008, http://www.khaleejtimes.com/DisplayArticleNew.asp?xfile=data/theuae/2008/April/theuae_April39.xml&section=theuae&col=.

27. *The National*, "Shisha and Internet Cafes Scrutinised," March 8, 2009, http://www.thenational.ae/apps/pbcs.dll/article?AID=/20090308/NATIONAL/113439722/-1/NEWS.

28. Andy Sambidge, "Dubai's e-Police Probe 222 Internet Crime Cases," *Arabian Business*, October 30, 2008, http://www.arabianbusiness.com/536556-dubais-e-police-probe-222-internet-crime-cases.

29. *Emaratalyoum*, "*Esabah takhtalis almukalamat aldawliyah wa fatayat yorawijna lilda'ara*" [Internet gangs steal international calls, girls market their sex services online], April 15, 2009, http://www.emaratalyoum.com/articles/2009/4/pages/14042009/04152009_4a6c7e4ba0894c5bb31-fe02a74c60295.aspx.

30. WAM, "Dubai Attorney General Refers Suspects in Deyaar Case to Courts," April 8, 2009, http://www.wam.org.ae/servlet/Satellite?c=WamLocEnews&cid=1238851046552&p=1135099400124&pagename=WAM%2FWamLocEnews%2FW-T-LEN-FullNews.

31. Vic Walter, Rehab El-Buri, Angela Hill, and Brian Ross, "ABC News Exclusive: Torture Tape Implicates UAE Royal Sheikh," ABC News, April 22, 2009, http://www.abcnews.go.com/Blotter/story?id=7402099&page=1.

32. Human Rights Watch, "UAE: Prosecute Torture by Royal Family Member," April 28, 2009, http://www.hrw.org/en/news/2009/04/28/uae-prosecute-torture-royal-family-member.

33. OpenNet Initiative Blog, "Middle East Countries Continue to Censor Content Deemed Offensive to Muslims," March 1, 2009, http://opennet.net/blog/2009/03/middle-east-countries-continue-censor-content-deemed-offensive-muslims.

34. Ibid.

35. OpenNet Initiative Blog "A Blind-Date with the Censors in UAE," June 20, 2008, http://opennet.net/blog/2008/06/a-blind-date-with-censors-uae.

Glossary of Technical Terms

2G is the second generation of telecommunication technology for mobile networking.

3G is the third generation of telecommunication technology for mobile networking.

403 (*403 Forbidden*) is the standard HTTP error code that occurs when a server will not allow a Web browser to access the file being requested.

404 (*404 Not Found*) is the standard HTTP error code that occurs when a server cannot find the file being requested.

ADSL (*asymmetric digital subscriber line*) is a technology that allows data to be sent over existing copper telephone lines.

Bandwidth is the amount of data that can flow in a given time.

Block page is the page delivered to the user when a request for a Web site is filtered, or blocked. Block pages take many forms and may be disguised as benign error pages or may bear the ISP's logo and further explanation of the block.

CCTV (*closed circuit television*) is the use of video cameras to transmit video from a specific place to a limited set of monitors. Signals for CCTV are not openly transmitted.

Circumvention refers to the general concept of using proxies and other tools to bypass Internet filtering.

Deep packet inspection is a form of computer network packet filtering that examines the data part (and possibly also the header) of a packet as it passes an inspection point, searching for protocol noncompliance, viruses, spam, intrusions, or predefined criteria to decide if the packet can pass or if it needs to be routed to a different destination, or for the purpose of collecting statistical information.

DNS (*domain name system*) is a hierarchical naming system for computers, services, or any resource participating in the Internet.

DNS tampering (*domain name system tampering*) is a method of blocking communication by preventing the conversion of domain names into IP addresses, effectively blocking access to the requested site.

Domain name   is a label identifying a specific computer, service, or resource on the Internet.

DoS attack   (*denial of service* attack) is an attempt to prevent users from accessing a specific computer resource, such as a Web site. DoS attacks (sometimes called DDoS, or *distributed denial of service*, attacks) usually involve overwhelming the targeted computer with requests so that it is no longer able to communicate with its intended users.

DSL   (*digital subscriber line*) is a family of technologies that provides digital data transmission over existing telephone wires.

EDGE   (*Enhanced Data rates for GSM Evolution*) also known as EGPRS or Enhanced GPRS is a GSM extension that improves data transmission rates by up to three times their original speed.

GB   (*gigabyte*) is a unit of digital information storage equal to 10^9 (1,000,000,000) bytes. However, this term is also often used to mean $1,024^3$ (1,073,741,824 bytes).

GPRS   (*general packet radio service*) is service for mobile devices that divides data into packets for transmission purposes. It can be used with 2G and 3G wireless telephone technology operating on the GSM standard.

GPS   (*Global Positioning System*) is a free global navigation satellite system that is used for both military and civilian purposes.

GSM   (*Global System for Mobile communications*) is a digital mobile phone standard used by as much as 80 percent of the global market. Its widespread use enables international roaming among different mobile phone operators.

HTTP   (*Hypertext Transfer Protocol*) is a set of standards for exchanging text, images, sound, and video by means of the Internet.

HTTP proxy filtering   blocks communication on the basis of the specific HTTP address or URL being requested.

ICP   (*Internet Cache Protocol*) is a set of rules used to coordinate Web caches (places where duplications of online data are temporarily stored, enabling faster access and reducing bandwidth).

ICP   (*Internet content provider*) is an online service provider that creates or provides informational, educational, or entertainment content.

ICT   (*information* and *communication technology*) is an umbrella term that includes all technologies intended for the manipulation and communication of information.

IP address   (*Internet protocol* address) is a numerical identification assigned to devices participating in a computer network utilizing the Internet Protocol.

ISP   (*Internet service provider*) is a company that provides users with access to the Internet.

IT   (*Information technology*) describes the use of computers, computer software, and other communications technologies to create and manage information.

IXP   (*Internet exchange point*) is a shared facility that allows ISPs to exchange traffic with one another through free, mutual peering agreements.

KB (*kilobyte*) is a unit of digital information storage equal to either 1,000 bytes (10^3) or 1,024 bytes (2^{10}), depending on context.

Kbps (*kilobits per second*) is a measure of bandwidth on a data transmission medium.

LGBT is an acronym that refers to the *lesbian, gay, bisexual,* and *transgender* community. Sometimes used to refer to anyone who is nonheterosexual.

MB (*megabyte*) is a unit of digital information storage equal to 10^6 (1,000,000) bytes.

MP3 (*MPEG-1 Audio Layer 3*) is a digital audio encoding format that compresses audio data by a factor of 12 without losing noticeable sound quality.

P2P (*peer-to-peer*) is a computer network that uses diverse connectivity between participants in a network and the cumulative bandwidth of network participants rather than conventional centralized resources where a relatively low number of servers provide the core value to a service or application.

Portal

- if **Web portal**: is an online interface that allows Internet users to collect and view information (e-mail, weather, stock prices, etc.) from various sources in a visually unified way.
- if **Intranet portal**: is a single network-specific hub that provides unified access to information and applications, often for a private company or organization.

Proxy (also **Proxy server**) is a server that acts as a go-between for clients (such as Web browsers or other applications) and other servers. Proxy servers enable anonymous online activity and increase access speed through caching.

Reverse filtering (also known as Geolocational Filtering) is a practice that occurs on the Web server hosting the content, as opposed to at a point along the way of the traffic flow, and is based on restricting requests based on geographical location of the originating Internet Protocol address Copyright holders who want to restrict access to their content in certain markets often use reverse filtering. Examples include hulu.com, BBC.com, and other sites that syndicate commercial video and audio content that is subject to licensing.

SMS (*short message service*), also known as *text message*, is a communication service standardized in the GSM mobile communication system, allowing the exchange of short text messages between mobile devices.

Social networking sites are Web services that focus on communities of users with shared interests. Popular examples include Facebook, Twitter, MySpace, and Orkut.

TB (*terabyte*) is a unit of digital information storage equal to 1 trillion (10^{12}) bytes, or 1,000 gigabytes.

TCP/IP (*Transmission Control Protocol/Internet Protocol*) is the set of standards governing data transmission over the Internet.

TCP/IP content filtering blocks communication on the basis of where packets of data are going to or coming from, and not on what they contain.

TCP/IP header filtering   blocks communication on the basis of the IP address and/or the port number (which gives clues as to the type of Web service being accessed) contained in the header of the data packet being sent.

Top-level domain   the group of letters (usually two or three, but can include more) that follow the final dot in a domain name. Example: in *opennet.net*, the top-level domain is *.net.*

URL   (*Uniform Resource Locator*) is a string of characters that specify where a particular resource is located online and how to retrieve it. Also known as a Web address.

User ID   (User *Identification*) is a unique string of characters that identifies users of password-protected online services, such as e-mail or social networking sites.

VCD   (*Video Compact Disc*) is a digital compression standard that enables the storage of video on a Compact Disc.

VoIP   (*Voice over Internet Protocol*) is a technology that allows for voice communication over the Internet.

WAP   (*Wireless Application Protocol*) is a global standard for the transfer of information without using electrical conduits (wires). It allows for access to the Internet using mobile devices.

Warez   (derived from the plural of "ware," as in software) refers to copyrighted material that is distributed in violation of copyright law.

White Hat   a person who attempts to infiltrate information technology systems or networks in order to expose weaknesses so they can be corrected by the systems' owners. Also known as an ethical hacker.

Index